To the Reader:

Scientology® applied religious philosophy contains pastoral counseling procedures intended to assist an individual to gain greater knowledge of self. The mission of the Church of Scientology is a simple one: to help the individual achieve greater self-confidence and personal integrity, thereby enabling him to really trust and respect himself and his fellow man. The attainment of the benefits and goals of Scientology philosophy requires each individual's dedicated participation, as only through his own efforts can he achieve these.

This book is part of the religious literature and works of the Scientology Founder, L. Ron Hubbard. It is presented to the reader as a part of the record of his personal research into life, and the application of same by others, and should be construed only as a written report of such research and not as a statement of claims made by the Church or the Founder.

Scientology philosophy and its forerunner, Dianetics® spiritual healing technology, as practiced by the Church, address only the "thetan" (spirit). Although the Church, as are all churches, is free to engage in spiritual healing, it does not, as its primary goal is increased spiritual awareness for all. For this reason, the Church does not wish to accept individuals who desire treatment of physical or mental illness but prefers to refer these to qualified specialists of other organizations who deal in these matters.

The Hubbard® Electrometer is a religious artifact used in the Church confessional. It in itself does nothing, and is used by ministers only, to assist parishioners in locating areas of spiritual distress or travail.

We hope the reading of this book is only the first stage of a personal voyage of discovery into this new and vital world religion.

Church of Scientology International

This Book Belongs to:

_____

_____

(Date)

The Organization Executive Course

and

Management Series

by

L. Ron Hubbard

POLICY INDEX

Bridge Publications, Inc.   NEW ERA Publications International ApS

Published in USA and International by
Bridge Publications, Inc.
5600 E. Olympic Boulevard
Commerce, California 90022

ISBN 0-88404-677-X

Published in United Kingdom and Europe by
NEW ERA Publications International ApS
Smedeland 20
2600 Glostrup, Denmark

ISBN 87-7336-761-3

OEC AND MANAGEMENT SERIES POLICY INDEX

Contents

Alphabetical List of Titles 3

Subject Index 81

Chronological List of Titles 485

Address List 597

How to Use This Book

This book has been designed to make finding the exact LRH policy you need or want as fast and simple as possible. In this volume, every issue contained in the Organization Executive Course (OEC) Volumes and the three Management Series Volumes has been indexed in three ways:

ALPHABETICALLY

by *SUBJECT*

and

CHRONOLOGICALLY.

All entries include both the *volume number* and *page number* where the issue can be found. For example, a policy letter appearing on page 70 of OEC Volume 0 would be listed as "0:70".

The divisional volumes and basic staff volume are referred to by their numbers, 0–7. The Management Series Volumes are denoted by "MS" (for *M*anagement *S*eries) followed by the volume number, 1, 2 or 3. For example, a reference appearing on page 297 of Management Series Volume 2 would be listed as "MS2:297".

Where a policy reference is in more than one volume, each of its volume and page numbers is given. For example, the listing for a reference appearing in OEC Volume 0 on page 321, in OEC Volume 3 on page 260 and in OEC Volume 6 on page 589 would be "0:321, 3:260, 6:589".

ALPHABETICAL LIST OF TITLES

When you know the title of the policy you are looking for, this list enables you to find it rapidly.

All policy titles are listed in alphabetical order. Titles beginning with words such as "the" or "an" are alphabetized *without* these words at the beginning. For example, THE AIMS OF SCIENTOLOGY is found under the letter "A" as "AIMS OF SCIENTOLOGY, THE"; it is not listed under "T".

Where two or more issues have the same title, the date of each is given in parentheses following the title, to assist in finding the one you are looking for.

The issue's title is followed by the volume number and page where it can be found.

SUBJECT INDEX

The second section of this volume consists of a complete subject index, enabling you to easily find the policy issues covering a specific subject. It can be used when you are looking for the issue or issues covering a particular area or situation, but don't know the titles or dates.

Many of the entries in this section include cross-references to policies on other, related subjects. By using these cross-references you can expand your knowledge of LRH policy and improve your effectiveness in doing your job and handling situations.

Each entry in the subject index is followed by the volume number and page number where the data you are looking for is located. The page number(s) given refer to the exact page or pages where the data is found, whether it is on the first page of the issue or not.

CHRONOLOGICAL LIST

When you know the date of a particular issue you are looking for, this is the section of the book to use. It lists all of the issues in the OEC and Management Series Volumes by date, starting from the earliest policies and coming forward to the most recent.

Where a policy has been revised, the date of the last revision is included in the entry.

———————

LRH policy is the tested and proven *key* to the success and expansion of any activity. With this index volume you have an invaluable tool for swift and easy location of the exact LRH policy you need. Use it!

The Editors

ALPHABETICAL
LIST OF TITLES

Alphabetical List of Titles

A

Ability Magazine	2:185
Academies, Internships and Grade Auditing	4:657
	5:858
Academy Certs Valid at SHs	5:510
Academy Checksheets	4:630
	5:759
Academy Checksheets, Supervisor Conditions	4:376
	5:781
Academy, Extra Weeks	3:152
	4:595
Academy Meters	4:471
Academy Processing	4:624
	5:197
Academy Schedule, Clarification Of	4:568
Academy Taught Processes	4:610
Academy Training (23 Oct. 59)	4:308
Academy Training (9 Oct. 61)	4:573
Academy Training Curriculum and Examination	4:557
ACC at Saint Hill	7:1346
Accounting Department, Washington	3:19
Accounting Policies of Scientology Companies	3:65
	7:1078
Accounting Records and Bills	3:375
Accounting System	3:104

Accounts	3:37
Accounts and PRO	3:69
	MS3:144
Accounts Clearance	3:163
Accounts: How to Do a Payroll	3:332
Accounts Information	7:623
Accounts Inspection	3:31
Accounts, Invalidating	3:399
Accounts Irregularities	3:123
Accounts Line	3:36
Accounts Policies (27 Jan. 60)	3:33
Accounts Policies (6 May 64)	3:126
Accounts Policing	3:73
Accounts Procedures	3:133
Accounts Unit	3:391
Acting Executive Director	7:609
Actions, Executive, for Handling Disastrous Occurrences	7:326
	MS3:306
Actions for HCO Secretaries Faced with Illegal Usage	7:1062
Actions to Start an HCO	6:773
Activities of Legal Department	7:1053
Ad	6:209
Ad and Book Policies, Text of Ads	2:266
	6:239
Ad Council and Ad Comms, Orders, Issue Of	7:905
Ad Council Income Planning	7:958

Addendum to HCO Policy Letter
of 7 September 1963,
Committees of Evidence,
Scientology Jurisprudence,
Administration Of   1:936
Additional Mag Policy   2:208
Additional Reges   2:452
Additional Staff Auditors   1:180
    4:844

Additions to HCO Div Account
Policy   2:290
Addition to HCO Gross Divisional
Statistic, Fully Hatted Org Staff
Members   1:106
Addresses   2:694
Addressing Department—Hats   2:684
Address Lists   2:710
Address Lists to City Offices   2:701
    6:789

Address Machines   2:695
Addressograph Equipment
Warning   2:699
Addressograph Tabbing—Libraries   2:693
Admin Degrades   0:73
    5:25
    7:489
    MS3:469
Admin High Crime   0:75
    1:917
    5:822
    7:491
    MS2:461
    MS3:471
Administering Justice   0:480
    1:733
Administration   7:402
    MS3:382
Administration Outside
Scientology   1:736
    7:1016
Administrative Procedure for
Reducing Overts   4:846
Administrative Side of PE
Foundation   6:364

Administrative Skill   7:438
    MS3:418
Administrative Stable Data   7:745
Administrative Traffic Trend   7:614
Administrator's Hat   7:624
Admin Know-How   7:403
    MS3:383
Admin Know-How No. 26   7:426
    MS3:406
Admin Know-How No. 30   7:434
    MS3:414
Ads and Copywriting   MS3:208
Ads and Info Packets   6:213
Advanced Course Regulations and
Security   4:813
Advanced Course Security Check   4:803
Advanced Course Violations   4:809
Advertisement for Field in
Certainty, Ability, etc.—Minor
Issues   2:189
    6:507

Advertisements, Continental
Magazines and Auditor   2:210
    6:219

Advisory Committee   7:885
Advisory Committees   7:903
Advisory Council   7:909
Advisory Council, The   7:889
Affluence Attainment   0:628
Aims of Scientology, The   6:519
    7:1021

All Auditors—Ministers,
Ministerial Board of Review   4:1190
    7:1220

All Class IV Orgs, OIC Cable
Change   1:670
Allocation of Quarters,
Arrangement of Desks and
Equipment   7:1333
Allowed Technical Services   4:121
    6:764

"All Pcs Undergoing Power
Processing . . ."   4:898
"All Preclears Are Expected
To . . ."   4:837

All Sea Org Orgs, OIC Cable
   Change   1:674
Alterations   5:468
Alter-Is and Degraded Beings   1:201
   7:389
   MS3:369
Always Register and Invoice   2:479
   3:141
   4:213
Amnesty   1:923
Amnesty, Cancelled Certs, Justice
   Comments   1:946
   5:348
Amnesty Policy   1:937
Analysis of Organization by
   Product, The   0:287
   MS1:226
Anatomy of Thought, The   MS1:3
And That Is Banking   MS2:389
Animals Forbidden in House   7:1352
Antibiotics, Administering Of   5:642
Antisocial Personality, the
   Anti-Scientologist, The   1:1014
"Any Staff Member . . ."   7:1166
AOs—OT Sections   4:804
Appearance and PRO   MS3:147
Appearances in Public Divs   0:339
   6:613
   MS3:154
Appearances Officer Hat Write-up   6:595
Appointment of Personnel   1:195
Appointment of Xerox Officer   1:419
Appointments and Programs   7:68
Appointments and Promotions   0:596
Appointments, LRH Comm and
   Executive Secretary and Others   1:199
Arbitraries   0:65
ARC Break Assessments on Staff   5:573
ARC Break Program, Additional
   Data   6:563
   7:881
ARC Break Registrar   6:547
ARC in Comm Course   4:549, 6:451

Areas of Operation   2:88
   6:59
Arrangement of the Academy, An   4:599
Artistic Presentation   2:263
Assembly Line for Produced
   Promo, The   MS3:192
Assignment, Model to Be Used   1:212
Assignment of Auditors, Rooms,
   Students   2:480
   4:294
Assignment of Tech Personnel   4:104
Association Secretary Duties   7:621
Attacks on Scientology   7:1024
Attacks on Scientology
   (Continued)   7:1026
Attacks on Scientology, Sex and
   Organizations   7:690
Attention Registrars and Book
   Administrators   2:329
   3:145
Audience Alertness and Tape
   Players   6:334
Auditing Allowed   4:313
Auditing and C/Sing below One's
   Training Level   4:664
   5:860
Auditing and Ethics   1:794
   4:1099
Auditing Discounts   2:474
Auditing Fees, Preferential
   Treatment of Preclears, Scale of
   Preference   2:520
   3:157
   4:888
Auditing Folders, Omissions in
   Completeness   1:640
   4:1194
   5:802
Auditing Hours Limited   4:870
Auditing Mystery Solved   5:277
Auditing Regulations   4:738
Auditing Reports   4:1182
Auditing Reports, Falsifying Of   4:1192
   5:288
Auditing, Rudiments Check Sheet   4:1168

Auditing Sales and Delivery
  Program No. 1   5:258
Auditing Supervisor and Auditing
  Instructors, Duties Of   4:315
Auditor and Org Individual Stats   4:118
Auditor and "The Mind's
  Protection," An   4:682
Auditor Assignment   4:670
Auditor Assignment Policies   4:923
   5:597
Auditor Estimation Test   4:1177
   5:201
Auditor Magazine: Policy and
  Format, The   2:249
Auditor Magazine Success   2:246
Auditor Recovery   4:970
   5:425
Auditors (31 May 68)   0:154
Auditors (20 Mar. 72)   4:1189

Auditors Association (28 Aug. 70)   6:730
Auditors Association (9 Feb. 71)   6:732
Auditor's Association Project in
  Your Area   6:726
Auditor's Code, The   4:1186
Auditor's Rights Modified   4:209
Auditor's Stats on F/N VGI   4:1188
Auditors Who Miss Withholds,
  Penalty   4:1196
   5:615
Auditor Training Prerequisite   4:659
   5:451
Authorized Processes   4:1052
Autographed Copies of Books by
  LRH   2:342
Automatic Evaluation Packet for
  PE Foundation   6:292
Axiom 28 Amended   1:319

B

Bad Clinical Results, Handling	4:842	Basic Staff Auditor's Hat	
Balancing Income–Outgo, Paper,		(20 Mar. 61)	4:1156
Postage and Printing	7:932	Basic Staff Auditor's Hat	
	2:176	(26 May 61)	4:1165
	3:269	Basic Study Missed Withhold	1:837
Barriers to Study	0:33	Battle Plans	0:706
Basic Certificates, Uncertified			7:458
Personnel	1:234		MS2:444
	5:351		MS3:438
Basic FBO Duties	MS2:322	Bean Theory, Finance as a	
Basic Financial Policy, HCO	3:21	Commodity	MS2:339
Basic Hat Pack	0:27	Beginning and Maintaining of	
Basic Management Tools	7:478	a Boom, The	7:858
	MS1:368	Bills Payments	3:317
	MS2:194	Black PR	MS3:26
	MS2:299	Blind Registration	2:564
	MS3:458		4:1032
Basic Organization	0:105		6:387
	MS1:193	Blow-Offs	1:724
Basic Principles of			4:1047
Promotion, The	0:344		5:547
	2:136	Board Decisions, Data	
	6:63	Evaluation, Raw Data, Judging	
Basics of Ethics, The	0:447	a Situation, Selection of Key	
	1:496	Personnel	7:770
Basics of Marketing, The	MS3:187	Board Minutes	7:1119
Basics of Statistics and		Board of Investigation	1:952
Management, The	0:679, 7:562	Board of Review	1:960, 7:1265

Boards of Investigation	1:958	Book Sales to Individuals from	
Boards of Investigation and		Pubs	2:348
Committees of Evidence,		Books and Marketing	MS3:164
Termination Of	1:959		MS3:217
Body Routing	6:228	Books Are Assets	MS2:381
Body Routing in Central		Books Are Dissemination	2:331
Organizations	1:121		6:234
	2:486	Books, Cost Of	2:324
	6:379	Book Section: Credits and Debits	3:118
Bonus	3:344	Books Make Booms	2:296
Bonuses (29 Apr. 65)	3:346		6:260
	5:408	Books Straight Talk	2:298
Bonuses (17 Oct. 66)	3:355		6:266
Bonuses for Service Delivery	3:352	Bookstore Officer Hat	2:300
	5:135	Boom Data, Publications Basic	
Book Administrator	2:319	Function	2:293
Book Auditor	2:166		6:257
	5:346	"Boom Formula" Cancelled	2:711
	6:840		6:103
"Book Buyers Should Be		Booming an Org Through	
Sold . . ."	2:280	Training	2:68
	6:506		4:336
Book Income	2:75		5:835
	6:243	Breakthrough, PR and Production,	
Booklets, Handouts, Mailing		Tone Scale Surveys	MS3:37
Pieces	2:178	Breakthroughs	MS1:15
	7:1304	Brief Outline of an HGC as	
Book of Case Remedies,		Currently Done, A	4:852
Application of Tech	5:732	Broad Public Questionnaire	6:596
Book Outlets of an Org	2:350	Building HCO	1:87
	6:261	Bulletin and Policy Letter	
Book Policy	2:321	Distribution	1:407
Book Promotion Design	2:338	Bulletin Board	1:347
	6:248	Bulletin Boards and Information	
Books (28 May 68)	2:310	Boards	1:351
Books (27 Feb. 71)	2:314	Business of Orgs, The	0:90
Book Sales Commission	2:354		7:880
	6:265	"By Their Actions . . ."	6:827

C

Cable, Don't Phone	1:457	Case Supervisor Statistic	4:1121
Call-In: The Key to Delivery and			5:703
Future Income	2:641	Cash-Bills Defined	MS2:404
	3:217	Cause	0:263
	4:276	Cause of Crime, The	7:1157
	7:865	Cause or Effect, The Quality of	
Campaign for Ethical Auditing, A	6:697	the Qual Division, a Qual Div	
Cancellation, Mimeo Distribution		Checklist for Quality	5:865
Changes (Sec ED Changes		CCHs	4:623
Distribution)	1:412	Celebrities	6:139
Cancellation of Assorted		Celebrity Centre	6:136
Directives	1:414	Celebrity Centre Magazine	
	7:1307	*Celebrity*	2:238
Cancellation of Certificates	1:856	Celebrity Centre Motto	6:137
	5:316	Celebrity Centre Purpose	6:138
Cancellation of Mail Lists to Field		Central Files and Procurement	
Auditors	2:703	(6 Apr. 57)	2:388
	6:713	Central Files and Procurement	
Captive Brains	7:1123	(15 May 57)	2:400
Car Parking	7:1367	Central Files and the	
Carrying Out Instructions	7:1178	Addressograph (Use Of)	2:651
Car Washing	7:1362	Central Files, Value Of	
Case and Letter Reg Project #1	2:637	The Gross Income of the Org	
Case Files	4:249	and Why	0:359
Case Gain, Completing Levels	5:593		2:673
Cases and Morale of Staff	1:800		6:89
	5:602		
	6:526	Central Organization and City	
Case Supervisor, Special Attention	4:1072	Office Tape Service	2:372

Central Organization Efficiency 0:230
7:600
Central Organization Minimum
Staff 7:212
Certificate and Classification
Changes, Everyone Classified 4:163
5:329
Certificate Cancellation 1:857
Certificate Display 5:301
Certificates (20 Dec. 58) 5:311
Certificates (31 Dec. 64) 5:342
Certificates and Awards 5:325
Certificates and Awards Revised
List 5:317
Certificates Handling 5:312
Certificates Release and Validation 5:305
Certification and Validation
Requirements 4:596
5:322
Certification Board Duties and
Responsibilities 5:91
Certification of Mission Students 5:199
6:755
Certification Requirements 5:321
6:509
CF/Addressograph, Handling of
New Names 2:660
CF and Address Change 2:659
CF and Address Presorting 2:676
CF–Promotion Liaison Hat 2:656
CFs, ARC Breaks In 2:677
6:554
Change of Organization Targets,
Project 80, a Preview 2:162
4:64
6:187
Changes in Basement Student
Facilities 7:1372
Change the Civilization Eval 4:427
Changing Workable Finance
Systems 3:95
MS2:371
Chaplain (2 Aug. 65) 6:518
Chaplain (2 Sept. 68) 6:523

Chaplain's Court, Civil Hearings 1:955
6:520
Charges 3:169
Chart of Abilities Gained for
Lower Levels and Expanded
Lower Grades 4:189
5:292
Charts, Routing and Publications,
The Enrollment Department 2:422
Checking Evals MS1:120
Checking Evaluations Addition MS1:122
Checklist for a Strategic Plan 7:475
MS3:455
Checksheet Format 1:281
5:503
Checksheet Rating System 4:612
Checksheets 4:632
Checksheets, Course 4:780
5:206
Check Signing 3:319
Check Signing Procedure 3:321
Chicago Area 6:704
Chinese School MS2:87
Choosing PE and Registration
Personnel 1:185
2:411
6:183
Christmas Bonuses for Staff 3:365
City Office 6:798
City Offices 6:782
City Offices, Successful Patterns 6:777
City Office System 6:796
7:270
Clarification, Auditing of Org
Executives 5:585
Clarification of Invoicing Items 2:482
3:142
Clarification of Public Relations
Post 7:175
Clarification of Sec ED 27 4:97
Class VIII C/S Qual Stat 5:676
Classes of Auditors 4:1166
Classification (13 Feb. 64) 4:170
Classification (23 Feb. 64) 4:171, 5:337

Classification at Upper Levels,
Temporary Measure 5:200
Classification for Everyone 4:168
5:333

Classification, Gradation and
Awareness Chart 2:517
4:186
5:191

Classification Is Required before
Moving to Next Level 4:776
Classification of Auditors, Class II
and Goals 4:875
Classification on GPMs 4:772
5:187

Classification Pass Marks 5:186
Classified Materials 4:825
Class II Training Only by
Academies and Saint Hill 4:593
Clay Table Training 4:374
Clay Table Use 4:879
Cleanliness and Tidiness of
Premises 1:520
6:594

Cleanliness of Quarters and Staff,
Improve Our Image 0:334
6:593

Clear Ads 6:160
Clear Bracelet Procedure 5:309
Clear Certainty Rundown:
Administration 4:975
Clear Certainty Rundown New
Service 4:998
Clear Certificates 5:374
Clear Checkouts in Continental
Orgs 4:908
5:236

Clear Checks and Re-Clear
Checks 5:243
Clearing 4:863
Clearing and OT Course
Reorganization 4:798
Clearing and Training 4:614
Clearing Course Folders 4:794
Clearing Course Regulation 4:795
Clearing Course Security 1:627, 4:792

Clearing Course, Submission of
Folders 4:790
Clearing—Free Needles 4:719
Clear Requirement 4:743
Clears, Invalidation Of 1:892
Clinical Procedure 4:831
Clipping Books MS3:98
CLOs, OTLs and Flag 7:417
MS3:397

CO and ED Penalty for False
Completion Stats 7:168
Co-audit 5:575
Co-audit Defined 4:687
Co-audits: How to Run Them 4:691
Code of a Scientologist 0:160
6:603
7:1047

Codes and Coding, Correct
Practice Policy 1:468
CO/ED Inspections 7:715
Collection from SPs and PTSes 1:764
3:190

Collection of Accounts 3:184
Color Flash System 1:373
Color Flash System Rewritten 1:352
Come-on Dissemination MS3:185
Command Intention and Your Post 0:256
1:286

Comm Baskets 1:371
Comm Center, Arrangement Of 1:350
Comm Cycle Additives 4:1175
5:667

Comment on Finance, A 3:26
7:924

Comments about Letter Registrar 2:622
Comments on Letter Registrar
Department 2:621
Committees of Evidence 1:935
Committees of Evidence,
Scientology Jurisprudence,
Administration Of 1:924
Comm-Member System, The 7:225
Comm-Member System, Routing
Policies Section, The 7:228

Comm Procedure Over Long
Distances   1:465

Comm Routing, How to Tie Up a
Whole Org and Produce
Nothing   0:386
    1:375

Comm Speed   1:364

Communication (13 Sept. 54)   1:299

Communication (30 May 68)   1:466

Communication Center   1:345

Communication Inspector Hat   1:383

Communications Functions   1:316

Communications, Registered Mail   0:379
    1:331

Communication, Stopping Of   1:902
    7:723

Competence   0:254

Complement   1:215

Completed Staff Work (CSW),
How to Get Approval of Actions
and Projects   0:401

Completing Conditions Formulas   0:666
    1:613

Completion of Cycles   7:778

Complexity and Confronting   0:36
    4:369

Compliance, How to Get One   7:824

Compliance Reports   7:708

Computer Ethics Points   MS2:464

Computers—Danger of
Relying On   MS2:466

Concerning Administration   7:292

Concerning Committees of
Evidence   1:933

Concerning the Separateness of
Dianetics and Scientology   2:143
    6:231

Condition Below Treason,
Confusion Formula and
Expanded Confusion
Formula   0:568
    1:588

Conditions Handlings   0:664, 1:603

Conditions, How to Assign   0:654
    1:566
    7:395
    MS3:375

Conditions of Liability and Doubt   0:574
    1:562

Conditions on Orgs or Divisions
or Depts, Clarification   0:652
    1:564

Conditions Orders, Executive
Ethics   0:659
    1:573
    7:698

Conditions Penalties, New
Employees and Persons Newly
on Post   0:566
    1:571

Conference Hats   7:918

Conference Planning Officer   7:920

Confessionals   1:633
    4:1109
    5:606

Confessionals—Ethics Reports
Required   1:645
    4:1197

Confessional Tech Policies   1:642
    4:985
    5:448

Confidentiality of Upper-Level
Rundowns   4:812

Confused Ideas   4:500
    5:464

Confused Presentation Denies
Service   7:1299

Confusion Formula, Additional
Data   1:615

Congresses   6:330

Congress Organization and
Increasing Interest and
Attendance   6:324

Congress Policies   6:333

Consequences of Miscramming   5:825

Construction Information   7:1370

Contests and Prizes 0:234
6:207

Continental and Area HCO
Finance Policies 3:244

Continental Liaison Officers
at WW 7:133

Continental Magazines to Model
after *Certainty* 2:209

Continuing Pc to Third Stage
Release 4:901

Contracts and Services 3:292
7:1070

Control of Statistics 0:686
7:521

Coordination Committees and
Management Committees,
Differences in Purpose and
Function 7:451
MS3:431

Coordination or Confusion, an
Exec Div Checklist for Quality 7:1425

Cope 1:59
7:791

Cope and Organize MS1:197

Copyright: USA 7:1077

Copywriting MS3:204

Corporate Address 7:1120

Corporate Names, Group Names 7:1118

Corporation Coordinator 7:1115

Correct Comm 0:391
MS2:236

Correct Danger Condition
Handling 0:605
1:582

Corrected Table of Conditions 0:567
1:575

Correction Division Purposes,
Ideal Scenes, Products, Statistics 5:58

Correction of HCO PL 23 Dec.
58, Qualification of HGC Staff
Auditors 5:832

Correction to HCO PL 26 May 65
II, Communications—Registered
Mail 1:332

Correction to Policy Letters on
Certification and Awards 5:350

Corrupt Activities 0:534
7:1036

Council and Ad Comms 7:896

Counterespionage 1:629
7:1033

Counting of Gross Income, The MS2:374

Course Administration 4:460

Course Administration, Roll Book 4:464

Course Checkouts, Twin Checking 4:766

Course Completion, Student
Indicators 0:32
4:379
5:215

Course Pattern 4:762

Course Schedules 4:453

Courses—Their Ideal Scene 4:424
5:516

Course Supervisors 4:399

Courts of Ethics 1:948

Cramming Section, The 4:364
5:773

Crash Program 1:515
4:311
5:168

Creating Overwhelming
Popularity MS3:157

Creating Survey Questions MS3:49
MS3:224

Credit and Discounts 3:164

Credit Collections Defined 3:137

Crediting of Auditor in Release
Logbook 5:355

Creed of the Church of
Scientology, The 6:315
7:965

Crime Additions 1:910

Criminal Mind, The 1:830
7:1147

Criminal Mind and the
Psychs, The 7:1155

Criminals and Psychiatry 7:1144

Critics of Scientology 1:782

C/S as a Training Officer, a Program for Flubless Auditing, A 5:694

C/Sing or Auditing without Folder Study 4:1117

C/S Qualifications 4:1129
5:715

C/S Series 11 4:1102

Current Office Work 1:369

Current Planning 4:61

Current Promotion and Org Program Summary, Membership Rundown 6:805

Curriculum Change 4:736

Cutative Prices MS1:212

Cutatives 4:23, 5:22

D

Danger Condition   0:585
                                          1:553

Danger Condition Data, Why
   Organizations Stay Small   0:598
                                          7:254

Danger Condition, Responsibilities
   of Declaring   0:590
                                          7:684

Danger Conditions, Inspections by
   Executive Secretaries, How to
   Do Them   0:592
                                          7:686

Danger Conditions, Technical
   Data for Review Auditors   5:775
Danger Condition, Warning, the
   Junior Who Accepts Orders
   From Everyone   0:589
                                          7:683

"Dangerous Auditor," The   5:589
Dangerous Environment, the True
   Story of Scientology, The   7:1039
Data and Situation Analyzing   MS1:18
Data Required as Reports from
   HCO Secs   7:1176
Data Series Auditing   MS1:86
Data Series PLs, Use Of   MS1:181
Data Systems   MS1:26
Date Coincidence   MS1:163
Dead File: Restoration to Good
   Standing   1:990, 2:671

"Dear Scientologist . . ."   6:581
Death Wish   1:1034
Debug Tech   MS2:144
Debug Tech Checklist   MS2:153
Declares   5:689
Defacing Books and Proper
   Addresses in Them   2:326
Definition of a Hot File   2:498
Definition of a Registration   2:497
                                          6:382
Definition of Release   5:225
Definitions   4:295
Deliver   0:282
                                          2:73
                                          4:80
                                          6:366

Delivering Public Division
   Courses   6:374
Delivering the Hubbard Key to
   Life Course, the Chicken and
   Egg Theory   1:912
                                          4:648

Delivery Duties   4:253
Departmental Actions   7:1198
Departmental Mini Programs:
   The Key to Achievement   MS2:278
Departmental Reports   7:55
Department of Enrollment   2:420

15

Department of Government Affairs	3:376
	7:997
Department of Government Relations (12 Aug. 60)	7:996
Department of Government Relations (22 Aug. 60)	7:1001
Department of Official Affairs (13 Mar. 61 I)	7:1004
Department of Official Affairs (13 Mar. 61 II)	7:1007
Department of Promotion and Registration	2:404
Department of the Chaplain, The	6:535
Department 1	1:112
Department 17 Course Checksheets	6:485
Department 17 Course Checksheets, Addition	6:489
Departments of FCDC	7:178
Departure Form	4:725
Dept of Promotion and Registration and CF–Promotion Liaison, The	2:654
Deputy CO or Deputy ED for Delivery and Exchange, The	7:877
Deputy FBO for Marketing of Org Resources for Exchange (D/FBO for MORE)—Purpose	MS2:395
Deputy FBOs for Marketing of Org Resources for Exchange (D/FBO for MORE)	MS2:384
Despatches, Speed Up Despatches, Staledate	0:381
	1:384
Despatches to Advisory Council	7:893
Despatch Lines	0:378
	1:370
Developed Traffic, the Delirium Tremens of Central Orgs	0:397
Dev-T (31 Jan. 65)	0:412
Dev-T (27 Oct. 69)	0:433
	7:412
	MS3:392
Dev-T Analysis	0:416

Dev-T and Unhattedness	0:439
	MS2:16
Dev-T Data, Executive Responsibility	0:419
	7:682
Dev-T Graphed	0:435
Dev-T Summary List	0:424
Dev-T Summary List Additions	0:429
Dianetic Assists	5:629
Dianetic Auditing	4:1094
Dianetic Auditor Course	4:628
Dianetic Certificates	4:636
	5:216
Dianetic Clear False Declares	5:291
Dianetic Contract	4:917
	6:435
	7:1096
Dianetic Courses, Wildcat	4:637
	6:720
Dianetic Registration	2:535
	4:920
	6:438
	7:1100
Dianetic Results	5:633
Dianetics	2:533
	4:1095
	5:595
	6:433
Dianetics and Results, Dianetic Counselling Groups	6:717
Dianetics and Scientology Are New	0:362
	MS3:136
	MS3:173
Dianetics: Its Relationship to Scientology	6:429
Dianetics, Right to Audit	5:368
	7:1103
Dianetics, Right to Teach	5:370
	7:1105
Different Types of Word Clearing, The	4:491
Dining Room for Staff	7:1353
Directives from a Board Member	1:399
Director of Administration Hat	7:594

Director of Enrollment, the Letter
  Registrar, Administration   1:307
   2:64
Director of Materiel   3:371
Director of Processing Hat   4:959
Director of Training Weekly
  Student Interviews   4:321
Director of Zoning Hat   6:837
Discipline, SPs and Admin, How
  Statistics Crash   1:1026
   7:510
Discounts   2:308
Discounts, Central Orgs, Books   2:305
   6:255
Dismissals and Post Changes   1:247
Dismissals, Transfers and
  Demotions   0:487
   1:251
Dissemination (15 Jan. 57)   6:151
Dissemination (2 May 57)   2:146
   6:153
Dissemination (24 Aug. 68)   4:120
Dissemination Drill   6:214
Dissemination Materials to Saint
  Hill   2:134
Dissemination Pieces, Stable Datum,
  Appearance, Layout and Design   2:274
Dissemination Tips   2:60
   6:166
Distraction and Noise   7:414
   MS3:394
Distribution Action   6:216
Distribution Division (Div 6)   6:61
Distribution Division Info Packet   6:211
Distribution of Bulletin Change   1:402
Div 5 Mini Qual Org Board   5:57
Div 6A Stat Renamed and
  Redefined: Bodies in the Shop   6:226
Division 2/Division 6 Registrar
  Publics   2:584
   6:411
Division 7, International
  Executive Division, Offices of
  the HCO Exec Sec and Org
  Exec Sec Described   7:93

Division Four Org Board, Ideal
  Scenes and Stats   4:136
Division Seven   7:103
Doctor Title Abolished   5:362
   7:1205
Documentation and the Dead
  Agent Caper   MS3:131
D of P Form   4:855
D of P Operates by OCAs   4:967
   6:301
"Doing a Quicksilver" Forbidden   0:264
   MS1:359
   MS1:467
Doing Work   MS2:63
Do-It-Yourself Therapy   6:452
Domestic Arrangements Changes   7:1345
Domestic Staff   7:1378
Dones   0:260
Don't Unmock a Working
  Installation   MS1:459
Doors   7:1375
Double Hats   1:205
Downstat Causes   7:513
Dramatization of Withholds on
  Vital Information Lines, The   5:800
Drills   7:800
Drills, Allowed   4:616
   5:188
Duplicating Functions   MS1:283
   MS1:450
Duration of SHSBC and Solo
  Course Requirements   4:785
Duties at Saint Hill—HCO WW   7:29
Duties of a Staff Member   0:165
Duties of HCO   1:34
Duties of Personnel Post   1:178
Duties of Sec'l ED   7:595
Duties of the Assoc Sec's Sec in a
  Central Organization   7:619
Duties of the Executive Director
  of the HASI (FC)   7:1167
Duty of Area Sec Re Personnel   7:182

E

Earned Flag Certificates	5:527	Employment Qualifications	1:158
"Economy," The	0:300	End of Endless Training, The	4:419
	3:78	Enemy Formula	0:573
Economy Wave	3:230		1:572
	7:613	Enemy Line, The	MS3:102
EC WW, Primary Duties Of	7:153	Enrollment in Suppressive Groups	1:894
Effective Hatting	MS2:123		2:434
Efficiency and Flaps	0:261	Enrollment on Self-Determinism	2:515
VIII's Nightmare, The	4:1097		4:323
	5:680		6:467
Eligibility for OT Levels	4:816	Enrollment on the Hubbard Key to	
Emergencies and Accounts		Life Course	4:655
Personnel	3:252	Entheta Letters and the Dead File,	
Emergency Headquarters	7:45	Handling Of	1:970
Emergency Library	2:697		2:661
Emergency, State Of	0:621	Environmental Control	0:251
	1:549		MS1:280
E-Meter Drills	4:626		MS1:445
E-Meters Allowed	2:381	Envisioning the Ideal Scene	MS1:144
	4:627	Equipment	0:189
E-Meters and Books for Academy			3:397
Students	2:341	Equipment of Organizations, The	0:186
	4:363		3:388
	5:723	Errors	MS1:38
E-Meters to Be Approved	2:377	Essay on Management, An	7:567
	7:1289	Establishing, Holding the Form of	
Employing and Discharging of		the Org	MS1:312
Personnel	1:245		MS2:119
Employment of Criminals			MS2:262
Forbidden	1:160	Establishment and the HAS	MS1:356

Establishment Officer, The	MS2:3	Ethics Officers	1:684
Estates Production Statistics	7:1402	Ethics Orders	1:979
Estates Restored to Dept. 21	7:1398	Ethics Penalty for Word Clearers	4:505
Estimated Purchase Orders	3:295		5:474
Esto Failures	MS1:304	Ethics Presence	0:247
	MS2:103		7:706
	MS2:254	Ethics Program No. 1	1:788
Estos	MS2:184	Ethics Program No. 1 Case	
Esto Series 30	MS2:126	Actions	5:599
Ethics (23 Jan. 59)	1:719	Ethics Protection	0:502
Ethics (18 June 68)	0:509		1:767
	1:786	Ethics Protection Conditions, Blue	
Ethics (4 Apr. 72)	0:525	Star, Green Star, Gold Star	0:662
	MS2:68		1:578
Ethics: Advanced Courses	1:637		5:366
Ethics and Admin, Slow Admin	0:244	Ethics, Review	0:491
	1:893		1:744
	7:701		4:354
Ethics and Executives	MS2:245		5:109
Ethics and Missions	1:795	Ethics, the Design Of	0:517
Ethics and Personnel	MS1:406		1:483
Ethics and Personnel, Adds To	MS1:451	Ethnic Surveys	MS3:68
Ethics and Study Tech	0:44		MS3:247
	1:899	Eval Correction	MS1:142
	4:481	Evaluation	7:818
Ethics and the C/S	1:839	Evaluation and Programs	MS1:167
	4:1130	Evaluation, Criticism Of	MS1:138
	5:716	Evaluation Success	MS1:173
Ethics and Word Clearing	4:504	Evaluation: The Situation	MS1:154
	5:473	Evening Foundations	7:312
Ethics Authority Section, Office		Evidence, Admissibility of, in	
of LRH	7:1263	Hearings, Boards or	
Ethics Chits (1 July 65)	1:703	Committees	1:954
	4:102	Examinations (18 Oct. 61)	5:163
	5:20	Examinations (5 Sept. 64)	5:174
Ethics Chits (15 Dec. 65)	0:549	Examinations (24 May 65)	5:114
	1:707	Examinations (12 Oct. 66)	4:478
Ethics Conditions: Hang-up at		Examinations of Academy	
Doubt	0:576	Students to Be Done by Director	
	1:605	of Processing	5:158
Ethics E-Meter Check	1:765	Examiner Bonuses	3:358
Ethics, Justice and the Dynamics	0:451		5:240
	1:486	Examiner's Form	5:282
Ethics Officer Hat	1:681	Examiner's Form—Additional	
Ethics Officer, His Character, The	1:687	Data	5:298

Examiner's 24-Hour Rule	5:279	Executive Responsibility for	
Examining Resources	MS1:177	Training Staff	0:220
Exam 24-Hour Rule			5:419
(Additional Information)	5:281		7:789
Exchange	MS2:222	Executives	7:585
Exchange, Org Income and		Executives and Governing Body,	
Staff Pay	0:317	Errors and Answers	7:321
	MS2:400		MS3:301
Exec Esto Hatting Duties	MS2:21	Executives of Scientology	
Execution of Evaluations	MS1:182	Organizations	7:746
Executive Council (21 Dec. 66)	7:913	Executives' Pay	5:402
Executive Council (26 Oct. 68)	6:86	Executive Success	MS2:291
	7:915		MS2:380
Executive Council Network	7:165		MS3:219
Executive Council Network		Executive, The	MS2:215
Disbanded, The	7:162	Executive Time Salvage and	
Executive Director Comm Lines	7:638	Conferences Curtailed	7:894
Executive Director Sec EDs	1:425	Exercise	0:225
	7:1317		5:639
Executive Division (2 Aug. 65)	7:71	Expansion of Your Org	7:849
Executive Division (21 Jan. 66)	7:96	Expansion, Theory of Policy	0:124
Executive Division Organization			7:354
and Its Theory and Purpose	7:105		MS3:334
Executive Facilities, Facility		Ex-Staff Free Service	0:175
Differential	7:343		3:173
	MS3:323		4:221
Executive Intention	MS2:228		5:432
Executive Letter Unit	7:1194		6:769
Executive Misbehavior	1:898	Extension Course Completion	6:508
	7:714	Extension Course Curriculum	6:501
Executive Posting Qualifications	MS1:471	Extension Courses	6:510
	MS2:307	Extension Course Students, Letters	6:504
Executive Responsibility for			
Technical Excellence	4:33		

F

Fable, A	7:1127	Field Activities	6:693
"Failed" Cases	5:657	Field Auditor Fees	6:734
Failed VIIIs	4:826	Field Auditor Rates	6:715
	5:785	Field Auditors	6:723
Failed PR	MS3:165	Field Auditors Become Staff	6:629
"Failure to Apply . . ."	7:694	Field Certificates	5:306
Failure to Follow or		Field Ethics	1:796
Apply Condition	0:653		6:724
	1:565	Field Office Communication	1:303
False Attestation	5:212		6:689
False Data Stripping	MS2:134	Field Offices	6:688
False Reports	1:869	Field Staff Member Commissions	6:643
Familiarity	MS1:29	Field Staff Member Courses	6:653
Fantastic New HGC Line, The	4:939	Field Staff Member I/C Hat, Field	
	5:608	Staff Members	6:639
Fast Courses	4:389	Field Staff Member Program	6:649
Fast Flow and Ethics	1:785	Field Staff Member Selection	
	5:139	Papers and Commissions	3:254
Fast Flow Grades Cancelled	5:255		6:645
Fast Flow Training	4:644	Files	MS2:46
	5:218	Files Accuracy	MS2:101
Fast Line Sec EDs and		Filling Posts	1:177
Admin Orders	7:1309	Films and Tapes Not Prohibited	2:374
FBO FP Adjudication	MS2:373		6:341
FBO Hat	MS2:332		7:1215
FC Communicator Basic Hat	1:304	Final HPA Exam, HCO Board	
FC Policy Letter (1 Jan. 57)	3:285	of Review	4:559
FC Policy Letter (5 May 71)	2:552		5:150
	6:386	Final Target Attachment	MS1:134
FEBC Graduate Policy	5:523	Final Targets	MS1:131

Finance Course, Vital Action 3:68
Finance Directives Cancelled 3:77
Finance Stress in an Org 3:85
7:724
Financial Enrollment Procedure 2:481
4:214
Financial Irregularities 3:97
Financial Lines and Legal Lines 7:1091
Financial Management (1 May 58) 3:20
Financial Management (3 June 59) 3:28
7:926
Financial Management Building
Fund Account 3:42
7:934
Financial Planning (26 Nov. 65R) 3:271
MS2:409
Financial Planning (15 Dec. 66) 7:947
Financial Planning Checklist for
the Promotional Actions of an
Organization 3:79
7:952
Financial Planning
Program No. 1 MS2:419
Financial Planning Regarding
Property Renovations and
Construction 3:281
7:961
Financial Planning—
Responsibility For MS2:406
Financial Planning Tips MS2:319
Financial Reports,
Washington, DC 7:887
First Financial Policy 3:72
First Policy 0:321
3:260
6:589
7:20
Fish and Game 7:1359
Fixed Public Consumption
of Product 7:507
Flag Banking Officer Purposes MS2:344
Flag Banking Officers MS2:317
Flag Executive Briefing Course 5:521
Flag External Expenses MS2:360
Flag External Expenses Addition MS2:363

Flag Rep Key Ingredients 7:1411
Flag Representative, Orders To 7:1416
Flag Representative, Purpose,
Duties and Statistic 7:1412
Flag Representative, Purpose Of 7:1407
Flag Rep Statistics 7:1419
Flash Colors and Designations 1:415
Fliers, Definition and Use MS3:293
Floating Needle on Former
Releases 5:233
Flowers 7:1344
Flowers, Care Of 7:1385
Flow Line for Personnel 1:157
4:38
Flows and Expansion, the Fast
Flow System 1:661
5:132
7:670
Flubless C/Sing 4:1118
F/Ning Auditors 5:702
Folder, The 4:1010
Folder Error Summaries 4:1007
Folders, Marking Of 4:1059
Follow Policy and Lines MS2:36
Former Saint Hill Staff 7:610
Form of the Org, The MS2:111
Form of the Org and Schedules MS2:116
Formulas 0:581
1:590
Foundation (16 Aug. 65) 6:478
Foundation (16 Sept. 65) 6:212
Foundation, The 7:297
Foundation and Day Orgs Separate 7:313
Foundation, Basic Course
Organization 6:473
Foundation, Basic Course
Organization Correction 6:477
Foundation Central Files Officer
and Address In-Charge 2:670
Foundation Course Change 6:480
Foundation Course Hours 6:484
Foundation Data, The 7:308
Foundation, Forming the
Foundation, The 1:757, 7:302

Foundation Income 3:171
7:316
Founder 7:1206
Founding Scientologist Certificate 5:335
Four Vital Training Data for
Training Hats and Registrar 2:488
4:302
FP Activation MS2:330
FP and Necessities MS2:402
Free Clear Estimates, Free
Clear Tests 2:490
4:841
Free Courses 3:148
Freeloaders (19 June 58) 1:248
3:183
Freeloaders (2 Dec. 69) 3:194
Freeloaders (13 Oct. 72R) 1:255
"Free Memberships for
Six Months . . ." 6:815
Free Release Check 2:531
3:162
5:120
Free Scientology Center 4:676
6:328
Free Services = Free Fall 2:451
3:170
4:220
Friday Cables 1:460, 7:622

FSM Awards 6:659
FSM Commissions 6:658
FSM Commissions, Payment
of Cancelled 3:261
FSM I/C Postings 6:670
FSM Penalty for Refunds,
Repayments And Bounced
Checks 6:664
FSM Section, Department 18
Statistics 6:671
FSM Selection Slips 6:651
FSMs FOLOs Commissions 6:662
Full Danger Condition Handling 0:611
MS2:205
Full Hatting 1:294
Full Product Clearing Long Form MS2:49
Full Table of Courses and
Classification, Classification
Correction 4:182
Fully Hatted Org Staff Members,
HCO Gross Divisional Statistic 1:105
Fundamentals of Administration
No. 2 7:780
Funds or Favors Received 4:1244
Furniture and Quarters 7:1332
Further Illogics MS1:14
Future Continental Officer Status 7:47
Future of Scientology, The 7:1151
Future Programs 7:1174

G

General Amnesty 1:951
General Form of Release Contract 2:418
7:1066
General Office Orders 2:336
3:381
Get Your Technical Division In,
Fully Manned and Functioning! 4:95
Gifts 7:1200
Giving the Pc Full Hours 4:850
Glossary of C/S Terms 4:1106
Goals Check 4:874
Good Service 0:276
2:435
Good Versus Bad
Management 7:340
MS3:320
Goodwill 0:332
6:625
MS2:297
MS3:168
Good Workers 0:156
5:580
Government Conflicts 7:1022
Government Project Stable Data 6:590
7:993
Gradation Program, Revised 4:181
Grade Award Insignia 5:356
Grade Chart Streamlined for
Lower Grades 2:460, 4:193, 6:419

Grades Above Clear 4:802
5:242
Grade Subsidy for Staff Forbidden
in Other Orgs 0:174
3:216
5:430
Gradient Scale of Personnel
Procurement 2:50
6:147
Graph Change, Ad Council
Statistic 7:908
Great "Charity" Swindle, The 7:1131
Grievances 7:886
Gross Book Sales—Definition 2:297
Gross Divisional Statistics 7:787
Gross Income/Corrected Gross
Income Ratio, Failed Cases
and Failed Students 2:111
3:87
4:153
5:659
6:555
7:861
Gross Income Senior Datum 0:358
2:672
7:851
Grounds Regulations, Staff and
Students 7:1384
Group Officer 6:845

27

H

Handle	7:721	Handling with Auditing	2:440
Handling Danger Conditions	0:610		4:927
	1:587		5:683
Handling Flubbed Pcs	5:655	HAS Apprenticing Actions	1:76
Handling of Bills	3:313	HAS Certificates	5:313
Handling of Bounced Checks			6:460
and Refunds	MS2:325	HAS Co-audit	6:453
Handling of Hubbard		HAS Co-audit and Comm Course	
Communications		(25 Mar. 59)	6:455
Offices, The	1:20	HAS Co-audit and Comm Course	
	7:1161	(3 Apr. 59)	6:457
Handling of Past-Life Auditing	4:257	HAS Co-audit Courses	6:459
Handling of Photographs	2:271	HASI Group Secretary	6:691
Handling of Purchased or Rented		HASI–HCO Relationship	
Mailing Lists, The	2:709	Discussed	7:195
	6:218	HAS Standard Actions	1:73
Handling of Telex Machines	1:458	HAS Troubles	1:81
Handling Overloaded Posts	7:801	Hat Checkout Sequence	1:277
Handling Policy, Plans,		Hat Checksheet Requirements	5:509
Programs, Projects and		Hat Knock Off	1:285
Orders Defined	MS1:100	Hat of PE HCO WW	6:314
Handling Situations	0:245	Hats (28 Feb. 57)	0:193
	7:703		1:266
Handling the Public Individual	0:323	Hats (17 Sept. 70)	1:280
	1:125	Hats (22 Sept. 70)	0:199
	2:80		MS1:202
	6:202		MS1:411
Handling the Suppressive Person,			
the Basis of Insanity	1:990, 4:82	Hats and Counter-Effort	MS1:213

Hats and Other Folders	0:194
	1:270
Hats, Basic and False	1:279
Hats, Not Wearing	0:572
	1:580
Hats of the Department of Promotion and Registration, The	2:55
Hats Program Pitfalls	MS1:448
Hats, the Reason For	0:196
	1:273
Hats—Vital Data	MS1:403
Hatting	1:295
Hatting and the Environment	0:207
	MS2:203
	MS2:310
Hatting Course Personnel	1:289
Hatting Officer	1:296
Hatting the Esto	MS2:14
Hatting the Product Officer of the Division	MS2:82
Hatting the Right Way	1:292
Hat Turnover	3:329
Have You Lived Before This Life? Sales	2:330
HCO Accounts Worldwide	3:23
HCO Administrator	7:26
HCO Area Secretary Hat Addition	5:552
HCO Area Secretary Hat Material	1:30
HCO Area Secretary Saint Hill	7:222
HCO Board of Review	4:550
	5:146
HCO Board of Review, Class II Awards	5:165
HCO Board of Review Duties	5:94
HCO Board of Review, Function and Practice	5:129
	7:1171
HCO Board of Review Goal	5:303
HCO Book Account (30 Nov. 64)	2:281
	3:187
HCO Book Account (17 June 68)	2:312
HCO Book Account Cash-Bills	2:315
HCO Book Account Policy, Receipt and Use of Membership Monies	2:285, 6:250
HCO Book Administrator Hat	2:327
HCO Cable and Despatch Designation System	1:451
HCO Communicator Basic Hat and Comm System, HCO Offices	1:355
HCO Communicator Has Program Checking Hat	7:1269
HCO Communicator Hat	1:358
HCO Communicator Writes from South Africa	3:374
HCO Confessionals	1:648
	4:995
HCO Continental	7:1182
HCO Cope Officer	1:79
HCO Corporations	7:1116
HCO Establishment Functions	MS1:298
HCO Exec Sec Condition	1:55
HCO Exec Sec Duties, Org Exec Sec Duties	7:695
HCO Executive Secretary Continental	7:24
HCO Files	3:287
HCO Forbidden Activities	7:183
HCO Income, Memberships— Tape Plays	2:289
	6:817
"HCO Is Entitled . . ."	1:26
"HCO Is Now Handling . . ."	7:174
HCO, Ltd. HPA/HCA Certificate Conditions	4:564
HCO Makes the Org	1:56
HCO May Do Confessional Lists	1:638
	4:973
HCO Monies and Book Stocks	3:186
HCO Office Designations and Personnel	1:27
HCO Order of Importance of Actions	1:33
HCO Organization, Future Plans	7:216
HCO Personnel Training	1:357
HCO Project Engineer: "Have You Lived Before?"	2:149
	7:591
HCO Puzzles	1:84

HCO Reception	1:133	HGC Cure, Intern Training and	
HCO Staff Qualification		Staff Auditors	4:903
Requirements	1:101		5:488
HCO Standing Order No. 5,		HGC Policy, Results or Else	4:838
Students	4:578		5:729
	5:167	HGC Preprocessing	
HCO Stat Penalty	1:94	Security Check	4:858
HCO (Sthil) Ltd. Course		HGC Processing Liability	4:861
Staff Transfers	4:1054	HGC Psychotic Applicants	4:1021
	5:665	"Hidden Data Line," The	4:347
HCO (Sthil) Ltd. Transport	7:1376	High Crime	1:890
HCO, the Elite Corps	1:88		4:18
HCO Theory of Communication	1:359		5:778
HCO Traffic	1:132	High-Crime Checkouts and Word	
HCO Volunteer Sec		Clearing	5:805
Policy Revised	6:707	High Ethics for High Conditions	0:661
HCO Washington, DC	7:28		1:577
HCO WW Changes Quarters		Hiring of Staff Auditors	4:836
and Address	7:27	Hiring Personnel, Line For	1:162
HCO WW Electric Stencil-Cutting		Historical Precedence of Ethics	1:774
Machine	1:405	Hold the Form of the Org, Don't	
HCO WW Internal Comm		Bring about Danger Conditions	0:582
Schedule	1:365		7:249
HCO (WW) Ltd., Central		Honest People Have Rights, Too	0:461
Org Activities	7:48		1:481
HCO WW Points of Concentration	7:36	Honesty and Case Gain	1:848
HCO WW Projects	7:30	Housing—Staff, Students,	
HCO WW Security Form 7B	1:620	Preclears	0:172
	5:560	How Ethics Gets Harsh	1:810
Healing Policy in Field	6:711	How to Build a Sauna	4:1224
Healing Promotion	2:158	How to Confess in HCO	7:1186
	4:864	How to Correctly Determine a	
Heed Heavy Traffic Warnings	0:380	Stat Trend	7:531
Held From Above,		How to Defeat Verbal Tech	
Double-Hatting	MS1:330	Checklist	0:23
Help Me Put in the New Lines	6:289		4:31
	7:197		5:804
HGC Admin Partial Hat, Staff		How to Do a Staff Job	0:232
Auditor Assignment	4:250	How to Do Surveys	MS3:45
HGC Allowed Processes	4:1056		MS3:220
HGC and Academy Prices		How to Do Theory Checkouts	
for Minors	3:146	and Examinations	4:395
HGC Auditing Policies	4:843	How to Fill Jobs	7:757
HGC Clearing	4:866	How to Find a Why on a Person	
HGC Cure (Continued)	4:907, 5:492	and Handle	5:791

How to Find and Establish an
Ideal Scene   MS1:50

How to Get Results in an HGC   4:949

   5:690

How to Handle Black Propaganda   MS3:77

How to Handle Work   0:399

How to Interview People   2:493

   4:40

   6:158

How to Maintain Credit Standing
and Solvency   3:245

   7:940

How to Organize an Org   MS1:199

How to Prevent an Ethics Officer
from Doing His Job   1:692

How to Procure People   2:601

How to Program an Org,
Corrections and Addition,
Sequence of Programs
Correction   7:369

   MS3:349

How to Program an Org, Saint
Hill Programs   7:362

   MS3:342

How to Raise Stats   0:684

   2:104

   4:127

   7:856

How to Raise Your Own Statistics
and Pay   0:688

How to "Sell Scientology"   6:164

How to "Sell" Scientology to
Your Friends   6:675

How to Study This Course   0:31

How to Write an ED or Order   7:711

How to Write Up a
Cramming Order   5:786

How You Are Limiting the Size
and Income of Your Org   4:407

   6:398

How You Can Increase the Size
and Income of Your Org   4:411

   6:402

How You Handle Demands
for Personnel   7:450

   MS1:465

   MS3:430

HPA Grants   6:705

HPA/HCA Policy   4:571

   6:783

HPA/HCA Requirement   5:319

HPA/HCA Training   4:586

HPA/HCA Written Examination   4:609

   5:173

Hubbard Communications Office
Organizing Board   1:19

Hubbard Key to Life Course
High Crime   1:911

   4:647

Hubbard Key to Life Course
Routing Forms   4:650

Hubbard Recognized
Scientologist   4:620

   5:194

Humanitarian Objective and
Gung-ho Groups   6:861

I

"I Am Worried about Your
Foundation . . ."   7:309
Ideal Ideal Scene, The   MS1:178
Ideal Org, The (20 May 70)   0:342
                                    6:618
                                    7:282
Ideal Org, The (12 Mar. 75)   MS1:152
Ideas and Compilations
  Branch WW   7:124
Illegal Pcs, Acceptance of,
  Addition Regarding Purification
  Rundown   2:585
                                    4:1039
                                    5:763
                                    6:412
Illegal Pcs, Acceptance of,
  High Crime PL   1:904
                                    2:581
                                    4:1037
                                    5:761
                                    6:407
Illegal Processing   4:1116
Immigration Tip   7:1094
Importance and Executives   7:23
Important Certification Change   5:315
Important Change in Reports   1:658
                                    7:39
Important Executive Action   7:512
Important Explanation, Auditing
  Restrictions   4:619

Important Information on Policy
  Letters   7:180
Income   2:399
                                    3:103
Income Cutatives and Salary Sum   0:301
                                    3:91
Income Data   2:532
Income Flows and Pools,
  Principles of Money
  Management   MS2:349
Income Records   3:383
Income Report Required   3:121
Income Sources (20 Mar. 57)   2:386
                                    3:101
Income Sources (1 Mar. 71)   MS2:328
Income Tax Reform   7:1063
Incoming Calls for LRH   7:1170
INCOMM   MS2:458
Indicators of Orgs   0:496
                                    1:750
                                    7:679
Individuals vs. Groups   MS3:150
Inept Students   4:301
Infinite Expansion   MS1:303
Information Boards   1:348
Information Collection   MS1:21
Information Concerning the WW
  Time Machine   7:692
Information Packets   6:217

Informing Public of Test Results   2:600

4:228

6:271

"In HCO Policy Letter . . ."   6:652

Injustice   0:521

1:811

Inspection Officer   1:191

Inspection of Hat Folders   1:268

Inspection of Low Stats   1:528

Inspections   7:636

Instability   7:810

Instant Impression   MS3:287

Instant Service Project   4:125

Institutional and Shock Cases,
Petitions From   1:798

2:549

Instruction and Examination:
Raising the Standard Of   4:327

5:175

Instruction Protocol, Official   4:287

5:143

Instructions to Attorney
or Solicitors   7:1061

Instructor Hats   4:322

Instructor's Conference
Report Form   4:755

"Instructors or HCO Staff
Processing . . ."   1:855

4:1246

Intensives for Staff   5:543

Intern Checksheets, Okays
to Audit   5:852

International Changes or Area
Changes of Address   2:708

International Officers at WW,
Alert Council   7:137

Interns   5:849

Internships and Case Supervisors   5:844

Internships, Electronic Attestation
Form   5:854

Internships Versus Courses   4:417

5:856

Intern Training   5:843

Inter-Org Exchange of Students
and Fees   3:208

5:123

Intervention   7:351

MS3:331

Interviews   1:824

2:586

4:979

5:764

6:413

7:730

Int Exec Div Relation to
Saint Hill Org   7:104

Investigatory Procedure   MS1:72

Invoice Form and Routing Forms   4:263

Invoice Routing   3:135

Invoice Routing, All Invoicing
Stations   3:136

2:292

Invoicing and Collection
of Money   3:119

4:215

6:383

Irrationality   MS1:58

Issue Authority for Mimeo   7:1279

Issue Authority for Translations
of Dianetics and Scientology
Materials   6:767

7:1321

Issue Authority Required
for Mimeo   7:1308

Issues—Types Of   1:429

7:1322

Issuing of Certificates   5:336

"It Has Come to My
Attention . . ."   2:401, 6:157

J

Job Endangerment Chits   0:551
    1:709
    7:329
    MS3:309

Jokers and Degraders   1:822

Justice (18 Mar. 65)   0:481
    1:734

Justice (12 Apr. 65)   1:741

Justice (24 Feb. 69)   0:513, 1:540

Justice Codes, HCO, Org Executive
    and Divisional Secretaries,
    Justice on, and Auditing Of   1:739
    5:583

Justice—Correct Application   0:520
    1:809

Justice of Scientology, Its Use and
    Purpose, Being a Scientologist, The   0:483
    1:939

Justice Policy Letters,
    Corrections   1:942, 7:1300

K

Keep Academy Checksheets Up to
  Date   4:459
                                5:209
Keeper of Tech, Office of LRH   7:1273
Keeping Admin Working   0:70
                                7:486
                           MS3:466

Keeping Dianetics Working
  in an Area   4:633
                                5:677

Keeping Scientology Working   0:7
                                  1:7
                                  2:7
                                  3:7
                                  4:7
                                  5:7
                                  6:7
                                  7:7
Keeping Stocks Up   2:307

Key Ingredients, The   7:405
                           MS3:385
Key Questions, Director of
  Success Duty, The   5:213
                              6:823
Keys   0:185
                              3:396

Key to the Organizational Chart
  of the Founding Church of
  Scientology of Washington, DC   7:189
Kha-Khan   1:838
Knowledge, Definition Of   0:270
Knowledge Reports   0:555, 1:713

L

Lamps and Security	7:311	Letter Writer's Code	2:620
Laundry	7:1355	Letter Writing, Amending CF and	
Leadership (3 Nov. 66)	7:332	Procurement, Paper Of	2:597
	MS3:312	Level 0 Comm Course	4:353
Leadership (29 Oct. 71)	MS2:218		6:471
Learning to Use Data Analysis	MS1:105	Liabilities of PR	6:620
Leaving and Leaves	0:177		MS3:3
	1:906	Library	5:724
Leaving Post, Writing Your Hat	0:198	Life Repair Block	4:145
	1:275	Line Design—HGC Lines,	
Legal Aid—HCO	7:1057	an Example	MS1:291
Legal and Dissemination	2:102	Lines and Hats	MS1:293
	6:82		MS1:452
	7:1095	Lines and Terminals	MS1:288
Legal and Promotion	2:133	Lines and Terminals, Routing	0:384
	7:1073		1:311
Legal, Tax, Accountant and			7:771
Solicitor, Mail and Legal		Logic	MS1:10
Officer	1:335	Lonesome?	6:686
	7:1081	Long Distance Phone Calls	
Legal, Tax, Accountant and		and Telegrams	3:314
Solicitor Mail, Incoming		Long Distance Program	6:52
and Outgoing	1:338		7:184
	7:1085	Look Don't Listen	MS2:39
Length of Time to Evaluate	MS1:111	Losses	7:929
	MS2:90	"Lost Tech" of Handling Overts	
Letter Policy	2:604	and Evil Purposes, The	1:914
Letter Reg, Body Reg	2:632		4:992
Letter Reg Hat	2:623		5:453
Letter Registrar Hat	2:605	Lower Grades Upgraded	5:254

M

Magazine Advertisement Policy 2:193
Magazine Motifs 2:223
Magazine Planning 2:221
Magazine Policy 2:186
Magazines (18 Feb. 61) 2:194
6:181
Magazines (14 Dec. 69) 2:215
6:221
Magazines (10 Aug. 72) 2:219
Magazines, Dating Forbidden 2:224
Magazines Permitted, All Orgs 2:211
Magic Formula, The 1:60
7:799
"Magic" of Good Management, The 7:628
Mail 1:324
3:200
Mailing List Policies 0:625
2:705
Mailing Lists and Field Auditors 2:683
6:696
Mail Line 1:323
3:199
Mail Opening 1:334
3:204
Mail Statistic, Dir Comm's
Functions 1:313
Main Weakness, The 1:111
Major Duty of the Hats Officer, A 1:291
Making an Executive MS2:58, MS2:240

Management and Activities of
Scientology Organizations, The 7:833
Management Coordination 7:454
MS3:434
Management Cycle 1:116
5:418
Management Tools Breakthrough 7:483
MS1:373
MS2:199
MS2:304
MS3:463
Manners 0:328
MS3:34
Manning Up an Org 7:448
MS1:324
MS1:463
MS2:272
MS3:428
Marketing Hat MS3:175
Marketing Posters MS3:295
Marketing, Promotion and
Dissemination, Defined MS3:174
Materials, Scarcity Of 4:463
Materiel Administrator Hat
(1 Dec. 58) 3:370
Materiel Administrator—Hat
(7 Mar. 59) 3:372
Matter of Orders, A 7:786
Medical Charts 5:635
Membership Attestations 6:814

41

Membership Monies	6:803	Mission Holders	6:743
Membership Policies	6:816	Mission of the LRH Comm	
Memorandum of Agreement	4:893	Network, The	7:1255
Message Placement	0:377	Mission Policies	6:744
	1:368	Mission Program	6:745
Meter Checks	5:226	Mission Promotion Musts	6:762
Method of Opening and		Missions, Multiple Ownership	6:768
Invoicing Mail	1:325	Mission Summary of Policy	6:749
	3:201	Mistakes	MS2:187
Method One Word Clearing	4:652	Mistakes, Anatomy Of	1:1033
	5:475	Mistakes and PTSness	1:1035
Mimeo	1:427	Misunderstood Words and Cycles	
	2:272	of Action	MS2:132
Mimeo and File Procedure	1:400	Model Hat for an Executive, A	7:753
Mimeo File Folders and Files	1:442	Modification of HPA/HCA,	
Mimeo Files (10 Feb. 71)	1:433	BScn/HCS Schedule	4:567
Mimeo Files (7 Feb. 73)	1:448	Money	MS2:219
Mimeo Files Product	1:437	"Moonlighting"	MS1:417
Mimeo Section	1:435	Moonripping	MS1:474
Mimeo Supply Conservation	1:440	Morale (16 Apr. 70)	6:524
Minimum Book Stocks	2:309	Morale (14 May 72)	0:299
Minimum Personnel of an Org	6:790		7:815
	7:252	Morale Note	7:744
Ministerial Ordination	5:302	More on Lines and Hats	1:276
Ministerial Qualifications	5:304	More on Marketing Basics	MS3:189
Miscellaneous Reports	1:850	More on Staff Member Reports	0:554
	4:261		1:712
	5:296	More Outpoints	MS1:84
Misrepresentation of Dianetics		Moving	7:1334
and Scientology	7:1110	Multiple Sit Eval Format	MS1:124
Missing Ingredient, The	MS3:7	Musical Chairs	1:211
Missing Scene, The	MS1:41	My Own Objectives	6:864
Mission Courses	6:748	My Program to Raise Your Unit	7:210

N

Names and the Local
  Environment   MS3:160
Naming Services and Products   MS3:284
Narrowing the Target   MS1:75
New Book   2:322
New Car Park   7:1387
New Case Supervisor Postings   4:1126
    5:708
New Corp—New Broom   7:605
New FSM Account   3:264
    6:667
New HCO WW Dept   6:163
New Hope for Justice, A   1:962
New Mimeo Line, HCO Executive
  Letter   1:406
New Org Board Design   1:147
New Org Board Design (2)   1:150
New Pattern of Organization, A   7:261
New PE and the New HAS
  Co-audit, The   6:462
New Post Formula, The
  Conditions Formulas   0:561
    1:557
New Posts   7:220
New Preclears   4:912
New Qual Stat, GDS Qual Div   5:73
New Road   7:1348
News   7:1049
New Saint Hill Certificates and
  Course Changes   4:746

New Status of Honorary Awards   5:343
New Students Data, Star-rated for
  New Students   4:757
New Students Sec Check   4:714
New Testing Promotion Section   6:273
New Type of Crime, A   1:908
New Work Arrangements,
  Outside Staff   7:1360
Nine-Division Org   6:81
1965 Saint Hill Objectives   7:67
"No Changes of Positions . . ."   7:1329
No-Gain-Case Student, The   1:1001
    4:341
No-Interference Area Clarified
  and Re-enforced, The   4:1111
"Noise" and Organization   1:152
    7:797
Noise, Session Interruption   4:897
"No New Charters or Contracts . . ."   6:690
Non-Existence Formula Expanded   0:578
    1:591
Non-Scientology Staff   0:152
Not-Dones, Half-Dones and
  Backlogs   7:431
    MS2:225
    MS3:411
"Now That the
  Proportionate . . ."   3:328
Numbering of Certificates   5:358
Numbering of Mimeo Issues   1:438

O

Objective One	4:871	Open Letter to All Clears, An	4:796
OCA Graphs	4:236		6:656
	6:307	Open Letter to All FSMs, An	6:673
OEC "Policy" Clarified	2:347	Operating at Risk	0:255
Offenses and Penalties	0:467	Operating Standard Rule, An	1:808
	1:861	Operational, Definition Of	0:190
Office of LRH	7:1209		7:1393
Office of LRH Supplies	7:1208	Opinion Leaders	MS3:17
Office of LRH WW		Oral Examination for HPA/HCA	5:172
Reorganization	7:1214	Order Board and Time Machine	0:375
Office of the Treasurer	3:63		1:518
Off-line and Off-policy—Your			7:677
Full In-Basket	0:404	Ordering People to Processing or	
OIC Board	1:660	Training	2:483
OIC Change, Cable Change	5:74		3:143
Okays to Audit in HGCs	4:946		5:103
	5:846	Order or Chaos, the Quality of the	
Old ACC Students	2:436	HCO Division, an HCO Div	
	6:220	Checklist for Quality	1:1057
Old Poem, An	0:532	Orders (7 June 61)	1:404
On Giving Checkouts	4:396		7:1288
Only Organization Offices Can		Orders (5 May 74)	0:144
Certify Clears	5:307	Orders and Responsibility	0:139
"Only 75 Copies . . ."	1:389	Orders During Absence	7:1179
	2:173	Orders, Illegal and Cross—How to	
	7:1283	Keep Out of Trouble	0:145
Only SSO Can TIP	5:435	Orders of the Day	7:727
On-Policy	0:28	Orders, Precedence of Personnel,	
	7:806	Titles Of	7:115
On-Policy Registration	2:561	Orders, Query Of	0:141

Orders to Divisions for Immediate
   Compliance   4:129
       5:267
       7:284
Orders to HCOs   1:53
Orders Versus Arbitraries   0:140
Order Versus Disorder   0:305
       MS1:342
       MS2:176
Org Affluences   7:853
Organization (19 Nov. 58)   1:143
       7:22
Organization (7 Mar. 69)   0:87
       7:776
Organizational Basics   0:89
       7:293
Organizational Enturbulence   0:68
Organizational Health Chart   2:47
       7:171
Organizational Indoctrination   1:265
       7:743
Organizational Intention   6:583
Organizational Suppressive Acts   1:988
Organization and Morale   MS1:230
Organization and Survival   1:86
       7:811
Organization at Saint Hill   7:87
Organization Chart   1:50
Organization, Definition Of   7:272
Organization Executive Course
   Checksheets   5:427
Organization GPM Unit   4:769
Organization Information Center   1:653
Organization Misunderstoods   0:39
       MS1:244
       MS1:421
Organization of a PE
   Foundation, The   6:315
Organization of a Scientology Org   7:239
Organization of Corporations   7:188
Organization of the Int Exec
   Division, Statistics of the
   International Executive Division   7:89
Organization of the Public
   Divisions   6:108

Organization Posts—Two Types   0:86
Organization Program No. 1   0:98
       6:92
       7:275
Organization Rudiments   1:503
Organization Secretary Hat   7:611
Organization, the Design of the
   Organization   0:95
       1:144
       7:246
Organization—The Flaw   0:66
       1:526
       5:138
       7:700
Organizing and Hats   MS1:220
Organizing and Product   MS1:218
Org Bd Cutatives   MS1:208
Org Board, An   1:151
       7:796
Org Board and Production   7:802
Org Board for the Department of
   the Chaplain   6:530
Org Board Knowledge   1:154
Org Division, Income Dept   3:131
Org Ethics and Tech   0:499
       1:754
       2:85
       4:99
       6:371
       7:844
Org Exec Course Introduction, The   0:3
       1:3
       2:3
       3:3
       4:3
       5:3
       6:3
       7:3
Org Image, The   0:335
       6:606
       MS3:140
Org Image Program No. 1 US   6:616
Org LRH Communicator Reports
   to LRH Comm Int   7:1235

Org Magazines: Policy and Format	2:228	Out-Ethics Indicators	0:533
Org "Move" Mags	2:225		7:1259
Org Officer	MS1:354	Out-Ethics Symptoms	1:835
Org Officers, Product Officers,			7:736
Estos	MS1:358	Outflow (6 July 59)	0:367
	MS2:185		1:306
Org Programing (6 Dec. 63)	3:124		2:117
	4:167	Outflow (9 Apr. 60)	2:610
Org Programing (24 Feb. 64)	4:172	Outline of Activities	7:1168
	7:930	Outline of PTS Handling	5:437
Org Reduction or Eradication	1:896	Out of Valence (OCA Graphs)	4:231
	7:916		6:299
Org Rudiment Reports to Me	1:514	Outpoints, More	MS1:126
Org Rudiments Section	1:521	Outside Auditing (20 May 57)	4:1243
Orgs Are Saint Hill FSMs	3:349	Outside Auditing (27 May 58)	4:1245
	6:642	Outside Funds or Gifts—Staff	
Org Services	6:722	Member Policy	1:729
Org Staff W/H Checks	5:574	Outside Pcs of Staff Members	1:619
Org, Suppression Of	1:254		4:1248
Original *Auditor* Journal		Outside Staff Duties, Assignment Of	7:1365
Policy, The	2:247	Outstanding Copyrights and	
OT Central Committee		Marks	7:1058
(11 Aug. 67)	6:843	Out-Tech (22 Nov. 67)	1:1032
	7:125		4:20
OT Central Committee			5:783
(30 Nov. 68)	7:152	Out-Tech (28 Aug. 68)	5:652
OT Courses	4:808	Out-Tech and How to Get It In	4:1078
OT Orgs	MS2:427		5:669
OT Regulations	4:793	Overfilled In-Basket—Bad News	0:420
	6:842	Overload and Hatting	1:293
OT Section Awards	5:365		7:809
OT WW Liaison Unit, OT Central		Owner of Materials, the Legal	
Committee	7:144	View	2:278
"Our First Lesson . . ."	4:299		7:1059
Our Goals	6:741	O/Ws and Evaluation	MS1:187
Our Role in the World	7:1012	O/W Write-ups	0:535, 1:843

P

Paint, Odorless	7:1388	PE Course	6:468
Pattern for City Offices	6:774	PE Course Abolished	6:321
Pattern of a Central		PE Handout	6:293
Organization, The	2:503	PE Literature	6:179
	3:231	Penalties for the Hiring or	
	4:44	Recruiting of Institutional or	
	7:199	Insane Persons	1:168
Pattern of District Office	6:784	People's Questions	0:322
Pay Card	3:337		2:598
Pay for Goals Finding	4:720		6:156
Pay of Executives	5:403	People Who Don't Do Their Jobs	0:422
Pc Application for Major Actions	2:546	Pep	5:640
	4:1029	Perfect Dissemination Program, The	2:154
Pc Application Form for Any			6:170
Major Auditing Action	2:542	Performance	0:259
	4:1024	Permanent Executives	1:228
Pc Examiner	5:246		5:406
Pc Folder and Its Contents, The	4:1013	Permanent Staff Exam	5:154
Pc Routing, Review Code	4:1060	Permanent Staff Member	
	5:115	Requirements	5:390
Pc Scheduling (19 Nov. 60)	4:248	Permanent Staff Members	1:221
Pc Scheduling (3 Nov. 65)	2:502		5:388
	4:252	Permanent Staff Privilege	1:229
Pcs Released Routing	4:1077		6:804
	5:119	Permanent Staff Requirement	
PE and Lectures	6:472	Changes	5:392
PE Change	6:318	Personnel	1:253
PE Comes after They Have Read		Personnel Control Officer	1:197
a Book	2:284, 6:242	Personnel Departure Requirement	1:183

Personnel Efficiency Foundation	6:313
Personnel Policies, Staff Post Qualifications, Permanent Executives to Be Approved	1:223
	5:394
	7:41
Personnel Policy	MS1:466
Personnel Pools	1:164
Personnel Prediction	MS1:454
Personnel Procurement	1:161
Personnel Programing (29 Aug. 70)	MS1:385
Personnel Programing (22 Jan. 72)	5:424
Personnel Records, Admin Certs	1:230
	5:338
Personnel Requirement	1:203
Personnel, Staff Status	0:209
	1:236
	5:411
Personnel Transfers Can Destroy an Org	MS1:381
Personnel Troubles	1:117
Persons Living In	7:1347
Petition	0:488
	1:742
Petitions	0:490
	1:753
Phone Bill	1:328
	3:144
Phone Costs, or How to Get Wiped Out	3:211
Phone Tips	1:339
	2:578
	3:213
	4:273
Photo Policy for Magazines	2:213
Photos, News and Statistics for Mags and *Auditor*	2:180
Physically Ill Pcs and Pre-OTs	5:622
Pink Sheets	4:446
Plan for California, The	6:710
Planning and Targets	MS2:435
Planning by Product	0:291, MS1:239

Pluspoint List	MS1:148
Policies: Dissemination and Programs	2:197
	4:69
	6:191
Policies in Force, Org/Assoc Secs, HCO Secs	1:517
Policies on Film Usage	4:526
	5:815
	6:343
Policies on Physical Healing, Insanity and Sources of Trouble	1:983
	4:880
	5:104
Policy and HCOB Alterations, High Crime	1:1031
Policy and Orders	0:132
	MS1:249
Policy—Certifying Clears	5:223
Policy Checkouts and E-Meter	5:780
Policy, How to Handle People Who Quote Policy to Show You They Can't Follow It	0:475
	7:773
Policy Knowledge Function	7:1243
Policy of HGCs	4:877
Policy on Payment for Training and Processing	2:478
Policy on Psychiatric and Medical Failures	7:1140
Policy on Sec EDs and Hats	1:269
Policy on Signatures in Publications	2:171
	7:1280
Policy on Technical Information	2:119
Policy: Source Of	0:111
Politics	0:157
	7:1014
Politics, Freedom From	0:159
	7:1020
Positioning Era, The	MS3:249
Positioning in PR	MS3:105
Positioning, Philosophic Theory	MS3:120
	MS3:181
Positioning Surveys	MS3:280

Post Changes	1:252	Press Relations	6:591
Post, Handling Of	0:238		7:1042
Posting	MS2:186	Press Releases	6:599
Posting an Org Board	1:61		7:1043
Post Protection, LRH		Pretended PTS	1:1045
Communicators	7:1258		4:1138
Post Purpose Clearing	5:461	PR Functions	MS3:167
Post Purpose Clearing for		Price Engram	2:428
Management Teams and			3:154
Executives	5:480	Prices Lowered Because of New	
Post Purpose Clearing Revived	5:478	Organization Streamline	6:368
Post Transfers	1:206	Prices, Upper Org	2:457
Potential Trouble Source Routing	1:1011		3:177
	5:121	Priority of Power Processing	4:900
Power Change Violation Repair		Private Mail and Telephone Calls	3:149
Formula	0:651	Private Pcs	4:1247
	1:581	PRO Actions	MS3:137
Power of Veto	7:888	PRO Area Control	6:624
Power Processes (28 Apr. 65)	4:885		MS3:40
	5:739	Problems	0:240
Power Processes (20 May 65)	4:891		7:673
Power Processing for the Public	4:902	Procedure for Certifying Clears	5:308
"Power to Forgive" Certificate	5:373	Procedure for Putting Auditors	
Practical Auditing Skills	4:579	on Staff	4:835
PR and Causation	MS3:72	Procedure on Setting up Central	
PR and Information	MS3:101	Orgs or City Offices	6:780
PR and Purpose	MS3:161	Processing	4:678
PR Area Control, Three Grades		Processing Administrator—Hat	4:241
of PR	MS3:41	Processing of Academy Students	4:563
PR Definition	MS3:16	Processing of Staff Members	5:546
Preclear Declare? Procedure	5:287	Prod—Org, Esto and Older	
Preclear Routing to Ethics	4:1073	Systems Reconciled	7:820
	5:118	Product as an Overt Act, The	0:294
Preparation of HPA/HCA			MS1:242
Certificates	5:323	Product Correction	MS2:74
Prepayments Used for Books	2:346	Production and Establishment—	
	3:207	Orders and Products	MS2:27
Presession Processes	6:174	Production and One's Standard	
Press Agentry	MS3:132	of Living	0:313
Press Book, The	MS3:96		MS1:350
Press Conferences,			MS2:284
Preparation For	MS3:94		MS2:367
Press Policies	MS3:124	Production Bugs	MS1:316

Production Quotas	MS1:326
	MS2:274
Product Officers	7:816
Product–Org Officer System Name Your Product	3:307
	7:443
	MS2:127
	MS3:423
Product–Org Officer System To Get You Have to Know How to Organize	7:446
	MS2:130
	MS3:426
Product–Org Officer System Want Your Product	3:309
	7:445
	MS2:129
	MS3:425
Product Orientation	MS1:376
	MS2:312
Professional Charges (10 Feb. 61)	2:410
	6:706
Professional Charges (14 June 62)	2:417
	3:151
	6:709
Professional Rates (29 May 62)	2:416
	4:218
Professional Rates (13 Nov. 76)	2:454
	3:175
	4:223
Professional Rates Restored	2:415
	3:150
	4:217
Professional Training to Be Done in Academy and Saint Hill Only	4:594
Program Drill	MS2:95
Programing (12 Sept. 59)	7:764
Programing (23 Oct. 59)	0:701
Programs, Use of, How to Save Useless Work	7:807
Project Engineering	7:586
Project Engineers, Three Types	7:590
Promotion	MS3:201

Promotional Actions of an Organization, The	0:346
	1:38
	2:90
	3:51
	4:105
	5:20
	6:65
	7:75
Promotional Functions of Various Depts	2:57
	3:227
	7:32
Promotional Letters	2:606
Promotion Allocations	MS2:357
Promotional Writing Fund	7:923
Promotion and Motivation	6:758
Promotion of Saint Hill, *Auditor* Issue Frequency	2:243
Promotion on PE Foundation	6:180
Promotion Plan, A	2:152
	6:161
Propaganda by Redefinition of Words	MS3:42
Proper Format and Correct Action	MS1:89
Proper Public Routing	6:113
Proportionate Marketing	MS2:379
	MS3:218
Proportionate Pay Plan Proposal	3:325
Provisional Certificate Expiry	5:372
Provisional Class VI Classification	4:761
PR Personality, The	MS1:419
	MS3:14
PrR Promotion	2:405
PR Texts	MS3:70
Psychiatrist at Work, The	7:1137
Psychosis	1:804
PTS Auditing and Routing	1:1012
	4:1084
	5:122
PTS Data	1:1036
	5:431
PTSness and Disconnection	1:1041
PTS People and Leaves	1:1050

PTS Personnel and Finance   MS1:460
    MS2:251
    MS2:354

PTS Sections, Personnel
    and Execs   1:1022
    7:372
    MS3:352

PTS Type A Handling   1:1037

Publications   2:135

Publications Depts and Orgs, How
    to Straighten Out   2:344

Publications Organizations Are
    Sales Organizations   2:355

Public Attacks, Legal Point   7:1092

Public Divisions, The   6:78

Public Divisions and
    Tech/Admin Ratio   1:208
    6:99

Public Divisions, The   6:78

Public Divisions Organizing
    Boards   6:19

Public Divisions Org Board   6:87

Public Exec Sec Privilege   6:101

Public Image   6:600
    7:1044

Public Meetings   6:322

Public Programs Officer, The   6:860

Public Project One   2:160

Public Warning on Psychiatry   7:1142

Publishing Policy, Books and
    Magazines   2:138

Purchase Order Filing   3:293

Purchase Orders   3:288

Purchase Order System   3:291

Purchasing and Check-Signing
    Lines Modified   3:278, MS2:346

Purchasing from Pubs Org   2:313

Purchasing Liability of Staff
    Members   0:183
    3:290

Purification Rundown: a Long-
    Range Detoxification
    Program, The   4:1237

Purification Rundown and
    Atomic War   4:1235

Purification Rundown Replaces
    the Sweat Program, The   4:1203

Purpose and Targets   MS2:438

Purpose of Ad Comm   7:895

Purpose of Class VIII, The
    (20 Oct. 68)   4:823

Purpose of Class VIII, The
    (23 Jan. 75)   4:828

Purpose of HCO WW, The   7:37

Purpose of the Department of
    Personnel Enhancement, The   5:379

Purpose of the Lead Auditor, The   4:1151

Purpose of the Saint Hill Special
    Briefing Course   4:728

Purposes of the Department
    of Registration   2:431

Purposes of the Qualifications
    Division   5:30

Putting an HCO There, How to
    Establish a Division   1:66

Putting New Personnel on the
    Job and Taking Over When
    People Quit or Are
    Transferred   1:181, 7:767

Q

Q and A Checksheet, Checksheet
  of the Hubbard Causative
  Leadership Course 7:440
                     MS3:420
Qual Goofs   5:228
Qual Has No Backlog 5:55
Qualification of Executives 1:222
                             5:393
                             7:769
Qualifications Division 5
  Functions   5:68
Qualifications Division 5
  Organizing Board   5:29
Qualifications of HGC
  Staff Auditors   4:1143
                     5:831
Qualifications of Permanent
  Staff Members   1:184
Qualifications Technical Actions 5:33
Qualities at the Top 7:720
Quality and Admin in
  Central Orgs   0:18, 7:837

Quality Counts   0:16
                     4:16
                     5:16
                     7:835
Quality of Division 6A, a Division
  6A Checklist for Quality, The 6:351
Quality of Division 6B, a Division
  6B Checklist for Quality, The 6:567
Quality of Division 6C, a Division
  6C Checklist for Quality, The 6:877
Quality of Presentation 2:174
                         7:1284
Quality of Service   1:792
                     4:933
                     5:248
                     6:548
Qual Library, The   5:725
Qual Senior Datum   5:52
Qual Stat Change, A New One 5:77
Quarters, Policy Regarding,
  Historical   7:1394
"Quickie" Defined   4:29
Quota Revision   7:608

R

Reading Statistics	0:677
	7:529
Reality of Products	MS1:254
Reality Test for Students	5:161
Real Why, The	MS1:82
Reason for Orgs, The	0:91
	4:159
Reasons Why Div 6s Don't Function	6:83
Rebates	2:523
	3:160
	4:895
	5:742
Reception	1:124
Reception Hat	1:123
Reception Log, In-the-Org List	1:130
Records of Bank Deposits	3:400
Recovering Students and Pcs	4:269
	6:550
Recruit!	7:783
Recruit in Excess	MS1:389
Recruiting Actions	MS1:393
Recruiting and Hiring	1:169
Recruitment Breakthrough	1:171
Red Tag Line, The	4:254
	5:284
Reduction of Refunds, C/Ses and Overload	4:1124
	5:706
Referrals to Field	2:385, 6:685

Refined Definition of PR, A	MS3:104
Reform Mailing Result	6:610
Refund Addition	3:259
	6:818
	7:1084
Refund Notice	2:181
	3:258
	7:1083
Refund Policy	3:242
	7:1068
Refunds and Repayments	3:262
	5:711
	7:1108
Registered Mail	1:337
Registrar (26 Sept. 56)	2:477
	4:834
Registrar (7 Nov. 58)	2:489
Registrar—Dir of Processing, the Most Frequently Lost Line	2:495
Registrar Hat	2:491
Registrar Lost Line	2:499
	4:848
Registrars' Advice Form	2:540
	4:1022
Registrars and Notes	2:569
	7:1107
Registrars, CF and Address	2:426
Registrars—Materials Available To	6:381
Registrar Statistic	2:551

57

Registrar Success	2:516
Registrar—Your Orders	2:702
Registration (25 Nov. 69)	2:538
Registration (22 Aug. 74)	2:576
Registration and Service	4:219
Registration Packet	2:633
Registration Pgm No. 2	2:570
	6:392
Regulations	4:747
	7:50
Regulations, Academies and Courses	4:473
	5:170
Regulations for Auditing of Staff and Students	4:681
	5:588
Rehab and Correction	5:674
Rehabilitation of Artists, The	6:135
Reissue of Materials	2:118
	7:1290
Relationship Between Design and Rough Layout, The	MS3:196
Release and Clear Checkouts	5:238
Release Checkouts (5 Aug. 65)	5:230
Release Checkouts (9 Aug. 65)	5:234
Release Checks, Procedure For	4:1068
	5:748
Release Declaration Restrictions Healing Amendments	4:474
	5:229
Release Declarations	4:1083
	5:235
Release Grades	4:1085
Release Pins	2:380
	5:357
Release Policies, Starting the Pc	2:525
	4:1064
	5:744
Releases	4:1063
Release Stages	4:1074
Releases, Vital Data	4:1057
Religion (29 Oct. 62)	7:1010
Religion (12 Feb. 69)	6:605
	7:1320
Religious Influence in Society	6:867
Religious Philosophy and Religious Practice	6:517
	7:995
Re: OIC Data	6:470
Reorganization (28 May 64)	7:52
Reorganization (9 June 64)	7:633
Repairing Past Ethics Conditions	0:668
	1:607
Repairs and Cleaning of My Office	7:1357
Repetition of Message	MS3:292
Reporting of Theft and Action to Be Taken	0:548
	1:706
	3:398
Reports to OIC	1:657
Requirement for Termination on the SHSBC and Enrollment on Solo Course	4:784
Requirements for Staff Posts	5:389
Re: Sec ED 29 (Tech Div)	4:98
Reserved Payment Account	3:315
Reserve Fund	3:401
Responsibilities of Assistant Org Sec	7:599
Responsibilities of Leaders, The	0:629
	7:376
	MS3:356
Responsibility	1:727
Responsibility Again	4:1050
	5:566
Responsibility, Control and Danger Conditions	0:619
	1:611
	7:738
Responsibility, Definition Of	0:269
Responsibility for HCO Files	1:391
Responsibility for Issue	7:1281
Responsibility for Results	4:55
Restoration of Local Control of Personnel Assignments and Comm Evs	1:260
Restriction on Saint Hill Area	6:708
Results of HCO Technical Investigation	1:749

Return Address	1:333
	2:340
Review	5:734
Review Complete?	5:251
Review Complete, Pc Attestations	5:245
Review of Departments	7:1373
Rewards and Penalties, How to Handle Personnel and Ethics Matters	0:504
	1:769
	7:500
Riches or Poverty, the Quality of the Dissem Division, a Dissem Div Checklist for Quality	2:715
Ridge on the Bridge, The	6:441
Rights of a Staff Member, Students and Preclears to Justice	0:477
	1:730
Rights of the Directors of Training and Processing, Staff Auditors and Instructors Regarding Preclears and Students	4:297
Rights of the Field Auditor, The	6:733
Robotism	1:816
Ron's Journal 1969 No. 3 Political Treatment	7:1134
Ron's Journal 33	6:494

Ron's Journal 35, From Clear to Eternity	4:988
Rooms, Emptying for Cleaning	7:1361
Routine 2-12	4:873
Routing	0:389
	MS2:234
Routing, Ad Comm Reports and Minutes	7:901
Routing and Handling of SHSBC Students	4:783
Routing Despatches	0:383
	1:372
Routing Forms, How to Write One	1:135
Routing of Bulletins and Policy Letters	7:35
Routing of Communication	7:21
Routing of Org Board Changes	7:177
Routing of Profiles	4:230
R6EW	4:789
R6EW and Clear	4:805
	5:250
R2-12, Validation	5:324
Rudiment Checklist for Orgs	1:509
Rudiments (ARC Break) Program	6:559
Rudiments Policy	4:1170
Rush Magazine Note	2:192

S

Safe Ground   MS3:99
Safeguarding Technology   0:21
    5:18
Safe Point, The   MS3:89
Saint Hill Course Changes   4:745
Saint Hill Course Goals   4:737
Saint Hill Enrollment, Materials,
    Courses, and Use of Class VI
    Processes   4:751
Saint Hill Graduates   4:59
Saint Hill Income Peaks,
    Reinforcement of *Auditor*
    Promotion   2:245
Saint Hill Org Board   7:57
Saint Hill Personnel   7:219
Saint Hill Projects Bonus and
    Quota System   7:606
Saint Hill Retread Fee   3:153
    4:730
Saint Hill Retreads   4:716
Saint Hill Solo Audit Course   4:777
Saint Hill Special Briefing Course   4:733
Saint Hill Staff Co-audit, The   5:568
Saint Hill Training Candidates
    from Organizations   5:404
Salary and Unit Pay   3:330
Sale and Conduct of Academy
    Courses   4:554
Sale and Handout of *Certainty*
    Minors   2:328

Sale of Bulletins and Tapes
    Forbidden   2:288
    3:130
Sanity   MS1:32
Sanity or Psychosis, the Quality of
    the Tech Division, a Tech
    Division Checklist for Quality   4:1253
Scarcity of Trained Auditors   4:910
Scholarships, No Discounts   2:456
    6:410
Scientologist, a Manual on the
    Dissemination of Material, The   2:20
    6:25
    7:966
Scientology Cleanup   1:722
Scientology Courses   4:324
    5:485
Scientology Courses Examination
    Policy   5:217
Scientology Library and
    Research, Ltd.   7:1189
Scientology Magazines (26 Jan. 59)   2:188
Scientology Magazines (2 July 59)   2:190
Scientology Magistrate   1:694
    5:456
Scientology Makes a Safe
    Environment   0:486
    6:592
    7:1019
Scientology Marriage Counseling   6:537

Scientology Missionary Hat	6:839
Scientology Organizations Communications System: Despatches	0:368
	1:374
Scientology Orgs Tax and Balance Sheets	3:402
	7:1086
Scientology Org Uniforms	3:393
Scientology Pins	2:378
	5:353
Scientology Technology	4:22
	5:651
Scientology Training, Technical Studies	4:613
Scientometric Testing	4:229
	6:272
Sea Org	7:151
Sea Organization Personnel	7:147
Sea Org Zones of Planning	7:145
Sec Checks on Staff	5:565
Sec ED, Change in Issue and Use	1:420
	7:1310
Sec ED Issue	7:1306
Sec EDs and HCO Exec Letters	7:1232
Sec EDs, Definition and Purpose, Cross-Divisional Orders	1:422
	7:1312
Sec EDs Okay (Continued), Policy Letter Changes and Origins	7:1315
Second Dynamic Rules	1:780
	4:479
Secretarial to the Executive Director Hat	7:598
Secretary to Training Department Hat (Temporary Hat)	6:505
Secret of Fast Courses, The	4:487
Section III OT Prerequisite	4:801
Security	1:386
Security Div 1	1:628
Security of Data	1:635
	4:806
Security of Employment	0:151
	1:249
Security of House	7:1354
Security of Persons Leaving Staffs	5:551
Security Risks Infiltration	1:623
Security Rules	5:556
Selectees Mailing, Selectee Advice Packets	2:635
	6:654
Self-Determinism in Central Organizations	7:627
Selling and Delivering Auditing	2:446
	4:954
Selling Techniques Forbidden	2:514
Senior Case Supervisor Requirements	5:713
Senior HCOs Area and Continental	1:98
	7:1224
Seniority of Orders	0:143
	7:722
Senior Policy	0:284
	2:103
	7:852
Senior Qual Network	5:69
Separation Order	1:763
Sequence of Hatting	MS2:33
Service (29 Oct. 59)	0:273
	4:42
	6:579
Service (27 May 71)	0:277
Service and Workload	0:279
	1:70
	7:803
Service Call-in Committee	7:873
Service Product Officer	MS1:332
	MS2:166
Service Routes for New Public	6:115
Service Routes into SO Orgs	6:121
Service Routes into the FSO	6:127
Services, Illegal Offering	6:756
Services Owing to Mission Holders	6:739
Setting up and Using a Reel-to-Reel Tape Player	4:531
SH FSM Bonus Awards	3:360, 6:661

Shipping Charges	2:343
	3:166
Shipping Department—Invoices	2:279
SH Pcs	5:274
SHSBC Unit Graduation	4:773
SH Staff Auditor's Purpose	4:1184
	5:591
SH–UK ANZO–EU Relationships	7:161
Signatures of Policy Letters	1:426
	7:1318
Signatures on Bulletins, Policy Letters and Sec EDs	1:390
	7:1286
Signs of Success	7:994
Sign-ups and Discounts	3:167
	5:363
"Since People Will Begin to Expect . . ."	2:484
	4:839
Single Declare	4:1100
	5:252
Situation, The	MS1:46
Situation Correction	MS1:140
Situation Finding	MS1:128
Six-Department System	6:792
	7:266
Six Power Processes	4:899
Sliding Scale of Pricing	2:458
	3:178
SLR Ltd. Tape Copying	2:371
Solo and Advance Course Checkouts	4:811
Solo Course Part One, Prerequisites	4:663
Solvency	7:950
Some Allowed Ads	2:269
	6:253
Some Tech Div Policies	2:528
	4:360
	7:1074
Source Acknowledgment	7:1222
Source to Cause	0:250
Space Allocation	7:1335
Space Planning	7:1336
Spatial Reorganization	7:1330
Special Briefing Course	4:717
Special Income	MS2:365
Specialization	7:812
Special Program, Fast Academies	4:372
Special Zone Department	7:1002
Special Zone Plan	6:831
Spectatorism	0:249
Speeding up a Slow Course	4:497
Speed of Service	0:275
	4:119
	7:850
Spheres of Influence	7:1180
Spot Checks	4:451
Squirrel Admin	0:61
	MS1:284
SSO Responsibility for Standard Staff Courses	5:443
Stability	0:67
	7:779
Stabilization of Clears	5:320
Stable Data for Instructors (24 May 57)	4:296
Stable Data for Instructors (4 Sept. 57)	4:300
Staff and Intern Auditors	5:833
Staff Auditing	5:550
Staff Auditing Requirement	5:544
Staff Auditor Advices	1:625
	4:1173
	5:586
Staff Auditor and Supervisor Procurement	4:117
	5:487
Staff Auditors (3 Mar. 59)	4:1145
Staff Auditors (9 Oct. 59)	4:1155
Staff Auditors (10 May 61)	4:1164
Staff Auditors (21 Aug. 64)	1:189
	4:1171
	5:581
Staff Auditor Training	4:853
Staff Auditor Training, Sequence of Training	5:399
Staff Bonuses	3:339
Staff Certificate Requirements	4:851

Staff Clearing	5:563
Staff Clearing—New Policy	5:553
Staff Clearing Program	5:570
Staff Co-audits	4:704
Staff Corrective Actions Requiring Auditing Actions	1:821
Staff Courses Mandatory in Orgs	5:514
Staff Intensives	5:558
Staff List, Notification to Payroll	3:331
Staff Meeting	0:173
Staff Member Reports	0:543
	1:699
Staff Members Auditing Outside Pcs	0:170
Staff Members Auditing Private Pcs	4:1249
Staff Members Ordered to Processing	5:555
Staff Pay (11 Nov. 74)	3:361
Staff Pay (30 Nov. 74)	3:363
Staff Personnel Allowance Saint Hill	7:1369
Staff Policy on Training and Indoctrination Courses	5:385
Staff Post, A	0:229
Staff Regulations	0:171
Staff Regulations, Auditing Versus Job	0:168
	5:576
Staff Regulations, Staff Intensives	5:578
Staff Section Officer Hat	5:381
Staff Status	0:213
	1:240
	3:191
	5:415
Staff Training	5:407
Staff Training Officer	5:496
Staff Training Program No. 2	5:499
Staff Transfers and Dismissals	1:250
Stages of Analysis, The	MS1:185
Standard Admin (9 Nov. 68)	0:51
	7:273
Standard Admin (4 June 71)	0:58
Standard Executive Actions	7:702

Star-rate Checkouts for Process	4:768
	5:184
Star-rates on Tech and Qual Staff	4:1183
	5:777
Start a Scientology Group in Your Area	6:716
Start That Practice!	6:681
State of Clear, The	2:469
	4:202
State of Emergency	7:1183
State of Orgs	1:69
Stat Interpretation	7:523
Statistical Judgment	7:516
Statistic Change, Gross Divisional Statistics, HCOs and Quals, OIC Cable Change	1:89
	5:81
Statistic Change HCOs and Qual, Definitions	1:95
	5:86
Statistic Change, Tech Sec Stat	4:157
Statistic, GDS Div Six	6:77
Statistic Graphs, How to Figure the Scale	0:675
	1:664
	7:505
Statistic Interpretation, Estate Statistic	1:524
	7:1389
Statistic Interpretation, Statistic Analysis	7:335
	MS3:315
Statistic Mismanagement	7:518
Statistic Rationalization	0:682
	7:400
	MS3:380
Statistics	5:54
Statistics, Actions to Take, Statistic Changes	7:497
Statistics and Org Board Copies	1:666
Statistics for Divisions	3:48
	7:898
Statistics, Management By	1:668, 7:514

Stat Push, The   0:692
                                                  MS1:318
                                                  MS2:266
Stat Push Clarified   0:696
                                                  MS1:322
                                                  MS2:270
Stat Recovery, an Analysis of
   Broad Outnesses   7:158
Stats and Progress Board   4:466
Stature   1:834
Status of Auckland   7:46
Status of PE Courses   6:465
Stickers for PABs Wanted   2:698
Strategic Planning   7:469
                                                  MS3:449
Structure of Organization, The
   What Is Policy?   0:114
                                                  7:660
Stuck In   MS2:44
Student Auditing   4:683
Student Auditing of Preclears   4:680
Student E-Metering   4:576
Student Folder, The   4:468
Student Intensives   4:669
Student's Guide to Acceptable
   Behavior   4:475
Students Terminating, Leave of
   Absence, Blown Students   4:366
Students Who Succeed   4:404
                                                  5:795
Student Training, Auditing
   Has Priority   4:713
Study   7:814
Study and Tech Breakthrough   5:787
Study Tech and Post   0:47
                                                  5:470
Study Time   0:222
                                                  5:421
Subject: Communication   1:297
Subproducts, How to Compile a
   Subproduct List   7:826
Substance and First Duty of
   HCO, The   7:1055
Successes of Scientology   6:821

Successful Class VIIIs   4:827
Success Through Communication   6:497
Summary of a Bulletin from the
   Academy in Washington, DC
   Concerning Training, The   4:541
Summary of Classification and
   Gradation and Certification   4:174
Summary of Outpoints   MS1:78
Sunshine Rundown:
   Administration, The   2:472
                                                  4:1002
Super Evaluation   MS1:175
Superior Service Image   4:124
                                                  5:56
                                                  6:585
Supervising Co-audit TRs   4:702
Supervisor Checkouts   4:393
Supervisor Know-How, Handling
   the Student   4:382
Supervisor Know-How, R-factor to
   Students   4:384
Supervisor Know-How, Running
   the Class   4:380
Supervisor Know-How, Tips in
   Handling Students   4:385
Supervisors   4:359
Supervisors Can Become
   Professors   4:416
                                                  5:434
Supervisor's Code, The   4:367
Supervisor's Duty   4:378
Supervisor's Stable Data   4:319
Supervisor Tech   MS2:98
Supplementary Evaluations   MS1:116
Supplies of Central Organization
   Forms   3:380
                                                  7:618
Supply Officer   0:184
                                                  3:395
Suppressive Acts, Suppression of
   Scientology and Scientologists   1:873
Suppressive Persons, Main
   Characteristics Of   1:1007

T

Tabulating Survey Responses	MS3:243
Tape and Record Production Hat	2:368
Tape Color Code	2:367
Tape Color Flash Code	7:1196
Tape Examinations	4:509
	5:171
Tape Prices	2:373
Tape Release	2:370
Tapes, How to Use	4:511
	6:336
Targeting of Divisional Statistics and Quotas	0:690
	MS2:230
Targets and Computers	MS2:440
	MS2:455
Targets and Production	0:704
	7:456
	MS2:442
	MS2:456
	MS3:436
Targets, More About	MS2:441
Targets, Types Of	MS2:431
Target Troubles	MS1:135
Target Types	MS2:437
Taxation	3:407
Teaching a Tape Course	4:516
Tech	0:262
Tech/Admin Ratio (24 Jan. 70)	1:207
Tech/Admin Ratio (23 Dec. 79)	1:216
Tech and LRH Comms	5:798, 7:1253

Tech and Qual Pre-examinations	5:210
Tech Certainty and High Stats	5:524
Tech Delivery Quality	5:653
Tech Delivery Situation	4:148
Tech Downgrades	4:26
	5:97
Tech Establishment Officer	4:150
Tech Estimate Line, The	2:592
	4:1040
Tech Films and Verbal Tech	4:519
	5:808
Technical and Administrative Divisions	4:39
Technical and Policy Distribution	2:125
	7:1291
Technical Council	4:68
Technical Degrades	0:14
	1:14
	2:14
	3:14
	4:14
	5:14
	6:14
	7:14
Technical Director and Administrator	4:56
	7:218
Technical Director Basic Hat	4:57
Technical Hat Checking	1:272, 7:1272

Technical Info for Continental
  Mags 2:196
Technical Lectures by
  Other Personnel 7:1191
Technical Personnel 4:93
  5:737
Technical Queries 4:502
  5:471
Technical Queries from
  R6 Graduates 4:775
Technical Specialist Courses 4:666
Technical Training Corps 5:533
Tech Recovery 4:1087
  5:752
Tech Services 4:207
Tech Versus Qual 4:1092
  5:757
Tech Volume and Two-way Comm 4:391
Telephone Answering 1:329
Telex Comm Clarity 1:467
Telex Discipline 1:472
Temperatures 5:638
Termination and Classification 4:721
Terminations 4:760
Terminations from the Saint Hill
  Special Briefing Course 4:729
Terror Stalks 7:1008
Testing 4:227
Testing Program Change 6:288
Testing Promotion Revised 6:283
Test Policy on MD Referrals, A 6:291
"The Following Are . . ." 7:25
"The Following Is a Letter . . ." 1:527
"The Organization Is As
  Apparent . . ." 2:54
Theory Checkout Data 4:333
  5:181
Theory of Scientology
  Organizations, The 0:81
  MS1:234
Theory of the New Grade
  Chart, The 2:467
  4:200
Theory Testing, Expiration Dates 4:326

"The Output of Special
  Letters . . ." 2:599
Thermostats in Buildings 7:1339
"The Symbol * on All
  Despatches . . ." 7:1175
"The Washington, DC, Central
  Organization . . ." 2:277
Things That Shouldn't Be 0:547
  1:705
Third Dynamic De-aberration MS1:261
  MS1:426
Third Dynamic Tech 0:55
Third Party, How to Find One 1:544
Third Party Law, The 0:510
  1:537
Three-Basket System, The 0:371
  1:354
Three Classes of People MS2:202
Three Service Branches, The 7:194
Tiger, A 1:787
Tips to HCO Communicators 1:362
To Advisory Council Worldwide 7:907
To a Roman Catholic 6:516
To Department Heads 3:24
  7:186
"To Ensure Speed and
  Accuracy . . ." 1:464
Too Little Too Late MS3:32
Tools of Management, The 7:461
  MS1:363
  MS2:188
  MS2:292
  MS3:441
Top Triangle, The MS2:232
To the Saint Hill Student:
  Instruction Targets 4:749
Traffic Regulations, Saint Hill 7:1381
Training MS1:401
Training Activities 4:715
Training Aids 4:597
Training and Interning
  Staff Auditors 5:528
Training and OT 2:471, 4:820

Training and Processing
Regulations, Tech Division,
Qual Division, Technical
Discipline, Students' Questions 4:350
5:840
Training, Classes of Auditors 4:587
Training Course Regulations 4:472
Training Department Organization 4:290
Training Drills Must Be Correct 4:591
Training of Clears 2:437
4:786
Training Policy 4:572
5:162
Training, Professional, New
Policy 4:565
Training Project Construction and
Preparation 7:1349
Training Quality 4:310
5:164
7:1188
Training Restrictions 4:309
Training, Saint Hill Special
Briefing Course 4:734
Training Sections 4:583
Training, Session Cancellation,
Auditing Section 4:671
Training—What It Is Today, How
We Tell People about It 4:547

TR and EM Films, Showing Of 4:537
5:820
6:347
Transferitis MS1:398
Transferring Funds 3:408
Transfers and Removals and
Permanent Postings Forbidden
Locally 1:257
Transfers from SHSBC to Solo
Audit Course 4:779
Translations 7:1319
Transport (8 May 64) 7:1379
Transport (13 May 64) 7:1380
Transport Arrangements 1:461
Transportation, Dir Admin
Responsibility 7:176
Treason Formula 0:571
1:576
Triple Grades 4:1098
Trips to Town 7:1368
Trouble 7:717
TRs Course and Auditing, Mixing
Major Actions 4:639
Twinning 4:431
Two-Bit FP MS2:364
Two Fine Magazines 2:191
Two Types of PTSes 1:1048
Types of Letters Established 1:393
Type Two PTS, The 1:1013

U

Unclassed Certificates—HAS,
HBA, HQS   5:360
Understanding and Tape Lectures   4:510
                                        6:323

Unevaluated Orders   7:726
Unhandled Drugs and Ethics   1:903
                                        4:972
                                        5:429

Units and Bonuses for Org Exec
Secs and HCO Exec Secs   3:350
                                        7:73

Untrained PR, The   MS3:92
Unusual Favors   1:895
Upper Org Central Files and New
Names to CF   2:678
                                        6:105

Upping Beginning Scientology
Enrollments   6:385
"Upside Down" Graphs   1:678
Urgent Mimeo Change   1:392
                                        7:1287
Urgent PrR   2:500
US Appointment and
Organizational Trend   7:1003
Use of Addresses in
Letter Writing   2:655
Use of Airmail and Air Freight   2:363

Use of *Big League Sales*   2:583
                                        6:409
Use of Demonstration, The   4:443
Use of "Dianetics,"
"Scientology," "Applied
Philosophy"   6:746
                                        7:1071
Use of I&R Form 1   1:533
Use of Recreation Facilities, 1964   7:1377
Use of Scientology Materials, The   6:143
Uses of Auditing, The   2:438
                                        4:925
                                        5:681

Uses of Auditing, Handling with
Auditing, Registrar Advice
Form, The   2:444
                                        4:931
                                        5:687
Uses of Orgs   7:391
                                        MS3:371

Using Orders or Policy to
Create Problems   0:476
                                        1:920
US Mission Holders   6:737
US Mission Queries   6:740
Usual, The   0:257
                                        7:718
Utilization   1:210

V

Validation of Certificates 1:720
2:609
6:702
Validation of Staff 5:386
Validity of Sec EDs 7:1285
Valid Processes 4:1053
Valuable Documents, Handling Of 1:1053
3:369
7:1054
Valuable Final Products 0:296
MS1:295
Verbal Tech: Penalties 0:24
4:32
Viability or Liability, the Quality
of the Treasury Division, a
Treasury Div Checklist for
Quality 3:411
Viability, the Make-Break Point
of an Org MS2:416
Viewpoint MS3:211
Violence 7:1143
Vital Data on Promotion 2:120, 6:54, 7:839

Vital Data: Power and Affluence
Conditions 0:642
1:594
7:553
Vital Necessity of
Hatting, The 0:216
MS1:308
MS2:107
MS2:258
Vital Org Activities 6:85
Vital Target, Trained Auditor
Program, A 4:386
5:493
Vital Training Data 4:304
Vitamin C 5:637
Vitamins (27 Dec. 65) 5:619
Vitamins (24 Oct. 71) 5:636
Voluntary Help 1:159
Volunteer Ministers 6:871
V Unit 4:740
V Unit, New Students, Saint Hill
Special Briefing Course 4:731

W

War, The   7:1129
Warning on New PE   6:281
Warning Signs   7:705
Wasted Planning   MS3:93
Weekly Book Stock Report
  Required   2:311
Weekly Secretarial Personnel
  Report   7:774
Weekly Staff Meetings   0:179
                                            7:739
"We Will No Longer . . ."   3:286
What an Executive Wants on His
  Lines   0:372
                                            7:602
What a Professional TR Course
  Must Consist Of   4:661
What Is a Checksheet   4:441
What Is a Computer?   MS2:453
What Is a Course?   1:287
                                            4:397
                                            5:507
What Is a Course High Crime   4:401
                                            5:511
What Is an Executive?   MS2:288
What Is Scientology?   6:165
What? No Auditors?   4:965
What's Coming Next   7:223
What to Tell New HGC Auditors
  to Process on Preclears   4:1045
What Was Wrong,   4:935, 5:263

What We Expect of a
  Scientologist   6:828
What Your Donations Buy   2:106
"When a New Post Is
  Created . . ."   1:267
"When a Verbal Direction Is
  Given . . ."   4:1046
"When in Doubt about
  Copyrighting It . . ."   2:175
                                            7:1060
"When the Success Story
  Stat . . ."   6:822
When You Need Reassurance   0:155
Who Can Be Processed, Who Can
  Be Trained   2:402
                                            4:306
                                            5:730
Who Can Order Printing   2:172
                                            7:1282
Who May See Technical Training
  Films   4:521
                                            5:810
Who or What Is a "C/S"?   4:1134
Who Should Take Which Class   4:303
Who-Where Finding   MS1:150
Why Hatting?   0:205
                                           MS1:301
                                           MS1:457
Why Is God, The   MS1:87

X, Y, Z

SUBJECT INDEX

Subject Index

A

aberration(s), aberrate(d), *see also* **reactive mind**

a chain of vias based on a primary nonconfront, 4:371

all evil stems from, 1:1027, 7:511

arbitrary is third dynamic aberration, 0:65

basis of, 0:36, 4:369

blowing huge holes in one's, 0:38

cause of products that are overt acts, MS1:244

definition, 0:38, 0:236, MS2:64

description of an aberrated condition, 0:38

example of, 7:673

false data or altered data and, 4:235, 6:306

handling for eradicating 10 points of third dynamic aberration, 7:795

have to de-aberrate a man before his whole social structure could be de-aberrated, 0:623

how sane person vs. aberrated person thinks, 0:236

musical chairs and flubbed hatting stemming from social aberration, 0:205

nonconfront and, 0:36, 0:38

only a few who are relatively unaberrated, 0:247

OT vs. aberrated universe, 0:617

people don't have to be aberrated, 0:156

personal aberration, undetected and unhandled, 0:40

position on lines and terminals scale and, MS1:289

primary aberration in situations that are being mishandled, 7:673

products that are overt acts are caused by, 0:39

secret of, 0:248

to be or unbe is the ability, to not quite be or to WAS is the aberration, 7:810

aberration(s), aberrate(d), *(cont.)*

unwillingness to do something and, 1:727

vias and, 0:38

ability(ies), *see also* **able; cause; competence; efficiency; skill**

amount of charge gotten off a case vs. ability gained, 5:260

auditing and, 2:438

chart of abilities gained, 4:189, 5:292

completing a cycle of action, handling the matter so it does not have to be handled again, 7:701

definition, 0:244

freedom depends on, 0:140

how to breed confidence in one's, 0:626

levels of able and extra-able beings, 0:95

purpose of HGC to improve, 2:402

to better conditions, 0:96

to complete cycles of action, 0:244

to confront, handle and control mest and people, 0:251–252

to hold a position in space, 0:205

to make things go right, 0:236–237, 0:252, 0:430

what your true ability depends on, 0:249

your greatest, 0:250

Ability **magazine,** *see also* **magazine**

advertise new books or one that has been out of print for some time in, 2:319

national magazine issued monthly, 1:396

sending to all libraries listed in CF, 2:693

when it should be issued, 2:185

Ability Release, ability gained, 4:191

able, who our promotion is aimed for, 2:427

absence, from post, 0:267, 0:471, 0:654

abundance,
  exchange in abundance, 0:317
  producing in abundance, 0:318, 0:642
  total abundance, 0:636

abuse(s),
  abolishing abuses against life and
    mankind, 0:160
  PRing an abuse into decay, MS3:9

Academy Levels,
  checksheets for, 4:631
  cover the data vital and necessary to understand
    and audit on them, 4:657
  prerequisites modified, 4:659
  student must be very in-ethics, 4:631
  student's checksheet must be short, 4:631
  trying to teach SHSBC instead of, 4:630

Academy(ies), *see also* course(s); instruction;
    student(s); study; Supervisor(s); train;
    training
  checksheets, secret of getting student through
    half a level in two weeks is, 5:759
  Chief Supervisor ideal scene and stat, 4:142
  clarification of schedule, 4:568
  competent auditors whose excellence promotes
    the, 0:350
  course, definition, 4:182
  Danger condition in, handling, 0:583
  definition, 2:505, 3:233, 4:46, 7:201
  demand Academy perform only miracles,
    2:112, 4:339
  Dept 17 courses vs., 6:488
  difficult student used as indicator, 1:1001
  dissemination value of, 2:68
  don't count on HGC income, count on much
    greater Academy income and guarantee
    continuance with fine training, 4:339
  don't process, 4:624, 5:197
  don't try to handle course environment with
    student auditing, 4:341
  downgrade of, 0:14
  E-Meters and books for Academy
    students, 4:363
  enroll pcs in the Academy whenever possible,
    2:69, 4:337
  goal of, 2:488, 4:302
  graduates came on staff as staff auditors then
    HGC auditors got promoted to
    executives, 4:386
  handling of a PTS or SP, 1:996, 4:89
  has a dissemination value about 150 times that
    of an HGC, 4:336

Academy(ies), *(cont.)*
  husband-wife teams trained to co-audit each
    other, 4:361
  if dissemination is very broad and good to
    general public, there will be Academy
    enrollments, 2:422
  long established data about dissemination
    value, 4:336
  magazines should say "enrolls any time" after
    every course in every Academy ad, 4:361
  may not loan, use or own meters, 4:573
  minors and, 3:145
  mission is to make auditors who can audit,
    3:152, 4:595
  must not fool with suppressive persons, 4:88
  no Academy courses may be given outside
    Academy premises, 4:361
  no persons may be admitted to an Academy or
    HGC who have not signed waivers (release
    forms), 4:360
  not a clinic, 2:488, 4:302
  one thing that can snap somebody around and
    completely change his life is finding his
    goal, 4:605
  only auditors in Academy, no cases, 4:304
  org income high when Academy good, 5:835
  outside auditing requirements for students
    enrolled in Academy, 4:563
  penalty for students violating auditing
    requirements while enrolled in an
    Academy, 4:563
  personal or case problems of students
    and, 4:304
  policy that each student own his own E-Meter,
    2:341, 4:363, 5:723
  processes that must be taught in the
    Academy, 4:610
  promotional purposes, 2:57, 7:32
  purpose is to train auditors, 4:626
  rates no meters for student issue, 4:471
  reasons for overlong attendance on Academy
    courses, 4:372
  relatively unteachable person is one whose goal
    is an overt against Scientology, 4:606
  remorselessly standardize and upgrade delivery
    in, 1:755, 4:100
  results just not happening, handling, 0:498
  run nonstandardly empties out, reason, 0:333
  sale and conduct of courses, 4:554
  schedules, day, evening and weekend, 4:182
  secret of getting students through is keeping
    ethics in in the Academy, 4:376
  sharp scheduling is mark of successful, 4:316

Academy(ies), *(cont.)*

sign in Academy to get graduates to join staff, 4:386

source of new personnel, 1:227

special program for fast Academies, 4:372

special schedule course room and, separate, 4:455

specialist courses available in, 4:666

spot a slow student at once and get correct Remedy A and Remedy B done, 4:376

standard schedules, Day and Foundation orgs, 4:453

state of should be first thought of Org Exec Sec every morning, 2:70, 4:338, 5:837

students must be trained on E-Meters from the start even if they only hold one in their lap whenever they are "auditor" or "student" (not coach) in a Comm Course TR, 4:576

students, should co-audit as they train, 4:688

students should only be allowed to use E-Meters approved by HCO, 2:377, 7:1289

Supervisor must not omit what an auditor actually uses in sessions whether it is covered in the level's training or not, 4:620

things you can only learn in an Academy, 4:568

time schedule, 4:600

"tough case" is only one you send to HGC, 4:344

trying to teach SHSBC instead of Academy level checksheets, 4:630

two-way comm and volume of auditing and training, 4:391

way the student body is divided up, 4:599

what a good academy looks like, 4:605

word of mouth and why it empties or fills, MS3:169

acceptable truth, MS3:9

acceptance, no org has to accept anyone, 4:896

accepting an almost, 0:429

accident(s),

auditing and, 2:438

why people cause themselves accidents, 0:452

accomplishment, morale depends upon, 1:63

accounting,

activities of Accounting Department, 3:19

administrative specialty, 7:434

beware of any person invalidating your accounts records or saying they or your system is bad, 3:399

bolster credit in emergencies, 3:253

collections from stations and, 3:107

disbursement files and, 3:391

accounting, *(cont.)*

freeloaders and, 1:255

give scheduling personnel a copy of the invoice, 3:159

goes PTS through various tax and government supervision suppressions, 7:372, MS3:352

going slack, 0:276

good service and, 3:70

how they apply the promote step of the Emergency Formula, 3:252

inspection of, 3:31

introduction of complex accounting contrary to policy is a suppressive act on laymen, 3:66, 7:1079

invoice filing system and, 0:276

invoices all sums for training and processing, payments on accounts, return of loans and other items not covered on other stations, 3:105

invoices payments, 2:481

keep good records and adhere efficiently to our system, 3:399

mail, handling of, 3:105

penalty for accounts policies not being followed and legible records not being kept, 3:123

policies of Scientology companies, 3:65, 7:1078

premeditated fraud and, 3:184

PRO and, 3:69, MS3:144–145

procedure for handling of deposit slip records, 3:400

procedure for handling, 3:104

promotion project for, 2:407

PRO, no substitute for knowing one's finance policy and following it, 3:70

records of bank deposits and, 3:400

remedy for delinquent, 3:184

require note, contract and release before invoice written, 3:119

result of falsely using Emergency Formula to turn down POs, 3:252

right to demand good technical service, 0:18

rules governing, 3:33

simplified system of, 3:37

specific, precise and definite policy in policy letters govern accounts income and accounts disbursement, 3:123

students and pcs sometimes elect to use advance paid credit in their accounts to buy books or meters, 3:207

three reasons why persons invalidate accounts, 3:399

tradesman dunning for a bill, handling of, 3:252

up to Accounts to get things paid for, 2:427

accounting, *(cont.)*

work very heavily in the income section and lightly in disbursement section, 3:392

Worldwide, handling of, 3:23

Accounts clearance,

certificates, awards and, 3:163

definition, 3:163

Accounts Files Administrator, post is created, 7:221

accounts policing, anatomy of, 3:73

accounts records,

items that may be considered accounts records, 3:375

longevity due to, 0:67

Accounts Unit, purposes, 7:59

accuser(s), accusing, *see also* **offense**

being confronted with one's, 0:515, 0:520

acknowledgment, acknowledge, acknowledging,

exec comm lines and, 0:372

failure or refusal to acknowledge, relay or execute direct legal order from International Board member, 0:470

failure to acknowledge direct and legal order from exec, 0:468

act(s)(ing),

definition, 1:196

destructive acts done out of fear, 0:454

good acts, definition, 0:453

how right or wrong it is, 0:453

I have no monopoly on the ability to observe and act, 0:140

not acting, 0:231

postings, state of Clear and, 1:199

slowing admin line by not acting NOW is suppressive, 0:244

status, can be demoted, 1:251

acting appointment, *see* **posting**

acting status, application for, MS1:472, MS2:308

action(s), *see also* **cycle of action**

any activity has a sequence of, 0:106

arranging personnel and organization to handle types of, 0:434

arranging sequences of, MS1:197

bad action, 0:480

be maximally right in your, 0:247

careless or other-determined, 0:301

completed staff work and, 0:402

complete the action, do it now, 0:245–246, 0:430

contrary to intentions and actions of remainder of team, 0:571

crashing misunderstood preventing, 0:39

data, not entheta, brings about action, 0:372

ethics actions, *see* ethics actions

action(s), *(cont.)*

fixing responsibility for, 0:419, 0:427

giving orientation to one's, 0:696

good vs. bad courses of action, rules or laws, 0:117

group types of actions into single posts, 0:88

how thetan can handle a vast volume of, 0:326

how to get approval of, 0:401

increasing speed of, 0:401

listing basic actions necessary to get out one's product, 0:308

one-man monopoly on, 0:87

one's actions not coordinating, 0:576

order of priority of staff action, 0:367

out of sequence, 0:307

overt act, *see* overt

planning out any, 0:108

putting off, 0:400

sequence of action, *see* sequence

staledating delays action, 0:425

stats and, 0:579

successful actions, getting them in, 0:643

what slows down approval and action, 0:401

actionable, auditing a Tech Specialist course rundown without training on authorized checksheet, 4:666

active,

efforts to look and sound active while loafing and goofing, 0:420

groups not active and vigilant as individuals die, 0:302

inactive, *see* inactive

active files, definition of, 2:704, 6:714

activity, activities,

any activity has a sequence of actions, 0:106

corrupt activities, 0:533

predicting survival or downfall of any, 0:297

trouble-free activities, 0:129

types of, 6:796

which could not be considered rational, 0:451

ad(s), *see* **advertisement**

Ad Committee, *see* **Advisory Committee**

ad copy, MS3:208

Ad Council, *see* **Advisory Council**

additives,

auditing comm cycle,
definition, 4:1176
examples, 4:1175

comm cycle additives,
definition, 5:668
examples, 5:667
not permitted in auditing, 4:1175

mannerisms, examples in auditing, 4:1175

Address (section of an org),

city office and, 0:619

entheta letters handled by, 1:974

failing to mail to CF list regularly, effect of, 0:359

handling of new book buyers, 0:619

is CF index as well as who gets magazine, 0:360

address(es), Address, Addressograph, *see also* **Central Files**

addresses to include all of Central Files accurately, 2:694

adjacent offices to CF and Letter Registrar and typists, 2:621

automatic equipment, 2:700

automatic feed and envelopes, 2:695

basic purpose and usefulness of, 2:695

can't find wrong addresses, 0:383

card file system of CF, 2:621

categories tabbed on, 2:652

Central Organizations should be changed by overpasting old data or address with a neat printed sticker, 2:326

change of address and, 2:397, 2:708

come from CF folders, 0:99

completing of old lists inclusion and category tabbing, 2:689

contribution to income, goodwill and success of the organization, 2:686

establishing an international headquarters of Scientology in the event of atomic war and, 2:697

facilitated by rubber stamps, 1:456

files,

cards to be run off, 2:695

constitute a geographical index, 2:684

must be accurate and be kept up-to-date, 2:684

Foundation and duties that need to be filled, 2:670

handling new addresses for bookbuyers, 2:706

how long post office in US keeps change of address card, 0:360

importance of getting known, 1:316

index file to Central Files, not just a general list, 2:694

inflow into, 2:689

mainly for people filing, 2:695

must be a total Central Files, 2:694

new addresses, handling, 0:619

no addresses of persons who have bought something may ever be retired, 2:703, 6:713

address(es), Address, Addressograph, *(cont.)*

not up-to-date and used is about the most costly error an org can make, 2:219

old addresses not used unless checked first with Addresso, 2:655

operator,

purpose, 2:684, 2:688

routing of the post, 2:688

placed under Letter Registrar, 2:659

plates for every public in comm with us, 1:316

plates tabbed in such a way they reflect CF *exactly,* 2:621

primarily for card files for use, 2:695

primary reason for unit decline and, 2:700

Addresses In-Charge,

card files and, 2:696

makes sure that all mailing projects are carried out, 2:690

procedure for ordering cards from, 2:653

purpose, 2:684, 2:688

address files, purpose, 2:200, 4:72, 6:194

addressing equipment, why you must have, 2:54

address list(s), *see also* **mailing list**

cause of ARC breaks, person's name in mailing address list twice or three times, 2:435

city offices and, 2:701, 6:789

must contain principal names of Scientology, Exec Councils of orgs and L. Ron Hubbard, Founder, 2:710

Address Unit, definition, 2:508, 3:236, 7:204

admin, *see also* **administration**

below administrative Why is an Ethics Why, MS2:245

Esto who does lots of, MS2:34

example of not handling, 2:440

if you can't get in admin, both tech and ethics are out, 1:1028

lines are most fundamental point of, MS2:170

no admin change, 1:1028

only works where tech is in, 1:5

time spent on C/Sing, FESing and FF table making should be deducted from pc's hours, 2:459

Admin Cramming (section), 0:392

furnished with packs of dev-t policies, 0:441–442

send anyone who is dev-ting to, 0:390, 0:442

admin cycle, MS1:23

admin degrades, 73–74

high crimes, 5:25, 7:490, MS3:470

standard policy, how it gets lost, 5:25

admin high crime(s), *see also* **high crime checkouts**

computerized system to verify, 7:493, MS2:463, MS3:473

computer verification of, 1:919

definition, 1:918, MS3:471–472

log of, 1:918

responsibility for, MS3:472

SSO and, 1:918

standard Word Clearing and star-rate checkouts on HCO PLs, 1:918

violations of, 1:918–919

administer, definition, MS2:216

administration, admin, administrative, *see also* **establish; management; organize; production**

bad administration, lack of know-how, lack of trained clerks and executives, can defeat utterly any plan or program no matter how urgent or beneficial, 7:779

below administrative Why is an Ethics Why, MS2:245

definition, 0:51, 0:58, 4:949, 5:690

degrade of, 0:73

Esto who does lots of, MS2:34

ethics and, 0:260, 0:527

expert knows where admin out it will be jammed at the top, 7:780

failing to apply it to society around us, result, 0:483

good, two distinct targets, 7:406, MS3:386

has right to raise hell over bad tech, 0:19

HCO PLs are senior in, 0:143

how it relates to quality in training and processing, 0:16

in essence you are wearing my administrative hat for that post, 0:238

keeping admin working, 0:70

keeps org from going broke, 0:18

key ingredients of, 7:408, MS3:388

know-how of handling orgs, 0:28

lines are most fundamental point of, MS2:170

most neglected and destructive admin action, 0:99

never send orders into out-admin area, 7:402, MS3:382

one knows and handles, produces, exchanges or dies, 7:437

one will survive as well as he can administer or handle administration, 7:436

administration, admin, administrative, *(cont.)*

only works where tech is in, 0:657

organizing and, 0:58

out-admin, 0:45, 0:47, 0:71, 0:260

outside Scientology, 1:736

overextended admin lines, 0:128

owed something by technical, 7:838

quality and admin in Central Orgs, 0:18

reason it is done, 0:684

resulting in production and exchange, 7:436, MS3:416

Security Checking is part of, 1:36

slow admin, 0:260

stability guaranteed by administrative skill, 0:67

standard admin, *see* standard administration

standard, comes from policy letters, 7:403, MS3:383

system, necessary to perpetuate any group, 7:406

systems which lack key ingredients, 7:409

tech and, 0:18, 0:527, 0:657

technical quality depends upon, 0:18

test of, 0:59, 0:61

to improve tech results, you must improve administration, 4:949

trouble with it because one doesn't know it or can't or doesn't use it, 0:551

true points of, 7:409, MS3:389

using Scientology admin and dev-t policies on the society outside Scientology, 7:1016

when admin out,
  org declines, 7:486, MS3:466
  tech is out, MS3:165, MS3:382
  tech out and ethics long ceased to exist, 7:402

why the subject appears difficult, 0:59

why we had to develop and learn it, 0:18

works where tech is in, 7:398, MS3:378

administration lines, point that fails, MS1:9

administrative department, most important is Promotion and Registration, 7:194

administrative directive, may only forward policy, 0:112

administrative know-how,

gap between plan and actuality will be found to be lack of, 7:407

man's happiness and longevity of companies and states depend upon, 7:411

Administrative Letter(s), definition, 1:414, 7:638

administrative orders, 1:414

administrative personnel,

functions of, 0:18, 7:838

high-crime checkouts and, 0:75–77

tech/admin staff ratio, 0:95, 0:98, 0:223, 0:416

administrative technology, admin tech, *see also* Hubbard Communications Office Policy Letter; policy; third dynamic tech

familiar with in order to evaluate, MS1:158

our tech of organization comes from Level VII, 0:482

what happens when it is used, 0:694

administrator(s), *see also* executive; leader; manager; officer; senior

definition, 7:438, 7:439, MS3:418, MS3:419

detection of a suppressive person, 7:392, MS3:372

skillful and well-taught, importance of, 0:67

squirrel administrator, 0:61, 0:63

test of, 7:438, MS3:418

too few trained and skilled who can get a show on the road, 7:435, MS3:415

why civilization develops so few, 7:434

Admin Scale, MS1:262–263, MS1:427–428

definition, 7:478, MS1:368, MS2:194, MS2:299, MS3:458

first true group tech, MS1:265

group sanity scale points must agree with, MS1:266

groups appear inefficient, unhappy, inactive when items not aligned, MS1:263

handling points found random or counter, MS1:264

strategic plan, applies to the top of the, 0:706, 7:458, MS2:444, MS3:438

admin staff, doing extra auditing time to prevent getting rusty, 1:180

admin/tech ratio, must never be more than two admin to one tech, 6:92

Admin Training Corps (ATC), vital to an org's future prosperity, 1:217

Admin Why, MS1:165; *see also* Why

admiration, that which is not admired tends to persist, 0:464

advance collections, obtained by industrious collection from "hot prospects" and other potential students and pcs, MS2:327

Advanced Clinical Course, former students, services for, 2:436, 6:220

Advanced Course(s), 5:250

above VA processes, 4:805

basic datum, 4:804

by invitation only, 4:808

checkouts, 4:811

gross violations, 4:809

noncompliance to instructions, 1:637

persons who have a history of carelessness with materials or bad or suppressive group connections are debarred from, 4:803

Advanced Course(s), *(cont.)*

procedure by which OT Sections are administered, 4:804

regulations, 4:813

Security Check, 4:803

security of data and materials, 4:753, 4:806

sources of failure on, 4:1115

Advanced Organization, MS3:429

allowed technical services, 4:121, 6:764

always mans up AO dept or div along with the SH one, MS2:273

exist to make OTs and support the Sea Org, 7:149

product of, 4:123, 6:76

responsibility for case folders of pcs and pre-OTs who have dropped the body, 4:258

Advance Program,

earlier called a Return Program, 4:1107

gets pc up to where he should be, 4:1107

on bright blue sheets, 4:1102

advances, have been in how to handle basics better, 0:65

Advance Scheduling Registrar (ASR),

Call-in Unit located under, to handle partially paids, 2:641, 3:217, 7:865

definition, 7:438, 7:439, MS3:418, MS3:419

detection of a suppressive person, 7:392, MS3:372

keeps two large, heavy books, 2:432

prime purpose of, 2:432

procedure for partially paid public call-in, 2:645, 3:217, 4:280, 7:869

receives folders of hot prospects, 2:431

uses prepared registration packets, 2:432

advertise, ads, advertising, advertisement(s), *see also* dissemination; promotion; message; word of mouth

advertising books in magazines, 0:303, 0:352

all ads carry the Pubs Org address, 2:348

basis of, MS3:190

common use of positioning in, MS3:122

Dept 4 properly presents services in ads, 0:348

Dianetics: Evolution of a Science ad, 2:269, 6:253

Dianetics: The Original Thesis ad, 2:269, 6:253

effectiveness, suitability and lawfulness of, 0:336

every magazine must carry an ad for every service rendered, 2:212

examples of ads with sales talk and lack of information, 2:266, 6:239

Foundation and, 6:213

general advertising of the org may not be paid for from the HCO Book Account, 3:188

advertise, *(cont.)*

info packets and, use of, 6:213

in mags, etc., to sell books and cassettes, 0:352

keynote is, what we can do for you and what you can do for others, 6:209

may be paid from the HCO Book Account but only for book ads, 3:188

model ad that can be used for anything including free course in local papers, 6:209

money to do wide advertising programs, 3:30, 7:928

must be factual and explicit, 2:266, 6:239

must be in accordance with long-standing policy, 2:210, 6:219

new books or one that has been out of print for some time, advertise in *Ability/Certainty,* 2:319

pcs that are walking advertisements, 0:351

PE ad, 2:270, 6:254

placing ads in the wrong media can be very costly as the money is wasted, 2:266, 6:239

policies on, 2:267, 6:240–241

PR and, MS3:108

Problems of Work ad, 2:269, 6:253

some allowed book advertisements, 2:269, 6:253

spatial vs. linear program, MS3:109

starting with core group, then rolling it out works best, MS3:115

text of ads, 2:266, 6:239

win an extension course, 2:189

word of mouth as a superior form of, 0:333, MS3:169

wrong way to advertise and run PE Course, 0:703

advice, reality in, 0:122

Advisory Committee,

assigns conditions, 7:906

composed of, 7:885, 7:896

conference routing and, 0:387

continuing Emergency-level GDS and, 0:583

D of P and, 4:960

Emergency assignments and, 7:903

exists for each division in the org and is advisory to the Ad Council, 7:117

grievances and, 7:886

Mandate of 1956 amended, 7:885

may only order directors, 0:583

meetings, 7:896, 7:906

orders, issue of, 7:906

purpose of, 7:895, 7:896

reports,

forwarded to Ad Council, 7:906

Advisory Committee, *(cont.)*

reports, *(cont.)*

minutes to the Association Secretary, 7:885

routing for, 7:901

slumps and, 0:596

statistics and, 7:898

who is represented, 2:57, 3:227, 7:32

Advisory Council,

assignment of Affluence and Emergency and, 7:900

assists Executive Council, 7:913

Boards of Investigation and, 7:910

chairman nominated and elected by, 7:910

composed of, 7:889, 7:909

coordination, why we have, 7:455

Danger condition assigned by, 0:584

despatches to, 7:893

dissident voice and, 7:911

Exec Secs may not be members of, 7:909

false reports and, 7:912

financial reports required in weekly reports, 7:887

function of, 0:128, 7:896

gross divisional statistics and, 7:898, 7:907

LRH Comm may veto any measure that is against policy, 7:913

majority, 7:892

may request removal of an Executive Secretary, 7:911

measures must be in issuable form, 7:914

members, removal of, 7:911, 7:914

minutes, 7:888, 7:891

not a governing body, 7:891

order of progress of meeting, 7:889

orders, issue of, 7:905

powers of, 7:891, 7:910

privilege, 7:912

promotional actions, 7:84

purpose of, 7:889, 7:909

quorum, 7:892

reports made to, 7:889, 7:891

representatives elected to, 7:909

rights of, 7:891

Robert's Rules of Order and, 7:912

Sec EDs issued by Ad Council may only change secretaries as personnel, 0:582

slumps and, 0:596

staff meeting minutes presented to, 0:173

statistic, 7:908

Thetan-Mind-Body-Product system, 0:128, 0:129

time of meeting, 7:889

aesthetics, ethics and, 1:32

affinity, *see* **ARC; ARC triangle**

Affluence condition,

Ad Council assignment of, 7:900

analyzing what is causing them and reinforcing them, 0:129

assuming there's nothing more that can be done in the sector that caused the, 0:648

attainment of, 0:628

boosting it up to a new higher point, 0:649

breaking an, 0:651, 0:653

cause of Affluence is still capable of causing it, 0:648, 1:600, 7:559

definition, 1:597, 7:556

description, 0:645

determining which stats need to be handled to maintain and strengthen the, 0:645

difference between condition of Power and, 1:594, 7:553

economize in, 0:564, 0:646

erroneous and misleading data regarding, 0:642

Exec Sec inspecting physical areas of, 0:655

first targets on battle plan where Affluence is going to be handled, 0:648

formula, 1:598, 7:557

graph showing Affluence, 0:643, 0:649

handling, 0:646, 1:598, 7:557

if you use Normal Operation Formula when you are in Affluence you will descend into Emergency, 0:583

most touchy condition there is, 1:598, 7:557

not maintained and org never really getting into Power, 0:642

period of for org, MS1:164

Power differentiated from, 0:643, 0:650, 0:651

program that started the, 1:599, 7:558

reason org can't hold an Affluence or high condition, 0:661

stat analysis and, 0:646

steps, 0:564, 0:646

strengthening or reinforcing it, 0:564, 0:648

where it can go off the rails, 0:648

Affluence Formula, *see* **Affluence condition**

afraid-to-do's, dev-t and, 0:415

aging, why president of the US ages about twenty years in one term of office, 0:201

agreed-upon actions, MS1:161

any policy, agreed upon, is better than points of individual decision on flow lines, 0:325

agreed-upon actions, *(cont.)*

bank-agreement made Earth a hell, 0:10

collective-thought agreement, 0:10

getting on-policy will build the agreement necessary to make a group, 0:28

group cannot function without agreed-upon policy, 0:408

individual must rise above avid craving for, 0:10

obtaining agreement and alignment necessary to generate group action and production which brings about success, 0:63

people agree to postulates they can understand and appreciate, 0:82

perfect org is not machine but pattern of agreements, 0:82

policy and, 0:60, 0:114–115, 0:132, 0:411

takes agreement to make a group, 0:28

with message is what PR is seeking to achieve, MS3:9

you cannot get a flow without, 0:324

agreement factor,

consists of, MS1:290

has to be established and group aware of it, MS1:290

Aides Council,

conference routing and, 0:387

three types of conferences held, MS2:13

Aides Order (AO),

definition, 1:431

may not abolish network, org or change form of org, 0:143

A–I hat, *see also* **hat,** 1:199–200

hat contents, MS1:202

aims, of Scientology, 6:519

airmail, locations not served by, 0:382

alignment, example of, 7:460, MS2:446, MS3:439

all auditors action,

procedure, 0:100

too many of these "all auditors" can cut an org to bits, 7:277

all-denominational, Scientology is, 0:153

all hands action,

stuffing–mailing cycle as, 0:103

used for every major program, 7:813

allocation,

cash-bills and, MS2:331

defined, MS2:317

Treasury Sec gives receipt and sees allocation check is banked, MS2:330

what staff who feel use of org allocation is incorrect may do, MS2:329

allocation, *(cont.)*

what the FBO looks at in order to make his allocation, MS2:329

when FP allocation amounts become due for transfer, MS2:330

allocation board, MS2:272, MS3:428

kept by Personnel Control Officer, 1:162

needed posts put up on an, 1:76

manning up an org, need an org board first and allocation board, 7:448

personnel request form requires one, 1:259

almost, accepting an, 0:429

alteration, alter(ed)(ing), *see also* **alter-is; change**

effect of altering basics of the technology, 0:126

HCOBs or PLs, altering content of, 0:24

of any meaning or action, handling for, 5:468

Org Exec Course material, alteration of, 0:4

people who continually alter policy, 0:406

policy not known or altered is death, example, 0:410

senior policy, alteration of, 0:468

sufficiently serious problem to destroy a course, 5:677

suppressives acting in an altered direction, 0:260

altered compliance, dev-t and, 0:424

altered data, aberration and, 4:235, 6:306

altered importance, definition, MS1:80; *see also* **outpoint(s)**

altered sequence, *see also* **outpoint(s)**

definition, MS1:78

investigation and, MS1:73

alter-is, *see also* **alteration; change**

comes after misunderstood word, 5:525

comes from can't apply, not not-know, 4:1080, 5:671

covert avoidance of an order, 1:201

definition, 7:389, MS3:369

degraded beings and, 1:201

following illegal orders or illegal local policies or alter-is, 0:471

lying, stupidity and, 0:536

minor alter-is of tech or policy, 0:467

of process, 1:1002

prime cause of, MS2:21

reported to Ethics promptly, 0:623

seriousness of technical alter-is, 0:545

student alter-ising or misadvising others on the use of study tech, 0:45

Alter-is Report, description, 0:543

Alternate Clear Route,

consists of doing Power, Solo auditor training, R6EW and then the Clearing Course at an Advanced Org, 4:1107

definition, 2:437, 6:424

altitude, being invalidated from, 0:247

amends,

Courts of Ethics and, 1:948

policy on, 0:545–546

we are not an Earthwide amends project, 0:507

America, *see* **United States**

American Medical Association,

attack on Scientology, MS3:124

use of black PR, MS3:79

amnesty, 1:701, 1:951

certificate cancellation and, 5:348

definition, 1:937

extending to non-Scientologists, 7:1016

intended to cover, 1:937

policy on, 0:545–546

restoring certificates, communications, cancelling infractions, 1:923

secondary purpose, 1:937

tertiary purpose, 1:937

what determines frequency of, 1:938

what is restored by, 1:937

who issued under and what it signalizes, 1:937

analysis, analyzing, *see also* **data analysis; evaluation; situation analysis; stat analysis**

data evaluation and, MS1:185

how to analyze a post, dept or org, 0:81–82

impeded by, MS1:61

less data the more precise analysis must be, MS1:22

obtained by, MS1:18, MS1:21

of dev-t, 0:416

of organization by product, 0:287

of traffic to increase income and efficiency, 0:417

statistic analysis, *see* statistic analysis

substantive data and, MS1:185

three types of data concerning, MS1:185

anarchy, everyone sets own policy, MS1:255

Anatomy of the Human Mind Course,

bridge from Book One to Scientology services, 6:443

has to be taught in PE Foundation, 6:466

PE and, 6:468

anger, compliance and ability to get mad, 0:246

announcement, births, marriages, divorces, 7:640

Annoyance Report, description, 0:544

answer(s), *see also* **response**

answer people's questions, 0:84, 0:166, 0:276, 0:370

letters, answering of, 0:370

people who cannot receive a comm so can't answer properly, 0:406

antagonism, in some cases stems from false data or outright lies, 5:440

antagonistic source(s),

handling of, 1:1043

most common cause is, 1:1043

antibiotic(s),

administering of, 5:642

cannot depress temperature by itself, 5:644

definition, 5:642

general rule when administering, 5:644

important three error situations, 5:643

intestinal bacteria and, 5:648

mainly effective against bacteria, 5:642

oldest are sulfa drugs, 5:646

operating rule is, 5:645

penicillin, 5:646

side effects, 5:645

virus diseases respond badly to, 5:642

vitamins given with, when, 5:647

antisocial personality(ies),

anti-Scientologist, 1:1014

attributes of, 1:1015–1016

cowed or ill associates or friends and, 1:1015

crime and criminal acts perpetrated by, 1:1014

criminal is antiself and, 0:456

one must examine the good with the bad before one can truly label the antisocial or social, 1:1019

reason for behavior lies in a hidden terror of others, 1:1017

understanding and ability to recognize could bring a major change in society, 1:1017

antithesis, definition of, MS2:137; *see also* **synthesis; thesis**

apathy,

due to off-line, off-origin comm, 0:394

when management unit is too big, individual becomes apathetic, 0:600

ape-think, 0:157

appeal, by staff member who is subject of transfer or removal, 1:261

appearance(s), *see also* **cleanliness; image; public relations**

ARC and, MS3:147

comes under Dept of Public Relations, 6:613, MS3:154

appearance(s), *(cont.)*

"cover appearance," definition, MS3:148

ethnic survey and, MS3:148

goodwill and, 0:333

important people and, 0:335

org board location, 0:339

part of everyone's hats is keeping a good mock-up in people, offices, classrooms, quarters, 0:84

posts of cleaners filled and cleaning scheduled so org is spotless, 0:356

pride and, 0:340, MS3:155

pride, primary reason for good appearance, 6:614

PRO and, what public think PRO person should look like, MS3:148

professional appearances, 0:334

publications, appearance of, 0:335

Public Exec Sec and, 0:339

public knows us by our mest, 0:84

reason it's in Dept 18A, 6:613

responsibilities regarding, 0:354

role in PRO, MS3:147

staff appearance, 0:166, 0:334, 0:335

staff member's responsibility for org physical appearance, 0:167

transferred to Public Divs, 6:616

Appearances Officer, purpose and duties, 6:595

applicant(s), *see also* **employment; hiring; recruitment**

location of the organization and, 1:171

log for employment, 1:172

misrouting of, 1:161, 1:172

someone on the line turning people away, 1:171

application, apply(ing), *see also* **use**

applying formula of condition one is in, 0:562, 0:628

applying Scientology, vs. "knowing about," 5:669

auditor is responsible for application of tech, 0:685

can't apply a policy, handling, 0:623

Crashing Mis-U blocking ability to apply data, 0:39

failure to apply,
our own admin, tech and justice procedures to society around us, result, 0:483
the tech, 0:64

getting technology applied, 0:8–12

honorary certificates and awards only given for achievement in, 5:345

if one is experiencing an adverse effect on a post or in life, 0:268

application, apply(ing), *(cont.)*

if you can get tech applied, you can deliver what's promised, 0:8

inability to confront things bars group member from using data, 0:63

job application file, 1:226–227

keeping Scientology working and, 0:8

of existing Scientology process or principle or book, 5:732

policy works if you apply it, 0:28

promotional actions regarding applications of Scientology, 0:354–355

results only occur when tech is correctly applied, 0:55

reversing dwindling spiral by applying tech and policy, 0:91–92

Scientology not applied exactly per HCOBs and tapes, result, 0:241

shortening time of application of auditing for financial or labor-saving considerations, 0:15

staff failing to apply policy, 0:59

third dynamic tech and, 0:56–57

applying, vs. "knowing about," 4:1078

appointee,

changing everything, 0:561

conditions and new appointees, 0:561, 0:566

I extend complete trust to an, 0:239

old post slumping under a new, 0:596

appointment(s), *see* **posting**

approval of, 1:223

Exec Council and, 7:914

exec does want on his lines, 7:603

executive, state of Clear and, 1:199

persons newly appointed to post, 1:571

preclear classification and staff, 5:576

procedure, 1:225

appointment list, org board vs., 0:414

apprentice(s)(ing), *see also* **deputy; education**

assigned to posts, not posted, 1:73, 1:76

auditor, done as org intern, 5:849

catch up all neglected apprenticeships, 5:850

certs issued when satisfactorily served, 5:509

definition, 1:77

done by deputy system, MS1:272

hats and, 5:509

importance of, 1:117

steps, 1:77

third dynamic psychosis is a denial of adequate experience to succeed, MS1:267

when one is posted to a post, 1:76

wog world takes five to twenty years or more for tradesmen, 1:77

Apprentice Scientologist, course outline, 6:750

approval,

button, 0:17

completed staff work and, 0:402, 0:424–425

"customer approval" of the team, 0:278

how to get approval of actions and projects, 0:401

lack of CSW slows down approval, 0:424

usually worked for harder than mere pay, 0:277

arbitrary, arbitraries,

breed of arbitrary that almost every outness is, 0:140

definition, 0:65, 7:323, MS3:303

orders vs., 0:140

we must not entangle our purposes with arbitrary laws which do not further our cause, 0:273

ARC (Affinity, Reality, Communication), *see also* **communication; reality; understanding**

practical policy agreed upon and followed provides ARC that is life of any group, 0:411

real force is dependent upon, 0:247

ARC break(s), ARC broken, *see also* **ARC triangle**

ARC broken field, handling, 0:498

ARC broken students and pcs, 0:493

assessments on staff, 5:573

Assistant Registrar and, 2:404

attacks and, 1:792

attacks on orgs and, 6:548

auditing a pc over, 4:1081, 5:672

Book of Case Remedies and, 5:733

bring about and restimulate desire to get even, 5:248

bypassed charge and, 5:248, 6:548

cause of, 0:245

collections and, 3:184

contribution and, 0:277

desire to get even, 1:792

end expansion if not handled, 0:100

ethics and, 1:746, 5:111

ethics injustice causes, 2:435

failing to answer a person's questions in letters causes, 2:435

field, failure to strenuously act to clean up, high crime for EC, 1:793

getting ARC broken Scientologists in, 0:353

inaccurate billing is most frequent source of, 2:435

ARC break(s), ARC broken, *(cont.)*

inadmissible in any ethics matter as defense or justification of misdemeanors, crimes or high crimes, 4:356

Letter Reg writing to offer service the person has already taken causes, 2:435

life ruds and, 0:103

long duration, 1:792

making it hard for people to help causes, 2:435

mechanisms, suppressive groups and use of, 4:83

most caused by bypassed charge, 4:933

most frequent source of, with the public, 0:276

not caught and handling, 7:128

overts and, 0:103, 0:277

person ARC broken, attacks, 5:248

person's name in mailing address list twice or three times causes, 2:435

plea of "ARC broken" is inadmissible in any ethics matter, 0:493

precede harmful intentional acts, 0:277

promotional actions and, 0:353

public and Ethics Officers, 1:793

reasons for ARC broken field, 2:555–556

refuse to repair, 1:993, 4:85

result of, 4:933

Review mistaking a withhold for, 5:38

sources of, with the public, 0:276

student left in, can't handle cramming, 5:210

taking pc off auditing once started causes, 4:252

the withholdy case and, 1:1004

when person in charge requests something be looked into and is given opinion or explanation, 7:786

when someone is not permitted to complete a cycle of action, 7:778

ARC Break Auditor, 5:67

ARC break mechanism, suppressive groups and use of, 1:9

ARC Break Program, *see also* **Rudiments Program**

actions of most successful team, 7:881

answer to heavy inflow is ARC Break Program to be gotten in, 6:756

definition, 7:881

EP of, 6:559

every ARC broken Scientologist or Dianeticist back in ARC with the org and Scientology, 6:559

ARC Break Program, *(cont.)*

expansion and wins are order of the day for an org that has program in full operation, 7:882

function, 6:563

org board position of, 6:560

refund/repayment line and, 6:564

Rudiments Officer and, 6:560

Rudiments Receptionist, duties of, 6:560

Rudiments Registrar and, 6:562

Rudiments Repair Auditor and, 6:561

Rudiments Survey and Research Clerk and, 6:561

run with in-tech can easily make thousands of dollars weekly in gross income and value of service delivered, 6:559

value of, 6:55

ARC Break Registrar, *see also* **Assistant Registrar**

bookbuyers and, 2:703, 6:713

contacts any person not enrolling or re-enrolling after declare of release, 6:547

people in CF ARC broken with the org and, 2:677, 6:554

refund and, 5:712

ARC Break Team, successful operating pattern of, 6:560

ARC triangle, *see also* **affinity; communication; reality**

Central Files folders and, 2:601

definition, MS3:7

duplication of type or class of appearance gives better, MS3:147

income comes from good ARC with the world, 3:103

Instructors and, 4:300

organization has to raise ARC with its community, MS3:157

PR surveys and negative ARC, MS3:37

PR totally built on, MS3:157

Arcturus, 0:19

area(s),

being cause over one's area, 0:249

reorganizing one's area to get tools within easy reach, 0:309

where stats just won't come up, 0:505, 0:584, 0:619

Area Cashier, definition, 3:131

Aristotle,

ethics and, 0:448

Greek philosopher, 1:497

army(ies),

electing a leader, 0:83

engaging in meaningless, often frantic and useless DO, 0:292

has a supposed product, 0:52

middle management, tactical planning and, 0:706

militia usually go down before regulars, 0:624

art,

misunderstood word and, 0:35

seeks to create an effect, 2:263

takes that bit more push for it to be effective art, 2:265

articles,

for outside publications must always mention specific text and its author, 7:1280

from tapes, how signed, 7:1280

no technical articles or letters by another person than LRH are permitted in Scientology publications, 7:1292

artists,

found as a magnet for persons with antisocial personalities, 1:1016

issuing projects involving, 0:355

rehabilitate old or faded artists, 6:135

as-isness, O/W write-ups and, 0:537

ask offs, aside from dead people, or people who want off the list or who move with no address change, there is no valid CF age, 0:360

assembly line, for produced promo, MS3:192

assessment,

on pc to find answer that would remedy the case, 4:1081, 5:672

to find outness in an auditor, 4:1081, 5:672

assets, books, meters, cassettes, films and insignia are, MS2:381

assignment board, 4:1061

assignment of posts, *see* **posting**

assist(s),

Auditing Assists, 5:630

Contact Assist, 5:629

for student doing badly on examination, 4:782

marriage counseling is classified as, 6:537

student assist, 5:210

Touch Assist, 5:629

use of, 5:629

assistance, *see* **help**

assistant, having exact write-ups of instructions to pass over to, 0:195

Assistant Org Sec, responsibilities and duties of, 7:599

Assistant Registrar, *see also* **ARC Break Registrar**

auditing job by mail, 2:657

definition and duties, 2:404

handles persons who have had ARC break with organization, 2:604

Association Secretary, Organization Secretary, *see also* **Executive Director**

duties, 7:1180

functions, 2:57, 3:227, 7:32

looking for dev-t, 0:398

promotion project for, 2:409

responsibilities for appointments, transfers or dismissals, 0:373

responsibility for financial management, 3:28

selected on basis of personal ability to promote and get show on the road, 2:59, 3:229, 7:34

task to get correct tech applied, 0:8

things to work hard to achieve, 7:210

two daily inspections, 7:621

weekly income reports entitled to, 3:121

Association Sec's Sec, list of secretarial admin duties to be performed, 7:619

A to E,

intention to force persons to go through steps as can salvage them, 5:348

relation to Dead Files, 1:978

staff or executives and, 1:989

students or pcs and, 1:989

suppressive person and, 4:90

atomic bomb, dangerous environment and, 0:486

atomic war, *see also* **war**

Purification Rundown and, 4:1235

attack(s)(ed)(ing), *see also* **enemy; opposition**

advocate total freedom, 7:1024

all attacks on Scientology were black propaganda from hidden fascist sources, 0:520

all statements attacking any political entity or ideology are withdrawn, 0:159

ARC broken person, 1:792, 4:933

expansion and, 0:100

from governments and monopolies, 0:8

handling of, effective and ineffective actions, 7:1026

how to meet any attack, 7:1029

inevitable when you hold up an image of freedom, 7:1026

investigation most effective in handling, 7:1027

I regard attacks on or criticism of orgs and staff as a personal affront, 0:276

attack(s)(ed)(ing), *(cont.)*

keynote of our campaign was to do right and keep our noses clean and thus render ourselves invulnerable to proper charges, 7:1022

look, investigate, defend, 7:1029

most successful response to meeting, 7:1024

never advertise, 7:1024

no results or bad results causing, 0:8

org PR area control and, MS3:158

people who attack, 7:1028

reply to any attack on Scientology, 7:1009

Scientology attacked by "public opinion" media, 0:10

should be in direction of enlarging one's scope and augmenting basic purpose, MS2:428

successful org will be fought, 0:64

true cause of is ARC breaks of long duration which transfer to us when we permit tech goofs, 6:548

United States inspiring Victorian State attacks in Australia, 0:159

attacker,

black PR and the, MS3:78

how he operates with black PR, MS3:79

attention, visualizing sequences and, MS1:73

attention-shifting drills, improve ability, MS1:73

attest(ed)(ing),

CSWs and, 0:427

false,

False Attestation Report, 0:544

don't go soft on penalty, 5:139

kills sign-ups if, 5:139

illegal for auditor to tell pc to attest, 5:245

now that we have ethics in and VIIIs in every org we can restore attestation, 4:387

permitting pc to attest to more than one grade at a time, 0:15, 5:15

attestation form, for final okay to audit a class, 5:854

attitude,

air and attitude of how hat is worn, 0:238

goodie-goodie attitude, 0:657

"nothing to do with me" attitude, 0:555

attorney,

appearing before Chaplain's Court, 1:957, 6:522

authorization to approach on behalf of the organization, 7:1061

audience, PR publication written for specific, MS3:12; *see also* **public**

audit(ed)(ing), *see also* **auditor; case; processing**

accidents and, 2:438

aimed at handling basic factors that stall a case cannot succeed unless it includes both, 4:993, 5:454

all bad results traced to inaccuracy in meter reading, 4:313

all roads lead to, 2:104, 4:127, 7:856

answer to human disability and travail, 4:926

ARC and, 4:549, 6:451

at own expense as amends project, 0:546

audit any process for which you have been certified, 6:722

bad processing, cause of, 0:301

below one's training level, 4:664

boasting as to speed of delivery in a session, 0:15

by a suppressive person, 1:992, 4:84

cases undergoing ethics actions, 4:1099

certificates delivered to all who earn them, 0:282

cheapest is to get trained and co-audit, 2:69, 4:337, 5:836

checkouts required before student auditing, 4:768

comm cycle additives,

definition, 4:918, 4:1176, 5:668

examples, 4:1175

conclusion for selling and delivering of, 2:449

conditions monitoring acceptance or establishment of number of weeks, 2:484

crime, falsifying auditor reports, 5:288

definition, 0:38

denial of, by a Comm Ev, 0:495

denied auditing or training until PTS person handles or disconnects, 0:493

Dianetic auditing lends itself to specific situations, 4:925

dishonesty and, 0:152, 0:153

done by OES in tiny org, 0:99

drugs and, 5:627

during ethics or justice action, 4:996

Eight Big Rules of, 5:37

ensuring pcs make each level fully before going on to next, 0:15

errors are gross, never slight, if a case doesn't move, 0:19

ethics actions and, 0:491, 1:794

ethics actions may only suspend training or deny auditing, 4:354

example of form for auditors, students, etc., to check out on auditing skills, 4:579

falsifying auditor reports is a crime, 4:1192

formal, definition, 4:549, 6:451

form vs. purpose, 4:319

audit(ed)(ing), *(cont.)*

for the preclear, 4:319

for use, 0:684, 2:104, 7:856

frowning on trying to prevent people from being processed, 0:153

good auditing, comm cycle used and muzzled, 4:1176, 5:668

good auditing worth far more than fees charged in HGC, 2:417, 6:709

goofs that would keep Scientology from working on every case, 0:18

guide to acceptable behavior for, 4:476

have good processing available and say so loudly, 0:626

having power as individuals due to, 0:484

HGC Admin responsible for economy of auditor auditing time, 4:250

high fee maintained to deter pcs while shunting them into Academy, 5:836

hours are coins, 4:253

how it is the primary solution to all problems, 0:242

how real gains for pcs are attained, 4:28

if auditor feels warm to the touch he can audit, 0:168

illness and, 2:438

important for org engaged in selling auditing in 25-hour lots to have regular HGC and staff, 2:447

in field of ability, auditing is king, 4:925

in the pursuit of the "new" one forgets the successful old, 2:438

introduction of mini list of processes for auditing requirements at each level, 4:420

is an award, 0:491

is king in field of ability, 2:438

is not limited action, 5:682

is problem in black and white, either it is done or it isn't, 0:19

is the service being supplied by org, 2:104

job vs., 0:168

Life Repair and, 4:145

lowest level of handling, 2:546, 4:1029

LRH is responsible for potential of, 0:685

major actions, 2:546

many uses to which it can be put, 5:681

matching of intern auditors in pairs, 3:158

may not be sold at half price or included in special offerings or packages, 2:474

medical care and, 2:438

medical examination and, 7:1100

minimum block of auditing which an org operating on the intensive system is allowed to sell in the HGC is a 12-hour block, 3:178

audit(ed)(ing), *(cont.)*

minimum of 25 hours per week must be delivered, 0:169

minors and, 3:145

mission and, 6:752

more desirable than anything else world has to offer, 0:332

more precise and organized than any so-called healing arts, 0:258

most expensive thing you can do is process the insane, 0:507

muzzled,
keynote for the beginning co-auditor, 4:708
lends itself perfectly to early Grade Chart processes, 4:708

never run a pc on a major action whose case is giving trouble, 2:546, 4:1029

no additives permitted on auditing comm cycle, 4:1175, 5:667

no-auditing and pc blows, remedy, 4:270, 6:551

no limit to what good auditing can do, 2:439

no "magic" touch, just skilled touch, 4:1082, 5:673

no mistakes which cannot be remedied, 4:682

no pc ever gets upset if actual error is spotted, 0:351

not owed to a staff member's family, 3:348

not to be accepted while working on TRs, 4:639

oldest rule in, 4:678

on a "locate the subject and word" basis, 4:335

only auditing can clean up community, 0:685

only one grade of auditing may be declared or attested to at one time, 4:1100

orders to, may not be made as sentence or used in an ethics court or by Comm Ev or any other reason, 4:354

org image and, 4:932, 5:588

org is an auditing factory that also trains people to audit, 0:675, 2:104, 7:856

OT Zero and TR 0 are key to good auditing, 4:1119

outside auditing, 0:170

O/Ws disclosed during, 4:995

pc application for major actions, 2:542, 2:546, 4:1024, 4:1029

pc has to have a new invoice to get audited, 4:1136

pc until case is handled, 5:686

people who have been scattered through one or another of the levels, handling, 0:283

person who has to be audited at once for desperate reasons, handling, 3:157

audit(ed)(ing), *(cont.)*

politics, ideology and, 0:157, 0:159

preferential treatment of preclears and, 3:157

pregnancy and, 2:438

pricing and, 2:449, 2:458

primary block on volume auditing, no two-way comm in training, 4:392

primary reason for case failures, 4:28, 5:99

problems in selling and delivering, 4:954

product of thoroughly audited pcs, 0:15

program for, 5:261

promotional actions and, 0:351

providing environment in which auditing is possible, 0:684

PTSes and, 1:1012

quality in, 0:16

real gains for pcs attained with lots of, 5:99

reasons for low hours, 5:277

receiving auditing while PTS, 0:470

refusing auditing, 0:153

regulations for auditing of staff and students, 4:681

relationship of ethics to, 4:127

requires an ability to confront and communicate and this is brought about on the TRs Course, 4:427

route to saner civilization, 5:858

Saint Hill Special Briefing Course regulations, 4:738

sales and delivery, orders to divisions, 4:129, 5:267, 7:284

scale of preference, 3:157, 4:888

sell hours, not result, 5:259

selling anything but hours asks the pc and Registrar to C/S, 2:446

selling by intensives, 2:458

service being supplied by org, 7:856

session, truly important data in, 5:671

shortening time of application of auditing for financial or labor-saving considerations, 0:15, 5:15

sign-up and, 2:447

single hours may not be sold, 4:867

skilled technical activity having precise steps and actions, 0:68

SP satisfied with when he gets worse, 1:1008

staff corrective actions requiring, 1:821

staff member(s),

don't add "processing" to handle people who don't work, 0:407

entitled to 2 hours study or auditing time per day, 0:222

hours for, 5:550

may buy auditing in the HGC, 5:578

audit(ed)(ing), *(cont.)*

staff member(s), *(cont.)*

may not be ordered to training or processing as a disciplinary measure, or to improve job performance, 0:168

may not be sent at org expense for processing, 0:174

no staff to audit private pcs, 0:165, 0:170

on a private basis, 4:870

org not processing its, result, 0:39

program for, 5:558

under Emergency condition may not have, 5:408

using org status to be trained or processed without completing contracts, 0:174

vital necessities regarding, 5:258

what can be run on any pc, 5:200

who should receive auditing, 0:156, 0:175, 0:213, 0:217

successes of, 2:449

suspension of, 0:495

system for selling, 2:446

team activity, 4:949, 4:1137, 6:718

test line is check on C/S and auditing quality, 4:234, 6:30

third dynamic auditing for production, MS2:24

three routes, 4:174

to *handle* a case one keeps at it, 2:442

Tone 40, definition and, 4:549, 6:451

TR Course not done concurrently with an auditing program, 4:641

training and, 0:684

training section, definition, 4:584

two types, 4:549, 6:451

two-way comm and volume of auditing and training, 4:391

understanding is higher than point of public entrance into processing, 0:323

uses of, 2:438, 4:925

US officials, processing of, 0:159

well-trained auditor gets no adverse reaction from auditing others, 0:268

what results depend on, 4:671

when to be satisfied with a pc's auditing, 4:27, 5:98

where there's pc to be processed, see that it's done, 0:273

why it really works, 0:38

why looking at or recognizing source of aberration in processing "blows" it, 0:37

winning attitude in, 4:929, 5:685

without folder study, 4:1117

you are raising your area little by little by auditing, 0:684

97

auditing commands, failing to clear every word of, 0:45

auditing discounts, 2:474; *see also* **discount(s)**

auditing folder,
HCO Why Finding worksheets and, 1:641
omissions, commonest, 1:640
Sec Check and Integrity Process Lists and, 1:641
Word Clearing worksheets and, 1:640

auditing program, Registrar must not sell, 4:1040

auditing report,
definition, 4:1182
should be as neat as possible, 4:1182

Auditing Section(s),
how they operate, 4:602
is not a practice section, 4:674
may not be treated as a practice section, 4:674
point to be driven home is section is not a training section, 4:604
processes to be used in, 4:675

auditing session, the truly important data in, 4:1080

auditor(s),
abusing "right to choose pcs" or advising others of "dog case," penalty, 4:209
acceptance of preclears, 4:1146
accepting unusual solution, 4:1088
administrative posts and, 4:844
admin people,
can qualify part time as, 0:223, 5:422
needed to back them up, 1:166
all auditors action, calling of, 0:100
assignment, 4:670
assignment for "on-call" auditing, 1:180
bad breath or body odor, 0:340
barriers to training, 4:320
best auditors made our best staff members, 2:414
biggest time wasters of a C/S are flubby, 5:850
big target, have trained auditors in plenty in orgs and field, 5:494
certain classes of, 4:599
Chaplain's main area of operation preventing people falling off org board is auditors, 6:523
chopped up by in session, 1:993, 4:85
clarification of "part-time" auditor, 2:206
classification more important than certification in judging skill, 5:342
classification of, 4:171
conditions orders from, 0:666
constant retraining within a level forbidden, 0:169

auditor(s), *(cont.)*
continuing to audit a person over and above the amount of hours paid for, 2:451
criteria for HGC auditors, 5:831
criticize auditors as a group, 4:85
C/S is the auditor's "handler," 4:1134
dangerous, 5:589
definition, 0:154, 2:162, 4:64, 4:175, 4:1078, 5:669, 6:187
delivering service without having a fully paid invoice to hand is Treason, 2:451, 3:170, 4:220
deserve the best on Solo levels, 4:820
diet, exercise and, 5:639
disseminate and purely preclears seldom do, 4:164, 5:330
D of P and, 4:904, 4:964
D of P responsibility for procurement of, 4:904
don't graduate those we wouldn't hire in HGC, 4:302
don't let an auditor on staff who has a bad needle on help, 4:54
drilling and, 4:924, 4:1082, 5:598, 5:673
estranging husbands and wives subject to Court of Ethics, 4:361
Ethics and, 5:587
for false reports, 1:626
for off-line directions, 1:626
exercise and, 0:225
F/Ning, definition, 5:702
failing to,
clear every word of every command or list used, 0:45
go from one level to next without becoming auditor for that class, 5:849
write clearly on worksheets or put down enough text, 0:47
write down disclosed crime, 0:555
fees charged, 5:193, 5:342
5-year contract, 5:530
forbidden to audit a rundown that he has not trained and been certified on, 4:664
forbidden to use noncertified staff auditors on HGC pcs, 5:833
fractured comm cycles and ethics-type case pcs, 1:625, 4:1173, 5:586
frequenting org premises for purposes of obtaining private preclears, 4:874
fumbling around and seldom getting results, handling for, 5:670
good, proven auditors assigned to audit good auditors, 4:923, 5:597
grade and class of pc and assignment of, 4:923, 5:597
grounds on which may refuse to process pc, 4:297

auditor(s), *(cont.)*

handling, 4:148, 4:910

handling to make auditors who can confront and communicate, 4:429

have to know the Auditor's Code, 4:569

HCO must pass on all auditors employed by HGC, 5:831

HGC Admin responsible for minimum change of auditors on pc, 4:250

HGC auditor, ideal scene and stats, 4:144

HGC, criteria for, 5:832

highest persons on control, make best staff members, 1:188

hire only full-time, 5:582

hiring of, 4:386, 4:835

how auditor can deprive staff of its pay and welfare, 0:302

how one can be an auditor but fail as a C/S, 0:65

how they are made and unmade, 4:304

if any pre-1960 auditor feels confused about his class, 5:332

if warm and breath can be detected, is in condition to audit, 0:168, 4:316

importance of, 0:154

incentive to be, 4:164, 5:330

individually practicing, often fails, 4:951

in-tech org services, a field full of well-trained auditors (and a good Div 6 and Div 2) are what give volume of delivery and GI and pay, 6:399

is either a staff auditor, working full time on units or he may not audit for the organization, 4:1171

lack of, handling, 4:965

lack of star-rates on staff auditors and interns, found to crash an HGC, 4:907, 5:492

lateness of auditor will result in his pay being docked, 4:1146

Lead Auditor, duties and purpose of, 4:1151

learned to audit by AUDITING, 4:420

learning only mechanical processes, not theory of mind, 0:65

leaving Cramming should go through the Examiner, 5:702

letter writing and, 2:607, 2:612

library and, 5:724

limping and fumbling, handling is the intern system, 5:851

magazine notices on validation of certificates, 2:609, 6:702

make the better executives, 4:386

making flubless, 5:694

matching intern auditors in pairs so they can crack their own cases, 2:521

auditor(s), *(cont.)*

may not use processes above his or her class, 4:164, 4:174, 5:330

messing up HGC, staff and field cases, effect of, 0:302

meter goes null on gradient scale of misses by, 4:314

minimum of 25 hours per week delivered by, 0:169

missing withholds is most destructive thing they can do, 4:1196, 5:615

misunderstood words and, 5:425

morale depends on completions, 5:700

must be certified for any rundown being audited, 5:860

must be full-time staff members, 1:189

must encourage in state and public and through all connections displacing psychiatric abuses with sane auditing, 7:1139

must hold a valid Certificate of Ordination, 4:1190

must not ever turn out a bad auditor, 5:164

need staff and post hats and need to be trained on them, 0:203

new, training required, 4:568

no bonuses of any kind may be paid for "completions," 4:1117

no mistake they can make which cannot be remedied, 4:682

not required to accept a pc, 4:896

not to continue auditing pc who has run out of hours, 4:263

Okay to Audit must be attested to in C&A, 4:946, 5:846

only auditors in Academy, there are no cases, 4:304

only classified auditor is truly a professional, 4:175

only disciplined or given courts or Comm Evs for violations of HCOBs, LRH tapes or issues, 0:145

only individuals in universe capable of freeing man, 0:154

only source of trouble are incompetent, 4:310

org major product, well trained auditors, 4:145

outline of duties of a staff auditor, 4:1145

outside auditing, 0:170

pcs may not be postponed for lack of, 4:250

penalty for unclear worksheets, 5:470

personnel pool for, 5:528

possession of certificate carries responsibility of knowing skills covered by it, 0:169

practical auditing skills, 4:579

auditor(s), *(cont.)*

preclear goes to Review, auditor to Review Cramming Section, 1:626

preclears he may refuse to release from HGC, 4:298

professional rates, 2:415, 2:416

professional, training route for (1964), 4:176

programing of, 5:529

program org must follow on staff auditors, 5:833

progress board, 5:531

project to get auditors starting successful practices, 6:681

promotional actions and, 0:351

psychiatry circulates rumors about auditors so it is only fair for the auditor to know exactly the status of psychiatry, 7:1139

qualifications for Post Purpose Clearing, 5:461

qualifications of HGC staff auditors, 4:1143

real auditor has to be able to *apply* the data, 4:1079, 5:671

real stars of staff team are auditors and HCO personnel, 1:60

reason for, 4:145

receives no better processing than he gives, 4:164, 5:330

refusing to audit, reason, 4:210

Registrar has no authority, 4:294

responses permitted if any query arrives concerning, 6:702

responsibility for blown students, 1:998, 4:90

responsible for application of the tech, 0:685, 2:105, 7:857

results of getting tech known and used by, 0:68

rights of staff auditor, 4:1146

routinely make Releases with Academy courses today, 2:519

schedule, 4:1146

seeking advice on cases, off-line, 4:1173, 5:586

sending to Cramming on each goof, 5:702

send to Review Cramming Section when pc goes to Review, 4:1174, 5:587

sent to Ethics for false report, 4:1174

sent to Ethics for not following instructions or taking off-line directions, 4:1174

shortage, basic Why of, 4:419

skills that make one worthy of the name, 4:613

slow auditors, 4:923, 5:597

special designations and insignia for, 0:154

SPs criticize auditors as a group, 1:993

staff auditor,
  basic staff auditor's hat, 4:1156
  rotation, 4:1155
  set up, 0:703
  staff auditors count as admin personnel, 0:95

auditor(s), *(cont.)*

staff trained,
  as, are clothed in ministerial suit, 7:1320
  as auditors, 4:386

statistics, 4:210, 5:74

statistics computed on the Examiner's Report, 4:1188

status measured by, 4:1189

student and staff hat come before tech, 5:422

students in the Academy are auditors, not preclears, 2:488

Tech Div has first call on all trained auditors, 4:96

Tech Services responsibility, 4:904

time is gold, 4:207

times of Technical and Qualifications overload, may be called upon, 5:737

trained,
  in skills of level or rundown could co-audit, 4:688
  make better executives, 5:493
  only by our orgs, 6:720
  scarcity of caused by, 4:910

training, approach, 4:320

training new, 5:525

training of Flag auditors, 0:290

two additional criteria for hiring, 4:961

uncertified, and results in HGC, 5:833

unclassed, cannot charge fee for auditing, 4:188

uncorrected error in auditor is perpetuated on every pc auditor audits, 0:11

uses processes of his class or lesser, 5:330

using a process on which they have high reality will obtain high results with the pc, 4:1045

waiting time is zero if Tech Services done and arranged well, 4:207

ways and means of settling rows amongst them, 6:683

way to make more, 4:666

we must not ever turn out a bad auditor, 7:1188

we will go as far as Dianetics and Scientology work in hands of, 0:337

what an ethical auditor does, 6:698

what causes them to have a lose, 4:928, 5:684

what is meant by "perfect on a meter," 4:313

whenever an org has a Tech or Qual backlog it is usual to call an "all auditors" action, 6:94, 7:277

when graduating should be capable of being employed, 4:568

when pc won't run, 1:625

when they may refuse to audit a pc, 4:209

who blow, reason for, 4:970

auditor(s), *(cont.)*

who fumbles around and seldom gets results, handling for, 4:1079

who get results are happy auditors, 4:1119

who gets no adverse reaction from auditing others, 0:268

who goofs seriously, 4:889

who let down have Why and misunderstood words, 4:970

why single practitioners can't expand their practices without overwork, 0:129

you don't "find" them, you make them, 4:966

Auditor Estimation Review,

ARC break review, 4:1179

auditing cycle review, 4:1178

continuous overt review, 4:1180

data duplication review, 4:1178

E-Meter review, 4:1177

knowledge of potential trouble sources, 4:1179

knowledge of suppressive person review, 4:1179

O/W review, 4:1180

pc in-session review, 4:1178

problem review, 4:1179

repetitive command review, 4:1178

Auditor Estimation test, 4:1177, 5:201

auditor judgment, lack of, 4:634

Auditor, **magazine,** *see also* **magazine**

ads must be aligned to the motif of the issue, 2:252

bonus for staff for every issue mailed on or within a week before the deadline for it, 2:245

change of address and, 2:708

classified ads and, 2:248

correspondent must be appointed in each Central Organization, 2:247

editor must follow management strategy in what to market and when, 2:251

feature news stories and, 2:254

finances and, 2:259

for each of the Saint Hills is originated and produced by the editor in the SH, 2:258

income peaks follow a good issue by about one month, 2:250

is not dated, it is numbered only, 2:255

issue authority, 2:257

issues of lighter weight and more varied vein can be issued through the year, 2:243

lists of names and, 2:254

LRH articles and, 2:253

mailing schedule, 2:245, 2:250

minimal types of ads that can appear in each issue of *The Auditor,* 2:251

Auditor, **magazine,** *(cont.)*

Minor issue reaches the broad Scientology public and tends to emphasize lower levels and pushing a person through his lower org to SH, 2:250

monthly *Journal of Scientology,* 2:249

must be excellent in early spring and early autumn and must go out to the whole list, 2:243

photos and, 2:254

plan and assemble a big important *Auditor* at least four months in advance of its issue date, 2:244

purpose, 2:250

reinforcement of *Auditor* promotion, 2:245

rigid rule on technical articles, 2:247

section made for vital statistics, 2:247

sent out by each Saint Hill org each month without fail, 2:250

size and layout of, 2:256

special editorial staff and provisions must exist for, 2:245

staff consist of Editor, Assistant Editor and Photographer, 2:258

standard features, 2:252

stresses the Training Route heavily, 2:250

success stories and, 2:254

supplements and, 2:256

survey and marketing tech must be fully used, 2:255

themes are planned months in advance, 2:251

vital statistics and, 2:254

way the Editor of *Auditor* in period of high stats ran her office and staff, 2:246

Auditor Recovery Program, 4:970, 5:425

Auditors Association, 0:354

call-in and, 2:647, 3:223, 4:282, 7:871

infiltration of, 6:728

opening up community, 6:726

org board, ideal scenes and statistics of, 6:730–731

project to set up, 6:726

relation to org success, 6:732

Auditor's Code, 4:1186, *see also* **auditor**

breaks, 0:468

evaluation of past-life identities or case states is violation of, 4:260

failure to follow, 4:638, 6:721

for SH staff auditors, 4:118, 5:914

HAS responsibility for enforcing, 1:32

Scientology Marriage Counseling and, 6:540

selecting staff auditor trainees and, 5:528

taking pc off auditing once started is breach of, 4:25

Auditor's C/S, definition, 4:1015

Auditors Night, 6:727

Auditor's Report Form,

definition, 4:1015

falsified, subject to a Court of Ethics, 4:679

turned in by every auditor, 4:672

written during session and turned in by auditor, 4:672

auditor's rights, major why of confusions in HGC is abuse of, 4:209

auditor training, prerequisite for, 4:659

audits, label all original records, 3:134

Australia, 0:159, 0:410

authoritarian rule,

antipathy I have to, 0:140

what determines to what degree it exists, 0:4

authority,

to handle routing, 0:409

to issue orders, 0:133–134

undermined by being made to commit injustices, 0:520

Authority and Verification Unit; Authority, Verification and Correction Unit International; AVC Int,

checksheets authorized by, 0:14

passing HCO PLs and HCOBs, 0:143

authorization,

command channel used upward for, 0:387

of checksheets, 0:14

policy authorizes people to issue orders, 0:133–135

automaticity, bank and, 0:449

automation, dream of industrialist is a totally automated activity, MS1:394

AVC, AVU, *see* **Authority and Verification Unit**

awards,

auditing and training are, 0:491, 1:744, 4:354, 5:109

Blue Star, Green Star and Gold Star, 0:662

cancellation of, for high crimes, 0:474

Fellow of Scientology, 5:326

function of the HCO Board of Review, 5:94

grade insignia, 5:356

HCO Board of Review and, 1:32

loss of, 0:495

may not be cancelled for crime, 0:474

may not be cancelled for misdemeanor, 0:470

may not be cancelled, suspended or reduced for error, 0:467

memorial, are medals or plaques, 5:345

obtained not as result of courses or examination, 5:344

only a Comm Ev can remove, 0:492

only ones that may be given, 5:343

Saint Hill FSM bonus awards to orgs or missions, 3:360

suspension of, for crimes, 0:474

awareness, *see also* **Grade Chart; observation**

52 levels from Unexistence up to the state of Clear, 2:517, 4:186

"level of awareness" means "that of which a being is aware," 2:517

other-intentionedness coming from unawareness, 0:509

person audited a bit below or at his level of, 2:517, 4:186

shutting down after misunderstood word, 0:39

what can the person be aware of is the level determiner, 4:619

awareness levels, 0:95, 5:191

Awareness Scale, org board and, 0:95–97

Axiom 28, 0:45, 1:319, 1:900–901, 4:483, MS3:72

B

Bachelor of Scientology (BScn),

goal, 4:567

qualification for, 5:148

training and examination and what it includes, 4:558

UK, certificate for, 5:317

backflash, definition, 0:372, 7:602

background, calling materials "background," result of, 5:275

background material, 0:14

backlog(s), backlogging; *see also* **half-done; not-dones**

activity, generates new work not concerned with reducing the backlog amount, 7:432

all auditors action for Tech or Qual backlog, 0:100

can increase itself by adding disorder that undoes things already done, 7:432

cure for, 7:432, MS2:226, MS3:412

definition, 7:431, MS2:225, MS3:411

destroy possibility of future production, 7:433, MS2:227, MS3:413

D of P and, 4:968, 6:302

doubles the work by addition of demand handling, 7:432, MS2:226

effect of, 0:426

example of handling, 2:441

generates new work not concerned with reducing the backlog amount, MS3:412

how org loads up with, 0:391

in Tech and Qual, effect on org, 2:441, 5:684

backlog(s), backlogging, *(cont.)*

most destructive thing in an org is a Tech or Qual backlog, 2:445

of pcs must be avoided, 5:493

one-hour wait (in Qual) is a, 5:55

prevents itself from being handled, 7:432, MS2:226, MS3:412

Quals never have, 5:55

result from not doing usual actions, 0:256

stat penalty for cramming backlog, 5:78

tech backlogs are primary menace in an org, 0:100, 6:94, 7:277

Tech or Qual backlog, 4:928, 4:932

two main classes are, 7:431, MS2:225, MS3:411

unusual actions will backlog one, 0:257

whenever an org has Tech or Qual backlog it is usual to call an "all auditors" action, 7:277

when pcs tend toward backlog the org increases its tech staff on a long range and starts heavily pushing courses on a short-range basis, 7:277

backwards evaluation(s), *see also* **evaluation(s)**

example of, MS1:179

how to do, MS1:179

bad, *see also* **evil; crime; crimes in Scientology; offense**

bank made to keep people who were not bad from going bad, 0:158

bank seeks to perpetuate the, 0:9

opposing what people think is bad, 0:337

reactive minds demand suppression of good and production of, 0:480

reason most people think discipline is bad, 0:521

bad, *(cont.)*

restrain just trifle more than a bank can compel a bad action, 0:480

so much bad in the best of us, 0:532

bad hats, PR and, 6:622, MS3:5

bad manners, 0:328

bad needle, definition, MS1:397

badness, safeguarding others from, 1:728

bad news,

formula to apply when being knocked about by, 0:420

leader doesn't have to know all the, 0:640

balance sheet, orders and, 3:405, 7:1089, MS2:318

bank, *see also* **reactive mind**

constructed to make very sure that no one ever succeeds in, 7:488

says that the group is all and the individual nothing, MS3:468

bank account(s),

Claims Verification Board (CVB) Account, MS2:324

FBO No. 1 Account, MS2:323

FBO No. 2 Account, MS2:323

FBO No. 3 Account, MS2:323

FSM Account, MS2:324

General Liability Fund, 3:401, MS2:323

HCO Book Account, MS2:324

Org Main Account, MS2:323

Org Reserve Account, MS2:323

Reserved Payment Account, MS2:324

Service Completion Award (SCA) Account, MS2:324

banking, 3:34

commodities and, MS2:390

example of, MS2:390–391

example of using receipts as currency, MS2:389

money is a negotiable receipt for deposited goods, MS2:389

what got current bankers in present predicaments, MS2:392

bankruptcy, *see also* **insolvency; solvency; viability**

corporations threatened with, 0:300

states that are going bankrupt and dying, 0:302

barrier(s), *see also* **stop**

confronting and drills in Esto tape series can push their way through, MS2:64

consist of, MS3:72

noncommunication consists of, 0:46

no objective worth obtaining was achieved without some, 0:92

removing barriers, 0:123, 0:283

Base Order (BO), definition, 1:430

basic(s),

ability to handle basics with such speed and certainty that it seems instinct, 0:54

all advances have been in how to handle basics better, 0:65

books and, 0:65

definition, 0:51

disorder vs., 0:307

effect of altering basics of the technology, 0:126

ethics, basics of, 0:447

get in one at a time, when personnel or place distracted, 7:415

how to know if basics are out in an area, 0:307

importance of knowing basics of post, 0:306

in our very oldest books, 0:65

knowledge of, 0:54, 0:65, 0:312

organizational basics, 0:89

out-basics, 0:306–307

person put in Estates to redo basics, 0:392

products, basics relating to, 0:290

standard admin and, 0:54

undercut to, MS1:343, MS2:177

when a personnel or place is distracted, get in only easy basics one at a time, MS3:395

basic courses, *see also* **Department 17**

description and purpose (1954), 4:290

how to organize them up, 6:473

Supervisors, what they must do, 6:482

basic nature, of man, MS1:396

basic purpose,

basic formula of living is having and following a, 0:123

cleaning away barriers, noncompliance and distractions from the, 0:123

description, 0:117

Basic Staff Certificate,

examination for, 1:238

permanent status and, 1:238

Basic Staff Hat, 0:27, 0:28

HCO people know it backwards and enforce it, 1:166

Basic Staff Proficiency Certificate, 5:351

Basic Technical Certificate, 5:351

basic words, use of, 6:750

basket(s), basket station(s), *see also* **in-basket**

Comm Center contains basket for each staff member, 0:369

in-basket, 1:354

location of, 0:378

basket(s), basket station(s), (cont.)

one puts one's baskets and one's "hands" into
lines and acts on lines, 0:326

out-basket, 1:354

pending basket, 1:354

piled high, reason for, 0:400

sizing up org by watching despatch lines
and, 0:418

three-basket system, 0:371, 0:378, 1:304, 1:354

battle(s), third party and national battles, 0:511

battle plan(s), *see also* **plan; program; project;
strategic plan(ning); tactical plan**

can become a liability, 7:460, MS2:446,
MS3:440

conditions formulas and, 0:664

definition, 0:696, 7:458–460, MS2:444–446,
MS3:438–440

example of what makes up your, 0:648

gradient scale of grand overall plan broken
down into segments, 7:460, MS2:446,
MS3:440

individual staff member responsibility for, 0:180

organizational planning and, 7:460, MS2:446,
MS3:440

policy concerning, 0:706

production and, 0:706, 0:707

short periods of time, 7:458, MS2:444,
MS3:438

staff meeting and, 0:180

starting each new week with a, 0:664

stat analysis and, 0:648

strategic planning and, 0:706, 0:707

test of an executive and, 7:460, MS2:446,
MS3:440

turning strategic planning into exact doable
targets, 7:459, MS2:445, MS3:439

be(ing),

one is what one is, not what one is admired or
hated for, 0:633

wrong personal org board to BE only, 0:292

beanstalk, 0:378

Bean Theory, MS2:339

be, do, have, 0:291–293

correct sequence of action, MS1:239

example of incorrect sequence, MS1:239

PR surveys and, MS3:37

survey questions and, MS3:55, MS3:230

Beginning Scientologist,

certificate for, 4:361

course outline, 6:750

behavior; *see* **conduct**

being(s); *see also* **individual; man; people;
preclear; thetan**

achieving a simple, powerful, effective
being, 0:38

attempting to put ethics in on their
dynamics, 0:457

basically good and attempting to survive, 0:457

competent higher-toned beings and compliance,
7:389, MS3:369

how reactive mind keeps beings from
growing, 0:117

in fair condition and compliance,
7:389, MS3:369

object of orgs, totally freed beings,
4:159

percentage of degraded to big beings, 7:390,
MS3:370

reactive minds can exert pain and discomfort
on a, 0:480

thinking of an org as an identity or a, 0:105

we are salvaging beings, 6:108

who can be depended upon to evolve beneficial
measures, 0:158

who try to weaken strong people, 0:205

work is done by living beings using good sense
and skill, 0:82

beingness,

anybody has a chance to go up in state
of, 0:234

doingness, havingness and, 0:291

how to materialize a real, 0:293

person who, having accepted a post, does not
know THAT he is a certain assigned
beingness is in Treason, 0:572

thetan's consideration on, MS1:407

benefactor(s),

defended by leaving, 5:548

person defends by leaving, 4:1048

betrayal, betray(ing); *see also* **trust**

after trust, 0:567

junior betraying exec, 0:420

of the functions and purposes of a group, 0:572

big; *see* **size**

Big League Sales, *see also* **registration**

example of handling public individual
and, 2:583, 6:409

PRs and, MS3:71

Reges who do not know or use, 2:570, 6:392

use of, 2:583, 6:409

bill(s), *see also* **debt; expense; financial planning**

cannot be paid without slip from inspecting executive certifying goods are on hand or work completed and satisfactory, 3:288

clean, well-dressed staff begets payment of, 0:334

disputed, handling, 0:326

don't incur until you have cash to pay it in the bank, 3:27, 7:925

each and every item on every bill must be covered by a purchase order, 3:291

exact way to pay, 3:248

example of measures taken to reduce, 7:929

fund shortage, how to handle, 3:288

goodwill and, 0:332

important points regarding handling of bills, 3:249

must be checked against the transaction in the regular business files, 3:391

never continue to use a private business firm after they become obnoxious about bills, 3:249

never contract unless money is immediately in sight to pay for them, 7:926

one files first and then reconciles the bill with one's records and what one has paid and then pays the bill, 3:392

pay every bill in Affluence condition, 0:564, 0:646

paying of, 3:35, 3:317

purchase or authorization record must come to hands of Disbursement Clerk before check may be written, 3:288

reporting and handling of, 3:110

Reserved Payment Account and bills in question, 3:315

routine bills, 3:289

routing and handling of, 3:313

statistic of bills owing, MS2:405

total accumulation of statements and purchases makes a true picture of what is owed, MS2:405

unpaid, can ruin your PRO in a whole town, 3:69

verifying correctness of, 3:288

billing,

inaccurate, 0:276

most frequent source of ARC breaks with public is inaccurate billing, 2:435

bill of particulars,

definition, 1:929

types of, 1:930

bills files, credit rating and correct payment comes from, MS2:47

bills statement, outstanding POs and, 3:293

binding, definition, MS3:194

biochemical substances, prevent case gain, 4:1205

biophysical handling, defined, 4:1206

Bismarck, Otto von (1815–1898), psychiatry, psychology and, 0:328

blackmail, 0:462, 1:631, 7:1035

black PR, use of, 6:621

black propaganda, 0:520, 1:809

campaign(s),

against Scientology, why it folded up, MS3:28

answer to, MS3:103

disprove every rumor, MS3:83

disprove false data, MS3:82

fill the vacuum, MS3:81, MS3:87

handle the interest level, MS3:83

how to impede or destroy, MS3:85

only counterattack handles, MS3:86

policy and rules for handling, MS3:29, MS3:81

study out the scene to find the source, MS3:84

technique of, MS3:29

definition, MS3:26, MS3:73, MS3:77, MS3:88

developed into fine art by British and German services in WW I, MS3:28

existing scene and, MS3:76

how it recoils on person using it, MS3:79

intention of, MS3:77, MS3:79

investigate and attack, MS3:87

sanctimonious hypocrites engage in, MS3:85

use of imagination in, MS3:75, MS3:4

where no data available people invent it, MS3:80

where PR and intelligence cross, MS3:29

blame,

being blamed sometimes blunts being cause, 0:249

blaming case is effect, 0:248

seeking to shift blame to innocent staff member, 0:472

blind, unhatted persons look sort of, 1:294

blindness, cause blindness, 0:242

blind registration, *see also* **Registrar(s); registration**

definition, 2:564, 6:387

example of, 2:564, 6:388

results and, 4:1035

what a Registrar needs to know, 4:1032

what the org delivers and, 2:565, 6:388

blind repair,

five areas of danger, 4:1008

when no FES is done, one is doing a blind repair, 4:1008

blood, we're playing for, 0:231

blow(s)(ing), *see also* **overt acts; withhold(s)**
5:547

auditors who blow, reason for, 5:425

caused by violations of and failure to use study tech, 0:47

co-auditors, handling, 4:699

criminal charges filed if any monies or org property is missing in consequence of, 0:177

definition, 0:203, 4:269, 4:1047, 6:550

five main reasons for student blows, 6:550

four reasons for most pc blows, 6:551

from course or session result from technical failures, 1:989

lack of grooved-in hats at the bottom of, MS1:206, MS1:415

nonattendee to staff study is a blown student, 0:224

org internal suppression causing, 0:102

people leave because of their own overts and withholds, 4:1048, 5:548

permitting blows without clearing overts and withholds, 4:1049, 5:549

preclear,
> four reasons for most, 4:270
> remedy for no-auditing, 4:270

reason behind, 0:177, 1:906

second phenomenon and, 4:330

staff member blow, actions taken upon, 0:177

student,
> five main reasons for, 4:269
> follow misunderstoods, 4:397
> handling of, 4:90, 4:366
> Super who taught him will be comm eved for out-tech, 4:403

student and pc, 5:734

traced back to PTS gone on leave to see antagonistic connections, 1:1050

blown students, handling of, 1:998

blow-offs,

explanation of departures, 1:724

why people leave, 1:725

Blue Seal, rating for field auditors, 5:312

blue star ethics protection, 0:662, 1:578; *see also* **ethics protection**

Board Executive Directives (BEDs),
definition, 1:430

Board Finance Officer,

finance stress and, 3:85, 7:724

should play it cool, require further decisions from the board and shepherd funds carefully, 3:85

board of directors,

how to write board minutes, 7:1119

reason for 90 percent of laws and directives passed by, 0:67

Board of Investigation, MS3:306

Advisory Council and, 7:910

appointed by local LRH Comm, 1:252

composed of impartial members who investigate disastrous occurrence, 7:326

composition of, 1:952–953

convened for improvement in org or stats, 1:952, 1:958

convened if any organization statistics level out, remain low, drop, 7:512

covering causes of statistics that level out, remain low or drop, 7:512

false attestation results in, 1:953

findings and recommendations, 1:953

less serious than Comm Ev, 1:953

members on two or more concurrently, 1:959

post changes and, 1:252

purpose, 1:952

termination of, 1:959

Board of Review, *see* **HCO Board of Review**

authority and what it can cancel, 5:129, 7:1265

Class II Awards, 5:165

composed of, 5:129

examinations and, 5:150, 5:168

examining status of Knowledge Reports, 1:715

function and practice, 1:960–961, 5:129, 7:1171, 7:1265

functions delegated to Dir of Processing, 5:159

reality test for students, 5:161

stable datum is, 5:129, 7:1171

Board Policy Letter(s) (BPL),

cannot be comm eved or given a court or disciplined for not following them, 0:145

contradicting HCO PLs or LRH EDs, 0:304

definition, 1:430

Board Technical Bulletin(s) (BTB),

cannot be comm eved or given a court or disciplined for not following them, 0:145

contradicting HCO PLs or LRH EDs, 0:304

definition, 1:430

bodies in the shop,

definition of statistic, 6:226

get lots of, 2:401

make sure lots move through, 7:630

body, bodies,

"bringing a body," 0:326

brought with a despatch, 0:326, 0:369, 0:416

body, bodies, *(cont.)*

capable of, 5:622

carbon-oxygen engine, 5:620

exercise and, 0:225

guiding in new body traffic, 0:352

keeping it clean and functioning, 0:251

pointing out channels on which bodies
flow, 0:389

spirit alone may save or heal, 6:515

Thetan–Mind–Body–Product pattern, 0:128–129,
0:654

when not exercised, goes downhill, 5:639

Body Registrar, *see also* **Registrar(s)**

functions of, 2:500

is a sign-up Registrar of individuals, 2:432

prime purpose of, 2:432

scheduling books and, 2:629

statistic of, 2:551

steps for answering forms or letters, 2:632

tests and, 6:276

where public traffic is large, additional Body
Reges must be posted, 2:45

body routing,

one of many channels for use by the Public
Divisions to introduce new public to
Dianetics and Scientology, 6:228

successful body router and, 6:228

body traffic, space planning and, 7:1330

Bolivar, Simon, 0:629–641

could not use men when they were begging to
be used, 7:381, MS3:361

did not aim for any solvency of states he
controlled, MS3:358, 7:378

did not get his troops or officers rewarded,
MS3:358

don't leave an enemy financed and solvent
while you let friends starve, 7:380

downfall, 7:378, MS3:358

first error, 7:377, MS3:357

glowed things right, until he no longer could,
7:377, MS3:357

greatest error, 7:379, MS3:359

liberator of South America, 7:376, MS3:356

two very real errors leading to his downfall,
7:378, MS3:358

weakened his friends and ignored his enemies,
7:379, MS3:359

Bongville, will be because Flag programs and
projects weren't going in, 7:424

bonus(es), *see also* **pay; units of pay**

authorization for, 0:546

awards to persons not org or mission
connected, 3:360

Case Supervisor, 3:355

Christmas bonuses, 3:365

claims and disputes, 3:356, 5:136

computation of, 3:340

Course Supervisor, 3:355

Cramming Officer, 3:355

D of P, 3:355

D of T, 3:355

Director of Certs and Awards, 3:356

Director of Review, 3:356

Director of Tech Services, 3:355

ethics files and, 1:702

Examiner, 3:356, 3:358

executive requirements for, 0:221

Management Status One checksheet and, 7:464,
MS2:191, MS2:295

only bonuses which may be awarded shall
consist of courses and intensives, 3:346

Qual Div, 5:135

Qual Sec, 3:356

Review Auditors, staff auditors and
interns, 3:355

rights to, 3:356

Saint Hill FSM bonus awards to orgs or
missions, 3:360

scale of, 2:576

staff in Affluence favored in, 5:408

Tech Div, 5:135

Tech Sec, 3:355

when a bonus cleans a person's ethics
files, 0:546

bonus eligible, management status checksheets
and, MS1:366

book(s) *see also* **book sales**

ads and sales are the keys to org survival,
2:295, 6:259

advertise books first, services second, 2:325

advertising books means Pubs mail order
business of individual book sales, 6:257

advertising depends on, 5:835

any money you get from book sales should go
to buy more books, 6:267

any time a Central Org requires special
handling from a Pubs Org, full postage
and handling charges are made, 6:255

are dissemination, 2:331

are the first line of promotion and
contact, 6:257

book(s), *(cont.)*

autographed copies by LRH, 2:342

basic approaches that get books into people's hands, 2:76, 6:244

basics are in our very oldest books, 0:65

best ambassador and spokesman, 2:298, 6:266

be sure books are on hand and deliver them, 0:282

big book distributors and how to handle, 2:306, 6:256

book sales,
> predict your future GI, 6:266
> to Scientologists and raw public the front line of expansion and org prosperity, 6:261

bring in org income, 2:78, 6:247

broad data on Scientology is in, 2:378

carelessness or inattention to book materiel can whittle down and then destroy the org GI, MS2:382

charges on, 7:834

costing formula for pricing a book by the *publishing* agency (not the seller), 2:268, 6:241

Department 16 should handle book ads, 2:294, 6:258

develop a new field so tours can work, 2:295

Dianetics books should advertise only Dianetics books, 2:143, 6:231

discounts,
> for bookstores, 2:305, 6:255
> only 10% to International and Lifetime Members, 2:306, 6:256

dissemination and, 6:234

distribution, you will not accomplish any security unless books are distributed, 2:331, 6:234

do make booms, 2:361

first line,
> of dissemination, 2:298, 6:266
> of promotion and contact, 2:293, 2:315, 2:705

have new people read, 2:401

heaviness and bulkiness of a book determines respect for it, 2:138

income sheets and, 3:76

it takes books to develop a new field so tours can work, 6:259

lifeblood of any Scientology organization, 2:302

local reprintings of books forbidden, 3:189

lowering the cost of a book decreases its sales volume in most cases, 2:139

mail order business of individual book sales, 2:293

make a personal contact all by themselves if put in the right places, 2:60, 6:166

book(s), *(cont.)*

make booms but they have to be sold first, 2:353, 6:264

making sure that interested people get books is making sure that they will continue their interest, 2:331

market and sell books and use the money to buy more books, 6:267

marketing and, MS3:164

maximum discounts on, 6:255

may never be given away by org or Pubs Org, MS1:212

may not be locally published without written authorization, 2:268, 6:241

merchandising and, 2:139

minimum book stocks, 2:309

misuses of Book Account policies, 2:300

money from book sales should go to buy more books, 2:299, 2:324

"more info" card put in the back of every, 0:625

must be invoiced whether charged for or not, 2:479, 2:552, 3:141, 6:386

must be marketed and sold or can't get word of mouth into public, 2:298, 6:266

must be subsidized by adding reserve monies to HCO Book Account from time to time, 2:312, 2:313

new, is heralded, reviewed (without giving all in it or its key) *and* advertised in magazines and flyers, 2:139

no book should be released with an improper address or price in it or lacking a Central Organization address, 2:326

no general service ads should be in public publication, only book ads, 2:294, 6:258

oldest Dianetics and Scientology books are brand new to bulk of humanity, 0:362

one even puts thicker paper in books which have less text, 2:139

order as many books as you possibly can without regard to fixed consumption considerations, 2:309

orgs must purchase books and standard stock items from Pubs Org for cash, 2:313

part of promo monies must always go to promoting raw public book sales, 2:298, 6:266

personal contact usually requires books to back it up, 2:60, 6:166

policies on, 2:267, 2:321, 6:240–241

prepayments used for books, 3:207

pricing policies, 2:305, 6:255

principal comm particles of Scientology organizations, 2:324

book(s), *(cont.)*

promotional actions and, 0:347, 0:349, 0:352

promotion and, 0:625, 2:76, 6:244

proper sequence for obtaining book sales that bring in org income, 2:75, 6:243

public, making sure that interested people get books is making sure that they will continue their interest, 6:234

public won't buy books until they are communicated with, 2:54

Reception sells books, 2:296, 6:260

refund overpayments, 0:282

reorganize book department if it doesn't slam back a book at every orderer within 24 hours of receipt, 2:705

reprinting submission procedure, 2:179, 7:1305

result of not selling books to raw public in volume, 2:298, 6:266

routinely, full inventories must be taken of all such materiel, MS2:382

Scientology books should advertise only Scientology books, 2:143, 6:231

"selling the trade," 2:306, 6:256

sequence of events of exact design to be followed in book sales, 2:338, 6:248

seven types of Scientology books, 2:338, 6:248

shall not be defaced by ugly rubber stamps, 2:326

shells and ammo in a planetary assault, 2:299, 6:267

shipping charges, 3:166

sin and a big one not to push them, 2:299, 6:267

some allowed advertisements, 6:253

spearhead of a planetwide offensive against the reactive mind, 2:299, 6:267

speed of flow of, 0:325

standard stock items must be purchased from Pubs Org for cash, 2:313

submission procedure, 2:179, 7:1305

test of reach and, 2:77, 6:245

those C/S should be an expert on, 0:65

trick in books is the "stock book," 2:314

two first reaches required of the individual in the public and, 2:77, 6:245

weekly book stock reports required, 2:311

what books have to do, 2:77, 6:245

what prices of books advertised must be, 2:267, 6:240

who the book outlets of an org are, 2:350, 6:261-262

why they sell Scientology, 6:151

written by staff, how signed, 7:1280

Book Account, *see* **HCO Book Account**

Book Administrator, duties and purpose, 2:319, 2:327

Book Auditor,

cannot legally charge fees or be a field staff member, 6:840

definition, 7:271

may be given a certificate on application to the Qualifications Division, 6:840

must be recognized as a valid practitioner of Scientology, 2:166, 5:346, 6:840

requirements for applying for certificate, 2:166, 6:840

bookbuyer(s), 0:349, 0:626

extension courses and, 2:280, 6:506

basic cycle of letter registration and, 2:625

drill for handling, 2:706

giving away the names of, 2:712, 6:104

line for, 2:712, 6:104

standard promotion to, 5:347

what to do if bookbuyer buys no service, 2:703, 6:713

Bookbuyer Letter Reg, 2:712, 6:104

book fliers, enclose in all letters out, 2:296, 6:260

Book of Case Remedies, The, Danger conditions and, 5:732, MS2:211

Book of Letter Scheduling,

definition, 2:628

game of Promotion and Registration, 2:629

Book One, *see also* **Dianetics: The Modern Science of Mental Health**

Anatomy of the Human Mind Course as bridge from Book One to Scientology service, 6:443

booming orgs where seminars used, 2:298, 6:266

children and babies and, 4:260

how to start a boom, 6:442

marketing of, must be done, 6:442

probable best sequence of services after, 6:443

promotion of, 6:444, 6:447

quantity and quality of training and auditing creates want and reach for their next service, 6:443

success in dissemination largely due to reality level, 6:441

book orderer, definition and handling, 2:390

book outlets, who the book outlets of an org are, 2:350, 6:261-262

book sales, *see also* **book(s)**

Book One boom and, 6:444

boom occurs about two or three months after book sales go up, 6:166

Central Org,
  boom occurs about two or three months after book sales go up, 2:60
  slump and how to detect when one is coming, 2:60

down means failure to advertise books in continental magazine, 2:194

front line of expansion and org prosperity, 2:350

income source, 2:386, 3:101, 3:103

individual book sales line, 2:348

key to org survival and expansion, 2:361

money used for book, tape and film replacement and bills, 3:244

oldest index of future business, 2:297

PES and, 0:99

predict your future GI, 2:298

promotion and, 0:303, 0:625

sales down means failure to advertise books in continental magazine, 6:181

slump and how to detect when one is coming, 6:166

bookstore, getting books and cassettes placed in, 0:352

Bookstore Officer,

cannot be transferred or demoted without the explicit approval of Flag Management, 2:302

importance of, cannot be underestimated, 2:302

key duties, 2:300

must truly realize that books make booms, 2:302

not getting needed backup must telex directly to WDC, 2:302

one of the most important posts in an org, 2:302

should use duties as a weekly checklist, 2:301

treats his books and stocks just as the Treasury Sec would treat his org cash, 2:302

boom(s); *see also* **expansion; prosperity; success**

basic staff hat made org boom, 0:27

beginning and maintaining of, 7:858

business has to be driven in on org for stats to rise greatly, 6:259

causes of, 0:59, 0:253

dissemination and income and hold the boom, be able to shift from II to I and back to Phase II, 7:430

boom(s), *(cont.)*

how to start a Book One boom, 6:442

in all the great orgs began with regular full mailing list magazines, 2:220

occur with books and tours that drive business in on orgs, 2:295, 6:259

org through training, 4:336

"secret" of how I could boom any org I was directly managing, 6:398

takes book advertising, book selling and tour personal contact work, 6:258

training and, 2:68, 5:835

training auditors and, 4:407

two outside actions that drive people in on orgs are books and tours, 2:294, 6:258

way paved for by earlier public book sales, 2:296, 6:260

what an org has to establish if it wants to, 1:60

what the whole forward thrust of any boom depends upon, 2:286, 4:336

boom formula, definition, 2:712, 6:104

booms and depressions, due to, MS2:3

boss(es); *see also* **executive; senior**

making your boss do full job of information collection, 0:401

bottleneck, created by staff when they jam an exec's line, 7:603

bounced checks,

corrected gross income and, MS2:326

gross income as reported on OIC is unaffected by bounced check collections, MS2:326

minus invoices are NOT deducted from weekly income total, MS2:326

procedure for handling, MS2:325

re-collected, having already counted as income once are not again counted, MS2:326

box, do not throw away, 3:381

BPL; *see* **Board Policy Letter**

brass, expecting high brass only to carry the load, 0:253

break,

depriving pc of full hours, 4:850

during session, 4:843

breath, if staff member's breath can be detected on a mirror he can do his job, 0:168, 4:316

Bridge, The, 0:96–97, 5:192

definition, 2:518

mentioned at end of DMSMH, 4:187

Bridge flow, *see also* **flow(s), flow line(s)**
    FSO and Bridge flow, 2:679, 6:106–107

    responsibility of SO Public Divisions in forcing the next lower Public Divisions to function, 6:122

    role of upper orgs in, 2:678, 6:105

brief(ing),
    failing to brief juniors, 0:424
    responsibility for briefing staff, 0:576

bright idea,
    evaluation handling often requires a, MS1:96
    examining resources and, MS1:177
    strategic planning is a very postgraduate form of, 7:470, MS3:45

"bright noncomprehension," cure for, 4:330

bright ones, 5:181

bringing a body, what it means, 0:326

Britain, British Empire; *see also* **England**
    cause of their decline, 0:505
    contraction of, 0:125
    inspection before the fact, 0:66
    Roman expansion and, 0:125

broke; *see* **insolvency**

broom, new brooms love to sweep clean, 0:597

B routing, 0:543

brutality, eradicating mental health abuses and, 0:160

brute, bully, 0:517

BScn, *see* **Bachelor of Scientology**

BTB; *see* **Board Technical Bulletin**

Buddhism, expansion of, 0:125

budget,
    calculation of, 3:28, 7:926
    use of money which is left after covering, 3:30, 7:928

bugged, definition, MS2:144

Building Fund Account,
    purposes of, 3:42
    signatories on, 3:42

bulk mail, *see also* **promotion**
    promotion to recruit personnel, 1:164
    supposed to be info and ad reg packs and magazines, 2:220
    what makes it up, 2:295, 6:259

bulletin board,
    no action to be taken to bar the public from viewing, 1:347
    special staff meeting notice posted on, 0:173
    status of bulletin board in Comm Center is official, 1:351

    who may post on Comm Center bulletin board, 1:351

bum(s); *see* **indigent**

bureaucracy; *see also* **government,** 1:70
    can build up where there are no realized or stated products, 0:292
    dev-t causing expansion of, 0:416
    how you get a, MS1:158
    organization disintegrating and turning into one, 1:163
    referral system and, 0:279
    superbureaucracy, cause of, 0:314

bureaux,
    divisional Esto and, MS2:8
    man is least efficient in his biggest bureaux, 0:624

business(es); *see also* **administration; company; management; organization; traffic**
    business tech outside of Scientology, description, 0:55–56
    confused promotion and loss of, 7:1299
    Dept 6 uses CF to limit to produce business, 0:349
    despatches take care of 99% of organizational business, 0:369
    drive in more business than can be driven off, 0:344
    enemies of a business, definition, 0:275
    failing by altering sequence of be-do-have cycle, 0:291
    failing, reason, 0:95
    injustice level of, 0:521
    never continue to use a private business firm after they become obnoxious about bills, 3:249
    orgs, business of, 0:90
    Org Exec Course data and, 0:3–4
    reversing conduct of declining governments and, 0:506
    working on basis of "fair exchange," 0:317

businessmen, Org Exec Course and, 0:129

business school, correct personnel pool, 1:164

business world, judges Scientology not on its scientific validity but on its financial credit rating, 3:245

busy(ness),
    but not much havingness, 0:293
    dev-t and, 0:391, 0:428, 0:441
    having all the data but being too busy to study it, 0:19
    no need to look busy if you are not, 0:399
    too busy to do one's job, 0:19
    wrong routing making people "busy" but nothing gets done, 0:387

button(s),

approval button, 0:17

definition, MS3:215

difference between buttons and message, MS3:215

ethnic surveys and, MS3:68, MS3:247

self-importance button, 0:9

bypass(ing); *see also* **Danger condition**

bypassing the line jams the terminal, 0:85

compulsive bypasser definition and handling, MS2:211

Danger Formula and, 0:562–563, 0:583, 0:590, 0:612, 0:613

definition, 0:562, 0:582, 0:590, 0:605, 7:684

don't bypass unless you are in a Danger condition, 7:250

effects of, 0:586, 0:590, 0:601–604

junior who accepts orders from everyone, 0:585

LRH studying whether or not HCOBs, PLs and actions by him were bypasses, 0:591

bypass(ing), *(cont.)*

making org smaller by bypassing subgroups and running individuals only, 0:599

necessity to bypass continuing, handling, 0:606

of command channels, 0:583, 0:585, 0:593

only time one should bypass command chain, 0:583

overwork due to, 0:590

permanent bypass, 0:585

person who secretly puts his superior into, 0:591

resulting in Non-Existence, 0:599

senior can bypass anyone in a Danger condition, 0:583

what happens if you bypass all the time, 0:583

when Estos bypass staff, result, MS2:34

when to, 0:584

why one should not, 0:592, 0:604

bypassed charge, withholds primary cause of, 4:933

bypassed definition; *see* **misunderstood word**

C

cable, *see also* telex

character of cables, 1:454

designation system, 1:451

don't phone, 1:457

message addresses, 1:451

Caesar, Julius, 0:125, 0:127

California, expansion plan (1962), 6:710

call-in, *see also* Call-in Officer; Call-in Unit

ARC broken public and, 2:647, 3:223, 4:282, 7:871

assist public persons in so arranging their own lines as to make coming to the org possible, 2:644, 3:220, 4:279, 7:868

Auditors Association and, 2:647, 3:223, 4:282, 7:871

blown public and, 2:647, 3:223, 4:282, 7:871

Chaplain and, 2:647, 3:223, 4:282, 7:871

coordination lines of, 2:648, 3:224, 4:283, 7:872

definition, 2:641, 3:217, 4:276, 7:865, MS2:173

delivery is the whole intention of, 2:643, 3:219, 4:278, 7:867

different types of public and, 2:646, 3:222, 4:281, 7:870

FSMs and, 2:647, 3:223, 4:282, 7:871

gimmicks, use of, 2:648, 3:224, 4:283, 7:872

handlings for different types of public, 2:646, 3:222, 4:281, 7:870

invoice assembly for, 2:642, 3:218, 4:277, 7:866

mailgrams, letters, promo and, 2:644, 3:220, 4:279, 7:868

phones and, 2:644, 2:646, 3:220, 3:222, 4:279, 4:281, 7:868, 7:870

Qual Sec and, 2:647, 3:223, 4:282, 7:871

call-in, *(cont.)*

re-sign line and, 2:644, 2:648, 3:220, 3:224, 4:279, 4:283, 7:868, 7:872

scheduling board and, 2:644, 3:220, 4:279, 7:868

three separate actions that must occur for, 2:642, 3:218, 4:277, 7:866

Tours use of, 2:646, 3:222, 4:281, 7:870

Call-in Officer,

coordination lines of, 2:648, 3:224, 4:283, 7:872

ensure org is prepared to handle public individual, 2:643, 3:219, 4:278, 7:867

Call-in Unit(s),

Advance Scheduling Registrar Call-in Unit, partially paids handled by, 2:641, 3:217, 4:276, 7:865
procedure for, 2:645, 3:221, 4:280, 7:869
product of, 2:645, 3:221, 4:280, 7:869
statistics of, 2:646, 3:222, 4:281, 7:870

ED/CO responsible for Call-in Units until Service Product Officer is appointed, 2:641, 3:217, 4:276, 7:865

gimmicks as a tool of, 2:648, 3:224, 4:283, 7:872

set up to handle partially paids located under the Advance Scheduling Registrar, 2:641, 3:217, 7:865

Tech Call-in Unit,
fully paid individuals called in by, 2:641, 3:217, 4:276, 7:865
procedure for, 2:643, 3:219, 4:278, 7:867
product of, 2:645, 3:221, 4:280, 7:869
statistic for, 2:645, 3:221, 4:280, 7:869

Cal-Mag formula, 4:1218

camera work, definition, MS3:194

115

camouflaged hole,
  covering up a, 0:232
  definition, 0:407, 1:276, 7:247,
    MS1:398, MS3:407
  dev-t made by, 0:232
  example, MS1:398
  untrained person on post and a, MS1:401
campaigns, planning campaigns, 0:119
cancellation,
  certificates,
    basis of, 5:328
    cancelled for technical degrades, 0:14
  high crimes and cancellation of certificates,
    classifications and awards, 0:474
  of HCOBs and HCO PLs, 0:143
can squeeze, wrong, 0:302
can't apply,
  alter-is and poor results come from, 4:1080
  what handles the condition, 4:1080
can't-have,
  definition, MS1:460, MS2:251
  PTSes and, MS1:460, MS2:251
can'ts, 0:372
Can We Ever Be Friends? use of in handling
    PTS conditions, 5:440
Cape Town, establishing an international
    headquarters of Scientology in the event of
    atomic war and, 2:697
capitalism,
  definition, 0:508
  why it has declined, 0:134–135
caprice, capricious, being free of capricious
    punishment, 0:481
Captain, green crew member and, 1:154
card file, *see also* **address(es); Address;**
    Addressograph; Addresses In-Charge
  list to be run off of Addressograph, 2:695
  procedure for ordering cards from Addresses
    In-Charge, 2:653
  without adequate card files of people in proper
    org hands, income is greatly reduced, 2:696
care, caring,
  around orgs my possessions are given
    good, 0:186
  civilization where it has become general not to
    care what is going on, 0:555
  company, corporation or state does not live or
    breathe and so it cannot care for
    anything, 0:186
  laziness and not caring about doing the job
    well, 0:255
  low pay due to careless actions or inactions,
    0:301–303
  what neglect or abandonment of staff or caring
    about staff can be indicator of, 0:693

carrier wave, definition, MS3:137
cars, proper washing and care of, 7:1362
case(s), *see also* **auditing; auditor; case gain;**
    preclear; processing
  all state of case established by D of P, never by
    Registrar, 2:484
  average case found rougher each year, 4:200
  better opened than left closed, 4:682
  blackness of cases is accumulation of case's
    own or another's lies, 0:536
  blaming case is effect, 0:248
  bogged cases routed to Review, 0:351
  by not doing the obvious things and doing them
    well, the case does not progress on
    anything new, 2:554
  clean up all, 5:729
  courses where attention dominantly on, are bad
    courses, 4:316
  cross programing of, 4:641
  cyclic, connected to a suppressive person, 4:84
  dangerous to leave a question with charge
    on it, 4:574
  Dept 12 responsibility for all cases in org
    area, 0:351
  Dept 13 makes sure no unsolved case gets
    past, 0:351
  difficulties, transfers and dismissals and, 5:576
  exist only in sessions, 7:767
  failure of cases and results lies in, 1:754, 4:99
  flubbed, clean up, 4:838
  four general groups, 4:197
  general questions are much more likely to be
    charged or to produce blows, 4:574
  good case condition, definition, 4:1122
  HGC product of resolved cases, 0:128
  how to handle, 4:929, 5:685
  incomplete cases, program to handle, 2:637
  is no excuse, 0:168
  no case change, 1:1028
  not running well, send to Review, 1:626,
    4:1174, 5:587
  of staff members require attention and case
    gain, 1:800, 6:526
  only six reasons they do not advance,
    4:1081, 5:672
  orgs exist to handle rough, 5:56
  pc blows and invalidation of case or gains,
    remedy, 4:270, 6:551
  pinning org advance down to its lowest staff
    member's case, 0:156
  poor case condition, definition, 4:1122

case(s), *(cont.)*

Qual is responsible for staff, 4:705

resistive, grades out is major factor, 5:275

roller coaster, definition of, 4:344

solution to ALL cases, 5:33

staff may not be transferred to another post or dismissed because of "case difficulties," 0:168

staff members and, excuses, 5:576

standard tech alone resolves all, 5:652

state of, and acceptance of students for training, 4:309

surest way in the world to bog a, 4:640

there are no cases in the Academy, 4:304

there are no different cases, 5:677

trouble means one of three things, 1:992, 4:84

unusual, 5:33

use only difficult case or student in the Academy as indicator of something worse, 4:341

which does not improve easily with auditing, 1:158

Case 1, description and handling, 4:197

Case 2, description and handling, 4:197

Case 3, description and handling, 4:197

Case 4, description and handling, 4:198

Case-Cracking Section, 0:624, 5:734

case gain(s), *see also* case

amount available not conceived, in aberrated state, to exist above him, 4:988

any level is itself capable of stable case gain, 5:593

classification designed to get maximum, 4:172, 7:930

degraded beings and, 1:201

honesty and in-ethics, keys to, 4:997

how Dept 3 prevents no case gain, 0:348

if a case doesn't move, errors are gross, never slight, 0:19

if a level does not, then the case is loused up on earlier levels, 5:593

no case gain in past = SP, 5:35

person must become aware of, to get, 5:191

personnel and, 1:198

quickie grades denied gain to tens of thousands, 0:7

six rough divisions of case gain, 4:988

speed of, 4:989

suppressive gets no, 1:203

to get, person must become aware of next level, 4:186

when tech is in, cases are gaining, 0:496

case level, pc classification may not be taken into account as a cause for demotion, suspension or dismissal, 0:168

case supervision, Case Supervisor, *see also* auditing; auditor

accomplished and properly certified auditor and person trained additionally to supervise cases, 4:1134

advance of cases, sole interest of, 4:1054

always writes his C/S instructions on a separate sheet of paper for the pc folder, 4:1102

auditor's "handler," 4:1134

below one's training level, 4:664

books, C/S should be an expert on, 0:65

case not running well, send to Review, 1:626

challenging with ferocity instances of "unworkability" of Scientology, 0:13

Class VIII in tiny org would have to be, 0:102

condoning neglect of duty, 0:47

C/Sing a level for which he has not been trained, 4:1129, 5:715

czar, should consider himself a sort of, 5:691

D of P does not have to be or know C/Sing, 6:301

ethics and, 4:1130, 5:716

Ethics Officer and, conflict of targets between, 5:718

F/Ning, definition, 5:702

failure, reason for, 5:23

finds false reports, auditor to Ethics, 1:626

firm rule is to C/S only with folders to hand, 4:1103

flubby auditors are biggest time wasters, 5:850

flubless, procedure, 4:1118

folder handling, 4:1103

gold certificate and, 5:713

gross case supervision errors, 4:1105

handling pc ethics, 4:1131

has Examiner question pc about sessions he has received, 4:1136

high crime not to write in preclear's folder what case-supervised instructions are, 4:1102

how one can be auditor but fail as, 0:65

how to tell if not working or overloaded, 5:706

inspections by, 5:695

interning,
auditors, 5:850
interns and, 4:904
internship checksheets, attest mandatory, 5:852

irreducible minimum C/S postings, 4:1124

limit that a C/S can handle, 5:709

must be certified to C/S any rundown to his class, 4:664, 5:860

case supervision, Case Supervisor, *(cont.)*

must not permit an unprogramed or un-C/Sed folder to exist, 4:253

not following C/S Series, effect of, 0:302

only disciplined or given courts or Comm Evs for violations of HCOBs, LRH tapes or issues, 0:145

operates now in Div 4, 5:256

overload and, 4:1124

overloaded, cause of out-tech, 5:706

past-life auditing and, 4:257

penalty for allowing unclear worksheets, 5:470

postings, irreducible minimum, 5:706

program for flubless auditing, 5:694–701

public Case Supervisor, ideal scene and stat, 4:1121

qualifications, 4:1129

quals for tech specialist rundowns, 5:860

reason for failed, 4:24

red tag line and, 5:285

relation to D of P, 5:489

requires retrain of HGC auditor for, 5:757

responsibility,
    for staff auditors and interns, 4:905
    on red tag line, 4:255

sees a process going wrong, 1:626

send auditor to Ethics for false report, 4:1174, 5:587

sending pc already in HGC to Review, 5:34

sends auditor to Ethics for off-line directions, 1:626

Senior C/S,
    duties of, 4:1126, 5:708
    ideal scene defined, 4:1122, 5:704
    located in, 5:708
    qualifications of, 5:713
    statistic definition, 5:704
    tech hierarchy and, 5:697

specialist rundowns, requirements for, 4:664

Staff Case Supervisor,
    entitled to have when, 5:709
    ideal scene defined, 4:1121, 5:703
    located in, 5:708
    statistic definition, 4:1121, 5:703

task to get correct tech applied, 0:8

Tech C/S, ideal scene and stats, 4:143

tech hierarchy and, 5:697

Tech (Public) C/S,
    ideal scene defined, 5:703
    located in Div 4, Dept 12, 5:708
    statistic definition, 5:703

test line is check on C/S and auditing quality, 4:234, 6:305

training and confessional tech, 4:986, 5:449

training officer, 5:694

case supervision, Case Supervisor, *(cont.)*

trouble in proportion to his own and his auditors' ignorance of tech, 0:68

types of, 5:706, 5:708–709

waste of, 5:707

watching for ethics record of pcs who have been C/Sed, 4:1104

who or what is a, 4:1134

without folder study, 4:1117

cash,

calculated from reconciled bank statements, MS2:404

definition of cash on hand, MS2:404

Dept 7 persuades payment of, 0:349

discounts given on cash sales only and sales or service paid in full, 3:145

received by staff, 1:729

cash-bills(ratio), *see also* **Executive Council; financial planning**

cash on graph defined, MS2:318

collective responsibility of an Executive Council, MS2:405

degraded beings and, 1:204

Executive Council and, 7:910, 7:914

FSM Account not included on the "cash" of, 3:264

improving by *trend* indicates Exec Council wearing its financial planning hat correctly, MS2:408

limit to expansion and, MS1:303

tell whether org is solvent, MS2:416

Casualty Contact, used in dissemination, 2:61, 6:167

catastrophe(s), *see also* **disaster; emergency; failure**

continued emergency inevitably results in, 0:584

dev-t and, 0:427

neglect of responsibilities resulting in catastrophe even when another manages to avert final consequences, 0:267

occurs by lack of prediction, 0:427

operating at risk, 0:255

steadily declining stat or series of noncompliances or offenses resulting in overwork for org seniors or near catastrophe, 0:622

those things planned for do not become, 0:427

cause, causative, *see also* **competence; efficiency**

any system which isolates causes disenturbulates a group and makes unusual solutions unnecessary, 0:241

being blamed sometimes blunts being cause, 0:249

being cause, 0:248, 0:249, 0:268, 0:685, 0:689

cause, causative, *(cont.)*

by not being cause you become an effect, 0:554

causing,
coming to cause-point on every post, 0:231
your own stats, 0:689

confusion between source and, 0:249

effective cause well demonstrated, 0:332–333

environment, being cause over, 0:263,
0:555, 0:689

hatted staff member cause over post,
0:216, 0:268

hatting and, MS1:308, MS2:107, MS2:258

importance of assuming cause on post,
0:230–231

Operating Thetan and, 0:248, 0:249

org will wither and die if you aren't
causative, 0:231

people who cannot see cause, cannot solve
problems, 0:242

people who know it isn't any use trying to do
anything about anything, 0:683

post and, 0:230, 0:231, 0:263, 0:268

PR and, MS3:72–73

spectators vs., 0:248

target attainment and, 0:248

you are and can be, 2:105, 7:857

cause blindness, 0:242

caved-in, caving in,

definition of caved-in, 0:457

post caving in on total effect person, 0:230–231

when person or group caves in, 0:457, 0:521,
0:525, 0:529

CCHs,

processes, not drills, 4:623

taught exactly as they are used in session, 4:591

ceiling,

having a real product that one does well brings
about an almost no-ceiling condition, 7:520

quality of the product and creating a demand
for it only determines the ceiling of the org
as a whole, 7:520

celebrity, *see also* **Celebrity Centre**

definition, 6:139

getting celebrity into Scientology would be
acceptable amends, 0:546

opinion leaders, MS3:18

rapid dissemination can be attained by
rehabilitation of celebrities who are just
beyond or just approaching their
prime, 6:139

who is eligible for services at Celebrity
Centre, 6:139

Celebrity Centre, *see also* **celebrity**

any org or mission contacting or giving service
to celebrities may do so where no Celebrity
Centre located nearby, 6:139

ensures beings in Power use their power to
create a safe space and thus bring about
destimulation, 6:136

expanded from a Sea Org mission to a full Sea
Org organization, 6:136

motto: real celebrities deserve the best in staff
and service and image, 6:137

purpose, 6:138

with small volunteer processing staff, can do
wonders for artists, 6:135

Celebrity **magazine,** *see also* **magazine**

motif should exactly fit CC's aims, 2:239

several things that should be taken into account
when putting an edition together, 2:238

Central Bureaux Order (CBO), definition, 1:430

central control point,

dual engagement it performs, 2:124, 6:58, 7:836

organization and, 2:124, 6:58, 7:836

what it puts an organization there to do, 2:123,
6:57, 7:836

Central Files, CF, *see also* **Address;**
Addressograph; central file folders;
mailing list

Addresses is the index file to Central Files, not
just a general list, 2:694

adjacent offices to Addresso and Letter
Registrar and typists, 2:621

alphabetical index of the people in
Scientology, 2:684

ARC broken public in, failure to deliver and,
2:677, 6:554

as an income-getting action, 0:99

aside from dead people, or people who want
off the list or who move with no address
change, there is no valid CF age,
0:99, 0:360

backlogged, result, 0:276

booming and using, only prosperity can result,
2:680, 6:107

change of address and, 2:708

city office and, 0:626

contain folders of persons who have *bought*
something, 2:621

cost to have a folder to file, 6:89

crash program for, 2:621

definition, 2:211, 2:508, 2:704

duties of person in charge of Central Files and
Procurement, 2:392, 2:400

examples of treasonable propaganda which
encourage the disuse and disposal of CF
files, 2:673

Central Files, CF, *(cont.)*

exceptions to CF no-retirement policy,
  2:704, 6:713

files,
  "active files" definition, 2:704, 6:714
  "hot file" definition, 2:492, 2:704, 6:714
  "inactive files" definition, 2:704

five classes of folders, 2:390

folder, definition of, 6:713

Foundation and duties that need to be
  filled, 2:670

FSO prospect names, 2:679, 6:106

gold-colored dummy file, uses of, 2:704, 6:714

gross income of the org and why, 0:359–361

handling for new names which have not bought
  anything, 2:660

handling of entheta letters and dead files,
  1:973–974

has no dead file, 1:974

if that folder has bought everything that org has,
  it is still worth 10% FSM commission, 6:90

inactive files, definition, 6:714

insolvency of orgs traced to failures to use
  whole CF for mailings of mags, 2:212

making CF into "hot" and "cold" files and
  failing to write the cold ones is a source of
  down stats, 2:435

names of persons who have not bought anything
  from the org may not be placed in Central
  Files, 2:201, 6:195

names should not be deleted unless the person
  is dead, 2:610

no CF folder may ever be retired from the files,
  2:703, 6:713

only route by which you get in gross income,
  2:674, 6:90

org's potential gross income, 2:673, 6:89

our policy is to rotate files, 6:150

people ARC broken with the org, time-honored
  way of handling, 2:677, 6:554

persons on any list of names submitted must be
  sent an intelligent information package at
  once, 2:201, 6:195

placed under Letter Registrar, 2:659
  police officer with regard to files, 2:392

policy changes about retiring folders,
  2:201, 6:195

prime purpose of, 2:433

procedure,
  for presorting, 2:676
  to write letters to, 2:601

promotional actions and, 0:349

Central Files, CF, *(cont.)*

Public Div actions mean "new names to CF,"
  2:674, 6:90

Public Divs and, 0:360

purpose, 2:200, 4:72, 6:194

questionnaires must never go straight into, 2:627

Registrar's responsibility for, 2:388

Release or Clear declaration copy always sent to
  CF, 2:668

report made by person in charge of, 2:395

Rudiments Survey and Research Clerk
  and, 6:561

schemes by which you get new names are
  almost as important as CF itself, 2:613

should include everyone who has *bought
  something from the org,* 2:610

SHs, AOSHs and AOs Addressos and, 2:678,
  6:105–106

system of routing invoice copies to, 2:621

there is no valid CF age, 2:674, 6:90

upper org Central Files and new names to CF,
  2:678, 6:105

value of, 0:359–361

what contributes to a messed-up field,
  2:677, 6:554

what it costs to have a folder to file, 2:673

what occurs when CF not kept filed
  up to date, 2:452

which tests are filed in, 6:272

work Address over so it is exact index
  of CF, 0:104

Central Files folder(s),

addresses for mailings come from, 0:99

giving away org's CF folders, 0:359

illegal to put tons of CF folders off line, 0:276

is direct product of Public Divs, 0:359

never decay unless person dies or asks to be
  taken off list, 0:99, 0:360

that has bought everything that org has, 0:360

value of, 0:359

what goes in it, 0:99

writing without person's folder before
  one, 0:276

Central Files Unit, definition, 3:236, 7:204

Central Organization(s), *see also* **organization**

Administrative Division, 2:506, 3:234, 7:202

administrative pattern of, 1:36

Association Secretary's Office, 2:503,
  3:231, 7:199

as successful as it gives good
  technical service, 7:1069

basic staff list, 7:213

biggest fault, 2:56

Central Organization(s), *(cont.)*

boom occurs about two or three months after book sales go up, 6:166

delirium tremens of, 0:397

dissemination to individuals is province of, 1:36

efficiency in, 0:230

first and last reason for the existence of, 1:189, 4:1171

fundamental changes and, 6:289, 7:197

HCO Area Office, 2:503, 3:231, 7:199

holding the form of, 2:511, 7:207

may not give special discounts, 2:306, 6:256

minimum staff of, 7:212

mission holders and field auditors vs., 0:273

must give higher, better services than feeder orgs, MS2:350

office will be a one-person office, occupying one room and possibly anteroom, 7:216

pattern of, 2:503, 7:199

phenomenon which costs it two-thirds of effort of its staff and execs, 0:397

program to raise your unit, 7:210

purpose and function, original intention, 6:583

putting in lineup without alteration or omission or additives, 7:198

quality and admin in, 0:18

self-determinism and, 0:230

should ensure all field auditors informed of current charges and terms, 2:417, 6:709

summary of all parts of, 4:44

Technical Dir and Administrator posts should be filled in addition to existing executive posts, 7:218

Technical Division, 3:232, 7:200

central reserves, what they are used for, MS2:318

Ceremonies I/C, VFP and statistic, 6:533

Ceremonies Records and Files Clerk, VFP and statistic, 6:533

cert, *see* **certificate**

certainty,

depends upon good training and exact application of the technology, 2:441

firm establishment and unchanging orders give, MS2:33

Certainty **magazine,** *see also* **magazine**

advertise new books or one that has been out of print for some time in, 2:319

communicates that the org exists, 2:54

national magazine issued monthly, 1:396

sale and handout of, 2:328

when it goes out and to whom, 2:54

certificate(s), cert(s), certification, *see also,* **awards**

administrative,
Hubbard Administrator, 5:327, 5:340
Hubbard Assistant Administrator, 5:327
Hubbard Executive, 5:327, 5:340

anybody has a chance to go up in certificates, 0:234

application for, 4:362, 5:340

apprenticeships and, 5:509

Basic Staff Proficiency, 5:351

Basic Technical Certificate, 5:351

basis of issue is competence, 5:328

before student or pc may have a certificate or an award of any kind he or she must have an Accounts clearance, 3:163

Beginning Scientologist, 4:361

BScn (UK) or Hubbard Clearing Scientologist (US), 5:317

C/S has final word on issuance, 5:853

C/Ses may not C/S specialist RDs without being certified, 5:860

cancellation, 1:856, 5:348
basis of, 5:328
can be restored after 500 hours of auditing, 5:316
HCO actions to take, 1:858
how to restore, 1:856
may be recommended by, 1:857
no Committee of Evidence needed, 1:857
only done by, 1:857
reasons for, 1:857
recommendations for, 1:857
recourse for, 1:857–858
steps A to E, 1:860
technical degrades and, 1:14, 5:14

cancelled, suspended or reduced, when certs may or may not be, 0:14, 0:73, 0:171, 0:467, 0:474, 0:492

chronological numbering, example, 5:358

classification, not certificate which permits use of processes, 5:331

"Competent Being," 7:442, MS3:422

Dean of Technology,
final authorization by, 5:714
issued when, 5:713

delivered to all who earn them, 0:282

display, what a staff member shall, 5:301

DScn (Commonwealth) or Hubbard Graduate Scientologist (US), 5:317

enrollment on a Dianetics Course does not guarantee, 4:636

examinations for, conducted by HCO Boards of Review, 5:146

Executive Qualification Certificate, 1:222

extension courses and, 6:509

falsely issued will be hidden or discredited, 5:45

FEBC, provisional and depend upon stat record of student on return to his org, 5:527

certificate(s), cert(s), *(cont.)*

FEBC, validation and endorsement of, 5:527

field certificates, 5:306

Founding Scientologist, 2:420, 5:335

gold seal, 5:342

HAS, description of, 6:460

HAS, *see* Hubbard Apprentice Scientologist

HCA, *see* Hubbard Certified Auditor

HCS, *see* Hubbard Clearing Scientologist

HDC, *see* Hubbard Dianetic Counselor

HGA, *see* Hubbard Graduate Auditor

honorary, 5:343

HPA, *see* Hubbard Professional Auditor

HPS, *see* Hubbard Practical Scientologist

HQS, *see* Hubbard Qualified Scientologist

HSS, *see* Hubbard Senior Scientologist

Hubbard Administrator, 5:327, 5:338

Hubbard Apprentice Scientologist (HAS), 5:306, 5:317

Hubbard Assistant Administrator, 5:327

Hubbard Book Auditor (HBA), 5:325, 5:331, 5:346

Hubbard Book Auditor is withdrawn, 4:165

Hubbard Certified Auditor (HCA), 5:317, 5:325, 5:336

Hubbard Clearing Scientologist (HCS), 5:317, 5:336

Hubbard Dianetic Counselor (HDC), 5:368

Hubbard Executive, 5:327, 5:328

Hubbard Graduate Auditor (HGA), (Saint Hill), 5:325

Hubbard Graduate Scientologist (HGS), 5:317

Hubbard Practical Scientologist (HPS), 5:317

Hubbard Professional Auditor (HPA), 5:317, 5:325, 5:336

Hubbard Qualified Scientologist (HQS), 5:336

Hubbard Recognized Scientologist (HRS), 5:194

Hubbard Senior Scientologist (HSS), 5:325

ideal scene and stats, 4:143

illegal, handling of, 5:328

issuing, 0:351

Level I, 5:336

Level V, VI, VII issued by HCO Board of Review, Saint Hill only, 5:336

loss of awards or, 0:495

may be withdrawn, 4:638, 6:721

ministerial certificates of ordination, 3:101

mission students and, 6:755

must rest only in clean hands, 5:316

nonclassed, available to, 5:360

numbering of, 5:358, 5:360

certificate(s), cert(s), *(cont.)*

permanent status and, 1:224

physical handling of, 5:312

policy reinstituted to speed up the issuing of, 4:596

present at course completion, 2:203, 4:75, 6:197

pretending Scientology certificates not actually held to obtain money or credit, 0:472

professional, extension course and, 5:321

release all paid up with Accounting, 5:305

requirements for, 4:596, 5:322

responses permitted if any query arrives concerning any auditor, 2:609, 6:702

responsibility possession of certificate carries with it, 0:169

R2-12 validation seals change, 5:324

Saint Hill Special Briefing Course, 5:350

Scientology One, 5:325

signature by the Examining Board, 5:342

staff certificates, 5:344

students and, 4:296

students paid in full for course for which certified, 5:311

suspension, 5:110, 5:328

suspension of freeloader's, 1:256

table (1964), 4:182

to audit any action, auditor must be certified, 5:860

validation of, 2:609, 6:702

validation seal and, 5:319

validity of, 5:328

when validated, 4:644

you can audit any process for which you have been certified, 6:722

Certification Board, chief responsibility, 5:91

Certifications and Awards Officer, ideal scene, purpose, stats, VFP, 5:67

CF, *see* **Central Files**

CF–Promotion Liaison,

Dir of PrR vs., 2:654

hat of, 2:656

responsible for quantity of mail going out, 2:654

chain of command, *see* **command channel**

Chaldea, 0:510

chance(s),

giving a removed person another, 0:239

if we don't do a good job now we may never get another, 0:85

I give a person on a post a lot of, 0:239

change(s), changing, *see also* **alteration; alter-is**

first persons to attempt large changes in org, 0:385

idea that man could not, 0:362

if you are trying to improve something make changes cautiously and keep a record of what is changed, 7:497

new appointee changing everything, 0:561

nothing can remain long in unchanging state, 0:117

operating basis, 0:563

particles and, 0:81–82, 0:108

people can, 0:239

procedure for locating *the,* MS1:50

something actually operating and solvent can outweigh the untested advantages of changing it, MS1:34

something seeking to remain level and unchanged contracts, 0:124

things enter org, get changed, flow out, 0:106

undoing changes which occurred just before slumped stat, 0:596

when you make a bad rearrangement and you have an incompetent personnel you have disaster, 7:498

Whys and, MS1:50

channel(s)(ed)(ing), *see also* **communication line; flow; flow line; line; route; routing**

basic purpose, channeling of, 0:123

command channel, *see* command channel

definition, 2:625

designating types of particles for, MS1:197

directing a channel toward attainment, 0:123

distractions removed from delivery channel, 0:283

going outside org and off channels to send a report, 0:623

justice keeps channel of progress a channel and not a stopped flow, 0:480

Letter Registrar and, 2:624

making channels on which things can flow, 0:389

needed within Public Divisions themselves if one is to create a flow, 6:115

skipping vital points on a, 0:426

what they consist of in an org, 0:123

where discipline is random and doesn't serve to, 0:123

chaos, *see also* **confusion; developed traffic; disorder; distraction; noise**

basic situation in this universe, 0:434

causes of, 0:119, 0:195, 0:484

definition, 0:115, 0:389

if people each wear any or all the hats, 0:196

chaos, *(cont.)*

merchant of chaos, 7:1039

nonproductive chaos, handling, 0:439

order vs., 0:389, 0:434, 7:413, MS3:393

personnel programing vs., MS1:386

result of no org boards, hats, programs known, MS1:217

Chaos Merchant, 1:990; *see also* **suppressive person**

Chaplain,

ARC Break Program and, 7:881

call-in and, 2:647, 3:223, 4:282, 7:871

complaints department, 6:518

holds services where required, regularly, on Sunday, or marriages, christenings or funerals, 6:518

if one is going to leave org, report it only to HAS and, 0:177

interview, 1:828, 2:590, 5:768, 6:417

main area of operation in preventing people from falling off the org board is auditors, 6:523

necessity in a PE Foundation, 6:475

primary duties of, 6:523

purpose and duties, 6:518, 6:535

reason for auditors being chosen as priority of the Chaplain, 6:523

requisites of good Chaplain, 6:525

responsibility for Chaplain's Courts and hearings, 1:955, 6:520

responsibility for staff auditors and interns, 4:905, 5:490

VFP of his dept, 6:535

when pcs and students cannot elsewhere be heard they always have recourse to the Chaplain, 6:518

Chaplain's Court,

attorneys and, 1:957, 6:522

Chaplain's Court Unit purpose and formation, 1:955

divorce matters, 1:956, 6:521

failure to abide by, 1:957, 6:522

for knowingly false statements made in Knowledge Reports, 0:557

hears civil matters, 6:520

jury, 1:957, 6:522

procedures for the unit, 1:957, 6:522

purpose, 6:520

recourse for individuals impeded in training or processing by 2D activities, 4:479

second dynamic activities and, 1:780

Unit formation, 6:520

what may be filed and addressed, 1:955, 6:520

wrongful dismissal taken up in, 0:552

Chaplain's Court Clerk, VFPs and
statistics, 6:532

Chaplain's Court Section, VFP and
statistics, 6:532

charge(s), *see* **offense**

charity, 0:508

charity auditing, 3:159

Chart of Abilities Gained, 5:292

Chart of Human Evaluation,
evil and, 0:526
personnel and, 1:66

charters, Clears and, 6:690

check(s),
conditions under which executive may sign
checks, 3:317

data necessary before any check can be
signed, 3:319

isolated, may not be presented for
signature, 3:317

no check will be signed unless the bill it is
paying and all purchase orders appertaining
thereto accompany it, 3:291

no staff member may be paid by check, 3:335

signing, 3:278, 3:317, 3:319, 3:321

transferring monies, never made out as payable
to any individual, 3:408

voided checks accompanied by a minus
voucher, 3:322

checkbook, assembly of, 3:134

checkers, people aren't, 1:206

checklist(s),
Dissem Div checklist for quality, 2:715

Division 6A checklist for quality, 6:351

Division 6B checklist for quality, 6:567

Division 6C checklist for quality, 6:877

Exec Div checklist for quality, 7:1425

for strategic plan, MS3:455

HCO Div checklist for quality, 1:1057

how to defeat verbal tech, 4:31, 5:804

Qual Div checklist for quality, 5:865

strategic plan, checklist for, 7:475

Tech Div checklist for quality, 4:1253

Treasury Div checklist for quality, 3:411

checkout(s),
done by Course Supervisor are to do with
the procedure and technology of
checkouts, 4:393

"double flunk" and, 4:437

Examiner should ask questions that require an
ability to *apply,* 4:374

checkout(s), *(cont.)*
give the student a situation and have him tell
you how he would handle it, 4:395

hat study and checkout done on post a bit each
day, 0:440

high-crime checkouts,
definition, 7:491, MS2:461
must be tough standard star-rate checkouts,
7:492, MS2:462
on PLs, 0:75–77

how to do, 4:329, 4:395

how to handle new issue to be star-rated, 4:396

minimum requirement for giving star-rate
checkout is having read or listened to the
material on which one is checking out
another, 4:396

most important part of student's hat is how to
do checkouts on his twin, 4:393

must also ask for demonstrations, 4:395

must consult student's understanding, 4:329

on Advanced Courses, 4:811

on policy by all administrative personnel,
MS2:461, 7:491

purpose of, 4:375

remedy for improper checkouts by
students, 4:394

sign-up sheet for, 4:694

staff member flunking, 1:241

system to be used, 4:333

theory checkout data, 5:181

turnabout system and, 4:435

twin checking system, 4:766

what to check out all seniors on, 0:279

when to order full checkout on PLs applying to
post, 0:406

checksheet(s), *see also* **course; training**
Academy,
designed to be covered in one week for, 5:781
evening courses, one month for theory and one
month for practical, 5:781
if student takes more than two weeks on
theory or practical, Supervisor placed in
Non-Existence, 5:781

A–I hat and, 0:199–200

any new HCOBs needed on particular level
must be added to, 5:209

any Scientology book, course pack or recorded
LRH lectures listed on checksheet must be
bought by the student for that course,
4:363, 5:723

authorization of, 0:14

basic Why of auditor shortage and, 4:419

crime to run a course without checksheet or to
change checksheet on student after
issued, 4:361

checksheet(s), *(cont.)*

cutative, 5:22

data and drills done in order, 4:441

definition, 4:441

degrading of, 0:14, 0:73–74

designed to be covered in one week for theory and one week for practical for each level 0 to IV, 4:376

examination of, 5:114

exec responsibilities for, 0:220–221

filing of, 5:505

form, 1:281

format, 5:504

full files must be kept, 1:283

hat, 4:442, 5:189

hat checksheet authorization, 1:14

hat material and, 4:617

how to issue, 1:281, 5:503

illegal to run any course in Scientology without, 4:442

issue types, 1:282

legal and, 4:616

length of in evening courses, 4:376

Management Series, MS2:190, MS2:294, MS3:443

Management Status One, 7:463, MS1:365, MS2:190, MS2:294, MS3:443

Management Status One vs. full pay or bonus eligible, 7:464, MS2:191, MS2:295

Management Status Two, 7:464, MS1:365, MS2:190, MS2:294, MS3:443

Management Status Three, 7:464, MS1:366, MS2:191, MS2:295, MS3:444

master, 4:442

material, definition, 1:287, 5:507

may not be changed once it is placed in a student's hands, 4:442, 5:189

new HCOBs needed on particular level must be added to, 4:459

new shorter checksheets demand study tech is applied, 4:419

not complete until C/S can attest, 5:852

packs made up from, 1:284

policy, 4:617

post, central authority to standardize, MS1:205

program to implement 0–IV checksheets, 4:421

Q and A, Hubbard Causative Leadership Course, 7:440, MS3:420

rating system, 4:612

seniority of issues, 5:504

standardizing post checksheets, 0:202

checksheet(s), *(cont.)*

students who fail to meet theory or practical checksheet times are sent to Cramming, 4:364

studied from volumes of PLs where these exist in the hands of the post holder, 1:284

Supervisor must inspect students' checksheets daily, 4:441

taking unlawful items off a student's checksheet is not illegal, 4:617

technical degrades of, 1:14

Tech Sec responsible for making up, 5:206

theory courses, 5:206

"through a checksheet" definition, 4:441

to mark out legal checkouts on a checksheet (cross them off) when not actually checked out is illegal, 4:617

up-to-date, responsibility of Tech Sec and D of T, 4:459, 5:209

vital points are star-rated, 5:206

when it is legal, 5:188

when OEC checksheet may be added to, 0:31

check signing,

lines modified, MS2:346

procedure of, 7:650

chicken and egg problem, solution of, 4:649

child, children, *see also* **second dynamic**

be-do-have cycle and, 0:291–293

contributing vs. not contributing, 0:529

feelings of obligation to parents, 0:529

must not withhold child from legal schooling, 2:402

processing should be limited to Scientology processes in early years, 4:260

threatening to run away, 0:177

trained-in criminality and, 0:529

Chinese school,

definition, 0:439, 1:277, MS2:87

dev-t handled by, 0:439

drill, MS2:87

each division first on own org board, then on org as a whole, MS2:17

handling for dev-t and unhattedness, MS2:16

on all staff, 1:63

org board and, 0:440, 0:442

two steps in teaching, MS2:87

chit, *see* **staff member report**

choice(s), choosing,

org board vs. random choices, 0:325–326

public never asked to decide or choose, 0:323–324

steps of making a decision or, 0:323

christenings, Chaplain and, 6:518

Christmas bonus, how to calculate, 3:365

church attendance, how the lowering of coincided with a rise in general immorality, 6:869

Church Services Section, VFP and statistic, 6:532

chute, down the, 0:449, 0:457

city office, 0:626

  address lists to, 2:701, 6:789

  conducts Communication Course for District Office, 6:788

  definition, 7:270

  disassociated from mission, 6:782

  first and last reason for, 1:189

  number of personnel, 6:790

  organized for, 6:790

  org board of, 6:797

  pattern for, 6:774, 6:777, 6:797

  procedure to set up, 6:780

  promotion and, 2:707

  purpose, 6:782

civil, definition, 1:968

Civil Committee of Evidence, description, 0:478

civil commotion, basic reason for, in US, 0:68

civil court, legal matters and, 0:477

civilization(s), *see also* **country; culture; Earth; group; man; society**

  change the civilization eval, 4:427

  corruption of be-do-have cycle contributes to dying civilization, 0:292

  decaying due to violation of basic economic law, 0:313–314

  decline or fall of, cause, 0:89, 0:119, 0:236, 0:505, 0:603, 0:665

  how it survives, gets better and lives on higher planes, 0:119

  how to make expanding civilization, 0:115

  inspection before the fact, 0:66

  may deteriorate when right to petition vanishes, 0:488

  new and better, how to get, 4:16, 4:657, 5:16

  Qualifications Cycle in which we adjust civilization, 0:96

  reason civilizations have died, 0:121, 0:512

  robot orgs and civilizations fail, 0:82

  route to a saner civilization, auditing, 5:858

  successful vs. perishing, 0:297

  troubles because it hasn't known about hatting, 0:393

  vanish because, 7:435, MS3:415

  we cannot look for justice at hands of, 0:481

civilization(s), *(cont.)*

  we're sole agency that can forestall erasure of all civilization or bring new better one, 0:231

  what any existing civilization is the sum total of, 0:277

  where it has become general not to care what is going on, 0:555

  which facilitate production and interchange, MS1:296

  without insanity, without criminals and without war, 6:519

civil law, no just civil law left, 0:483

civil matter(s), no recourse to tech in Ethics hearings, 1:969

clarification, failure to get order clarified, 0:430

clarity, programing and, 0:705

class(es), classroom,

  briskly and punctually scheduled classes, 0:350

  disturbing a, 0:468

  table of certificates and classes, 4:76, 2:204

  two courses to one class, theory and practical, 4:188

Class and Grade Chart, major and time-honored route for all to travel, 6:115; *see also* **Grade Chart**

Class II,

  reason for training only by Academies and Saint Hill, 4:593

  reexamination, when it may occur, 5:166

  steps taken in order to complete, 5:165

Class II Auditor, as a Blue Star, 0:662

Class IV Auditor, as a Green Star, 0:662

Class V,

  internship, description, 5:844

  Saint Hill, 5:510

Class VII Case Supervisor, internship, description, 5:844

Class VIII,

  big point is that pc's case or a pre-OT's is prepared and set up for any major action, 4:1029

  Dianetics prerequisite, 4:826

  failed, 4:827

  flawless, flubless, smooth-as-silk specialist in standard tech, 4:828

  lower-classed auditor, and, 4:828

  prerequisites modified, 4:659

  purpose, 4:823

  reason it's being taught, 5:652

  retread, 4:827

  sharp rapid STANDARDIZATION of auditing and case supervising with 100 percent gains, 4:387

Class VIII Auditor(s),
  as a Gold Star, 0:654
  crack standard tech people, 5:675
  functions in a tiny org, 0:102
  retreads and, 5:785

Class VIII Case Supervisor,
  internship, description, 5:844
  most awful thing that can happen to, 5:680
  must examine a returning VIII graduate, 5:680
  stat is number of names in CF, 5:676

classification, *see also* **certificate(s)**
  adopt for preclears as well as auditors, 4:164, 5:330
  automatic disqualification for, 4:680
  award, not owed anyone, is for proficiency, 5:187
  course completion, definition of, 4:361
  delivered quickly to those who pass, 0:282
  depends upon examination by area HCO Board of Review, 5:336
  designed to get maximum case gains for pc, 4:172, 7:930
  entirely at the discretion of HCO, 5:344
  Free Scientology Center and, 0:350
  general written examination for, 4:335
  in addition to certification, 5:325
  issued with honors, 5:326
  Level 0, 5:194
  Level I, 5:336
  Level II, 5:336
  Levels II, III and IV, 5:200
  Level V, VI, VII, 5:336
  more important than certification in judging an auditor's skill, 5:342
  none may be assigned by reason of course attendance and examination only, 4:611
  not certificate that permits use of processes, 5:331
  on the basis of processes flattened, 5:337
  pass marks, for all classes, 5:186
  pc classification may not be taken into account as cause for demotion, suspension or dismissal, 0:168
  pc must be trained in classification matching grade, 4:187, 5:192
  permits use of processes or being run on processes, 4:165
  preclears, done on basis of process flattened, 4:171
  provisional, students can charge fees with, 4:97

classification, *(cont.)*
  purpose of, 4:174
  re-awarded as Saint Hill classifications, 5:344
  rules of, 4:174
  staff aspiring to next classification, handling, 0:169
  student failing, 5:734
  table (1964), 4:182

Classification, Gradation and Awareness Chart, 2:517, 2:632, 4:177, 4:186, 4:1107, 5:191, 5:331; *see also* **Grade Chart**

classified material,
  authorized places to do, 4:825
  Class VIII students taught, 4:825

class revision, table of certificates and classes, 6:198–199

clay demonstration(s), clay table training,
  doing orgs, org board, post, steps to get product, etc., in clay, 0:89, 0:309, 0:407, 0:415
  example of, 4:374
  procedure for, 4:374
  purpose of, 4:374
  requires expert usage, 4:879
  use by Central Organizations, 4:879
  which actually does demonstrate will produce marvelous change in that student, 4:375
  whole theory of, 4:444

clay pigeon, 0:521, 0:525

Clay Table Administration Processing, 1:182

Clay Table Processes, drugs and, 4:655

clean hands, happiness and survival and, 0:458

cleaning cleans,
  definition, 0:431
  missed withhold of nothingness and, 4:314

cleaning stations, 0:339, 7:1400

cleanliness, clean(ing), *see also* **appearance; image**
  goodwill and, 0:333
  HGC quarters clean, 0:351
  image and, 1:520
  income and, 0:334
  of office and quarters, 0:84, 0:165, 0:334
  of premises, 6:594
  of staff, 0:166, 0:334, 0:339, 0:340
  promotional actions and, 0:350, 0:354, 0:356
  respect and, 0:340

Clear(s), clearing, *see also* **Dianetic Clear**
  ability gained, 4:192
  alternate route, 4:999, 4:1107, 6:424

Clear(s), clearing, *(cont.)*

auditing and training of, 4:786, 4:1000

being made today with NED, 2:470

being who no longer has his own reactive mind, 2:469

bigger responsibilities given and expected of, 4:796, 6:656

Book One definition of Clear is valid, 2:469, 4:202

CCRD for cases originating past-life Clear, 4:258

CCRD given to establish whether or not state achieved, 4:975

certifying, 5:223, 5:307

charters and, 6:690

checkouts or estimates, no charge for, 2:490, 4:841

checks, 5:243
    Continental Orgs and, 5:236
    policy if checkouts are bad and nonfactual, 5:238

Clear estimates and Clear checkouts, procedure on informing of, 2:600

Clearing Course for those who don't go Clear on NED, 4:203

color flash for, 4:791

crime to invalidate the state of, 4:796, 6:656

definition, 4:202

democracy only possible in nation of, 0:83

direct award, not provisional, 5:365

estimates and Clear checkouts procedure, 4:228, 6:271

executive postings and, 1:199

executives preventing people from becoming, 1:200

HGC may only, 4:877

HGC plan, 4:866

invalidation of, high crime, 1:89

may only be issued by, 5:374

New Era Dianetics and, 4:1107

no privileges beyond being declared Clear, 4:796

numbers, Advanced Orgs responsible for, 5:374

only person you could completely trust is a, 0:243

open letter to all, 4:796, 6:656

org's primary role, 4:998

past-life Clear and Dianetics, handling, 4:259

person whether goes Clear on NED or not, can begin his Solo Auditor Course in his home org, 6:425

pin, 5:345

plan for, 6:741

procedure for certifying, 5:308

Clear(s), clearing, *(cont.)*

processing sold on basis of estimate to, 4:839

PTS Rundown and, 5:440

realizing need for training as an auditor, 4:786

Release vs., 4:202

re-sign line for, 4:978

stabilization of, 5:320

stalled, handling, 4:978

training and, 4:614

training of, 2:437, 4:786

what it takes to clear people, 4:16

within reach of every Scientologist, 4:16

Clear ads, list of ads which pull best of all ads of whatever kind, 6:160

Clear bracelet,

issued on, 5:318

procedure, 5:309

Routine 3D and, 5:320

silver, 5:327, 5:356

Clear Certainty Rundown,

cases that originate past-life Clear and, 4:258

delivery line, example of routing, 4:999, 4:1000

object of, 4:998

sold in blocks of 5 hours, minimum, 4:977

who it's given to, 4:975

who it's not given to, 4:198

who may deliver, 4:978

Clearing Course, *see also* **Clear**

all staff have right to demand releasing and, 0:20

auditor is very important in clearing planet and universe, 0:154

CCRD and Sun RD vs., 4:198

engaging in out-ethics activities while on, 4:792

folders, 4:790, 4:794

for those who don't go Clear on NED, 4:203

only things that will count in long run, 0:16

our target, 0:657

person connected to suppressive group may not be enrolled in, 2:434

regulations, 4:795

reorganization, 4:798

security, 1:627, 4:792

submission of folders, 4:790

taking off brakes for a cleared Earth, 0:498

what it takes to clear people, 0:16

cliché, used to handle all down stat situations, 0:682

clinic, Academy is not a, 4:302

clinic types, recruiting of, 0:302

clipping(s),
  book, defined, 7:640
  description and use, MS3:98

cliques, use of justice and, 1:962

CLO, *see* **Continental Liaison Office(s)**

clothing, *see also* **uniform(s)**
  clean and functioning, 0:251
  keep attire as presentable as possible, 0:166
  uniforms, 0:334

clues, why criminal leaves clues, 0:452

CO, *see* **Commanding Officer**

coach(ing),
  definition, 4:295
  instruction of, 4:300
  theory coaching, definition, 4:334, 5:182

co-audit,
  benefits of, 4:687
  blown or blowy co-audit twins, handling, 4:699
  bugged sessions, handling, 4:700
  charge for professional co-audit, 4:689
  cheapest way to get auditing, 5:836
  co-auditors do not leave their pcs, 4:698
  definition, 4:687
  doingness activity, 4:692
  economical, 4:163, 5:329
  evenings and weekends, 5:334
  folders, handling of, 4:696
  handling co-auditor in trouble, 4:696
  how to run, 4:691
  interrupting co-audit sessions, 4:697
  logbook kept by Supervisor, 4:698
  must be well organized, 4:691
  nonprofessional, definition, 4:688
  not a study or theory, 4:692
  operating tone of, 4:693
  orgs cannot offer nonprofessional co-audits on Grades, NED, 4:689
  personnel needed for, 4:691
  professional, 4:688
  public co-audit may only do supervised itsa, 2:203, 4:75, 6:197
  purpose, 4:687
  Qual, when to send co-auditors to, 4:700
  red tags on co-audit, handling, 4:700
  responsibility of co-auditors, 4:708
  rooms for, 4:693
  rundowns taught on course, 4:666
  scheduling must be tight, 4:694

co-audit, *(cont.)*
  session admin, 4:698
  staff co-audit, 4:689
    during working hours, 5:577
    most advantageous method to move staff up Bridge, 4:689
  stats, 4:701
  St. Hill, 5:575
  student can get all of his Grades and New Era Dianetics, 4:689
  Supervisor, 5:571
  TRs and Objectives, 4:695
  twinning and, 4:693
  what makes them thrive, 2:204, 4:76, 6:198

Co-auditor Route, 4:175

Co-audit TRs,
  definition, 4:702
  steps in training a person on Co-audit TRs, 4:702

code(s),
  applications for certificate and pledging codes, 4:362
  common errors in using, 1:468
  definition, 1:469
  HCO Ethics Codes, *see* HCO Ethics Codes
  Justice Codes, *see* Justice Codes
  moral codes, 0:455
  of discipline, offenses and penalties, 1:861
  of good conduct laid down out of experience, 0:455
  of offenses and discipline, 0:467
  policy on, 1:468
  right conduct and, 1:774
  theory of, 1:469

Code of a Scientologist, 0:160–161, 6:603, 7:1047

Code of Reform, questionnaire, 6:598

cognition, entitled to have cognitions so long as these do not bar the route out for self and others, 0:22

collapse, collapsing,
  booming a collapsing org, 0:57
  early orgs: why they crashed, 0:10
  keeping leader from collapsing through overwork, bad temper or bad data, 0:640
  lower condition person industriously collapsing own post stats and stats of adjacent posts, 0:657
  offbeat use or ignorance or nonapplication = collapse, 0:59
  offenses concerning, 0:267
  resuming post one has left because it collapsed, 0:597
  when you get a total collapse, 0:325

collation, definition, MS3:194

collection(s),

ARC breaks and, 3:184

delinquent, stem from two sources, 3:184

Dept 7 and, 0:349

from staff liable for training or processing debts, 0:174

from suppressive persons and potential trouble sources, 1:764

HCO and, 1:35

income source, 3:101

money must be taken on sign-up, 3:119

recruiting and handling FSMs to collect past debts, 0:349

suppressive persons and potential trouble sources and, 3:190

Collections Section, definition, 3:131

collective think, 0:158, 2:123

in finance always less wise than individual reason, 3:43

colonialism, 0:508

colony, colonies,

England and, 0:595

Germany and, 0:449

color flash,

Conditions Orders published on, 0:659

divisional, 1:373

for despatches and letters, 0:369

for hat folders, 0:166, 0:194

for staff member reports, 0:543

marking system for types of messages, 7:1163

NED for OTs, 4:812

OT, 4:791

speed priority and, 1:352–353

staff responsibility for following the, 0:166

types of messages, 1:22, 1:352

white paper, use of, 0:369

come-on,

creating interest in your prospects, MS3:185

definition, MS3:186

thetan is a mystery sandwich, MS3:185

comm, *see* **communication(s)**

command,

for one org to command another, they must be similar, 0:122

I believe that to command is to serve and only gives one right to serve, 0:238

only privilege position of command conferred on me was right to serve, 0:278

command, *(cont.)*

what to do to live life of command or near to command, 0:638

whim of those in command, 0:467

command channel(s), command chain(s), chain of command,

bypass of, 0:583, 0:585, 0:592

Danger conditions only occur when there are fundamental disagreements on, MS2:210

disagreements on, 0:591

graph readings and, 0:679

hats, org boards and, MS1:223

hold org firm by holding firm its lines and, 0:582

jumping proper terminal in a, 0:590

orders and, 0:387, 0:592

routing, 0:387

use of, 0:387

why it is vital to follow them, 0:593

command comm cycle, he who gives the order gets an answer, 7:708

Commanding Officer, *see also* **Executive Director**

interview, 1:828

penalty for reporting false stats, 7:168

statistic of, 7:168

Commanding Officer Conference, conference routing and, 0:387

command intention, your post and, 0:250

command line, *see also* **communication line**

confused with a comm line, MS2:58, MS2:240

definition, 7:479, MS1:369, MS2:58, MS2:195, MS2:240, MS2:300, MS3:459

how to clear your, 0:593

paying no real attention to, 0:604

unmocking a section or dept by sloppy command lines, 0:593

command policy, for projects, CLOs and orgs, when it has to be handled, handle the hell out of it, 7:721

command post, PTS or chronically ill or NCG and top command posts, MS1:460, MS2:251

command types, have to be able to supervise and handle ethics, 7:720

Comm Center, *see also* **baskets; comm station(s); comm system; communication(s)**

arrangement of, 1:350

baskets labeled in comparison to organizational chart, 1:350

bulletin board in, 0:173

daily pickups to and from the, 0:165

Comm Center, *(cont.)*

description, 0:369–370

establishment of, 1:316–317

in larger orgs, divisional Comm Centers may be instituted, 1:376

not in reception room, 0:501

"off line" and "out of comm," 1:346

useful only when, 1:345

commendations, Bs of I and, 1:959

commercial, commercialism,

British Empire was a commercial one, 0:600

no commercial development to distribute goods to common people, 0:506

self-defeative, 2:441

commercial firm(s), *see* **business**

Comm Ev, *see* **Committee(s) of Evidence**

commission(s),

forbidding another to sell books for the purpose of monopolizing commissions costs one his bonuses, 2:354, 6:265

for processing sold at professional rates, 6:633

offenses concerning taking, 0:471

payment of FSM commission, 6:632

committee(s),

Advisory Committee, *see* Advisory Committee

appointing committees of Scientologists to advise on improvements of civilization, 0:355

"ethics committees," 0:450

Committee of Evidence, Comm Ev, *see also* **ethics**

actions taken on committee members found to be slack, negligent or biased, 1:936

admin high crimes and, 7:493, MS2:463, MS3:472

anyone can request one on himself for anything, 0:524

Area Committee of Evidence, definition, 1:925

auditors abusing "right to choose pcs" or advising others of "dog case," subject to, 4:209

auditors and preclears, violations resulting in, 4:175

bill of particulars and, 1:929

called on student or pc for offenses covered in Justice Codes, 0:478

can recommend suspension or remove certificates or awards or memberships or recommend dismissal, 4:355

cannot be comm eved for not following BPLs, BTBs or targets or orders that violate HCO PLs, 0:145

can restore lost pay in cases of injustice but not damages, 0:478

Committee of Evidence, Comm Ev, *(cont.)*

Central Org Committee of Evidence, definition, 1:925

chairman, definition and duties, 1:927

Civil Committee of Evidence, 0:478, 1:731

committing offenses or omissions that bring one's senior, staff member, unit, dept, org, or zone official to personal risk and/or a Comm Ev, civil or criminal court, 0:472

composition of, 0:487

contempt or disrespect shown to a, 0:469

Continental Org Committee of Evidence, definition, 1:925

convening authority's actions, 1:931

convening of, 0:487

crimes and, 0:583

Danger condition and, 0:585

Danger Formula and, 0:562–563

definition, 0:484, 1:926

demotion and, 0:487, 0:492

denial of auditing or training, 0:495

destroying documents required by Comm Ev or refusing to produce them, 0:469

disciplinary actions for PTSness undertaken by a, 0:493

dismissal and, 0:487, 0:492, 0:524

disputes and civil or criminal matters, 1:930

District Committee of Evidence, definition, 1:926

do not seek to name member of senior org in Comm Ev requested by anyone in junior org, 0:478

dropping tech off checksheets, 1:801, 6:527

Emergency condition and, 0:622

endorsement of, 1:929

example of protecting person from viciousness and caprice, 1:939

executive councilman and, 1:731

executive postings not making visible progress up the Gradation Chart ordered to a, 1:199–200

fact-finding body, 0:484

failure to appear before a, 0:469

filing of, 1:930

findings, 1:929

Fitness Board and, 0:524, 1:814

for absence from post resulting in stats crashing, 0:267

for discounting or giving away org services or materials, 0:303

for false attestations, 1:869

for false reports, 1:869

for following off-policy issues or orders, 0:145

Committee of Evidence, Comm Ev, *(cont.)*

for letting people be hit with wrong
conditions, 0:519

for no-reports, 1:869

for not auditing staff cases to good wins, 1:801

for refusal to report, 1:869

for resistance to full tech delivery, 1:801

for staff accepting student or pc for personal
profit or favors, 0:171

for treasonable neglect, 0:220

for using color combination of LRH issues for
any other purpose or counterfeiting, 0:113

for violations of study tech, 5:470

form of issue for, 7:1303

formation of, 1:931

getting in ethics by, 0:513

Gold Star, Green Star and, 0:662

HCO Continental Committee of Evidence,
definition, 1:925

HCO personnel and, 0:477

illegal orders and, 1:285

independent disciplinary actions, 1:933

is not a court, 0:484

justice and, 0:477, 1:924–925

levels of ethics actions and, 0:494–495

may not be convened because of an error, 0:467

may not order to auditing or training, 0:491,
1:744, 5:109

member, definition and duties, 1:927–928

modifying findings, 0:495

most severe form of ethics action, 0:492, 1:745,
4:355, 5:110

nobody can be suspended or punished by
convening of, 0:485

no one can be comm eved for querying an
order in proper form, 0:142

not a court, 1:940

not auditing staff cases to good wins, 6:527

offense, halting or editing Flag Rep
comm, 7:1408

Office of LRH passes on all findings, 0:492

offloads require a, 0:524

on a charge of out-admin, 0:260

one assigns condition or Comm Ev, 0:524

only Comm Ev can recommend suspension or
remove certificates, awards or memberships
or recommend dismissal, 0:492

only given for things that violate policy, 0:145

pay reduction, demotions, transfers, fines or
dismissal may only be done after, 7:1300

pcs may not request Comm Ev for causes
occurring during intensive, 0:478

penalty for falsely testifying, 1:930

Committee of Evidence, Comm Ev, *(cont.)*

permanent staff may not be demoted,
transferred or dismissed without, 1:238

petitions and, 0:489, 1:743, 1:753

potential trouble sources and, 4:356

power restored to an org to convene and
conclude locally, 1:260

protested, handled by Review Comm Ev, 1:261

publication of, 1:930

purpose, 0:487, 1:251, 1:931

recommendations for use, 1:924

recourse and, 0:492, 0:522

removal from post requires a, 0:523, 0:584

requesting a Comm Ev of HCO when staff
member believes he has been falsely
wronged, 0:478

requesting Comm Ev when one is pressured to
follow illegal order, 0:147

Review Comm Ev, definition and duties, 1:930

rules for interested parties, 1:928

secretary, definition and duties, 1:927

some are guilty, most are innocent, 0:483

students may not request Comm Ev for causes
occurring during course, 0:478

summary of procedure, 1:931

suspension and, 0:492, 0:495

technical terminals can only be given Comm
Evs for violations of HCOBs, LRH tapes or
issues, 0:145

to clear name or repute, 1:814

transfers and, 0:487, 0:492, 0:584

types of, 1:924–926

types of bills, 1:930

what may and may not be used as
evidence, 1:928

when Comm Ev is held and all evidence is
forwarded to Sea Org for review, 0:662

when senior exec may be called as witness in
matters of recourse requested by
junior, 0:478

who may convene, 1:943

why it is not as acceptable as a hearing, 0:603

witnesses, rules for, 1:929

wrong in its findings, recourse, 0:523

WW Committee of Evidence, definition, 1:926

Comm-Member System,

A Routing, 7:228

B Routing, 7:228

C Routing, 7:228

direct communications system between the staff
member of one org and only the exact staff
post in another org without vias, 7:228

Comm-Member System, *(cont.)*

D Routing, 7:228

is result of experience already tested, 7:226

new system authorized, 7:225

orders and, 7:229

routing and, 7:228

special benefit to public is improved service ability of their local orgs, 7:227

commodity, commodities, *see also* **product; service**

area not producing interchangeable commodity, 0:297

desirability and quality of one's, 0:598

handling highest commodity—life itself, 0:656

promotion without adequate delivery of service or, 0:347

scarcity of, 0:506

that are more desirable than anything else world has to offer, 0:332

common sense,

exec lacking, 0:266

top management depends on, 0:134

commotion, HCO deputizing other Scientologists in times of, 0:478

comm station(s), *see also* **baskets**

appearance, 1:304, 1:355

comm centers, description, 0:369–370

every person must have basket station, 0:378

not organized so as to be easily used, 0:426

provide for each post, 1:64

responsibility of, 1:316

route to hat only, give its dept, section and org, 0:383

Scientology orgs comm system: despatches, 0:368

three-basket system, 0:371, 0:378

comm system, *see also* **baskets; bulletin board; Comm Center; communication(s); communication line(s); information board(s)**

belongs to Dir Comm, 1:315, 1:355

plan can have errors, 1:359

planning must be adequate to volume and needs, 1:359

purpose of, 1:355

use airmail, air letters, cables, telegrams, 1:457

communication(s), comm, communicating, *see also* **ARC; ARC triangle; despatch; letter; message; particle; telex; traffic**

answer people's questions, 0:84, 0:166, 0:276, 0:322, 0:370

antisocial personality and, 1:1015

appearance and tone of, 0:335

communication(s), *(cont.)*

as basic of administration, includes, 7:409

Axiom 28, 0:45–46, 1:319

basic step of administration, 7:408, MS3:388

basket for each person in the organization, 1:304

booms and correct comm, 0:393

cable and telex placement, 1:368

cannot occur without stable terminals, MS1:298

channels must center in one room, 1:345

channels of communication used in PR, MS3:72

comm baskets, 1:371

Comm Center, *see* Comm Center

comm discipline, 0:391–392

Comm Ev offense for anyone in an org to halt or attempt to halt the communication of a Director of Special Affairs, an LRH Comm or a Flag Rep, 7:723

comm line, *see* communication line

component parts of, 0:46, 1:319, 4:483, MS3:72

correct comm, 0:391, MS2:239

customs and, 1:21, 7:1162

daily pickups to and from Comm Center, 0:165

definition, 0:46, 1:319

demanding comm be in proper form, 0:392

Dept 2 promotional actions, 1:40

Dir Comm puts lines there, sees that they flow fast, 1:315

dynamics out of, 0:456

Emergency Formula and, 0:625

entheta forbidden on long-distance, 1:473

executive and, 0:372, 0:387, 0:388, 0:389, 0:391

exists to be replied to or used, 0:330

extraordinary locations and stale date, 0:382

failure to communicate, 1:902

failure to make tech bulletins and policy letters distinctive in appearance, 1:393

falsifying comm from higher authority, 0:472

fast comm most easily done by comparisons, MS3:120

fast flow, not inspected by seniors, 0:386

first action of executive is to demand correct comm, MS2:236

first action of HCO, 1:35

flow of, 0:196

formula, 0:46, 0:122, 1:319, 4:483, MS3:72

forwarding proper communication to its proper destination, 0:405

from org to public, letters, magazines, 1:316

from public to org, 1:316

handling of packets, 7:1162

communication(s), *(cont.)*

having standard lines and routes for particles to follow, 0:392

HCO's first action is, 0:377

high crime to cut basic comm lines of Scientology, 7:1242

how the lines are severed, 7:575

how to speed up, 1:472

implies somebody is reached, MS3:8

into disorganized area without first organizing it, result, 0:433

intraorganizational despatch, 0:368

Intraorg Comm Section, 1:317

items in progress must be locatable on visible lines, 1:369

leave current work and communications in open baskets near desk, 1:369

levels of communication upon which certain materials of Scientology can be communicated, 6:143

levels of skill in, and the STCC, 6:497

lie will either blunt or end, MS3:8

LRH Comm sees that Ron's comms fly, 0:356

mail and despatch delivery, 1:365

management can instantly improve the tone of any organization and its efficiency by hooking up and keeping wide open all communication lines, 7:574

may not contain entheta or misemotion, 7:235

message placement, 1:368

must be very precise in order to have impact, 1:29

must streamline if expect answers back, 1:300

network of, 7:418, MS3:398

never make despatches or comm material vanish off lines and into desk, 0:195, 0:378

no-communication, 0:417

no logistics on telex or telephone lines, 1:466

noncommunication consists of barriers, 0:46

nonsuppressive comm, 0:392

nonurgent comm on telex lines, 1:465

no real comm, only dev-t, cause of, 0:408

one does not accept comm that does not belong to him or is not post business of originator, 0:392

order of importance, 1:316

org board and, 0:370

origination of comm that should have been originated by someone else, 0:413

outflow to general public using any comm particle or body, 0:367

packets, handling of, 1:21

people who cannot receive comm so can't answer or respond properly, 0:406

communication(s), *(cont.)*

pickup and delivery times, 1:304

PR is supposed to be a communication technique, MS3:7

primary factors are positiveness and speed, 1:465

priority of, 7:1163, 1:22, 1:306

procedure over long distances, 1:465

promotional actions and, 0:348

PRO work and comm formula, MS3:149

refusing to communicate, refusing to act, are alike crimes of omission, 6:43, 7:984

registered mail, 0:379

removing particles off the line, 0:432

request put in writing, 0:369

responding to, 0:370

right to give and receive, 1:1041

routing of, *see* routing

send them to a function, not a person, 1:303, 6:689

send to the department from which you want something, 6:689

should be good and not offend, 0:335

social personality and, 1:1019

speed of, 1:317, 1:364

SPs fail to relay or report, 1:993, 4:85

staledate, 0:381

stopping of, 1:902

supervision of internal system, 1:317

system parallels the org board, 1:317

telex comm cycle, 1:476

terminals and, 0:196, 0:433, MS1:298

theory of, stable datum, 1:359

to members of special interest groups vs. individuals, MS3:152

two-way comm cycle vs. content, 0:330

types to be handled, 1:345

understanding and, 0:46

vocabularies have to be increased before comprehension and communication occur, 0:41

why one cannot avalanche data onto the heads of partially trained, poorly comprehending people, 6:144

wrong address or names misspelled, result of, 0:338

Communication Course, consists of, 6:455

communication cycle,

additives, 5:667

auditor and fractured comm cycle, 5:586, 4:1173

communication formula, 1:901;
  see also **Axiom 28**
  admin high crimes and, 7:493
  definition, 0:46
  form of issue for, 7:1303
  management–labor problems evolve from the, 0:122, 7:668
  offense, halting or editing Flag Rep comm, 7:1408
  pay reduction, demotions, transfers, fines or dismissal may only be done after, 7:1300
  unused, 0:424

Communication Inspector, duties and purpose, 1:383

communication line(s), comm line(s), *see also* **channel; flow line; line; route**
  confused with a command line, MS2:58, MS2:240
  definition, 7:480, MS1:370, MS2:58, MS2:196, MS2:240, MS2:301, MS3:460
  despatches and, *see* despatch
  erroneous data jams it, 0:85
  example of not really finding a, 0:578
  exec hatting someone at a distance on his, 0:390
  Executive Director,
    books, 7:646
    business mail and, 7:647
    carriers of data and commands, 7:659
    copy of every magazine and brochure and pamphlet published by orgs, 7:644
    if good and complete and well handled, position becomes very easy to deal with and all will go well, 7:659
    magazines, 7:644
    presents and, 7:640
    Sec EDs, 7:638
    SO #1 and, 7:646
    watched carefully, 7:646
  finding comm lines that apply to one's post and insisting one be put on those lines, 0:576
  four things exec wants on his incoming comm lines, 0:372
  generalities omitted on, 0:85
  general public to the general public, 2:24, 6:30–34
  group has the right to exile anyone it discovers to be guilty of tampering with any communication line, 7:575
  HASI members and, 2:36, 6:41–48, 6:48–51
  holding them rigidly in place, 0:230
  how our lines can stay freer and faster, 0:403
  it must be possible to locate any active despatch on the, 0:378
  jamming a, 0:85

communication line(s), *(cont.)*
  keep current work visible and where it belongs on the, 0:378
  keep them taut and crisp, 7:651
  kept in endless foment, 0:400, 0:431
  letters go on, 0:377
  lousy source of data, 0:388
  main reasons the comm lines to the Executive Director exist, 7:653
  member HASI to member HASI, 6:37
  member of the HASI to a preclear, 6:38
  natural law of, 7:578
  only few situations require acknowledgment to order over long lines, 0:372
  org is number of terminals and comm lines united with common purpose, 0:81
  public comm lines and org image, 0:335, 6:606, MS3:140
  putting org there by providing comm lines amongst group and from org to public and public to org, 0:408
  removing particles off the, 0:432
  rounding up comm lines that relate to one's post, 0:578
  routine despatches go on, 0:377
  Scientologists to the general public, 2:29, 6:34–37
  seeing that terminals and comm lines exist, 0:82
  several ways to jam, MS1:238
  sizing up org by watching despatch lines and baskets, 0:418
  slow, 0:432
  straightening out comm lines of each post, 0:442
  to speed a comm line remove mest from it, 7:762
  trained Scientologist to member of the HASI, 2:32, 6:37
  trained Scientologist to preclear, 2:33, 6:38
  trained Scientologist to trained Scientologist, 2:33, 6:38–41
  two paramount data in handling, 0:404
  used to detect areas of potential slump, 7:657
  watching products vs. watching comm lines, 0:388
  why execs get themselves onto all, 0:388

communication routing, *see also* **comm system; communication; communication line**
  command channel, 1:378
  conference, 1:378
  horizontal fast flow, 1:377
  lots of staff and no income, conditions present, 1:379

communication routing, *(cont.)*

table, 1:378

three types, 1:377

why a scramble occurs, 1:378

Communications Officer, responsible for relaying anything or anyone that is received at or sent by Saint Hill, 7:220

communications personnel, 0:326–327

Communications Release, ability gained, 4:190

communicator,

accepting an almost, 0:429

communicator's title, 7:348, MS3:328

definition, 7:346, MS3:326

exec actions, 7:348, MS3:328

HCO Area Secs were LRH's first, 0:101

policing compliance is a vital function, 7:348, MS3:328

primary duties, 7:346, MS3:326

purpose, 7:348, MS3:328

three depts, the secretary, deputy and communicator in division, 0:601

why comm runner can move on lines with impunity, 0:326–327

communism, *see also* **socialism**

based on squad mentality, 0:134

business world under threat from, 0:55

everyone starving to death in, 0:82

most individually oppressive form of government, 0:601

only criticism of communism that Communist will tolerate, 0:600

oppresses up stats and rewards down ones, 0:507

simply old-fashioned today, 0:507

why it is unlikely to produce good society, 0:134

would be huge joke in insane asylum, 0:157

community, exchanging with the, 0:298

company, companies, *see also* **administration; group; organization**

"company property" idea is stupid and dangerous, 0:186

does not live or breathe and so it cannot care for anything, 0:186

down-trending,

OEC and, 3:4, 7:4

reversing any down-trending company, 0:4

essentially a collection of small org boards combined to operate together as a large org board, 0:108

few individuals have concept of structure of entities such as their, 0:41

government interference with, 0:506

company, companies, *(cont.)*

national maps and leading companies change many times a century, reason, 0:41

socialism unmocks companies, 0:598

squad mentality and, 0:134

staying level or seeking to grow smaller, 0:123

successful company deserves fruits of its success, 0:508

United States,

government vanishes regularly and only companies keep civilization going, 0:599

putting companies in Danger condition, 0:599

West still permits companies, 0:598

what they rise or fall in direct relationship to, 0:89

comparative(s),

example of, MS1:164

in evaluations, MS1:164, MS1:166

competence, competent(ly), 1:86; *see also* **ability; cause; efficiency**

definition, 0:251, MS1:445, MS2:65

demanding high competence on post, 0:258

environmental control and, 0:251

getting work being competently done, 0:590

hatting and, 0:206

having a hat, being hatted and demonstrating, MS1:302, MS1:458

incompetent, incompetence,

competence vs., demonstrated in his environment, MS1:445

competent person vs. incompetent, 0:251

correct action when faced by urgent necessity arising from, 0:87

definition and results of, 0:252

"incompetent" sciences, 0:258

psychiatry, psychology and, 0:40

increased by, 0:64, MS1:287

insanity has to do with motive not competence, 7:1143

people,

can't build up competent people by invalidating, 0:247

person can really never do more than he can do, 0:87

why a competent individual tends to take work all on himself, 0:87

production in training is the evidence of the demonstration of competence, 4:436

sanity and insanity are matters of motive, not rationality or, 0:296

standard admin is the key to, MS1:287

we hold posts as competent teammates, 0:235

"Competent Being," certificate as, 7:442, MS3:422

competition, is a trick of the weak to fetter the strong, 0:273

complaint(s), *see also* Chaplain

    department, Chaplain is also the complaints department, 6:518

    handling, 2:396

    primary public complaint, 0:322

    taken to HCO personnel, 0:477

    those who do their work least well have the greatest number of, 0:229

    what to say when somebody complains too hard about an org, 0:276

    where auditor has given auditing for fees less than those charged by Central Org, handling, 2:417, 6:709

complement,

    assigning a, 1:215

    definition, 1:215

completed intensive, definition, 4:210

completed staff work, CSW,

    always demanded by Executive Director when asked to make any decision or okay anything, 7:658

    conclusions or solutions not acceptable from junior to senior, only data, 0:240

    CSWP, definition, 0:390, 0:403

    definition and description, 0:402

    enforcing CSW, 0:392

    incomplete staff work, effect of, 0:401

    "Is this already covered in policy?" 0:404

    junior,

        must state or initial "This is okay" on all work, actions or projects, 0:419

        that don't CSW but load you up with problems they should have solved, 0:390

    lack of, 0:424

    policy on, 0:401–403

    problems and, 0:390–392

    reducing dev-t and increasing speed of action, 0:401

    requiring only an approved or not-approved, 0:424

completion(s), complete, completing, *see also* compliance

    accepting incomplete cycles as complete, 0:430

    ARC break occurs when someone is working on a cycle of action and is not permitted to complete it, 7:778

    complete action now, 0:244, 0:430

    definition, 4:29, MS1:333, MS2:167

    failing to follow through and get completions, 0:430

    incomplete courses, reason for, 0:223

    no bonuses of any kind may be paid for, 4:1117

    only report completions, 0:428

completion(s), complete, completing, *(cont.)*

    procedure for, 2:449

    promotional actions and, 0:350

    quick vs. results, 4:1189

    reverse of quickie, 4:29

    statistics,

        high stats from concluding actions, 0:244

        Intern Sup's stat, 5:532

        plummeted, things discovered, 4:1090

    student indicators and course completion, 0:32, 4:379

    targets and, 0:428

complexity, complexities,

    admin and, 0:59

    basic law of, 4:369

    blowing huge holes in one's, 0:38

    comm system or procedures too complex to be useful, 0:426

    confront,

        complexity vs., 0:36–38, 0:51

        when no-confront enters, chain may be set up which leads to total complexity and total unreality, 4:371

    engaging upon trivial complexities, 0:51

    misunderstoods and, MS2:133

    study and, 0:36

    why mental mass accumulates in vast complexity, 0:37

compliance, comply(ing), complied, *see also* completion

    accepting an almost, 0:429

    altered compliance, 0:424

    checking compliance, 0:595, 7:1212

    command channel used upward for, 0:387

    counter-intentions in the way, 0:246

    definition, 0:706

    done target, MS3:439

    ethics presence and persistence and, 0:246

    example of how to get, 7:824

    failure to comply with a direct and legal order from an exec, 0:468

    false compliances come about because a staff membei under threat or duress seeks to protect himself by false reporting, 7:824

    false report detection and handling, 7:1212

    harsh discipline may produce instant compliance but smothers initiative, 0:515

    how to get one, 7:824

    insisting original order be returned with the, 0:430

    lack of skills to detect lack of compliance, 0:67

compliance, comply(ing), complied, *(cont.)*
LRH Communicator,
responsibility for, 7:1211
sees that Ron's EDs are complied with, 0:356
make it easy to accept a report of a
done, 7:825
misunderstood orders will not be properly
complied with, 0:431
noncompliance, *see* noncompliance
not safe to falsely infer or report target
done, 0:146
ounce of PR is worth a ton of ethics, 7:1262
point where "reasons it can't be done" are not
a square one problem but simply Q and A
and a flagrant will not, 7:825
really a done target, 7:459, MS2:445
repeating targets and, MS2:441
report,
definition, 7:479, 7:708, MS1:369, MS2:195,
MS2:300, MS3:459
stalled or bogged targets, handling, 7:710
what it isn't, 7:708
square one, find out why they're not yet at, and
get them there fast, 7:825
staff member ordering and complying only in
his favorite area, 0:425
strategic plan and, 0:706
telex, reported by, and then same information
sent by despatch, 0:432
time machine use in checking
compliance, 7:1212
too timid to refuse to comply to off-policy
order, 0:147
verify it personally, 7:825
with policy, and good public relations, 7:1260
composition, inextricably linked to a
message, MS3:297
comprehension, *see* **understanding**
compromise, I never compromise with a situation
to be agreeable, 0:238
compulsive bypasser,
Danger condition and, 0:617
definition and handling, MS2:211
computer(s),
able to detect noncompliance in writing and
getting done programs, 7:456, MS2:442,
MS2:456, MS3:436
authorization of orders from, MS2:459
can keep track of things and operate to catch
things, MS3:436
danger of relying on, MS2:466
definition, MS2:453
equipment, responsibility for, MS2:459
ethics points, list of, MS2:464

computer(s), *(cont.)*
false data fed into, MS1:11, MS2:466
high crimes and, MS2:459
keep track of things and operate to catch things,
7:456, MS2:442, MS2:456
management and, 0:704, 0:705
no better than the organization that feeds it,
MS2:466
programs, what based on, MS2:458
speed of particle flow and, MS2:453
targets and, MS2:440, MS2:455
use of to boost efficiency and production,
MS2:453
user, definition, MS2:453
concept,
of right and wrong, 0:452–453
understanding ceases on going past
misunderstood word or, 0:39
conclusion(s),
how right or wrong it is, 0:453
never accept from a junior, 0:241
condemn, to protect dishonest people is to
condemn them to their own hells, 0:461
condition(s), *see also* **repair of past ethics
conditions; statistics; various conditions by
name**
ability to better, 0:96
acting fast to get stat up before a condition has
to be assigned, 0:653, 0:661
Affluence, 1:560
applying formula of condition one is in, 0:562,
0:628
assign(ing) conditions,
assign a condition or a Comm Ev, 0:523
assigning moderate conditions at first by current ups and downs of graphs, 0:655
below Normal assigned to org, div or dept
applies to all staff, 0:654
by graph, 1:567, 7:396, MS3:376
exec responsibilities for, 0:653, 0:659
expansion and, 0:655
finish week by assigning it condition and writing up formula, 0:657
getting in ethics by condition assignments,
0:518
Gold Stars, Blue Stars and Green Stars, assignment of own condition and, 0:525,
0:662
how to, 1:566
levels of ethics actions and, 0:494–495
one gets the conditions he fails to assign,
7:399, 7:825, MS3:379
only on the basis of graphable statistic, 7:904
reason for, 0:655, 0:658
requires all graphs to be accurate, 0:655
status reasoning and, 0:678

condition(s), *(cont.)*

weekly, 0:669–670

what should be done before any condition is assigned, 0:515

what you are assigning conditions to doesn't exist or doesn't expand, handling, 0:655

why you assign and enforce, 1:570

assignment of, for divisions, departments, sections, units and individuals, 7:903

battle planning needed actions without taking condition into account, 0:664

ceasing to apply formula when one is out of the condition and in another, 0:562

clarification on orgs, divisions or departments, 1:564

Comm Ev offense, hit with wrong conditions, 1:484

completing conditions formulas, 0:666, 1:613–614

Conditions by Dynamics, 0:530

Confusion, 1:588

Expanded Confusion, 1:588–589

constant condition, if you want to hold a, 7:497

cycles of lowered and raised, 0:252

Danger, 1:558–559

assessment, 1:587

mechanism of, 1:611

Why finding, 1:587

definition, 7:481, MS1:371, MS2:197, MS2:302, MS3:461

desire to change one's, 5:353

difference between Affluence and Power, 1:594, 7:553

doingness which will bring about changed condition will be reflected in one's stats, 0:665

downstats breaking high conditions and claiming ethics protection, 0:661

dropping one condition below condition one is *actually* in, 0:667

Emergency, 1:559

ethics,

high ethics for high conditions, 0:661

hitting people with conditions is small part of, 0:519

Examiner and attesting to completion of, 0:670

example of assigning a condition to a stat, 7:563

Executive Council, set and declared by, 7:913

executive may assign any condition to immediate juniors, 1:573

exempted from a general condition, 0:662

existence, three conditions of, MS2:49

condition(s), *(cont.)*

expansion and, 0:124, 0:655

explaining away a, 0:655

failure to,

follow or apply, 0:562, 0:653

handle can hang person up later, 1:607

flow one to the next, 0:672, 7:563

getting ethics in and, 4:973

getting person to apply to his life, 0:668

good physical condition, definition, 4:1121

hang-up at Doubt, 0:576, 1:605

hitting real condition that applies, 0:657

how to never get ethics condition for months, 0:144

it is important to understand bad conditions don't just happen, 6:867

judgment and, 0:680, 7:563

list of, 0:562–565

lower-condition person industriously collapsing own post stats and also stats of adjacent posts, 0:657

management tool, 0:648

moderate conditions, 0:655

no rote method of determining condition of stat, 0:680

Non-Existence, 1:558

Expanded, 1:591

when HCO Exec Sec automatically assigned Non-Existence, 1:55

Normal Operation, 1:559–560

only a few working to push it up, 0:661

operating state of existence, 0:680

past conditions, 0:619, 0:668, 1:611

Power, 1:560

Power Change, 1:560–561

protesting assigned condition, 0:654, 0:668

reason org can't hold Affluence or high condition, 0:661

reciprocity, 1:570

repairing past ethics conditions, 0:668

scale, too large or small will obscure the true condition of a stat trend, 7:532

sequence of, 0:583

short application and a long application of conditions formulas, 7:562

SP found at root of every bad, 0:498

State of Emergency, *see* State of Emergency

statistic,

volume of, has little to do with, 0:677

when won't come up, you drop condition down, 0:657

status,

think and, 0:678

when you let status reasoning get into stat assignment of conditions, the org has had it, 7:530

condition(s), *(cont.)*

steps,

one has "no handling" for condition if one doesn't do steps to handle, 0:667

one has to do, in order to improve one's condition, 1:603

person must do, to get through, 0:667

success story written after attesting to a, 0:670

table of conditions, 0:567, 1:575

tool to change future of stats, 7:564

transfer while in low, 0:566

Treason, technical degrades and, 1:14

upgrading individuals from general condition, 0:654

viewing actual condition is vital step to resolving it, 0:122

weekly,

assignments of conditions, 0:671–679

condition assignments must be accurate, only in that way can one maintain expansion, 7:530

conditions formula steps added to battle plan, 1:603

one only considers two things, 7:529

whole rationale of, 1:566

why it is vital to accurately and honestly ascertain condition one is in and apply that formula and do it, 0:667

wrong condition, incorrect condition,

assigning, 0:302

being in Affluence, thinking it was Power and applying wrong condition, 0:651

effect of assigning and applying, 0:643, 0:665

false condition assignments, 0:643

incorrect condition assigned, handling, 0:426, 0:668

letting people be hit with, 0:519

not correctly designating the condition he is in, 1:604

using condition lower than you are in, result, 7:250

condition formula(s), *see also* **various condition formulas by name**

acting like natural laws, 0:578

applying formula of condition one is in, 0:562, 0:628

battle plan and, 0:664

ceasing to apply it when out of condition and in another, 0:562

completing, 0:578, 0:666

failure to apply formula of condition one is in, 0:562

flow, one to next, 0:666, 0:680

followed scrupulously and steps taken reported one by one, 0:614

formula evasion, 0:426

list of, 0:561–565

condition formula(s), *(cont.)*

misunderstoods in application of, 0:671

new post formula, 0:561

not reading or verifying formula has been done, 0:302

one has to *do* formula steps to improve one's condition, 0:665

past ethics conditions,

completing old incomplete formula, 0:669

repairing, 0:668

scale,

definition of, 7:563

make up a, 0:680

short and long application of, 0:679

stats rising before completing, 0:667

three Danger Formulas, 0:612–613

weekly condition handling steps added at beginning of battle plan, 0:664

write-ups, 0:664, 0:666, 0:669–670

wrong condition formula, incorrect condition formula,

what happens if one does not correctly designate condition he is in and apply its formula, 0:665

wrong or no formula being applied, 0:426

conditional target(s), *see also* **target(s)(ing)**

definition, MS2:432, MS2:435, MS2:437

example of, MS2:432

Conditions by Dynamics, procedure, 0:550

Conditions Order(s),

definition, 7:698

description, 0:659

published on divisional flash color, 1:573

students and pcs subject to, 1:574

conduct, behavior,

code of good conduct laid down out of experience, 0:455

ethical conduct, what it includes, 0:456

individual,

freed of aberrations reacts more decently, 0:158

restimulated, acts worse, 0:158

is dramatization and above the awareness of the person, 4:619

long unchanged pattern of, 0:574

past vs. present, 0:152

professional, 0:102, 0:103, 0:333

reversing conduct of declining governments and businesses, 0:506

sane and insane, cannot tell difference between by, 0:252

Scientology has definite set of standards of, 0:152

standards of conduct staff are expected to uphold, 0:153

conduct, behavior, *(cont.)*
    survival and, 0:453
    unethical conduct is conduct of destruction and
        fear, 0:454
    uniform yardstick for, 0:455
conductors (railroad), 0:197, 0:199
conference(s),
    data vs. opinions and, 7:918
    executive time and, 7:894
    Flag Representatives and, 7:1410
    hats, 7:918
    kept to a minimum, 0:369
    members, vital actions of, 7:918
    objection to planning of, handling, 7:920
    org form and, 1:277
    planning hat and, 7:918
    planning member of, 7:920
    routing, 0:387
    why they fail, 7:918
Confessional(s), *see also* HCO Confessional(s);
        Security Checking
    antisocial overts or intentions disclosed,
        handling, 4:986, 5:449
    anyone refusing should be turned over to Ethics
        Officer, 4:986, 5:449
    benefits, 1:644
    broad general clues about suspects, 5:607
    course or school and, 4:406
    failed case pc, handling, 1:643
    getting ethics in and, 4:973
    HCO may not do, 5:606
    honest students and, 4:406
    Knowledge Reports and, 1:851
    leaving staff and, 1:214
    ministers and, 5:448
        minister report of pc overts, triple purpose
            served by, 1:646
        who misses withholds on parishioner,
            4:986, 5:449
        with red tag pcs, handling, 1:643
    omission of Confessional tech and failed
        execs, 1:642
    org trouble vanishes when used correctly by
        Dept 3, 4:973
    parishioner who knowingly withholds during an
        HCO Confessional, 4:986, 5:449
    penances, 1:643–644
    persons doing, checked out and drilled, 1:635
    policies, 1:642
    red tag, Solo auditor handling, 1:643
    reports,
        required, 1:645
        use of pc reports to Ethics Officer, 1:646
        writing of, 4:1197

Confessional(s), *(cont.)*
    students and, 5:797
    suspects, 1:634
    Tech and Qual may do them, 1:633, 5:606
confidence, confident, 1:86
    becoming more confident in life, 0:206
    clean, well-dressed staff inspires, 0:334
    person made more confident by being given a
        post, 0:205
    public confidence in Scientology depends on our
        promoting and maintaining excellent credit
        everywhere, 3:253
confidence check, definition, 0:469, 1:863
conflict(s),
    caused by third party, 0:510–512
    none which cannot be resolved, 0:512
    on-policy orgs have least internal conflict, 0:28
    squad mentality, causing, 0:134
    target has the junior position to policy, MS1:135
confront(ing), *see also* look; observation
    ability to confront,
        mest and people, ability to confront, handle
            and control, 0:252
        preclear improvement, and 4:305
    administrator or staff member must be able
        to, MS1:287
    basic law of, 4:369
    complexity vs., 0:36–38, 0:51
    criminals lie rather than be made to, 0:527
    evil,
        basic thing man can't or won't
            confront is, 4:370
        confront of, 0:37, 0:525, 0:648, 1:836,
            MS1:168
        lowest confront there is, 0:648,
            7:398, MS3:378
    facing past and misdeeds, 0:152
    failure to apply tech due to not
        confronting, 0:64
    group size and, 0:600
    if one confronts his post he will see there are
        things to do, 0:259
    inability to confront, effect of, 0:63–64
    mest, ability to confront, MS1:445
    nonconfront,
        aberration and, 0:38
        mental mass and, 0:37
        preventing success, 0:63
    not confronting the accused with all charges and
        his accusers, 0:514
    of outpoints, MS1:168
    O/Ws and evaluation, MS1:187

confront(ing), *(cont.)*

people,

less confront, the more false data he has accumulated and will accumulate, MS2:137

who can't confront can have trouble communicating, reading meters, studying or even detecting what is going on, 4:427

who can't confront, symptom—not to make anyone else confront, 4:433

problem, to take apart requires only to establish what one could not or would not confront, 4:370

public relations personnel and, MS1:419, MS3:14

service facs and, 0:9

solving inabilities to, 0:64

standard admin complicated by inability to confront and do actions called for by policy, 0:59

suppressive person, why he is a no-confront case, 0:657

unreality and no-confront, 0:37

vias vs., 0:51

confusion, Confusion, confused, *see also* **developed traffic; disestablishment; disorder; distraction; noise**

anything in org is your job if it lessens confusion if you do it, 0:83

arranging personnel and organization to handle types of actions and, 0:434

between ethics and justice, 0:448

between source and cause, 0:249

blows off when order is entered, 1:31

causes of, 0:81, 0:108, 0:195, 0:230

condition, 0:308–312, 0:567
Expanded Confusion Formula, 1:588–589
formula, 1:588
formula for a group, 1:615

definition, 0:106, MS1:194

Formula, Expanded Confusion Formula and, 0:568–570

generated by posts not held, 7:412, MS3:392

greatest single confusion that can exist in subject of organizing, 0:132

handling, 0:64, 0:82, 0:308–312, 0:434

handling, example, 4:500, 5:464

human leaders and, 0:641

major source of dev-t is ignorance or failure to grasp confusion and the stable datum, MS3:392

materials, when they are issued above the acceptance level of an audience, a confusion results, 6:28, 7:969

misunderstood word and, 5:464

never Q-and-A with, 1:31

confusion, Confusion, confused, *(cont.)*

no confusions when lines, terminals and actions exist for each type of particle, 0:82

oppressive, confused and overworked org, reason for, 0:554

order vs. disorder and area which is in, MS2:182

organizational pattern lessens overburden and, 0:82

org board,
classifies types of, and gives stable terminal to each type, 7:413, MS3:393
confusion vs. org board, 0:106, 0:433

Personnel people, when they do not know all the hats, 0:280

portion of org in confusion, reason, 0:4

post not held by someone will generate, 0:433

product vs., 0:106, 0:308–309

sources of, in an organization, 1:30

unstable terminals and, 0:436, 0:437

way to take a lot of confusion out of orgs, 0:383

when combined strength of "org" is only that of one person in state of confusion, 0:325

confusion and the stable datum,

applying principle of, 0:433–434

ignorance or failure to grasp, major source of dev-t, 7:412

org board and, 0:433

Problems of Work and, 0:65, 0:200, 0:433

congress,

attendees and, 6:326

Congress of Scientologists, 1:23, 7:1164

Distribution Division function on the 1966 org board, 6:104

must answer people's questions, 0:320, 2:598, 6:156

organization and increasing interest and attendance, 6:324

policies that apply, 6:104

something should be done to get the people there, like Hello-Okay—locational processing on the whole group, 6:326

conscience, guilty, 0:461

consequence(s),

afraid of consequences, should one tell truth, 0:454

detecting people who fear responsibility or consequences of their most ordinary actions, 0:412

I give instructions based on prediction of, 0:140

out-ethics on a dynamic has disastrous consequences on other dynamics, 0:459

consideration, communication and, 0:46

conspiracy,

pushing someone up in whose leadership they have faith, 0:640

totalitarian conspiracy using "mental health" to control populations, 0:336

constitution, 0:41, 0:68

construction, constructive, 1:488

contracts for, 3:292

easier to destroy than construct, 0:63

good vs. evil in relation to destruction and, 0:452–453

ideas, 0:10

sane are constructive, 0:296

survival of life forms depends on, 0:63

two rules regarding renovations and construction, 3:281

Consultant, definition, 4:295

consultant policy, evils resulting from, 4:1171

consumption,

got into production that equalized or tended to exchange, 7:436

production vs., MS1:61

Contact Assist, 5:629

contacts, PES and, 0:99

contempt,

holding Scientology materials up to, 0:472

showing contempt to Comm Ev when before it, 0:469

contests,

minority-type prizes, never offer in Scientology, 6:207

must be planned so that every entrant gets a prize or the prize, 6:207

policy and, 6:207

prizes and, 0:234

context,

definition, MS1:135

targets out of, MS1:135

continental directives, 1:414

Continental Executive Council, what caused collapse of HCOs in orgs, 7:162

Continental Finance Office expense, definition, MS2:352

Continental Flag Banking Officer, definition, MS2:352

continental letters, 1:414

Continental Liaison Office(s) (CLOs),

activities of, MS3:400

continental Whys to remedy to get Flag programs and projects in, 7:425, MS3:405

definition, MS2:351

duties, 7:420,

example, 7:422, MS3:402

to observe, first duty of, 7:419, MS3:399

Continental Liaison Office, *(cont.)*

expense, MS2:352

fits at (1) Observation and (4) Supervision per Key Ingredients, 7:418

mission to find out Why or remedy already found Why, 7:421, MS3:401

operation, example of, 7:420, MS3:400

purpose of, 7:417, MS3:397

reason for, 7:425, MS3:405

reserves, MS2:352

supervise getting programs and projects in and done, 7:418, MS3:398

when a CLO doesn't report or backlogs, it gets Bongvilles, 7:424, MS3:404

Continental Liaison Officer,

appointed to WW for six months, 7:139

authority and functions, 7:133

junior to Exec Secs in his cont zone and has to take their orders, 7:139

primary duty, 7:134

statistics, 7:133, 7:140

Continental LRH Communicator, resolves disputes on divisional secretary recruitment, 1:170

continental office, city office and, 0:626

Continental Order (CO), definition, 1:431

Continental Organization(s),

how many orgs it should have under it, 0:597

purpose and function, original intention, 6:583

Continental Pubs Liaison Officer,

duties, 2:359

representative for Pubs in his continental area, 2:359

continuous overts, suppressive person and, 1:1005

contract(s),

Dianetic auditing, 7:1096

ending of, model to be used, 1:214

entered into by staff member with no purchase order, handling, 3:290

failure to produce satisfactory statistic is violation of, 1:194

for services, 3:292, 7:1070

freeloader account of person who went to higher org, 1:256

general form of release contract, 7:1066

legal matters and, 0:477

policy on purchases and, 0:183

processing, stipulations of, 7:1066

recruitment contracts, stacked at Reception, 1:172

requests for contractual approval, none will be entertained unless passed upon in affirmative by administrative head of corporation requesting, 7:1070

contract(s), *(cont.)*

security checking persons whose contracts expire
without renewal, 0:177

signing, 0:213, 0:217

staff contract breakage, 0:104, 0:214,
1:241, 3:192

submitted in writing by the other party and
signed by him before any work is
done, 3:285

training and,
begins or renews a five-year staff contract,
0:174, 0:176
full-time training and, 1:169
person to be trained by org at no or discounted
fee must sign 5-year contract in
advance, 4:222

warn new staff of seriousness of contract
breakage, 1:256

contraction,

Britain and, 0:125

causes of, 0:115, 0:116, 0:117, 0:534

expansion vs., 0:124, 0:131

formula for salvaging contracting org, 0:534

leads to death, 7:355, MS3:335

org, how it determines its own state of
expansion or, 0:318

out-ethics causing, 0:534

reasons for, 0:102, 0:115, 0:130, MS1:303

survival vs., 0:124

trends used to warn of, 0:677

contrary fact(s), *see also* **outpoint(s)**

definition, MS1:84

examples, MS1:85

contribution(s), contributing, contributism, *see
also* **exchange**

being part of important team is return
contribution, 0:278

child,
contributing vs. one who isn't, 0:529
psychology and, 0:529

description, 0:277

for groups, 6:848

staff member,
permitting to receive without
contributing, 0:527
what they are expected to contribute, 0:278

control,

ability to control mest and people, 0:251

arrogance and force may win dominion and
control but will never win acceptance and
respect, 0:328

definition, MS1:308, MS2:107, MS2:258

dominance of others is a control symptom,
2:413, 6:185

control, *(cont.)*

E-Meter registers bad control, 2:411, 6:183

England and, 2:413

environment, control of, 0:251, 0:253,
0:255, 0:555

executive and, 0:266
does not relax control of, 7:427

failure of individual members to control their
fellows, 0:557

group survival and control of
environment, MS1:447

importance of, 0:555

income,
control equals income, 6:183
falls or vanishes without control, 1:185
proportional to control exertion of our
personnel, 2:413, 6:185

interviews and, 2:493, 6:158

knowingness must be included with,
2:411, 6:183

militant control, too much, 0:338

mission of techno-space society is to subordinate
individual and control him, 0:462

of one's environment, MS1:445

org at cause can reach and, MS1:308,
MS2:107, MS2:258

personnel,
bad control personnel on Reg and PE posts
will waste whoever is driven in,
2:412, 6:184
best control personnel must come into closest
contact with public, 2:413, 6:185
priority of personnel by degree of ability to
control, 1:185, 6:183

responsibility and, 0:619

Scientology does not work in absence of official
control, 0:159

staffs should be tested on, 2:413, 6:185

Upper Indoc,
best test for control, 2:411, 6:183
for the whole staff, 1:185
whole staff can have its control level raised by,
2:413, 6:185

we exert upon public brings about a better
society, 6:183

controversy, tool that can drive your message into
the mind, MS3:107

convening authority,

acts when it has facts, 0:485

definition, 1:926

endorsement of Comm Ev findings, 1:929

has no other duties on committee
convened, 1:926

misdemeanor offenses reclassed as crimes
by, 0:470

other duties allowed at higher echelons, 1:926

recourse requested of, 0:492

conversion, titles for six-department system, 6:792

cooperation,

orders and, 0:144, 0:146

what it depends upon, 0:144

coordinating committee,

agenda, 7:452

definition, 7:451, 7:452, MS3:431, MS3:432

difference between management committee and, MS3:431

exists to clear orders and, 7:452, MS3:432

membership, 7:451, MS3:431

rules,

list of, 7:453, MS3:433

regulations and, must be set up, 7:452, MS3:432

coordination, coordinating,

basic management tools and, 7:484, MS2:200, MS2:305, MS3:464

call-in and, 2:648, 3:224, 4:283, 7:872

council, committee,

what it is and what it does, 7:451, MS3:431

why we have Executive Councils, Advisory Councils, staff meetings, mini programs, 7:455, MS3:435

dull policies providing agreement as basis for, 0:115

elements of, 7:454, MS3:434

essence of management, 7:454, MS3:434

exec coordinating activities, 0:372

manager has to use the tools of, 7:455, MS3:435

master elements of, 7:460, MS2:446, MS3:440

one's actions not coordinating because he does not have lines to give or receive information, 0:579

strategic plan and, 0:707, 7:459, 7:470, MS2:445, MS3:439, MS3:450

cope, coping, *see also* **organizing; Phase I; single-handing**

all right to, MS1:197

becoming an overwhelm, 0:204

by all means but spend some of that time organizing, 7:518

cope sort of hat, description, 0:201

coper goes outpoint found—correct it; and never finds or corrects Why these outpoints, 7:270

definition, 0:201, 7:270, MS1:204, MS1:413

demand to cope increases if you remain in it, MS1:204, MS1:413

departures from hats and, MS1:204

end product of, MS1:198

government operating in, example, MS1:413

handling, 0:201–202, 0:204, MS1:204, MS1:413

cope, coping, *(cont.)*

if you don't have stats and they're not collected, posted, used, prepare to do an awful lot of, 7:519

lack of hats and, MS1:413

organize and, 0:201, 0:204

president of US and, 0:201

remaining in cope, 0:202

what it really is, 1:59

without organizing also, result, MS1:197

copyright,

ads and, MS3:208

approach should be fresh and truthful, MS3:204

hard sell, MS3:206

HCO Secretaries must make certain that all LRH materials published are properly copyrighted in the name of LRH, 7:1292

homework, MS3:204–205

illegal copyright, handling, 7:1058

importance of, 7:1055, 7:1062

infringement, handling, 7:1062

legal matters and, 0:477

neglect or omission in safeguarding, 0:473

no org copyrights are permitted of LRH materials, 2:126, 7:1292

positioning and, MS3:205

responsibility for, 7:1055, 7:1057

safeguarding, 7:1059

surveys and, MS3:209

to leave one copyright outstanding anywhere is unthinkable, 7:1058

use of copyrighted materials, 7:1062

viewpoint, MS3:205–206

when in doubt about copyrighting it, copyright it, 2:175, 7:1060

corporate,

address, 7:1120

Legal Dept responsibility for, 7:1053

status, must be in excellent condition, 7:1027

corporation(s), *see also* **business; company**

bankruptcy and, 0:300

legal matters and, 0:477

Corporation Coordinator,

definition, 7:1115

functions and purposes of, 7:1115

correct(ness), *see* **right(ness)**

corrected gross income, *see also* **gross income; income**

causes of the gap being too wide between GI and CGI, 2:11, 3:87, 7:861

divided by staff, least that it has to be, 0:314

correction, correct(ed)(ing),

correctly reported outnesses that threaten org NOT being corrected, 0:517

correction, correct(ed)(ing), *(cont.)*

don't correct pc who needs no, 5:675

errors are dealt with by corrections of person, reprimand or warnings by seniors, 0:467

how org corrects itself, 0:95

of tech, staff and orgs, belongs to Snr Qual N/W, 5:69

org's product, correction of, 0:292

product of "corrected auditor" missing, 0:293

Qual Div keeps Scientology working through, 5:865

quality and viability of, 0:292

recognizing and correcting bad spots in org, 0:544

that which is produced or produces, 0:290

Correction Division, *see* **Qualifications Division**

correction list, definition, 4:1015

corrupt, corruption

delivering part or corrupted version of what was ordered, 0:317

effects of corrupt activities, 0:534

in police and court systems, 1:962

of be-do-have cycle, 0:287

persons trying to pervert policy and corrupt tech, 0:92

sign of culture on way out, 0:454

SPs corrupting tech, 0:90

corrupt activities,

effect of, 7:1036

handling, 7:1036

cost(ing),

definition, MS1:275, MS2:341

product cost related to whether or not it is used, 0:337

to be real must take into account expected capacity or ideal scene of the activity, MS2:341

cost accounting, formula, MS2:416

counter-effort, 0:587, 0:588

definition, MS1:213

lack of a hat is most usual, MS1:213

counterespionage,

org and, 1:629, 7:1033

reward for, 1:630, 7:1034

counterfeiting, of mimeo issues, 0:113

counter-intention(s),

compliance and, 0:246

ethics vs., 0:509

mechanisms to mask, 1:786

counter-policy,

independently set, MS1:261, MS1:426

mechanism of 3D aberration, MS1:261, MS1:426

varieties of, MS1:261, MS1:426

counter-postulate, 0:576

counter-purposes, effect on a group, MS1:265

counter-solution, org stuck on track with, 0:405

country, *see also* **civilization; culture; group; nation; society**

all follow principles which apply to the individual, 0:297

best guarantee of stability, 0:67

booms and depressions, probable basis of, 0:253

down-trending, OEC and, 3:4, 7:4

few individuals have any concept of structure of entities such as their, 0:41

never looks so good as when it is already about to fall apart, 0:599

overthrown in areas where administrative skill is missing, 0:67

reason things do not run well in a, 0:199

reversing any down-trending country, 0:4

survival of, 0:297

value of, 0:297

what they rise or fall in relationship to, 0:89

courage,

having enough to face own past and misdeeds, 0:152

Socrates and, 0:448

course(s), *see also* **Academy; checksheet; instruction; student; study; Supervisor; training**

abbreviating an official course in Dianetics and Scientology, 1:14

Academy, standard Day and Foundation org schedules, 4:453

admin degrades and, 0:73

altering, 5:677

anyone can be signed up for a course, 2:486, 6:379

as FSM prizes, 0:337

attention on case and, 4:316

authorized for Central Orgs, 4:184

basic reason students remain long on, 4:327

can be run two ways, 5:516

clay table healing to be taught in HPA, 4:76

Comm Ev offense to allow out-ethics activities in, 4:425

completion, definition of, 4:361, 7:1075

course(s), *(cont.)*

consists of, 4:397, 4:427, 5:507

cost and length of rise as they increase in class, 4:169, 5:334

crime to run a course without checksheet or to change checksheet on student after issued, 4:361

definition, 1:287, 4:182, 4:417, 5:856

deliver it and certify you have, 0:283

do not teach processing in HAS courses, 2:203, 6:197

don't try to handle course environment with student auditing, 4:341

each has progress and stat boards, 4:466

empty, causes of, 4:461

enroll any time of any day, 4:361

essence of twinning and, 4:434

extension courses, 4:554

fast, secret of, 4:490

50 percent on auditing, 50 percent on case gain is stress in any course, 4:179

final valuable product of, 1:288

flubbed instruction perpetuates error on every pc that auditor audits thereafter, 4:11

future depends on, 5:486

good, sound examination and speed of courses, 4:395

graduate, becomes auditor by auditing, 5:849

graduation and, 4:384

handle course environment with good data, good 8-C and discipline and HCO justice machinery, 4:341

handling for misunderstood words, 4:385

hat checksheets done as, 5:509

how courses run when in-ethics, 5:516

if you want full course, provide a well-supervised course, 4:324

illegal to,
give a retread course away, 4:389
run without checksheet, 4:442

income source, 3:101

incomplete courses, reason for, 0:223

indoctrination courses, 5:385

in-ethics, 4:424

internships and, 4:417, 5:856

invoicing for, 0:222, 0:303

large, more than 18 students, needs Course Admin, 4:460

magazines should say "enrolls any time" after every course in every Academy ad, 4:361

course(s), *(cont.)*

materials, 4:442, 5:698

mission courses authorized, 6:748

motto of good course, 4:461

must culminate in teaching a definite skill or skills, 2:205, 4:77, 6:199

natter stems entirely from students' noncomprehension of words and data, 4:329

no Academy courses may be given outside Academy premises, 4:361

no-case-change students and, 1:1001

only those students enrolled on a course may purchase the course pack for that course, 4:363

org far better off selling courses, 0:100

out-ethics and, 4:424, 5:517

overlong, 4:417

policy of gradient course costs, abandoned as unsuccessful, 2:202, 4:74, 4:324, 6:196

poor course will become an empty course, 5:485

practical,
sections of courses and twinning, 4:434
will include, 5:206

product of, 4:417, 5:856

proficiency denoted by a class seal, 5:326

put a course there, 4:398, 5:508

reasons for overlong attendance on Academy courses, 4:372

requires an ability to confront and communicate and this is brought about on the TRs Course, 4:427

roll book,
filed in val docs when full, 4:464
purpose and description, 4:464

roll call, materials, stats, etc., must be part of staff courses, 0:222

schedule, 4:425
day, evening and weekend, 4:182

secret of getting students through is keeping ethics in in the Academy, 4:376

seeing that intro lecture and nonclassed courses use no words that will be misunderstood, 0:352

senior part of the establishment, 1:289

slow,
how to speed up, 4:497
progress, handling, 1:12
spot a slow student at once and get a correct Remedy A and Remedy B done, 4:376

course(s), *(cont.)*

  specialist,

    full panorama of other rundowns and actions available on, 4:666

    where available, 4:666

  squirreling on Academy course, 0:12

  student,

    disruptive of course discipline may only be ordered to Ethics, 4:365

    enrollment for, 4:554

    indicators at course completion, 4:379

    may not request Comm Ev for causes occurring during a, 0:478

    who drift off courses or who are very slow lack somebody to talk to, 4:391

  study time and, 0:222

  successful, 1:288

  supervision failures throw out whole tech delivery of an org and staff, MS2:98

  Supervisor,

    does not offload his course into Ethics or Cramming, 4:400

    R-factor to students, 4:384

    responsibility to eradicate any barriers or hindrances presented which distract student from studying, 4:381

    Supervisor's Code, 4:367

  teach,

    balance of repetitive processes, auditing cycle and meters at HCA level, 4:76

    Clay Table Clearing in HCS courses, 4:76

  technical degrades and, 0:14

  Technical Div may not provide a library as substitute for students buying their own textbooks or course packs, 4:363

  theory,

    checkouts and, 4:395

    routine practical and, belong on, 4:418

  three zones of responsibility in course management, 4:324

  "tough case" makes a lot of commotion so one may think they are "everybody" on course, 4:343

  training,

    partial-paids and unpaids without noticing, 0:302

    policies and, 2:202, 4:74, 6:196–197

  trouble and tendency to alter-is material comes from trying to force a "tough case" to get gains, 4:343

  twinning mandatory on courses where essence of the course is to train the student in practical application of the data, 4:434

  200 fully paid students routinely on courses, 4:410, 6:401

  two ways it can be run, 4:424

  VFP of, 4:398, 5:508

  well-run,

    described, 4:417

    result of, 5:856

course(s), *(cont.)*

  what is a, 0:222, 0:302, 1:287

  when offering training put a course there, 1:288

  when tech courses can be considered in programing staff, 0:222

  Why behind failed courses, 4:431

  zones of responsibility in course management, 5:485

Course Administrator,

  course roll book and, 4:464

  duties of, 1:288, 4:398

  filing of student folders, 4:468

  master checksheet kept up for each course, 4:442

  progress and stat boards and, 4:466

  purpose, 4:460

  responsible for student files, 4:468

course graduate, definition, 4:417

course supervision, *see also* **Supervisor(s)**

  done by OES in tiny org, 0:99

  making it available to all crew or staff, 0:222

Court of Ethics, *see also* **ethics; justice**

  cannot be given for not following BPLs, BTBs or targets or orders that violate HCO PLs, 0:145

  Comm Ev is not a, 0:484

  committing offenses or omissions that bring one's senior, staff member, unit, dept, org, or zone official to personal risk and/or a Comm Ev, civil or criminal court, 0:472

  convened by, 1:948

  convened solely on, 1:949

  disciplinary actions for PTSness undertaken by a, 0:493

  disciplinary actions ordered, 1:948

  dismissals or offloads require a, 0:524

  false evaluation and, MS1:176

  falsified auditor's report is subject to, 4:679

  for Word Clearers who accumulate MUs, 4:505

  Green Star may not be given a, 0:662

  levels of ethics actions and, 0:493–494

  may not order to auditing or training, 0:491

  may not order transfer, demotion or dismissal, 1:950

  no recourse from, 1:950

  not a fact-finding body, 1:949

  not seeking recourse, result, 0:523

  one report received during State of Emergency can bring about a, 0:545

  potential trouble sources and, 4:356

  psychiatric influence on, 0:521

Court of Ethics, *(cont.)*

PTSes and, 1:950

reasons for,

absence from post without competent replacement, 0:267

alter-ising or misadvising others on use of study tech, 0:45

amends project that comes off time machine undone, 0:546

auditor failing to clear every word of every command or list used, 0:45

failing to write clearly on worksheets or put down enough text to make it understandable, 0:47

failure to employ study tech, 0:44

following off-policy issues or orders, 0:145

out-tech, 0:45

permitting auditor to write incomprehensibly or omit data, 0:47

releasing materials broadly to a wrong public, 0:45

report of error, misdemeanor or crime on any staff member in area in State of Emergency, 0:621

verbal tech, 0:24

violating policy or tech, 0:145

reasons for convening, 1:949–950

recourse and, 0:522

required to remove from post and/or to send before a Fitness Board, 0:524

staff going by MUs and, 5:470

students, preclears and, 1:745, 5:110

who summoned by, 1:948

wog and society's "courts," 0:485

Word Clearers who accumulate MUs and, 5:474

court systems, composed of, 1:962

covert invalidation, is social level of an SP, 1:1008

coward, inevitably a liar, 0:454

cramming, Cramming Section,

Admin Cramming, *see* Admin Cramming

administrator needs to know plus and minus of, 5:825

auditors leaving Cramming go through the Examiner, 5:702

compliance reports, 5:702

C/S who lets an auditor struggle without a, 5:702

C/Ses not cramming or getting crammed auditors, Supervisors and Cramming Officers, effect of, 0:302

detects deviation from policy, 7:487, MS3:467

excellent auditors and, 4:966

flunks on checkouts and, 1:241

if examination is not passed, student remains in Cramming, 4:365

instruct, cram, retrain, offload system, 0:442

cramming, Cramming section, *(cont.)*

must exist in org which sells auditing, 4:946, 5:846

no cramming for HGC auditors and auditor scarcity, 4:148

outpoints and, 5:79–80

purpose of, 4:364, 5:773

retread vs., 5:79

section of Dept of Review, 5:773

should exist in every org, 5:653

staff member is sent for remedies if flunks are continual, 3:192

student upset by a flunk and, 5:210

students who fail to meet theory or practical checksheet times sent to Cramming, 4:364

teaches students what they have missed, 4:365, 5:734, 5:774

trains *only* to a specific result, 4:365

twin checking, 5:774

when a student is sent to Cramming his twin is borrowed from course to see that the student goes through his requirements, 4:365

who is sent to, 4:364, 5:773

Cramming Officer(s), 0:302

bonus, 5:135

ED or CO, OES or Chief Officer, HES or Supercargo and HAS subject to Comm Ev if there is no, 5:79

failure on functions will throw out whole tech delivery of an org and staff, MS2:98

F/Ning, definition, 5:702

ideal scene, 5:64

must sign Okay to Audit, 4:946, 5:846

product, 5:65

purpose, 5:64

statistics, 5:65, 5:75

tech hierarchy and, 5:697

cramming order,

definition, 4:261, 5:296

handling for tech queries, 4:502

how to write, 5:786

Crashing Mis-U, *see also* **misunderstoods**

debug tech and, MS2:147

False Data Stripping and Crashing Mis-U Finding, MS2:141

crazy, *see* **insane**

credit,

bad credit rating comes from negligence in Accounts, not from the lack of industry of the Registrar, 3:246

basically a matter of confidence, 3:245

credit, *(cont.)*

cases can be handled on, 5:735

companies, injustice level of, 0:521

credit collection,
    industrious collection action by Div 3 is all it
        represents, 3:137
    what it includes, 3:137

discounts vs. credit purchases, 3:145

do not invite, 3:120

downgrading Scientology credit ratings by
    careless or false statements is serious and
    should be regarded as such, 3:253

extended must be in form of legal promissory
    note, 2:569

extending vs. not extending credit, 0:507

extend only when the down payment covers all
    cost or the past credit record guarantees
    future payment, 3:185

for students and pcs, 4:216, 6:384

giving credit is seldom done except in
    Qual, 0:276

good credit is a primary dissemination
    line, 3:245

has everything to do with confidence and
    reliability, 3:245

rating, bills files and, MS2:47

rating, bills paid in such way that org is in
    excellent credit repute, 0:350

when it has gone bad, it takes making money
    and brilliant PRO actions to restore a good
    credit image and it must be restored, 3:70

credo,

of a good and skilled manager, 7:583

of a true group member, 7:582

creed,

Church of Scientology, 6:515, 7:965

of Scientology, posted in public areas, 7:1320

crew, *see* **staff**

crime(s), *see also* **ethics; justice; offense; overt**

abusing statistical management, 0:696

accepting for training or processing at higher
    levels persons who have not made lower
    levels, 1:792, 4:933, 5:248, 6:548

accessory to, by failing to report it, 0:557

additions, 1:910

always other crimes when you get
    false report, 0:658

an increase in, caused a rise in number of
    police without subsequent decline in actual
    moral aberration, 6:869

answer to crime is raising IQ, 7:1156

antisocial persons freely confess to most
    alarming, 1:1016

ARC broken person leaving org unhandled,
    permitting, 1:793, 5:249

crime(s), *(cont.)*

by student, penalty for, 0:478

cannot live a happy life when one is
    committing, 1:836

case on post, 1:910

changing a checksheet on a student after it's
    issued, 7:1075

collective petition is crime under ethics, reason,
    0:488, 1:742

Committee of Evidence and, 0:474, 0:593

committing a problem, 1:910

committing a solution which becomes a
    problem, 1:910

computer crimes, list of, MS2:464

contributing to a, 0:469

corruption of the be-do-have cycle and, 0:287

Court of Ethics and, 1:948

critics of Scientology and, 1:782–783

de-aberrating crime from society, 0:206

definition, 0:296, 0:455, 1:491

delivering service or goods to person who has
    not been invoiced or registered to
    receive it, 4:219

encouraging crime when you let person give
    nothing for something, 0:527

examples of, 1:908–909

exchange and, MS1:295

failing to write down disclosed crime in
    worksheet or report, 0:557

four general classes of, 0:467–474

gotten off in session, 4:1110

government by riot and intimidation finds rising
    crime rate, 0:481

hiring or recruiting institutional or insane
    person, 1:168

insane and, 0:296

Instructor teaching or advising method not
    contained in HCOBs or on tapes,
    4:350, 5:840

invalidating the state of Clear, 4:796

knowingly withheld by pc until in session,
    actionable, 4:995

knowing of outness or crime and failing to
    report, 0:557

list of, 1:864–868

new kind of, 1:908

offenses which are treated in Scientology as
    crimes, 0:470

omitting to handle criminality can make one as
    guilty of resulting crimes as if one
    committed them, 0:527

one remedy for, 7:1157

crime(s), *(cont.)*

people who engage in black PR have, MS3:85

permitting an ARC broken person to leave an org unhandled, 1:793

perpetrated by antisocial personalities, 1:1014

personnel without purpose commit, MS1:407

persons with undeclared crimes, 1:722

punishment for, 0:474

reclassed as high crimes, 1:883

refusing to communicate, refusing to act, are alike crimes of omission, 6:43, 7:984

running a course without a checksheet, 7:1075

seriousness of, 0:545

sign of a culture on way out, 0:454

SP characteristics found back of, 1:1009

stems from lack of belonging, MS1:408

to be without money, biggest crime one can commit in society, MS3:144

to invalidate the state of Clear, 6:656

training person at higher level who hasn't proven himself, 4:934

two crimes in this universe, one is being there and the other is communicating, 2:613

types of relating to ARC broken public, 6:549

welfare and, 0:204

when misdemeanor offenses may be reclassed as, 0:470

when person has no purpose and value he will commit crimes, 0:204

world without, 0:458

Crime Report, 0:544

criminal(s), criminality,

accuses others of things which he himself is doing, 1:830, 7:1147

actions proceed unless checked by more duress from without not to do an evil act than they themselves have pressure from within to do it, MS2:68

almost every modern horror crime committed by a criminal who had been in and out of the hands of psychiatrists, 7:1144

antisocial and antiself, 0:456

anything that a criminal seeks to obtain can be obtained without crime if one is bright enough, 7:1155

attempting to put ethics in on himself, 0:452

becoming very angry if not prevented from hurting others, 0:480

caged like some wild beast, 0:455

characteristics of, 0:480, 0:526

civilization without, 6:519

compose about 20% of the race, 1:783

coverup for, 1:836

criminal(s), criminality, *(cont.)*

crimes unreal, do not read, 1:633

criminally insane politicians, 0:451

criminal think, 0:527

deciding to rise above aberrations and get busy and go straight, 0:557

definition, 1:830, 6:827, 7:1147

desiring society in which criminal is free to do as he pleases, 0:480

does not survive well, 0:455

due to no ethics presence, 0:527

dynamics out of communication, 0:456

easy step to insanity from, 1:728

E-Meter check for, 1:160

employment of, 1:160

ethics being applied by criminal hands, 0:527

evil intentions and, 1:832

exchange and, 0:317, 0:527

handling, 0:526–531

hate anything that helps anyone, 1:783

individual rights were not originated to protect criminals, 0:461

individuals with criminal minds tend to band together since the presence of other criminals about them tends to prove their own distorted ideas of man in general, 7:1148

intent, person dramatizing, 1:733

is in protest against his own survival, 7:1150

is not much benefited by the giving off of current withholds and is not likely to reform because of this, 1:832, 7:1149

lack of ethics permits criminal impulse to go unchecked, 0:527

leaves clues on scene, 0:452, 1:487

must not triumph with new found tools of destruction, 0:462

no matter what harm he is doing to others, is also seeking to destroy himself, 7:1150

not only antisocial but antiself, 1:491

offenses normally considered criminal, 0:470

only sees others as he himself is, 1:832, 7:1149

org full of staff members who aren't properly apprenticed and hatted goes criminal, 1:78

out-ethics person is potential or active criminal, 0:456

policy regarding, 4:881

psychopathic, 0:518

relentlessly seeks to destroy anyone it imagines might expose it, 7:1148

criminal(s), criminality, *(cont.)*

rich political and financial criminals are not happy, 0:459

rip-off and, 0:317

Scientologists deserve protection from, 1:989

seeking to destroy himself, 1:833, 7:1150

society run by, 0:456

source of trouble, 5:105

there would be no criminals at all if the psychs had not begun to oppress beings into vengeance against society, 7:1157

trained-in criminality, 0:529

TRs and 8-C and even ARC Straightwire indicated as first steps to handling a criminal, 7:1149

unhatted persons becoming, 0:206, 0:391, 0:527, MS1:458, MS2:69

criminal acts,

committed by SPs, 1:993, 4:85

handling, 0:526–531

criminal charges, filed if person blew and monies or org property missing, 0:177

criminal exchange, definition, 0:527

criminal mind,

individuals with criminal minds tend to band together, 1:831

seeks to destroy anyone it imagines might expose it, 1:831

criminal record,

persons with criminal record refused training or processing, 4:360

student, rejection for acceptance of training and, 4:309

critic,

approach to somebody who complains too hard about an org, 2:435

defense of a power to a, 0:640

definition of, 4:327

handling, 1:783

investigation of, 1:782

never discuss Scientology with, 1:784

recommended approach to the, 0:276

sample dialogue, 1:783–784

three points of fault, MS1:53

criticism, criticizing, 5:175

attainment of one's standards is not done by, 0:251

become better evaluators by process of, MS1:138

correct and not capricious, MS1:138

correspondence, done by, 4:846

I regard attacks on or criticism of orgs and staff as personal affront, 0:276

criticism, criticizing, *(cont.)*

pretending withholds which are actually, 1:993, 4:85

refusing to speak ill of Scientology or criticize it to outsiders, 0:153

Crosby, Bing, 0:506

cross-chit, Exec Secs and secretaries can, 0:582

cross order(s), cross ordering, *see also* **illegal order**

cross-ordering an LRH evaluation, 0:146

disciplined for issuing or following a, 0:146

due to failure to record an order, 0:431

effect of, 0:425

hobbyhorses and, 0:425

orders, illegal and cross, 0:145

orders of higher superior changed by immediate superior, 0:623

seniors with an unreality on the problems of juniors can paralyze them with floods of orders, 7:149

cross programing, 4:641

cross purpose(s), individuals working at, 0:325, 0:405

cross selection, field staff member and, 6:634

cross target, dev-t and, 0:425

crusade, post in Scientology org is a, 0:85, MS1:238

C/S, *see* **Case Supervisor**

C/S instruction, always written in duplicate, 4:1102

C/S Series 53, lists general things that can be aberrated in thetan, 4:1081, 5:672

CSW, *see* **completed staff work**

Cuba, why experiments of totalitarian communal states starve and fail, 0:186

cultural decay, isn't haphazard, it was caused, 6:867

culture(s), *see also* **civilization; country; group; man; organization; society**

dwindling spiral of current culture, freeing oneself from, 0:451

group expanding into decadent culture, 0:253

group that inherits the, 0:253

moral codes and, 0:455

primitive, rituals of human relationships and, MS3:34

signs of culture on the way out, 0:454

world will come our way as fast as we attain a superior culture, 0:481

cure(s), acceptable cure, 0:453

currency, *see* **money**

customer(s), *see also* **public**

actions which drive customers off, 0:338

anything which delays or puts customer or product on wait is enemy, 0:275

expects staff member to contribute his specialized services to those who seek them, 0:278

influx of, unsettling an area, 0:252

losing customers by inaccurate billing, 0:276

status and, 0:338

Tech can never tell Dissem Div when or how many customers to bring in, 0:344

customs,

communication and, 7:1162

(government function), suppression and, 0:66

cutative(s),

checksheet, processes, intensives, grades, 4:23, 5:22

definition, MS1:208

cutative(s), *(cont.)*

example of cutative org board in government, MS1:210

income cutatives, 0:301

org board, how it occurs, MS1:209

policies in full force, 4:24

cutting, definition, MS3:194

cycle(s), cycle of action, *see also* **action**

completing or ending cycles of action, 0:244–245, 0:260, 0:431

ending cycles consists of seeing that it stays handled, 7:703

how an unfinished one comes about, 0:248

how to handle factors that prevent completion of, MS2:133

misunderstood on any given subject can prevent completion of, MS2:132

suppressives cannot complete, 0:260

Cycle of Production, 0:95

D

damage(s),

careless or malicious and knowing damage caused to projects, orgs or activities, 0:574

Comm Ev can restore lost pay in cases of injustice but not damages, 0:478

equipment damaged, who is liable for, 0:186–187, 0:189

failure to follow policy and, 0:115

failure to take responsibility and failure to act with initiative in circumstances which, not handled, bring damage to others or serious overwork, 0:662

making up damage one has done, 0:574

occurring because urgent message was not marked RUSH, 0:381

of org materiel, 0:468

property owner awarded damages, 0:172

staff member debited for damages on post vacated, 0:198

using fact of leaving to damage org or staff, 0:178

Damage Report, 0:543, 0:544

Danger, *see also* **condition(s)**

additional actions to take, MS2:210

assessment, 1:583–584, 1:587, MS2:208

compulsive bypasser handling and, MS2:211

conditions, 1:553

  Book of Case Remedies and, MS2:211

  misunderstoods and, MS2:211

  only occur when there are fundamental disagreements on a command channel, MS2:210

consequence of not doing both formulas, MS2:207

correct Danger handling, 1:582

Danger, *(cont.)*

Disagreement Check and, MS2:210

ending a Danger condition, 1:586

end ruds check and, MS2:207

example(s), 1:554

  of correct Why found, MS2:208

finding the Why, MS2:208

First Dynamic Formula, 1:583

  example of, MS2:209

  steps of, MS2:206

formula, 1:553

  3 May PL and, MS2:207

full study of, MS2:211

if full tech were totally applied, could move one up the line out of the condition of being human, MS2:212

if person refusing to follow First Dynamic Formula, HCO moves in with full investigation and takes action per what it finds, MS2:210

Junior Danger Formula, 1:583

  definition, MS2:206

mechanism of, 1:611

O/W write-up and, MS2:207

result of full Danger handling done, MS2:211

Sec Checking and, MS2:210

Second Formula, definition, MS2:206

semi-heavy ethics period and, MS2:206

Senior Formula, steps of, MS2:206

steps of full program which can be applied to junior who has been assigned Danger, MS2:207

tech on Danger when seen against responsibility, 1:612

there are three Danger Formulas, MS2:205

155

Danger, *(cont.)*
Trouble Area,
Questionnaire and, 1:584, MS2:207
Short Form and, MS2:207
who may assign, 1:556
Why finding, 1:587
wrong Why handling, MS2:209

Danger condition, *see also* **bypass**
assigned when,
Emergency condition continued too long,
0:583, 0:585, 0:606
senior exec suddenly has to wear hat of head
of activity because it is in trouble, 0:606
stat plunges downward very steeply, 0:606
stats continue to go down or continue at dangerous level, 0:587
being human and, 0:618
brought about by violation of Power Change
condition, 0:651
bypass(ing) and, 0:583, 0:594, 0:619
carried on too long drops to
Non-Existence, 0:599
command channel disagreements and, 0:616–617
correct Danger condition handling, 0:605
Dir I&R assigned Danger if Ethics Officer had
to be shot from guns, 0:656
disagreement,
and, 0:591, 0:696
cure, 5:775
occurs only when there are fundamental disagreements on a command channel, 7:685
don't infer Danger condition that doesn't show
on graph, 0:587
ending Danger condition when production has
increased, 0:609
ethics investigation and, 0:585
First Dynamic Danger condition assigned to
each individual connected with the,
0:585, 0:605
formula, *see* Danger Formula
graph description, 0:677
handled on bypass, 7:250
handling, 0:583, 0:605, 0:611
handling for anyone proposing assignment of a
Danger condition to a section with rising
statistics, 7:1235
hearing and Comm Ev on anyone whose
negligence or noncompliance brought
situation about, 0:585
how a junior who accepts an order from anyone
can cause one, 7:683
if declared one of course does the work
necessary to handle the situation that is
dangerous, 7:684
inspections by Exec Secs and, 0:592
junior who accepts orders from everyone, 0:593

Danger condition, *(cont.)*
low leadership survey grade person putting
wherever he is in, 0:591, 7:685
LRH assigning a, 0:587
mechanism of, 7:738
moral, 7:251
moving from Non-Existence into a, 0:562
Org Exec Sec actions taken during, 0:590–591
O/W write-ups and, 0:612–613
past Danger condition never assigned, result,
0:619–620
person not even up to Danger because nobody
knows they are even bypassing him, 0:578
responsibilities,
control and, 0:619
of declaring a, 0:590
right way to handle Danger condition assigned
one, 0:610
second danger condition and handling, 7:1236
senior,
can bypass anyone in a, 0:583
exec suddenly finding himself wearing hat of
head of activity, 0:606
Trouble Area,
Questionnaire, 0:607–609
Short Form, 0:608–609
what to do when several Dangers and Non-
Existences have been assigned, 0:574
when it is over, 0:590
when it is very bad to assign a, 0:587
who may assign a, 0:588
why orgs stay small, 0:598
Why should be found for individuals in a,
0:608, 0:613–614

Danger Formula,
applies when orders bypass those responsible,
7:353, MS3:333
bypass and, 0:562–563, 0:583, 0:585,
0:592, 0:594
correct formula not done, 0:605
executive applies to neglected area,
7:428, MS3:408
Junior Danger Formula, 0:606
Second Danger Formula being applied but real
Danger Formula not, 0:605
steps, 0:562–563, 0:585, 0:605–606, 0:612,
0:614–616

dangerous, position near power is delicious but
dangerous, 0:640

dangerous auditor, specific actions or omissions
that make such are, 5:589

dark age(s),
cause of, 0:125

dark age(s), *(cont.)*

when society produces little and has to feed many, 0:506

darkness,

plunging the world into, 0:483

we can stand in the sun only so long as we do not let deeds of others bring darkness, 0:462

data, *see also* **information**

absence of, MS1:157

alarming, 0:401

applying the data, *see* application

auditor omitting data, 0:47

comes from tabulation of actions and amounts in orgs, 0:123

comm lines are a lousy source of, 0:387

completed staff work and, 0:401

computer cannot detect false or imperfect data save by system of considering repeated reports correct, MS2:466

cooked data, 0:120

Crashing Mis-U blocking off further ability to study or apply data, 0:39

data, not entheta, brings about action, 0:373

decrying suppression of data which would help mankind, 0:160

definition, MS1:20, MS1:90, MS1:91

determining the value of, MS1:16

economy of, MS1:155

emerging after the fact, MS1:157

failure to inform senior of relevant data, 0:424, 0:430

false data, *see* false data

false reports and ignorance of, 0:139

forwarding fragment of alarming data without collecting whole picture, 0:401

how too little or erroneous data can jam a line, 0:85

inability to confront things bars group member from using, 0:63

junior, data from, 0:240, 0:241

lacking data and assigning wrong cause, 0:413

less you have the more precise analysis must be, MS1:22

masses of, MS1:141

normal admin flows contain enough, MS1:22

obtain(ing),
analysis of situation by analyzing, MS1:18
information for analysis of, MS1:21

offenses concerning, 0:469

omitted,
definition, MS1:78
when to look for, MS1:78

data, *(cont.)*

one studies area, takes data he can get, develops what he can't, applies what he finds, 0:300

only value is if evaluations are done on it, MS1:161

opinion vs., 0:373

orders and, 0:122

prediction from, MS1:155

quantity of, MS1:21

raw data, use of in selecting and promoting personnel, 0:120

reason, depends on, MS1:12

regarded from the angle of outpoints is a lack of consistency, MS1:91

required in evals, MS1:156

selective and right target, MS1:175

Sherlock Holming of the trail that gave the Why, MS1:91

solution given can only be as good as data offered, 0:409

substantive, MS1:185

suppression of operational data and management, 7:574

to be logical, MS1:12

too little on comm lines, MS1:238

two bad systems, MS1:26

valid, MS1:16

validity of, which monitors logic, MS1:156

way to analyze, MS1:17

when faulty, MS1:12

where there is none available, people invent it, MS3:80

written by others on application, use and results are permitted, 7:1292

wrong,
and impure intent, MS1:156
solutions made without full data, 0:401

data analysis, *see also* **analysis; situation analysis; stat analysis**

barriers to being able to use, MS1:105

compares to operating experience, MS1:19

correct sequence, MS1:22–23

definition, MS1:15

grading data for outpoints, MS1:19

instant result, MS1:19

learning to use, MS1:105

necessary to logic system, MS1:16

no substitute for correctly done data analysis, MS1:104

quality of, MS1:19

reason one does, MS1:69

data evaluation, definition, MS1:185; *see also* **evaluation**

data files, separate from stats, MS1:163

Data Series,
  admin degrades and, 0:74
  definition, 7:482, MS1:372, MS2:198, MS2:303, MS3:462
  illegal to randomly place on a checksheet, MS1:181
  in its use one enormously increases one's effectiveness and enormously reduces the worry and stress, 7:819
  intelligence and, MS1:154
  must be studied in sequence, MS1:181
  tech found to be out in orgs, 7:818
  used to its full potential, MS1:138

Data Series Evaluator's Course,
  verbal tech and, MS1:174
  why you should do it, 0:147

data trail,
  examples of, MS1:91
  fixated on the history of something, MS1:141
  use of to find situation, MS1:140

date(s), dated,
  despatches and, 0:369, 0:382
  looking into people's baskets for despatch and letter dates, 0:416

date coincidence, investigatory tech and, MS1:165

dateline,
  outstanding purchase orders and, 3:293
  pay bills up to a certain date always, 3:248
  paying by dateline and other accounts policies prevent bad credit, 3:70

Date/Locate, False Data Stripping and, MS2:142

datum,
  comparable magnitude to, MS1:15
  evaluation of importance, MS1:155
  subject with which to compare it, MS1:15

day course, length of and hours per day, 4:182

Day organization, *see also* **Foundation organization**
  accounting functions for both Day and Foundation are handled by the Day org, 3:172, 7:317
  and Foundation orgs have their own staffs, 7:314
  definition used to determine income of, 3:171, 7:316
  during Day org hours the Day org executives and personnel have full possession and use of org premises and facilities, 7:313

Day organization, *(cont.)*
  FP *must* be kept separate, 3:172, 7:317
  HCO Book Account sales counted as stat of the org that makes the sale regardless of whether person is on Day or Foundation lines, 3:171, 7:316
  only one set of bank accounts for Day and Foundation and all income is banked in these accounts, 3:172, 7:317
  separate invoice machines, one for the Day org and one for Foundation, 3:171, 7:316
  staff study and, 0:222
  stat belongs to that org, Day or Fdn, whose production it measures or reflects, 7:314

D/CO or D/ED for Delivery and Exchange,
  bridge between D/FBO for MORE and the FBO, 7:878
  ensures call-in occurs and org's exchange with public kept in, 7:878
  makes sure the public gets signed up and serviced, 7:878
  primary function, 7:878
  sees that org operates at the highest level of exchange, 7:877

de-aberrate, one would have to de-aberrate a man before his whole social structure could be de-aberrated, 7:377

dead agent(ing),
  caper,
    best tool to handle black PR campaign, MS3:29
    Scientology vs. psychiatry and, MS3:9
    used to handle black PR campaign on Scientology, MS3:28
  definition, MS3:9, MS3:82
  documentation and, MS3:131
  packs,
    definition, MS3:95
    press conferences and, MS3:95
    use of in handling black PR, MS3:83
  use of in handling counter-PR, MS3:9
  vital PR function, MS3:99

dead cat, asserting one's own importance is about as acceptable as dead cat at wedding, 0:330

dead file(s)(ing),
  accusative reports handled by, 1:970
  Address Section and, 1:974
  Ethics,
    actions on receiving folder or letter marked with the Entheta stamp, 2:65
    clearance before being trained or processed and, 2:667
    Officer to equip contact points with rubber stamps for, 2:666
  expired memberships, 1:976

dead file(s)(ing), *(cont.)*

fast flow system of management, 2:666

first place to look in cases of trouble, 2:669

handling restoration to good standing of, 1:980

how does person ever get out of, 2:669

how to,
get out of, 1:978
route entheta letters, 2:664
set up, 2:663

include, 1:972

intention of the system, 1:976

Letter Reges and, 1:976

nonco-op category vs., 1:973

not done to Scientologist for reporting breach of ethics, 1:970

notes from students or pcs now on course or in HGC containing entheta routed to Ethics for Court of Ethics, 2:669

potential trouble source order not given Dead File routing unless person refuses to disconnect or handle, 2:668

Release and Clear,
declarations and, 2:668
declares, routing of, 1:977

restoration to good standing, line for, 2:671

routing of, 1:973–976

suppressive persons and groups, handling of, 2:668

system described, 1:971, 2:662

until Release or Clear declaration is issued, 2:669

use of as opposed to SP orders, 1:972

what it doesn't cover, 2:664

who is assigned to, 2:663

Dean of Technology, requirements, 5:713

death, dead, die, dying, *see also* **succumb; suicide**

bad policy, bad mores, and you have a dying group, 0:411

bad policy or laws or actions based on rumor causing, 0:117

civilizations dying because too few present making things go right, 0:236

contraction leads to, 0:125

corruption of be-do-have cycle contributes to dying civilization, 0:288

dying in ditch, 0:506

environment and, 0:207, 0:208

groups not active and vigilant as individuals die, 0:302

infinity or immortality vs. pain and, 0:452

it's no fun being dead, 0:249

most wrong person can be on first dynamic is dead, 0:453

death, dead, die, dying, *(cont.)*

org will wither and die if you aren't causative, 0:231

policy not known or altered is death, example, 0:410

reason every great civilization that is dead died, 0:121–122

rejuvenation, 0:118

saying that dying is unimportant, 0:302

survival and, 0:452

value of saving a being from death in each lifetime, 0:528

when you're dying of malaria you don't usually complain about the taste of the quinine, 0:449

without discipline group and its members die, 0:450

working for dream of dead people in dead world, 0:302

death camp school, 0:40

death wish,

anyone who doesn't wear his hat in a group and doesn't do his job is obviously dramatizing, 1:1034

definition, 1:1034

debt(s), *see also* **bill; expense**

Dept 7 collects outstanding notes by monthly statements, 0:349

head of government who got into most debt became hero, 0:505

running into debt, 0:317

unfilled staff contract and, 0:174

debug,

definition, MS2:144

demanded by computer when target not done in expected time, MS3:437

first step of handling is to demand production, MS2:146

inspection *always* done as first step in any debug, MS2:155

most wide trap debugger can fall into, MS2:146

second stage of, MS2:147

target not done in expected time, debug will find, 7:457

tech, MS2:145

why do you debug something, MS1:183

debug evaluation, perfect, MS1:104; *see also* **evaluation**

debug tech,

applies from the very small expected action to the huge expected project, MS2:152

checklist, MS2:155
assessed on meter or administratively used, MS2:151, MS2:154

debug tech, *(cont.)*

EP of, MS2:154

how to handle steps done off the
meter, MS2:154

object of, MS2:153

purpose of, MS2:154

restriction on administrative use of, MS2:154

use of, MS2:153

Crashing Mis-Us and, MS2:147

end phenomena of, MS2:152

evaluation and, MS2:152

handling must be in direction of at least 50
percent production, MS2:152

history of, MS2:144

insolvency and, MS2:145

inspection steps and, MS2:145

justifications and, MS2:151–152

locating and correcting disordered areas, 0:307

look don't listen and, MS2:146

personal handling and, MS2:146

procedure, MS2:145

repair list, use of, MS2:151, MS2:154–155

sequence of, MS2:154

study of time and motion and, MS2:146

vital executive tool, MS2:145

Volunteer Minister's Handbook and, MS2:146

when to use, MS2:145

decay(ed),

evil, illness and decay often go hand in
hand, 0:452

off-policy and, 0:59

reason orgs have decayed, 0:66

Western government, reason for decay of, 0:504

decent,

decent people are in favor of justice, 0:480

justice developed to protect the, 0:456

where decent, pleasant things on this planet
come from, 0:10

deception, not a legitimate PR action, MS3:100

decision(s), decide, deciding,

acceptance without decision, 0:323

applicable only to sphere of one job, 0:373

being causative, correct and decisive on posts,
0:230–231

be right on majority of, 0:231, 0:246

demands for, 0:372

by staff and executives, 7:602

depending on exec for petty decisions, 0:373

don't be wrong on any important
decisions, 0:231

Doubt Formula steps allow one to make up his
mind, 0:576

decision(s), decide, deciding, *(cont.)*

execs who refer to others to make a, 0:260

first thought of exec handling despatch
requiring, 0:404

how multiple decision points can work, 6:205

if public is being asked to decide about coming
into an org full of individual decision
points, you get a total collapse, 6:204

indecision, reason for, 0:576

individual decision points, 0:325, 0:326

is close to a thetan's identity, 0:326

judgment and decision are needed in every staff
post, 0:82

knowable decisions, 0:325

making decisions, 0:230, 0:231

multiple decision points, 2:83

never put in an individual random decision point
on a chart, 6:204

organizations,

full of individual *decision points* not covered
by group understanding is no org at all
and will fail, 2:82, 6:204

will flow and prosper as long as the decisions
to be made are known already,
2:83, 6:205

org board and, 0:326–327

people demanding I make decisions they should
be making, 0:374

policy and requests for decisions, 0:325,
0:326, 0:404

postulate or decision too close to a thetan's
identity, 2:83, 6:205

predictable vs. unpredictable, 0:327

PTS person is unable to come to a, 0:573

public individual never asked to decide or
choose, 0:323, 0:324

steps of making a, 0:323

decision point, individual or multiple, 0:326

declaration, auditors outside org bringing in their
pcs for examination and Release
declarations, 0:351

declare (ethics), leaving and leaves and, 0:177

declare, Declare?,

defined, 4:1060, 5:115

only one grade of auditing may be declared or
attested to at one time, 4:1100

out-ethics activities in course rooms and, 4:425

procedure, 5:287, 5:296, 5:689

routing pcs recommended to Ethics and also to
Declare?, 5:119

several grades at once, 5:254

single, only one grade declared at a time, 5:252

Success and, procedure, 4:261

decline, *see also* **collapse; contraction; down statistic; slump**

from rewarding nonproduction, 0:506

governments and, 0:505

reason for decline of Scientology network in late 60s, 0:15

student and auditor cycle of, 4:823

what underlies decline and fall of civilizations, 0:505, 0:603, 0:665

dedicated, we'll survive because we are tough and are dedicated, 7:13

dedicated losers, definition and handling, MS2:202

defeat,

group harder to defeat than individual, 0:87

refusing discouragements and, 0:114

defense, defend(ing),

be decent and effective and do our jobs and the sharpest spears cannot touch us, 7:1022

continuously defending your dept, unit or org means there must be something knocking it down, 0:410

defending and retaining in employ anyone who does his job, 0:151

ethics action and, 0:145, 0:492, 0:524

Job Endangerment Chits and, 0:551–553

knock off frantically trying to cope or, 0:651

of a power to a critic, 0:640

only way to defend anything is to attack, 6:32, 7:973

resorting to defense to control situation when directly attacked, 0:520

defensive PR, MS3:9

definition,

new Scientology basic definitions, 2:162, 4:64, 6:187

wrong, cause stupidity or circuits followed by overts and motivators, 4:335

degradation, degrade,

falsely degrading auditor's technical reputation, 0:472

inevitable when right to serve is interrupted or denied, 0:278

people find losing post or job degrading, 0:205

sexual promiscuity, covetous pervert and, 0:454

technical degrades, 0:14

way out of trap of, 0:458

degraded being(s),

alter-is and, 1:201

cash-bills ratio and, 1:204

characteristics of, 7:390, MS3:370

definition, 1:203

degraded being(s), *(cont.)*

detecting and ejecting them, 0:656

find instruction painful, as have been painfully indoctrinated in the past, 7:389, MS3:369

handled only at OT III, 7:389, MS3:369

in area where suppression has been very heavy for long periods, 1:202

not an SP, but is so PTS that he works for SPs only, 7:389, MS3:369

not natively bad, simply so PTS for so long, 7:390, MS3:370

very degraded beings alter-is, 7:389, MS3:369

degraded scene, definition, MS3:76

degree(s),

honorary, Doctor of Scientology, 5:326

must not issue degrees of an academic nature, 2:402

delays, on customer, product or flows of a business, 0:275

delirium tremens, of Central Orgs, 0:397

deliver, delivering, delivery, *see also* **auditing; course; exchange; processing; production; service; training**

Accounts, admin personnel and, 0:18

balling up lines, retarding growth and keeping everyone marking time, 0:282

battle plans and, 0:708

better than was ordered and more, 0:318

boasting as to speed of, 0:15

bring up to your dissemination, 2:85, 6:371, 7:846

CCRD, who may deliver, 4:978

ceasing to deliver, effects of, 0:10

competent use of targeting in battle plans and, 7:460, MS2:446, MS3:440

completed intensives and courses are keynote to an org's prosperity, MS2:280

definition of, 0:282

dissemination and, 0:499

distractions removed from delivery channel, 0:283

effective delivery, 0:282, 0:283

exchange, four conditions of, 0:317

expansion and, 0:123

Flag Rep report, 7:1419

getting an org or individual to deliver effectively, 2:74

GI increase and, 7:858

give them what we promised if it was promised, 0:404

giving something more valuable than money was received for, 0:317

goods, deliver the, 0:16

deliver, delivering, delivery, *(cont.)*

goodwill and, 0:332

human race will move to degree you deliver, 0:283

hurry and rush of modern age no excuse for not, 5:260

if org can't deliver auditing it will shortly find no pcs apply, 0:100

if you can get tech applied, you can deliver what's promised, 0:8

Instant Service Project, 4:125

in-tech org services, field full of well-trained auditors (and a good Div 6 and Div 2) are what give volume of delivery and GI and pay, 4:408, 6:399

limit to expansion and, MS1:303

low, cause of, 0:689

making it more possible to, 0:564, 0:646

minimum of 25 hours per week delivered by auditor, 0:169

not done swiftly, cheerfully and effectively balls up the lines, retards growth and keeps everyone marking time, 4:80, 6:366

only tough thing to do is NOT to deliver, 4:154

orgs' purpose and, 0:91

prepare to, 0:563

procedure for, 0:282–283

promotion, 0:347
without adequate delivery, 1:39

promptly and with courtesy, 0:317

quality and, 0:17, 0:318, 0:333, 0:499

remedy for dropped auditing volume, 7:159

remorselessly standardize and upgrade in HGC, 4:100

remove barriers to, 0:283

rip-off vs., 0:317

Scientology works, training, processing and results, 7:1293

seeing that everything org is allowed and able to deliver for which demand exists is available, 0:355

senior endangering, 0:266

senior policy, 0:284, 4:145

shortcutting tech delivery is fatal, 1:801, 6:527

straight nonsquirrel product, delivery of, 0:125–126

technical quality and, 0:16, 0:17, 0:18, 0:333

to get an org or individual to deliver effectively, handling, 4:81, 6:367

tolerating poor delivery, effect of, 0:689

tours are vital to, 0:265

we always deliver what we promise, 0:284, 0:404, 2:103, 7:852

deliver, delivering, delivery, *(cont.)*

went out with fast flow and quickie lower grades, 5:277

what is promised, 4:937, MS1:277

when promotion has promoted a response, tell what it is, how much it costs, how easy it is and when he should get it and *deliver,* 2:73, 4:80, 6:366

without proper invoice or payment, result, 3:120

you will go broke if persist in taking fee and delivering for half a year, 4:97

delusion, position on lines and terminals scale and, MS1:289

demand, *see also* **want**

anti-demand factor, 0:126

attempted servicing in absence of, 0:130

creating amount of org proportionate to its final product demand, 0:292

creating demand, 0:131

ethics system and, 0:126, 0:131

expansion and, 0:123

internal demand determines condition of group, 0:318

monetarist's idea is to decrease demand, 0:315

nation expanding demand for its products, 0:124–125

orgs shrink by not creating new demand, 0:130

policy is calculated to ensure continued and widening demand, 0:126

public demand for service is largely dependent upon goodwill, 0:332

quantity of product sufficient to satisfy, 0:292

SP is an anti-demand factor, 0:126

demand directive, definition, 7:353

democracy, democratic,

aberration and, 0:157–158

collective-think of reactive banks, 0:158

inflation and income tax given to us by, 0:9

in organizations, MS1:236

is a collective-think of reactive banks, 7:1015

only possible in nation of Clears, 0:83, MS1:236

prosperity difference between democracy of US and England and super-socialism of Russia, 0:598

reason it caves in, 1:988

Scientology gives us our first chance to have real, 0:158

why one shouldn't be democratic about selecting leader, 0:83

will emerge when we have freed each individual of the more vicious reactive impulses, 7:1015

would be huge joke in insane asylum, 0:157

demo kit, *see also* **demonstration**

basic purpose of, 4:443

basic use is during a checkout to demonstrate understanding, 4:445

definition, 4:443

demonstration,

checkouts must also ask for, 4:395

definition, 4:443

glibness vs., 4:333

history of, 4:443

how the data is USED, 5:179

is key, 5:181

may be done before groups of students but only if the demonstration is translated under supervised student doingness, 4:584

person being tested demonstrating how the data is *used*, 4:331

theory study and, 4:444

you can show somebody how to do things far better than you can tell him, 4:513, 6:338

demotion(s), demote(d), *see also* **dismiss; removal; transfer**

as a student or pc, 0:492

Comm Ev required for, 0:487, 0:492

deputy or acting appointment, demotion of, 0:487

dismissals, transfers and, 0:487

Emergency condition and, 0:477

for treasonable neglect, 0:220

HCO justice prevents wrongful demotion, 0:477

may not be demoted for committing an error, 0:467

may only be done after a Committee of Evidence, 7:1300

never demote an upstat, 0:505

nobody can be demoted without cause, 0:482

pc classification not taken into account in, 0:168

permanent staff member may not be demoted, transferred or dismissed without a full Comm Ev, 1:238

recourse, 1:251

staff members, may request without ethics action, 1:241, 3:192

three things required prior to, 1:253

when someone can be demoted, 0:485, 0:487

where it fits in levels of ethics actions, 0:495

wrongly demoted, handling, 0:487

department(s), dept(s), *see also* **division**

actions of, 7:1198

analyzing a, 0:81

area not producing something valuable enough to interchange will not be supported for long, 0:298

department(s), dept(s), (cont.)

each of the six depts has a promotional purpose in addition to all its other purposes, 7:32

equipment must be specifically assigned to, 0:189

every dept has an assigned stat, 0:690

every job has all depts of org board, 0:95

expansion of, 0:96, 0:115

figuring out the subpurpose of, 0:118

heavy traffic warnings and, 0:380

how to know duties of, 0:440

individual has his 7 (or 9) divs and his 21 (or 27) depts, 0:3

interchange and, 0:298

judging state of dept by state of basket station, 0:378

levels written on org board above, 0:96

list of promotional actions of each, 0:346–355

names of the, 0:346–355

once basic purpose known, only two things should be necessary, 7:600

org board must exist, be real and say what depts, units and staff do, 0:410

policy and size of, 0:115

problems unhandled by dept or post receiving them causing confusion, 0:231

purpose and function of, 3:24

quicksilver personnel scene crashing stats in, 0:266

responsibility for work or production of every, 0:690

sections (number of) in a, 0:96, 0:601

self-determinism defined as it applies to, 0:230

specialization and, 0:196

survival of, 0:297

Thetan–Mind–Body–Product pattern, 0:654

three depts, secretary, deputy and communicator in div, 0:601

tightly run, 0:231

too underloaded will be upset, 1:63

too undermanned and overloaded will empty, 1:62

two things necessary once basic purpose of post or dept is known, 0:230

unmocked by sloppy command lines, 0:593

used for things it was not organized to do, 0:426

value of, 0:297

when you look at dept names, you can see what is missing in your own life, 0:95

Department 1 (Department of Routing and Personnel), *see also* **hat; hatting; posting; recruitment**

appearance of org and staff transferred out of, 6:613, MS3:154

beat down reason why we can't hire anyone, MS1:387

first post of new Exec Esto, MS1:305, MS2:104, MS2:255

generation point of org, 1:112

main weakness, 1:111

mind, MS3:375

name change, 0:339

org board, posts and keeps it there, 1:112

principal functions, 1:112

promotional actions, 0:347
list of, 1:39–40

PR trainees and, 1:39

reserve Registrar personnel and, 1:39

responsible for hatting, 1:294

vital, 1:112

what happens when Dept 1 goes out, 1:113

Department 2 (Department of Communications), *see also* **Comm Center; comm system; Director of Communications; HCO Communicator**

body, MS3:375

oversees stationery and typing quality, 1:40

promotional actions, list of, 0:348, 1:40

responsibility for easy and fast comm lines for public to the org, 1:316

see that no mail or packages leave their org with no return address, 2:340

Department 3 (Department of Inspections and Reports), *see also* **ethics; Inspections and Reports; justice**

duty to inspect low stats, 1:528

exempted from Annoyance Reports, 0:544

first target, 1:810

keeps copies of execs' orders, 0:375

product, MS3:375

projects routinely inspected by, 0:376

promotional actions, list of, 0:348, 1:40

sections and duties of, 0:518

sees that the org is there and functioning, 1:40

Department 4 (Department of Promotion and Marketing), *see also* **Department of Promotion and Registration; marketing; promotion**

always bend toward Promotion in filling posts, 0:101

promotional actions of, 0:348

Department 5 (Department of Publications), *see also* **books; magazines** promotional actions of, 0:349

Department 6 (Department of Registration), *see also* **Department of Promotion and Registration**

always bend toward Registration in filling posts, 0:101

promotional actions of, 0:349

Department 7 (Department of Income),

actions of, 3:37

description, 3:126

has three sections which must not tangle and cross and why, 3:131

may release to field staff members in an area lists of overdue accounts in that area, 6:636

procuring money is the main function of, 3:129

promotional actions of, 0:349

Department 8 (Department of Disbursements),

actions of, 3:39

good credit of companies or person being disbursed to is full responsibility of, 3:127

promotional actions of, 0:349

safeguarding credit and solvency is the main function of, 3:129

what they receive from FP, 3:298

Department 9 (Department of Records, Assests and Materiel), promotional actions of, 0:350

Department 10 (Department of Tech Services), *see also* **call-in; Call-in Unit(s); Director of Tech Services,** 2:641, 3:217, 4:276, 7:865

always bend toward Tech Services in filling posts, 0:101

promotional actions of, 0:350

Department 11 (Department of Training), *see also* **Academy; course(s); Director of Training; training**

goals, 4:290

minimum functions, 4:253

promotion project for, 0:350, 2:407

Department 12 (Department of Processing), *see also* **Director of Processing; Hubbard Guidance Center**

promotional actions of, 0:351

promotion project for, 2:406

Department 13 (Department of Validity),

awareness level, 5:65

created to permit personnel to be improved, MS1:386

functions, 5:68

ideal scene, 5:65

part-time study and, MS1:387

Department 13 (Department of Validity), *(cont.)*
promotional actions of, 0:351, 5:45
purpose, 5:65
statistics, 5:65
valuable final product, 5:65
Department 14 (Department of Personnel Enhancement),
anatomy, 5:380
awareness level, 5:59
custodians of Word Clearing, 5:379
finding disagreements, 0:591
functions, 5:68
ideal scene, 5:60
operating basis, 5:380
ordering students and pcs to, 0:491
promotional actions of, 0:351, 5:45
purpose, 5:60
repair crew, 5:380
responsible for, 5:379
results just not happening, handling, 0:498
statistics, 5:60
valuable final product, 5:60
Department 15 (Department of Correction),
awareness level, 5:63
functions, 5:68
ideal scene, 5:63
product and VFP, 5:63
promotional actions of, 0:351, 5:45
purpose, 5:63
statistics, 5:63
Department 16A (Department of Public Book Sales),
needs free intro courses, 6:485
promotional actions, 6:71, 0:352
Department 16B (Department of Body Routing), promotional actions, 0:352, 6:71
Department 16C (Department of Public Contact), promotional actions, 0:352, 6:71
Department 16D (Department of Public Introductory Services), promotional actions of, 0:352, 6:71–72
Department 17,
course,
checksheets, KEEPING SCIENTOLOGY WORKING and TECHNICAL DE-GRADES PLs not included on and why, 6:489
definition, 6:485
EP, 6:486–487
how it is put together, 6:485–486
how to survey for public's needs and wants, 6:490
must address public needs and wants, 6:486

Department 17, *(cont.)*
naming, 6:487
not training professional Scientologists; getting them to BE Scientologists, 6:488
paid services are those services which give the public what is needed and wanted to handle their ruins, 6:673
product—people into org and going up the Bridge, 6:487
surveying and, 6:491
Department 17A (Department of Public Registration),
bookbuyers who do not buy service and, 2:703
prime purpose of, 2:431
promotional actions of, 0:353
Department 17B (Department of the Hubbard Dianetics Foundation), promotional actions of, 0:353
Department 17C (Department of Public Services), promotional actions of, 0:353, 6:72
Department 17D (Department of the Chaplain), *see also* **Chaplain**
org board (1979), 6:530
promotional actions, 0:353, 6:72
to be established in all Class IV Orgs, 6:530
VFP and statistic, 6:531, 6:535
Department 18,
statistics and, 6:671
third FSM section statistic, 6:672
value of new statistic, 6:672
Department 18A (Department of Public Relations),
appearance of org and staff and, MS3:154
promotional actions of, 0:354, 6:72–73
Department 18B (Department of Clearing), promotional actions of, 0:354
Department 18C (Department of Success), promotional actions of, 0:354
Department 19 (Office of the Executive Director), promotional actions, 0:355, 7:84
Department 20 (Department of Special Affairs), promotional actions, 0:356, 7:85
Department 21 (Office of LRH), promotional actions of, 0:356, 7:85
department head(s), director(s), *see also* **executive**
can't be in charge if thing one is in charge of doesn't exist, 0:654
establishing quotas for weekly divisional stats, 0:691
handling staff member who has too many hats, 0:166
how one is judged, 7:758

department head(s), director(s), *(cont.)*

must never begin a practice of yanking people off post to do things that aren't hat, 7:759

procuring personnel, 1:226

requirements for permanent status, 1:223

responsibilities,
for appointments, transfers or dismissals, 0:373
for notifying payroll of staff under him, 3:331
for providing his personnel with materials of their job whatever these may be, 7:761
of, 7:186

should have hat folder, 0:193

size of dept, 0:601

what expected from each, 3:24, 7:186

Department of Accounts,
definition, 2:510, 3:238, 7:206
promotional purposes, 2:59, 7:34

Department of Body Routing, *see* **Department 16B**

Department of Certifications and Awards,
prime purpose, 5:31
records kept, 5:410

Department of Clearing, promotional actions, 6:73

Department of Communications, *see* **Department 2**

Department of Correction, *see* **Department 15**

Department of Disbursements, *see* **Department 8**

Department of Enrollment, purpose of, 2:420

Department of Estimations, use of dead files, 1:976

Department of Examinations, prime purpose, 5:30

Department of Government Affairs,
formed, 3:376
headed and directed with a minimum of personnel, 7:997
new department formed, 7:997

Department of Government Relations,
mailing pieces of, 7:996
may not use org personnel for typing and mailing, and may only use org personnel for reception, switchboard and despatch purposes, 7:1001

Department of Income, *see* **Department 7**

Department of Introductory Services, *see* **Department 16D**

Department of Materiel,
definition, 2:509, 3:237, 7:205
promotional purposes, 2:58, 7:33
promotion project for, 2:407
purpose of Materiel Administrator hat, 3:370

Department of Official Affairs,
actions, 7:1004
Dept of Government Relations retitled, 7:1007
description, 7:1104
exists as an extension of the Office of the Continental Association Secretary and purpose, 7:1004
maxims, 7:1006
operations and, 7:1005

Department of Personnel Enhancement, *see* **Department 14**

Department of Processing, *see* **Department 12**

Department of Procurement,
duty of Procurement personnel, 2:602
purpose of, 2:601
requirements of Procurement personnel, 2:602

Department of Promotion and Registration,
Book of Letter Scheduling is the game of, 2:629
CF files and addressing plates and, 2:56
definition, 2:506, 3:234, 7:202
description, 2:426
full complement, 2:55
hat(s), 2:55
of this department and how they can be combined in many ways, 2:55
in continuous crash program of mailings, letters out, getting new lists and names, 2:427
is not a scheduling agency, 2:502, 4:248
key department of dissemination and has full responsibility for it, 2:56
promotional purposes, 2:57, 7:32
promotion program for, 2:405
three distinct categories, 2:404
works for present time income hard and rightly, 6:287

Department of Public Book Sales, *see* **Department 16A**

Department of Public Registration, *see* **Department 17A**

Department of Public Relations, *see* **Department 18A**

Department of Public Services, *see* **Department 17C**

Department of Records, attends to deposits, 3:131

Department of Registration, *see* **Department 17A**

Department of Review,
prime purpose, 5:31
red hot on doing Remedy A, Remedy B and S&Ds that never miss, 4:630

Department of Routing and Personnel, *see* **Department 1**

Department of Success, promotional actions, 6:73–74

Department of the Chaplain, *see* **Department 17D**

Department of the Hubbard Dianetics Foundation, promotional actions, 6:72

Department of Training, *see* **Department 11**

Department of Validity, *see* **Department 13**

departure(s), *see also* **squirreling**
    deterrents to departures, 0:116
    from ideal scene, how to spot, MS1:56
    outpoints and, MS1:58

deposit, always have in the bank deposit book the original deposit slip, 3:400

depression(s) (economic), *see also* **down statistic**
    basic economics eventually catches up with weird false pretenses, 0:315
    causes of, 0:253, 0:506
    dev-t and, 0:393
    great depression in the US and England, 0:506
    off-policy actions followed by, 0:145

deputy, deputizing, *see also* **apprentice**
    definition, 1:196
    demotion of, 0:487
    deputy, appointment cancelled in State of Emergency, 0:622
    every key post should have, MS1:273, MS1:454
    four divs in a portion, the Org Exec Sec, a deputy and a personal secretary, 0:601
    HCO deputizing other Scientologists, 0:478
    org composed of groups of six persons; manager, deputy and four, 0:600
    postings, state of Clear and, 1:199
    rule for, MS1:438
    staff approaching deputy to see if they should approach exec, 0:602
    status, can be demoted, 1:251
    training as prior to posting, purpose for, MS1:399
    used to run the same post, MS1:273

derived, definition, 0:52

design,
    art forms, MS3:196
    composition and "eye trail," MS3:197
    definition, MS3:194
    delivers emotional impact, MS3:197
    purpose, MS3:196
    relationship with rough layout, MS3:196

desire(s), What is desired product that will also be desired by others? 0:260

desk,
    cable or telex, placement of, 0:377
    letting despatches (or letters) stack up on your, 0:370
    neat and orderly, 0:82, 0:165
    policing one's desk and lines, 0:390
    putting active work, despatches or comm material in drawers, 0:195, 0:378
    sitting at desk handling despatches, exec remains ignorant, 0:388
    staff members that must have a, 0:378
    taking comm particles off another's desk, 0:432
    three-basket station located by, 0:378
    wearing holes in heels resting them on, 0:400

desk workers, exercise and, 0:225

despair, with regard to one's post area, 0:311

despatch(es), *see also* **communication; letter; particle; telex; traffic**
    active despatches, handling of, 0:378
    address it to the post not the person, 0:368
    Advisory Council, despatches to, 7:893
    all answers dated, 1:385
    already covered by policy, 0:405
    answering letters, how to do, 1:376
    arrow indicating first destination, 0:383
    body presented with, 0:326, 0:369, 0:416
    color flash system for, 0:369
    copying despatches, 0:382
    daily pickups to and from Comm Center, 0:165
    dating of, 0:369, 0:382
    definition, 7:480, MS1:370, MS2:196, MS2:301, MS3:460
    delayed internal and external despatches, handling, 0:381–382
    designation system, 1:451
    entheta despatch, handling, 0:414
    "everybody says" despatches, 0:405
    every person must have a basket station, 1:370
    example of how to set up a, 0:368
    exec(s),
        forwarding misrouted despatch, what it means, 0:409
        sitting at desk handling despatches remains ignorant, 0:388
        who work hard but have fantastic staff despatch volume, 0:407
    existing only because originator has not handled situation, problem or executive order, 0:397
    external despatches, 0:381
    extraordinary locations and staledate, 0:382, 1:384
    filed where it can be retrieved, 0:307
    form, 1:372, 1:374

despatch(es), *(cont.)*

forwarding fragment of alarming data without collecting whole picture, 0:401

get work done better than conferences, 7:894

handing out despatches and work to correct hats vs. to anyone handy, 0:196

handled daily, 0:370

handwritten, 0:369

held until completed or handled, 0:369, 0:372

held up on lines, 0:432

hiding those that should be visible, 0:378, 0:416

how to get your despatch to arrive, 0:383

how too little data can jam a line, 0:85

if I find myself handling a piece of traffic, I handle it, 0:400

if you have a request, put it in writing, 0:369

improper despatch, 0:405

internal, 0:381

intraorganizational, 0:368

it must be possible to locate any active despatch, 1:370

knowingly going by MUs in, 0:47

let originator do the work, 0:406

letters go on comm lines, 1:368

line does not keep executive informed, MS2:59, MS2:241

locating despatches on lines, 0:378, 0:416

major part of an executive hat is "routing," 1:372

meaning of symbol * on all despatches, 7:1175

message,
form, 1:452
replies, 1:453

misrouted despatch, handling, 0:383

never make them vanish off the lines and into a desk, 0:195, 0:378

nonsense despatch, 0:405

not originating when one should, effect of, 0:413

only one copy goes and comes back, 0:368

original(s),
goes and comes back, 1:374
only return with "done" or "can't be done," 0:369

originated despatches, 0:370, 1:376

passed in manner to deny info on record, 0:426

pointing out channels on which despatches flow, 0:389

procedure for writing, 0:368

production vs., 0:41

put any vias at top, 0:383

despatch(es), *(cont.)*

querying for policy where policy already exists, 0:404

removing particles off the line, 0:195, 0:378, 0:432

repeated traffic, 0:431

responding to communications, 1:376

route to the hat only, 1:372

routine, 1:368

routing of, *see also* routing, 0:383, 0:386, 1:304–305

rush, 0:377, 0:381, 1:368

safeguarded against public or unauthorized interference, 1:386

Scientology orgs comm system: despatches, 0:368

sign name but also hat you're wearing when written, 1:372

sizing up org by watching despatch lines and baskets, 0:418

speed of flow of, 0:275, 0:325, 0:432

speed up, 1:384

staff member writing despatch to himself but routing it to somebody else, 0:412

staledate, 0:381, 0:425, 1:384
external despatches, 1:384
internal org despatch en route more than three days must be reported, 1:384

swiftly delivered and in accurate form, 0:347

taking care of 99% of organizational business, 0:369

telex vs., 1:472–473

that should go in your hat, 0:369

unanswered, 0:417

vital part of any staff member's duties is proper routing, 1:372

volume, 0:407

when converted to air letter, 1:455

when not getting answered or actioned, don't keep issuing more of the same, 7:415, MS3:395

when you get a misrouted despatch, 1:372

which don't concern or belong to one, handling, 0:166, 0:390

written requests, put it in writing, 1:375

despatch system(s), *see also* **communication station**

description, 0:85

staff responsibility for following the, 0:166

destiny, what your destiny depends on, 0:13

destruction, destructive, destroy(ing),

acts are good which are more beneficial than destructive along dynamics, 0:453

anyone following destructive reinterpretation of policy is as guilty as misinterpreter, 0:141

committing destructive acts on the job, 0:459

criminal and madman must not triumph with their new found tools of, 0:462

destructive acts done out of fear, 0:454

dev-t destroys real production, 0:391

easier to destroy than construct, 0:63

forwarding purpose not destructive to majority of dynamics, 0:236

freedom of speech does not mean freedom to harm by lies, 0:461

good when enhances survival, 1:488

hidden actions of insane can destroy faster than environment can be created, 0:252

highest ethic level would be long-term survival concepts with minimal destruction, along all the dynamics, 0:451

insane person and, 0:296

man puts ethics in on himself by destroying himself, 0:452

misinterpretation of policy resulting in, 0:141

mistake to use individual rights and freedom as arguments to protect those who only destroy, 0:461

most neglected and destructive admin action, 0:99

no construction without some destruction, 0:453

offenses concerning, 0:467

orders, query of and destructive orders, 0:141–142

persons who wish to destroy civilizations, 0:297

person who accepts a post or position and then doesn't function as it, will upset or destroy some portion of an org, 0:569

products of governments are mainly destructive, 0:252

psychiatrists' destructive tech, effects of, 0:68

secret desire to destroy causing failure, 0:63

staff member's goof can destroy whole org, 0:409

unethical conduct is conduct of fear and, 0:454

weapon capable of destroying all life on this planet, 0:451

willful destruction of Scientology property, 0:472

destructiveness, difference between insanity and sanity is, 7:1143

destructive order, 0:102, 0:141, 0:265

detention, ethics actions do not carry detention, 0:495

detoxification,

defined, 4:1237

long-range, Purification Rundown, 4:1239

developed traffic (dev-t), *see also* **confusion; destruction**

Admin Cramming vs., 0:390, 0:442

analysis of, 0:416

area giving dev-t, persons supposed to be stable terminals are not holding their posts, 7:413

bureaucracies expanding due to, 0:416

busy but only handling dev-t, 0:427

camouflaged holes make, 0:232

cause(s),

is unhattedness, MS2:236

or sources of, 0:288, 0:391, 0:401, 0:405, 0:414, 0:416–417, 0:421, 0:433, 0:438, 0:441

Chinese school vs., 0:439

comes from people with no product, MS1:240

complete and only major source of, 7:412, MS3:392

completed staff work vs., 0:401

costs us services of 66% of our personnel, 0:397

definition, 0:397

delirium tremens of Central Orgs, 0:397

destroys real production, 0:391

doing other jobs and hats than one's own, 0:232, 0:408, 0:431–432

due to lack of visible record of our posts and functions, 0:195

essential part of training is study of *The Problems of Work*, 7:412, MS3:392

Esto vs., 0:393, 0:441`

executive handling dev-t forced to work harder than if post empty, MS3:393

expression of untrained, unhatted staff, MS2:236, MS2:239

failing to recognize dev-t and handling it anyway, 0:427

graphed, 0:435–438

handling of, 0:427–428, 0:434, 0:623

hatting failing to produce rapid comprehension of dev-t, handling, 0:442

HCO generating dev-t, 0:440

heavy ethics and, 0:393

heavy traffic warnings and, 0:380

in area giving dev-t, persons supposed to be stable terminals are not holding their posts, MS3:393

interrupting staff unnecessarily, 0:83

is just accumulations of not-knowns and afraid-to-dos, 0:415

Is this okay? 0:419, 0:427–428

large staff, no effectiveness, 0:397

developed traffic (dev-t), *(cont.)*

    lists of types of, 0:424–427, 0:429–432

    log,

        each staff member keeps, MS2:17

        kept of, 0:416, 0:427–428, 0:440

    low responsibility and, 0:397

    malice seldom in it, 0:394

    missing terminal and, 0:436

    musical chairs, 0:433

    noncompliance, 0:417, 0:424

    off-line, *see* off-line

    offloads and, 0:393

    off-origin *see* off-origin

    off-policy staff and, 0:391, *see* off-policy

    org board and, 0:414–415, 0:426

    origination of comm that should have been originated by someone else, 0:412

    overt product and, 0:294

    overwork and, 0:391, 0:427

    packs, consist of, MS2:16

    people,

        who are not stable terminals, executive who goes on handling forced to work harder than if post empty, 7:413

        who originate traffic they have no business with and send it to wrong terminals, 0:391

    pieces of paper that don't belong to one, handling, 0:390

    policies, list of, 0:439–440

    policing dev-t, 0:391, 0:427–428

    program for handling, MS2:18

    reasonableness and, 0:416, 0:430

    reducing dev-t, 0:401, 0:414

    referral causing, 0:400, 0:430

    results from failure to hat, MS1:407

    routing and, 0:404, 0:405

    Sahara sandstorms of, 0:390

    sending dev-t back to sender, 0:616

    sending skimpy information and demanding a solution, 0:401

    senior datum in all dev-t policy, 0:420

    single-handing caused by, 0:391

    spotting sources of, 0:552

    stable terminals vs., 0:433–434

    staff not grooved in on the lines mainly deal in, 0:426

    technology and Estos, MS2:20

    types of, 0:424–427, 0:429–432

    unhatted(ness), MS2:16

        causing, 0:391, 0:393, 0:414, 0:426, 0:439, 0:441

        dev-t, nonproducing org and out-ethics, 0:525

developed traffic (dev-t), *(cont.)*

    unstable terminal and, 0:436, 0:437

    unwilling personnel causing, 0:397

    using dev-t as excuse to cut lines, 0:427

    using Scientology dev-t policies on the society outside Scientology, 7:1016

    very little is caused by viciousness or mean intent, 0:415

    Why of, MS2:16

devotion, requires active contribution outwards from the power as well as in, 7:388

Dev-t Chit, issuing of, 0:440, 0:442

dev-t log, 0:416, 0:428, 0:440

dev-t merchant, unload from staff, 1:181

dev-t packs, 0:439–440, 0:442

Dev-t Report, description, 0:542

D/FBO for MORE, *see also* **Flag Banking Officer (FBOs)**

    authority is to see that promotion or sales hats are worn fully, MS2:395

    definition, MS2:384

    driving more business down on the org than it can waste, 7:878

    gets assets into full use so resultant exchange with public brings about prosperity, MS2:399

    in an org, reports stats weekly to his continental senior, MS2:388

    key duties, MS2:385

    located in Dept 21 under the FBO, MS2:385

    major purpose of, MS2:397

    safeguarding assets and making sure they are not neglected or abused, MS2:399

    statistics, MS2:386

    substats, MS2:387

    what the tools of the D/FBO are, MS2:398–399

Dianazene, definition, 5:619

Dianetic Assessment List, definition, 4:1015

Dianetic Assists, 5:629; *see also* **assist**

Dianetic Auditor's Course, in arranging or establishment of, what must be observed, 4:628

Dianetic Certificate, 5:216

Dianetic Clear, *see also* **Clear**

    evaluating for, actionable, 5:291

    false declares, 5:291

Dianetic Clear Special Intensive, replaced by CCRD, 4:998

Dianetic Counseling Group,

    best solution to field auditor as a one-man band, 6:717

    will tend to stabilize any practice area, 6:718

Dianetic Internship, description, 5:844

Dianetics,
  advances have been in how to handle basics better, 0:65
  altering it, 4:633
  auditing, demonstrates mental anatomy, 4:1094
  basic discovery was exact anatomy of the human mind, 6:430
  being living examples of what it can do, 0:335
  big stable datum in, 4:635
  books of comparable magnitude in Scientology, 6:233
  can handle insanity with relative ease once the physical injuries and illnesses of the patient are cured medically or when the patient is only lightly ill, 7:1134
  courses, who may deliver, 6:720
  definition, 6:295
  degrading of, 0:14–15
  derivation, 4:918
  description of, 7:1097
  Distribution Center and HCO was mainly concerned with advertising and handling of materials, 6:233
  exteriorization and, 5:633
  fast course on *technique* slide by on philosophic data, 4:387
  four points of greatest potential failure, 5:678
  healing practice supplementing medical treatment, 5:595
  history of, 6:430
  how it spreads through training, 4:461
  if it isn't working, it is being varied, 5:679
  insane pcs and how they are handled, 2:536
  is a healing practice supplementing medical treatment, 2:533
  made the first Clears, 2:468
  misrepresentation of, 7:1110
  more and more tech "leaks" into general knowledge, 0:3
  never suffered from lack of programs, 0:701
  newness of, 0:362
  new news to bulk of world's population, MS3:136, MS3:173
  no new subject, 4:634
  only way it can be sold short, 4:937, 5:265
  order of magnitude between Scientology and, 6:431–432
  originally designed to handle the apparent basic cause of psychosomatic illness, 5:632
  past-life Clears and, 4:259
  people all fired up about getting Dianetics MUST be given Dianetics and not shunted toward another different service, 6:443

Dianetics, *(cont.)*
  policies effective immediately to protect good name of Dianetics, 6:746, 7:1071
  policy is not to engage on auditing sick pcs without medical advice or treatment as required, 2:536
  policy on, 2:533, 4:1095, 5:595, 6:433
  problems of early Dianetics, 5:677
  psychoanalysis vs., 4:919
  registration for, signs to be prominently placed, 4:920, 6:438
  reinstituting full use and delivery of, 0:15
  relationship to Scientology, 6:430
  results only occur when tech is correctly applied, 0:55
  road out of the witch pit, 0:362
  route from aberrated or normal to capable human being, 6:429
  Scientology,
    separate subjects, 5:633
    when to use, 5:633
  selling hours and courses vs., results, 5:259
  separate subject to Scientology, 2:143, 6:231
  speeds up reaction time, 4:923, 5:597
  supplements medical treatment, 4:1095
  we get into muddy water whenever we as org violate basic philosophy of, 0:65
  we will go as far as Dianetics and Scientology work in the hands of auditors, 0:337
  what any person not recovering health after Dianetic auditing should be given, 2:533, 6:433

Dianetics Case Supervisor, 4:1127

Dianetics Course,
  checksheets for, 4:631
  enrollment on does not guarantee a certificate, 4:636
  wildcat–unauthorized–handling of, 4:637

Dianetics: Evolution of a Science,
  advertisement, 6:253
  tech of arbitraries, 0:65

Dianetics: The Modern Science of Mental Health, *see also* **Book One; Dianetics; ridge on the Bridge**
  advertisement, example, 6:446
  best forward vanguard in our possession, 2:332, 6:235
  Book One boom and selling books, 6:442, 6:444
  books of comparable magnitude in Scientology, 2:145
  bridge between the uninformed and the informed public on the subject of Scientology, 2:332, 6:235

Dianetics: The Modern Science of Mental Health, *(cont.)*

contains today a perfectly workable therapy, 2:332, 6:235

C/S should be an expert on, 0:65

definition of Clear is valid, 4:202

if people do not read this book, they just will not have broken through, 6:236

sells more copies around the world than the average bestseller in any given year, 2:332, 6:235

why it was written, 2:331, 6:234

Dianetics: The Original Thesis,

advertisement, 6:253

C/S should be an expert on, 0:65

dictates, be maximally right in your, 0:247

dictionary(ies),

library and, 5:724

should be available to students, 5:182

didactic approach, 0:324

diet,

exercise and, 0:225

fads, 5:641

sugar and, 5:640

differences, definition, MS1:3

difficulty, difficulties, *see also* **problem; trouble**

how foundations of our difficult times were laid, 0:336

stems from no responsibility, 4:1051, 5:567

what any and all org difficulties trace to, 0:221

dilettante(s), dilettantism

definition, 0:497, 1:751, 7:680

described, 7:680

pantywaist dilettantes, 0:12

dimensions, arbitrary but workable rule regarding demonstrating something in two dimensions, 4:444

ding, definition, MS3:162

directive(s),

Ad Council and, 7:909

administrative directives, 0:112

cancellation of assorted directives, 1:414

Ethics interrogatory, 1:417

HCO Ethics Orders, gold paper with blue ink, 1:416

may not abolish network or org or change form of org, 0:143

may not alter or cancel any PL or HCOB, 0:143

one issues urgent directives when the situation is rough and simply demands a directive when things look like they will get rough, 7:353

directive(s), *(cont.)*

reason for 90% of directives passed, 0:67

valid only so long as they do not contradict HCO PLs, HCOBs, 1:404

director, *see* **department head product officer of department,** MS2:7

direct order, example, 7:352

Director of Administration,

function of, 7:594

hat and purpose, 7:624

spheres of responsibility, 7:624

task is to make existing policies stick, 7:594

Director of Certificates and Awards,

bonus, 5:136

responsibility for staff auditors and interns, 4:905

responsibility for staff training, 5:490

statistics, 5:76

Director of Clearing,

before public leaves org he is issued with materials of an FSM and made a field staff member, 6:652

should plan to hold regular field staff member courses, teaching Dissem Drill and policy letters governing an FSM, 6:653

what orders in orgs are, 6:649

writes each field staff member enclosing record of all selectees and asks him to compare his records of his selectees with yours, 6:651

Director of Communications, Dir of Comm

delayed internal and external despatches, handling, 0:381–382

functions, 1:314

lines that cross divisions are dummy run by Dir Comm under guidance of HCO Esto, MS2:36

purpose, 1:316

puts the lines there and sees that they flow fast, 1:315

responsible for OODs, 7:728

Director of Disbursements,

actions of, 3:39

FP activation and, 3:299

FSM Account and, 3:264

good credit of companies or person being disbursed to is full responsibility of, 3:127

no bill may be paid by Disbursements without checkup, 3:288

safeguarding credit and solvency is the main function of, 3:129

Director of Disbursements, *(cont.)*

sees that FBO transfer check is deposited in FSM Account, 3:265

Director of Examinations,

responsibility for staff auditors and interns, 4:905

responsibility for staff training, 5:490

statistics, 5:75

Director of Inspections and Reports, Dir I&R,

delayed internal and external despatches, handling, 0:381–382

should inspect course roll book from time to time, 4:465

utilization survey and, 7:450, MS3:430

Director of Materiel, transportation and, 3:371

Director of PE,

informs Addressograph of new people, 6:365

responsibility, 6:470

Director of Personnel Enhancement, holds keys to staff and org success, 5:379

Director of Processing, Dir of Processing, D of P,

all state of case established by D of P, never by Registrar, 2:484

better auditor than Director of Training, 4:93, 5:737

cannot direct Reg in cutting back numbers of people to be processed, 2:480

cannot take pcs, 0:169, 0:703

check pc out for missed withholds, 1:515

contending co-auditors must seek out the, 0:478

directing Reg on sign-ups, penalty, 4:294

doesn't audit pcs, 4:961

duties of, 4:904, 4:959

finance report, 4:214

goes wholly on idea of more auditing to raise graph or IQ, 4:967, 6:301

grounds on which may refuse a preclear already registered, 4:297

has no right to direct Reg in signing up pcs, 4:294

has to know how to read OCA, IQ, aptitude and other tests, 4:967, 6:301

ideal scene and stat, 4:143

interview, 1:826, 4:245, 4:261, 4:963, 4:981, 5:766, 7:732

job is to get people processed, 4:967, 6:301

job, "To raise OCAs with paid-for processing . . ." 4:967

may increase required hours before technical acceptance of pc, 2:500

may not accept a pc for processing if Reg to D of P line is out, 2:499

Director of Processing, *(cont.)*

may not assign himself to audit full intensives, 5:577

may not order disruptive student to Review, 0:491

outside pcs, check for missed withholds and pull them, 4:311

pcs he may refuse to sign out or release, 4:298

primary duty to keep all his auditors auditing, 4:253

principal duties, 5:489

provides excellent service to pcs and gets them through their case actions, 7:875

purpose, 4:959

receives invoice from pc or no processing, 3:119

responsibility for,

amount of auditing time put in on pcs, 5:488

getting auditor trainees, 5:528

procuring staff auditors, 4:117, 4:904

staff auditors, 5:487

staff case state, 5:571

staff training, 5:490

red tag line, 4:255, 5:285

seeing that pcs get gains, 0:409

should submit projects for inflow to OES, 4:964

staff auditor setup, 0:703

stats, 4:210

task to get correct tech applied, 0:8

to teach field auditors HGC routines to get them up to HGC qualifications level, 5:831

two types of D of P interviews, 2:588, 6:415

writes letters to possible pcs, 0:351

Director of Promotion and Registration, drills and clay table for, 2:623

Director of Registration,

responsibility for staff auditors and interns, 4:905

what he does when he receives a copy of a selection slip sent in by field staff member, 6:654

Director of Review,

bonus, 5:135

responsibility for staff auditors and interns, 4:905

responsibility for staff training, 5:490

statistics, 5:75

Director of Routing, Appearances and Personnel, opened on time and properly locked up at closing is responsibility of, 7:311

Director of Success, suppressed in doing his job, handling, 5:214

Director of Tech Services,

Advanced Org, responsible for folders of pcs and pre-OTs who have dropped body, 4:258

gets pc tested when new OCA test called for by C/S or D of P, 4:236

ideal scene and stats, 4:136

not keeping track of number of hours pcs have paid for, 0:303

responsibility on red tag line, 4:255, 5:285

stat, 4:210

Director of Training, Dir of Training, D of T,

accepting students on course without seeing invoice, 0:303

cannot direct Reg in cutting back numbers of people to be trained, 2:480

defense of org, LRH or track of Dianetics and Scientology and, 4:296

directing Reg on sign-ups, penalty, 4:294

end-of-week interviews, 4:321

finance report, 4:214

get auditors graduating, 1:515

get personal with your students, 4:311

get students winning, 1:515

grounds on which may refuse student already registered, 4:297

has no right to direct Reg in signing up students, 4:294

high crime to have anyone supervising without full use of study tech, 4:402

ideal scene and stats, 4:141

inquiries from prospective students brought to attention of, 4:292

interviews, 4:292

makes sure students own their own meters, 5:723

making sure students are taught only straight tech, 0:408

may not order disruptive student to Review, 0:491

may reject a student for health or security reasons, 2:500

promotional actions of, 0:350

provides excellent service to students and get them through their courses, 7:875

reason may refuse to send student to Examiner, 4:298

responsibilities, 4:290
for precise course schedules, 4:453
for procuring Sups, 4:117
for Supervisors, 5:487

trying to wear an ethics hat, 0:384

up to the D of T to make sure his students own their own meters and are using E-Meters per policy, 4:363

uses spot check as a tool, 4:452

Director of Zoning, purpose of, 6:837

Dir I&R, *see* **Director of Inspections and Reports**

Dir of Comm, *see* **Director of Communications**

disagreement(s), *see also* **agreement; danger condition**

caused by unknown policy or policy set by wrong source, 0:131

cure, 5:775

Danger conditions occur due to, 0:591
disagreement with, 0:475

nobody knowing what policy is, so in disagreement the org disintegrates, 0:405

policy,
unknown or set by wrong source leads to, MS1:249

Disagreement Check,

Danger Formula and, MS2:210

First Dynamic Danger Formula and, 0:616

when it's done, MS2:31

disassociation, definition, MS1:79

disaster(s), *see also* **catastrophe; failure**

definition, MS1:70

formula to apply when being knocked about by, 0:420

frequent disasters, cause of, 0:42

governments and, 0:505

operating at risk, 0:255

outpoints and, MS1:70

small neglected bits cause the, 0:261

disbursement(s),

against the FP sums, 3:299

done by check and check alone, 3:110

government and, 0:505

Disbursements Division, actions of, 3:39; *see also* **Department of Disbursements**

disbursements file, for consistent, consecutive, current, repeating folders, 3:391

Disbursements Section, 3:126; *see also* **Department of Disbursements**

good credit of companies or person being disbursed to is full responsibility of, 3:127

safeguarding credit and solvency is the main function of, 3:129

disbursement voucher,

handling for, 3:133

monies transferred to Reserved Payment Account are subject of, 3:316

packaging of monthly machine copies, 3:134

procedure for handling, 3:127

rules, 3:34

discipline(d), disciplinary, *see also* **punishment**

bringing off victory by cooperation and, 0:624

cannot be disciplined for not following BPLs, BTBs, or targets or orders that violate HCO PLs, 0:145

code of, 0:467

crimes may not be handled by direct discipline, 0:474

destroyed by injustice, 1:811

direct, 5:348

disciplinary laws also injure and restrict those who do not err, 0:461

disciplining those who are hurting others and giving them a way to change so they can eventually win too, 0:484

Emergency Formula and, 0:563

expansion and, 0:123

failing to confront accused with report and his accuser before discipline is assigned, 0:515

failure of group began with lack of or loss of, 0:450

false report leading to unjust discipline of another, 0:472, 0:515

for following cross order or not following HCO PLs or HCOBs, 0:146

guide to severity of, 0:494, 0:495

harsh, 1:542

harsh discipline, effects of, 0:515

if all were honest there would be no disciplinary threats, 0:461

inequitable and often unjust before Justice Codes, 0:477

injustice vs., 0:449, 0:521

justice means Comm Evs, internal enforcement and, 0:477

must be based on truth, 0:515, 1:542

near ultimate help can only be given with near ultimate discipline, 0:656

need for, MS1:8

needful in a group, 1:815

none of it carries physical punishment or detention, 0:495

only the already decent can be disciplined, 1:1027, 7:511

our discipline is capable of driving person around bend, 0:493

positive, 1:542

discipline as stable datum, 0:515

random or doesn't serve to channel, effect of, 0:123

reason most people think it is bad, 0:521

recourse after an illegal disciplinary action, 0:492

discipline(d), disciplinary, *(cont.)*

self-discipline to correct out-ethics, 0:601

standardization of, 1:734

stiffening discipline, 0:563

use to hold the edges of a channel, not to stop the flow, 1:1027, 7:511

used in getting policy followed, 0:120

when it is safe to use discipline, 0:522

when state of discipline does not exist, whole group caves in, 0:450, 0:521

who to discipline, 0:122

why Scientology must also have power and authority to bring total discipline or it will not survive, 0:660

wog discipline is simply harsh injustice, 0:521

discomfort,

caused by hat "worn" without contributing to team or without contributing one's real efforts, 0:277

reactive minds exert pain and discomfort on a being, 0:480

disconnect, disconnection,

evidence of, 1:863

examples, 1:1044

first law of condition of Power is don't disconnect, 0:564

how it is done, 1:1044

when it's used, 1:1043

discount(s), *see also* **prices**

credit purchases and, 3:145

do not apply to credit purchases, 2:329

illegal discounts, 0:303

largest single discount only is given, 3:164

may be given on cash sales only and sales or service paid in full, 2:329

no credit extended to orgs for books, E-Meters and tapes, 2:308

only one discount counts at a time, 3:164

package and discount rates, 2:346

policies,
regarding, 3:167
adopted, 5:363

professional discount is not given to persons who buy courses just to get a professional rate and then don't attend the course, 3:176

relatives of staff and students are not entitled to discounts, 3:164

sliding scale and, 2:458

student, effect on auditing sales, 4:954

there may be no hidden discounts, trick reductions, whims or favors given in pricing, 3:155

what is okay to offer, 2:474

discourtesy,

in request for justice, favor or redress, 0:488

misdemeanor, 0:468

discoveries, from pluspoints and outpoints, MS1:76

disease,

caused by, 5:642

when may be processed, 1:984

disestablish(ment), *see also* **chaos; confusion; disorder; disorganization; establish; establishment; organize**

definition, MS1:299

do not disestablish a working installation, MS2:37

orders kicking around and, MS2:28

org whose admin or body lines are being violated will, MS2:37

disgrace,

applying Emergency Formula to post of somebody who left in disgrace, 0:565

HCO justice prevents wrongful disgrace, 0:477

dishonest(y), *see also* **honesty; lie**

case gain can be prevented by, 1:848

condemning dishonest people to their own hells, 0:461

culture itself encourages, 4:405

definition, 0:152

dishonest people have sacrificed their rights, 0:152

illness, unhappiness and, 0:528

incompetence and, 2:112, 7:862

is nonsurvival, 0:454

only one way out for dishonest person, 0:461

when you have incompetence, you generally get dishonesty, 3:88, 6:556

dismiss(al)(ed), *see also* **demotion; removal; transfer,** 1:814

all data presented before the fact of, 1:250

approval of, 1:223

being free of dismissal by rumor, 0:481

Court of Ethics or Comm Ev required for, 0:487, 0:492, 0:523

Emergency condition and, 0:477

exec does want on his lines, 7:603

executives and, 0:373

for committing degrades, 0:14, 0:73

HCO justice,

PLs forbid staff being sacked, 0:487

prevents wrongful dismissal, 0:477

instruct, cram, retrain, offload system, 0:442

levels of ethics actions and, 0:494

dismiss(al)(ed), *(cont.)*

may only be done after a Committee of Evidence, 7:1300

model to be used by PCO, 1:214

nobody can be dismissed without cause, 0:482

no senior can "balance the budget" by wholesale dismissals, 0:482

only reason for or way to bring about, 0:151, 0:168

pc classification may not be taken into account in, 0:168

people who do not work are, 0:151

permanent,

member may not be demoted, transferred or dismissed without a full Comm Ev, 1:238

staff status and, 5:413

persons who do not do their work and, 1:249

procedure for,

in cases of insubordination or other acts, 1:250

temporary status, 1:237

PTS staff and, 0:493

recourse, 1:251

Review Comm Ev and, 0:524

sack every junior who will not put in ethics in their area, 0:421

staff cannot be "removed from post, sent before the Fitness Board and dismissed," 0:524

staff case difficulties and, 5:576

staff status and, 0:487

steps for, 1:245

students and, 0:491

sudden removals can do more harm than good, 0:523

Temporary staff status, procedure, 5:412

test of who deserves promotion or the gate, 0:121

three things required prior to, 1:253

transfers, demotions and, 0:487

trying to get others dismissed, reason for, 0:206

when the crime warrants it, 0:474

who to dismiss, 0:151

without following proper procedure, 0:552

wrongful dismissal, 0:477, 0:487, 0:552

"You're fired" can be incorrect order and can be queried, 0:141

disorder(ly), *see also* **chaos; confusion; disorganization**

area,

lapsing back into, 0:312

which is in Confusion and, MS2:182

basics vs., 0:307

condition of Confusion and, 0:568

handling, MS2:176

disorder(ly), *(cont.)*

justice, vs., 1:924

lawless and disorderly condition in society, effect of, 0:483

locating and correcting disordered areas, 0:308

orderly service is preferable to disorderly service, 0:273

order vs., 0:305

disorganization, disorganized, *see also* **chaos; confusion; disorder**

behind bad morale, MS1:232

communicating into disorganized area, 0:433

disordered person operating in disorganized area, 0:305–306

handling, 0:308–311

poor product and, MS1:218

reversal of policy and orders causing, 0:132

what it consists of, 0:196, 1:273

dispersal,

other-intentionedness coming from, 0:509

suppressive person and, 4:82

dispersal factor, suppressive person and, 1:990

display book, *see* **press book**

disputes, Chaplain's Court used to resolve, 1:956, 6:520

disrepute,

offenses resulting in, 0:468

PR used to bring about, MS3:4

disrespect, to Comm Ev when before it, 0:469

dissatisfied with results, will be found that Dianetics and Scientology were not being used on them, 7:1110

Dissem Div, *see* **Dissemination Division**

dissemination, disseminate, *see also* **advertising; promotion; word of mouth**

Book One, 6:442

success in, 6:441

books are, 2:331

breakthrough, 2:162

on basic auditing, Central Org planning and, 4:64, 6:187

bring your delivery up to, 1:754, 4:99

by means of come-on strengthens reach, MS3:185

conditions of a perfect dissemination program, 6:170

definition, MS3:174

destroyed by eating up exec's time and patience, 0:373

Dianetics: The Modern Science of Mental Health and, 2:332

disseminate publicly at the level of Scientology One only, 4:67, 6:190

dissemination, *(cont.)*

do not bring down to quality of delivery, 2:85, 6:371, 7:846

do not disseminate to groups or professionals in the social "sciences," 6:611

don't try to persuade, penetrate, 2:62, 6:168

effect on broad public through advertising Foundation services and in coaching field staff members, 6:212

examples of books selling Scientology, 6:151

failure to apply study tech in, 0:45

Flag Rep report, 7:1419

how to obtain higher level of, 0:232

how to sell Scientology to your friends, 6:675

if very broad and good to general public, there will be Academy enrollments, 2:422

increasing demand by, 0:129

Letter Registrar correspondence policy, 2:197, 4:69, 6:191–192

level of Scientology One only, 2:165

LRH hat of, 0:233

making auditors and, 4:120

making money and, 7:926

manual on, 6:25, 7:966

methods of, 7:833

money, making, 3:27, 7:925

most grooved comm line in Western society is selling, 2:155, 6:171

motto, 2:62, 6:168

never stop dissemination to iron out legal, 2:102, 6:82, 7:1095

perfect dissemination program, 2:154

personal contact best method of, 2:60, 6:166

point of agreement assists, MS3:69, MS3:248

policy and guideline used to guide both the creation and authorization of every dissemination piece, 2:274

policy, you can survive with Scientology, 2:146

prime target of the SP, 1:1007

program to increase dissemination, activities and income of all organizations, 7:48

Project 80, 4:64, 6:187, 2:162

promotional actions and, 0:348–349

purveying a little piece or several little pieces of tech ends the cycle and terminates the reach, MS3:185

questions answered in books, 2:331

rationale of main points of selling, 2:155, 6:171

reduced by lines stacking up and becoming tangled, 0:404

registration packet and, 2:633

releasing materials broadly to wrong public, 0:45

dissemination, *(cont.)*

sales talk can be outrageously strong and will appeal, 2:155, 6:171

salesman and, 2:156

sees more people in a day than other people see in a month therefore, he is himself an excellent comm particle, 6:172

Scientologists to the general public, 6:34, 7:975

soft sell, 0:499

SPs recommend ineffective, 1:1008

steps that plotted and used will sell Scientology, 6:675

students disseminate better, 0:100

successful,

method of selling books, 6:151

you have to have an APPARENT goal that is understandable to the audience or person at his tone level and with which he will agree, 6:168

technical facts of, 6:676

tips, 2:60, 6:166

total mission would be to teach the salesman to confront and communicate to bodies, 6:173

to those who have problems not those who have solutions, MS3:152

upping dissemination, by adherence to good, steady programing that wins, 0:703

what the perfect program would do, 2:154, 6:170

what we would like the general public to say to the general public about Scientology, 6:30, 7:971

why books sell Scientology, 6:151

you are wasting most of your time answering questions which are answered in books, 6:234

you do not bring your dissemination down to your quality of delivery, 0:499

you will fail to interest people in our work if you do not clear on them help, control and communication, 6:676

Dissemination Division (Div 2), Dissem Div,

actions that good pay is composed of, 0:688

any staff member may inspect using the Dissem Div inspection checklist, 2:110

can look into and tell what staff pay, cash-bills, PR area control is like, 2:721

checklist,

poor quality characteristics, 2:715

Power quality characteristics, 2:715

Treason quality characteristics, 2:715

difference between it and Public Div, 2:109

handles people who have bought something from an org, 2:88, 2:109

inspection checklist, 2:110

Dissemination Division (Div 2), *(cont.)*

org can be starved along on its Public Divisions until it builds or rebuilds its Dissem Division, 2:720

programing division for the public, 2:555

promotional actions for, 2:92

small things that can break it internally, 2:721

statistic, 2:551

Tech can never tell Dissem Div when or how many customers to bring in, 0:344

Thetan–Mind–Body–Product pattern, 0:654

when they do their work well they are worth diamonds, 2:721

Dissemination Drill,

coaching of, 6:214

has four exact steps that must be done with a person you are disseminating to, 6:214

dissemination formula, 6:369, 6:637

Dissemination Phase, 0:624

dissemination policy of Scientology, 6:153

Dissemination Secretary,

actions which deprive staff of pay, 0:302

building power quality, 2:720

drills and clay table for, 2:623

promotional actions and, 0:348–349

dissident, Dept 11 routes to Ethics, 0:350

distance,

exec hatting someone at a, 0:390

formula of communication and, 0:46

distraction(s), *see also* **confusion; developed traffic; noise**

executive's actions to handle, MS3:396

first inkling of is no-reports, noncompliance, slow compliance, 7:415, MS3:395

from Scientology, get rid of, 1:756, 4:101

get rid of distractions from Scientology in your org, 7:848

individuals or areas least well organized are most affected by, 7:414, MS3:394

new programs causing, 0:702

of personnel or area, executive's actions to take, 7:416

reasons for place being distracted, 7:415, MS3:395

removing of, 0:123, 0:283, 0:501

when a personnel or place is distracted, get in only easy basics one at a time, MS3:395, 7:415

distribution,

all materials released, used or sold must be straight Scientology as given in the writings or lectures of LRH, 2:126, 7:1292

formula is "Issue the correct data properly, correct use when delivery is poor or nonexistent," 2:129, 7:1295

distribution, *(cont.)*

new mimeo distribution symbols, 1:408–409

non-remimeo, 1:407

Scientologists at Saint Hill, 1:412–413

Sec ED, 1:412

technical and policy distribution, 2:125, 7:1291

what the HCO Sec passes on and makes available for issue, 2:125

distribution action, free information packets and, 6:216

Distribution Center, HCO and, was mainly concerned with advertising and handling of materials, 6:233

Distribution Division (Div 6), *see also* **Public Divisions**

actions that good pay is composed of, 0:679

advertising and, 6:212

cannot do its job where standard tech badly done, 6:824

deleted from Org Divs and expanded into three divisions under a new Executive Secretary, 6:81

gross divisional statistic is a triple statistic, 6:77

handles the people who have never bought anything from an org, 6:59

if were allowed to cannibalize off CF, there'd be no growth, 6:60

keep a statistic on which mailing lists respond the best and which info packet communicated the best, 2:709

mags don't belong in Division 6 as they go to people in CF, 6:59

mailing lists, purchased and/or rented and, 2:709

new unreached bodies = Division 6, 6:60

purposes of, 6:61

reasons why they don't function, 6:83–84

specific functions and, 6:61

stat most given attention is the increase of names in CF, 6:59

Distribution info packet, full info packet for newcomers and Foundation, 6:211; *see also* **info packet(s)**

Distribution Secretary, not having FSMs or training or paying them, 0:302

district office, pattern of, 6:784

Division 1, *see* **Hubbard Communications Office**

Division 2, handles people who have bought something from an org, 6:59

Division 2, *see also* **Dissemination Division**

Division 2, Registrar,

may route people to Division 6 for intro services or Department 17 services, 6:411

public of, 6:411

Division 3, *see* **Treasury Division**

Division 4, *see* **Technical Division**

Division 5, *see* **Qualifications Division**

Division 6, Registrar,

public of, 6:411

wherever public on their lines are ready to commence major services they may sell them, 6:411

Division 6, *see* **Distribution Division**

Division 6A, *see* **Public Contact Division**

Division 6B, *see* **Public Servicing Division**

Division 6C, *see* **Field Control Division**

Division 7, *see* **Executive Division**

divisional comm center, description, 0:369

divisional files, definition of, MS2:47

divisional order, definition, 1:430

Divisional Organizer,

authority of, 7:121

correspondence and, 7:122

directives and, 7:123

purpose, 7:120

seniority and, 7:121

statistics, 7:121

urgent directives and, 7:123

divisional secretary,

fully responsible for the personnel in their division, 7:774

may recruit or hire staff for his own division, 1:169

recruitment disputes resolved by the Continental LRH Comm, 1:170

divisional summaries, checked out by Hats Officer, 1:278

division head, division(al) secretary, *see also* **executive secretary; various divisions by name**

Advisory Council and, 0:582

always some individual assigned as responsible for work or production of every, 0:690

analyzing stats within a, 0:646

area not producing something valuable enough to interchange will not be supported for long, 0:298

businesses failing due to lacking a, 0:95

Chinese school on div org board, 0:440, 0:442

conditions on orgs or divs or depts, 0:652

condoning circumstances or offenses capable of bringing div to state of collapse, 0:472

Danger condition can be assigned by, 0:588

division head, *(cont.)*

disorganization will empty it out of personnel, 1:62

Divs 4 and 5 contain five times as many personnel as all others, 0:96

each division to have completed org board, 1:152

equipment must be specifically assigned to, 0:189

establishing quotas with div secretaries, 0:691

Esto operating in a, 0:393

Exec Council and, 0:355

falling apart or slowing up, handling, 0:441

four divs in a portion, 0:601

hat from the top down, MS2:29

interchange and, 0:297

managing by stats, 0:679

org boards, 0:95–96, 0:440–441

production unit, every div is a, 0:502

reporting things that need improving to, 0:623

requesting withdrawal of ethics chit, 0:549

responsibility for briefing staff, 0:579

seven divisions of a Scientology org, 7:89

size of, 0:596

specialization and, 0:196

statistics, 0:502, 0:654, 0:690

steps one takes to establish, 1:67

straightens up and improves when, 5:759

targeting of divisional stats and quotas, 0:690

Thetan–Mind–Body–Product pattern, 0:654

too overloaded will empty, 1:62–63

transfer inside any, 4:94, 5:738

value of, 0:297

waiting for orders, 0:135

which blows up, MS1:405

divorce, Chaplain's Courts and, 1:956, 6:521

do(ing), done(s),

accepting reasons why something cannot be done, 0:430

afraid-to-do's, 0:415

armies engaging in meaningless, often frantic and useless DO, 0:288

be-do-have, 0:287–288

datum that can put you on road to OT doing what you're doing and right where you are, 0:268

definition, 0:259

doing what Ron says, 0:626

doing work of post results in effective exchange, 0:259

do work that comes your way when it comes, 0:399, 0:430–431

do(ing), done(s), *(cont.)*

establish product then find out what to do to achieve it, 0:287

exec getting people to get work done, 0:373, 0:388, 0:406

exec getting things competently done, 0:594

fixation on DO without any product in view, 0:288

getting the job done, 0:239, 0:428

having to have before they can do, 0:427, 0:624

if one confronts his post he will see there are things to do, 0:259

if one knows tech of how to do something and can do and uses it, he cannot be adverse effect of it, 0:268

inability to get things done due to nonapplication of ethics, 0:660

infinity of wrong ways to do something, 0:58

lots of motion but nothing done, 0:387

people who just watch and don't do anything, 0:248

people who know it isn't any use, 0:683

persistent inability to actually do one's hat, 0:443

person who doesn't know what he's doing, 0:306

person who isn't noisy but never gets anything done, 0:237

person with understanding of what he is doing, 0:307

right way to do things can exist, 0:58

select as exec person who can get work done, 0:82–83

there's plenty of work to do, 0:399

what is necessary in order to get anything decent done, 0:10

why it is of considerable interest to staff what other staff do or don't do, 0:302

will to do amongst Scientologists, 0:693

work not organized so that it could be done, 0:306

working out the DO resulting in each product, 0:288

doable, doability,

clarity and doability of targets, 0:704

operating targets must be, 0:705

doctor(s),

on the third and fourth dynamics, 6:833

procedure for sending Dianetic pc to, 4:920, 6:439

secretly attending criminals or peddling dope, 0:455

term stained by its preemption by medical doctors and psychiatrists, 7:1205

Doctor, title abolished, 7:1205

Doctor of Scientology (DScn), 5:326

certificate for, 5:317

qualification for, 4:552, 5:149

doers,

misunderstood word and, 0:34–35

selecting talkers of big deeds, 0:664

D of P, *see* **Director of Processing**

D of T, *see* **Director of Training**

"dog pc," simply problems in repair, 4:209

dog's breakfast, how to straighten it out, MS1:200

doingness(es),

exactly-targeted which get strategic planning executed, 7:472

how they become bad, 1:727

without taking responsibilty, cause of, 1:728

doing work, barriers to, MS2:64

doll, use of in practical training, 4:780

dominance, of others is control symptom, 2:413, 6:185

donation,

what your donation buys, 2:106

would not be acceptable amends, 0:546

door,

keep the door open, only if it's just a crack, 1:808

open with nobody on post, 0:165

double assign, definition, 0:410

double flunk, definition of, 4:437

double-hatting,

advice to I/C vertical double-hatted, MS1:331

held from above (HFA), MS1:330

two types, MS1:330

level, MS1:330

vertical, MS1:330

Doubt, *see also* **condition**

assigned to person who accepts false report and disciplines another unjustly, 0:515, 1:542

automatically assigned to freeloader, 1:256

false data can cause hang-up on Doubt Formula, 1:606

formula, 1:563

handling for somebody hung up at Doubt, 1:606

hang-up at, 0:576, 0:671

if PTS, stuck in problem, 1:605

only wanting the title, MS3:408

PTS condition can hang one up at Doubt, 1:605

when in doubt, do the usual, 7:718

when it exists, 0:575

downfall,

cause of org downfall, 0:203

predicting downfall of any activity, 0:297

down org, Emergency Formula for, 6:812

down spiral, begins when responsibility has failed, 0:139

down statistic(s), downstat person(s),

actively working the other direction, 0:661

agreement with stats being down is suppressive, 0:682

answer to stats that won't go up, 0:531

area with consistently down stats, handling, 0:621

bad indicator, 0:496

breaking high conditions, 0:661

can't sneeze without a chop if one's stat is down, 0:503

causes of, 0:276, 0:384, 0:514, 0:652

caving downstat in by rewarding him, 0:529

chronic low-stat person is working to keep stat down, 0:657

chronically ill person and, 0:507

claiming ethics protection during high conditions, 0:661

crimes and, 0:587

don't get reasonable about, 0:505

early orgs, why they crashed, 0:9–10

ethics actions, 0:502, 0:503, 0:505

exec who tolerates, 0:659

factor which made downstat group downstat, 0:556

false perception leading to false stats, 0:514

false reports causing, 0:514

finding excuses for, 0:682

fixed idea or cliche being used to handle, 0:682

getting in trouble if one's stats are down, 0:694

handling, 0:239, 0:505, 0:556–557, 0:587–594, 0:596

held down, 0:587

hope is byword of down and outer, 0:255

I have only seldom raised a chronically down stat with orders or persuasion or new plans, 0:505

idleness, inattention and, 0:587

if stat is down and won't come up, I find another person, 0:239

industriously collapsing own post stats and also stats of adjacent posts, 0:657

injustices and, 0:515

low stat personnel gets rid of good staff, 0:656

only reason stats are down is because somebody didn't push them up, 0:682

down statistic(s), downstat person(s), *(cont.)*

org downfall, what it traces to, 0:203

overwork for org seniors or near catastrophe due to steadily declining stat, 0:622

penalize nonproduction and down stats, 0:504

person who whenever he takes over a post the stat collapses, 0:657

question one can ask of any group not doing well, 0:556

quicksilver personnel scene causing, 0:264, 0:266

rationalizing a, 0:682

reasons an area is downstat, 0:514–515

resuming a post one has left because it collapsed, 0:597

reward the up stat and damn the down, 0:508

sagged stats, 0:56, 0:203, 0:653

Section 5 investigates social areas of, 0:506

source of, 0:276

SP collapsing stats, 0:519

stat continues to go down, handling, 0:563

takes a series of serious blunders to reduce stats, 0:622

tolerating low individual stats, effect of, 0:689

traced to, MS1:403

transfer and, 0:587, 0:653

upstat vs. downstat group, 0:556

when something seeks to remain level and unchanged, it contracts, 0:124

when stats won't come up, you drop the condition down, 0:657

why one must never pour in more and more personnel when stat goes down, 0:624

why person collapsing stats is in Liability, 0:657

downgrade, of Academy and SH courses, 0:14

dramatization, dramatize,

bank and, 0:9

defined, 5:800

freeing a person into anarchy of dramatizing his aberrations, 0:630

man dramatizes his inability to get his ethics in, 0:449

overt acts dramatized by turning out bad product, 0:294

person dramatizing his criminal intent, 0:480

dream(s),

druggie's dream, 0:314

planner is seldom an actual member of the group, 7:569

way to make come true, MS1:180

drill(s)(ed)(ing),

attention-shifting, MS1:73

definition, MS1:287

done to accustom them to the actions that will be necessary in doing processes, 4:623

five violations of logic, MS1:12–13

for new bookbuyers, 0:626

group drills, MS2:44

Group Processing, can be run in seminars by staff, 6:327

handling for auditor who squirrels, fools about with pc, fumbles, 4:1079, 5:670

handling for can't apply, 4:1080, 5:671

have several purposes, 7:800

only allowed practical drills on any Scientology course, 4:616, 5:188

org board and, 0:392, 0:394

slow auditors should be, 4:924, 5:598

standard admin and, 0:64

to groove in team action, 7:800

way to educate people, MS1:8

drop a ball, motto, 6:742

dropped time, *see also* **outpoint,**

definition and examples, MS1:79

drug(s), *see also* **Purification Rundown**

designed by US Army, 0:451

firm policy regarding unhandled drugs, 4:972

learning and, 4:655

"nothing to do with me" attitude caused by, 0:555

proven to prevent case gain, 4:655

sign of a culture on way out, 0:454

therapy and, 0:362

unhandled, 1:903, 5:429

Drug Rundown, optional or conditional Grade Chart step, 4:195

DScn, *see* **Doctor of Scientology**

DTS, *see* **Director of Tech Services**

dummy, definition, MS3:194

duplicating functions,

product of this in an org, MS1:450

right way to handle, MS1:450

duplication, duplicate, *see also* **understanding**

great tension exists at points of nonduplication, 0:122

of effort, 0:231

Duplication Unit, 0:659

duplistickers, 0:627

duress,

applying more duress from without not to do an evil act than one has pressure from within to do it, 0:526

techno-space society and, 0:462

duty, duties, *see also* **function; hat; post**

assigned additional duty, handling, 0:197

condoning neglect of, 0:47

Crashing Mis-U blocking understanding of, 0:39

HCO policies and, 1:34

how to know duties of divs, depts and posts and flow lines of org, 0:440

insisting post originate or do duties of that post, 0:392

list of staff member duties, 0:165

neglect of, 0:47

no other duties more important than remedying the reason one has so many other duties, 7:422

offenses concerning one's, 0:467

"other duties" and "noise," reasons for, MS3:401–402

permitting staff origination on matters relating to, 0:173

Post Purpose Clearing and, 0:136

proper routing as vital part of one's, 0:383

questions concerning, handling, 0:166

senior must know all which come under his orders, 1:277

dwindling spiral,

freeing oneself from dwindling spiral of current culture, 0:451

reversing the, 0:91

universe and the, 4:160

dynamic(s),

accomplishing optimum survival for oneself and others on all, 0:452

dynamic(s), *(cont.)*

acts are good which are more beneficial than destructive along, 0:453

all beings are attempting to put ethics in on their, 0:457

best program will reach and do greatest good on greatest number of, 0:702

Conditions by Dynamics, 0:530

continuing to have trouble in area or on the dynamic on which previously messed-up or incomplete handling was done, 0:668

ethics and justice exist to keep dynamics in communication, 0:457, 0:458

ethics, justice and the, 0:451–460

Exchange by Dynamics, procedure, 0:529–530

forwarding a purpose not destructive to majority of, 0:236

greatest good for greatest number of, 0:146, 0:238, 239, 0:575

highest ethic level and, 0:451

individual's dynamics in communication, 1:492

man is basically good, 1:487

one must have done to other dynamics those things which other dynamics now seem to have power to do to him, 0:457

out-ethics person has dynamics out, 1:491

person cannot go out-ethics on a dynamic without it having disastrous consequences on his other dynamics, 0:459

they do not operate singly without interaction with the other dynamics, 0:458

what happens if the dynamics go out-ethics, 0:458, 1:493

wrecking first and second dynamics by abandoning third, 0:301

E

Earth,

bank-agreement made Earth a hell, 0:10

everyone on Earth has problems, 0:153

rivers and seas supporting less and less life, 0:258

we are not an Earthwide amends project, 0:507

we're sole agency that can forestall erasure of all civilization or bring a new better one, 0:231

world's "sciences" causing decaying Earth, 0:258

East, differences between West and, 0:598, 0:603

East Grinstead, preventing bad will with local property owners, 0:172

East India Company, 0:599

echelon(s), evaluation of, MS1:118

economist, seeking to gratify politicians or aggrandize some false philosophy, 0:314

economy(ics)(izing), MS3:219; *see also* **exchange; finance; income; money**

actions to take to handle, 3:230

Affluence Formula and, 0:564, 0:646

basics of VFPs are true for any economic system, 0:298

capitalism, *see* capitalism

contributism and, 0:277

crackpot economics, 0:315

definition, MS2:220, MS2:291, MS2:380

depression, *see* depression

Earth's people are all part of economic machine, 0:151

Emergency Formula and, 0:562, 0:625

exchange is heart of, MS1:258

economy(ics)(izing), *(cont.)*

having more economics and time to do our job, 0:13

inflation, *see* inflation

is a sign of increasing prosperity, 3:246

most effective trap of modern slave master, MS2:223

offbeat products and, MS1:257

probable basis of national economic booms and depressions, 0:252

receiving and spending money, field known as economics, MS2:219

strict economy of materials and contracture carried out at Saint Hill, 7:613

stripping false economic data from area not prospering, 0:313

what to do when times get worse or conditions are not the best, 0:300

EC Worldwide,

collective actions, 7:156

first and foremost concern is Personnel, 7:156

ED, *see* **Executive Directive; Executive Director**

education(al), *see also* **hatting; study; training**

barriers to study, 0:33

basic education, what has happened to it, 0:41

crawling with bad texts and noncomprehension, MS1:246

de-aberrating just by education contained in Scientology, 0:38

false, MS1:4

perverted by psychiatrists and psychologists, 0:555

teaching of personal appearance, manners, cleanliness, 0:340

educational-type ad, 6:180

effect,

becoming cause over environment instead
of, 0:689

blaming case is, 0:248

by not being cause you become an, 0:554

communication cycle and, 0:46

criminal society where individual is supposed to
be effect of everything, 0:555

effect vs. able to have effect upon one's
environment, 0:251

experiencing adverse effect on post or
in life, 0:268

sex is, 0:248

total effect, 0:231, MS2:429

two ways to be total effect, 7:601

Effective Public Relations, see also **Department of
Public Relations; public relations**

good textbook on PR, 7:1261

main faults of text, MS3:70

tech of PRO area control, 6:624

textbook on PR, MS3:40, MS3:70

effectiveness, effective(ly),

decadent society measures men by how pleasant,
not how effective they are, 0:237

delivering effectively, 0:282, 0:283

don't fall into our own new rituals so hard that
we are no longer brave and effective, 0:273

don't protect the ineffective, 0:232

promotion must be huge and effective, 0:344

what you need to know to be totally
effective, 0:410

efficiency, efficient, *see also* **ability; cause;
competence**

analyzing traffic to increase, 0:417

Central Orgs efficiency, 0:230

flaps and, 0:261

government and, 0:624

how to increase, 7:258

model of, 0:400

not fettering ourselves beyond increasing our
own, 0:273

orgs have to be more efficient to
pay well, 0:705

size and, 0:602–603, 0:624

what happens when group is not alert or, 0:261

effort(s),

duplication of, 0:231

life is a group effort, 0:458

phenomenon which costs Central Org two-thirds
of effort of its staff and execs, 0:397

production and, 0:277

effort(s), *(cont.)*

results are effect of your own efforts, 0:249

shoulder to shoulder effort, 0:273

Egypt, became a badlands, 0:510

8-C, Instructors and, 4:300

ejection jitters, 7:744

elect, election,

elect leaders temporarily and reserve right of
recall, 0:83

human group is likely to elect only those who
will kill them, 0:158

electricity, twelve factors in producing, 0:291

electronic attestation form, 5:854

eligibility, OT levels, 4:816

Elliot addressing machine, 0:627

embezzlement, 0:471, 0:533

emergency(ies),

a nonplanned department is a total
emergency, 7:759

activity not coming out of the, 0:563

Ad Comms and assignment of, 7:903

Ad Council assignment of, 7:900

are made actively, 0:587–588, 1:555

assigned only on OIC statistics and not by
rumor or opinion, 7:1300

basis of any, 0:417

condition, calling of, 7:1300

continued emergencies, cause and results of,
0:583–584

created by staledating, 0:425

definition, 7:614

do things right when they should be done and
emergencies do not occur, 7:622

emergency promotion, 0:346

examples of, 7:615

handling, 1:293

handling for anyone assigning Emergency
condition to an Affluence statistic, 7:1235

how they are classified, 7:615

how to prevent an, 0:623

lack of supplies and, 0:380

misrouting and bad assignment of
hats make, 7:759

noncompliance and, 0:417, 0:587

occurs only in presence of poor planning, 7:261

only time it occurs is when someone earlier has
erred, 7:615

people sitting on hot emergencies, 0:391

quicksilver personnel scene and, 0:266

stem from omission of action at a proper time,
1:460, 7:622

emergency(ies), *(cont.)*

why we must be able to recognize, assign and handle any, 0:624

Emergency condition, *see also* **Emergency Formula; State of Emergency**

Ad Comm that never takes effective action to remedy continuing Emergency-level GDS, 0:586

assigned when OIC graphs show a declining condition, 0:477

assignment of personal condition of Emergency for up to three weeks, 0:469–470

Comm Ev and, 0:358

continuing, handling, 0:563, 0:585–588, 0:606

Danger condition assigned when it has continued too long, 0:583, 0:585, 0:606

Emergency-type people have to have before they can do, 0:624

ending an, 0:621

ethics is heavy in Emergency on down for all, 0:661

government bureau and, 0:624

graph description, 0:677

heading for another, by not changing operating basis, 0:563

level at high or level at low are alike Emergency, 0:677

never pour in more personnel when a stat goes down, 0:624

personal conditions of Emergency reduce pay or units one third, 0:470

post just vacated by a promoted person going into Emergency or Danger within 90 days, 0:596

promotion and, 0:357, 0:625

senior exec made to look bad by continued Emergency on a lower echelon, handling, 0:587

sole evidence used to assign an, 0:477

surest way to bring about or continue an, 0:623

suspension of Justice Codes, 0:477

taking over post in Normal Operation and getting it into, 0:597

when staff members may be subjected to demotion, transfer or dismissal, 0:477

Emergency Formula, 1:559

applied to post of somebody who left in disgrace, 0:565

books are your first line of promotion, 2:705

elementary Emergency Formula for a down org, 2:705

for a down org, 6:812

how Accounts tendency to promote emergencies reverses the formula, 3:252

Emergency Formula, *(cont.)*

mailing lists and promote step, 2:705

neglect or gross errors resulting in need to apply, 0:468

promotion and, 0:357, 0:625

reporting formula steps taken, 0:621

steps, 0:563, 0:625

emergency headquarters, handling in event of atomic war, 7:45

Emergency Officer, 0:304

emergency traffic, brings about sudden rushes, the peaks, the overloads and the flaps, 7:614

Emergency, State of, *see* **State of Emergency**

E-Meter(s),

ability to run and read, important datum in an auditing session, 4:1080, 5:671

Academy rates, no meters for student issue, 4:471

advance paid credit in accounts sometimes used to buy, 3:207

anyone objecting to an E-Meter check should be refused entrance, 4:360

authority to manufacture, 2:377, 7:1289

D of T to make sure students own their own meters and are using as per policy, 4:363

drills must be used which stress only meaningful and significant instant reads coming at the end of the full question, 4:592

emphasis on accuracy in reading, 4:861

finding disagreements using, 0:591

goes null on gradient scale of misses by auditor, 4:314

only meters authorized for use in Dianetics and Scientology, 2:381

only register at reality level of the being, 4:1109

people who can't confront can have trouble communicating, reading meters, studying or even detecting what is going on, 4:427

policy for Academies that each student own his own, 2:341, 4:363

reads, suppressive person and, 4:87

registers bad control, 2:411, 6:183

staff auditor responsibility for, 4:1149

student must own his own, 4:627, 5:723, 7:1010

students in Academy should only be allowed to use E-Meters approved by HCO, 2:377, 7:1289

used in organization must be approved by HCO, 2:377, 7:1289

vitamin E and, 5:619

E-Meter case, FDA and, 0:485

E-Meter check(s),

C/S okay not required, 1:765

E-Meter check(s), *(cont.)*

directs who to investigate, 1:765

for criminal records, 1:160

overts and withholds checked before departing an org, 1:183

refusing an, 0:468

theft or insecurity and, 1:241, 3:192

what it consists of, 1:765

E-Meter drills,

should stress only meaningful and significant instant reads coming at the end of the full question, 4:592

use of, 4:607

E-Meter instruction films, *see also* **films; Technical Training Films**

are not for public showing and may not be shown to the public, 4:537

may be shown only to paid students and paid retread professional auditors, 4:537

showing of, 5:820

staff auditors, Case Supervisors and Course Supervisors may view them only if signed up for retread and may only view in the course of being retreaded, 4:537

E-Meter reads, suppressive person and, 1:995

E-Meter training, divided into four stages, 4:576; *see also* **training**

empire,

no empire stands still, they expand or shrink, 7:657

what they rise or fall in direct relationship to, 0:89

employee, *see* **staff**

employment,

application forms, 1:161, 1:172

conditions for security of job, 1:249

criminal records and, 1:160

E-Meter check for undetected current-life crimes, 1:160

forbidden category, 1:160

handouts, 1:164

log for applications, 1:172

notice boards, 1:164

preparedness program, 1:164

qualifications, OCA below center line, 1:158

security of, 0:151

special mailings to personnel pools, 1:164

termination,
  form and procedure, 5:397
  of, 1:226

employment agency, correct personnel pool, 1:164

endocrine system, study of, 4:1217

End of Endless Int RD, remedy to stabilize pc after exteriorization, 4:197

end rudiments check, 0:613

endurance,

asserts the truth of unkillability, 7:706

ethics presence and, 0:246

enemy(ies), *see also* **attack; opposition**

anything which stops or delays the flows of a business or delays or puts a customer or product on WAIT is an enemy of that business, 4:119, 7:850

as time goes on I even love my, 0:239

controlling all news media and governments, 0:336

definition of enemies of a business, 0:275

delivering an effective blow to enemies of group one has been pretending to be part of, 0:574

don't leave enemy financed and solvent while friends starve, 0:633

eradication of enemies on public lines, 0:335

eradication of, org image and, 6:606, MS3:140

how enemies or opposition come about, 0:117

how one knows their enemies, 2:123, 6:57

how to identify, 7:844

knowing your friends vs. your enemies, 0:89

lacking integrity, word of mouth and workable tech, 0:337

person who enters a Scientology group to sell other-answer is an, 0:509

person who is seeking to make org less viable and trying to contract and destroy it, 0:89

rendering enemies powerless to stop us, 0:239

taking on color of an, 0:574

Enemy Formula,

formula, 1:572

step for, 0:573

enemy line,

definition, MS3:102

example of how it works, MS3:102

examples re Scientology and handling, MS3:103

energy, sugar and, 5:640

enforced overt have, definition, MS1:460, MS2:251

enforcement, enforce(d), enforcing,

basic programs or standing orders or policy go out by not being enforced, 0:425

Ethics Officer gets condition he failed to enforce, 0:656

how and why you assign and enforce conditions, 0:658

learning and enforcing policies which bring success, 0:119

enforcement, enforce(d), enforcing, *(cont.)*

men will keep accounts straight only because you can muster bayonets to enforce that they do, 0:246

engineer (railroad), hat worn by, 0:197, 0:199

England, *see also* **Britain**

"aristocratic" tradition, 0:506

colonialism and Victorian England, 0:508

control and, 2:413

depression, causes of, 0:506

dwindling in size to degree it taxes individual and seeks to govern him, 0:598

Joe Cockney vs. government of, 0:600

engram, definition, 6:430

enroll(s)(ing)(ment),

course quality and, 5:485

excellent training is soundest possible promotion mirrored in numbers enrolling, 0:350

financial enrollment procedure, 2:481

high enrollment–low income, 0:655

high letters out–low enrollment weeks later, 0:655

improper, effect on student, 4:460

no applicant accepted for training or processing who is not there on his or her own self-determinism, 2:515, 6:467

of students, 4:292

Registrar's hat in, 4:214

when somebody enrolls, consider he has joined up for duration of universe, 0:13

enslavement, *see* **slavery**

entheta,

long-distance comm line and, MS2:196, MS2:301, MS3:460

definition, 0:373, 1:972, 2:663, 7:603

forbidden on long-distance comm line, 1:473

improper despatches and, 0:405

long-distance comm line vs., 7:480

obtains all its apparent power by being parasitic on theta lines, 5:108

on comm lines, MS1:238

parasitic on theta lines, 1:987

sole stock in trade of the SP, 1:1008

SPs give fragmentary or generalized reports that cave people in, 1:993, 4:85

entheta despatch, let it drop right there, 0:414

entheta letter(s),

CF handles by, 1:973–974

circulation and routing of, 1:975

definition, 1:970, 2:661

ethics actions on, 2:665

entheta letter(s), *(cont.)*

Ethics should order a hearing on person answering an, 2:666

executive handling on such forwarded him by staff member, 2:667

how to route, 2:664

impolite "petition" is handled as an entheta letter always, 2:661

penalty for answering, 1:975

routing of, 1:973–976

entheta lines, handling of, 1:973

enturbulation, enturbulence, enturbulate, *see also* **ARC break; upset**

definition of enturbulence, 0:68

Dept 3 sees that suppressives and enturbulative elements do not block dissemination, 0:348

exec getting area confusion and enturbulation of wobbly post incumbent, 0:434

executive enturbulence, 0:427

flaps, causes of, 0:261

of society around us, 0:483

Enturbulence Report, 0:554

environment,

becoming cause over your, 0:263, 0:555, 0:689

command of the, 0:498

control of, 0:251, 0:253, 0:255, 0:555

control of, begins with, MS1:445

dangerous, 6:592, 7:1019, 7:1039

ethics removing counter-intentions and other-intentionedness from, 0:509

getting someone located in his, 0:569

hatting and, 0:207, MS2:203, MS2:310

hidden actions of insane can destroy faster than environment can be created, 0:252

maintain friendly relations with the, 0:321

man as successful as he adjusts it to him, MS1:445

man thrives only in the presence of a challenging, 1:568

"nothing to do with me" attitude, 0:555

one's standards are directly related to one's desire to have a controlled environment, 0:251

only good tech and justice can make org environment safe, 6:592, 7:1019

org adapting to environment so as to expand, 0:52

predictable environment, 0:327

safe environment, making of, 0:486, 0:519

solving yesterday's, 1:991, 4:83

state of a person's living, including working, environment, 0:313

threat of, 0:207, 0:486

environment, *(cont.)*

thriving only in presence of challenging environment, 0:656

equalitarianism,

description, 0:315

economic theory, MS1:352, MS2:286

equipment, *see also* machine

assigning responsibility for, 0:186–187, 0:189

cleanliness and appearance of, 0:84, 0:165

description of equipment it would take to give a congress with tapes, 6:334

disposing of, 0:187–188

handling for damage or neglected equipment, 3:388

inoperational, 0:306, 0:307

Inventory Officer and, 0:189

logging things one is using in and out, 0:306

misuse or abuse of, 0:543

must be specifically assigned to divisions and departments, 3:397

nonoperational things not kept around, 0:190

operational, definition of, 0:190

order vs. disorder, 0:305

putting things away when one is done with them, 0:306

responsibility of in an organization, 3:388

standard of living and, 0:313

stock cards and, 3:388

the worse your equipment, the less comprehension, 6:325

Title A, Title B and Title C, 0:187

turning over equipment of post being vacated, 0:198

err(ing),

one does not expect exec to front up to personnel who err, 0:544

processing only erring staff members, 0:156

targets of all disciplinary laws are the few who err, 0:461

error(s), *see also* mistake; overt product

Bolivar's errors, 0:629–635

case is not an excuse for, 0:168

Comm Ev may not be convened because of an, 0:467

definition of an error, 0:467

disasters, cause of, 0:261

driving in more business than mistakes can waste, 0:344

due to no familiarity with HCO PLs, 0:55

efforts by juniors to look and sound active while actually loafing and goofing, 0:420

example of, MS1:38

error(s), *(cont.)*

example of how small error leads up to a flap, 0:261

examples of auditing goofs that would keep Scientology from working on every case, 0:18–19

fatal error in promotion, 0:357

fear of making, 0:231

inspection before the fact, 0:66, 0:244, 0:430

list of, 1:861

neglect or gross errors resulting in need to apply Emergency Formula, 0:468

no amount of conditions applications in your org or area is going to prevent a mistake in some other org or area, 0:679

observation, "being reasonable," MS1:30

product flubby, 0:294

repeated error offenses brought into category of misdemeanor, 0:467

resulting in financial or traffic loss, 0:468

staff member goofs roll up and knock my hats sideways, 0:233

staff member's goof can destroy whole org, 0:409

statements that are accurate, on-policy, and do not ARC break public with errors, 0:350

State of Emergency and, 0:621

takes series of serious blunders to reduce stats or bring about public or press smear campaign, 0:622

uncorrected error in auditor is perpetuated on every pc auditor audits, 0:12

viewing situations, MS1:77

when person has no purpose and value he not only goofs, he will commit crimes, 0:204

willing to be hanged for our mistakes, 0:231

Error Report, description, 0:544

establish(ed)(ing)(ment), *see also* Establishment Officer; hatting; organization form; organizing board

administration and, 0:58–59

building up an org, 0:89

"clearing post purpose" is another way of saying "Get the policy that establishes this post and its duties known and understood," 0:136

concentration points in putting org together and keeping it viable, 0:41

consists of, MS2:4

continuously creating your dept, unit or org or defending, reason, 0:410

courses are senior part of, 1:289

definition, MS1:29

delivery and, 7:859

establish(ed)(ing)(ment), *(cont.)*

establishing something that produces, 0:290

Esto admin is way to slow down establishment, MS2:41

examples of, MS1:356

Exec Dirs who reg instead of getting Reges and putting an org there, 0:693

first step in establishing anything is valuable production and income, 1:66

holding the form of the org, MS1:312, MS2:119, MS2:262

how to establish an org, 0:53, 0:292

in small org, MS2:8

largest building blocks it takes to make big org, 0:601

lines are a major part of, MS2:36

manning it up, MS2:106, MS2:257

may not be expanded without, MS2:9

only way a HAS can maintain and increase establishment, 1:76

planning, direction and persistence in application of, MS2:125

points to have in to be a success, MS2:13

poorly established departments and divisions, 1:68

product–org officer system and, MS2:3

putting org there, 0:291, 0:292

starting new suborganization, 0:130

Why for failures to establish the org, 1:78

Establishment Officer(s), Esto(s), *see also* **establish; hatting; organizing board**

achieving product of established producing executive, MS2:40

admin is way to slow down establishment, MS2:41

Assistant MAA, functions, MS2:34

backed up by good courses and course supervision will eventually bring it all straight, MS2:100

backs off from an area, reason, MS2:14

basic problem is getting somebody to do his job, MS2:63

bypassing staff, result of, MS2:34

case requirements, MS2:10

checklist for, MS2:23–24

Conditions by Dynamics, 0:530, MS2:72

conference, functions, MS2:12

cover whole area with short cycles you can complete on each person individually, MS2:44

desk sign, MS2:25

dev-t and, 0:393, 0:439–443, MS2:20

Establishment Officer(s), Esto(s), *(cont.)*

divisional Estos, list of, MS2:6

duties, 0:393

Establishment Officer I/C, 0:443

Esto's Esto, functions, MS2:6 hatting and training of Estos comes under, MS2:9

Ethics Officer function, 0:439

exchange all awry, handling, 0:529–530

Exchange by Dynamics, 0:530

Exec Esto's MAA, functions, MS2:12, MS2:34

files and, MS2:46, MS2:48

first action, MS1:313, MS2:120, MS2:263

first job, MS2:238

first thing they run into in unhatted area, MS2:16

full training outline, MS2:9

gets hatted while he produces, MS2:14

going on duty and training part time, 0:442

good Esto looks, MS2:39

hallmark of, MS2:38

has to know how to clear up "products," MS2:28

has two hats, MS2:11

hat from the top down, MS2:82

hats, organizes, trains, sets up files, lines and does all establishment actions people need to *really* establish a division and maintain it, MS2:184

have to be able to train, hat, groove in and make functioning people, 7:720

how many Estos are needed, 0:393

how to get Estos to hat people, MS2:123

how to make an executive, MS2:62, MS2:244

how to recruit new Estos, MS2:103, MS2:254, MS1:304

if cannot or do not follow exact procedure required in policy or routing forms or admin patterns will tear things up faster than can be gotten in, MS2:36

if person is too confused or out-ethics, alert HCO and not place them, MS2:186

In-Charge, functions, MS2:6 primary duty, MS2:21

(in Europe) must know foreign language translated tape HCOBs, PLs and expertise, MS2:11

In-Training, bringing unusual remedies to his senior, handling, MS2:23 correct actions for handling, MS2:23 example of incorrect Why finding, MS2:22

Establishment Officer(s), Esto(s), *(cont.)*

involvement in production cycles and, MS2:11

lines within a division are the business of Estos of that division, MS2:37

Long Form Product Clearing done on Esto before he does it on staff, MS2:49

looking to see the scene and find the Why and establish, MS2:42

must follow policy and lines, MS2:36

must hat for the product, MS2:28

must wear Esto hat in any given situation, MS2:14

new piece of Esto tech, MS2:187

not well enough or firmly enough hatted, handling, 0:443

operates in a division under its secretary but under a senior establishment officer, MS2:238

org board, MS2:4

performs duties of the depts of HCO for that division, MS2:238

Personnel goofs, 0:280

primary targets, MS1:309, MS2:108, MS2:259

Product Clearing and, MS2:57

purpose, MS2:3

quality of skill directly reflected in, MS2:9

reason for failure, MS1:304, MS2:103, MS2:126, MS2:254

remedies to use on an individual unable to do his post, MS2:65

remedy for handling exchange, MS2:71

requirements for, MS2:126

result of cycle of outpoint, handle, outpoint, handle, outpoint, handle, MS2:42

R-factor to execs when Exec Esto goes into an org where there are no Estos, MS1:304

right answer is establish faster and more firmly, MS2:40

sample program to cure dev-t and get org hatted and producing, 0:441–443

Section, definition, MS2:6

Service Product Officer and, MS2:175

skill in rapidly finding a Why, MS2:21

standard action to survey hats, MS2:28

straightening out comm lines of each post, 0:442

test of, MS2:8, MS2:44

time required to handle situations, MS2:42

training breakdown will defeat all his best-laid plans, MS2:98

training of Estos is secondary to getting them to do, MS2:125

training requirements for, MS2:126

Establishment Officer(s), Esto(s), *(cont.)*

when all looks black, handling, 0:531

when stats won't go up, MS2:73

when they get pulled into operating the division, MS2:21

where departmental Estos exist, lines linking up departments are handled by Esto Conference of that division, MS2:37

who tries to do it with admin will fail, MS2:40

Estates Branch, MS3:352

calculation of square paces stat, 7:1402

cleaning stations and, 7:1400

duties, 7:1398

in Dept 21, 7:1398

listening to Town and Country Planning tends to go PTS, 7:372

only odorless paint may be used, 7:1388

operations, 7:1399

person put in Estates to redo basics, 0:392, 7:1401

promotional actions, 7:85

statistics, 1:524, 7:1389, 7:1402

"useful space," definition, 7:1389

Estates Bureau, description (1967), 7:1391

Estates Manager, responsibilities (1967), 7:1391

estimated purchase order,

definition, 3:296

form, 3:303

several EPOs against one final PO, handling of, 3:299

system, steps on how to activate it, 3:300

Esto, *see* **Establishment Officer**

Esto system,

manning it up, MS1:307

reconciliation with prod–org system, 7:821

when established, 7:821

eternity,

looking at eternity as far as case is concerned, 0:304

one is rising to, in Scientology, 4:990

thetan and, 0:302

threatening somebody with oblivion for eternity by expulsion, 0:494

ETH?, definition, 4:1060, 5:115

ethics, ethical, *see also* **Ethics Officer; Ethics Section; HCO Ethics Codes; justice**

absence of true ethics, result, 0:456–457, 0:518

"acceptable social behavior" and, 5:248

actions,

individual takes on himself, 1:487, 0:448–449

levels of, 1:747–748, 5:112

actions that are part of standard ethics, 0:44

ethics, ethical, *(cont.)*

act or conclusion, how right or wrong it is, 0:453

admin and, 0:260

admin degrades, 0:73–74

admin high crime, 0:75–77

aesthetics go with, 1:32

all auditing failures are ethics failures, 4:679

Aristotle and, 0:448

as a tool, 0:449

auditing and cases undergoing ethics actions, 4:1099

auditor sent to,
  for false report, 4:1174, 5:587
  for not following instructions or taking off-line directions, 4:1174, 5:587

bank automaticity and, 0:449

basic nature of man and, 0:449

basic personality and basic intentions of individual are good, 0:452

basics of, 0:297, 0:447

became a problem in orgs when quickie auditing began, 1:800–801, 6:527

being hard on anyone discoordinating or blunting purposes, damaging or omitting lines and disestablishing terminals, 0:89

blind spot, 0:449

blunting of demand prevented by, 0:130

Board of Investigation, 0:304, 0:424

breakthrough in solving subject of, 0:448

Buddhist form, 1:774

can't sneeze without a chop if one's stat is down, 0:503

Case Supervisor and, 4:1130

chain lightning, 0:494

chits, 5:20

clay pigeon, staff member who does not know ethics policy is a, 0:521

Committee of Evidence, *see* Committee of Evidence

completing conditions formulas, 0:666

computer ethics points, MS2:464

concepts of right and wrong, 0:453

Conditions by Dynamics, MS2:72

conditions, *see* condition

consists of, 1:486

Court of Ethics, *see* Court of Ethics

courts may not order to auditing or training, 1:744

crimes, *see* crime

criminal and, 0:452, 0:526

C/S and, 5:716

ethics, ethical, *(cont.)*

C/Ses to make every staff member Ethics Upstat, 5:599

C/S, ethics handlings and, 1:839

deciding to rise above aberrations and get busy and go straight, 0:555

defending and retaining in employ anyone who does his job, 0:151

definition, 0:447–448, 4:404

demotion, *see* demotion

design of, 0:516

design of, developed to aid an individual, 1:492

designed to keep in tech and policy, 1:280

digging oneself out with, 0:449

discipline, *see* discipline

dishonest conduct is nonsurvival, 0:454

dishonesty, *see* dishonesty

dismissal, *see* dismissal

down the chute, 0:449, 0:457

downstats going the other way, 1:577

duress leveled by, 1:770, 7:501

during high condition, penalties for breaking Power, Affluence and Normal, 1:577

dynamics and, 0:451–460

dynamics in communication to degree applying ethics in life, 1:492

easier to hit with than to program, MS1:207

Emergency condition and, 0:563, 0:621

encouraging crime when you let person give nothing for something, 0:526

ethical conduct is survival, 1:488

ethical failure at the top or just below it can destroy and make an organization downstat, MS2:246

"Ethics Committees" and, 0:450

ethics, justice and history, 0:447, 0:448

ethics, justice and the dynamics, 0:451

ethics offense to issue orders altering lines without clearance from the Office of LRH, 7:772

Ethics Program No. 1, 1:788

Ethics Section in Department 3, 1:484

evil conduct is nonsurvival, 0:453

evil, illness and decay often go hand in hand, 0:452

exchange factor out, effect of, 0:528

executioner, person becoming his own, 0:452

exists primarily to, 5:248

exists to get tech in, 0:496, 0:502

expulsion, 0:494

failure of cases and results lies in lack of an efficient ethics section, 7:846

failure to apply ethics to himself, justice enters in, 1:491

ethics, ethical, *(cont.)*

failure to assign or enforce conditions penalties, 1:565

failure to follow or apply condition, 1:565

False Purpose RD, any person found to be omitting or refusing to deliver, called before a Committee of Evidence, 4:993

False Purpose RD delivery and, 5:454

fast flow and, 1:785

field and, 1:796, 6:724

file complaints on upstats with a yawn, 1:767

files, evaluation and, MS1:175

fine-edged tool, 1:761, 7:306

fine line between tech and, 0:509

finger faltering on the trigger, 0:658

folder, definition, MS1:371, MS3:461

future race and, 0:451

gets case resurgences by finding the *right* SPs, 1:40

getting away with murder so long as one's stat is up, 0:503

getting own ethics in, 0:449, 0:672

gigantic overt—to have tools and not apply them, 0:500

good and evil, 0:452, 1:487

goofing up during Affluence goes overboard three times, 1:577

gradient levels of, 0:494

handles field auditor misuse of tech, 1:719

handling for pc with incorrect suppressive person or group found, 5:122

handling in relationship to C/Sing, 1:841

handling of PTSes remains with, 1:1012

handling pc ethics, 4:1131

harsh, 1:810

has its own tech, 1:688

having ethics just boiled down to conditions, 0:554

HCO responsibility for field and org ethics, 1:37

heavy ethics,
being used on wogs, 0:247
in Emergency on down for all, 0:661
nonapplication of ethics, results, 0:660
not having led to any spectacular recovery, 0:441
reason for, 0:391, 0:392

heavy in-baskets, inability to get things done, down stats, failures, all stem from nonapplication of ethics, 7:699

heavy, reduction of staff and, 1:810

high ethics for high conditions, 0:661, 1:577

high ethics level, 0:451

historical precedence of, 1:774

ethics, ethical, *(cont.)*

history of, 1:497

hitting with ethics vs. programing and giving someone full hat, 0:204

ideals, morals, ethics and survival, 0:455

if out, tech won't ever go in, 7:306

if person is doing his job ethics is considered in, 0:502

if we are to live in this universe, we are going to have to get in ethics and clean it up, 0:658

image vs., 6:614

individual can be trusted with, 0:450

individual who lacks ethics technology, 1:497

in-ethics and affluence attainment, 0:628

in-ethics and prosperity, 0:534

injustice causes ARC breaks, 2:435

interviews done on a preclear, routing, 1:851

investigates when seeing tech stats drop, 4:103, 5:21

investigation by stats, MS1:165

investigation, *see* investigation

I try afterwards to patch up whoever had to be shot, 0:239

job of, 1:752, 7:681

juniors not putting in ethics but leaving it all to exec, 0:420

justice, *see also* justice
solution of ethics and justice lay in their separation, 0:448
when it is used, 0:448

keeping of one's word, 0:454

lack of, permits the criminal impulse to go unchecked, MS2:69

letting SP collapse stats, shooting offense, 1:485

levels of ethics actions in degree of severity, 4:357

light touch, 1:746–747, 5:111

loss of certificates or awards, 0:495

man and, 0:447, 0:449

man is basically good, 1:487

means to the end of getting tech in, MS2:211

missions and mission holders, 1:795

missions will get help from orgs, 6:754

must keep the door open, only if it's just a crack, 1:808

never report, relay, or condone a false GI statistic, MS2:375

new hope for justice, 1:963

no absolute right or wrong, 0:454

no Comm Ev, court or executive may sentence anyone to auditing, 5:410

no direct routing of preclear to, 4:1073

ethics, ethical, *(cont.)*

no ethics change, 1:1028

no ethics presence in an org, criminality shows its head, MS2:68

noncompliance to Advanced Course instructions, 1:637

normal level of an unhatted, dev-t, nonproducing org is out-ethics, MS2:68

Normal Operation and, 0:563–564

no secret standards in Scientology, 0:153

not having guts enough to handle discipline, 0:500

only exists to get technology in, 1:750, 7:679

only in-ethics can deliver standard tech, 0:534

only SPs will blow, 0:501

optimum solution to any problem, 1:486

orgs where ethics is tight grow in numbers, 1:568

originated by terminal other than C/S, 5:717

out-ethics, 1:486

out-tech, handling, 0:498

out when PR won't go in, MS3:166

pcs who ask for rebates and, 3:160

people with low ethics enturbulate and upset a group, MS2:246

people with out-ethics withholds cannot see, MS2:246

personal thing, 0:448

Personnel and Ethics, how they work together or conflict, MS1:409

personnel files help to decide what to investigate, 1:192

philosophy and, 0:448

Plato and, 0:448

preclears and, 1:840, 1:851

presence, 0:246–247, 0:526

primary reason for existence, 6:548

primary tool, 1:492

principle of VFP and, MS1:296

production and, 1:768

promising to be good is never good enough, 0:497

protection, 1:767

protest from ethics actions worded as a petition, handling, 1:753

purpose of, 0:496, 0:509, 1:751, 1:786, 1:969, 7:680

put in provides environment in which auditing possible, 4:127

"putting a head on a pike," 0:496, 1:750, 7:67

putting in ethics where individual appears incapable of keeping his own in, 0:691

Pythagoras and, 0:448

ethics, ethical, *(cont.)*

quality of service and, 4:933

quickie and, 4:30

quicksilver personnel scene, 0:265

reason for heavy ethics actions occurring, MS2:68

reason ship or org can't hold Affluence or high condition, 1:577

removing counter-intentions and other-intentionedness from environment, 0:509

repeated out-tech and out-admin, consequences, 1:900, 4:482

reporting of theft, 1:706

reports of offenses other than the pc's, 1:851

results of nonapplication, 1:574

Review and, 5:774

reward, *see* reward

right and wrong conduct, 1:487

role—after all else fails, 1:59

routine action of, 4:355

routing pcs recommended to Ethics and also to Declare?, 5:119

running a course and, 4:461

sack every junior who will not put in ethics in their area, 0:421

secret of getting students through is keeping ethics in in the Academy, 4:376

situations found in session, handling, 1:851

Socrates and, 0:448

soft ethics and fast flow, 5:139

soft sell and, 0:499–500

sole purpose of, 1:951

so powerful in effect that a little goes a very long ways, 4:356

staff members or executives who fail to set an example of high ethical standards, MS2:246

students and pcs are subject to Conditions Orders from their Supervisors and auditors, 7:699

study tech and post, 0:45, 0:47

substituted as an effort to get up production, MS1:200

summary, standard ethics actions, 4:481

suppressive person, *see* suppressive person

survival assured only by knowledge and application of ethics, 1:495

symptoms of orgs, 0:497

takes far more ethics and far steeper enforced penalties to make org work than Scientologists have been using, 0:421

target, 1:767

Tech Div and, 4:96, 4:102

tech of ethics is tech of survival, 0:457

ethics, ethical, *(cont.)*

tech of survival, 1:492

tech will not go in when ethics is out, 1:484, 1:761, 1:842, 1:1028, 4:1133, 5:719, MS3:165

tech works only where ethics is in, 0:502, 0:656–657

time machine, 1:683

training for anyone on Ethics post, 1:67

tried and true methods of getting it in, 4:973, 1:635

unethical conduct is conduct of destruction and fear, 0:454

use ethics to protect upstats, 1:485

use of to produce image compliance is murderous, MS3:155

viewpoint, 1:752, 7:681

way out of trap of degradation and pain, 0:458

we are not in business of being good boys and girls, 0:503

we don't hang people because we started to hang them and so must do so, 0:496

what to do where it is out, 1:815

when a group prospers, MS2:247

when individual starts trying to put ethics in on himself, 0:448–449

when people violate their own ethics they begin to decay, 0:452

when person does something out-ethics, 1:492

when you can't get check-signing line in, call Ethics, 3:322

where it has to be heavy you find, MS1:409

who to investigate, 1:768

whole failure of cases and results lies in lack of an efficient Ethics Section in an org, 2:85, 6:372

whole subject has become almost lost, 0:451

why ethics? 1:760, 7:305

why exists, 1:493, 1:767, 1:792

why people can't put in, MS1:165

wild rumors, handling, 0:498

withdrawing and withholding from area harmed, 0:457

you won't lose any people because of ethics, 2:87, 6:373, 7:848

Ethics (section of org),

alter-is or technical omissions or offenses reported to, 0:623

ARC broken students or pcs and, 0:493

average fair to poor stat staff member, handling, 0:503

Dept 11 routes dissidents quickly to, 0:350

excellent vs. bad stat, when Ethics gets interested, 0:502

Ethics (section of org), *(cont.)*

failure of cases and results, reason, 0:499

far worse threat than mere wog law, 0:493

gets case resurgences by finding right SPs, 0:348

getting tech and policy in and getting org going, 0:549

if tech is out, only Ethics can bat down the reasons it can't be gotten in, 0:498

industrious in ratio to number of bad indicators, 0:496

Kha-Khans and, 0:503

levels of ethics actions used by, 0:494–495

light touch, 0:493

low-stat fellow gets a court if he sneezes, 0:503

never finally shut off possible demand, 0:127

never gets reasonable about lack of expansion, 0:498

our lines are too powerful and direct, 0:493

person not doing his job becomes Ethics target, 0:502

purpose of, 0:549

recourse and, 0:492

responsibility for cleaning ethics files, 0:545

sending all ethics matters discovered to, 0:352

SPs and PTSes routed to, 0:351

staff member reports and, 0:543–544

that we exist here could restrain fellow who could push button on atomic war, 0:493

time machine and, 0:375–376

upstats and, 0:505

verbal order reported to, 0:376

viewpoint of, 0:498

we can all too easily make person feel guilty by just whisper, 0:493

when Ethics is fascinated with staff member's smallest misdemeanor, 0:503

withdrawal of ethics chit, procedure, 0:549

ethics action(s),

best defense against any, 0:524

Comm Ev is considered most severe form of, 0:492

does not carry physical punishment or detention, 0:495

for misunderstoods, 0:47

hang up in past ethics actions, 0:668–669

light touch, 0:493

listed in degree of severity, 0:494

may only suspend training or deny auditing, 0:491

must parallel purposes of Scientology and its orgs, 0:502

ethics action(s), *(cont.)*

need not be very heavy to produce most startling results, 0:494

not carrying on past point where result has been achieved, 0:617

not necessarily taken because chit has been filed on one, 0:553

PTSness and, 0:493

when tech is in, ethics actions tend to be dropped, 0:502

Ethics Authority Section, 0:545

ethics bait, definition and handling, 0:529

ethics chit(s), *see also* **ethics report; Knowledge Report; report; staff member report**

Ethics Officer adjudication, 1:707

filed on instances of dirty offices and grounds, 6:594

Job Endangerment, 1:274

Non-Enturbulation Order, 1:704

Tech or Qual personnel and, 1:703

what to do when recipient feels chit is incorrect, 1:707

Ethics clearance, needed for those in dead files, 1:976

Ethics Codes, *see* **HCO Ethics Codes**

students and pcs undergoing review and, 4:352, 5:842

ethics files,

amnesty and, 0:546

cleaning the files, 0:545–546, 1:701

do all the work, 1:682

freeloader lists and, 1:256

removing Knowledge Reports from, 0:557

staff member reports filed in, 0:545

what they are comprised of, 0:554

ethics folder(s), 0:545–546

definition, 7:481, MS2:197, MS2:302

Ethics Hearing(s),

called for answering entheta letters, 1:975

convened by, 1:949

Danger condition and, 0:585

hearing in area where stats just won't come up, 0:588

Job Endangerment Chits and, 0:551–553

never hold hearing on upstat, 0:505

noncompliance with standard, on-policy order and, 0:592

prevention of, 1:250

purpose and procedure, 1:949

staff member, following a warning given by an executive, 1:250

system of chits and hearings being out, 0:554

Ethics Hearing(s), *(cont.)*

taking over post in Normal Operation and getting it into Emergency or Danger, 0:597

Ethics interrogatory,

description, 0:615

used for, 1:417

Ethics Interview Officers, for each Ethics Officer in org of more than 100 staff members, 1:55

Ethics investigation, Danger Formula and, 0:563

Ethics Officer (E/O), *see also* **Masters-at-Arms (MAAs)**

actions to be taken when theft occurs, 0:548

activities, 1:681

basic duties of, 0:519

CF folders and, 2:704, 6:714

character of, 1:687

Clearing Course security and, 4:792

combining LRH Comm-HCO Area Sec-Ethics Officer, 0:101

condition(s),

assigning wrong conditions, 0:302

he gets conditions he failed to enforce, 0:656

hitting people with conditions is small part of Ethics, 0:519

upgrading individuals from, 0:652

verifying that condition formula is complete, 0:670

conduct, 1:690

conduct of duty regulated to safeguard good auditing and training, 5:249

Confessional tech and, 4:986, 5:449

C/S and, conflict of targets between, 5:718

Director of Inspections and Reports and, 0:656

entheta letters handled by, 1:974–975

Ethics functions, 1:687

Ethics Hearings and, 1:949

fast flow pattern and, 1:972

filing, 0:551, 0:552, 0:659

firm policy, 1:685

full-time, 1:55

greatest enemy, 1:688–689

handling of clearance on dead file public, 1:976

hat, 1:681

high-crime checkouts violations, action of, 0:76–77

how to prevent from doing his job, 1:692–693

interviews, 1:827, 5:767, 6:416

investigation of down statistics must include inspection of Qual checkout log, MS2:462–463

making environment safe, 0:519

may become PTS, 1:1022

may convene Court of Ethics, 1:948

Ethics Officer (E/O), *(cont.)*

minimum for SH org, 1:684

must be ministers, 1:643

must know his policy, 1:485

no direct routing of preclears to the Ethics Officer except through Qual Div and Review, 5:118

order to handle things in, 1:690

penalty for not being trained ministers, 1:643

protecting ethics upstats, 0:519

PTS or chronically ill or NCG and EO/MAA posts, MS1:460, MS2:251

Public E/O, 1:685

purpose, 1:681

quality of service and, 4:934

ratio of Ethics Officers in org, 1:684

reporting what you know and find to, 0:554

reports, 5:297

responsibility for,
staff auditors and interns, 4:905
staff training, 5:490

routes roller coaster cases to Review, 1:1011

second E/O for org of more than 100 staff members, 1:55

security of data and, 4:806

Staff E/O, 1:685

staff member reports and, 0:554

Student/Pc E/O, 1:685

suppressive reasonableness, 1:688

three zones, 1:685

Ethics Order(s),

form, 1:416

how to write, 1:967

PTSes and SPs and, 1:968

putting a head on a pike, 0:498

run out group engrams, 1:967

upgrading individuals from general condition assignment, 0:652

what they must state, 1:979

when absence of personally issued Ethics Conditions Orders may constitute grounds for removal of exec, 0:659

which go to dead files, 1:978

ethics presence, 0:246–247, 0:526

reason an exec gets compliance, 7:706

way to continue to have is to be maximally right in your actions, decisions and dictates, 7:706

X quality made up partly of symbology, partly of force, some "now we're supposed to's" and endurance, 7:706

Ethics Program No. 1, 0:103

case actions, 5:599

ethics protection, 0:519, 1:767, 5:366

blue star, green star, gold star, 1:578

given only upstats, 1:577

ethics report, *see also* **ethics chit; Knowledge Report; report**

definition, 1:970, 2:661, 4:262

ethics scene, inactivity and, MS1:169, *see also* **scene**

Ethics Section,

CF folders and, 2:704, 6:714

entheta letters handled by, 1:974–975

fast flow pattern and, 1:972

handling of clearance on dead file public, 1:976

ethics system, forerunner of, 1:734

ethics tech, *see* **ethics**

Ethics Why, MS1:165, *see also* **ethics; Why**

ethnic(s),

definition, MS3:68, MS3:148, MS3:247

org and, MS3:68, MS3:247

putting reality in with the public, MS3:69, MS3:248

survey and org image, 6:614

surveys,
how and why they are done, MS3:69, MS3:248
majority opinion, MS3:69, MS3:248
needed to control, govern or have influence upon an area, MS3:68, MS3:247
org image and, MS3:155
use of in programs and mock-up, MS3:69, MS3:248

values,
not knowing, MS3:68, MS3:247
of public, vital to PRO, MS3:138
what it consists of, MS3:68, MS3:247

evaluate(ing),

ability to, puts one at cause, MS1:130

faulty, examples of, MS1:90

heart of is a cool, cold knowledge of the Data Series, MS1:98

length of time to, MS1:111

methods used by intelligence systems, MS1:90

people who cannot evaluate an area, MS1:187

when some situation is nonroutine, MS1:183

when something won't resolve to a debug, MS1:184

evaluation(s), *see also* **analysis; investigation**

after you get the "who or where," MS1:150

anyone doing target must read whole evaluation, MS1:137

art of, MS1:128

backwards, example of, MS1:179

cancel a failing eval fast, MS1:174

carry name and post of person responsible for program, MS1:136

evaluation(s), *(cont.)*

common bug, MS1:120

consistency of, MS1:89

criteria for outness in, MS1:138

cross-ordering LRH evaluation, 0:146

debug tech and, MS2:152

definition, MS1:155

different types of, MS1:170

duties of person responsible for
    passing, MS1:138

echelons, system by which is done, MS1:118

end product of, MS1:158

evaluator has to learn to think like
    an idiot, 7:819

examples of, MS1:150, MS1:155

examples of lack of evaluation in orgs and
    results, 7:818

existence and soundness of, 0:705, 7:457,
    MS2:443, MS2:457, MS3:437

expansion program and, MS1:169

final objective of, MS1:133

four final targets, MS1:132

get the show on the road, MS1:161

good or bad, MS1:166

handling, MS1:96

hard and fast rule of insisting upon, MS1:120

if used to delay putting something there or
    getting something done, MS1:183

incomplete when you see a Who-Where as
    a Why, MS1:151

incomplete Whys and, MS1:150

length of time to evaluate, MS2:90

long times required to evaluate traced to an
    individual Why for each evaluator, MS2:90

made complex, MS1:187

mandatory statement in policy section, MS1:182

matter of skill, MS1:154

mental exercise if program never done, MS1:131

multiple situations, MS1:122

needing a catastrophic sit in order to, MS1:179

new way to think, MS1:130

no achievement in improvement toward the ideal
    scene, reasons for, MS1:116

preserving or acquiring resources, MS1:177

program and execution integral
    part of, MS1:133

proper form, MS1:89

recognizing outpoints and speed of, MS1:168

requires data, MS1:156

resources and, MS1:177

review of, MS1:142, MS1:157, MS1:173

sequence for, MS1:165

evaluation(s), *(cont.)*

should have someone who can personally
    contact people getting the targets done,
    MS1:137

something that can be operated, MS1:166

speed of, MS1:168

standard pattern, MS1:108

success depends on, MS1:137

supplementary, MS1:116
    can rescue long series of apparently fruitless
        evaluations, MS1:119
    local environment and, MS1:116
    relay points and, MS1:116

test of, MS1:132

thumbnail, some strategic plannings are result
    of, 7:471, MS3:451

trick on, MS1:157

"who or where" and, MS1:150

why they fail, MS1:131

why things are evaluated, MS1:183

without vital data concerned, MS1:176

word cleared on it, MS1:137

evaluator(s),

ability, mandatory, MS1:131

corrective actions, MS1:188

cramming and, MS1:188

definition, MS1:155

evaluators can be on a "whole org" kick,
    MS1:122

failed, overts and withholds in abundance,
    MS1:187

long times required to evaluate traced to an
    individual Why for each evaluator, MS1:111

procedure to handle O/Ws on, MS1:188

qualification for, MS1:155

remedy for bogged O/Ws handling, MS1:188

repute of, MS1:131

resources, take stock of, MS1:177

slow because evaluation not done in sequence,
    MS1:165

test of, MS1:167

evening course, scheduling of, 4:182

event(s),

generating public interest and goodwill, 0:332

goodwill and, MS3:168

PR events or capers, wasted planning and,
    MS3:93

success of and preparation, MS3:33

truth, stupidity and, 0:535–536

eviction, by HCO order, 1:732

evidence,

admissibility of in boards or Comm Evs, 1:954

courts convened on stats and known, 1:949

evidence, *(cont.)*

definition, 1:928

withholding evidence, 0:469

evil, *see also* **bad**

anything more destructive than constructive, 1:488

basic thing man can't or won't confront, 4:370

collective-think is, 0:158

confront of, 0:37, 0:526, 0:657

eradicating evil men do to themselves, 0:462

inability to confront evil leads people into disregarding it or discounting it or not seeing it at all, MS2:68

man seeks to check evil impulses by inhibiting his own skill and strength, 1:805

only road out is processing, 1:1027, 7:511

opposite of good, 1:488

stems from aberration, 1:1027, 7:511

strength has two sides, one for good and one for evil, 0:516

when going on some evil course man attempts to restrain himself and caves himself in, 0:526, MS2:68

evil intention,

as reason for failure, 5:467

one must not permit men to hide evil intentions under protection of freedom, 0:462

evil purposes,

FPRD and, 1:915

handling of, 1:914

evolutionary group, we are essentially an, 0:273

examination(s), 0:351, *see also* **study; training**

done on theory and practical checksheets, 5:114

85% pass basis for, 4:335

Examiner must not be used as subject on which student auditor demonstrates degree of auditing skill, 5:172

fast flow student and, 4:644

fast flow system of management and, 5:210

flunks and HCO Board of Review, 5:95

for any classification, 5:174

GAEs constitute a flunk, 5:208

good, sound examination, 5:168–169

honest and factual exams will make people happy, 5:239

how correct examination is done, 4:331

how many passed per week per student, 5:163

how to do theory examinations, 4:395

HPA/HCA, shall cover, 5:158

examination(s), *(cont.)*

if not passed, student remains in Cramming, 4:365

incorrect, way to find, 5:240

incorrectly flunked or passed upsets students, 5:208

method of, 5:207

number Releases and Clears soaring, income remaining same, 5:239

oral examination, 5:322, 5:323

example of, 5:151

marks on, 5:150

Permanent staff status, example, 5:154

raising the standard of, 4:327

required before being allowed on internship, 5:857

requirements for anyone giving, 5:217

student,

failing, 5:163

may not discuss, 4:478

who feels he has been incorrectly failed, handling, 4:478

tape,

asking for verbatim wording drives students to copy, 4:509

demand understanding, 4:509

exams, asking for verbatim wording, 5:171

written examination,

example of, 5:151

marks on, 5:150

Examiner(s)(ing), *see also* **checkouts**

asking end phenomena question for grade, 4:1100

asks for examples of action or application, 5:179

asks what the words mean, 5:179

bad indicators present, pc back to HGC, 5:256

bonuses and fines for, 3:358, 5:135, 5:240

case level of, 4:813

C/S has Examiner question the pc about the sessions he has received, 4:1136

data about not examining above level applies very severely to theory checkout as well as to practical and general instruction, 4:332

Dept 13 makes sure no untrained student or unsolved case gets past, 0:351

duty of, 5:246

every auditor leaving Cramming should go through, 5:702

expiration dates and theory testing, 4:326

final classification exams, must require, 5:197

full-time, required for Tech Div, 4:96

going to Examiner and attesting to completion of a condition, 0:670

goofs, 5:228

invalidate or evaluate, must never, 5:247

Examiner(s)(ing), *(cont.)*

meter check on all attests, 4:234, 6:305

metered exam given after each session, 5:246

must verify any red tag handled within 24 hours, 4:256

pc does not arrive in good shape, 4:824

Pc Examiner,
ideal scene, 5:66
product, 5:66
statistics, 5:66

post requires greatest honesty, 5:239

purpose, 5:66

refuses to examine any two or more grades at a time, 5:257

Student Examiner,
ideal scene, 5:66
product, 5:66
statistics, 5:66

student upset on flunking, 5:210

theory and practical, purpose, 4:322

theory checkouts and, 4:395

24-hour rule, 5:279

what Examiner does when he/she does not declare a pc, 5:36

what he must require for final classification, 4:624

Examiner's Report Form,

additional data, 5:298

auditor's stats are computed on, 4:1188

definition, 4:1015

example, 5:282

Examining Board, 5:342

Exchange by Dynamics, procedure, 0:530–531

exchange(d), exchangeable, *see also* **finance; income; money; production**

auto industry and, 0:318

children and, 0:529

civilizations which facilitate production and interchange and inhibit crime and fraud, 0:297

conditions of, 0:317–318

consumption and production and, 7:435, MS3:415

crime, fraud and, MS1:295

criminal exchange defined, 0:527

criminal exchange is nothing from the criminal for something from another, MS2:69

doing work of post results in effective exchange, 0:259

exchangeability, definition, 0:296

exchange condition I try to operate on, 0:318

exchange factor out, effect of, 0:528

fair exchange defined, 0:317

exchange(d), exchangeable, *(cont.)*

four conditions of, MS2:400

fourth principle is produce in abundance, deliver and get paid for it, MS2:401

getting org producing products which exchange for valuables, 0:443

goodwill or friendship as, 0:528

income, staff pay and, 0:317

maintains inflow and outflow that gives person space around him and keeps bank off him, 0:528, MS2:70

offer valuable service in return for, MS3:178

one exchanges something valuable for something valuable, MS2:223

one has to produce something to *exchange* for money, MS2:70

organization, involved in, MS3:178

partial exchange, definition, 0:317

produce in abundance and try to give better than expected quality, 0:318

short-changing, 0:317

survival of any group depends upon, 7:435, MS3:415

to *exchange* something, one must find or create a *demand*, MS:224

valuable exchangeable product, 0:296

viability and, 0:89

with community and org value, MS3:158

with the community, 0:297

exchangeability, VFPs and, MS1:295

exclusion, things which set a group on a course for, MS1:270

excuse(s), no excuses for staff not doing their jobs, 0:521

exec, *see* **executive**

Exec Esto, Exec Esto Org Officer, *see also* **Establishment Officer**

actions taken, MS1:306, MS2:105, MS2:256

always holds form and lines of org, MS2:25

first product of, MS1:358, MS2:185

functions, MS2:6

holding line of hatting Estos and success, MS2:24

how he holds Esto stable as an Esto, MS2:25

if cannot or do not follow exact procedure required in policy or routing forms or admin patterns will tear things up faster than can be gotten in, MS2:36

must follow policy and lines, MS2:36

org board position and functions, MS2:6

responsible for quantity of establishment and quality and performance of Estos, MS2:9

responsible to get product conference operating and competent, MS2:12

who tries to do it with admin will fail, MS2:40

Exec Sec, *see* **Executive Secretary**

execution, execute(d), *see also* **compliance**

any idea no matter if badly executed is better than no idea, 0:702

battle plan execution, 0:708

orders given are to be executed and reported done, not nearly done or almost done, 0:429–430

person whose disagreements are too many and who doesn't execute, 0:591

program execution, 0:701–703

targets and, 0:704

executioner, when person becomes his own, 0:452

executive(s), *see also* **administrator; leader; manager; senior**

abilities needed, 0:260, 0:704–705

able to write clean, concise programs, 7:456, MS2:442, MS2:456, MS3:436

accepting an almost, 0:429–430

accepting reasons why something cannot be done, 0:430

accepts help conditionally until demonstrated to be help, 7:427, MS3:407

acting only on verified information, 0:520

acting status, MS1:472, MS2:308

actions to be taken to handle soft sell, 2:86, 6:372

activate programs without consulting, 1:379

administration, result of missing key ingredients, 7:409

administrator who does not know and enforce dev-t policies, 7:324

all he has to do to expand org or part of it, 7:669

answer to an overburdened post, 7:748

anyone in charge of anything should know the workings and functions of every unit, MS3:301

any person, head of dept or above is deemed an executive, MS2:245

appointments, 1:199

arranges personnel and organization to handle types of actions and confusions, MS3:393

auditing of, 5:552, 5:585

basic elements of correct comm, MS2:236–237

basic management tools, list, 7:484, MS2:200, MS2:305

battle planning and, 0:706–708

beingness, in order to achieve, what one would have to do, MS2:216

be maximally right in your actions, decisions and dictates, 0:246

executive(s), *(cont.)*

body or person who carries the laws into effect or superintends the enforcement of them, MS2:215

bonus and Management Status One checksheet, 7:464, MS2:191, MS2:295, MS3:444

bonuses, requirements for, 0:221

breakthrough and management tools, MS3:463

briefing staff, 0:373, 0:424, 0:579

bypass and, 0:582, 0:604, 7:260

cannot confront evil, on way to being suppressive, 1:569

can only go so high without being precise in use of tools, MS2:190, MS2:294, MS3:443

can't be in charge if thing one is in charge of doesn't exist, 0:654

catastrophe, what exec should do when hit with, 0:427

checksheet a MUST for, MS3:420

climbing status stairs in terms of influence and zones of control, MS1:365

common denominator is ability to communicate, MS2:218

competence and, 0:221

competently handle any post or machine or plan under him, 7:427, MS3:407

condition(s),

continued emergency inevitably results in catastrophe for exec, 0:581

Danger condition, declaring and handling of, 0:592, 0:606

exec assigned condition he should have assigned, 0:653

exec in Non-Existence, 0:578

how exec brings about Danger condition, 0:593

conditions assignment and, 7:698

conditions, one gets the conditions he fails to assign, 7:825

conferences and time salvage, 7:894

confusion and stable datum, 0:433

coordinating committee and, 7:452

coordinating committee, perpetually in charge of it, MS3:432

cope by all means but spend some of that time organizing, 7:518

Danger Formula and 3 May PL, MS2:207

data an executive wants is in statistics and reports and briefings, MS2:59, MS2:241

datum to apply in a formed activity, 7:429, MS3:409

executive(s), *(cont.)*

debug tech is a vital executive tool, MS2:145

definition, 1:573, 7:698, 7:746,
MS2:215, MS2:288

demanding correct comm as a first action, 0:391

deputy and, 0:601

despatches, handling of, 0:388, 0:389,
0:404, 0:407

detecting people who fear responsibility or
consequences of their most ordinary
actions, 0:412

developed traffic and, 0:405, 0:417, 0:427,
0:433–434

dev-t logs, 0:416, 0:428

disastrous occurrences, actions for handling,
7:326, MS3:306

discipline, only use of is to continue to make
processing possible, 7:511

discouraging or forbidding Confessionals,
5:448, 4:985

discussing rather than acting and
handling, 7:1198

dismissals and, 0:372, 0:373

distraction, actions to take to handle, 7:416

doesn't deserve secretaries or communicators,
they earn them, 7:343, MS3:323

Doubt, only wanting the title of, 7:428

downfall of most executives is lack of
information and files, MS2:46

duties of, 0:383, 0:389, 0:405, 0:406, 7:750

eating up exec's time and patience destroys
harmony, dissemination and income, 0:372

entheta and, 0:372

ethics offense to fail to use tools of
management, 7:485, MS2:201,
MS2:306, MS3:465

ethics presence and, 0:246–247

evaluation revealed what breakdown in
orgs is, MS2:245

evaluations done by inspection on the spot,
MS2:61, MS2:243

every Exec Sec has products of his/her portion
of org, 1:566

example of confused comm line with command
line, MS2:58, MS2:240

example of correct flow lines,
MS2:59, MS2:241

exchange principles, 0:318

"exhausted executives," key to, 0:201

expecting only high brass to carry load, 0:253

failed, what found, 1:642

failing,
it will be found that, 5:480
to apply the exact policies of Scientology
ethics, 7:694

executive(s), *(cont.)*

failing, *(cont.)*
to hold firm the form and channels of the org,
their own posts and org will be a
confusion, 0:582, 7:249

false reports and, 0:420

false reports, who accepts is doing his job
backwards, 7:825

fastest way for technical exec to get into
trouble, 0:241

financial matters and, 0:372, 0:374

fire-breathing product officer will be
followed, MS2:290

first action is to demand correct
comm, MS2:236

first duty of, 0:404

first job of, MS1:311, MS2:110, MS2:261

first test, competence, MS2:218

first thing needs to know is he has tools with
which to manage, MS2:199,
MS2:304, MS3:463

five persons under exec, 0:601, 0:603

formula to apply when being knocked about by
one's lines, bad news, disasters and feeling
PTS, 0:420

four things they want on their lines, 7:602

fronting up to personnel who err, 0:544

fully trained, will raise stats, MS1:401

gets people to get the work done,
7:426, MS3:406

getting dev-t knows what posts are not being
held, 7:412, MS3:392

getting job done, 0:421

"GI push" and, 0:693

going on assumption that all want things to go
right, 0:246

good executive,
arranging personnel and organization to handle
types of actions and confusion, 0:434
how to be a, 0:58

group size and, 0:600, 0:603

handling dev-t of people not being stable
terminals is forced to work harder than if
post empty, 7:413

handling for area giving excessively developed
traffic, 7:413, MS3:393

handling for distraction, MS3:396

handling for entheta letter forwarded to him by
staff member, 2:667

harder exec works on bypass, more section he is
working on will disappear, 0:593

hardest job any top exec has, 0:384

hardest job is teaching staff the lines and
terminals and getting them followed, 7:771

executive(s), *(cont.)*

HAS's responsibility for is, 5:552

has to know how to change gears,
7:430, MS3:410

has to pay attention to the basic law about
standard of living, MS2:286

hat knockoff, 0:280

hats, responsibilities for, 0:221

hatting those around him and at a
distance, 0:390

heavy ethics and, 0:247

high crime, to penalize auditors, C/Ses,
Tech/Qual or Ethics Officers, 4:985

how exec can make mistakes, 0:372

how exec handles project he doesn't know
much about, 0:87–88

how head of an organization or division who is
not going to make it operates, 7:518

how to attain ideal scene with,
MS2:62, MS2:244

how to clear your command lines, 0:591

how to know one, MS1:404

ideal scene for, MS2:61, MS2:243

if flow lines wrong he will never be a product
officer but only a comm clerk, MS2:58,
MS2:240

if one thinks by taking it easy on staff he will
make points he is very mistaken, MS2:289

if overworked, seek to contract the org to
reduce the traffic, 7:242

if you bypass an area, you must assign a
Danger condition, MS2:207

if you're wrong other fellow gets wrapped
around pole for complying, 0:246

ignoring nonproducers and overt product
makers, 0:316

impersonating an, 0:472

in combat with senior management
body, MS2:228

incomplete staff work and, 0:401

in conflict with Flag, CLO or policy, MS2:228

in disciplining is concerned with those who
would stop or hinder the flow and those
just plain idle or stupid, 1:1027, 7:511

information and, 0:372, 0:373

inspection and, 7:688

inspection of org and its staff, 1:379

inspects areas of Dangers and Affluences, 1:567

instant hat for, MS1:375

instant-hat type of checksheet for, 7:485,
MS2:201, MS2:306, MS3:465

intention, plays a major role in successful
production of org or activity, MS2:228

executive(s), *(cont.)*

invalidating people, effect, 0:247

investigation, *see* investigation

is one who does and backs off spots
continually, 7:427

Is this OK? 0:427

junior(s),
always demand facts from, 0:241
conclusions from, 0:241, 0:242
execs failing to brief their, 0:424
may not OK anything done or to be done below their level unless immediate junior has
also stated or attested with initial that it is
OK, 0:419, 0:427
never act on junior's data until you have fully
investigated situation, 0:241
never solve problem junior presents, 0:240
not getting exec's orders executed, 0:420
number of juniors exec can handle,
0:601, 0:603
order only your immediate juniors, 0:584
who accepts orders from everyone, 0:592

junior who accepts orders from anyone,
result, 7:683

lack of exec responsibility, 0:427

lack of foresight or initiative, 7:400, MS3:380

lack of knowledge of post, exec becomes effect,
7:321, MS3:301

lazy executive only disciplines staff,
1:1026, 7:510

letting people get on with it, 0:88

letting things run as long as they run
well, 0:587

Liability condition if he does not handle fully
once he does see an outness, 7:428,
MS3:408

line(s),
being hit back by lines you are trying to
handle, 0:420
having put lines there, exec must see that they
exist and go on existing, 0:409
in exec's area stacking up and becoming tangled, 0:404
what they should look like, 0:373

list of basic management tools, MS3:464

Long Form Product Clearing run on leading
executives, MS2:56

low leadership score and, 1:197

main duties are observation, evaluations and
supervision, MS2:60, MS2:242

make it easy to accept a report of a
done, 7:825

making an, MS2:58, MS2:240

making channels on which things can flow and
putting terminals there to handle or change
them, 0:389

executive(s), *(cont.)*

management tools, breakthrough was discovering executives did not look upon these as tools, 7:483

may assign any condition to immediate juniors, 1:573

may not be removed for issuing Conditions Orders, 1:573

misbehavior,

engaging in activities for which he could be blackmailed, 7:714

placing personal interests and situations above interests of the group, 7:714

sex and, 7:714

misbehavior of, 1:898

missing Key Ingredients of administration, result, MS3:389

mistakes due to no familiarity with HCO PLs, 0:55

most important zone of ethical conduct in an organization is at or near the top, MS2:246

most valuable product of, MS1:216

must challenge with ferocity instances of "unworkability," 2:13, 3:13, 4:13, 5:13

must develop sensitivity to indicators of outnesses, MS3:407

must know and be able to use tools of third dynamic tech, MS2:188, MS2:292, MS3:441

must not permit bypass and misrouting, 0:582

must work off datum "get people to get the work done," 7:745

never put person with bad study history on key exec post, 0:114, 7:660

noncompliance,

add ferocity against, 0:247

exec seldom hit unless he has had noncompliance on his lines, 0:427

exec who tolerates, 0:659

handling, 0:592

make penalties for noncompliance and false reports too gruesome to be faced, 0:420

no real effective attention on recruitment, training, apprenticing, hatting, future execs, reason for, 0:693

nothing wrong with working hard as, 0:411

not insisting on execs being trained, 0:303

observation by (1) stats, (2) reports, (3) inspections, MS2:60, MS2:242

OEC Volumes, execs should own whole set, 0:27

off-line, off-policy, off-origin despatches and, 0:407, 0:416

executive(s), *(cont.)*

of the organization are never off duty wherever they are, 7:585

on a product he names it, wants it, gets it, gets it wanted, gets in the exchange for it, MS2:60, MS2:242

one who does and backs off spots continually, MS3:407

only use of discipline is to continue to make processing possible, 1:1027

only wanting the title, condition of Doubt, MS3:408

order(s),

command channel and, 0:592

exec seldom orders the impossible, 0:372

follower of destructive order is far more guilty than issuer, 0:142

insisting that original order(s) be returned with the compliance, 0:430

issuing unreal orders, how to avoid, 0:88

make clear, precise, communicative instructions and, 0:431

when you issue orders you are using power and force, 0:247

"Order Board" and, 0:375

organization, preservation of, 7:428, MS3:408

org board, knowing the, 0:280, 0:409

outnesses, must develop sensitivity to indicators of, 7:427

overloaded execs who are near the top should also have an organized personal staff, less numerous, but still with the basic org board fully covered, 7:781

overwork(ed),

having more than four subordinates, result, 0:603–604

how to prevent, 0:602

when execs cannot afford to expand, 0:130

when exec will feel overworked, 0:389, 0:602

overworked executive is trying to handle more than five other people directly, 7:258

paused statistics and, 7:499

pay, 5:402, 5:403

pay attention to the basic law about standard of living, MS1:352

penalizing auditors, C/Ses, Tech/Qual or E/Os for following HCOBs or HCO PLs, 5:448

penalty for any found to be interpreting, altering or cancelling tech, 4:214, 5:784

penalty for discouraging or forbidding Confessionals, 1:642

people afraid of taking responsibility are not execs, 0:260

people want exec to make the mistakes, 0:372

executive(s), *(cont.)*

permanent, defined, 7:42

permanent, requirements for, 1:223

personal org board, MS1:198

personally or by representative inspects continually, MS2:60, MS2:242

Personnel Department and, 7:757

personnel, work-organization potential, 7:427, MS3:407

planning and, 0:266, 0:372

policy regarding misbehavior of, 1:898

policy, seeing that it is followed, 0:404, 0:406, 0:407

post, requirements for, 5:390

posting qualifications for, MS1:471, MS2:307

Power Quality Checklist good for an inspection, 2:721

primary hat, 7:753

privileges and responsibilities of their posts, must insist upon, 7:249, 0:582

put hats on people, 7:753

putting in new lines and posts or making changes in old ones, 0:384

Q and A, who indulges in, 7:440, MS3:420

quicksilver personnel scenes and, 0:264–267

reason an exec gets compliance, 7:706

reasons a great many persons fail as execs, 7:321, MS3:301

referring to others to make decision, 0:260

regging for the bonus, 0:302

report, taking action on any single, 0:520

require junior to initial "This is okay," 7:682

required to take FEBC, 5:521

responsibility for training staff,
    penalty, 7:789
    reward, 7:790

responsibility(ies) of, 0:260, 0:629 MS1:376, MS2:312
    for staff, penalty, 5:419
    for staff, reward, 5:420
    for training staff, 5:419, 5:421

responsibility to see that persons in his area get their personal ethics in and keep them in, MS2:245

rise and sudden downfall of, 7:23

role of, 7:603

routing,
    as major duty of exec, 0:383, 0:389
    one of exec's first duties is, 0:390

executive(s), *(cont.)*

properly and seeing that others do, 0:404

salary, expenses or travel may not be paid by an org while the exec or staff member is absent obtaining higher grades, 0:174

secondary hat, 7:753

secret of exec success, 0:260, 7:701

seeking popularity, 0:315

selected on the basis of personal ability to promote and get the show on the road, 2:59, 3:229, 7:34

Senior Danger Formula and, 0:612

senior exec, made to look bad by continued Emergency on a lower echelon, handling, 0:587

senior executives with ability to make money should have facilities, 7:343, MS3:323

seniority of, 7:117

serious fault in any is unawareness of the coordinated functions of terminals, 7:771

serves more than the lowest staff member, 7:761

severing somebody's responsibility line, 0:619, 1:611

should know the workings and functions of every unit, 7:321

should not write critical or confusing despatches, 7:754

single-hands while he trains his staff, 7:426, MS3:406

situations existing where exec writes despatches and gets no action or answers, 7:415, MS3:395

soft sell going on in org, actions to take, 7:847

solution to off-line, off-origin comm, MS2:239

solvency is not made by high execs, 0:357

someone from whom others are willing to take orders, MS2:218

source of overwork and woe, 1:204

stable datum for, 7:746

stable terminal for his staff and assistants, MS2:215

stable terminals, solving areas by reinforcing, 0:434

staff, *see* staff

staff respect the one that makes them work, MS2:289

standard of living and, 0:315, MS1:352, MS2:369

statistic(s),
    don't confuse exec's efforts to get stats up with suppression, 0:519
    handle org by stats only, 0:584
    head of a part has stat of that part, 0:654

statistics and, 7:91, 1:555

executive(s), *(cont.)*

steps for getting in ethics on a staff member, MS2:247–250

study time and, 0:222

subject which makes executives harassed, 7:433, MS2:227, MS3:413

suppressives often rise up to being in charge, 0:518

supreme test of, 7:427, MS3:407

target policies and, 0:88, 7:777

temper lightning with sunshine occasionally, 0:247

temporary defined, 7:42

test of, 0:708, 7:460, MS1:167, MS2:446, MS3:440

there to ensure people produce in viable quantity with no overt products, MS2:288

Thetan–Mind–Body–Product system, 0:128

to command is to serve and only gives one the right to serve, 0:238

tools, use of, 7:461, 7:463

tools with which to manage, MS1:373

top of org board being forced to act at lower levels, 0:132

top-stat executives, what they actually do, 7:427, MS3:407

trained auditors make the better executives, 4:386

training, failure of any exec is traceable to, MS1:403

training program, 7:463, MS2:190, MS2:294, MS3:443

two jobs, 7:745

two necessary ideas, 5:480

unable to assimilate straight Scientology, 0:12

understanding added to competence, ideal character of, MS2:218

untrained, will depress stats, MS1:401

unusual solutions and, 0:146, 0:405

upper triangle of Scientology symbol particularly applicative to, MS2:232

urgent directive,
defined, 7:326
when findings of Board of Investigation actually become law, 7:327

valuable exec, symptom of, 0:394

warning signs of imminent danger, 7:705

way to be popular is by doing your job well and raising the general income thereby, 7:758

executive(s), *(cont.)*

way to decrease traffic and workload of org, 0:279

what a successful exec understands, MS1:404

what an exec wants on his lines, 0:372

"what-do-I-do's" flying up to head of org, 0:412

what it takes to make one, 7:1438

when accepts "done," 7:479, MS2:195, MS2:300, MS3:459

when an exec can call himself fully competent, 7:321, MS3:301

when he does something of any importance to others, he ought to say so, 0:373

when to beware of being told it is "on-policy" or "an LRH order" or "in bulletins" or "on LRH tapes," 0:146

while learning post, exec should spend bulk of time in study, 7:321, MS3:301

who aren't trained auditors have the highest mortality rate, 4:387, 5:494

who cannot confront evil, en route to becoming suppressive, 7:398, MS3:378

who can't evaluate, MS1:154

who do not handle matters so as to complete them, 1:893, 7:701

who does not know all the hats and their duties, 1:71

who does not know and enforce dev-t policies is letting the org down, MS3:304

who doesn't handle but puts something on wait is irresponsible, 0:260

who goes on handling dev-t of people not being stable terminals is forced to work harder than if post empty, MS3:393

who is only handling unworn hats that result in no stats, 7:518

who tolerate noncompliance, false reports or down stats, 7:698

why and how they get repeatedly pulled into an area, 7:738

winding up as an, 0:689

wise exec gets in policy on a gradient, 7:404, MS3:384

worker-oriented, 7:428, MS2:289, MS3:408

you get compliance because you have ethics presence and persistence and can get mad, 7:706

you have to know the ground and the business, 0:589

Executive Committee, conference routing and, 0:387

Executive Council (EC),

appointments and, 7:914

assigned unreal and vicious condition, result, 7:916

collective responsibility, 7:914

composed of, 7:909

conditions set and declared by, 7:913

coordination, why we have, MS3:435

deadlock in, 7:913

financial planning and, 7:910, 7:913

first business of, 1:57

highest governing body of an org, 7:913

LRH Comm may veto any measure that is against policy, 7:913

managing by stats, 0:679

may remove members of Ad Council, 7:914

measures from Ad Council and, 7:914

permitting offering services it can't deliver would only come from personal case failures or no gain, 6:756

promotional actions of, 0:355, 7:84

PRO should have direct access to the, 0:338

Public Exec Sec member of, 6:86

purpose of, 7:913

responsible for org as a whole, 7:910

unfilled as posts, result, 7:916

when Public Divisions become inactive or hopeless or slothful then people inflow drops, 6:756

which has no operating HCO, 1:58

working toward more initiative and independence of action by every, 6:584

Worldwide, 7:165

executive councilman, Comm Ev and, 0:478

Executive Courts of Ethics, 1:948–949

for failure to employ study tech, 0:45

Executive Directive (EDs),

decays in one year, 7:713

definition, 1:430, 7:1323

issued, should better things, 7:711

LRH Comm sees that Ron's EDs are complied with, 0:356

may not alter or cancel any PL or HCOB, 0:143

sample program to cure dev-t, 0:441–443

should exist in Mimeo Files, 1:435

three things have to be missing that make EDs necessary, 7:712

two basic rules of, 7:712

Executive Director (ED),

bulk of the job of, 7:642

comm line,
books, 7:646
business mail, 7:647
carriers of data and commands, 7:659
if good and complete and well handled, position becomes very easy to deal with and all will go well, 7:659
presents, 7:640
Sec EDs, 7:638
watched carefully, 7:646

coordinates work of Prod Off, Org Off and Exec Esto, MS2:5

HASI (Founding Church), duties of, 7:1167

how lines can be jammed, 7:650

inspections that embrace establishment and production observations and, 7:715

interview, 1:828

LRH Communicator as deputy of, 0:173

management of org, cheek by jowl with FR, 7:292

must have control of his org to achieve the product of a flourishing, prosperous org, MS2:278

org being run on day-to-day basis by, MS1:172

penalty for reporting false stats, 7:168

penalty for stopping the communication of, 1:902

primary commodity is data, 7:643

purposes, 7:57

responsibilities for appointments, transfers or dismissals, 0:373

responsibility for getting auditor trainees, 5:528

responsibility for making sure Staff Section Officer is posted, 5:443

restimulation by reason of comm lines or hats and why, 7:648

Sec EDs, 1:425

sequence of hats ED gradually unloads as org takes over, 7:449, MS2:273, MS3:429

sphere of influence is too large to be handled on a part-time basis, 7:652

staff meeting and, 0:173

stationery must always be top grade, 7:647

statistic of, 7:168

symptoms of not handling the post, 7:652

territory and lines and errors that can be made, 7:652

usually also the Product Officer, MS2:7

verbal comm and, 7:649

veto power of, 7:888

what they are mainly concerned with, 7:643

who has no HCO are first ones that need Sec Check, 4:974

Executive Division (Div 7),

checklist for quality, 7:1425
use of, 7:1438

consists of three departments, 7:71

coordinators and, 7:94

full setup for an, 0:601

keynotes of the division, 7:72

management and coordination of org depends upon, 7:1425

modified organization of division, 7:93

pattern of, 7:105

promotional actions, 7:84

Executive Establishment Officer, 0:442, 0:443

Executive Ethics Hearing, 0:549–550

Executive Letter Unit,

function of person in charge, 7:1194

purpose, 7:1195

Executive Qualification Certificate, 5:393, 7:769

Executive Secretary (Exec Sec),

actions taken at a time when Saint Hill started its soaring climb out of the doldrums, 7:695

advisers and, 7:94

Board of Investigation, convene if statistics level out, remain low, drop, 7:512

condition of Treason for not knowing and keeping in gross income senior datum, 0:358

Danger condition can be assigned by, 0:592

Executive Council and, 7:913

GDSes of his or her divisions, responsible for, 7:914

gross income senior datum and, 2:672, 7:851

inspection, should walk through his divisions and inspect once a day, 7:702

inspections and, 0:592–595

may not be member of Ad Council, 7:909

not a desk job, 0:592

ordering and chitting only secretaries, 0:582

orders of, 7:910

organization not expanding, fault is with Exec Secs, 7:695

performance of duties that must be understood, 7:695

removal of, may be requested by Ad Council, 7:911

responsible for state and activities of his or her division, 7:910

stats, summary of what is being done when org's stats are down, 7:697

Executive Secretary Communicator,

authority of, 7:101

bypass and, 7:101

conditions assigned only on basis of graphs, 7:99

conduct of, 7:99

handling of despatches for Exec Secs, 7:96

has no Advisory Council seat, 7:97

high crime to use authority to subvert an Exec Sec, 7:101

how many are needed, 0:601–602

is a valid Executive Hearing Officer, 7:101

may be employed by Exec Sec in any fashion on Scientology business, 7:100

OIC and, 7:96

prime concern, 7:100

purpose, 7:96

executive status,

levels, designation of, MS1:366

staff status and, MS1:366

Executive Status One, 5:428

checksheet, ethics offense to fail to use tools properly, MS3:465

checksheet, instant-hat execs and managers, 7:485, MS2:201, MS2:306, MS3:465

definition, 7:464, MS1:366, MS1:375, MS2:191, MS2:295, MS3:444

ethics offense to fail to use tools properly, 7:485, MS2:201, MS2:306

Executive Status Two, 5:428

definition, 7:464, MS1:366, MS2:29, MS2:191, MS3:444

requirements, MS1:367

Executive Status Three, 5:428

definition, 7:464, MS1:366, MS2:191, MS2:295, MS3:444

exercise, 0:225, 0:439

importance of, 5:639

exhausted, working frantically, totally exhausted and yet producing nothing of value, reason, 0:439

existence,

conditions of, MS2:49

dynamic principle of, 0:452, 1:487

three major conditions of, MS1:107

existing scene(s), *see also* **scene**

compared to ideal scene, MS1:63

definition, MS3:75

estimating what post's existing scene is, 0:294

estimation of by product, MS1:242

ideal scene vs., MS1:52

existing scene(s), *(cont.)*

moved up markedly toward ideal scene, MS1:131

person must have an ideal scene with which to compare, MS1:29

Expanded ARC Straightwire, ability gained, 4:190

Expanded Confusion Formula, 0:311, 0:569–570

Expanded Dianetics Case Supervisor, 4:1127

Expanded Grade 0, ability gained, 4:190

Expanded Grade I, ability gained, 4:190

Expanded Grade II, ability gained, 4:190

Expanded Grade III, ability gained, 4:191

Expanded Grade IV, ability gained, 4:191

Expanded Grades,

Academy Levels contain data necessary to audit, 5:858

attested by pc declaring full statement of, 5:292

how they are attested to, 4:189, 4:657

Expanded Lower Grades, harmonic into the OT levels, 4:1107

Expanded Non-Existence, formula, 0:579–580, 1:592–593; *see also* **condition; Non-Existence**

expansion, expand(ing), *see also* **boom; growth; prosperity; success**

accelerating expansion, 0:124

actions to take, 7:1237

affluences and, 0:129

all policy is built on expansion, 7:356

almost impossible to run nonexpanding org with ease, 0:130

basic ingredient of, 0:434

basic purpose and, 0:117

bigger we get, the more economics and time we will have to do our job, 0:13

Buddhism and, 0:125

company needs a demanded product to expand, 7:354, MS3:334

conditions assignment and, 0:655

contraction vs., 0:124, 0:130

correct expansion, definition, 0:127

demand and, 0:125, 0:129

Ethics never gets reasonable about lack of, 0:498, 1:752, 7:681

exchange and, 0:89

expansion planning of facilities, 0:336

fair exchange does not guarantee any, 0:318

first sound move is to secure the ground you're standing on, 7:67

formula of, 0:115, 0:124

greatest liability in expansion of orgs is promotion (of staff), 0:596

expansion, expand(ing), *(cont.)*

group taking on more area, 0:253

growing to degree we can manifest superior order, 0:481

guarantee of, 0:318

HAS is the key, 1:83

HCO Ethics Codes and, 0:481

how HCO makes an org expand, 1:53

how org determines its own state of, 0:318

how to be ten times your size with a lot more pay, 0:626

how to expand and prosper, 0:584, 0:591

how to expand an org, 7:293

how to predict for, MS1:455

impossible where prediction is out, MS1:455

increase in living, 7:669

ingredients of, 7:464

into a decadent culture, 0:253

Keeping Scientology Working PL points 1–10 and, 0:13

key to, 0:318

level statistics and, 7:498

make-break point of, 7:457, MS2:443, MS2:457, MS3:437

make-break point of expand or not expand, 0:705

no limit to, MS1:303

nonexpansion, cause of, 0:115

nothing remains exactly the same forever, MS3:334

often gets pinned by false economy in personnel, MS1:382

only interrupted by inattentive or poor service resulting in ARC breaks in the field which if not handled end expansion, 6:95, 7:278

organization and, 0:123

organization pattern and, 7:260

organization will expand if you make Auditors and Supervisors make Scientology work, 7:849

org board and, 0:96

org image and, 0:335

org must expand to survive, 0:130

org should only increase in size as things get better and never when things get worse, 0:624

org which keeps its field cleaned up and active on the Bridge or as FSMs will expand, 6:564

overexpand, several ways one can, 7:358, MS3:338

expansion, expand(ing), *(cont.)*

overexpansion, 0:128

ownership and, 0:187

personnel mishandling and, MS1:384

plan for California (1962), 6:710

policy and, 0:115, 0:124, 0:125

policy interpreted against, MS3:336

poor org image and effect on, 6:606, MS3:140

positive orders and directions on positive programs inevitably cause, 7:333, MS3:313

product and, 0:124–125

proper expansion, when org can hold its territory without effort, 7:357

proper organization for expansion builds in blocks of six, 0:602

reason why we are alive and expanding, 0:337

requires expansion of all factors, 7:360, MS3:340

Scientology orgs are designed for, 0:130

space planning and expansion, 7:1336

statistics, level stats and, 7:498

survival and, 0:125, 0:129, 0:644

theory of policy and, 7:354, MS3:334

things either expand or they contract, MS3:334

third dynamic tech and, 0:56

trend is overall measure of expansion or contraction and is most valuable of stat messages, 7:528

trends used to estimate, 0:677

twelve ingredients of, 7:464, MS1:366, MS2:191, MS2:295, MS3:444

war and, 0:125

what an org must do to, 0:89

whole reason you assign conditions, 1:567, MS3:376

wider zones of responsibility, MS1:365

without order nothing can grow or expand, 0:480

expansion formula, 7:661, 7:668

expansion program(s),

definition, MS1:169

lines for, MS1:170

long-range actions and, MS1:169

LRH Comm and, MS1:171

mostly has to do with policy, MS1:172

repeating targets and, MS1:171, MS2:441

expeditor(s),

model assignment to be used in posting, 1:212

musical chairs and, 1:206

expeditor pool,

assign all new personnel to it, 1:73

filling it up, 1:74

new staff through SS I and II while in, 1:76

expense(s), expenditure(s), *see also* **bill; cost**

damage or expense occurring because urgent message was not marked RUSH, 0:381

executive and staff expenses may not be paid by an org while staff absent obtaining higher grades, 3:216

missionaire's expenses and how they will be issued by local FBOs, MS2:360

missionaire extravagance condoned by local FBO becomes expense of his own org, MS2:361

no exec or staff may be sent at org expense for processing, 0:174

org must obtain more potential than it spends, 0:53

policy for anyone advancing money or committing Flag to expenses without a Flag PO or FP, MS2:361–362

experience,

code of good conduct laid down out of experience of race, 0:455

leadership and, 0:122

lines and terminals (hats) outlined in policy are based on, 0:384

orders and, 0:122

policy and, 0:28, 0:112, 0:114, 0:116, 0:117, 0:118, 0:122

experiential track, suppressive persons have poor, 1:1009

expert(s), 5:798; *see also* **professional; specialist**

counter-intention and, 0:509

must be hatted and trained for org post, 0:202

post hats and, MS1:205, MS1:414

seeking to get own stats up at any cost, 7:489, MS3:469

expertise, obscures lack of full post hat, MS1:414

explaining Scientology, sell a book, 6:808

explanation, example, MS1:82

expulsion,

allowing out-ethics activities in course rooms and, 5:517

without recourse leads to desperation and revolt, 1:808

ex-staff members, right of appeal, 1:250

ex-student, has no recourse beyond refund, 1:1000, 4:92

Extension Course, 0:353

assuring then they will read and understand the books, it is necessary to get them into an extension course, 6:234

Extension Course, *(cont.)*

bookbuyers and, 2:280, 6:506

books and, 2:331

completion and certificates, 6:509

enrollment on, 6:511

exist so that anyone interested in learning the basics of Dianetics and Scientology may do so in his own home, 6:510

for old-timers, new people, professional students, bookbuyers and HAS students, etc., 6:510

goal and purpose of, 6:510

how they are designed, 6:510

how to give the students a more definite end of cycle and sense of accomplishment, 6:508

Extension Course, *(cont.)*

how to promote, 6:512

how to write, 6:502

introductory level on the Classification, Gradation and Awareness Chart, 6:510

procedure for handling lessons sent in, 6:505

special training books by correspondence, 2:338, 6:248

what it consists of, 6:511

Extension Course Director, certifications, student completes and, 5:321

extension course student, letters to, 6:504

exteriorization, remedies to stabilize pc after, 4:197

extortion, when charity is, 0:508

extraordinary solutions, lead to auditing failures, 4:671

F

fable, 7:1127

facilities,

    expansion planning of and org image, 6:607, MS3:141

    investing in service facilities, 0:564, 0:646

facility differential, defined, 7:343, MS3:323

fact(s), *see also* truth

    accepting incomplete cycles as complete, 0:66, 0:429

    always demand facts from junior, 0:241

    Convening Authority acts when it has the, 0:483

    definition, MS1:5

    inspection before the, 0:244

    opinions masquerading as, MS1:5

    penalty after the fact has occurred, 0:66

    seeing things that don't exist and reporting them as "fact," 0:514

factors,

    theory of VFPs and, MS1:296

    which govern production, MS1:226

Factors, The, 0:277, 0:297

fad, of "the other person doesn't matter," 0:301

failed cases, medically ill or injured, 5:623

failed purpose,

    all you have to do to restore life and action is to rekindle the failed purpose, MS2:428

    behind every stop there is a failed purpose, MS2:428

    remedy for, MS2:434

failure(s), fail,

    applying conditions without being hung up in past failures, 0:669

    bank says we must fail, 0:10

failure(s), *(cont.)*

    causes of, 0:53, 0:63, 0:95, MS1:286

    dev-t and, 0:393

    drawing up list of unsuccessful things, 0:651

    due to nonapplication of ethics, 0:660

    group failure began with lack of or loss of discipline, 0:450, 0:521

    how thetan fails and becomes weak, 0:51

    if we fail, it is improbable job will ever again be done, 0:239

    incorrect usage of be-do-have sequence and, 0:291

    orders occur where responsibility has failed, 0:139

    organization(s),

        causes of failures, 0:53, 0:63

        early orgs, why they crashed, 0:10

        robot orgs and civilizations fail, 0:82

    post failures, reason for most, 0:562

    real Why of any governing body failure when it is sincerely trying but failing is that it is operating on wrong Whys, 7:165

    Scientology failed in hands of non-Scientologists, 0:159

    sign of threatened failure in an org, 1:60

    students who can't even read a despatch, 0:302

    tech failure, effects of, 0:19

    those who are quite happy to have everything fail and go wrong with no protest from them, 0:237

    to organize, 0:88

    we only fail when we do not help, 0:84

    when all else fails, do what Ron said, 0:104

    why of, 7:431, MS2:225, MS3:411

    why we mustn't fail or permit others to, 0:239

fair exchange, 0:317–318

    fair play, justice and, 0:520

false attest(ation),

    Committee of Evidence for, 1:869

    examples of, pcs, 1:870–871

    false swearing on signed statement or form, 0:469

    hang them if it's a, 0:419

    never issuing anything falsely as it will be hidden or discredited, 0:351

    persons found guilty, penalty, 5:212

False Attestation Report, description, 0:544

false data,

    aberration and, 4:235, 6:306

    arbitrary and, 0:65

    buries itself as person may firmly believe that it is true, MS2:142

    can cause a hang-up on the Doubt Formula, 0:576–577, 1:606

    comes off in gradients, MS2:136

    do not continue past a point where the false datum has blown, MS2:141

    effectively block someone's understanding of true data, MS2:143

    handling for person who has false data on Scientology, 5:440

    handling for someone prone to accepting false data, MS2:138

    indicators of, MS2:135

    in some cases antagonism stems from, 5:439

    on tech of doing one's post and on what purpose of post is, 0:577

    overts and, MS2:137

    people whose estimate of the environment is totally perverted and, MS2:135

    phenomenon additional to misunderstood words, MS2:135

    primary reason people cannot be hatted, MS2:135

    procedure for False Data Stripping, MS2:138

    result of, MS2:137

    service facsimiles and, MS2:138

    sources of, MS2:135

    Straightwire and, MS2:138

    textbooks that reek with, MS2:135

    the less a person can confront, the more false data he has accumulated and will accumulate, MS2:137

    theory of, MS2:136

    verbal hatting is main source of, MS2:134

    what to do if person collides with more false data on a subject, MS2:141

False Data Stripping,

    Auditor's Code and, MS2:142

    Crashing Mis-U Finding and, MS2:141

    Date/Locate and, MS2:142

    end phenomena of, MS2:141

    must utilize basic workable texts in, MS2:135

    new students and, MS2:143

    on or off the meter, MS2:136

    overrun and, MS2:142

    procedure, MS2:138

    Repair List, when to use, MS2:143

    repeated as often as necessary until person is finally duplicating and is able to use correct tech, MS2:136

    repeated use of, MS2:142

    requirements for administering, MS2:136

    rudiments and, MS2:142

    solves problem of inability to hat or train, MS2:135

    who can do it, MS2:136

    Word Clearing and, MS2:142

false done(s),

    example of, MS1:136

    how to prevent, MS1:137

false evaluation(s),

    example of, MS1:136

    how to prevent, MS1:137

    penalty for, MS1:176

falsehood(s), 0:484; *see also* **false report; outpoint(s); pretense**

    contrary facts and, MS1:80

    definition, MS1:80

false perception(s),

    definition, 0:514

    one sees things that don't exist and reports as "fact," 1:541

false pretenses, obtaining loans or money under, 0:47

false reports, *see also* **false data; lie**

    acting on, 0:515

    basis of all troublesome third party activities, 1:540

    Committee of Evidence for, 1:869

    criminals and, 0:527

    dev-t and, 0:424

    Doubt condition assigned person who accepts and disciplines another unjustly on basis of, 0:515

    handling for, 0:549, 0:553

    in attempt to fend off wrath, 1:819

    injustice and, 0:520

false report(s), *(cont.)*

Instructor obscuring source of tech, 4:350, 5:840

Knowledge Reports, knowingly false statements made in, 0:557

lacking of skills with which to detect, 0:67

leaving, leaves and, 0:177

make penalties for false reports too gruesome to be faced and enforce them, 0:420

method of self-protection, 0:248

missions and, 7:825

only occur where ignorance of data or avoidance of orders occurs, 0:139

order of the day in society, 1:962

out-ethics indicator, 0:533

penalty, 4:1193, 5:289

personal security undermined by, 0:515

policy, 1:542

PR should counter with minimum documents or evidence, MS3:131

running back investigation by following chain of, 0:514

smoke screen for idleness or bad actions, 0:527

source of upset in area, 1:542

suppression by giving false reports on others, 0:513

target has been done, MS1:136

targets and, 0:146, 0:647, MS2:429

third party tech and, 0:513

where they are sometimes found to exist, 0:587

why does he false report instead of just doing the thing required? 7:824

willful and knowing false report, handling, 0:549, 0:553, 0:557

wog world and, 0:421

familiar(ity),

achieving apparency of, MS3:121

if one has no familiarity with how a scene (area) ought to be, MS1:29

with scene being handled, MS1:158

family, *see also* **second dynamic**

staff auditors auditing family and friends, 0:170

using best one knows of Scientology to help family, 0:160

fascism, led by and applied to idiots, 0:157

fast flow grades, cancelled, 5:255

fast flow hiring, MS2:109–110, MS2:260–261; *see also* **hiring; recruitment**

hatting and handling of personnel, MS1:311

recruitment and, MS1:310

fast flow system, 7:670

clay representations, must be done, 5:219

definition, 5:218

designation, 5:220

don't confuse with quick auditing, 4:937, 5:265

drug cases, handling, 5:220

example of how it works, 7:671

horizontal fast flow, 0:386

OIC system and, 5:133

pattern for handling particles, 1:971

principle of traffic flows, 1:661

statistics as indicators, 7:671

student,
defined, 5:476
examination and fast flow management system, 5:210
Method One Word Clearing and, 4:196
not fast flow, 5:219

system of management, 1:661, 5:132, MS2:59, MS2:241

training, definition of, 4:644

what it depends on, 0:660

fatigue, vitamin C and, 5:637

favor(s),

discourtesy, malice or threat in a request for, 0:488

letting org get ripped off for some personal favor, 0:534

no report cause for dismissal, 4:1244

policy concerning receiving favors from pcs not known or followed, results, 0:410

received by staff, 0:171, 1:729

unusual, 1:895

using org position to procure personal or non-Scientology funds or unusual favors, 0:471

FBI,

conduct of, 1:963

criminal mind and, 1:830

planned wholly on terrorism, 1:963

FBO, *see* **Flag Banking Officer(s) (FBOs)**

FCDC, *see* **Founding Church of Scientology of Washington**

FDA, *see* **Food and Drug Administration**

fear, afraid,

destructive acts, lies and, 0:455

of taking responsibility, 0:260

person secretly afraid of others will not hat them or hats them wrongly, 0:206

feature news shot, definition, 2:213; *see also* photograph(s)

FEBC, *see* Flag Executive Briefing Course

fee(s),

inter-org transfers and, 5:123

mission or field auditor may not charge less for services than Central Org, 3:151

Saint Hill Special Briefing Course retread fee, 3:153

seeking to charge for little services that should be free, 0:303

staff made to refund fees illegally received, 0:171

taking private fees while on staff to audit outside pcs, run private courses, coach or audit students or org pcs, 0:471

feeder line, lower level, healing, 4:864

Felis Domesticus, 0:39

Fellow of Scientology,

definition, 5:326

issued by LRH for contribution to knowledge of Scientology, 5:318

field, *see also* public

ARC breaks and, 0:498

ARC broken with the org, time-honored way of handling, 2:677, 6:554

Central Files and what contributes to a messed-up field, 2:677, 6:554

ethics and, 1:796, 6:724

getting failed cases in field in for Review, 0:352

handling of traffic from new field, 0:129

make your posts or post real to, 0:166

never ask anyone in field to decide or choose, 1:125

organizational prosperity is dependent on success of Public Divisions in building an enormous, active field, 6:108

org has to service the, 0:685

Public Divisions keep the whole field alive, 6:109

working out org in relation to field and public in clay, 0:415

field auditor(s), *see also* Auditors Association

field auditing, ethical standards of, 6:697

acceptance of appointment as field staff member, 6:629, 6:630

auditing alone, result, 6:718

basic hats he would have to wear, 6:717

Blue Seal rating for, 5:312

bringing order and key rehabilitation process, 6:694

field auditor(s), *(cont.)*

can be a field staff member to more than one org but is actually on the staff of the nearest org to his address, 6:636

Central Orgs vs., 0:273

definition, 2:391, 7:271

Dianetic Counseling Group is solution to being a one-man band, 6:717

D of P to teach them HGC routines, 5:831

fees, 6:715, 6:734

get them back on staff, 5:834

goodwill of, 6:726

HCO campaign regarding, 6:699

HGC pcs and, 1:190

included wholly into the general activity, 6:833

may charge more for services than the Central Org, 2:410, 2:417, 6:706, 6:709

may not charge less for services than the Central Org, 2:410, 2:417, 3:151

may not run Power Processing or AO Class VIII rundowns, 6:723

may teach PE Course, 4:184

no staff of church should refer any person to any field auditor anywhere, 2:385, 6:685

organization, forbidden to release in whole or in part any mailing list of Dianetics and Scientology, 6:696

organizing or allowing gathering or meeting to protest orders of a senior, 0:471

orgs and missions, cooperation between, 6:579

policies on physical healing, insanity and sources of trouble, 6:711

practicing around Saint Hill, 6:708

prices and, 6:369

proper procedure in being requested to heal physical disability, 6:711

responsibility for keeping themselves informed of current charges, 2:417, 6:709

rights, 6:733

route for training, 5:528

single Scientology practitioners, problems of, 0:334

starting a group blows disorder out of society, 6:693

steps to follow for Scientology to go well in an area, 6:693

supposed to charge the same as the organization, 2:417

with a private practice who wishes to retain it should advise his Public Executive Secretary of the nearest official org and explain why, 6:635

field centers, established with Saint Hill graduates, 5:337

Field Control Division,
checklist for quality, 6:877
functions of, 6:109

Field Control Secretary, promotional actions, 6:72

field staff member(s),
are to demand org services, 6:674
awards,
should only consist of courses, never auditing, 2:474
to orgs or missions from Saint Hill, 3:360
to persons not org or mission connected, 3:360
book sales and, 6:633
call-in and, 2:647, 3:223, 4:282, 7:871
Central Org, city office or pioneer office, that is, any official org in Scientology that is part of the Central Org system is a field staff member of Saint Hill and may select students and preclears for Saint Hill, 6:642
collecting outstanding notes, 0:349
comes under the same discipline as any other org staff member and is subject to the same codes of ethics, 6:634
commissions,
disbursement of, 3:255
discounted or cut-rate items, MS1:212
do not depend upon administrative facts but upon actual presence of student or pc in org taking service and directed there by the field staff member, 3:256
count as admin personnel, 0:95
definition, 7:271
Dir Disbursements responsible for administration and orderliness of FSM Account, 3:264
eligible person may become a field staff member, 6:643
files and, 6:668–669
FSM Account checks are exempt from once a week check-signing rule, 3:279
making them financially successful, 0:354
must not place any lists in the hands of, 2:706
newsletter to, 0:99
no field staff member who selects a person for training or processing may remain unpaid, 3:256
org must not place any lists in hands of, 0:626
payment line should be dummy run, 3:266
persons of SP group membership or declared SP may not be, 2:434
person who has done services at a Saint Hill, an AO or the Flag Service Org is appointed one, 6:635–636

field staff member(s), *(cont.)*
PES and, 0:99
policy on payment of commissions, 3:254
procedure for paying commissions, 3:254, 3:265
program, 6:649
promote and select people for authorized specials that they can receive commissions for, 3:261
promotional actions regarding, 0:354
provisional, 6:631
purpose, 6:630
selects a person to be trained or processed after direct personal contact with the person and issues to that person a paper stating the contacted person has been selected, 6:631
supplied with book lists and org rate card, 6:633
system will recruit you new general staff members which you'll be needing regularly as you grow, 6:639
two different lines: one to selectees, one to names sent in, 6:654
Field Staff Member I/C, 3:255, 6:646
appointed at Flag, in each FOLO and in all orgs, 6:670
Dir Disbursements must keep FSM I/C informed whenever a refund or repayment is paid, 6:664
settles any dispute claims from field staff members, 6:634
fight, third party must exist and develop it, 1:535
file(s), filing,
accuracy of, MS2:101
best to file many things under projects rather than company names, 3:287
bills, credit rating and correct payment comes from, MS2:47
cause of more downfalls than desks and quarters and sometimes even personnel, MS2:46
Central Files, *see* Central Files
complete files, why you must have them, 2:54
definition of Central Files folder, 2:704, 6:713, 7:482, MS1:372, MS2:198, MS2:303, MS3:462
divisional, definition of, MS2:47
earliest date at the bottom, progressing towards the latest date at the top, 2:398
Esto responsible for organizing, establishing and maintaining files even when there is a Files I/C, MS2:48
ethics action taken on finding a misfiled particle, MS2:101
Ethics Files, *see* Ethics Files
ethics, *see* ethics files
examples of misuse, MS2:46
exceptions to CF no-retirement policy, 2:704, 6:713
failing to file or removing Knowledge Reports from, 0:557
financially vital to an org, MS2:47

file(s), *(cont.)*

full of experience MS1:166

handling and use of, 0:306–307, 0:310

hot files,

handling of, 2:390

should be identified very easily, 2:398

Inspection Officer reports in, 1:191

items get misfiled for four reasons, MS2:101

location of, MS2:48

longevity due to file keeping, 0:67

memory and, MS2:48

mimeo file folder prepared, 1:442

nebulous issues, how to file, 1:192

never record before you file, 3:387

non-current files should be cleaned out and filed in dead storage, 3:392

of staff member reports, 0:545, 0:554

personnel, *see* personnel files

personnel have to know their alphabet forwards and backwards, MS2:47

person's name, file by, 1:191

PL and HCOB files almost totally monitor training and processing and admin quality, MS2:47

prefile boxes, 2:398

purchase orders, 3:293

Registrar and, 2:388

remedies for misfiling, MS2:101

staff,

file is closed out, 1:192

transfer, folder is shifted to new post, 1:192

state of HCO files is responsibility of HCO Communicator, 1:391

steps of organizing, MS2:47

systems whereby "certain files are held out" should be discouraged, 2:424

there are no "miscellaneous files," MS2:47

valuable to an org, MS2:48

file folder, ARC triangle and, 2:601

file system, used by HCO offices, 7:1162–1163

fill the vacuum,

black PR campaign handling, MS3:81

handle black PR campaign by continuing to, MS3:87

right answer to proving a negative rumor, MS3:83

film(s), *see also* **Technical Training Films**

abuse of and penalties, 4:529, 5:818, 6:346

designation of, 4:529, 6:346

distribution of, 5:818

general public showing, 5:816

film(s), *(cont.)*

glossaries must be provided for each film, 4:529, 5:818, 6:345

instruction, when may be viewed, 5:820

introductory films and tapes are a MUST for proper public information, 2:374, 6:341, 7:1215

may not run halfway through, 5:821

points that should be understood, 2:374, 6:341

policies on usage, 4:526, 5:815

policies set to govern the use and exhibition of general public films, 4:528, 6:344

policies to enable students to view Technical Training Films in an environment conducive to study, 4:526, 6:343

showing technical training films, 5:815

to cease to use tapes and films for fear of misunderstood words is a fatal decision, 2:374, 6:341, 7:1215

violations and penalties as covered in licensing and leasing agreements, 4:538, 6:348

final target(s), *see also* **evaluation(s)**

attachment for, MS1:134

list of, MS1:132

finance, *see also* **financial management; financial planning**

actions that are vital to PRO in an org, 3:70

anyone who permits, neglects or forwards financial irregularities with org finances is, to put it very mildly, tampering with his own future, 3:97

bank accounts and, 3:110

basic financial policy, 3:21

becomes org management only where it ceases to handle finance as a commodity like beans and where org managers themselves fail to grasp and understand financial realities, MS2:342

best understood as a commodity in terms of beans, MS2:339

changing workable finance systems, 3:95

credit unions, 0:693

D of P and, 4:961

don't leave enemy financed and solvent while friends starve, 0:633

effectiveness of financial control and what it depends on in orgs, 3:278, MS2:346

exec and, 0:372, 0:374

exec does want finance matters on his lines, 7:604

finance units frowning on new demand expenses, 0:130

first financial policy is income is more important than disbursement, 3:72

first rule is income greater than outgo, MS2:339

finance, *(cont.)*

governing policy, MS2:353

greater loss is income lost or never made, MS2:342

greater the income, the greater opportunity for this banker (FBO) to loan (invest in FP) for more service capacity, MS2:394

HCO office and, 7:1162

how to handle, 3:26–27, 7:924–925

image and, 0:339, 0:340

invoice line, 0:282

issuing of Finance Directives cancelled, 3:77

loss by illegal discounts or giving away services or materials, handling, 0:303

money problems answered by making lots of money, 3:26–27, 7:924–925

odd financial deals, 0:693

offenses concerning, 0:467, 0:468

only properly issued policy letters are to be followed in finance matters, 3:77

org monies misdirected in this life could very well guarantee a very nasty next, 3:98

org personnel may not solicit payments from staff or public on behalf of others, MS2:327

penalty for OES, Treas Sec, Flag Banking Officer or any Div 3 member not done the Finance Course pack star-rate, 3:68

penalty for terminal who does not comm ev an individual staff member who discounted or gave away services or materials, 3:93

people put on the finance special post ONLY handle the subjects of finance emergency, 3:85

policies, 3:244, 7:834

programs and, 0:702

PTS or chronically ill or NCG and finance lines, MS1:460, MS2:251

purchasing liability of staff, 0:183

question that must be answered before one can adjust or arrange finance or any org board, 0:292

reason for change of status of HCO Continental Sec and Continental Director, 7:47

reason for troubles is dropping the 25-hour intensive, 2:446

reason why staff pay got so undermined, 3:96, MS2:372

Registrars may not discuss, 2:426

saving money on paper, postage and printing, 3:269

second interest is financial, being most direct index of whether or not promotion is reaching people, 7:1176

security, how it is obtained, 7:834

finance, *(cont.)*

seeking extraordinary solutions for, outside Scientology is sign of poor management, 3:125, 4:173, 7:931

stable data, 3:46

stress,
compartmenting off the financial stress works only if the rest of the org flat out DELIVERS and produces in every division to do so, 3:86

how to handle in an org, 3:85, 7:724

summary of key terms used regarding Church of Scientology finances, MS2:350

trouble in an org comes from undermanning, undertraining and underproducing, MS1:392

unshakeable policy that no person who is PTS or chronically ill or who gets no case gain may be on Finance or Registrar lines or in top command posts, MS2:354

what causes financial emergencies to occur, 3:129

when an org is dealing with this society, it can go as far as it has financial resources, 3:98

where finance lines were very sour a PTS person was on those lines, MS2:355

why marketing, books, recorded LRH lectures, other audiovisual properties, films, insignia, meters and related items are in the FBO Network, MS2:395

Finance Office,

immediate seniors, MS2:333

org board location, MS2:332

Finance Secretary, 0:171

finance systems, changing workable finance systems, 3:95, MS2:371

financial control, make all the money you can, spend less than that, 3:246

financial emergency, test entire staff for knowingness and control, 1:185

financial irregularity,

financial loss occasioned by illegal discounts or giving away services or materials shall be recompensed to the org by the guilty individual, 3:93

when one uses an org for personal rip-off, he is cutting his own throat, 3:97

financial management, *see also* **finance**

basic principle of, 7:926

control point must be on purchasing and contracting, not on paying bills, 3:29, 7:927

drill for financial manager, 3:30, 7:928

guaranteeing the survival of the organization within the economic framework of the society, 3:30, 7:928

guarantees solvency, 3:20

hat of, 7:926

financial management, *(cont.)*

hat worn by, 3:20

manager must be tough and learn how to say no, 3:30, 7:928

must be real, 3:30, 7:928

must help general dissemination by maintaining good credit, 3:245

purpose of, 3:20, 3:28

who done by, 3:28

financial planning (FP), *see also* **finance**

actions for, 3:272, MS2:410

action taken, 3:298

added to the line is FBO's prepared statement of summarized income sources, MS2:328

additions to FP Program No. 1, MS2:423

Bank Reconciliation Section and, 3:274, MS2:412

carefully planned and results, MS2:419

checklists for promotional actions,
Dissem Sec, 3:80
Estates Branch, 3:84
Field Control Sec, 3:84
HCO Area Sec, 3:80
Public Contact Sec, 3:82
Public Servicing Sec, 3:83
Qual Sec, 3:82
Tech Sec, 3:80
Treasury Sec, 3:80

Collections Section submits Income Note Collections Summary, MS2:412

data required for, 3:273, MS2:411

definition, 3:271, MS2:406, MS2:409

Dept of Disbursements receives, 3:298

Disbursement Section furnishes data without which financial planning is impossible, 3:273, MS2:411,

Exec Council sees that pricing is not too high and not too low, 0:355–356

Executive Council action, 3:275, 7:910, 7:913, MS2:413

Executive Council responsibility, MS2:407

FBO is final approval authority for org's FP, MS2:407

five conditions that make FP very easy, MS2:319

FP line, MS2:322

gives you your make-break point in an org, MS2:416

having to have before they can do, 0:427

how one uses the funds one has to keep things running well and make more income, MS2:342

how to use FP Program No. 1, MS2:422

financial planning (FP), *(cont.)*

income note collections summary, 3:274

is "how do we stay solvent?" MS2:364

know finance pack, MS2:319

monitoring point in FBO's judgment of how much to give the org for FP, MS2:373

necessity and, 3:295

neglecting necessities, MS2:320

object, orientation and action of, 3:295

on investigation what FP troubles trace to, MS2:402

operates to create and maintain viability, 3:295

planning hat worn by Executive Council, 3:271, MS2:409

procedure, MS2:407

produce as an activity, MS2:319

property renovations, construction and, 3:281, 7:961

schedule, 3:272, MS2:410

separate out different types of expenditure, MS2:319

thrown out by presenting isolated checks for signature, 3:317

two rules regarding renovations and construction, 7:961

unusual pay arrangements, 1:169

using FP to neglect duty, handling, MS2:321

valuable tool that determines the "course" of your org, MS2:423

wages for new staff, 1:163

what the organization has to first assess, MS2:419

where complete org officer system exists FP can be delegated to them to do, MS2:407

findings,

definition, 1:929

of court or Comm Ev, 0:495, 0:523

fine,

for losing a key, 0:184

mission found processing any org pc within 2 years of pc's last service, 3:174

not acceptable amends, 0:546

not fined for committing an error, 0:467

one week's pay, 0:661

only way to fine or reduce pay of staff member, 0:358

finishing, definition, MS3:194

fireball,

definition, MS2:61, MS2:243

how to make, MS2:62, MS2:244

firm(s), try not to deal with firms who fail to send correct statements, 3:294; *see also* **company**

first dynamic, *see also* **self**

material in HCOBs applies to, 0:55

most wrong person can be on the, 0:453

"nothing to do with me" attitude, 0:555

Power Formula for the, 0:645

wrecking first and second by abandoning third, 0:301

First Dynamic Danger Formula, First Dynamic Formula, *see also* **Danger**

assigning each individual connected with Danger condition a, 0:585, 0:605

Ethics investigation on person who does not follow formula completely, 0:605

example of, MS2:209

if person refusing to follow, HCO moves in with full investigation and takes action per what it finds, MS2:210

junior and, 0:606

Senior Danger Formula and, 0:612

steps of, 0:606, 0:612, 0:615–616, MS2:206

sucking in a bypass from not applying, 0:581

Trouble Area Questionnaire, 0:607–608

Trouble Area Short Form, 0:606–609

use of, 0:612

first dynamic tech, 0:55–56

first phenomenon, definition, 4:330

first policy, maintain friendly relations with the environment and public, 3:260, 6:589, 7:20

Fitness Board, 0:524

fixating, total effect and, 0:231

fixed consumption,

definition, 7:507

example of, 7:507

only sure way to proceed, 7:509

fixed idea,

being used to handle all downstat situations in one's life, 0:682

definition, MS1:32–33

example of, MS1:32

method of handling a down stat, 7:400, MS3:380

reason a fixed idea can get so rooted, MS1:33

fixed income scene, Why for, 4:407, 6:398

Flag Banking Officer(s) (FBOs), *see also* **D/FBO for MORE**

abilities, MS2:344

allocation-production ratio statistic of, MS2:403

appeal line, MS2:402

basic duties, MS2:322

be prepared to take action of the strongest kind when he finds stocks missing, MS2:382

chief concerns, MS2:338

Flag Banking Officer(s), *(cont.)*

collection of bounced check procedure, MS2:326

duties, MS2:333

ensures all income is properly and legibly invoiced by the org, MS2:325

final FP authority, MS2:329

finance office representative in every bureau, Continental Liaison Office and every org, SO and Scn, MS2:317

FP activation and, 3:299

income,

collected on which service is undelivered is really unearned income, MS2:373

demand and tracing and summarizing of present and past income sources, MS2:328

increased allocation-production ratio concern of, MS2:329

know HOW an org makes money and keeps its reputation with excellent delivery, MS2:344

know policy expertise used in making money, MS2:344

know that lack of Word Clearing and hatting will make a financially irresponsible org, MS2:345

located on org board in Dept 21, MS2:317

maintains second bank account for transfers of money for International Management expenses, MS2:322

must see that Word Clearing on all finance policies occurs both in himself and in the org, MS2:345

not let org run on unearned income, MS2:373

org cash collections and, MS2:322

procedure for handling bounced checks, MS2:325

products, MS2:332

purposes, MS2:333, MS2:344

safeguards incoming monies, MS2:325

sees to the org's solvency by ensuring income is greater than outgo, 7:878

service capacity utilized is the depository for an FBO, MS2:394

solvency of orgs and areas and, MS2:318

spends money out of FBO No. 1 Account, only transfer checks are drawn on it, MS2:323

statistics, MS2:318, MS2:333

what must be known about orgs in order to wisely allocate funds, MS2:340

what the FBO pays from his own funds, MS2:318

when office established, procedure followed, MS2:317

Flag Banking Officer local expense, definition, MS2:353

Flag Bureaux, Flag, FB,

actions are not piecemeal, but directed at whole orgs, MS2:282

big, broad situations are spotted and the Whys found, 7:419, MS3:399

definition, MS2:350, MS2:351

international Whys applying to all orgs and, 7:425, MS3:405

issues,
Flag Bureaux Data Letter (FBDL), definition, 7:1324
Flag Conditions Order (FCO), definition, 7:1324
Flag Divisional Directive (FDD), definition, 7:1324
Flag Mission Order (FMO), definition, 7:1324
Flag Order (FO), definition, 7:1323
Flag Personnel Order (FPO), definition, 7:1324
Flag Program Order (FPGMO), definition, 7:1324
Flag Project Order (FPJO), definition, 7:1324

make Flag planning become an actuality in orgs, MS3:397

plans and makes projects for type of org or all orgs and for applications of orgs to various publics, MS3:399

Flag Bureaux Data Letter (FBDL),

definition, 1:431

description, 0:724

seniority of, 0:143

Flag Command Bureaux, definition, MS2:351

Flag Command Bureaux News Letter, description, 0:724

Flag Conditions Order (FCO),

definition, 1:431

description, 0:724

Flag Divisional Directive (FDD),

definition, 1:431

description, 0:724

HCO PLs or LRH EDs vs., 0:304

Flag Executive Briefing Course (FEBC),

curriculum, 5:521

graduate is expected to, 5:523

intention of, 5:521

nominated future execs required to take, 5:521

provisional certificates and, 5:527

recall of, 5:523

student, validation of certificate, 5:527

trained on, vs. those not trained, MS1:401

Flag External,

in no event will external Flag bills be cash reimbursed, MS2:361

revised policies governing externally incurred Flag bills, MS2:360

Flag Field Staff Member (FSM),

may present his selectee to a Registrar of a Flag or FOLO Tours when it appears in his area for final regging and payment of the donation, 6:662

may take his selectee to a Flag Service Consultant (FSC) in a Flag Operations Liaison Office (FOLO) or to the CO or Purser of a FOLO for final regging and payment of a donation, 6:662

Flag Mission Order (FMO),

definition, 1:431

description, 0:724

Flag operated tour, that signs up prospects is another form of a remote Flag Reg, 6:662

Flag Operations Liaison Office, definition, MS2:351

Flag Order (FO),

definition, 1:430

description, 0:725

Flag Personnel Order (FPO),

definition, 1:431

description, 0:725

Flag Program Order (FPGMO),

definition, 1:431

description, 0:725

Flag Project Order (FPJO),

definition, 1:431

description, 0:725

Flag Representative (Flag Rep, FR),

can get eval in in org without reference to the ED/CO, 7:292

communication and command lines, 7:1407

compliances and, 7:1414

conferences and, 7:1410

does the actual staff contacts and sees that they comply with the target that applies, 7:1416

duty to enhance image of Flag, 7:1408

ethics,
justice and ethics actions taken on, 7:1412
powers of, 7:1413

have to be able to observe, 7:720

investigation requests and, 7:1410

lack of, shortens reach of Pgms Chf to three feet instead of several thousand miles, 7:292

line for evaluation request, 7:1418

may call for a mission, 7:1410, 7:1417

observation is key ingredient of, 7:1408, 7:1411

orders to, 7:1416

org checklists and inspections, 7:1407

penalty for stopping the communication of, 1:902

Flag Representative, *(cont.)*

plans and makes projects for type of org or all orgs and for applications of orgs to various publics, 7:419

production program and, MS1:170

purpose, 7:1407, 7:1412

reports, what they should consist of, 7:1413

responsible for enhancing Flag's PR, 7:1408

routine line for orders, 7:1416

seniority of, 7:1412

short-term organization and, MS1:172

statistic, 7:1409, 7:1414, 7:1419, 7:1421

verify reports of dones or get dones done, 7:479, MS2:195, MS2:300, MS3:459

Flag Service Organization, Flag, FSO,

continued expansion wholly depends upon all lower orgs sending more and more public up the Bridge, 6:127

definition, MS2:351

nearest service org to Flag and International management for financial support, MS2:349

Power condition and, 0:645

quantity, quality and viability of Flag training, 0:290

word of mouth, PR and, 0:333

Flag Ship Order (FSO),

definition, 1:431

description, 0:725

flap(s), see also **enturbulation; upset**

causes of, 0:261;

definition, 4:140

staff, having produced poorly or poor quality of basic product, then invites a flap, 7:520

flat ball bearings,

Dept of Correction quickly repairs any, 5:45

handled by Review, 1:971

Qual Div handles, 5:36

quickly repairing any, 0:351

Review gets, 5:52

flattery, not very useful, MS3:35

flaw, basic flaw in organization, 0:66

flier(s),

become an altered importance for Div 2s, and an unusual and costly solution to get gross income up, MS2:358

definition, MS3:293

doesn't have to teach anything, merely creates want, MS3:293

Letter Reg and Publications Shipping Unit are users of fliers, MS3:293

not handed out in streets, MS3:293

offers product, describes it, says how to get it,

flier(s), *(cont.)*

pictures it and hard sells it, MS3:293

reason one produces fliers, MS3:294

shipped out regularly to Scientologists and book buyers, 0:349

stacks made available in cases in Reception, MS3:293

flourish and prosper, 7:1154

how to really flourish and prosper, 0:318

flow(s)(ing), *see also* **Bridge flow; channel; flow line**

agreement is needed to have a, 0:325

anything which stops or delays flows of a business is an enemy, 0:275

communication flowing correctly, 0:196

conditions flow one to next, 0:680

confusion defined as unpatterned flow, 0:106

consists of a number of individual routes, each of which must be known by Public Divisions staff if they are to accomplish their purpose of moving people up the Bridge, 6:121

copy of flow line that travels up hierarchy of service orgs, 6:121

difference between order and chaos, 0:389

example, 6:204

exchange flows of org messed up, 0:526

flow items, things undergoing change, 0:106

FSO and Bridge flow, 6:106–107

if body and despatch lines flow, org will prosper, 0:385

independent, unagreed-upon decision points and, 0:325

individual decision not laid out by policy stops the, 0:325

justice is one of guards that keeps channel of progress a channel and not stopped flow, 0:480

making channels on which things can flow, 0:389

necessity of stable points which do not flow in order to handle things which do flow, 0:106

organizing board and, 0:106, 0:107, 0:108

perpetual combination of, MS1:196

pointing out channels on which bodies, materials, products or despatches and letters flow, 0:389

policy establishes points of agreement that permit flows of traffic, 0:475

random choices stopping the, 0:325

rapidity of particle flow alone determines power, 0:325, 0:432, 1:127

role of upper orgs in Bridge flow, 6:105

flow(s)(ing), *(cont.)*

speed of particle flow, 0:66, 0:275, 0:325, 0:432

stable items vs. flow items in org, 0:106

takes a lot of counter-effort to jam org's, 0:587

visualize sequence of, MS1:196

why an org won't flow traffic when policy is out or not formed, 0:325, 1:126

work out by dummy run, 1:63

flow chart, 0:200, *see also* **organizing board**

flow line(s), *see also* **channel; communication line; flow; line; route**

any policy, agreed upon, is better than points of individual decision on, 0:325

example, 2:82

green staff is unaware of, 0:384

HCO and, 1:58

horizontal fast flow, 0:386

if wrong, executive will never be a product officer but only a comm clerk, MS2:58, MS2:240

isolating and eradicating stops on, 0:275

space planning and, 7:1336

which way they should be made to operate, MS2:349

flub, solution to a flubbing staff member, MS1:376, MS2:312,

F/N VGI session at the Examiner,

definition of, 4:1122

if drops from 90 percent, overhaul, 5:691

remedy for low, 5:93

FO, *see* **Flag Order**

folder(s),

analysing, 4:1103

Clearing Course folders, 4:794

Clearing Course submission of, 4:790

C/Sing or auditing without folder study, 4:1117

double folder danger, 4:1103

ethics folder, 0:545–546, 0:552

example of, 4:1010

firm rule is C/S only with all folders to hand, 4:1103

hat folder, *see* hat folder

HGC Admin handling of, 4:1061

high crime for C/S not to write in preclear's folder what case supervised instructions are, 4:1102

it now becomes a LIABILITY to have out-admin in pcs' folders, 4:1105

loss of or omissions in, Comm Ev offense, 4:1195

folder(s),

may only be two numbered series of folders for any pc or pre-OT, 4:1011

most common omissions in, 4:1194

must be marked, 4:1059

mustn't get too fat, 4:1011

NED for OTs, 4:812

new folders, how to make and numbering of, 4:1011

old and those of pcs not currently on auditing lines are carefully preserved in secure storage rooms, in alphabetical order, 4:1012

omissions in, 4:1194, 5:802

provided for each pc, 4:1010

reviewing, 4:1104

student, what it consists of, 4:468

three,
classes of, 0:194
types of, 1:271

Folder Error Summary(ies),

can be sold directly or removed from hours bought, 4:1008

cost of, 4:1007

credited on auditor's stat, 4:1188

done by students, especially interns well taught, learning practical tech or auditors, 4:1007

has value and is valuable to the pc to get one done, 4:1008

usefulness and when used, 4:1007

Folder Pages, importance of, 4:1194, 5:802

folding, definition, MS3:194

FOLO FSC, commissions and, 6:663

Food and Drug Administration, 0:410, 0:485

foot traffic, org relocated where there is lots of, 0:356

force(s),

channeling of, 0:63

ethics presence and, 0:247

freeing a society from things you see wrong with it and using force to demand it do what is right, 0:630

is dependent upon ARC, 0:247

physical universe forces can be channeled and used only with tech, 0:63

real force is dependent upon ARC, 7:707

used in order to expand, 0:124–125

used only to shut down false anti-demand factors, 0:127

foresight,

heavy traffic warnings and, 0:380

policy and, 0:117

to make stats go up, 0:683

form(s), supplies of organizational forms kept and stored ready for issue, 3:380

form letters, letters sent out are to be individual letters, 2:606

Former Release Check, described, 5:33

forming org(s), 0:95

field staff members and, 6:635

formula(s),

communication formula, 0:45–46

for expansion, 7:661

Formula of Policy, 7:665

short and long application of conditions formulas, 7:562

to apply when being knocked about by one's lines, bad news, disasters and feeling PTS, 0:420–421

why some people never really get on post, 1:590

formula evasion, 0:425

Foundation Bulletins, description, 0:725

Foundation organization,

accounting functions for both Day and Foundation are handled by the Day org, 3:172, 7:317

advertising and, 6:213

bank accounts, Day vs. Foundation, 7:317

comm stations, 7:301

Day and Foundation orgs,
have their own staffs, 7:314
stats are kept and computed separately, 7:314

definition used to determine income of, 3:171, 7:316

does its own collections, 3:172, 7:317

during Foundation hours Foundation org personnel have full possession and use of org premises and facilities, 7:313

Estos and, MS2:9

financial planning kept separate from Day org, 7:317

for ease of recognition invoices are additionally marked with large "F" letter, 3:171

FP *must* be kept separate, 3:172

hats which are doubles, 7:298

HCO Book Account sales counted as stat of the org that makes the sale regardless of whether person is on Day or Foundation lines, 3:171, 7:316

hours of the org, 7:313

invoicing and invoice machines for, 7:316

Foundation organization, *(cont.)*

minimum posts to be filled, 7:298

not under the Day org, 7:313

only one set of bank accounts for Day and Foundation and all income is banked in these accounts, 3:172

purpose, 7:297

ratio for posting of staff, 7:300

responsibility for handling lights for the Foundation, 7:311

schedules and use of personnel from any division doubled in technical, 7:308

second org board is posted for, 7:298

separate invoice machines, one for the Day org and one for Foundation, 3:171

services,
delivered to public, 7:297
provided to the Day org's staff members, 7:312

size of, 7:312

staff obtain their services in the Day org, 7:312

staff study and, 0:222

statistic belongs to that org, Day or Fdn, whose production it measures or reflects, 7:314

steps to inspect and debug income and service, 7:309

until Foundation warrants CF Officer and Address In-Charge, Day Org CF Officer and Address In-Charge to cater for Foundation posts as well as Day posts, 2:670

what success depends on, 7:297

will get and keep students only if run on tightly timed schedule, 6:484

Founder, title formed and Executive Director title resigned, 7:1206

Founding Church of Scientology of Washington (FCDC),

list of departments of, 7:178

purposes of various posts and departments, 7:190

Founding Church Policy Letter, description, 0:725

Founding Scientologist,

certificate, 2:420, 5:335

right to auditing, 4:170

right to use processes up to and including Class IV if trained before 1964, 4:180

what it entitles one to, 4:171, 4:177

Found Report, description, 0:543

Four Seasons of Manuela, 0:629

FP, *see* **financial planning**

FPRD, refusal to deliver, 1:915

France,

cause of their decline, 0:505

revolt and, 0:631

fraud,

definition, 0:296

exchange and, MS1:295

Free Auditing Check, blown students and pcs and, 4:271, 6:552

freedom, free(d)(ing),

being free of capricious punishment, dismissal by rumor and constant post change, 0:481

criminally inclined desire a society in which criminal is free to do as he pleases, 0:480

depends on ability, 0:140

does not mean freedom to injure man, 0:461

don't stand in road of, 0:462

evil intentions being hidden under protection of, 0:462

for honest people, 1:481

freeing,

man or society, results of, 0:462, 0:629–630

of things is the reverse unstated dramatization to the slavery enjoined by the mechanisms of the mind, MS3:356

getting out of labyrinth, 0:21

government by riot and intimidation finds rising crime rate and sinking freedom, 0:481

honesty and, 0:461–462

how setting people free is done, 0:90

individual,

freed of aberrations reacts more decently, 0:158

rights, liberties and, 0:461–462

keep people on route and they will be, 0:21

last free men and women on Earth, 0:85

last time night's curtain began to fall on, 0:85

man cannot be free while there are those amongst him who are slaves to their own terrors, 0:461

must be something to free men *into,* 0:629–630

no humanoid is free while aberrated in body cycle, 0:623

object is totally freed customers, 0:91

of speech does not mean freedom to harm by lies, 0:461

one of the buttons that gets us forward, MS2:439

only individuals in this universe capable of freeing man, 0:154

orgs are in business of setting people free, 0:90

politics, freedom from, 0:159

reverse unstated dramatization to the slavery enjoined by the mechanisms of the mind, 7:376

freedom, *(cont.)*

Scientology,

brings total freedom, 0:660

for a free people, 0:159

supporting freedom of religion, 0:160

suppose Scientology could really free men from pain and suffering, 0:153

unless there is something to free men into, the act of freeing is simply a protest of slavery, 7:376, MS3:357

US Constitution and freedom of speech, 0:68

we can stand in sun only so long as we do not let deeds of others bring darkness, 0:462

we're in business of going free, 0:503

when we will bring it to this planet, 0:140

working for freedom of speech, 0:160

Freedom, description, 0:715

Freedom Release, ability gained, 4:191

freeloader(s), 0:104

account of person who went to higher org without handling his contract, 1:256

Accounts compiles the list of, 1:255

certs and awards are suspended, 1:256

contract breakers and, 3:194

definition, 1:255

ineligible for further services at any org until corrected their overt, 1:255

list, 3:194

retroactive as far back as org has any record, 1:255

specifics composed of, 1:255

not acceptable back on lines without permission of Continental Justice Chief and Int Justice Chief, 3:195

statements, 1:255

technical posts and, 1:248

free membership, *see* **membership,** 6:815

program, 0:354

free pass, if pc presents a letter from me for a former Release check, 4:1066

Free Release Check, 5:120

Free Scientology Center auditors are deputized as, 6:478

groups and commissions, 6:847

invoicing of, 3:162

is not paid by the FOLO but by Flag on the arrival of the selectee at Flag per FSM policy, 6:662

list of steps that lead up to need of org services and how they are utilized, 6:673

may be requested by the Department of Income to collect overdue accounts on which 10 percent commission of any sums collected will be paid by the org, 6:636

Free Release Check, *(cont.)*

no field staff member who selects a person for training or processing may remain unpaid, 6:647

on the arrival of the selectee at the Flag Service Org for service, the FSM will receive, direct from Flag, without fail, 10 percent of the donation, 6:662

open letter to all FSMs, 6:673

Free Scientology Center,

auditors deputized as deputy field staff members, 6:478

is the student clinic, 6:328

when open, 4:676, 6:328

Free Scientology Center Registrar, 0:350, 4:676, 6:328

route into org in Div 6, 4:683

source of pcs for student auditors and interns, 4:683

student clinic, 4:676

free service(s),

exchange in abundance is not, 0:317

giving away services or materials, 0:303

result of giving, 3:159

seeking to charge for services that should be free, 0:303

Freud libido theory,

libido theory (1894), MS3:3, 6:620

Freud, Sigmund, 2:332, 6:235

developed psychoanalysis, 4:919

friend(s),

deciding who are one's friends, 0:574

don't leave enemy financed and solvent while friends starve, 0:633

empowering your, 0:637

info packets being sent to, 0:352

knowing your friends vs. your enemies, 0:89

man who breaks faith with, 0:454

people tend to believe their, 0:333

selling out one's, 0:534

staff auditors auditing family and, 0:170

survival and, 0:455

using Scientology to help friends, 0:160

friendliness, goodwill and, 0:332, 0:333

FSM, *see* **field staff member(s)**

FSM Account, *see also* **field staff member(s); FSM awards**

checks are exempt from once a week check-signing rule, MS2:347

established to make it easy to pay out FSM commissions instantly, 3:264, 6:667

how the line is run, 6:668

how to set up, 3:264

FSM Account, *(cont.)*

not included on the "cash" of the cash-bills stat, 3:264

replenishing the account, 3:264, 6:667,

set-up for, 6:667

signatories, 3:264, 6:667

FSM awards, *see also* **field staff member(s); FSM Account**

no one may claim an award or bonus or contest prize by reason of multiple missions or multiple orgs or several individuals, 6:659

who they are paid to, 6:659

FSM commissions, *see also* **field staff member(s); FSM Account**

may not be paid on unauthorized discounts or illegal cut-rate items, 3:261

procedure for payment, MS2:330

FSM contest bonuses, who is eligible for, 6:660

FSM Newsletter, description, 0:725

FSO, *see* **Flag Service Organization**

FSO Public Divisions, *see also* **Bridge flow; routes**

have additional responsibility of ensuring the lower orgs are functioning and moving people in volume up their service routes, 6:127

see that the next lower Public Divisions (AO) are functioning and that AO Public Divisions are forcing the next lower Public Divisions (SH) to function, 6:128

full-time training,

penalties for pirating staff on, 5:497

requirements for, MS1:389

fully paids, called in by Department of Tech Services, 2:641, 3:217, 4:276, 7:865

function(s), *see also* **duty; hat; post**

betrayal of functions and purposes of group, 0:572

divisions must not cross in, 0:479

exec knowing functions, 0:280

list of major duties in tiny org, 0:99

losing functions through promotions, 0:198

memory is inadequate in supervision of posts and, 0:195

must functions of org, 0:99

nearly every function of Central Org was at one time new program, 0:701

never noticing there is org there that has posts and, 0:383

not necessary to have stable terminal do only one thing, 0:106

organizing functions and work, 0:88

staff inattentive to functions halts expansion, 0:101

function(s), *(cont.)*

    taking causativeness over, 0:231

    unawareness of, 0:383, 0:384

    why full statement of function of every post is necessary, 0:231

fundamental, definition, 0:52

Fundamentals of Thought, "Book One" of Scientology, 6:231

funerals, Chaplain and, 6:518

future, *see also* **survival; viability**

    Affluence condition and future commitments, 0:564, 0:646

future, *(cont.)*

    being who is guilty knows he is offending against future of all, 0:493

    inferring that nothing including one's own future fate and that of other fellow is important, 0:302

    it will all come out all right, 0:155

    we have a trust which, if we fail it, condemns ourselves, our friends, our future, to continued oblivion, 0:239

    what future of this planet depends on, 0:13

    what our personal futures depend on, 4:62

G

GAE, *see* **gross auditing error(s)**

gain(s),

desired to achieve by the use of Scientology, 2:378

most rapid gain financially that any individual could make from getting trained or processed would be the salesman, 2:156, 6:172

game,

figuring out if you want to play that game or not, 0:238

for Scientologists to play, 6:448

formula for game of life, 0:119

not playing some minor game in Scientology, 0:13

only game in which everybody wins, 0:234, 0:235

what happens when game is over, 0:638, 0:645

"games condition,"

twinning and, 4:437

with field auditors, 5:834

gardening, caring for plants and cut flowers, 7:1385

gateway, into Scientology, 2:378

GDS, *see* **gross divisional statistic(s)**

generalities, generality,

combined with a false report and intended to upset somebody, 1:737, 7:1017

demanding full particulars, not half-reports or, 0:392

"everybody says" despatches, 0:405

make suppressive persons hard to detect, 1:1009

generalities, generality, *(cont.)*

petitions and, 0:488

strategic planning and, 0:706

targeting and, 0:691, 0:705

when you have critical data omit "everybody" generality, 0:85

General Liability Fund, 3:401

Genghis Khan, 0:518

genius,

belief that it takes genius to run org successfully, 0:40

organizational, composed of, MS1:197

Germany,

financed Lenin, 0:511

Hitler and, 0:127, 0:449

smashed by the psychiatrist, 0:68

GI, *see* **gross income**

gifts,

receiving favors or gifts from pcs, 0:171, 0:410

restrictions on, 1:729

gimmick,

Call-in Unit tool, 2:648, 3:224, 4:283, 7:872

definition, 2:648, 3:224, 4:283, 7:872

glibness, demonstration is key to, 4:333

glib student, basic anatomy of, MS2:137

glossaries, must be provided for each film, 4:529, 6:345

Glutz PR, MS3:102

goal, *see also* **purpose**

as desirable as contains truth or true advantage along the dynamics, 7:570

companies or governments are usually a dream, dreamed first by one man, then embraced by a few and finally held up as the guidon of the many, 7:568

exec ought to tell people his, 0:373

goal, *(cont.)*

first and primary goal of org, 0:17

inherent in definition of management itself, 7:568

LRH hat, 0:233

no objective worth obtaining was achieved without some barriers arising or industrious dedication, 0:92

pretended goals and management, 7:578

strategic plan and, 7:470, MS3:450

two categories of, 7:569

Goals-Problem-Mass, (GPM),

best way to run, 4:172

common denominator is "no responsibility," 5:566

made up of, 5:566

theory, 5:566

gold seal, 5:342

Gold Star, 0:525, 0:662

Certificate, 0:663

ethics protection, 1:578

good, 1:488

achieving group which is basically good, 0:158

definition, 0:453

does not always triumph, 0:455

evil and, 0:452

greatest good for greatest number of dynamics, 0:146, 0:238, 0:239, 0:480, 0:575, 0:702

man is basically, 0:158, 0:452, 0:453, 0:526, 6:515

our ethics must be proportional to our ability to do good, 0:421

reactive mind and, 0:9, 0:480

right and wrong, good and evil, 0:452–454

so much good in worst of us, 0:532

someone promising to be good is never good enough, 0:497

strength has two sides, one for good and one for evil, 0:517

survival and, 0:452, 0:453

thetan is good, 0:480

things do not run right because one is, 0:518

good acts, definition, 0:453

good indicator,

graphs are a, 0:655

rising stats and, 0:496

good manager, ignores rumor and only acts on statistics, 1:1026

goodwill,

activities which generate public interest and, MS3:168

building goodwill is job of every staff, MS3:169

goodwill, *(cont.)*

definition, 0:332, 6:625, MS2:297, MS3:168

demand for service and future income dependent upon, MS3:168

dirty quarters and slovenly staff depress, 6:593

dirty quarters, sloppy, "help yourself" service and an unfriendly staff, destructive to goodwill, 6:626, MS2:298

events and, 0:266

exchange and, 0:527

PR and, 0:332–333, 0:334

producing product returns pay and, 0:296

promoted by, MS3:169

psychiatrist or psychologist and, MS3:34

source of, MS3:169

what generates goodwill, 6:625, MS2:297

word of mouth and, 6:626, MS2:298

goof, *see* **error**

gossip, I pay no attention to, 0:151

"got to's," 7:1138

govern(ing), *see also* **management**

England governing individual colonial citizens, 0:599–600

how Russia governs people, 0:599

no political system is any better than those who use it to govern or be governed, 0:157

seeking to govern individuals through income tax, "benefits," etc., 0:598

what happens when state begins to govern individual, 0:603

governing body,

real Why of any failure when sincerely trying but failing is that it is operating on wrong Whys, 7:165

reasons any conference or board become bogged, 7:322, MS3:302

government, *see also* **bureaucracy; politics**

accounting summaries done for governments, not for management, 0:594

activities connected with, 7:1007

antisocial personalities and, 1:1014, 1:1019

attacks from, occur only where there are "no results" or "bad results," 0:8

bad repute, causes of, 0:40

best guarantee of stability, 0:67

bursting into uncontrolled violence, 0:522

by riot and intimidation, 0:481

catering to royal governments as focus of production, 0:506

centralized government, 0:598, 0:632

conflict with, 7:1022

government, *(cont.)*

dead for very long time before fact is discovered, 0:53

decay of Western governments, 0:504

dependence on spy reports, police reports, etc., 0:413

disaster and, 0:505

divine rightness in judicial matters, 0:450, 0:522

efficiency of, 0:624

Emergency condition and, 0:624

employing persons of Leipzig, Germany death camp school, 0:40

errors, only two that one can make in face of danger from, 7:998

"Ethics Committees" and, 0:450

example of operating in cope in the, MS1:413

exchange condition of, 0:317

formula to revive dead government, 0:53

highest skill is murder, 0:83

inflation created by, 0:452

interference, 0:66, 0:506

making money, 0:528

Marx neither knew nor solved basic problem of, 0:601

misuse, neglect or abuse of PR tech and, MS3:19

money and force and power of the, MS3:22

"moonlighting" on the, MS1:417

most individually oppressive form of, 0:601

nine factors causing troubles for, 0:40

officials, lack of organizational know-how and, 7:407, MS3:387

only two errors one can make in face of danger from governments, 3:377

politicians, *see* politician

PR continually recoiling on, MS3:20

products, 0:252, MS1:446

why final product is riot, war and a polluted planet, 0:40

run on rumors and false reports, MS1:68

seeking to govern individuals, 0:598

selling Scientology to, 0:354

suppression and, 0:66

taking in its own laundry, 0:83

three functions of, 0:505

use of force vs. opinion leaders, MS3:20

violence gets a government nowhere, 7:1143

whose policies are unreal are perishing, 0:411

why they don't work, 0:82

governors, US putting them in Danger condition, 0:599

GPM, *see* **Goals-Problem-Mass**

gradation,

purpose of, 4:174

rules of, 4:174

Gradation Chart, *see* **Grade Chart**

Grade Chart, *see also* **Classification, Gradation and Awareness Chart**

Alternate Clear Route, 2:465

following this chart one can make Release and then Clear, 2:518

Happiness RD and, 2:462

Int Rundowns and, 2:464

introductory and assist actions, 2:461

lineup of affected by declining case state in society, 4:200

lower grades, 4:193

main change, 2:468, 4:201

omitted and quickied actions, 0:7

optional or conditional steps, 2:461, 4:194, 6:420

position of HRD on, 4:195

programing and, 2:464

cases divide up into four general groups, 6:423–424

individual programing done against the, 4:198

programing and C/Sing of cases for a staff co-audit done against, 4:706

promotion, anyone writing promo, engaged in Reg or Letter Reg or Div 6 work would have to be fully briefed on, 2:559–560

PTS RDs and handlings not assigned to specific point on, 4:197

purpose of co-audit and, 4:687

relative positions of NED and Scientology lower grades, 2:468

road map upward, 2:517

Scientology DRD or NED DRD, 2:462

stalled Dianetic Clear and, 2:464

theory of the new Grade Chart, 2:467, 4:200

use of in answering forms sent in by public, 2:632

grades,

abilities gained for, 5:292

above Clear, checked only when, 5:242

award insignia, 5:356

cutative, 5:22

declaring several at once was never authorized, 5:254

grade subsidy for staff forbidden in other orgs, 0:174, 5:430

issuing data or information to wrong grades or unauthorized persons or groups, 0:469

lower, must be gotten back in, 4:935, 5:263

grades, *(cont.)*

obtained by flattening the process of that level, 4:177

overwhelming the pc with high levels, 0:473

permitting a pc to attest to more than one at a time, 1:15, 2:15, 3:15, 4:15, 5:15

placed before NED on Grade Chart, 4:201

policy, 5:250

possible to have several F/Ns, 5:253

public interested in co-auditing, 4:689

purpose was not to produce a Clear, 4:203

running only one process for, 1:15, 2:15, 3:15, 4:15, 5:15

sale of,
in intensives, 2:427
sell only auditing hours for, 5:258

staff members must be audited up through, 5:408

technical degrades and, 0:14

upper, requires lower grades fully rehabbed, 4:1087

"quickie grades," 2:14, 5:14, 5:274–275, 5:277

Grades Case Supervisor, 4:1127

grade subsidy, staff members and, 3:216

gradient(s), gradient scale,

can raise an org by, MS2:430

definition, MS1:203, MS1:412

false data comes off in, MS2:136

field of doingness and, 0:34

new people and principle of gradient scales, 2:401

organizing by, MS1:203

scale of OT, MS2:429

survival is graduated scale, 0:452

too steep study gradient, effects of, 0:34

graduation, when held and how conducted, 4:384

graph(s), graphing, *see also* **statistic**

accumulating graph described, 0:691

Affluence condition, illustration, 0:643, 0:649

condition assignments and, 0:655, 0:677, 0:679, 0:680

daily stat graph, 0:689, 0:691

definition, 7:481, MS1:371, MS2:197, MS2:302, MS3:461

dev-t graphed, 0:435–438

discrepancies,
amongst graphs, 0:655, 0:657-658, MS3:378
where found, some graph is false, handling, 7:398

don't infer Danger condition that doesn't show on a, 0:584

dreaming up a figure and putting it on, 0:694

graph(s), graphing, *(cont.)*

false graph, 0:658, 1:570

good indicator, 0:655, 1:567

must be based on actual figures, 0:655

quotas set with idea of creating continually rising graph, 0:691

reading of, 0:655, 0:679–680
line going steeply up, 0:645
place you are on a chain of command monitors all graph readings, 7:562
Power can't be judged from one line on, 0:643
recent ups and downs, 7:396
trends and discrepancies and, 7:396
viability monitors all readings, 7:562
what to look for, MS3:376

scale(ing),
correct scaling, 0:676, 0:679
how to figure scale, 0:675

shifts of comm lines, functions, policies, equipment, duties, locations quite often far more responsible for graph shifts, 7:498

trend,
monitors all graph readings, 7:562
viability and, 0:679

upside-down, 1:678

why ups and downs must be plainly visible, 0:675

Greece, Greek(s),

cause of their decline, 0:505

philosophers, ethics, justice and, 0:448

Green Form, covers things bugging a case, 4:1081, 5:672

Green Form 40 Expanded, 6:421

Green Star, 0:525, 0:662,
ethics protection, 1:578

green-on-white, *the* tried and true way to go about something, 7:488, MS3:468

grooved in, *see* **hatting**

gross auditing error(s), (GAEs),

Auditing Supervisor or Instructor action when seeing one, 4:672

cancellation of session may only occur in the presence of a, 4:673

comm cycle additives are, 4:1176, 5:668

how a person gets one, 4:604

list of, 4:673

penalties for in training (1962), 4:317

gross book sales; *see also* **book sales**

primary stat of a Pubs Org, 2:297

redefined, 2:297

gross divisional statistic(s), GDS(es), *see also* **statistic**

Ad Council and, 0:582

analysis, 0:646, 0:648
will get confirmed by data, MS1:121

common reasons for declining, 7:787

doing comparison of each set of stats in same or related activity, 0:646

internally controlled in an org, 7:787

primary divisional statistic, 3:48

quotas set with div secretaries for, 0:691

reading by the day, 0:677

targeting of, 0:690

Treasury Division, 3:49

understanding what has put GDS up or down, 0:646

what they consist of, 0:688

gross income, GI, *see also* **income; money**

causes of GI/CGI gap being too wide, 2:111, 3:87, 4:153, 5:659, 6:555, 7:861

Central Files and, 0:359

definition, MS2:326

future predicted by book sales, 2:298, 6:266

"GI push," 0:693

hatting and, 0:216

how to count, MS2:374

key to high GI, 2:577

list of several distinct sources of GI in an org, MS2:280

low gross income, what is behind it, MS2:220

made from high division stats, 7:517

most usual reasons for dwindling GI statistics, 7:513

only route by which you get in, 0:360

prediction of collapse based on high Qual income, 5:54

reasons for deteriorated org GI, 2:445

Registrar statistic of, 2:551

senior datum, 0:358, 2:672, 7:851

totally under own control of an org, 7:519

when managing by statistics one does not manage by gross income only, 7:516

where it comes from and why, 2:673, 6:89

gross income divided by staff, 0:261, 0:688

Gross Income Executive International,

responsible for issuing directives establishing pricing scale, and for updating them as needed, 3:178

group, *see also* **business; civilization; company; country; culture; man; organization; society; team; third dynamic; world**

absence of hats is reason why things don't run well in, MS1:411

accepting unworkable tech, 0:9

accomplishing many times the work only one can do, 0:87

agreed-upon policy and, 0:411

agreement needed to make a, 0:28

alliances with suitable groups, org image and, 6:606, MS3:140

at effect, 7:407, MS3:387

awareness of org group as team of people with similar purposes, 0:439

bad policy, bad mores, and you have a dying group, 0:411

bank says group is all and individual nothing, 0:10

betrayal of functions and purposes of, 0:572

bits of third dynamic, each opposed, 0:273

buffer against injustice, 0:522

can be seen to have three spheres of interest and action, 7:570

cataclysms or political or social catastrophes or upheavals, planning for, 0:64

collective-think and, 0:158

common denominator of a group is the reactive bank, 0:10

composition of, 0:253

conditions and,
asking for reentry to the, 0:574
Confusion Formula for, 1:615
delivering effective blow to enemies of, 0:574
evaluating one's group as to intentions and objectives, 0:575
joining, remaining in or befriending group which progresses toward greatest good for greatest number of dynamics, 0:575

control of environment, 0:253, 0:556, 0:557

cooperating with groups used in dissemination, 2:61

correct actions to take when faced by urgent necessity arising from incompetence of a group or other causes, 7:776

credo of a true group member, 7:582

definition, 7:271

depressing group's standard of living, 0:314

discipline,
is needful in a group, 0:525
when it does not exist, whole group caves in, 0:450, 0:521

do not disseminate to, 6:611

don't seek the cooperation of, 6:835

elect or select only those who would kill them, 0:83, 0:158

group, *(cont.)*

ethics,

group and, 0:451

group taking action against individual when he fails to put in his own ethics, 0:449

tolerating and ignoring loafers or out-ethics cats in group, 0:556

every action a PR takes concerns, MS3:14

exact formula to put group into action, 6:88

exchange *see* exchange

expansion and,

expanding into a decadent culture, 0:253, MS1:447

org image and, 6:607, MS3:141

fail to form in absence of purpose, 6:686

failure of individual members to control their fellows makes group hard for all to live and work with, 0:557

failure, causes of, 0:63

field staff member and, 6:635

greatest source of confusion, seniors who knock hats off and lines out, MS1:290

group member *see* group member(s)

how to make into an organization, MS1:290

idea that group could evolve truth, 0:9

ideal group member, 1:816

ignoring real producers of the, 0:316

individual and, 0:599–602

is composed of, 0:253

justice and, 0:448, 1:741

know-how of handling them, 0:28

life is a group effort, 0:458

low standard of living, why, MS1:352

major failure is to fail to organize, 0:88, 7:777

man's systems are based on, 0:96

management which will hide data is operating toward a decline of the group, 7:575

new group or company should be established first as safe point and then as an operating point, MS3:90

only the aberrated group, the mob, that is destructive, 2:10, 3:10, 4:10, 7:10

organization and, 1:86, 6:856

organized so as to permit flows and accomplish specialized actions which are completed in themselves, 7:776

our power as group striking innocent and guilty alike, 0:483

outward signs of badly organized group, 1:86

person in charge trying to do all actions himself can break up a, 0:87

person who publicly rejects is no longer member of, 1:989

group, *(cont.)*

personalities who do not want group to succeed, 0:62

pleasant and effective, 0:135

points of success or failure must agree with, MS1:266

policy and, 0:28, 0:55, 0:132, 0:410-411

popularity and usefulness depend upon, MS3:97

positive, enforced orders, given with no misemotion are the need of a group if it is to prosper, 7:333, MS3:313

promotional actions and, 0:354

prospering *see* prosperity

purposes, 6:716

question one can ask of any group not doing well, 0:554

recruiting for, 6:695

responsibility for viability, MS1:66

right to exile anyone it discovers to be guilty of tampering with any communication line, 7:575

running away from, 0:177

sanity depends upon, MS1:57

sanity scale for, MS1:266

selecting a leader, 0:83

senior to group exec is not counted as member of group, 0:603

size of,

how many individuals can effectively compose a group, 7:257

importance of, 0:598–603

large organization composed of groups, small organization composed of individuals, 7:254–599

proper size of, 7:256

shrinking and becoming weak, 0:117

small group can make it if they are very alert and efficient, 0:261

social or public groups, do not lecture or disseminate to, MS3:150

specialized, served by reporters, MS3:152

success by efforts of individuals and, 7:1015

success of, 0:63

survival of,

depends upon, 0:253, 0:451, 7:435, MS1:447, MS3:415

Group Sanity Scale and, MS1:269

talking to groups used in dissemination, 2:61, 6:167

tend to perpetuate conditions they are formed to combat, MS3:151

third dynamic tech and, 0:55

three divisions of action which are interactive and interdependent, 7:570

tone scale of, 7:573

traffic between the group and the goal maker should be direct and clean of all "interpretations" unless management wishes to destroy the group, 7:570

group, *(cont.)*

true group, 0:140, 6:854

understanding all groups, 0:89

unregistered, has no right to use Scientology materials, 6:691, 6:701

upstat vs. downstat group, 0:556

urgent necessity arising from incompetence of group, 0:87

VFPs and successful groups, MS1:258

vicious character of, 0:158

ways to audit a group in collapse, 7:238

what can destroy them, MS1:72

what they rise or fall in direct relationship to, 0:89

when you accuse wrongly and punish unjustly the group caves in, 0:521

where there's a group to be helped, see that it's done, 0:273

who attack Scientology are consistently erring, 7:1092

why group is harder to defeat than individual, 0:87

why we are capable of power as a group, 0:484

will be poor and fail if, MS1:215

group clearing, by pulling false report, false attestation, no report, refused report, 1:871

group member(s), *see also* **individual; staff**

enforcing action and mores of group, 0:556

failure of individual members to control their fellows, 0:557

honesty and, 0:152

how he can measure his progress, 0:253

insisting other group members control their environment, 0:253

lessening group members' sense of their own power, 0:604

preselecting group individuals, 0:556

senior to group exec is not counted as member of group, 0:603

snarling because he is overwhelmed, 0:602

tolerating and ignoring loafers or out-ethics cats in group, 0:556

waiting for orders, 0:135

group member(s), *(cont.)*

will not identify or phrase VFPs, MS1:258

what happens when new group member doesn't get trained up, 0:261

group morale,

handling of, 6:525

morale of each individual affects, 6:524

what increases, 6:524

Group Officer, duties and responsibility of, 6:845

Group Processing, PES and, 0:99

Group Secretary,

duties, 6:691, 6:700

requirements for post, 6:691, 6:700

growth, grow(ing), *see also* **expansion**

agreed-upon policy and, 0:408

if we reverse conduct of declining governments and businesses, we will grow, 0:506

programs, growth of, 0:702

reactive bank keeps beings from growing, 0:117

without order nothing can grow, 0:480

guilt(y),

first step toward freeing a man from guilt of self, 0:462

follower of destructive order, 0:142

following destructive reinterpretation of policy, 0:141

future political slavery where we all have numbers and our guilt, 0:462

omitting to handle criminality, 0:527

some are guilty, most are innocent, 0:483

striking innocent and guilty alike, effect, 0:483

we can make person feel guilty by just a whisper, 0:493

guilty conscience, 0:461

"Guk Bomb," formula, 5:619

gung-ho, definition, 6:716, 6:846

Gung-ho Group(s),

humanitarian objective, 6:861

motto: "A community that pulls together can make a better society for all," 6:716

purpose, 6:846

Third Party Law and, 6:859

H

Hagen, Victor W. von, 0:629

half-done(s), 7:431; *see also* **backlog**

  causing attention to drift off targets, 0:647

  how org loads up with, 0:391

  reasons for, MS2:225

handle(d), handling, *see also* **program; project**

  ability to confront, handle and control mest and people, 0:252

  become simple with right Why, MS1:146

  being hit back by lines you are trying to handle, 0:420

  criterion for, MS1:166

  definition, 2:440, 4:927, 5:683

  do every piece of work that comes your way when it comes, 0:399

  everything you don't handle comes back and bites, 0:400, 0:431

  examples of not handling, 2:440

  executive, handling project he doesn't know much about, 0:88

  feeling there was "no handling apparent," 0:664

  how to confront and handle confusions which invite a squirrel solution, 0:64

  how to handle work, 0:399–400

  improvised "handling," effect of, 0:73

  one has "no handling" for the condition if one doesn't do steps to handle, 0:665

  patching it up vs., 0:244

  post(s),

    how to never be faced with post situations for which there seems to be "no handling," 0:665

    mishandled items drive one off, 0:389

  problem forwarded only with full recommendation for handling, 0:392

handle(d), *(cont.)*

  public individual, handling of, 0:323–327

  routes of handling are not orders to handle but directions to go, 0:82

  Scientology helps people to come up to handling their problems, 0:153

  situation handling, 0:244–245

  "special handling," 0:404

  successes come from anticipating the situation and handling it, 0:64

  target handling, 0:248

  terminatedly handle, 0:244–245, 0:281

  when demands to rehandle occur, 0:280

  Why opens door to, MS1:146

  why people refer things they should handle to others, 0:391

  "Will it cause less confusion to handle it or to slam it back onto its proper lines?" 0:83

  "Work out how this problem should be handled and recommend," 0:390

"handle or disconnect,"

  definition, 1:1042

  E/O's advice is to handle, 1:1043

hang(ed),

  being willing to be hanged for our mistakes, 0:231

  labeling as a suppressive is our hanging, 0:496

  we don't hang people because we started to hang them and so must do so, 0:496

happiness, happy, unhappiness, unhappy, *see also* **success**

  achieving happiness, 0:458, 0:459

  comes from self-determinism, production and pride, MS2:65

  ethics tech and, 0:458

happiness, *(cont.)*

honesty and, 0:528

is power and power is being able to do what one is doing when one is doing it, MS2:65

liar and, 0:458

man is not happy unless he is honest, 4:406

pleasure and, 0:459

right to serve and, 0:278

salaries accurately and punctually paid to keep staff happy, 0:350

staff and, 0:604

unhappiness, unhappy,

chaos and unhappy org, cause of, 0:196

from wearing other hats than your own or being ignorant of what other hats are being worn, 0:197

shrinking and unhappy org, 0:693

unused people become unhappy, 0:639

why people are unhappy in an area which is not *well* disciplined, 0:515

Happiness Rundown, 6:421

auditor course, prerequisites modified, 4:659

major route for public into the org, 4:198

position on Grade Chart, 4:195

harassment,

how to avoid feeling harassed, ordered around and oppressed, 0:140

off-policy orders and, 0:145

harbinger of evil tidings, 1:1015

hard sell, *see also* **soft sell**

ads must be, 2:230, 2:251

definition, 2:132

Hardship Section, 5:735

harm, hurt(ing), *see also* **injury**

disciplining those who are hurting others, 0:484

freedom of speech does not mean freedom to harm by lies, 0:461

person dramatizing his criminal intent can become very angry if not prevented from hurting others, 0:480

reports collect and point out bad conditions before those can harm org, 0:544

Scientology can help you if you haven't done things to hurt its people, 0:153

trying to hurt one's fellow human beings, 0:152

HAS, *see* **Hubbard Apprentice Scientologist; HCO Area Secretary**

HAS Co-audit,

as a route to Release, 6:452

consists of, 6:459

how it is run, 6:455

importance of, 6:453

HAS Co-audit, *(cont.)*

PE Course is a training activity for, 6:462

processes, 6:456, 6:463

Section, definition, 2:504, 3:232, 4:45, 7:200

society, our method of progress into, 0:231

HASI,

individual service organization, 7:196

stable data for negotiation and discourse to any government official or on any government project, 6:590, 7:993

three service branches and, 7:194

HASI Assoc Sec Administrative Order,
description, 0:715

HASI Assoc Sec Technical Order,
description, 0:715

hat(s), *see also* **hatting; post**

activities greatly improved by, MS1:214

adjacent area dumping its, 0:514

A–I,

contents of, MS1:202

hat, 0:199–200

always give back hat you stole for moment, 0:83

any hat is better than no hat, MS1:207, MS1:416

assembling folder for newly created post, 1:267

based on experience, 0:384

basic staff hat, 0:27, 0:28, 0:200

checked out against an org board, 1:277

checkout on,

exact sequence for, 1:277

when to order full checkout of person on PLs applying to post, 0:407

checksheet,

authorization, 1:14

length of, 1:282

collect a complete hat folder when someone leaves, 1:179

combined hats, 0:101

complete, 0:193, 0:194

completeness and size of the product make the seniority of the hat, 7:796

contents of, 1:270, MS1:411

contributism and, 0:277

cope vs., 0:201

criminal or antisocial conduct occurs where there is no, MS1:271

defined by a product, 1:151, 7:796

definition, 0:196, 0:199, 1:266, 1:268, 1:273, 1:280, 7:480, 7:796, MS1:202, MS1:222, MS1:370, MS1:403, MS1:411

deliver service each hat calls for, 0:279

departures from and cope, MS1:204, MS1:413

hat(s), *(cont.)*

description, 0:199

designates particular status and duties, MS1:202

despatch which should go in your hat, 0:369

development of, MS1:202

double, triple, quadruple hat wearing, 1:205

dumping of, 0:47, 0:426, 0:514

each person wearing all hats and wearing them all differently, 0:408

each person wears his own, 1:273

engineer hat example, 0:197, 0:199

Estos establish and maintain the, 0:393

every post, 1:63

evolving one's own hat, 0:415

examples, MS1:222
  lack of hats, MS1:213
  problem in hats, MS1:294

executive(s),
  knowing all the hats, 0:280
  responsibilities for staff hats, 0:221, 0:409

failure to know or wear and org lines, MS1:294

false,
  definition, 1:279
  steps to correct, 1:279

folder,
  blue, 1:270
  contents of, 1:266
  incomplete, penalty for, 1:268
  issued for new staff, 1:178

full hat contains the usual, 0:257

general staff hat, 0:200

gradient scale of, MS1:412

handing out despatches and work to correct hats, 0:196

having too many, handling, 0:166

HCO Sec must recapture hat of removed person, 1:182

held from above, 1:205

how to combine hats per Org Program No. 1, 7:278

ideal scene and, 0:204

inspection of, 1:268

keynote of, 0:278

knock off, 0:280, 1:71, 1:285

lack of, 0:199, 0:203, 0:204, 0:294, MS1:201–202
  absence of is reason why things don't run well, MS1:411
  blows and, 0:203
  counter-effort and, MS1:213
  full training on, MS1:206
  in orgs, MS1:207
  real WHY behind org sags and troubles, 7:792
  when person has no hat he lacks purpose and value, 0:204
  Why of departures from ideal scene, MS1:207

hat(s), *(cont.)*

leaving post without turning over, 1:291

lengthy and complex hats, 0:415

letting somebody steal your hat, definition, 0:197

LRH's hats, 0:233

main outnesses, MS1:448

measuring stick for a worn hat is a stat, 7:518

mini hat, 0:217

modernized by the board and person being removed or transferred, 1:252

more to org than one person wearing all hats, 0:384

most common reason why they aren't worn, 1:276

most important piece of your, 0:401

not wearing, condition of Treason, 1:580

one for every post regardless of the number of bodies, 1:28

org board and, 0:201
  omitted hats, MS1:219

org slumps traced to lack of, MS1:202

originating for another hat than one's own, 0:413

outlines the actions necessary to accomplish a production, 1:151

overload due to lack of, 0:204

part of everyone's hats is keeping good mock-up in people, offices, classrooms, quarters, 0:84

person lacks purpose and value without a, MS1:416

personnel demands vs. hat inspections, 7:450

point which isn't wearing its, 1:276

post checksheets and packs as, MS1:205

product, every hat has a, 0:199, MS1:202

production and, 1:210

reason for, 0:196, 1:270

reason they fall into disuse, 1:277

redefined, 7:794

relation of GDSes and hats, 7:793

result of no org boards, programs and, MS1:217

results of hatting people and getting lines running the way they are supposed to, 7:1178

seniors made responsible for, MS1:205

service and, 0:277, 0:278

smooth organization and, 1:273

specialty, MS1:411

staff hat,
  auditors and, 0:223
  no post or staff hat folder, 0:220

hat(s), *(cont.)*

staff member goofs roll up and knock my hats sideways, 0:233

study of, 0:440, 0:443

technology of hats, 0:199

turnovers, policies covering, 0:266–267

two reasons to wear a, 1:276

types of, MS1:403

undercut, 0:307

unhatted people go bad, 1:68

wearing of,

air and attitude of how hat is worn, 0:238

each person wearing his own, 0:196

every Scientologist on staff potentially wears every hat in org, 0:84

failure to wear your hat, 0:432

hat has to be worn as I would wear it, 0:238

if you wear several hats do them, not other hats, 0:232

ignorant of what other hats are being worn, 0:197

in tiny org everyone wears all the hats, 0:595

making other people wear only their hats, 0:197

not wearing hats, 0:572

why ordering someone to wear his hat is altered sequence, 0:294

you are wearing my admin hat for that post, 0:238

went out when ethics came strongly in, 1:59

write-up, checksheet and pack, MS1:207

hat check(s),

administrative pattern of org must be hat checked into solid existence by HCO, 1:36

hat drill, 1:31

technical,

definition, 1:272, 7:1272

HCO guarantees technical excellence by, 1:35–36

procedure, 1:272

purpose of, 1:272

unpopular with a staff member, reason for, 1:31–32

hat checksheet,

authorization of, 0:14, 2:14, 5:14, 7:14

done as a course, 5:509

hate, one is what one is, not what one is admired or hated for, 0:633

hat folder,

description and importance of, 0:166, 0:193, 0:194, 0:195

getting thick to point where it cannot be used, 0:194

no post or staff hat folder, 0:220

Post Purpose Clearing and, 5:462

review them periodically, 0:166

turnover of, 3:329

hat inspection, done for every personnel demand, MS1:465

Hats Assembly Unit, 1:74

Hats Officer,

absence of, 0:221

checks out divisional summaries of actions, 1:278

duty, 1:291

hat campaigner who never lets up, 1:75

hats by checkout everyone, 1:74

should have list of clients, 1:296

hatting, hat(ted)(ness), unhatted(ness), *see also* **education; establish; Establishment Officer; instant hat; study; train**

ability to handle basics with speed and certainty, 0:54

basic sequence of, 0:217, MS1:309, MS2:108, MS2:259

before full posting, 0:261

beware the product officer who won't give time off for, 7:447, MS2:131

cause over post due to, 0:216, 0:268

definition, MS2:196, MS2:301

demanding hattedness, 0:392

Dept 1 responsible for, 1:294

down stats traced to failure in, MS1:403

environment and, 0:207, MS2:203, MS2:310

equals control, MS1:308, MS2:107, MS2:258

essence of, MS1:167

Esto and, 0:393

Estos and staff, cycle of, MS2:11

examples,

how to, 1:295

LRH getting Estos effective at hatting, MS2:124

exec hatting someone at distance, 0:390

experts vs., MS1:414

failures to, 0:74, 0:221

False Data Stripping enables person to be hatted, MS2:135

first situation, MS2:82

full hatting, 1:294

going on producing while being hatted, 0:440

gradient is, 1:294

HCO not having enough people devoted to, 0:393

helps person to hold his post, 0:206

how to get Estos to hat people, MS2:123

if staff don't get hatted, they're condemning themselves and the planet to death a thousand times over, MS2:204, MS2:311

hatting, *(cont.)*

instant, 1:294

laws of, 0:205–206, MS1:301, MS1:457

mini, 1:294

no real attention on hatting, reason, 0:693

on-the-job, MS2:17

org or division from the top down, MS2:29

out-basics, examples, 0:306–307

overload and, 1:293

person is greatly strengthened by, MS1:302, MS1:458

person is responsible for his own, 1:294

person not fully hatted liable to ethics action, 1:294

personnel goofs and, 0:280, 7:804

Post Purpose Clearing and, 5:461

  clearing the purpose is essential to, 1:292

Product Clearing,

  hat on product before doing anything else, MS2:29

  not possible over quickie Product Clearing, MS2:31

production and, 0:277, 0:281

product officer of the division, MS2:82

reason why persons who should have handled things haven't and, 7:809

refresh your memory regarding your duties, 0:166

refusing to get hatted, result, 0:207–208

right direction to, MS2:29

sample program to get org hatted and producing, 0:441

senior responsibility for, 1:295

sequence of, 1:292, MS2:17

Situations One through Thirteen, MS2:82–84

staff learn and do their job or they go, 0:406

staff sent to special outside schools for brief training periods, 0:223

study time and, 0:222

surveying hats, standard Esto action, MS2:28

system for handling overload and hatting, 7:809

those who cannot be hatted also don't learn from their own mistakes, MS2:187

trying to hat people in totally safe space with no threat to them whether they get hatted or not, 0:207

unhatted, unhattedness,

  criminality and, 0:391, 0:527

  dev-t and, 0:391, 0:393–394, 0:415, 0:439, 0:441

  out-ethics and, 0:526

  persons don't go idle, 0:390

  persons look sort of blind, 1:294

hatting, *(cont.)*

persons not hatted becoming weak and criminal, 0:206

person will get ill, 0:529

single-handing caused by, 0:391

stability and, 0:205

traffic volume and, 0:280

why unhatted org is a madhouse, 0:391

verbal, main source of false definitions and false data, MS2:134

where hatting continues to fail, handling, 0:443

why hatting, 0:205–206

Hatting Officer, *see* **Hats Officer**

hat write-up, *see also* **hat**

changing post, 1:275

  leaving post, writing your hat, 0:198

  to pass over to newly acquired assistants, 0:195

  writing up one's hat and breaking in successor properly, 0:596

has no further authority than advice, 0:200

in hat folder, 0:193, 0:194

Power condition and, 0:564

what happens if you don't write up your whole post, 0:564

what to include in, 0:198

have,

be-do-have, 0:291–293

having to have before one can do, 0:427, 0:624

HCA, *see* **Hubbard Certified Auditor; HCA/HPA**

HCA/HPA, *see also* **Hubbard Certified Auditor; Hubbard Professional Auditor**

certificate,

  red seal validation of, 5:322

  restored at Level III, 5:333

certification of, 5:322

extension course, 5:322

given international standing but are different classes, 5:331

graduate, 5:323

retread, 5:325

HCO, *see* **Hubbard Communications Office**

HCO Administrative Letter(s),

definition, 1:430

green ink on salmon paper, 1:395

HCO Administrator, definition, 7:26

HCO Area Office, definition, 7:1180

HCO Area Secretary,

amount of distraction and orders thrown at HAS, 1:78

ARC break assessments on staff, 5:573

construction of HCO itself done by the HAS, 1:79

HCO Area Secretary, *(cont.)*

Data Series, must know, 1:81

demanding new personnel on key outflow posts, 0:586

duties of, 1:30, 1:73, MS1:299, MS1:356

elite post, 1:82

ethics and, 1:32

Ethics Officer and, 0:101

expeditors, put on writing letters, 0:586

first product of, 1:79

freeloader list, assistance in compilation of, 1:255

ideal org and, 6:618, MS1:152

ignore all goofy demands and refer sensible ones to the HCO Cope Officer, 1:74

illegal orders and recourse, 1:81–82

long-term, MS1:357

LRH's first communicators, 0:101

off-policy orders knock the hat of the HAS off, 1:81

only way a HAS can maintain and increase establishment, 1:76

organizing officer of HCO, 1:80

Org Exec Course, should have at least an, 1:66

org ruds and, 4:311

penalty for stopping the communication of, 1:902

point where an org makes or breaks, 1:73

post has to establish the org, so itself must be very stable, 1:81

processing for, 1:82

promotional functions of Div 1, coordinates and gets them done, 0:347

PTS or chronically ill or NCG and HAS post, MS1:460, MS2:251

purpose, 1:30

put on post to get an org there, 1:75

put the org there as well as confirm the org that is there, 1:73

recourse of, 1:82

reporting steps of Emergency Formula taken, 0:621

responsibility for, 1:56
    execs, 5:552
    staff auditors and interns, 4:905

stability is the watchword of, 1:83

stable HAS wearing hat = stable org producing, 1:73

staff leaving org, report it only to Staff Chaplain and, 0:177

staff training and, 5:490

troubles, Why, 1:81

HCO Area Secretary, *(cont.)*

TTC and, 5:534

who isn't a policy expert in both knowledge and application is not long for this world, 1:82

works to put an establishment there, MS1:356

HCO Area Secretary Saint Hill, duties, 7:222

HCOB(s), HCO Bulletin(s), *see* **Hubbard Communications Office Bulletin**

HCO Board of Review, 0:147, 0:557

auditors,
    qualification and, 4:1143
    passed for HGC employment, 5:831

awards and, 1:32

basis of authority, 5:94

duties and line regarding certification, 5:94

function of, 1:841, 4:1132

goal, 5:303

handling of flunks, 5:95

necessary in every area where training is done, 7:1173

responsible for, 4:550

stable datum, 5:95

take exam for Class II and III off the HCO Area Sec, 4:311

three classes of people and, MS2:202

HCO Book Account, 0:627

book stock, great care must be taken to buy enough to have stock available to mail in response to ads, 2:282

cash-bills,
    cash and bills of account never intended to be included in org's cash-bills figure, 2:315
    cash-bills stat definition, 2:315

checks may be signed with FBO presence not required, 3:279, MS2:347

D/FBO for Marketing of Org Resources for Exchange,
    HCO Book Account now monitored by D/FBO for MORE, 2:290
    mandatory signatory, 3:279, MS2:347

disbursements and, 2:281, 3:187

examples of illegal uses, 2:291

invoicing and, 3:187

loans, bonuses or commissions, none paid from this account, 2:286, 6:251

monies used only to buy books, 2:344

pins paid for out of, 5:345

policy on use of account, 2:290–291

postage and, 3:188

receipt and use of membership monies, 2:285, 6:250

regulations, 2:286, 6:251

HCO Book Account, *(cont.)*

sales,

all book sales invoiced to HCO Book Account, 2:281

counted as stat of the org that makes sale regardless of whether person is on Day or Foundation lines, 3:171, 7:316

signatories and, 3:187

use funds to buy good mailing lists of people who buy health and mental books, 2:702

what began the account, MS2:396

HCO City Secretary, definition, 6:707

HCO Communicator(s), *see also* Director of Communications

daily pickups to and from Comm Center, 0:165

functions, 1:355–356

tips to, 1:362

HCO Confessional, *see also* Confessional; HCO Security Check; Security Check

abuse of and handling, 1:648–649

actions, 4:996

circumstances under which it is done, 1:649, 4:996

definition, 4:995

justice, 1:649

procedure, 1:649, 4:996

proper administrative handling of, 1:648

HCO Continental, duties, 7:1182

HCO Continental Office, basic functions of, 7:1180

HCO Cope Officer,

defends the establishing functions of the HAS, 1:80

grabs all the nonsense the HAS is getting, 1:74

product officer of HCO, 1:79

way for HAS to cope with torrent of distraction and orders, 1:79

HCO Division Checklist for Quality, 1:1057

optimum operation, 1:1063

poor quality, 1:1060–1061

Power quality, 1:1057–1060

Treason quality, 1:1061–1062

HCO Establishment Officer, MS2:36

HCO Ethics Codes, HCO Codes, *see also* Justice Codes

acting outside of, 1:251

advancement as staff member and org depends on, 0:481

agreement to abide by, 1:730

description and value of, 0:481

end insecurity and fear, 1:734

maximum protection lies in knowing, 1:735

part of expansion programing, 1:735

HCO Ethics Codes, *(cont.)*

right, wrong and, 1:734

Scientologists and staff members in accepting posts or membership agree to abide by, 0:477

student and, 0:491

your job, position, reputation, org, Scientology, and, 1:734

HCO Ethics Orders, gold paper with blue ink, 1:416

HCO Executive Letter,

definition, 1:406, 7:639

distribution, 1:406

Ethics Files wiped out by, 0:545

white paper with blue ink, 1:416

HCO Executive Secretary, HCO Exec Sec, HCO ES, HES,

basis for appointment, 7:914

bonuses and, 7:73–74

combining LRH Comm-HCO Area Sec-Ethics Officer, 0:101

duties of, 0:99, 0:339

duties of in a tiny org, 6:93, 7:276

functions that MUST be covered for org's basic survival, 0:99

income-getting actions of org, 0:99

Organization Program No. 1 and, 6:92, 7:275

promotional actions and, 7:84

reporting steps of Emergency Formula taken, 0:621

responsibility for,

performing and reporting actions where no LRH Comm, 7:1241

staff training program, 5:502

Thetan–Mind–Body–Product pattern, 0:654

when automatically assigned a condition of Non-Existence, 1:55

who has no HCO are first ones that need Sec Check, 4:974

HCO Executive Secretary Continental, purpose and primary business, 7:24

HCO Executive Secretary International, would supervise all Executive and HCO Divisions including Saint Hill's via local HCO Exec Secs, 7:87

HCO Executive Secretary World Wide,

copy of hat write-up to, 0:198

primary duties, 7:154

HCO Expeditor(s), 0:586

HCO income, book sales, ACCs, congresses, tapes, records and memberships invoiced to credit of and deposited in accounts of HCO, 2:289, 3:186, 6:817

HCO Information Letter, info letter,
blue ink on white paper, 1:393

HCO Justice Codes, *see also* **HCO Ethics Codes**
acting outside of, 1:251
suppressive acts and, 1:996, 4:88

HCO monies, *see* **HCO income**

HCO office(s), *see also* **Director of Communications; Hubbard Communications Office; HCO Communicator**
communications and, 1:20
purpose of, 1:20
routing, 1:20
secretarial functions for LRH, 1:20
stable terminal for any area operation, 1:20
three types of, 1:27

HCO organization chart, 1:50

HCO PL(s), HCO Policy Letter(s), *see* **Hubbard Communications Office Policy Letter**

HCO Project Engineer, *(Have You Lived Before?)*
attitude of project, 7:592
procedure for, 2:149
purpose, 7:591

HCO Secretary, *see also* **HCO Area Secretary**
Comm Ev convened by Office of LRH through the, 0:487
duty regarding KSW PL, 0:7, 0:8
refuting purchase or contract made with no purchase order, 0:183

HCO Secretary's Communicator, duty regarding KSW PL, 0:7

HCO Secretary World Wide, International Officers formed at WW under HCO Sec, 7:137

HCO Security Check, done to verify past-life identity of pc, 4:258

HCO Technical Advice Letter, description, 0:717

HC Outpoint–Pluspoint List, MS1:86

HCO World Wide,
highest priority activities, 7:36
list of staff and their duties when officially inaugurated, (10 July 1959), 7:29
new department created herewith; it is PE Foundation HCO WW, 6:163

HCO World Wide Security Form,
Form 7A, 5:565
Form 7B, 5:560, 5:565
Security Check used for any organizational reason, 5:556

HCS, *see* **Hubbard Clearing Scientologist**

HCS/BScn, qualifications for, 4:551

HDC, *see* **Hubbard Dianetic Counselor**

HDG, *see* **Hubbard Dianetic Graduate**

head on a pike,
definition, 1:818
putting a head on a pike, 1:750
when this is done, 7:679

headphones,
course tapes must always be listened to through high quality, high fidelity, 4:31
listener, high fidelity headphones and, 4:31

healing,
arts, auditing vs., 0:258
field auditors and policy on, 6:711
field, policy bars entrance of the, 0:126
legal position of, 4:1096
mental and spiritual causes, 4:880
one is dealing with two things, spirit and body, 5:626
physical exams and, 1:983
proper procedure for, 1:983, 4:880
we are not in the field of, 4:1094
what resolves it, 2:158

health, exercise and, 0:225

hear, misunderstood words and ability to, 0:44

hearing, why Comm Ev is not as acceptable as a, 0:603

heavy druggie, Purif and Objectives done on, 4:194

heavy ethics, *see* **ethics**

heavy traffic,
comes under heading of emergency, 7:614
warning, 0:380

heckling, 0:472

hell,
bank-agreement made Earth a, 0:10
to protect dishonest people is to condemn them to their own hells, 0:461

help,
believing people can be or deserve to be helped, 0:152
criminals and, 6:827
help people, 0:84
man suspects all offers of, 6:519, 7:1021
near ultimate in helping, 0:656
only fail when we do not help, 0:84
person must be helped to achieve what *he* wants, 2:498
posts are responsibilities we hold to help, 0:234
public objecting to us when we fail to, 0:84
reaction to, 1:970

help, *(cont.)*

refusing to accept for processing anyone one feels he cannot honestly help, 0:160

Registration personnel help people to get, 2:497, 6:382

Scientology can help if you haven't done things to hurt its people, 0:153

Scientology does not owe its, 6:519, 7:1021

SPs vs., 0:656

staff helping one another, 0:167, 0:235

two-way flow, 1:798

using best one knows of Scientology to help family, friends, groups and the world, 0:160

where there's a group to be helped, see that it's done, 0:273

help factor, 5:684

determination to *handle* cases and, 2:441, 4:928

help wanted, notice for, 1:161

Hemingway, Ernest, 0:299

hero,

doesn't always win, 0:455

head of government who gets into most debt became, 0:505

HES, *see* HCO Executive Secretary

"hey you," lack of coordination and, 7:455

"hey you! org board,"

commonest cause of org collapse, MS1:218

definition, MS1:218

HGC, *see* Hubbard Guidance Center

HGC Admin, *see also* Hubbard Guidance Center

all auditor-pc-room-time assignments done by, 4:250

ideal scene and stat, 4:139

must not take away low-priority pc's auditor once he has started his auditing, 4:252

responsible for,

filing miscellaneous reports, 4:261

connecting up the folder, the pc, the auditor and the room with NO auditor time loss, 4:253

economy of auditing time and minimum change of auditors, 4:250

safeguarding folders and caring for the folder library and state of folders, 4:253

HGC Clerk, ideal scenes and stats, 4:139; *see also* Hubbard Guidance Center

HGC PC Technical Estimate Interview, purpose of, 6:414; *see also* Hubbard Guidance Center

HGS, *see* Hubbard Graduate Scientologist

hidden data, information, particularly estimates of situations and reasons why, must be published so staff can see them, 7:649

hidden data line,

causes of, 5:699

definition of, 4:347

if it isn't written it wasn't said, 4:349

to believe there is makes an ARC break, 4:348

high crime(s), *see also* crimes

actions which violate KSW PL are, 0:7

admin degrades, 0:73–74, 5:25, 7:490

admin high crime checkouts, 5:822
Qual responsibility, 5:823
staff member responsibility, 5:823
violations, 5:823

admitting a famous person to higher-level processing who has not fully attained lower-level processing, 1:793

cancellation of certificates, classifications and awards for, 0:73, 0:467, 0:474

computer,
crimes may be reclassified as, MS2:465
program or system and, MS2:459

Course Supervisor and, 4:394

Courts of Ethics and, 1:948

cramming must include, 4:978

failure to,
EC failure to act to clean up "ARC broken field," 5:249
take responsibility and failure to act with initiative in circumstances which, not handled, bring damage to others or serious overwork, 0:662
use study tech, 4:402–403, 5:513

following or obeying or issuing any verbal or written order or directive which is contrary to or changes or "abolishes" anything set up in HCO PLs or HCOBs, 0:143

Hubbard Key to Life Course, delivering without having successfully completed it, 1:911–912, 4:647

list of, 1:880–883

penalties, 7:489

seriousness of, 0:545

standard admin and, MS2:462

Supervisor and study tech, 4:402, 5:512

technical degrades and, 0:14

technical high crime checkouts,
cramming must include, 5:806
where these have fallen out, 5:807
Word Clearing requirements, 5:806

high-crime checkouts, 0:75–77, 1:890; *see also* admin high crimes

High Crime Report, description, 0:544

hiring, *see also* applicant(s); employment; recruitment

ad, person who comes in or calls in response to, 1:162

hiring, *(cont.)*

Affluence condition and, 0:646

anyone hiring should be familiar with, MS1:395

application forms, design of, 1:172

auditors, two additional criteria, 4:961

executives and, 0:373

fast flow,
  hatting and handling of personnel key in, MS1:311
  recruitment and, MS1:310

first organizing action would be, MS1:313, MS2:120, MS2:263

institutional cases or persons with psychiatric history or insane, 1:168

line to be followed for, 1:162

location of the organization and, 1:171

musical chairs, answer to, 0:280

network representative and, 1:169

points on a checksheet for, 1:245

project prepare line, 1:172

requirements for retaining staff, 1:169

simultaneous, example of, MS1:391

State of Emergency and, 0:621

third dynamic psychosis is a refusal to employ people, MS1:267

three things required prior to, 1:253

Hitler, Adolf,

attempts at self-restraint, 0:457

caved himself and Germany right in, 0:449

suppressives and, 0:518

why he lost his war, 0:127

homework, ideal scene and, MS1:178

honesty, *see also* **dishonesty; truth**

consists of, 0:296, MS1:295

exec persuading out-ethics person to be more honest and ethical, 0:462

honest people,
  freedom is for, 0:461, 0:462, 1:481
  have rights, 0:152, 0:461, 1:481

if world were honest, justice and need for it would vanish, 0:519

man,
  is not happy unless he is honest, 4:406
  why no man who is not honest can be free, 0:461

must be maintained by Pc Examiner, 5:287

opens the door to case gain, 1:849

primary requirement on test lines, 4:234, 6:305

processing and, 0:152

honesty, *(cont.)*

road to sanity, 0:528, MS2:70

road to truth, 4:210, 4:1193, 5:290

sanity is basically honesty and truth, 4:235, 6:306

study and, 4:404

survival and, 0:455, 0:461

using one's own honesty to protest unmasking of dishonesty, 0:462

hope(s),

byword of down and outer, 0:255

harming others and blighting their, 0:454

horizontal fast flow routing, 0:386, 0:387

Host Interview, 1:829, 6:418

hot files, *see also* **Central Files**

definition, 2:492, 2:498, 2:656, 2:704, 6:714

handled in such a way as to *help* the person achieve his goal, 2:498

nothing may be filed in, that has not already been answered by a Letter Registrar, 2:704, 6:714

hot prospect,

definition, 2:431

how to answer forms so as not to lose, 2:632

hour(s), *see also* **time**

off post during appointed hours, 0:151

person can only work so many hours in day, 0:644

spending 3 or 4 hours trying to locate piece of paper, 0:306

staff schedule requirements, 0:165, 0:168, 0:169

housewife, takes over a woman's club, 6:834

Housing Officer, 0:593

housing unit, definition, 4:140

How to Improve Your Marriage Course, part of standard marriage handling, 6:543

HPA, *see* **Hubbard Professional Auditor**

Hubbard Administrator, 5:327, 5:338

Hubbard Apprentice Scientologist (HAS),

certificate, 5:313, 5:317, 6:460

course, confers no classification, 4:176

Hubbard Assistant Administrator, certificate, 5:327

Hubbard Book Auditor (HBA),

certificate for, 5:325

offer made in mailings to persons who have bought books, 5:346

Hubbard Certified Auditor (HCA), *see also* **HCA/HPA**

certificate for, 5:317, 5:325

Level II replaced by Hubbard Qualified Scientologist, 5:333

Hubbard Certified Auditor (HCA), *(cont.)*

may train person to level of Hubbard Apprentice Scientologist, 5:330

qualification for, 5:146

written examination, when a student is released from, 5:173

Hubbard Clearing Scientologist (HCS), *see also* **Bachelor of Scientology**

certificate for, 5:317

qualification for, 5:148

Hubbard Communications Office (Div 1), HCO,

accounts and, 7:1165

anyone in HCO should have done student's mini hat, 1:67

approval of E-Meters and, 2:377, 7:1289

Area Office, definition, 1:28

auditors employed by HGC, must pass all, 5:831

begins to function only when, 1:84

Bring Order, 1:83, 1:731

can recruit other staff, 4:89

checks sent to HCO for signing and issue, 3:114

collections and, 1:35

communication,

comm lines must be very precise, 1:29

communications and, 7:1161

exist to expedite Scientology communications, 7:1165

first action of is communication, 0:377, 1:35

has the incoming and outgoing flow lines, MS1:299

is communications office, 1:394

is really hCo, MS1:298

message placement, 0:377

puts in comm systems and takes the lag out of them, 1:33

competent HCO, getting it there and keeping it there, 1:57

Continental, definition, 7:1182

Continental Office,

definition, 1:27

plans for, 7:216

copyrights, trademarks, registered marks and rights of all materials of Dianetics and Scientology, holds all, 7:1171

covert criticism of, 1:31

cycle of building, 1:87

definition, 7:1116, MS1:298

dev-t and, 0:391, 0:441

duties and policies of, 1:34

Elite Corps, 1:88

equipment and supplies they are entitled to, 1:2

establishment,

establishes the org, MS1:300

Hubbard Communications Office (Div 1), HCO, *(cont.)*

Esto performs duties of depts of HCO for div he's in, 0:393

Estos, HCO is to back up, MS2:11

expected to establish the org, 1:66

fastest way to expand an org, 1:88

how HCO makes an org expand and prosper, 1:53

puts an org there and keeps it manned and working, 1:57

steps to establish HCO, 1:67

trying to operate before it itself is established, 1:66

what an HCO that builds itself can build, 1:87

ethics and,

has right to do Sec Checks, 4:973

investigatory procedure PLs that MUST be known to HCO, 4:1109, 5:606

may not do Confessionals or Sec Checks, 4:1109

most ethical division in the org, 1:88

out-ethics indicators, 0:533

should learn full investigatory procedure, 1:633

evictions, handling, 0:478–479

exterior view to Central Orgs, 1:33

external lines, 1:28

failure of, 0:391, 0:393

to police dev-t, was downfall of, MS2:236

field,

and org ethics and, 1:37

field auditors, campaign regarding, 6:699

financing of, 7:1162

first product of an HAS, 1:79

functions, MS1:298

actions of, 1:34

actions that good pay is composed of, 0:688–689

create the org and hold it there, 1:56

elementary actions of, MS1:298

first duty, 1:132

HCO Secs may not do, 7:183

make LRH's postulates stick, 1:392, 7:1287

most important one in HCO, 7:1055

my communications, 1:394

order of importance, 1:33

handles,

future, 1:33

Secretarial and Reception for Association Sec, 7:174

hats and, 7:1162

how to build an effective HCO, 1:74

inefficient, poorly organized or posted, out-ethics indicators of, 7:125

internal lines, 1:28

issues,

appearance, authorship and handling, 1:394

types of, 1:394

justice and, 0:477, 0:480, 0:487, *see also justice*

agency of Scientology, 1:730

Hubbard Communications Office (Div 1), HCO, *(cont.)*
    justice and, *(cont.)*
        Committee of Evidence, *see also* Committee of Evidence
        internal justice in orgs, 1:730
        one who withholds crimes until he gets in session, penalty, 4:996
        originates Committees of Evidence, 1:869
    LRH,
        extended pair of eyes for, 1:20–21, 7:1161
        reputation and, 7:1165
        secretarial functions for, 7:1161
    makes majority of the troubles orgs have tend to vanish, 1:635
    mass dissemination organization, 7:196
    may deputize any staff, 1:989
    meter checks, 1:633
        may only do meter checks, 4:1109
        omitting use of meter, 1:635
    Mimeo Section transferred to HCO Dept 2, 1:435
    more of a trouble-shooting unit than a secretarial office, 7:1161
    no non-HCO person may enter, 1:132
    not fully formed, result, 1:64
    office filing system and, 7:1162
    order,
        bringing and maintaining, 0:478–479
        Bring Order, 1:83, 1:731
        to bring order it itself must be orderly, 1:29
    organizational statements sheet and what it contains, 3:386
    organization chart, 1:50
    organizing board, 1:19, 7:1161
        placed one inch higher on org board, 1:150
        report to HCO org board which does not reflect reality of your posts, 0:166
    owns all the addresses in all orgs, 1:58
    peculiarly subject to being hit, 1:66
    personnel,
        demands and, 7:450
        real stars of staff team are auditors and HCO personnel, 1:60
        should have Staff Status II and specialty post hats and data, 1:66
        training, 1:355
    policy,
        issued by, 0:111
        preparation and distribution of HCOBs and PLs and, 1:22, 7:1163
    principle in staffing, 1:28
    product–org system,
        reverses in HCO, 1:80
        shortcomings of HCO with, MS2:3
        why not formed because of org officers, MS1:354
    products are part of Product 1, 1:65
    promotion and, 1:33
        promotional actions, list of, 1:39–40
        promotion project for, 2:408

Hubbard Communications Office (Div 1), HCO, *(cont.)*
    purpose, 7:1161
    putting at risk by false attestation, 1:869
    puzzles,
        backlogs, 1:84
        handling, 1:84–85
        no staff, 1:84
    quality set by, 1:36
    reasons for HCO disappearing in orgs, 1:132
    Reception,
        Dept 1 is not org Receptionist, 1:132
        purpose, 1:133
        Receptionist handles routing forms and traffic, 1:132
    routing and, 7:1161
    rudiments,
        gets org ruds in, 1:514
        must establish org rudiments section, 1:521
    schedule of, 7:1165
    security and, 1:36
    Senior HCO, 7:1224
    separate organization, 1:58, 7:1164
    special projects, example of, 7:25
    stability and, 1:24, 7:1165
    stable terminal for any area operation, 7:1161
    staff qualification requirements, 1:101
    Staff Staff Auditors run staff through and pick up missed withholds, 1:515
    statistics,
        how HCO loses, 1:94
        penalty, 1:94
        recruitment stat penalized double value for any ineffectiveness in Qual, 1:93
    students and pcs must report matters covered under the Justice Code to, 0:478
    system for locating and handling of PTS or SP in Academy, 1:996–997, 4:89
    technical hat checking and, 1:35–36
    terminal, first principle of, 1:24
    Thetan–Mind–Body–Product pattern, 0:654
        BODY of HCO, Dept 2, 1:566
        MIND of HCO, Dept 1, 1:566
        PRODUCT of HCO, Dept 3, 1:566
        THETAN of HCO, HAS, 1:566
    tough case is reported to, 1:1002
    use of checks vital, 1:636
    what it needs when nonfunctional, 1:84
    Worldwide,
        definition, 1:27
        purpose of office staff, 7:37
Hubbard Communications Office Bulletin(s), HCOB(s), *see also* **technology**
    altering,
        cannot be amended, 1:1031
        content, 0:23
        high crime, 1:1031

Hubbard Communications Office Bulletin(s), *(cont.)*

apply to first dynamic, 0:55

color scheme, 1:392–393, 7:1287

definition, 0:112, 1:429, 7:1322

distribution of, 1:407, 7:180

HCO Area Sec to hat check on personnel to whom they apply, 7:1287

LRH studying whether or not HCOBs, PLs and actions by him were bypasses, 0:591

Mimeo Files, should exist in, 1:435

only HCOBs may revise or cancel HCOBs, 0:143

orders,
HCOBs remain senior to all tech orders, 7:722
seniority of, 0:143, 0:523
valid only so long as they do not contradict, 7:1288

prepared and distributed by HCO, 1:22, 7:1163

sale of forbidden, 3:130

senior data on which we operate, 0:143

signatures, 1:390

statements attacking any political entity or ideology are withdrawn, 0:159

survival and, 0:55

total defense to plead one followed correctly interpreted HCO PLs, HCOBs, EDs or LRH issues or tapes, 0:145

verbal tech categories, 0:23

violations,
Comm Ev for violation of publishing or counterfeiting of, 0:113
following, obeying or issuing any verbal or written order or directive which is contrary to or changes or "abolishes" anything set up in HCO PLs or, 0:143
laying oneself open to discipline for not following, 0:146
of HCOBs, LRH tapes or issues, result, 0:145

when it becomes policy, 0:112

Hubbard Communications Office Policy Letter(s), HCO PL(s), *see also* **administrative tech; policy; technology**

apply broadly to all orgs and Scientologists, 0:112

basic principle underlying all, 0:123

be sure policy you are being shown applies in matter under discussion, 0:147

cannot be comm eved or given court or disciplined for not following BPLs, BTBs, or targets or orders that violate HCO PLs, 0:145

color scheme, 1:392–393, 7:1287

Hubbard Communications Office Policy Letter, *(cont.)*

data in HCO PLs won by hard experience, 0:56

definition and description, 0:111, 0:112, 0:716, 1:429, 7:1315, 7:1322

distribution of, 1:407, 7:180

exec should send number and date of PL and ride it until it is in, 7:403

expiration, cancellation, revision or change of, 0:113

HCO Area Sec to hat check on personnel to whom they apply, 7:1287

LRH,
LRH Communicator can assign projects based on, 7:1233
written or authorized by, 0:111

Mimeo Files, should exist in, 1:435

orders,
seniority of, 0:143, 0:523
valid only so long as they do not contradict, 7:1288

overlooked PL can become a project, 7:1233

prepared and distributed by HCO, 1:22, 7:1163

remain senior in admin, 7:722

sale of forbidden, 3:130

signatures of, 1:390, 1:426, 7:1318

standard admin, source of, 0:59

survival and, 0:55

third dynamic tech, 0:55–56

when to ask for date of it and to see a copy of it, 0:551

where staff member puts HCO PLs received, 0:166, 0:194

Hubbard Communications Office portion, 0:654

Hubbard Consultant, course fulfills tech training requirements for admin personnel, 1:165

Hubbard Dianetic Auditor (HDA), 5:326

Hubbard Dianetic Counselor (HDC),

certificate application, 5:368, 7:1103

pledge required to be signed and, 5:368

Hubbard Dianetic Graduate (HDG),

certificate,
application, 5:370, 7:1105
to obtain must have witnessed the, 5:370

internship, 5:845

Hubbard Executive, certificate, 5:327, 5:338

Hubbard Graduate Auditor (HGA), certificate, (Saint Hill), 5:325

Hubbard Graduate Scientologist (HGS), *see also* **Doctor of Scientology**

certificate, 5:317

qualification for, 5:149

Hubbard Guidance Center (HGC),

acceptance of psychotic persons for processing in the HGC is forbidden by Board Minutes, 4:1021

auditors,
criteria, 5:831, 5:832
"Okay to Audit" system is mandatory, 5:846
requirements to be done in Cramming, 5:846

cramming, Qual Sec responsible for overall tech quality, 5:612

definition, 2:505, 3:233, 4:46, 7:201

does own pc repairs, MS1:291

dummy run line, 4:944, 5:613

E-Meters used must be approved by HCO, 2:377, 7:1289

error showed up, 5:492

income, must not count on them for, 2:69, 4:337, 5:836

line,
fantastic new line, 4:939–940, 5:608
new sequence, 4:941

major Why of confusions traced to abuse of "auditor's rights" in choosing pcs, 4:209

may offer only what their staff auditors can deliver, 2:205

minimum functions, 4:253

minors and, 3:145

orgs are not huge HGCs for staff, 0:168

persons who cannot be accepted for processing, 4:1021

present lines subject to, MS1:291

procurement of pcs done by, 4:944, 5:613

product of resolved cases, 0:127

promotion,
promotional actions and, 0:351
promotional purposes and, 2:58, 7:33

psychiatric clinic, is not a, 2:402

purpose of, 2:402, 4:959

results,
falling off to degree uncertified auditors used, 5:833
HGC irresponsible for cases, 4:55
not happening, handling, 0:498
or else, 5:729

two chief seniors in area are, 4:943, 5:612

use only certified auditors on preclears, 5:833

vital datum, 4:907, 5:492

well done auditing hours over 600 a week, what to do, 4:943, 5:612

what to put attention on in, 0:16

Hubbard Key to Life Course, 4:645

chicken and egg theory of, 4:648

delivering of, without having been through it oneself, 4:647

drugs and, 4:655

enrollment on, 4:655

first hard fact of, 4:648

only possible way to export it rapidly, 4:649

prerequisite for, 4:655

routing forms for, 4:650

steps to be taken by an org in order to deliver it, 4:648

Hubbard Life Orientation Course, 4:645

Hubbard, L. Ron (LRH),

an individual, 7:1201

antipathy to authoritarian rule, 0:140

attacks on or criticism of orgs or staff considered as personal affront, 0:276

being asked for "orders," 0:144

board member, 7:1202

capitalism, get no idea that I beat any drum for, 0:508

comm lines kept wide open for research data, 0:9

criticizing ideology does not mean embracing its opposite, 0:157

crystal ball and, 0:594

defending and retaining in employ anyone who does his job, 0:151

doing what Ron says, 0:104, 0:627

don't act unless it is obvious roof is falling in, 0:239

effects on orgs of violation of KSW PL with LRH off lines, 0:7

exchange condition I try to operate on, 0:318

Executive Director, 7:1202

first order given to org, 0:335

floods of requests for decisions cuts my lines, 0:230

"For God's Sake Build a Better Bridge," 0:97

give a person on post a lot of chances, 0:239

"greatest good for the greatest number of dynamics," 0:238

handling neighborhood bully, 0:517

hats, hatting,
has to be worn as I would wear it, 0:238
hats of, 0:233
illiterate crew, hatting, 0:207
my job, 0:230

Hubbard, L. Ron, *(cont.)*

high stats from concluding actions, 0:244

in handling something I figure out if I want to play that game or not, 0:238

inspections and, 0:594

instructions, give them based on prediction of consequences, 0:140

job is not an administrative job in Scientology, 7:1164

LRH Comms and, 0:356, 0:595

mapping general strategy, 0:230

most stark truth I have ever uttered, 0:208

never compromise with a situation to be agreeable, 0:238

no monopoly on ability to observe and act, 0:140

only when success is bought by enslavement or rewards are given to bums or thieves will you find me objecting, 0:508

operate on a "sixth sense," 0:594

patching up whoever had to be shot, 0:239

perfect, I don't try to be, 0:594

person whose dept or area is running well has my full support, 0:151

petitions and, 0:489

"policy letter" is not Scientology org policy unless written or authorized by, 0:111

possessions given good care around orgs, 0:186

post,
    if person can't handle, I find another who possibly can, 0:239
    if person has been trusted with, I also trust him to handle it, 0:238
    resuming post I had left because it collapsed, 0:597
    what I say when I appoint or confirm Scientologist on post, 0:230

proved man is basically good, 0:452

quoting from works of, 7:1222

reason you see me get cross, 0:140

right, try to be right more often than wrong, 0:594

rules, don't care how many you break if they're broken to give unselfish service to one another and public, 0:273

rumors, I pay no attention to rumors or gossip, 0:151

sacking people who consistently don't do their work, 0:151

serve,
    only privilege position of command conferred on me was right to, 0:278

slaves, I rebel at making, 0:231

source of Dianetic and Scientology tech, know-how and org form, 0:658

Hubbard, L. Ron, *(cont.)*

staff member goofs roll up and knock my hats sideways, 0:233

statistic, if stat is down and won't come up, I find another person, 0:239

studying whether or not HCOBs, PLs and actions were bypasses, 0:587

technology,
    development of first and third dynamic tech, 0:55–56
    I find or develop tech of what I do, 0:300

traffic, if I find myself handling piece of, I handle it, 0:399

Trustee, 7:1201

we at top of Scientology work hard, 0:103

what would happen if I started working for pay outside orgs, 0:170

"What would Ron do in this situation?" 0:238

when I find a hat forced upon me, handling, 0:587

where I get *my* orders from, 0:140

work, philosophy about, 0:151

Hubbard Practical Scientologist (HPS),
    certificate for, 5:317

Hubbard Professional Auditor (HPA), *see also*
    Hubbard Professional Auditor/Hubbard Certified Auditor (HCA/HPA)

certificate, 5:317, 5:325

grants, no further may be issued, 6:705

may train person to level of Hubbard Apprentice Scientologist, 5:330

qualification for, 5:146

written examination, when a student is released from, 5:173

world supports me only so long as I do my job, 0:151

Hubbard Professional Auditor/Hubbard Certified Auditor (HPA/HCA),

auditing, must know two types of, 4:557

certificate,
    red seal validation, requirements for obtaining, 4:596
    requirements for obtaining, 4:564
    restored at Level III, 4:168
    what it should include, 4:610
    who holds actual certificate may train any person to the level of Hubbard Apprentice Scientologist, 4:164

course, none may be offered or run outside a Central Organization, 4:571

examination,
    oral, 4:559
    written, 4:560, 4:609

Hubbard Qualified Scientologist, replaced by, 4:168

materials to be used for compiling checksheets, outline of, 4:587

Hubbard Professional Auditor/Hubbard Certified Auditor (HPA/HCA), *(cont.)*

meters, Sec Checks and hidden standards, important that students become familiar with early in training, 4:573

qualifications for, 4:550

student,
what they are expected to pass, 4:574
when students, or auditors doing HPA/HCA retread are expected to graduate, 4:586

teaches up to Class IIa, which is the equivalent of HPA/HCA and results in the award of that certificate, 4:587

training,
of and what must be included, 4:557
requisites, 4:547
schedules, modified, 4:567

Unit 1 and what it consists of, 4:567

Unit 2 and what it consists of, 4:567

Hubbard Qualified Scientologist (HQS), 5:333

confers no classification, 4:168, 4:176

course,
how it is run, 6:481
Review, when student is routed to, 6:482

Hubbard Recognized Scientologist,

Auditors Report and, 4:620

checksheets and what they include, 4:620

TRs with meter and, 4:620

twin checking and, 4:622

Zero Certificate Course, 4:621

Hubbard Senior Scientologist (HSS), 5:325

human, humanoid, *see also* **man**

being vs. machines and automation, MS1:394

disability, auditing is answer to, 5:682

not free while aberrated in body cycle, 0:630

rights, 0:160

humanities, 4:634

using Scientology as philosophy in, 0:161

hurt, *see* **harm; injury**

husband-wife teams,

co-auditing and, 4:360

penalty for stopping the communication of, 1:902

personnel, final say in placement of, 1:163

takes company in PE Foundation, 6:462

training and, 4:360

I

I&R Form 1,
>   authorization of before issuing and enforcing
>   recommendations, MS1:451

>   done on area demanding personnel,
>   MS1:306, MS1:451

>   routing and handling of, MS1:451

>   rule, 1:533

idea(s), *see also* **dream; plan**
>   any idea is better than no idea, 0:702, 7:765

>   anyone is entitled to have, so long as these do
>   not bar route out for self and others, 0:22

>   bank dramatization and "new ideas," 0:10

>   constructive ideas are individual, 0:10

>   definition, MS3:194

>   fixed idea to handle all down stat
>   situations, 0:682

>   new ideas needed only in emergency
>   promotion, 1:38

>   outside wild queries or ideas, handling, 0:404

>   PRO is creature of ideas, 0:338

>   takes years for new ideas to "leak" into public
>   consciousness, 0:3

ideal(s), 0:455

idealization, white PR and, MS3:74

ideal organization, 0:342–343
>   definition, 6:618, 7:282, MS1:152

>   end product is not just an ideal org but a new
>   civilization already on its way, 7:283

>   how one is built, 7:283

>   image one builds toward, 6:619, MS1:153

ideal scene(s), 0:204, 0:441–442; *see also* **existing
   scene; scene**
>   ARC Break Auditor and, 5:67

>   attaining depends on, MS1:137

ideal scene(s), *(cont.)*
>   by trend it shows the overall tendency
>   to approach or depart from the ideal
>   scene, 7:527

>   clean statement of purpose is, MS1:54

>   concept of, MS1:128

>   could not envision, MS1:145

>   departure,
>   from ideal scene, low stats show, 7:518
>   handling a departure from the ideal
>   scene, MS1:54
>   most glaring departure from ideal
>   scene, MS1:179

>   evaluating, start from, MS1:178

>   executive,
>   how to attain with an, MS2:62, MS2:244
>   ideal scene for, MS2:61, MS2:243

>   existing scene,
>   ideal scene vs., MS1:52
>   moved up markedly toward, MS1:131

>   experts put so far from reach, MS1:52

>   have some idea of and want it, MS1:128

>   how to work out an, MS1:54

>   idealized scene, definition, MS3:76

>   if one doesn't know the ideal scene or
>   situation, MS1:29

>   importance of, MS1:178

>   irrationality and departures from, MS1:58

>   must be able to envision to find
>   situation, MS1:144

>   operating with incorrect, MS1:61

>   person must have an ideal scene with which to
>   compare, MS1:29

>   products, work out the correct ones to
>   know, MS1:106

>   program, will occur if program is
>   done, MS1:179

ideal scene(s), *(cont.)*

Qualifications Division ideal scenes, 5:58
  Certs and Awards Officer, 5:67
  Cramming Officer, 5:64
  Department of Correction, 5:63
  Department of Personnel Enhancement, 5:60
  Department of Validity, 5:65
  Examiner, 5:66
  Intern Supervisor, 5:64
  Medical Liaison Officer, 5:62
  Personnel Programer, 5:61
  Qual Establishment Officer, 5:59
  Qual Interview and Invoice, 5:65
  Senior C/S, 5:59
  Staff C/S, 5:60
  Staff Librarian, 5:63
  Staff Training Officer, 5:60
  Word Clearing Section, 5:61

rationality and, MS1:58

reapproach to the ideal scene for a group is by a gradient approach, 7:527

require homework, MS1:178

something that can be attained, MS1:145

statistics,
  effect of wrong stats on, MS1:63
  low stats show a departure from, 7:518
  production stats for, MS1:63
  staticizing of, examples, MS1:64–65
  valid statistic is best indicator of, 7:527

take what was desired and make it into, MS1:179

testing for correctness, MS1:61

viewpoint has a lot to do with the, MS1:95

what is retarding achievement of, MS1:128

when an org or division has departed from its ideal scene it cannot be made to recover in an instant, 7:527

work out with care, MS1:178

Ideas and Compilations Branch WW, transferred, 7:124

idée fixe, in addressing groups you are talking to an, MS3:150

identities, definition, MS1:3

ideology, 0:157, 0:159

idiot, "learn to think like an," MS1:109

idle(ness),
  down stats and, 0:587, 0:657
  false reports serving as smoke screen for, 0:527
  made to appear as best way of life, 0:315
  unhatted persons don't go idle, 0:390

Idle Report, description, 0:543

ignorance, ignorant, *see also* **stupidity**

exec remaining ignorant, 0:388

false reports and, 0:139

hats not worn and, 1:276

indicator of gross ignorance by exec of his org board, 0:409

insanity and, 0:252

lack of observation and, 0:255

no majesty and innocence like, 0:596

of human leaders in general, 0:641

policy,
  collapse caused by those ignorant of, 0:59
  continued ignorance of senior policy, 0:468
  labor–management hurricanes caused by ignorance of, 0:134
  staff ignorant or neglectful of, 0:59, 0:405

rights, ignorance of one's, 0:521, 0:525

squirrel admin due to, 0:59

trouble when ignorant or destructive people get into org issuing orders or "setting policy," 0:145

I HELP, field auditor fees, 6:734; *see also* **field auditor**

ill(ness), *see also* **potential trouble source**

auditing and, 2:438

chronically ill person, 0:507

definition, 2:403, 4:307, 5:731

dishonesty and, 0:528

evil, illness and decay often go hand in hand, 0:452

freeing the spirit prevents, 4:865

insane are very physically sick, 0:528

lower level of resolution, 4:864

persons,
  no one who is chronically ill may be accepted for processing by the HGC, 2:402
  not hatted or made to produce will get ill, 0:529
  suspected of purely medical illness should be referred to a doctor for competent treatment if such exists, 4:360
  who is chronically ill is a suspect, 4:1110

policy to send chronically ill to medical care, 2:402

psychosomatic, 0:152

staff member with severe temporary illness or physical injury may receive auditing during working hours, 0:168

studying absent masses and, 0:33

terminally ill, 2:581
  preclear, Comm Ev offense to accept, 4:1037, 6:407

when may be processed, 1:984

why people develop strange incapacitating illnesses, 0:452

illegal order(s), *see also* **cross order**
  definition, 0:145
  following, 0:102, 0:146
  forbidding anyone to write Knowledge
    Reports, 0:556
  if it seems kind of stupid it is probably
    off-policy or out-tech, 0:147
  immediate superior endangering your job
    with, 0:623
  Job Endangerment Chit and, 0:384
  junior staff member accepting illegal
    orders, MS2:229
  making oneself a party to, 0:523
  recourse and, 0:522
  reporting of, 0:623
  small play about senior trying to issue
    junior an, 0:148

illegal preclear(s), *see also* **preclear**
  acceptance of,
    Comm Ev offense to accept for
      processing, 1:904, 2:581
    high crime, 4:1037, 5:761, 6:407
  definition, 1:904–905, 2:581
  handling of, 2:582
  Office of Senior C/S Int and, 1:905
  petition may be made, 4:1038, 5:761, 6:408
  promise to audit not binding on org, 1:905
  Purification Rundown, and, 4:1039, 2:585,
    5:763, 6:412

ill feelings, in orgs, cause of, 0:413

illogic(s), *see also* **outpoint**
  beings operating on, MS1:87
  feeling angry, frustrated, helpless, MS1:129
  primary, MS1:11
  three more points of, MS1:14
  tool for rational thinking, MS1:129

illogical,
  fear of being, MS1:129
  five primary ways to become, MS1:11

image, *see also* **appearance; cleanliness; public
  relations**
  built by *action*, not just statements, 6:601,
    7:1045
  cleanliness,
    of quarters and, 0:356, 1:520,
    org image and, 6:593
    quarters and neat, professional-looking staff
      can increase income about 500%, 6:593
  creating without its costing more than one can
    afford, 6:613, MS3:154
  don't tear up org or distract it while working to
    build image, 6:601

image, *(cont.)*
  examples of poor org image, 6:614
  ideal org and, 0:342
  important to maintain org image, 1:520
  improve our, 0:334
  Inspection Officer and org image, 1:520
  LRH Comm sees that Ron's comms fly,
    look well and that Ron's EDs are complied
    with, 0:356
  org image, 0:335–338, 0:339–341, 0:356, 5:56
  projection into the public, org image is, 6:613,
    MS3:154
  public,
    comm lines and org image, 0:335
    knows us by our mest, 0:84
    poor public image, result of, 6:606
  reasons for deterioration of org image, 2:445,
    4:932, 5:688
  staff idling in Reception and org, 0:338
  use of press agentry in forwarding, MS3:134
  ways to upgrade, 6:617
  zones which comprise, 6:606

imagination,
  black PR and, MS3:75
  use of in PR, MS3:10, MS3:74, MS3:99,
    MS3:100

Immediate Registrar, definition and duties, 2:404

immigration, Scientology books and, 7:1094

imperialism, 0:508

importance, important,
  ability to apply data and, 4:1080, 5:671
  asserting one's own, as acceptable as a dead cat
    at a wedding, MS3:35
  good manners and granting importance, MS3:34
  of people, 0:329–330, MS3:35
  saying nothing is important, 0:302
  when individual can't work or doesn't see
    himself as important enough to bother
    about, 0:600

important person, org environment and handling
  of, 0:338

impression,
  first impression public gets is impression that
    stays, MS3:287
  instant impression survey, MS3:287
  message must be something which can be
    absorbed at a glance, MS3:289

improve(ment), improving,
  appointing committees of Scientologists
    to advise on improvements of
    civilization, 0:355
  fair exchange does not guarantee any
    expansion or, 0:318

255

improve(ment), improving, *(cont.)*

political system which suppresses right to improve, 0:157

who to report things to that need improving, 0:623

inactive,

SPs persuading people to be, 0:90

what encourages people to hide and be, 0:515

inactive file, definition, 2:704, 6:714

inactivity,

ethics scene, MS1:168

nobody ever does nothing, MS1:168

in-basket, *see also* **basket; out-basket**

described, 1:354

dev-t and, 0:415

empty, keep it, 0:378, 1:369

executive, 0:406–407, 0:409, 0:420

full continuously, what it means, 0:407, 0:416, 0:420

handling, two paramount data in, 0:404

having an, 0:371, 0:389, 0:392

heavy due to nonapplication of ethics, 0:660

off-line and off-policy, your full in-basket, 0:404–411

org would run better if Exec Secs had no, 0:595

should not contain anything twenty minutes after delivery, 1:364

spending part of each day clearing all traffic, 0:389

taking comm particles out of another's, 0:432

telex or cable, do not place in, 0:377

tied down to an, 0:409

in-charge(s), in charge, *see also* **executive; senior**

attacked, what happens when those in charge are directly attacked, 0:520

can't be in charge if thing one is in charge of doesn't exist, 0:654

five staff and their in-charge as a unit, 0:601

functions and work, has to be able to organize, 0:88

insane, what happens when they are put in charge, 0:253

orders, waiting for, 0:132, 0:135

person in charge trying to do all actions himself, 0:87

routing and, 0:105

suppressives often rise up to being, 0:518

what an in-charge does, 0:105

inclusion,

major point in all great organizations, MS1:269

plans of inclusion are successful, MS1:271

income, *see also* **exchange; finance; gross income; money**

analyzing traffic to increase income, 0:417

ARC Break Program run with in-tech can easily make thousands of dollars weekly in gross income and value of service delivered, 6:559

auditing and, 4:128

battle plans and, 0:708

blocked Registrar lines and, 7:847

book sales and, 2:75, 6:243

bottleneck,
is fixed ratio of outflow–inflow, 2:67
of income, 1:310

cleanliness,
dirty quarters depresses, 6:593
income depressed by dirty quarters and slovenly staff, 0:333–334
of quarters and neat, professional-looking staff can increase your income by about 500%, 0:334

competent use of targeting in battle plans and, 7:460, MS2:446, MS3:440

control equals, 2:411, 6:183

cutatives, 0:301

definition of, for Day and Foundation orgs, 3:171, 7:316

Dept of Income promotional actions regarding, 0:349

destroyed by eating up exec's time and patience, 0:373

dev-t vs., 0:391

directly proportional to number of trained auditors and sharp Course Supervisors, 7:783

exchange, org income and staff pay, 0:317–318

Executive Council shuts off all but promotionally vital POs when income far down, 3:275, MS2:413

expert handling of people, 2:399

first rule of finance, income greater than outgo, MS2:339

first step in establishing anything is valuable production and, 1:66

fixed income, how to break the back of, 1:310, 2:67

Flag Rep report and, 7:1420

Foundation org, steps for inspection, 7:309

from books, kept ready to buy new stocks when old stocks are exhausted, 2:324

future income is largely dependent upon goodwill, 0:332

income, *(cont.)*

GDSes, income depends wholly on the org's, MS1:392

goodwill and future income, MS3:168

greater than outgo, 0:289, 7:834

HASI income and where it comes from, 3:103

high when Academy good, 5:835

how almost perfectly run org will fail to get in income or give service, 0:156

how you are limiting the size and income of your org, 4:407, 6:398

if communication can flow correctly then work gets done and org can get in income, 0:196

inflow, outflow and, 0:367

largely depends upon the outflow of letters, 3:328

large percentage of comes from signing up *again* people who are already in the org, 2:642, 3:218, 4:277, 7:866

letters out statistic, income parallel to, 1:314, 7:847

list of where it comes from, 2:399

lots of staff and no or decreasing income, 0:388, 0:416

low, one should at once suspect having PTS or NCG persons on key finance post and handling, MS2:356

mail income defined, 3:74

manning organization in correct sequence and, MS3:429

moonripping and, MS1:474

more vital to pressure income up than to save money by financial planning restrictions, 3:275, MS2:413

neat, fast, no-wait, efficient reception followed by confident registraring can quintuple any org's income, 2:486, 6:379

organization,
if manned in correct sequence income has chance to stay abreast, 7:449
which has consistently low income, MS2:253

outflow, from the Registrar and CF, auditors, 2:399

policing of, 3:73

poor org image and effect on, 0:335, 6:606, MS3:140

poor, look at Dissem Division hard, hard, hard and checklist inspect it and get flubs remedied fast, 2:721

PRO actions which, if neglected, would result in heavy income losses, 0:335–338

production and, 0:502

program maxims and, 0:702

promotional writing and, 7:923

income, *(cont.)*

promotion without adequate delivery of service or commodity vs., 0:347, 1:39

proportional to control exertion of our personnel, 1:187, 2:413, 6:185

PTS or NCG persons on finance posts and, MS1:462

Public Divisions and, 6:108

reduction of, 0:197, 0:333–335, 0:338

Registrar,
action which increases income is interviewing students and selling them professional auditing, 6:414
activity is direct monitor of, 2:492

sale of books, memberships and tapes, 2:399

senior datum, 7:851

service and, 7:847

slump,
follows mail volume slump, 1:307
steps to take to handle slump, 7:848

sources of, 3:101

staff,
denying themselves, 5:544
determines the income, 0:318

think Academy, 2:70, 4:338

tours are vital to, 0:266

traced to sales expertise alone, neglecting promotion and delivery give no beans, MS2:340

train and post enough C/Ses and watch go up, 5:707

training makes most profitable, 4:461

two divisions that directly influence—Public Div and Dissem Div, 2:109

two-thirds comes from having well kept Central Files and Address and FSM files, MS2:47

unusual solutions and, 0:405

use of computer and, MS2:453

volume of income of an org is in direct proportion to number of phone calls and letters of an org, 2:613

weekly income reports from departments and, 3:121

what it depends on, 0:317

when you have people who cannot control people on PE and Registration posts, income falls or vanishes, 2:411, 6:183

where income came from to start orgs, 7:1217

where it comes from, 3:103

without adequate card files of people in proper org hands, income is greatly reduced, 2:696

income breakdown, 3:35

Income Division, *see also* **Department of Income**

actions of, 3:37

is a recording, compiling and billing section and attends to banking and bank records, 3:385

income records, advices, procedure and policy, 3:383

Income Section, *see also* **Department of Income**

description, 3:126

procuring money is the main function of, not merely recording it, 3:129

should have a way of dividing up all incoming data so it can be readily summarized onto reports, 3:383

income sheet,

Certs and Awards log and, 3:76

definition, 3:74

made available by the Accounts Dept to the posting agencies, 3:108

Qual I&I and, 3:75

reported weekly, 3:121

income sources, 2:386, 2:399, 3:101

income tax,

is a suppressive effort to crush individuals and businesses and deprive the state of national gross product (since none can expand), 3:406, 7:1090

reform and, 7:1063

income tax agency, failing national prosperity and inflation and, MS1:462, MS2:253

INCOMM,

admin high crimes, computerized system to verify, 0:77, 7:493, MS2:463, MS3:473

definition, MS2:458

product of, MS2:458

purpose of, MS2:458

representatives of, MS2:458

incompetence, incompetent, *see also* **competence**

basic reason behind, 1:819

definition, MS1:446

indicator(s),

at course completion, 0:32

auditing and, 0:32

bad, definition, 0:496, MS1:24

definition, 1:661, 5:132, 7:670, MS1:22

ethics gets good indicators in by getting tech in, 0:497

graphs and, 0:655

must be watched for in situation analysis, MS1:22

of orgs, 0:496, 1:750, 7:679

out-ethics indicators, 0:533

stats as an, 0:496, 0:681, 0:692, MS1:163

symptoms which tell how things are ethicswise, 0:497

technical gains and, 0:496

indicator(s), *(cont.)*

what neglect or abandonment of staff or caring about staff can be an indicator of, 0:693

what occurs when you push the indicator, 0:692, MS1:318, MS2:266

indigent, bum,

"hope" is byword of down and outer, 0:255

rewarding downstat, 0:50, 0:505

individual(s), *see also* **being; group member; man; people; preclear; public; staff; thetan**

bank says group is all and individual nothing, 0:10, MS3:468

basically good, 0:158, 0:453

becoming more alive, 0:123

believing or pretending something was done to one that prompted or justified his out-ethics action, 0:449

building block of any political system, 0:157

can be trusted with ethics, 0:450

cause, you are and can be, 0:685

communism vs., 0:600–601

competence, increase of, 0:64

competent individual, why he tends to take work all on himself, 0:87

constructive ideas are, 0:10

criminal society and, 0:555

decent, pleasant things on this planet come from individual actions and ideas, 0:10

determinism and, 0:448

directly responsible for a stat, MS2:230

dishonest person, only one way out for, 0:461

disseminate to individuals with problems, MS3:150

do not say that investigation of person or the past is step toward slavery, 0:462

down the chute, 0:449

dynamics in communication, 0:457

ethics,

is native to the individual, 0:448

tech exists for the individual, 0:451

freedom and, 0:461, 0:462

government seeks to run the, 0:598

group(s),

composed of individuals, 0:253

justice and action taken on individual by group when he fails to take ethics actions himself, 0:448–449

size and the individual, 0:599–602

handling for individual who has failed to win back confidence from teammates, 7:811

handling the public individual, 0:323–327

having power as individuals due to processing, 0:484

individual(s), *(cont.)*

honesty and, 0:461, 0:462

"individual liberty," what happens where it is abused, 0:461

loses out in misorganized society, 0:4

machine age vs., 0:462

ninety-two percent do not belong to groups, MS3:151

noncomprehension of basic words with which he is working, 0:40

not properly posted, isn't performing the duties of the post, is not trained or hatted, is soft, 7:811

OEC applies to the, 0:3

one of primary tools individual uses to dig himself out, 0:449

org board and, 0:3

org vs. bunch of individuals working at cross purposes, 0:405

person who cannot reveal his own acts, 0:462

personal security of, 0:515

point individual starts downhill, 0:449

Power condition for, 0:644

protesting revelation of improper acts of others, 0:462

quarrels between individual and org, 0:512

restimulated, acts worse, 0:158

right to petition, 0:488

Russia seeks to run the, 0:598

single unit (individual) is basis of a mass, 0:157

slave to his own conscience, 0:461

survival; *see* survival

techno-space society vs., 0:462

thinking he is not important enough to bother about, 0:600

to succeed, survive and expand in influence must have formulated basic policy, 7:663

unsuccessful, 0:3

we know the jailer—the person himself, 0:462

what happens when state begins to govern the, 0:603

when he starts trying to put ethics in on himself, 0:449

who do not understand pass on slanderous rumors, MS3:77

who objects to Scientology, what to ask him, MS3:152

who takes but does not give, 0:318

why a person caves in, 0:457

with personal sense of order, 0:305

working at cross-purposes, 0:325, 0:405

individualism,

obsessive individualism and a failure to organize, result, 4:796, 6:656

Russian state and, MS3:23

individuality,

teamwork vs., 0:82

total individuality and total mechanization, 0:82

indoctrination courses, 5:385

in-ethics, course, 4:424

infiltration, primary motive for, 1:630, 7:1033

inflation,

definition, MS2:390

democracy has given us income tax and, 0:9

government actively creating, 0:452

individuals being eaten up by, 0:302

moonlighting and, MS1:417

ratio of the amount of money against the goods, MS2:392

selling auditing and, 4:957

sign of culture on way out, 0:454

what it is all about, 0:318

inflow, *see also* **outflow**

exchange maintains inflow and outflow that gives person space around him and keeps bank off of him, 0:528

outflow,
holier, more moral, more remunerative and more effective than, 1:306
inflow, vs., 0:367

quantity of personal letters determines the inflow, 2:610

rises higher in proportion to outflow, the better the promotion is, 1:308

influence,

person who exerts wide primary influence on affairs of men, 0:629

zero of influence and vacuum for trouble, 0:457

info failure, 0:424

inform(ed),

juniors failing to inform seniors of data they have, 0:424

people not keeping themselves informed of what's going on, 0:144

information, info, *see also* **data**

acting only on fully verified information, 0:520

collection of and PRs, MS3:101

command channel used upward for, 0:387

exec comm lines and, 0:372

failure to forward complete information, 0:424

given information and the purpose, anybody can make a decision, 0:231

how one obtains, MS1:21

information, info, *(cont.)*

inflow of, from other org members, 0:367

infoing exec after the fact, 0:373

inspections as real source of, 0:388

irrelevant vs. relevant information, 0:430

maintaining origination lines to inform others what you are doing, 0:580

placed on time machine, 0:382

poor relay of, 0:432

security and, 0:579

sources of, 0:388

to handle any post you have to have and furnish, 0:578

up-to-date org board as a source of, 0:388

what an exec does want on his lines, 7:603

information board(s),

have no official status, 1:351

may contain personal notes, 1:348

placement of, 1:351

posting of information relating to exact job, 1:348

student information board, 1:348

information letter, info letter, *see* **HCO Information Letter**

information packet(s), info packet(s), info package,

CF–Promotion Liaison hat and, 2:658

Distribution Division can keep a statistic on which communicated the best, 2:709

may not contain or lead the person toward confusing words or terms, 2:201, 4:73, 6:195

must stress only one thing, 2:398

never inform someone of the road to freedom without also informing him of how and where to get it, 6:217

points to be adhered to, 6:217

selected mailing lists and, 2:709

ways you will lose person sent an, 2:201, 4:73, 6:195–196

what to do when a person responds to, 2:709

infraction sheet, 4:316

initiative,

failure to act with or show, 0:662

harsh discipline smothers it, 0:515

take the initiative and take action instead of referring it, 0:399

to make stats go up, 0:683

understanding and, 0:144

injury, injure, *see also* **harm**

freedom for man does not mean freedom to injure man, 0:461

working quietly and silently to help injured person, 0:153

injustice, *see also* **HCO Ethics Codes; justice**

actions taken on others without investigation and without confronting them with their accusers or data, 0:514

ARC breaks with public due to, 0:276

authority undermined by being made to commit injustices, 0:520

Comm Ev can restore lost pay in cases of injustice but not damages, 0:478

cumulative and unremedied, 0:515

description, causes, handling, prevention, 0:521–525

discipline and, 0:477, 0:415, 0:421

dishonesty and, 0:152

Doubt assigned person who accepts and disciplines another unjustly on basis of false report, 0:515

false reports and, 0:515, 0:520

ignorance of rights and, 1:811

injures discipline, 1:815

man wreaks injustice with punishment, 0:449, 0:521

operating on unsubstantiated reports, 0:520

permitting it by not knowing or ignoring one's rights, 0:525

personal security undermined by, 0:515

PTS condition and, 0:515

recoils on those who deal in it, 0:520

recourse from, 0:481, 0:522

third party actions and, 0:513

through bad metering on meter checks, 1:766

when it occurs, 1:815

wrongly accusing and punishing unjustly, result, 0:521

innocence, innocent,

justice developed to protect the, 0:456

some are guilty, most are innocent, 0:483

striking innocent and guilty alike, 0:483

there is no majesty and innocence like ignorance, 0:596

In-Person Scheduling Book, definition, 2:629

inquiry, how Australia got into inquiry mess, 0:410

insane, insanity, *see also* **mad; suppressive person**

about 15 to 20% of the human race apparently is, 1:804

accepting unworkable "tech," 0:9

insane, insanity, *(cont.)*

actions are not "unconscious," 1:804

actions of, 0:252, 0:296

acts are not unintentional, MS1:446

anatomy of, MS1:36

apparent pattern of behavior, 1:806

are just one seething mass of overt acts and
withholds, 0:528

belong to the psychiatrist, 4:1094

characteristics of suppressive person and, 1:804

civilization without, 6:519

definition, 1:168, 1:805, 2:403, 4:307, 5:731

difference between sanity and, 7:1143

easiest ways for a C/S to detect, 1:805

handling situations which no longer
exist, 1:991, 4:83

in Dianetics insanity is shown to be common
physical illnesses, 7:1134

madman only goes *toward* but never really
arrives, 0:237

maintain own stability by unstabilizing everyone
else, 1:211

matter of motive, MS1:295

most expensive thing you can do is process
the, 0:507

must reach–can't reach, must withdraw–can't
withdraw is total basic insanity, 7:1138

no person who is insane may be accepted for
processing by the HGC, 2:402

now defined as anyone who disagrees with the
social autonomy, 7:1135

on part of receiver of VFP, MS1:295

persons, handling, 5:105, 5:625

point where a thetan goes mad, 0:509

policies regarding, 5:105

product of the, 0:252, 1:804, MS1:446

psychiatry's product of, 0:125

quite happy to have everything fail and go
wrong with no protest from them, 0:237

real cycle of behavior, 1:806–807

refusal to allow others to be, do or
have, MS1:268

sanity and insanity are matters of motive, not
rationality or competence, 0:296

Scientology and, 0:152

sign of a culture on way out, 0:454

technology to handle, 1:806

treatment of, 1:984

very physically sick people, 0:528

violence practiced for its own sake is just
insane, 7:1143

insane, insanity, *(cont.)*

who real crazy people in universe are, 0:237

working endlessly to make things go wrong and
prevent anything from going right, 0:237

insane preclear,

definition, 7:1101

handling of, 7:1101

"in-session," correct definition, 5:653

insight, MS1:92

policy, orders and, 0:114, 0:122

insignia,

Clear bracelet, 5:327, 5:356

Dept 5 gets insignia in stock and ensures broad
issue, 0:349

Grade VII Clear, 5:356

ministerial, 5:327

OT bracelet, 5:327, 5:356

Release button, 5:327

sales of, income source, 3:101

Scientology pins, 5:327, 5:356

special insignia for auditors, 0:154

when preclear has attained Grades V or VI,
5:356

insolvency, insolvent, *see also* **bankruptcy;
solvency; viability**

condition where outgo exceeds income, 3:129

debug tech and, MS2:145

how to understand whether you should be
solvent or insolvent, 0:357

org appearing busy and overworked while
producing little, 0:441

org getting insolvent, handling, 0:374

staff transferred out of an org tending toward,
1:170

without promotion one has, 0:347, 1:39, 5:41

inspection(s), inspect(ing), *see also* **investigation;
look; observation**

always done as the first step in any debug,
MS2:155

areas in order of sequence, 7:636

areas of Dangers and Affluences, 0:655

as a real source of info, 0:388

assessing the subproduct lists against a direct
inspection of the area to which it applies,
7:828

Assoc Sec to do two daily inspections, 7:621

before the fact, 0:66, 0:244, 1:526

by direct inspection, an executive learns who is
or isn't on post, 1:379

by outpoints against factor of orderliness, 0:307

comm lines, analysis of, 0:416

C/S, study out terminals and lines, 5:695

inspection(s), inspect(ing), *(cont.)*

example of, 7:686

fast flow depends on total flow without inspection, 0:660

graph posted for inspection, 0:691

intention is to hat, don't hit personnel, 1:528

KOT expected to do org inspections, 7:1274

locating and correcting disordered areas, 0:308

looking into people's baskets, 0:416

low stats, 1:528

morale factor and, 7:716

nothing will substitute for, 0:595

noticing something nonoptimum without mentioning it but only inspecting it silently, 0:494

of grounds and premises, 6:594

only physical inspection will reveal other crimes going on in area where false graph originated, 0:658

operating targets and, MS2:433

personally or by representative an executive inspects continually, MS2:60, MS2:242

personal quarters, inspection of, 0:311

procedure, 0:308, 0:592

reason for, 0:308, 0:593

senior who doesn't inspect or get inspections done does not know, 0:593

steps, debug tech and, MS2:145

two types of actions a CO/ED does, 7:716

viewing actual condition is vital step to resolving it, 0:122

vital targets and, MS2:432

ways of how to inspect, 7:686

when all areas and departments of Saint Hill to be inspected, 7:636

Inspection and Report Form, *see also* **I&R Form 1**

personnel demands and, MS2:105, MS2:256

Inspection Officer,

does regular Friday inspection of grounds and premises, 6:594

duties of, 1:191

investigating things that shouldn't be, 0:547, 1:705

landlord presenting claim against Scientologist, handling, 0:172

training for, 1:67

Inspection Section,

duty to inspect low stats, 1:528

familiar with stats and stat interpretation, 1:528

first section's function, 1:484

I&R Form 1, 1:529, 1:533

Inspection Section, *(cont.)*

in Department 3, 1:484

in small orgs has one person, 1:484

second section is Ethics, 1:484

time machine and, 0:375

instability, persons having rough time or giving others one, not actually on post, 7:810

instant hat, *see also* **hat; hatting**

checksheet for execs and managers, 7:485, MS2:201, MS2:306, MS3:465

instant hatting, 0:308, 0:439, 0:440

Management Status One checksheet and, 7:463, MS2:190, MS2:294, MS3:443

instant impression, definition, MS3:287

"instant" opinion, definition, MS3:121

instant purpose clearing, definition, 5:461

Instant Service Project, 4:125

institution, institutionalized,

definition, 2:403, 4:307, 5:731

illegal pcs and, 4:1037

persons with record of being committed in an institution refused training or processing at the organization, 4:360

institutional, institutionalization,

case, definition, 1:168

history, definition, 1:904

processing not allowed on people with history of, 1:984

institutional background, no person who has institutional background may be accepted for processing by the HGC, 2:402

institutional history,

definition, 2:581

preclear with, Comm Ev offense to accept, 6:407

instruction, instruct(ing) (in a course room), *see also* **course; training**

clear, precise orders and, 0:431

course natter stems entirely from noncomprehension of words and data, 4:329, 5:177

demanding things student has not yet reached, result, 5:176

done on a gradient scale, 4:329, 5:177

flubbed instruction perpetuates error on every pc that auditor audits thereafter, 4:11, 5:11

I don't try to force job to be held by streams of instructions once failure is apparent, 0:239

I give instructions based on prediction of consequences, 0:140

instruct, cram, retrain, offload system, 0:442

learn each part well by itself, 4:329, 5:177

instruction, instruct(ing) (in a course room), *(cont.)*

offenses concerning, 0:467–468

proper instruction attitude, 0:12–13

proper source of, 4:1173, 5:586

protocol, issued at beginning of Dianetics, 4:287

raising the standard of, 4:327

result of demanding things student has not yet reached, 4:328

staff may not employ staff time to instruct, 0:168

why proper instruction is vital, 0:12–13

Instructor, *see also* **Supervisor**

how they must teach, 5:177

invoices and, 3:119

must challenge with ferocity instances of "unworkability," 3:13, 5:13

obscuring source of tech, guilty of false report, 5:840

responsibility is to graduate students who have accurate knowledge of the subject, 5:170

teaching or advising method not contained in HCOBs, tapes, etc., crime, 5:840

Instructor's Code (Supervisor's Code), *see also* **Course Supervisor; Supervisor**

challenging with ferocity instances of "unworkability" of Scientology, 0:13

closer to test evaluation than the Auditor's Code, 6:273

Keeping Scientology Working PL and, 0:12

must be alert for, 1:1001

responsibility for blown students, 1:998

student trying to wear instructor's hat, 0:413

training and, 4:304

insubordination, offenses concerning, 0:468

Insurance Officer, 0:548, 1:706

Int Admin Officer, duties, 7:137

integrity,

enemy is lacking, 0:337

expansion and, 0:100, 0:337

goodwill and, 0:332

PR and, 6:608, MS3:142

Integrity Checks, *see* **HCO Confessional; Security Check**

intelligence,

covert, MS3:26

Data Series and, MS1:154

definition, MS1:3, MS3:27

exposure is basic threat of, MS3:27

increasing ability and, 4:306, 5:730

power of, MS3:27

intelligence, *(cont.)*

PR and, MS3:26, MS3:29, MS3:73

purpose of HGC to improve, 2:402

tech, PR man should know something about, MS3:26

intelligence actions, 1:629; *see also* **counterespionage**

organization and, 7:1033

intensive(s), *see also* **audit(ing); processing**

admin time,

deducted from intensive hours purchased by pc, 3:179

spent on C/Sing, FESing and FF table making should be deducted from hours purchased, 2:459

buying enough, 4:1042

completed, definition, 4:210

cutative, 5:22

definition, 2:458, 3:178

for staff, 5:543

sell grades in, 2:427

sliding scale of pricing of, 2:458

25-hour intensives should be delivered in one week, 4:250

intention(s),

communication and, 0:46

evaluating oneself or one's own group, project or org as to objectives and, 0:575

man is basically well-intentioned, 0:453

strength and, 0:517

interchange, principles of, 0:296–298; *see also* **exchange**

interest,

best way to handle, 6:676

living off interest from loans, 0:508

programs must accumulate, 0:702

interested party(ies), *see also* **Committee of Evidence**

definition, 1:928

do not seek to name exec councilmen as, 0:478

failure to appear before Comm Ev as an, 0:469

false witnesses become, 1:930

no senior exec in org may be named as interested party in matters of recourse requested by a junior, 0:478

Interiorization Rundown, 4:197, 6:423

intern(s),

checksheets for, 4:631

definition, 4:417, 5:849, 5:856

may not be paid units for being, 5:834

"Okay to Audit," means, 5:852

professional staff auditors vs., 5:833

use no interns in HGC, 5:833

who they may audit, 4:683

internal noise, definition, 7:454, MS3:434

Internal Requisition Form,
    filled in when supplies needed, 3:395
    use of, 0:185

International Board, policy letter passed as resolution of, 0:111

International Board Members, passing HCOBs and HCO PLs, 0:143

International Communications Officer,
    duties, 7:137

International Declarations Officer, duties, 7:138

International Ethics Officer,
    duties, 7:137
    protesting assigned condition and sending copies of all stats and order to, 0:652

International Executive Division,
    another Saint Hill Division, 7:104
    how it was handled by a Coordinator, 7:91
    newly formed up, 7:87
    statistics, 7:90

International Finance Office, definition, MS2:351

International Justice Chief (IJC),
    failing to advise him of serious charges in Knowledge Reports, 0:557
    must approve removals, 1:257
    only terminal for suppressive person, 1:885
    staff member may not be comm eved, removed, dismissed or routed off staff without approval of, 1:257

International Management, definition, MS2:350

International Management expenses, definition, MS2:352

International Promotion Officer, duties, 7:137

International Technical Officer, duties, 7:138

internship(s), *see also* **course**
    being used to teach course again, 4:417
    consist of, 4:417, 5:856
    courses and, 4:417, 5:856
    cramming and Word Clearing make excellent auditors, 4:966
    definition, 4:417, 5:849, 5:856
    done in Div 5, 4:417
    electronic attestation form, 5:854
    established in Central Orgs, St. Hill Orgs and Advanced Orgs, 5:844
    Flag and, 5:851
    follow LRH PLs and HCOBs and keep arbitraries off the line, 5:859
    graduate, definition, 5:856
    heavily into theory, reason for, 4:418
    must audit high hours, 5:850

internship(s), *(cont.)*
    overlong, 4:417
    product of, 4:417, 5:856
    purpose of, 4:418, 5:857
    remedy to streamline them, 5:857
    requirements for HGC auditors, 4:946, 5:846
    student must pass exam on course materials before routing onto, 4:418
    Type A definition, 4:543
    Type B definition, 4:543
    Type C definition, 4:543

internship graduate, definition, 4:417

Intern Supervisor,
    auditor trainee's top boss, 5:530
    ideal scene, 5:64
    keeps checklist of trainee's program, 5:531
    makes full training report weekly, 5:843
    OES may appoint or transfer, 5:843
    product, 5:64
    purpose, 5:64
    responsibility for auditor trainees, 5:528
    statistics, 5:64, 5:532
    tech hierarchy and, 5:697

interorg exchange, definition, 3:208, 5:123

interorg bills, definition, MS2:405

interorg comm, remedies, 7:158

interorg transfer,
    definition, 3:208, 5:123
    most common cause of, 3:209, 5:124
    policy regarding, 3:209, 5:124

interpretation, interpreting,
    leave nothing to, MS1:8
    meaning shifted by reinterpretation, 0:141
    of policy, 0:126, 0:141
    read exact issue or book for yourself and don't listen to interpretation that seems far-fetched, 0:147
    verbal tech and, 0:23

interrogation, ethics actions and, 0:494

interrogatory, 0:494

intervention,
    I don't act unless it is obvious roof is falling in, 0:239
    routine, 7:351, MS3:331

interview(s),
    actions to do when interviewing someone, 4:40
    beginning intensives, for pcs, 4:858
    control and, 2:493, 6:158
    Host, Flag and some other orgs, 4:984, 7:735
    how to, 2:493

interview(s), *(cont.)*

list of, 2:586

people, how to, 6:158

preprocessing Security Check, 4:858

purpose of, 2:493, 4:40, 6:158

Qual Consultant, provided by, 4:982, 7:733

types of, 4:979, 5:764, 7:730

   Chaplain, 1:828, 2:590, 5:768, 6:417

   Director of Processing, 1:826, 2:588, 4:244, 4:963, 5:766, 6:415, 7:732

   Director of Training's end-of-week interviews, 4:321

   Ethics Officer/MAA, 1:827, 2:589, 5:767, 6:416

   Executive Director/Commanding Officer, 1:828, 2:590, 4:983, 5:768, 6:417, 7:734

   Host, 1:829, 2:591, 5:769, 6:418

   Qual Consultant, 1:827, 2:589, 5:767, 6:416

   Registrar, 1:824, 2:586, 4:979, 5:764, 6:413, 7:730

   Solo Consultant, 1:827, 2:589, 4:982, 5:767, 7:733

   Technical Estimate, 1:825, 2:587, 4:980–981, 4:1041, 5:765, 6:414, 7:731

when prospect comes in, what to do, 2:611

wronged, ARC broken public, Chaplain interviews, 4:983, 7:734

intimidation, government by riot and, 0:481

in-training, new people on post serve as, MS1:200

intro services,

are the answer to an FSM's prayers, 6:674

definition, 6:673

Introductory and Assist Actions, 6:420

introductory courses, vs. Dept 17 courses, 6:485

introductory lecture(s), intro lecture(s),

advertise it heavily, 6:475

follow up with letter, 6:482

free, 0:303, 0:347

handing out invitations to, 0:352

stresses value of Scientology and communication, 6:480

used to sell courses or processing, 6:480

using no words that will be misunderstood, 0:353

invalidation, invalidate,

antisocial personality deals mainly in, 1:1015

auditor ceases to audit well, 4:828

effect of, 0:247

self-invalidation defined, 0:247

when rehabbing can act as, 5:674

you should not minimize yourself as cause, 0:249

inventory, 0:187

Inventory Officer, 0:189, 3:397

investigation, investigate(d), investigating, *see also* evaluation; inspection; observation

always investigate for true cause of trouble, 0:240

background of person guilty of technical degrades investigated, 0:14

best answer is to organize our own corps for investigation, 7:1028

Danger condition and, 0:585

dead files and, 1:976

done at effect, MS1:76

done on person who does not follow First Dynamic Danger Formula completely, 0:605

effectiveness in handling attacks and, 7:1027

ethics, by stats, MS1:165

examples, MS1:74

full data on how to do given in *The Volunteer Minister's Handbook*, MS2:146

HCO should learn full investigatory procedure, 1:633

Inspection Officer investigating things that shouldn't be, 0:547

investigate someone with steady down stat, 0:505

levels of ethics action and, 0:494

necessary in face of, MS1:72

never act on junior's data until you have fully investigated situation, 0:241

of person or the past is not step toward slavery, 0:462

on personnel on whom noncompliance or crimes are discovered, 0:586

outpoints and, MS1:157

primary block to, MS1:73

required by Flag or CLOs requested on Flag Rep lines, 7:1410

running back investigation by following chain of false reports, 0:514

Section 5 investigates social areas of down stats, 0:506

sequence and, MS1:73–74

skill behind intelligent action, MS1:72

solve only problem you find after careful investigation, 0:240

tech, getting ethics in and, 4:973

technical, 1:749

when too many chits occur in staff member's file, 0:553

"who-where" needed for, MS1:151

Investigations Checksheet, *The Volunteer Minister's Handbook* and, MS2:146

investigation personnel, communication's personnel vs., 0:327

investigatory tech,

date coincidence, MS1:165

what happens when it is used, 0:694

why people can't put in ethics, MS1:165

invitation, OT courses are by, 4:808

invoice(ing),

accepting students on course without seeing, 0:303

addresses culled back from old invoices, 2:705

all books issued anyone must be invoiced whether charged for or not, 2:552, 3:141, 6:386

any item for which there would ordinarily be a charge must be invoiced, 2:482

anyone who ever buys anything from org is invoiced, 0:99

auditors or Supervisors who deliver service without fully-paid invoice to hand, 3:170

clarification of invoicing items, 3:142

confidence checks and, 0:469

corrections done on additional invoices or vouchers, 3:133

definition, 3:74

Dept 7 gets all mail orders invoiced and/or collected, 0:350

description and routing of the various copies, 3:135, 3:136

five stations in an organization, 3:104

Free Release Check and rehabilitation, 3:162

getting one's mailing list off old invoices, 0:625

handling for minus invoices, 3:133

HCO Account done on a separate invoice machine, 2:281

how copies are distributed, 2:292

invoice line for books ordered, 0:282

membership funds and, 3:188

must be legibly done, 3:107

no charge, 2:482

no-charge activity and, 3:119, 3:142

no-charge invoice, Sup must reject, 4:461

no exceptions, 3:142

no service or sale may be given without invoicing or registration, 4:219

one copy of kept by Shipping Department, 2:279

packaging of, 3:134

people ordered to processing or training and, 3:143

permitting delivery without proper invoice or payment, result, 3:120

preclears,

may not be extended into unpaid courses or hours of processing by debit invoice, 3:164

must be invoiced by Registrar whether charge is made or no charge, 6:386

procedure for invoicing, 0:99, 0:282, 2:489

invoice(ing), *(cont.)*

rules, 3:34

staff must be invoiced for course, 0:222

students,

may not be extended into unpaid courses or hours of processing by debit invoice, 3:164

must be invoiced by Registrar whether charge is made or no charge, 6:386

"pass" to enter course, 4:460

survey done out of, MS3:178

system of routing invoice copies to Address and CF, 2:621

where copies of invoices go, 0:99, 0:626–627

Invoice Form, use of in tracking pc paid auditing hours, 4:263

invoice packets, kept secure and made available for use in audits, MS2:327

Invoicing Section, definition, 3:131

invoicing stations, Treas Div controls and polices each day, 3:75

IQ (intelligence quotient),

can change, 0:3

how to raise, 6:296

lower IQ, the more individual is shut off from fruits of observation, 0:9

Scientology has already taken people toward higher, 0:21

irrationality,

departures from ideal scene and, MS1:58

in government, MS1:59

man and, MS1:60

irreducible minimum,

law of, MS1:441

posts and, MS1:219

irresponsibility, irresponsible, *see also* **responsibility**

demands for decisions are indicative of, 0:372

exec who doesn't handle but puts something on wait is, 0:260

glorious irresponsibility of orders, 0:140

letting unwilling, irresponsible person on our lines, 0:398

referral is, 0:260

issue(s), *see also* **mimeo issue**

Aides Order (AO), definition, 7:1324

Base Order (BO), definition, 7:1323

Board Executive Directive (BEDs), definition, 7:1323

Board Policy Letter (BPLs), definition, 7:1323

Board Technical Bulletin (BTBs), definition, 7:1323

issue(s), *(cont.)*

Central Bureaux Order (CBO),
definition, 7:1323

Continental Order (CO), definition, 7:1324

divisional order, definition, 7:1323

Flag Bureaux Data Letter (FBDL),
definition, 7:1324

Flag Conditions Order (FCO), definition, 7:1324

Flag Divisional Directive (FDD),
definition, 7:1324

Flag Mission Order (FMO), definition, 7:1324

Flag Order (FO), definition, 7:1323

Flag Personnel Order (FPO), definition, 7:1324

Flag Program Order (FPGMO),
definition, 7:1324

Flag Project Order (FPJO), definition, 7:1324

Flag Ship Order (FSO), definition, 7:1324

HCO Administrative Letter, definition, 7:1323

Mission Order (MO), definition, 7:1324

numbering of, 1:438

order of seniority, 1:282

issue(s), *(cont.)*

Orders of the Day (OOD), definition, 7:1325

Sea Org Executive Directive (SO ED),
definition, 7:1323

Station Ship Order (SSO), definition, 7:1324

Technical Individual Program (TIP), issue type,
definition, 7:1324

types of, 1:429, 7:1322

Issue Authority, I/A,

all foreign translations must have, 6:767, 7:1321

for all mimeo, reasons for, 7:1308

for mailing piece or handout of any Central Org
or city office, 2:134

OODs and, 7:729

parties involved must okay issue, before it goes
to I/A, 7:128

too tough, causes ARC breaks, 0:276, 2:435

"Is this okay?" 0:419, 0:427

ivory tower,

doesn't exist in PR, MS3:101

executive and, 0:594

most ivory of, 5:709

J

jam(s), jammed, jamming,

 by demanding to be on routing lines exec can jam lines, 0:388

 comm line, ways it can be jammed, 0:85, 0:430

 exec resolving jams that impede things, 0:373

 floods of requests for decisions cuts my lines by jamming them, 0:230

 jamming exec's lines, result, 0:373

 lack of supplies causing flow to jam, 0:380

 takes lot of counter-effort to jam org's flows, 0:587

janitor, promotion and, 0:346

Japan, how US might have won war with Japan in six weeks, 0:116

Jews, passivity earned them slaughter, 0:518

job, *see also* post

 description of, 1:266

 failure to provide begets revolt, MS1:408

 handling for people who aren't doing their jobs, 7:605

 how to hold in Scientology org, MS1:237

 solvency is made by doing one's own, 1:49

 what is your job in an org, MS1:236

job card, system used for renovations, 7:1399

Job Endangerment Chit(s), *see also* ethics chit(s); report(s)

 chits by seniors, 7:330, MS3:310

 definition, 0:384, 1:709

 description, 0:544, 0:552–553

 file, when falsely reported upon, 7:331, MS3:311

 immediate superior endangering your job with illegal orders or alter-is, handling, 0:623

Job Endangerment Chit(s), *(cont.)*

 on somebody ordering you to do things not your hat, 1:274

 threatened with punishment if one files a, 0:552

 vexatious filing, 7:330, MS3:310

 what to file, 7:330, MS3:310

 when and where to file, 0:197, 0:384, 0:544, 0:551–553, 0:579, 1:709–710, 7:329, MS3:309

Joburg Org, misplaced CF address list, 0:359

Joburg Security Check,

 staff members and, 5:565

 staff right to demand that any or all staff be given a, 0:20

jokers and degraders, 1:822

judgment,

 conditions formulas and, 0:679

 leadership that will lack, 0:122

 lies in how much external restraint to apply, 0:480

 needed in every staff post, 0:82

 stat management and, 0:679

judicial, body that judges or applies the laws to particular cases, MS2:215

junior(s), *see also* staff

 always demand facts from, 0:241

 checking junior's graphs daily, 0:691

 comm-member definition, 7:229

 completed staff work and, *see* completed staff work

 conclusions not acceptable from, 0:241

 efforts to look and sound active while loafing and goofing, 0:420

 ethics and, *see* ethics

269

junior(s), *(cont.)*

exec may assign any condition and improve any condition he assigns to any person immediately junior to him on his command channel or within his own office or area, 0:659

exec not putting on hats of his, 0:409

failing to inform seniors of data they have, 0:424

First Dynamic Danger Formula and, 0:606

group size and, 0:598

how to keep out of trouble, 0:145

illegal orders and, 0:145

making all juniors into workers or privates, 0:134

may complain to Dir Comm re staledate, 0:382

may not name senior exec as interested party in recourse action, 0:478

must follow the orders of their own seniors or Danger condition results, 7:683

never take a generality from, 0:241

no top management can predict what policy will be set by its, 0:134

one has to exert some control over his equals, juniors and superiors, 0:555

order(s),

accepting orders from everyone, 0:589

action on receiving, 0:375

duplicate order and never fail to clarify if you have misunderstood, 0:431

goes from a senior to junior, 0:134

issuing orders unknown to senior and across his lines, 0:425

lumping all juniors into order-receivers, 0:134

not getting exec's orders executed, 0:420

protection from off-policy orders, 0:145–146

subjected to harassment and forced to obey off-policy order, 0:145

verbal order reported to Ethics, 0:376

problems presented by, 0:207, 0:240, 0:427

sack every junior who will not put in ethics in their area, 0:421

secretly putting his superior into bypass, 0:587

seniors let down by, handling, 0:552

seniors' responsibility that juniors have hats, 0:202

severing their control of their area by not doing their job, 0:619

smarter than the senior, 0:589

steps of full program which can be applied to junior who has been assigned Danger, MS2:207

"This is Okay," 0:419, 0:427

time machine and, 0:382

junior(s), *(cont.)*

when to beware of being told it is "on-policy" or "an LRH order" or "in bulletins" or "on LRH tapes," 0:146

why juniors are juniors and have seniors, 0:593

writing up overts and withholds and any known out-ethics situation, 0:606

Junior Danger Formula, *see also* **Danger**

consists of writing up one's overts and withholds, then doing First Dynamic Formula, 0:612

definition, MS2:206

jury, Chaplain's Court, 1:957, 6:522

justice, *see also* **ethics; HCO Ethics Codes**

accepting any accusation and acting upon it, 0:514, 0:520

acting on false reports, 0:514

administering justice, 0:480, 1:733

auditor of the group, 1:741

balance of power and, 7:1302

basic intention of, 0:456

becomes less needful and milder as technology develops, 5:348

breakthrough in solving subject of, 0:448

cannot be trusted in hands of man, 1:963

channel of progress and, 1:733

Civil Committee of Evidence and, 0:478

Comm Evs and, 1:933

Committee of Evidence, *see* Committee of Evidence

confronting accused with accusation and accuser, 0:514, 0:515

contending auditors must seek out the D of P, 0:478

correct application, 0:520

court, *see* court

Court of Ethics, *see* Court of Ethics

criminally inclined protest and complain that justice exists, 0:480

definition, 0:448, 0:477, 0:520, 1:730, 1:811

demotion, *see* demotion

developed to aid an individual, 1:492

developed to protect innocent and decent, 0:456, 1:491

discipline, *see* discipline

dismissal, *see* dismiss

Div 1, depends upon for authority and power, 1:944

don't react to Scientology justice as though it were "wog" law, 0:485

equal justice for all, 0:160

establishing truth of accusation before action is taken, 0:515

ethics and,

ethics, justice and the dynamics, 0:451–460

justice, *(cont.)*

ethics and, *(cont.)*

justice used only after failure of individual to use, 0:458

justice used until person's ethics render him fit company for his fellows, 0:456

solution lays in their separation, 0:448

substituting justice for ethics, 0:456

example, 1:483

external restraint, how much to apply, 0:480

external threat and internal pressure, 1:733

failing to apply it to society around us, result, 0:483–484

fair and equitable treatment for group and individual, 0:521

fair play and, 0:520

function must exist, 1:483

going on being wogs if we don't use our justice, 0:485

greatest good for the greatest number and, 1:733

Greek philosophers and, 0:448

group's use of, 0:450

harsh injustice vs. required discipline, 0:522

having superior law code and legal system which gives real justice to people, result, 0:483

HCO is justice agency of Scientology and Scientologists, 0:477, 0:487, 1:730

history and, 0:447–448, 1:497

honesty, *see* honesty; dishonesty

how to be just, 0:121–122

impeding justice, 0:469

in the absence of, there is no progress and no team, 1:250

is expected and has definite use, 0:450, 0:521

keeps channel of progress a channel, 0:480

law, *see* law

look up person who rails against justice most, 0:480

LRH hat of, 0:232, 0:233

man cannot be trusted with, 0:450, 0:456, 1:498, 7:1143

must be fast and cheap, 1:968

must exist to protect producers, 1:483

necessary action, 1:484

necessary to any successful society, 0:518

need for, lies in the public and lower levels, 5:349

new hope, 1:962

not operating on isolated reports, 1:809

Office of LRH issues all authorities for, 7:1301

only overt in handling justice, 0:480

justice, *(cont.)*

opinion and, 0:521

oppression, identified with, 0:456, 0:517

order and, 1:733

our justice rehabilitates in long run, 0:484

overts disclosed in session, not used for justice, 1:634

penalty, *see* penalty

person who rails against, 1:733

personal security and, 0:515

petition and, 0:488, 1:742

points needing correction in uninformed person concerning our justice, 0:483

police, *see* police

policy letter corrections, 1:942

primary breakdown of any justice system, 0:516

protects staff member's reputation and job, 0:477, 0:481, 0:502, 0:503

psychiatry's justice procedures, 0:521

punishment, *see* punishment

purpose of, 0:456, 0:457, 0:483, 0:517, 1:741

reason for, 1:939

reasons for it straying, MS1:72

recourse, *see* recourse

renewed faith in, 1:542

rights of a staff member, students and preclears to, 0:477–479, 1:730

right to be tried only by seniors in rank or status, 0:524

runs out group engrams if good, 1:924

safeguards rights of Scientologists, prevents injustice, prevents punishment by whim, and brings order, 0:477–479

sentence, 0:491, 0:495

should serve as a means of establishing guilt or innocence and awarding damages to the injured, 1:924

Spanish Inquisition and, 1:963

SPs snarl about, 1:994

staff member report, *see* staff member report

state of discipline and, 1:811

suing fellow staff member or righting wrong, procedure, 0:478

suppressive person cries for protection of, 1:988

taking justice in own hands, 0:479

thetan invented bank to keep others good, 0:480

third dynamic psychosis is the substitute of violence for reason, MS1:268

third party and, 0:513

threat included in request for, 0:488

truth and, 0:520

two lessons learned, 1:483

used for political gain, 1:962

justice, *(cont.)*

used incorrectly increases disorder, 1:924

used until, 1:491

use of Scientology justice, 0:483

vs. personal security, 1:924

weighing value of person against alleged crime, 0:516

what every upset is traceable to, 1:940

what happens to Scientologist who fails to use Scientology technology, 1:940

what it consists of, 0:515

when it becomes end-all in itself, 0:450

when it would not be needed, 0:456, 0:458

when justice enters in, 1:491

when to use group justice procedures, 0:456

whole task of justice is to defend the honest man, MS1:279

without understanding there will be no, 0:483

wog law and courts, 0:327, 0:485

work for greatest good of greatest number, 0:480

wrongful disgrace, demotion, transfer or dismissal, 0:477, 0:487

Justice Codes, *see also* **HCO Ethics Codes**

assignment of Emergency suspends the, 0:477

Justice Codes, *(cont.)*

discipline before the, 0:477

HCO, org executive and divisional secretaries, justice on, and auditing of, 5:583

reason for, 0:483

Scientologists and staff members in accepting posts or membership agree to abide by HCO Codes, 0:477

secure job, a peaceful org, 0:487

students, pcs and, 0:477, 0:487

when they are in full force, 0:477

Justice Department, 1:963

justification(s), justifying, 0:464

believing or pretending something was done to one that prompted or justified his out-ethics action, 0:449

debug tech and, MS2:151–152

excuses for leaving are usually simply justifications, 0:177

thrusting aside all, 0:236

Justinian I, 0:637

juvenile delinquency, 0:291

K

Keeper of Tech and Policy Knowledge,
Boards of Review and, 7:1265
business of, 7:1274
Continental, org inspections and, 7:1274
establishment of Qual and, 7:1273
network structure, 7:1274
posting C/Ses and, 5:709
purpose and channel used, 7:1273
reason for the post, 7:1276
stats, 7:1276

Keeping Admin Working,
definition, 7:487, MS3:467
what it means, 0:70–72

Keeping Dianetics Working, 4:633

Keeping Scientology Working (KSW),
example of correct handling, 0:11
example of not keeping Scientology
working, 0:11
points one to ten of, 0:8
policy on, 0:7
safeguarding tech, 0:21
unswerving and relentless application of, 0:70
verbal tech, how to defeat it, 0:23
verbal tech penalties, 0:24

key ingredients,
cycle of management and, 7:417, MS3:397
of administration, 7:408–409, MS3:388–389

Keynesian economic theory, creating
want, MS1:62

Key Officer, 0:184

Key Question,
negative answer, handling, 5:214
One, 5:213
Two, 5:213

key questions, 6:823

keys,
handling for person receiving keys, 3:396
penalty for loss of, 3:396
penalty if space taken over and key not
returned, 3:396
policy on issue of, 0:184

Key Word Clearing, *see* **Method Six Word
Clearing**

Kha-Khan,
awarded by, 1:838
definition, 1:768, 1:838
description, 0:503
taking away lives of, 1:838

Khrushchev, Nikita, 0:19

King, 0:116

know(n)(ing),
being in the know on current scene, 0:144
handling project one doesn't know much
about, 0:88
if one is experiencing adverse effect on post or
in life, then he does not know or has not
applied tech or policy covering it, 0:268
not knowing that makes men stupid, 0:327
part of knowing is "In a given situation what
should be decided?" 0:327
policy,
make it easily knowable, 0:115
to be known must exist and be findable, 0:410
trouble with policy or admin because one
doesn't know it, 0:551
staff members are seldom willful, they are just
unknowing, 0:552–553
taking this planet just as we are and with no
more than we know, 0:273

know best,

    lawyers, accountants and, 0:421

    out-admin and, 0:71

know-how, lack of, result, 0:67

knowledge, knowingness

    ability to investigate and, MS1:74

    before 1949 man's knowledge of himself, the spirit and the mind was a black barbarism, 0:362

    decrying the suppression of, 0:160

    definition, 0:270

    deliver means good reality and useful knowledge and skill to every student, 0:283

    means self trust, 4:411

    must be included with control, 2:411, 6:183

    not knowing makes men stupid, 2:84, 6:206

    ours is superior, 0:481

    part of knowing is, in a given situation what should be decided, 2:84

Knowledge Report(s), *see also* **ethics chit; ethics report; report**

    concerning dev-t, 0:428

    definition, 1:700

    description, 0:544, 0:556–557

    enforced as, 1:713

    handling of blown students and pcs and, 4:272

    illegal orders and, 0:523

    references, 0:555

    reposting of areas and, 1:154

    written during HCO Confessional, 4:995

knownness, PR and, MS3:73

KRC triangle,

    acts like ARC triangle, MS2:233

    defined, MS2:232

KSW, *see* **Keeping Scientology Working**

L

labeling, as a suppressive, 0:496

labor, *see* work

laborers,
   no laborers in Scientology org, 0:82
   people afraid of taking responsibility are, 0:260

labor-management problems, 0:122, 0:134

labor-management upsets, come from three points, MS1:254

labyrinth,
   route along terminals that never agreed is a, 0:82
   Scientology will take man out of the, 0:21

La Mar, 0:634

Lateness Report, 0:554

laundry, handling of, 7:1355

law(s), *see also* policy; regulation; rule
   administrative specialty, 7:434
   basic, confused with incidental fact, MS1:6
   conditions formulas acting like natural laws, 0:581
   disciplinary laws, 0:461
   good vs. bad laws, 0:117
   having special value of aligning other data, MS1:7
   having superior law code and legal system, 0:483
   ignorance of the, 0:68
   in current society manager or exec has no recourse to, 0:587
   morals are laws, 0:455
   no just civil law left, 0:483
   one survives so long as he is true to himself, his family, his friends, the laws of the universe, 0:455

law(s), *(cont.)*
   pressure group laws, 0:117
   principle of VFP and, MS1:296
   reason for 90% of laws passed, 0:67
   regarding org boards, MS1:208
   something with which one thinks, MS1:6
   sweeping away unreal, unapplicable and impeding laws and policies, 0:117
   two senior data, 1:968
   we must not entangle our purposes with arbitrary laws which do not further our cause, 0:273
   what it is based on, 0:297
   wog law vs. Scientology ethics and justice, 0:485, 0:493

Law of the Omitted Data, black PR and, MS3:80

lawyer, attorney,
   legal matters and, 0:477
   missing post hat, 0:203
   out-ethics and trouble from, 0:421

laziness,
   giving something a "lick and a promise," 0:255
   musical chairs and, 0:280
   off-line or off-policy despatches and, 0:409
   unhatted org is lazy and refers everything to someone else, 0:390

Lead Auditor, duties and purpose of, 4:1151

leader(s), leadership, *see also* administrator; executive; manager; officer; senior
   alliances with suitable groups and, 0:335–0:336
   bad leaders whose groups disintegrate, why, 7:333, MS3:313
   being or working under a, 0:629

275

leader(s), leadership, *(cont.)*

brilliant one, refuses to disconnect from opinion leaders and connects with previously opposing opinion leaders, MS3:21

choosing a, 0:83

definition, 0:629 7:332, MS3:313

elect leaders temporarily and reserve right of recall, 0:83

enemy vs., 0:640

examples of outcome of unhatted, MS1:216

experience and, 0:120

failure to contribute to strength and longevity of work, health and power of a power, 0:640–641

floods of requests for decisions denies us materiel and, 0:230

good leadership, results of, 7:334, MS3:314

how to elect one, MS1:236

how to move off point of power, 0:640

keeping leader from collapsing through overwork, bad temper or bad data, 0:640

mistakes of Simon Bolivar, 7:376, MS3:356

providing things to win and enemies to conquer, 0:638

push power in direction of, 0:640

remote leadership, 0:122

responsibilities of, 0:629

result if group led by someone whose programs and orders are positive, 7:332, MS3:312

seven things about power, 0:639–640

soundest leadership, 0:122

value of, 0:83

what sound leadership comes from, 7:668

where leadership levels of a movement come from, 0:120

who are not hatted results in, MS1:215

who lets staff force him to wear their hats, 0:412

workable formula used "instinctively" by most successful, practical political leaders, 0:630

leadership survey, 0:587

lease(s), policy on personal leases by staff, 0:171

leave(s), leave of absence,

as a privilege, 0:200

complete hat folder allows one to be relieved in orderly fashion for a, 0:193

falsifying the reason for, 1:907

from course, students and, 4:475

of absence, definition of, 4:366

of absence, incorrect handling for PTSes, 1:1050

leave(s), leave of absence, *(cont.)*

persons are entitled to annual leave, 0:265–266

policy on, 0:177–178

secretly planning to, 1:906

Security Checks and, 0:178

tours used to take longer leaves, 0:265

lecture, by others on application, use and results are permitted, 7:1292

lecturer(s),

furnishing lecturers to groups, 0:353

successful approach, 6:762

ledger,

list of items that are charged to what columns on the ledger sheet, 3:116

sheet, photolithoed form, 3:109

legal,

by keeping legal aspects straight, you will be able to help the many and not be messed up by a few, 7:1074

communications and routing of legal matters, 7:1053

control is part of the functions of justice which belongs to HCO, 2:133, 7:1073

corporate structure is part of the Office of LRH, 2:133

goes PTS being in contact with SP courts and with SP or PTS attorney firms, 1:1022, 7:372, MS3:352

keep nose clean legally, 7:1074

never stop dissemination to iron out legal, 7:1095

policy regarding legal activities, 2:133, 7:1073

PR and legal situations from people who have complaints stem from two reasons, 7:1111

role in restraining black PR campaign, MS3:29

routing of communication received from legal, accounting or government, 7:1085

sign-ups, legal aspects of, 7:1074

who is owner of all tapes, publications, bulletins and materials of Scientology, 2:278

Legal Department, activities of, 7:1053

legal matters, definition of, 1:730

Legal Officer,

all legal-type letters, government letters, accounting notices, etc., go to Legal Officer, 7:1081

is hereby authorized to have a clerk, 7:1081

purpose, 7:1082

legislative, body that deliberates and enacts laws, MS2:215

Leipzig, Germany, death camp school, 0:40

leisure class, 0:506

letter(s), *see also* **communication; despatch; telex**

answer person's questions, 0:84, 0:166, 0:276, 0:370

any letters are better than no letters, 2:612

applicant letter, 2:396, 2:398

ARC triangle and, 2:601

auditor's letter writing role, 2:597

auditors used to write procurement letters, 2:607, 2:612

basic cycle of letter registration, 2:625

code of letter writer, 2:620

copies filed in Central Files, 2:393

correctly addressed with right name and not sent to several addresses for same person, 0:335

Dept 11 writes letters to possible students, 0:350

Dept 12 writes letters to possible pcs, 0:351

don't *sell,* just write a *person,* 2:611

enclosure pieces, 2:394

example of handling an ARC break in, 2:619

examples of, 2:615

extension course students receive handwritten notations on their papers or despatches, 6:504

failing to answer a person's questions causes ARC breaks, 2:435

false reports and, 2:623

"friendly and agreeable responses," 0:335

go on comm lines, 0:377

handling of, 2:393

how to answer, 2:632

how to write, 2:611

if they aren't dead and still have a body and are written to they will come in for training or processing, 2:614

if you are only interested in the org making money you'll get a much lower response, 2:614

if you write them enough letters they'll still come in, 2:614

if your whole target is addressed to their end of the communication line you'll get response, 2:618

included in Dead Files, 1:972

laws of, 2:601

Letter Registrar finds individuals who want something and writes that person letters that help him or her to get it, 2:623

letting them stack up on your desk, 0:370

looking into baskets and drawers for, 0:416

no form letters sent out, 2:606

no letter may be written containing actual results of tests, 2:600, 4:228

letter(s), *(cont.)*

no want of any kind expressed or inferred-no Letter Reg letter is written, 2:624

of complaint, handling, 2:396

one subject per, 1:303, 6:689

order of importance in handling, 1:314

pointing out channels on which letters flow, 0:389

power of org is proportional to its speed of particle flow, 0:325, 0:432

procedure for writing students, 2:601

procurement letters,
Central Files and, 2:389
how to write, 2:389
number which must be written, 2:389
procedure for handling, 2:612
staff auditors must write, 2:389

prospect letter, 2:396

public who did PE Course but haven't gone further, 6:385

quantity is more important than quality, 2:614

quota being set for, 0:681

referring to test results obtained on a person in any way must be given in person by a qualified person, 2:600, 4:228

R-factor, 2:614
definition, 2:615
dependence upon an earlier factor, 2:614

routing of, 1:326, 2:393, 3:202

sample procurement letters, 2:603

Secretarial Unit typing answers to, 0:370

should not cross the words Dianetics and Scientology, 2:143, 6:231

size not quality of mailing list and number of mailings and letters to it determines gross income, 0:358

special, output of, 2:599

technical letter, handling, 2:396

test results may not be sent in a, 6:271

three main lines of, 2:604

three types of, 2:389

unanswered from public, 1:313

unanswered letters, 0:694

used to get public to phone in, 3:211

volume of income of an org is in direct proportion to number of phone calls and letters of an org, 2:613

when they are not answered, 1:313

when they don't go out in volume, 1:313

white paper used for letters to the field, 0:369

write like you have new news, 0:363

write the person, not the air, 2:611

writing, staff auditors and, 4:1153

letter of appointment, example sent to field auditors, 6:639

Letter Registrar(s),

Addresso gives card files from Addresso plates to, 2:621

adjacent offices to CF and Addresso, 2:621

ARC breaks and, 2:624

basic cycle of letter registration and, 2:625

Book of Letter Scheduling and, 2:628

cannot work without a complete file, 2:424

Central Files, Address and typing pool transferred under, 2:659

change of address and, 2:708

clay demos and, 2:630

code of, 2:620

correct project for, 2:627

definition and duties, 2:404

Div 2 and, 0:360

drills and clay table for, 2:623, 2:630

entheta letters handling, 2:630

example of destructive order affecting the, 0:141

faces individuals only, 2:623

failing to answer person's questions, 0:276

handle all outgoing procurement letters from organization, 2:622

handling for field staff member's contact who writes in, 2:625

hat of, 2:605, 2:623

high reality factor and, 2:622

hot prospect files and, 6:714

how to answer no want for training or processing, 2:704

how to handle letters which have a dead file dummy in CF, 2:667

how to handle tech questions, 2:627

keeps Body Reg informed of who is expected in, 2:500

letters out statistic vs. false report, 2:623

must be an expert on programs (such as books available, Academy training, HGC processing, memberships), 2:624

mystery and, 2:628

never heavily acks any intention to reach expressed by a person, 2:628

not producing, evidence of, 0:681

nothing may be filed in a hot prospect file that has not already been answered by a, 2:704

no want for training or processing, how to answer, 6:714

no want of any kind expressed or inferred/no Letter Reg letter is written, 2:624

Letter Registrar(s), *(cont.)*

offering service person has already taken, 0:276

outflow of origin and, 2:501

picks up the individual response and puts it in the channel and pulls it in, 2:623

prime purpose of, 2:431

program to recover incomplete cases, 2:637

purpose of, 2:623

qualifications for, 2:630

quota is secondary aspect to effectiveness of getting people cleared and trained, 2:622

registers by getting people to schedule courses and intensives, 2:628

report of statistics, 2:631

responsible for all cases in connection with organization and on org mailing lists, 2:622

routes hot prospects to Advance Scheduling Registrar, 2:431

should be sure letters have very high "R" factor, 2:605

steps for answering forms or letters, 2:632

system of, 2:621

take personal interest in person's case, 2:622

user of fliers, MS3:293

where volume of letters require it more than one Letter Reg should be posted, 2:452

whole duty of, 2:624

works to accumulate questionnaires and mail from those responding to promotion, 0:349

would have to be fully briefed on Grade Chart and C/S Series HCOBs, 2:559–560

writing to offer service the person has already taken causes ARC breaks, 2:435

writing without person's folder before them, 0:276

Letter Registration Section,

definition, 2:507, 3:235, 7:203

summary of, 2:508, 3:236, 7:204

letters of credit, procedure for, MS2:360

letters out statistic,

down, handling, 0:586, 0:691

example of rationalizing down stat, 0:682

high letters out—low enrollment weeks later, 0:647

Letter Writer's Code, 2:620

level(s) (auditing and training),

abilities recovered in levels are marked above dept names, 0:96

deliver case gain and completed level, 0:282, 0:283

ensure pc makes each level fully before going on to the next, 4:15

give processing called for at pc's level, 0:283

level(s) *(cont.)*

if you skip a person on one level several levels up, he or she will experience only an unreality and will not react, 2:517

introduction of mini list of processes for auditing requirements at each level, 4:420

levels of able and extra able beings, 0:95

org board and, 0:96

pc wanting next level of auditing, 0:32

remaining, 0:124, 0:130

requirements of one level must be met before proceeding to next, 4:179

technical degrades and, 0:15

Level of Awareness, definition, 4:186, 5:191

Level 0,

basic point of, 5:196

course checksheets, what to include on both theory and practical, 5:194

examinations, 5:195

on pc who has never been processed, 0:283

vocabulary, 5:195

Level I, 5:336

Level II, 5:333, 5:336

replaced by Hubbard Qualified Scientologist, 4:168

Level III, 5:333

HCA/HPA restored to, 4:168

Level IV, 5:200

Level V, 5:336

Level VI,

meter check for classification, 5:226

must include, 5:207

Level VII, 5:336

tech of organization comes from, 0:482

Liability condition, formula, *see also* **condition(s)**

assigned when, 1:562

executive and, 7:428, MS3:408

false graph and, 0:658

formula, 1:562

jailed person and, 0:668

noncompliance = Liability, 0:528, 0:655

seniors who don't see to hatting, MS1:404

steps, 0:574

when it is assigned, 0:574, 0:647

why person collapsing stats is in, 0:657

liberty, individual liberty, 0:461, 0:462; *see also* **freedom**

libido theory, 6:620, MS3:3

librarian, duties of, 5:725

library,

containing materials of one's field, 0:310

library, *(cont.)*

dictionaries and, 5:724

emergency, definition, 2:697

tabbing on Addressograph plates, 2:693

lie(s), lying, *see also* **dishonesty; false data; false report**

any lie will either blunt or end the C (communication), MS3:8

definition, 0:534

false reality, MS3:8

freedom of speech does not mean freedom to harm by lies, 0:461

hidden, lying source can cause authority to act, 0:520

hostile PR is usually, MS3:9

investing a lie with power, 0:484

liar, 0:454, 0:458

never use lies in PR, MS3:8

PR practitioners and, MS3:7

safe ground in PR and, MS3:99

stock in trade of PRs has been, MS3:7

universal population stuffed with, 0:91

where lies are sometimes found to exist, 0:587

why lies are told, 0:454

life, live(s), living, *see also* **survival; viability**

acquiring potential of creating or helping to create far better life for all, 0:89

adverse effect on post or in life, reason for, MS2:193

applying conditions to one's, 0:668–671

awareness levels missing from one's, 0:95

basic formula of living, 0:123

beings living lives of quiet correctness, 0:236

bored wandering through, 0:292

decrying and doing all one can to abolish any and all abuses against life, 0:160

dynamic principle of existence, 0:452

dynamics and, 0:457, 0:458

ethics and, *see* ethics

expansion and, 0:123–124

experiencing adverse effect on post or in life, 0:268

formula for game of life, 0:119

full of dangerous, violent, live situations, 0:635

group effort, 1:493

handling highest commodity/life itself, 0:648

happy productive lives, 0:454

hats and, 0:199, 0:206

how to determine what's missing from your, 0:95

idleness made to appear as best way of, 0:315

in a far nowhere, 0:526

is a group effort, 0:458

life, *(cont.)*

machines can't do man's living for him, 0:314

man or girl on the post is one who puts life in it, 0:231

none survive alone, 1:493

only gets easy when small bits are handled, 0:261

optimum solution to any problem presented by, 0:458

org board applied to one's, 0:95

"people should live a little," 0:497

people who cry and moan that life has "done them in," 0:152

points of decline traced to, MS1:88

reason things do not run well in, 0:199

routinely running away from, 0:177

secret of being successful in life, 0:562

short span of men's lives, 0:56

standard of living, 0:313–316

to live at all, one has to exert some control over his equals, juniors and superiors, 0:555

two-pole activity, MS3:120

wanting to get more able in life and to live better life, 0:152

way out in life is way through, 0:300, 3:78

way to save time and lives is do it right in first place, 0:255

your post and, 0:268

Life Repair,

ability gained, 4:189

no policy that it must be done on all pcs, 4:145

limping scene, successful org vs., 0:62

line(s), *see also* **channel; communication line; flow line; routing; terminal**

actions and lines to be product officered by Service Product Officer, MS2:174

admin personnel keep lines moving, 0:18

altering lines, 0:384, 0:385

altering without clearance, ethics offense, 1:311

are a major part of establishment, MS2:36

are based on experience, 0:384

being hard on anyone damaging or omitting the, 0:89

change of requires clearance from the Office of LRH, 1:311

command and communication, D of P must know and enforce, 4:960

command line, definition, MS1:369

communication line, definition, MS1:370

completed staff work and, 0:401, 0:402

line(s), *(cont.)*

control of, 0:389, 0:390

declining stat due to lines out or being misrouted, 0:385

definition, 7:479, MS1:369, MS2:195, MS2:300, MS3:459

despatch lines, 0:378

dev-t and, 0:426, 0:427

Estos establish and maintain the, 0:393

example of dummy running lines to find and handle blocks, 7:848

example of problem in, MS1:294

executive,

demanding to be on routing lines, 0:388

seeing that lines are followed, 0:409

seldom hit unless he has had noncompliance on his lines, 0:427

what he wants and doesn't want on his lines, 0:372

what his lines should look like, 0:373

executive's lines, result of jamming, 7:603

external, 1:28

formula to apply when being knocked about by one's, 0:420–421

hats and commonest reason lines don't go in, MS1:453

having standard lines and routes for particles to follow, 0:392

HCO not having enough people devoted to getting in, 0:392, 0:393

heavy traffic warnings and, 0:380

hit back by lines you are trying to handle, 0:420

holding org lines and chain of command firm, 0:581

how our lines can stay freer and faster, 0:401, 0:403

how to adjust, 1:69

if people won't work, they throw out lines, 0:475

importance of org lines, 0:384

improperly set overload seniors, MS1:291

internal, 1:28

invoice line for books ordered, 0:282

jam in five ways, 1:360

jammed or blocked lines,

by forwarding improper despatches, 0:405

bypassing line jams terminal, 0:85

covert block on lines, 0:380

exec's lines jammed, result, 0:373

how exec can jam all lines, 0:388

irrelevant info causing, 0:430

no-supply block, 0:380

only exec can string lines and coordinate actions and resolve jams that impede things, 0:373

too little data causing, 0:85

too much traffic jams a line, 0:85

line(s), *(cont.)*

juniors issuing orders unknown to senior and across his lines, 0:425

knowledge of org board and, 1:154

linking up departments are handled by Esto Conference of that division where departmental Estos exist, MS2:37

most frequently lost line, Registrar to D of P in signing up preclears, 2:495, 2:499; *see also* Registrar

most fundamental point of administration, MS2:170

must be in neat pattern or power in them recoils, 0:389–0:390

must be in, in an exact known pattern, 1:311

must cross divisions to function, 5:491

org consists of coordinated purposes, terminals and, 0:89

org whose admin or body lines are being violated will disestablish, MS2:37

organization consists of coordinated purposes, lines and terminals, 7:293

person who is barely able to perceive lines, 0:433

personnel promotions and, 1:275

policing of, 0:389, 0:390

preservation of, 1:269

promotion (of staff) tends to lose lines, 0:198, 0:596

putting one's baskets and "hands" into the, 0:326

reducing income by not knowing posts and, 0:197

removing particles off line, 0:195, 0:378, 0:432

routing new staff onto post, 1:178

scale concerning lines and terminals, MS1:288

shifting of, most serious threat to stability of org, 1:311

soggy feeling, cause of, 1:276

SPs cutting dissem lines, 0:90

suppression on, 0:425

that cross divisions are under control of Dept 2 HCO, MS2:36

things I want on my lines, 0:372, 0:374

to function must cross divisions, 4:906

two types of, 1:28

when delivery balls up the, 0:282

why one doesn't put his decisions on the, 0:326

within a division are the business of Estos of that division, MS2:37

linear recruitment, MS1:391; *see also* hiring; recruitment

lines and terminals scale,

awareness and, MS1:288

causes for positions on the scale, MS1:289

list,

assessed for evaluators, MS1:111

for evaluators, MS2:90

Listing and Nulling list, definition, 4:1015

literature, should not cross the words Dianetics and Scientology, 2:143, 6:231

little-brown-church-in-the-vale mock-up, 1:754, 4:99

living, basic formula of, 7:669

loafing,

efforts by juniors to look and sound active while loafing, 0:420

how I buy "loafing time," 0:399

reporting people loafing when they should be working, 0:623

tolerating loafing, effect of, 0:680

loan(s), 6:724

living off interest from, 0:508

org execs corrupted by, 1:796

received by staff, 1:729

staff may not borrow money from past or present students or pcs, 0:171

Local Org Reserves, definition, MS2:353

location, *see also* position

establishment and, 0:289

extraordinary locations and staledate, 0:382

Locational, Confusion Formula and, 0:568

log(s), logbook(s),

dev-t log, 0:427, 0:440, MS2:17

system for locating things, 0:310

logbook, for preclear gradation, 4:177

logging, things one is using in and out, 0:306

logic,

ability to reason, MS1:10

breakthrough, MS1:11

"Bright and Stupid," 7:1155

dedicated to being, MS1:129

definition, MS1:10

finding datum of comparable magnitude to the subject, MS1:15

logic and illogic are the stuff of survive and succumb, MS1:28

mind, capable of being, MS1:16

must have several conditions, MS1:12–13

pluspoints show, MS1:148

validity of data which monitors, MS1:156

what is necessary to be, MS1:15

logistics, not legitimate telex traffic, 1:473

London,

HCO office in, 7:1161

PABs are printed and distributed from, 7:1162

Long Distance Program, 6:52

The Way We'll Clear (Continent)
Program, 7:184

longevity,

due to sound knowledge and use of Scientology
policy and structure, 0:69

how org establishes its own level of, 0:318

Long Form Product Clearing, *see also* **Product
Clearing; Short Form Product Clearing**

form for, MS2:49

must be done on an Esto before he does it on
staff, MS2:49

steps for, MS2:49

long-term organization, MS1:172

look(ing), *see also* **confront; inspection;
observation**

person who cannot or will not look, 0:694

you can never guess at what holds some things
up, you have to look, 0:594

losers, definition and handling, MS2:202

loss, lost,

financial loss by illegal discounts or giving away
services or materials, handling, 0:303

misinterpretation of policy resulting in, 0:141

of certificates or awards, 0:495

of equipment, who is liable for, 0:186, 0:187,
0:189

of keys, 0:184

"Orders, Query Of" and, 0:141–142

staff member debited for losses on post
vacated, 0:198

things getting lost and people not knowing
where things are, 0:306

Loss Report, description, 0:543

low units, main sources of, 7:212

lower grades,

abilities gained, 5:292

contain solutions to what makes a humanoid
human, 5:260

LRH, *see* **Hubbard, L. Ron**

LRH Communicator(s),

absence of, out-ethics indicator, 7:1259

Ad Council and Exec Council measures
and, 7:913

admin high crimes and, 7:493,
MS2:463, MS3:473

as deputy of Executive Director, 0:173

as staff meeting chairman, 0:173

basic duty of, 7:1260

LRH Communicator(s), *(cont.)*

Boards of Review and, 7:1265

can assign projects based on policy
letters, 7:1233

cannot operate at all unless supported by strong
HCO, 7:1226

dismissal of Temporary staff status
personnel, 5:412

duties of, 0:173, 0:250, 7:1229

every org must have one, 7:1239

example of Correction Form, 7:1248, 7:1251

examples of why all orgs should have LRH
Comms and how it improves
statistics, 7:1255

Executive Letter Unit and, 7:1194

expansion program and, MS1:171

first and primary duty, 7:1240

gets compliance on LRH EDs, programs,
projects and orders, 7:1243

gets policy followed and in such a way as to
expand the org and not stop flows, 7:1243

gives I/A to all OODs items before
publishing, 7:729

handling for discovery of departure from
policy or tech on the part of author of an
issue, 7:1268

handling of Sec EDs, 7:1315

how to get form clearance, 7:1247

issue authority, 7:1267

job to see there is an HCO there and
operating, 1:57

lines, result of censorship of, 7:1267

log, 7:1211

LRH PR actions done, 7:1261

may never again be an EC member, 7:1240

may not be comm eved in their own org and
may only be comm eved in a senior org
and only if the orders are their own
executive seniors', 7:1258

may not wear additional hats outside
Dept 21, 7:1239

new basic duties, 7:1246

no HCO (Div 7, 1, 2) part of org,
handling, 0:648

observing and reporting is a PR action
and, 7:1262

office has seals and signatures and can pass an
ED only as "not against policy," 7:1240

orders and, 7:1234

org builders, 7:1257

org with an LRH Comm, prospers, 7:1244

out-ethics indicators of, 0:532

LRH Communicator(s), *(cont.)*

penalty for attempting to remove or transfer a duly appointed LRH Comm in violation of policy, 7:1258

penalty for stopping the communication of, 1:902

positive way to expand an org is to have an LRH Comm who gets the org on-policy and in-tech, 7:1256

primary function, 7:1234

primary stress is on tech quality, ethics adherence, org form and policy, 7:1268

production, 7:1223

program checking and, 7:1269

promotional actions of, 0:173

purpose, 7:1231

purpose of LRH Comm N/W, 7:1229

pushing project home, 0:595

raises LRH's PR value with staff, 7:1260

reason he cannot get compliance, 7:1246

reporting off-policy or out-tech order to, 0:147

responsibility,
    for lines, 7:1241
    for LRH image, 7:1260
    for premises, 7:1231
    for staff training program, 5:502

result of getting in orders and know-how in tech and admin, 7:1245

sees that Ron's postulates stick, 0:355

Senior HCOs and LRH Comm N/W, 7:1224

should come down with hearings on noncompliance and false reports and demand on false reports the removal of the offender from that post, 7:1243

should not flinch at the idea of putting in HCOBs, books and tapes just because he is not a classed auditor, 7:1253

size of org required to have LRH Comm single-hatted, 0:101

split-off of old HCO Area Sec hat, 0:101

tech and, 7:1253

troubles, reasons for and handling of, 7:1223

up to the LRH Comm Network to expand Scientology orgs, 7:1255

verify reports of dones or get dones done, 7:479, MS2:195, MS2:300, MS3:459

LRH Communicator(s), *(cont.)*

vitally important for every org, 7:1229

what is found where trouble occurs, 7:1243

when an LRH Comm may issue his own orders from policy, 7:1234

while pushing to get compliance, puts in train a correction checklist which he keeps to hand, 7:1246

who accepts false reports is doing his job backwards, 7:825

who doesn't uphold or increase LRH PR, 7:1261

LRH Communicator Continental, 0:147

LRH Communicator International, handling for receiving report on a Danger condition assigned to a rising statistic, 7:1236

LRH Communicator log, 7:1211

LRH Communicator WW, three things to give first priority to, 7:153

LRH Executive Directive (LRH ED),

definition, 1:429, 7:1322

destructive issues being accepted and followed even when they contradict HCO PLs or, 0:304

total defense to plead one followed correctly interpreted HCO PLs, HCOBs, EDs or LRH issues or tapes, 0:145

LRH image,

easy to obtain compliance when present, 7:1260

LC to establish, maintain and improve local, 7:1260

LRH Personal PR,

actions done by LC, 7:1261

basic duty of LC, 7:1260

LRH Programs No. 1, where issued, stats recovered, 7:793

LRH Property, Building and Plans Branch,

formation and purpose (1967), 7:1391

Plans Section, responsibilities, 7:1391

LSD, recruiting only heavy LSD and clinic types, 0:302

luck, counting on or trusting to, 0:255

lunatic, characteristic of, 5:835

LX Lists, out of valence and, 4:231

lying, definition, 1:844

M

MAA, *see* Master-at-Arms

MAA interview, definition, 1:827, 6:416; *see also* Ethics Officer

machine(s), machinery, *see also* equipment

can't do man's living for him, 0:314

difference between live org and, 0:81

established and corrected machine, 0:287

just tools, 0:314

perfect org is not machine but pattern of agreements, 0:82

products of, 0:288

standard of living raised by, 0:314

we live so long as our share of economic machinery runs, 0:151

machine age,

only casualty is individual and his freedom, 0:462

standard of living and, 0:314

mad, *see also* insane; insanity; suppressive person

percentage of any org that is, 0:40

point where a thetan goes mad, 0:509, 1:786

we are not mad, 0:462

with no exteriorization of his interest, one simply goes mad, 0:630

Madison avenue, depression and, 0:506

madness,

basic characteristic of, MS3:78

we must be able to work undisturbed by madness at our doors, 0:486

magazine(s), mag(s), *see also* *Ability* magazine; Auditor magazine; Celebrity magazine; Certainty magazine

additional policy, 2:208

Address is CF index as well as who gets the, 0:360

magazine(s), *(cont.)*

Advance! 2:219

advertisements,

ads must be aligned to the motif of the magazine, 2:230

advertising pieces for other items or services, 2:138

books advertised in, 0:303

carry six kinds of ads every issue, 2:216

Dept 4 properly presents services in ads in, 0:348

entheta or flaps never advertised on org lines, 2:216, 6:222

never make promises in ads or articles that the technology or the org cannot fulfill, 2:252

not used to advertise unofficial orgs or auditors or groups, 2:186, 2:216, 6:222

policy on, 2:193

priority ads in Scientology magazine, 2:190

six kinds of ads every issue, 6:222

what ads appear in every issue, 2:229

who is responsible for the ads, 2:210, 6:219

any mag is better than no mag, 6:224

backbone of org promotion, 2:219

communicate to the public by, 2:54

condensing wins into data of interest for, 0:355

content, 2:229

carries the org address and phone number, 2:216, 6:222

certificate validation notices, 2:609, 6:702

church news and format, 2:231

contain LRH articles in every one, 2:230

continental magazines to model after, 2:209

copyright and, 2:212

dated materials are subject to being inserts, 2:224

dignified but enthusiastic, 2:186

magazine(s), *(cont.)*
content, *(cont.)*
follow management strategy in what to market and when, 2:225
HCO PLs and HCOBs appearing in, 0:112
inserts and, 2:232
list of completions and graduations, 2:231
must not carry squirrel tech, 2:216, 6:222
names, mastheads and, 2:233
notices on validation of certificates, 2:609, 6:702
PE news and, 2:194, 6:181
planned, repeating format will standardize and popularize the magazine, 2:248
public must be given stable data and standard articles from tapes or texts they recognize, 2:186
success stories are usually inserted in the magazine shooting boards by the org, 2:231
different texts and, 2:212
don't promise spectacular results or something that the org cannot fulfill, 2:230
dummies, definition, 2:247
editor duties, 2:236
every org puts out a magazine, 2:215, 6:221
excellence of training bragged about in, 0:350
format has no *weight* in terms of ounces or pounds, 2:138
has to be on-policy and go out regularly, 2:220
helps sell only those people already sold, 2:218, 6:223
how it is used to procure public, 2:54
how they are financed, 2:235
insolvency of orgs traced to failures to issue mags on time, 2:212
internal "house organ," 2:216, 6:222–223
keep out of releases local names of SH and orgs, 2:208
key tool of marketing and org's major comm line to its field, 2:228
mailing of,
how to mail and distribute them, 2:235
issued on schedule, 0:348
on time, 2:54
regularly mailed, all at once, on-schedule, on-policy mags are the backbone of an org's promotion, 2:237
sent out to whole mailing list frequently, 2:325
what happens if it is not sent regularly, 2:56
when all org mags should be mailed, 2:234
when Major and Minor mags go out, 2:228
mailing list and, 2:211
Major issue,
definition, 2:190
orders on how many Major magazine issues must go out, 2:702
policy concerning, 2:199
sample, 2:235
to members every two months, 2:215

magazine(s), *(cont.)*
maxim is any mag is better than no mag, 2:218
Minor issue,
definition, 2:190
orders on Minor issues to go out, 2:702
policy concerning, 2:198
sample, 2:235
to whole of CF list on in-between months of Major issue, 2:215
motifs,
each issue has to have its own, 2:221
importance of, 2:221
reason for, 2:223
move mag, *see* move magazine
names and addresses of city offices carried in, 0:627
never mention staff member in news or tidbits, reason for, 2:186
no surer way for an org to collapse than to curtail its magazine issue, 2:215, 6:221
not in themselves a primary publications media, 2:138
people do not respect things issued in magazines; they respect the same things in books, 2:138
policies concerning,
for printing of lists of names, 2:247
Major and Minor issues, 6:192–193, 6:221, 6:260, 6:453
what technical may be printed in continental mags, 2:196
printing,
binding and, 2:232
format that can be read, 2:186
size and paper and, 2:232
promotion of testing program, 2:194, 6:181
promotional actions concerning, 0:348, 0:350, 0:355
quality of, 2:220
reason for, 2:228
review and discuss and direct attention to things and make them desirable, 2:138
rush notice, 2:192
spectatorism and, 0:248
squirrel data starts trouble with regular customers, 2:186
stats rise six weeks after a good mag is mailed, 2:237
submission procedure, 2:179, 7:1305
three types that should be used by Pubs Org and orgs, 2:348
timeless, 2:224
translations and, 2:234
ways to improve your org mag, 2:233
when an org ceased to send its mag out to *all* its CF it promptly started to go broke, 2:219
when an org moves to a new building special treatment is given in org's magazine, 2:225

mail, *see also* **inflow; letter; outflow**

Accountant and, 1:325, 3:201

Accountant's baskets for, 3:201

accounting or governmental must be approved by the Legal Officer before leaving the org, 1:338

all, personal or otherwise, opened by mail opener, 3:199

applicant mail, definition, 2:388

consists of letters from individuals, 2:624

delivery of, 1:366

distribution of in org, 7:220

fully distributed within an hour of receipt, 1:364

handling of, 1:323–324, 1:334, 3:105, 3:200, 3:204

Invoice Clerk handling of, 1:325, 3:201

lacking return address to be returned to department sending, 2:340

Legal Officer and, 1:335

losing the mail covertly, 0:574

method of opening and invoicing, 3:201, 3:204

must be secure in the extreme, 1:323

opening of, 1:334

order of importance, 1:324, 3:200

org is alive as it gives and receives pieces of, 1:307

priority of answering, 1:324

private letters, handling of, 3:149

procurement letter, definition, 2:389

promotional action of Dept 2, mailings prompt and on schedule, 1:40

prospect mail, definition, 2:388

receipt and logging functions, 1:316

registered mail, 0:379, 1:331, 1:337

Registrar directly responsible for three types of, 2:388

return address on, 1:333

routing of communication received from legal, accounting or government, 7:1085

security and, 3:199

sent from an org must bear the return address of that org, 2:340

students' and pcs' sent to Tech Services, 1:334, 3:204

surface mail, 1:456

volume,

gives about a six-weeks warning on income, 1:307

importance of, 2:64

is good datum as gives about a six-weeks' warning, 2:65

principal route to solvency, 1:307

mail, *(cont.)*

volume, *(cont.)*

quality vs. quantity and, 1:307

rising always presages an income rise, 2:64

slump always followed by an income slump, 1:307

watch volume in and out to determine how you're going to be doing a bit into the future, 2:64

whether personal or otherwise, opened by the mail opener, 1:323

mail clerk,

promotion and, 0:348

purposes, 2:684, 2:686

mailing(s),

addresses for mailings come from CF folders, 0:99

all hands onto any stuffing-mailing cycle, 0:103

appearance and tone of, 0:335

correctly addressed with right name and not sent to several addresses for same person, 0:335

duplistickers, 0:627

promotional actions concerning, 0:348, 0:349, 0:352

size not quality of mailing list and number of mailings and letters to it determines gross income, 0:358

mailing list(s), address list(s),

acquiring, 0:352, 0:625–626

book promotion and, 2:705

buying new mail lists, 0:130

correct project for Letter Registrar, 2:627

culled addresses back from old invoices, 2:705

Distribution Division keeps a statistic on which mailing lists respond the best and which info packet communicated the best, 2:709

Emergency Formula and, 2:705

gross income senior datum and, 2:672, 7:851

handling of purchased or rented, 6:218

info packets and, 2:709

list of purchased and/or rented mailing lists, 2:709

longstanding policy that org may not give out its mailing lists, 2:711, 6:193

never letting go of address or mailing list and keeping them all properly corrected and up-to-date and in proper categories for ready use, 0:352

not placed in hands of FSMs, 0:626

only names which are removed from, 0:99, 0:360

mailing list(s), address list(s) *(cont.)*

organization is forbidden to release in whole or in part any mailing list of Dianetics and Scientology, 2:683, 6:696

person's name in list twice or three times, 0:276

policies regarding, 0:625

procedure after purchase of each list, 6:218

procedure for handling purchased and/or rented lists, 2:709

promotion and, 6:812

promotion procedure for mailing lists bought or sent in, 2:626

purchased and/or rented mailing lists, 2:709

selling org prospect lists to a squirrel, 0:533

size vs. quality of mailing list, 0:358

mail order, 0:303, 0:349

special skill to mail order book business, 2:314

maintenance, checklists used, 7:1399

major change, if all else fails, go back to, MS1:160

majority,

be right on majority of decisions, 0:247

handling bad situation according to greatest good for majority of dynamics, 0:239

when majority rules, minority suffers, 0:83

majority opinion, ethnic surveys and, MS3:69, MS3:248

Major magazine, *see also* **magazine; Minor magazine**

definition and editorial policy, 2:229

policies on, 6:192–193, 6:221, 6:260, 6:453

major target, definition, MS2:427, MS2:437; *see also* **target**

make-break point, 7:457

expand or not, MS2:443, MS2:457, MS3:437

malice, malicious(ly),

careless or malicious and knowing damage caused to projects, orgs or activities, 0:574

false reports on others maliciously intended, 0:515

in request for justice, favor or redress, 0:488

seldom any malice in dev-t, 0:394

spreading tales and making accusations out of, 0:513

trying to hurt with malicious talk, 0:152

malnutrition, definition, 5:640

man, mankind, *see also* **being; group; individual; thetan**

auditor is only one who can give man truth, 0:154

awareness levels on org bd cover human states, 0:96

man, mankind, *(cont.)*

basic nature of, 0:449

basically good, 0:158, 0:452, 0:457, 0:526, 1:487, 1:805, 6:515

before 1949 man's knowledge of himself, spirit and mind was a black barbarism, 0:362

best news man has ever had, 0:363

bringing self-determinism back to, 0:230

can't, cannot,

be free while there are those amongst him who are slaves to their own terrors, 0:461

be trusted with justice or punishment, 0:449, 0:456, 0:521, 7:1143

or won't confront evil, 0:37

character and basic nature of, MS1:396

condition of being, 0:618

de-aberrating a man before his whole social structure could be de-aberrated, 0:630

does not really seek discipline with justice, 0:449

doing himself in, 0:247, 0:452

doubtful man will evolve another workable system than Scientology, 0:21

down the chute, 0:458

drowns in irrationality, MS1:60

environment, adjusting of, 0:251

ethics, *see also* ethics

man has not had workable way of applying ethics to himself, 0:457

putting ethics in on himself, 0:450, 0:457

when going on some evil course he attempts to restrain himself and caves himself in, 0:526

freedom for man does not mean freedom to injure man, 0:461

freeing man from restimulators of reactive patterns, 0:630

governments, armies and big research bureaus allow no human equation, 0:82

greatest weapon is his reason, 0:451

happiness and longevity of companies and states depend upon organizational know-how, 7:411, MS3:391

idea that man could not change, 0:362

in danger all the time, 0:618

individual rights were originated to bring freedom to honest men, 0:461

invalidation of, 0:248

it's not knowing that makes men stupid, 0:327

knowledge of before 1949, MS3:136, MS3:173

labyrinth man is caught in, 0:21

machines can't do man's living for him, 0:314

man, *(cont.)*

man's systems are based on groups and masses of people, 0:96

manners and, 0:328

no humanoid is free while aberrated in body cycle, 0:630

one would have to de-aberrate a man before his whole social structure could be de-aberrated, MS3:357

personalities who do not want group or org to succeed, 0:62

racial degeneration, 0:251

real men are full of dangerous, violent, live situations, 0:634

solving himself to extinction, 2:264

successful as he adjusts environment to him, MS1:445

survival and, 0:454, 0:459

suspects all offers of help, 6:519

thing man can't or won't confront is *evil,* 4:370

thrives only in presence of challenging environment, 0:648

use of justice, MS1:72

vicious mental technology evolved by, 0:9

wants to belong, MS1:410

war, famine, agony and disease has been the lot of, 0:10

what one could do if he lacked ability to free man wholly from his reactive patterns, 0:630

who breaks faith with his friend, 0:454

who is true to his ideals, 0:455

why we're here, 0:480

wreaks injustice with punishment, 0:449, 0:521

management, *see also* **administration; manager**

absence of skilled managers, common denominator for, MS1:320, MS2:268

accounting summaries done for governments, not for management, 0:594

admin people are the management people, 1:166

art of managing as practiced in the past required too much hard labor on the manager, 7:567

at its best when, 7:459, MS2:445, MS3:439

basics of, 0:679–681

basic tools of, MS1:368

between the pressure of the group to attain the goal and the clarion call of the goal maker to go forward, 7:571

body, what it is and what it does, MS3:431

breakthrough, MS1:373

cause blindness is basic problem of, 0:242

management, *(cont.)*

computers and, 0:704

concerns itself with the accomplishment of goals otherwise determined, 7:568

coordination, essence of, 7:454, MS3:434

cycle of, 7:417, MS3:397

definition of, 7:568, MS1:263

detectable points of bad management, 7:342, MS3:322

difference between brilliant and mediocre, 7:461, MS1:363, MS2:188, MS2:292, MS3:441

direct index of management quality and how it is expressed, MS2:349

easy for thetan to postulate a fact and so arduous to move it into MEST universe existence that management tends to be impatient, 7:527

echelons, MS1:364

essence of good management is caring what goes on, 7:340, 7:473, MS3:320, MS3:453

false reports, lack of compliance or failed performance vs., 0:67

fast flow, 7:670–671

financial planning a vital part of management, MS3:320, 7:340

Flag Rep report, 7:1420

flow lines and, 0:275

general plan of, 7:897

good goal can be attained by poor management, 7:568

good versus bad management, 7:340, MS3:320

gross divisional statistics and, 7:900

group size and, 0:600–602

heart and soul of, MS1:186

if unit such as a bureaux, a Continental Liaison Office, an OT Liaison Office is any good, result in nearest service org, MS2:349

improve the tone of any organization and its efficiency by hooking up and keeping wide open all communication lines, 7:574

income tax vs., 0:506

in management unit in Scientology, the real VFP, MS2:287

key tools of, 0:648

labor vs., 0:122, 0:132–134

laws by which management can raise the level of its own efficiency and production and activity of a group, 7:574

letting things run as long as they run well, 0:587

management, *(cont.)*

list of tools of, 7:478, MS2:194, MS2:299, MS3:458

local management using a single week's statistics, 7:530

middle,
management, 0:704, 0:707
strategic planning gets bugged most often because, MS3:436

mismanagement, what it would consist of, 0:118

of courses, 5:485

only if you use the single week can you properly, locally manage, 0:678

power of is effective in ratio to cleanness with which it relays between goal maker and the group, 7:577

pretended goals and, 7:578

primary,
failure of, isolated, MS3:161
function of management is discovery and publication of the reality of circumstances, situations and personnel, 7:575

PRO should have direct access to, 0:338

puts goal into effect, provides the ways and means, coordination and execution of acts leading toward goal, 7:568

quicksilver personnel scene vs., 0:264

real VFP of, MS1:353

remedy for bad management, 7:342, MS3:322

remote governing body would use a trend of divisional stats to interpret it, 7:523, 7:527

right way to handle it is to program it, 7:527

Scientology does not work in absence of official control, 0:159

seeking extraordinary solutions for finance outside Scientology is sign of poor, 4:173, 7:931

Senior Executive Strata above middle management, 7:462, MS2:189, MS2:293, MS3:442

skilled stat trend recognition is an essential ingredient of skilled management, 7:535

sole criteria by which skill in management is estimated is financial volume and solvency, 7:628

statistic,
analysis, core of, MS1:185
must be studied and judged alongside the other related statistics, 7:516
trends and remote management, 7:532

statistical management, 0:679–681, 0:696

strategic planning,
gets bugged most often because, 7:456, MS2:442, MS2:456
must be done by upper-level planning body if management is to be effective and succeed, 7:470

management, *(cont.)*

success of founded on, MS1:214

suppression of operational data and, 7:574

tactical, of a strategic planning is bit of an art in itself, MS3:452, 7:472

team,
failing, it will be found that, 5:480
two necessary ideas must have, 5:480

telex one of the basic tools of, 1:472

tenets of, 7:581

to be effective and succeed if, MS3:450

tools of, MS1:363

top management, *see* top management
sets policy, MS1:254

trend monitors all graph readings, 0:679

unless one knows how to read statistics correctly and how to correctly determine a stat *trend*, prediction and management by stats will be way out in left field, 7:531

upper management bodies, putting HCO there, 1:58

various echelons of, 7:462, MS2:189, MS2:293, MS3:442

violating management by trend, 0:648

ways a no-cause attitude towards statistics expresses itself, 7:518

what it takes to bring about effective, coordinated management, 7:453, MS3:433

workable science of, 7:580

management body,
three indicators which point to possible out-ethics, 7:1259
what it is and what it does, 7:451

management committee,
definition, 7:451, MS3:431
organizes and runs things, 7:452, MS3:432

Management Cycle, 1:116, 5:418

Management Series, checksheets for, 7:463, MS2:190, MS2:294, MS3:443

management status,
checksheets, MS1:365
from lower-level to upper-level, MS1:365

Management Status One, checksheet, instant-hats an exec on basic tools of management, 7:463, MS2:190, MS2:294, MS3:443

Management Status Two, checksheet, profound review of basic management tools and upper-level tools, 7:464, MS2:190, MS2:294, MS3:443

Management Status Three, checksheet, more profound review of basic and upper-level management tools and twelve ingredients of expansion, 7:464, MS2:191, MS2:295, MS3:444

management tools,
    failure to use, ethics offense, MS1:375
    foundation of organization, MS1:375

management unit, *see also* **Flag**
    VFP of (in Scientology), 0:316
    when it is too big individual becomes apathetic, 0:600

manager(s), *see also* **administrator; executive; leader; senior**
    actions a manager does to have high financial volume, 7:628
    bypassing manager and directly seeking to govern individuals, 0:598
    considered successful or unsuccessful by measure of balance sheets, 7:632
    credo of a good and skilled manager, 7:583
    financial volume and solvency are final test of any manager of a Scientology organization or area, 7:628
    first thing needs to know is he has tools with which to manage, 7:483, MS2:199, MS2:304, MS3:463
    good manager ignores rumor and only acts on statistics, 7:510
    group size and, 0:598–604
    instant-hat type of checksheet for, 7:485, MS2:201, MS2:306, MS3:465
    middle management, 0:704, 0:707
    must know and be able to use tools of third dynamic tech, 7:461, MS2:188, MS2:292, MS3:441
    no recourse to law or the culture, 0:587
    stat pushing and, 0:687, 0:692–695, 0:696–697
    tools with which to manage, MS1:373
    use the tools of coordination, 7:455, MS3:435
    US putting managers in Danger condition, 0:599
    we are all managers of particles (in Scientology org), 0:82
    what a manager is for, 7:454, MS3:434
    what must be known about orgs in order to wisely allocate funds, MS2:340
    when accepts done, 7:479, MS2:195, MS2:300, MS3:459
    working manager deserves his pay, 0:508

managerial, definition, MS2:216

manic-depressive, 1:994
    potential trouble source gone mad, 4:86

mankind, *see* **man**

manners, 0:165, 0:328–330, 0:340
    bad,
        are condemned, MS3:34
        examples and results of, MS3:35

manners, *(cont.)*
    excellent, points to observe, MS3:36
    good,
        developed by man to oil machinery of human relationships, MS3:34
        more widely known and respected than PR tech, MS3:35
        reason they are less apparent than once were, MS3:36
        requires two-way comm cycle, MS3:36
        sum up to, MS3:34
    other terms to describe, MS3:34
    primary tech of PR, MS3:34

manning,
    done against production, MS1:306
    of org done against production, MS2:105, MS2:256
    planned, MS1:325

manual, "The Scientologist: A Manual on the Dissemination of Material," 2:20

Manufacture of Madness, 0:521

marital-type ad, 6:180

marketing, Marketing, *see also* **dissemination; promotion**
    action, keynotes are, MS3:175
    basics of, MS3:187
    books and, MS3:164
    creates demand, MS3:219
    cycle of, MS3:190
    definition, MS3:174
    distribution planning and, MS3:190
    don't,
        market with generalities, MS3:217
        plan books to be printed without liaison with, MS3:217
    duty of, MS3:189
    essence of, MS3:211
    formula for naming a service, MS3:284
    hat, MS3:175
    includes all actions from, MS3:190
    magazines are a key tool of, 2:228
    management strategy in what to market and when, 2:187
    Marketing Bureau, motto is, MS3:175
    most attacked and suppressed line in any org or management unit is promo and marketing, MS3:191
    naming services and products, MS3:284
    of Book One must be done, 6:442
    one finds or strengthens or creates a demand, MS2:380
    one markets what is there right now in existence that can be delivered, MS3:189

marketing, *(cont.)*

one must push harder toward largest bulk of future business, MS2:379

pictorial or written materials done for, MS3:211

PR and, MS3:190

primary block as it relates to finance and, MS2:388

promotion is an essential part of, MS3:201

purpose of, MS3:175

scale that tells target proportion of finance and effort to allocate in marketing, MS2:379

shotgun marketing definition, MS3:190

stable data, MS3:187

supposed to create want and demand, MS3:189

surveying a name, MS3:285

two vital data are, MS3:189

two ways a catastrophe can be caused in, MS3:213

whole story of success told in few words, MS2:291

marriage(s),

held by the Chaplain, 6:518

how they can be saved, 0:511

marital quarrels, 1:536

Marriage Counseling,

Auditor's Code and, 6:540

both partners should take part in on own determinism, 6:542

definitions sheet, 6:544

depicted in "The Married Couple," 6:537

end phenomena, 6:540

handling misemotion in, 6:542

How to Improve Your Marriage Course and, 6:543

OTs and, 6:541

procedure, 6:537

repair, 6:541

requirements for delivery, 6:537

setups ordinarily unnecessary, 6:541

Marriage Counselor, VFP and statistic, 6:533

married couple, when only one takes an intensive, 4:843

Marx, Karl, 0:600–601

mass,

education in absence of, mental reactions, 0:33

mental, 0:37

mass accumulates in a complexity because one would not confront something, 4:370

mass purchases, should be submitted in writing by the other party and signed by him before any mass purchase is engaged, 3:285

Masters-at-Arms (MAAs),

Esto MAAs, Assistant MAA, functions, MS2:34

Esto MAAs, Exec Esto's MAA, functions, MS2:12, MS2:34

PTS or chronically ill or NCG and EO/MAA posts, MS1:460, MS2:251

material(s),

all material of Academy and SH courses is in use, 0:14

announcement of material available, 2:278

books, meters, cassettes, tapes, films and insignia are assets greater than hard money, MS2:382

calling them "old" or "background," result of, 5:275

courses and, 4:462

C/S responsibility for course, 5:698

data should be channeled to the right sources, 7:1292

degrade of, 0:14

discounting or giving away org services or, 0:303

dissemination materials to Saint Hill, 2:134

for course include, 5:507

for dissemination to public can be rewritten and published so long as no confusion as to origin generated, 2:118, 7:1290

going to field, printing vs. mimeo, 7:1279

having orderly collection of references or library containing materials of one's field, 0:310

heavy traffic warnings and, 0:380

issues of materials of mine under other names without credit is the most destructive action that can be undertaken, 7:1290

knowing what materials one works with are, 0:306–307

labeling material "background," "not used now" or "old," 0:14

literature must state Scientology is religious philosophy, 7:1320

needed for courses, 4:397

no-supply block, 0:380

number of times over the material equals certainty and results, 4:442

of Scientology are designed to communicate, 6:143

one would not issue Scientology materials of considerable weight to people incapable of assimilating them, 6:28, 7:969

pointing out channels on which materials flow, 0:389, 0:390

points on downgrade of materials, 2:139

material(s), *(cont.)*

policies governing release, 7:1292

refer to, to handle tech query, 4:502

released broadly to wrong public, 0:45

rules regarding the use of, 6:145

scarcity of and wrecked courses, 4:463

trouble training personnel traced back to lack of, MS1:400

when issued above the acceptance level of an audience, a confusion results, 6:28, 7:969

which may be added to a course, 4:442

workable and proven materials of Dianetics and Scientology only may be released, 7:1293

Materials Supply Clerk, ideal scene and stat, 4:138

materiel,

Estos establish and maintain the, 0:393

keeping materiel of org bright, 0:356

offenses concerning org materiel, 0:468, 0:543

responsibility of accounting for, 0:198

used for things it was not organized to do, 0:426

Materiel Administrator,

duties and post purpose, 3:372

purpose of, 3:370

meaning(s),

of policy shifted by reinterpretation, 0:141

unless precise meanings are given, then organization becomes very confused activity, 0:135

mechanization, total, 0:82

media, mass media,

definition and fault of, MS3:22

enemy controlling all news media, 0:336

PR men operating in, MS3:3

Scientology attacked by "public opinion" media, 0:10

skills needed by PRO to comm to the, MS3:167

special interest PRs and, MS3:8

medical, policy on psychiatric and medical failures, 7:1140

medical care, auditing and, 2:438

medical chart, description, 5:635

medical examinations, auditing and, 7:1100

Medical Liaison Officer,

ideal scene, 5:62

product, 5:62

purpose, 5:62

reports defined, 4:262, 5:297

statistics, 5:63

medical professions, their future vs. Scientology, 1:986–987

medicine, is always noting odd phenomena it finds but never uses in practice, 7:1092

meeting,

disrupting a, 0:468

eviction of person from, handling, 0:478–479

member(s),

definition of, 7:271

person does not have to know Scientology to be a, 0:152

refusing to vote while member of Comm Ev, 0:469

Scientologists may be members of any political group, 0:159

membership(s),

at end of six-month period person is told his free membership is expiring and is then sold a membership, 6:815

dead files and, 1:976

definition, 2:508, 3:236, 7:204

discounts and, 3:167

encouraging broad public memberships, 0:354

expansion of and org image, 0:336, 6:607, MS3:141

expired memberships go into Qual Div, 2:667

free,

for six months are open to all Scientologists, 6:815

memberships, 0:354

funds, invoicing and, 3:188

good service is keynote to whether they will buy or not, 6:815

handling, 2:397

income from, 2:399, 3:103

money,

monies separately banked, 3:244

separate, 6:803

no grade, certificate or classification qualification, 6:807

no refunds, 6:818

only a Comm Ev can remove, 0:492

Registrar must demonstrate savings of, 2:516

Scientologists and staff members in accepting posts or membership agree to abide by HCO Codes, 0:477–478

signature is adequate attestation, 6:814

types of, 6:805

memorial awards,

medals or plaques, 5:345

pins are the more usual, 5:345

memory, memorizing,

beware of memorizing things without understanding them, 0:31

memory, *(cont.)*

inadequate in supervision of posts and functions, 0:195

phones have no, 0:379

refresh your memory regarding your duties, 0:166

mental health, mental healing,

helping clean up and keep clean field of, 0:160

org/Scientology image and, 6:600, 7:1044

totalitarian conspiracy using "mental health" to control populations, 0:336

mental hospital(s), discovery of undisclosed tenure in a, 0:468

mental technology, vicious tech man evolved, 0:9

merchant of chaos, 7:1039; *see also* **suppressive person**

Merchant of Fear, 1:990; *see also* **suppressive person**

mere explanation,

definition, MS1:82

stats and, MS1:82

message(s), *see also* **communication**

agreement with, what PR is seeking to achieve, MS3:9

comm cycle and, 0:330

damage or expense occurring because urgent message was not marked RUSH, 0:381

definition, MS3:74, MS3:215

handling, 0:399, 0:400

must be repeated over and over, MS3:102, MS3:138

must have comm line first, MS3:36

placement of, 0:377

PR and, MS3:167

priority of, 1:22, 7:1163

PRO must know it and provide means of getting it carried, MS3:137

right message in the right form to the right public gets the result, MS3:13

subject, should contain only one, 1:299

what should be included, 1:300

messenger(s),

accepting an almost, 0:429

speed of service and, 0:275

mest,

ability to confront, handle and control it, 0:252

made to help too much, 6:834

messed up or in state of disorder, handling, 0:569

neat and orderly, 0:84, 0:165

public knows us by our, 0:84

meter check, *see also* **E-Meter**

for classification at Level VI, 5:226

on all attests at the Examiner, 4:234, 6:305

required at Success, 4:234, 6:305

what they consist of, 4:1109

metering, *see also* **E-Meter**

all bad results traced to inaccuracy in, 4:313

because auditor TRs and metering were out auditors have not been producing uniformly spectacular results, 4:428

incorrect, examples, 4:314

poor,

most fruitful source of missed withholds, 4:314

what brought it about, 5:653

unusual solutions by auditor and, 4:313

usual to check in Cramming, 5:653

what is meant by "perfect," 4:313

Method One Word Clearing, 6:421

Academy and OEC training, 5:475

action taken to clean up all misunderstoods, 5:475

case setup, 5:477

Danger conditions and, MS2:211

how to get, 5:477

prerequisite for Academy or OEC/FEBC training, 5:476

result of, 5:475

when it can be done, 5:476

middle management, *see also* **management**

above level of service orgs, 7:462, MS2:189, MS2:293, MS3:442

concerned with implementation of strategic planning, 7:459, MS2:445, MS3:439

definition, 0:707

handles many orgs and their functions, MS1:365

management status checksheets and, MS1:366

planning and, 0:704, 0:707

militant control, org's vitality and, 0:338

military science, technology of masked management, 7:578

Mimeo Files,

deficient or disorderly, 1:445

different cabinets for different types, 1:444

exact duties of, 1:433

file drawers, 1:444

file folder prepared, 1:442

filing procedure, 1:400

full policy, HCOB, ED files exist in, 1:435

maintain salvage measures, 1:445

object of, 1:433

product of, 1:437

steps of making, 1:448

mimeo issue(s),

color flash for, 0:113

Comm Ev for violation of publishing or counterfeiting of HCO PL or HCOB or their color combinations or signatures, 0:113

routing it correctly, 0:383

seeing that they look well when completed, 0:348

seniority of orders, 0:143, 0:523

mimeo, Mimeo,

all must have issue authority, 7:1308

composed of two units, 1:435

conservation is mandatory, 1:441

copies of any item run off on mimeo machines, 7:1283

different classes of issue, 1:442

distribution symbols, 1:408–409

does NOT belong in Promotion, 1:435

end product of, 1:433

excessive xerox or photostat expensive, 1:445

for small org, done by liaison to Continental Liaison Office, 1:436

handling of rare items or old original issues of historical value, 1:447

HCO issues, appearance, authorship and handling, 1:394

HCO, if it has a mimeo and an address file can always set wheels in motion when stats go down, 2:273

if Address is plated and in some kind of shape you can do a lot with specialized promotion, 2:272

look well when completed, Dept 2 promotional action, 1:40

machine, Roneo, 1:428

master copy stamped as such and DO NOT REMOVE, 1:394

mimeograph has uses, but it has to be a guarded use, 2:176

no org could prosper without a mimeo machine, 2:272, 1:427

org has two choices, 1:436

permission to mimeo, 1:411

photolitho machines, 1:427

procedure, 1:400

quality and essential communication are targets of Mimeo, 1:441

restrictions on use of, 2:173

routing forms, other forms run off in Mimeo, 1:435

spare copies, 1:446

stencil files, 1:444

mimeo, Mimeo, *(cont.)*

supply conservation, 1:440

types of HCO issues, 1:394

use of mimeo restricted, 1:389

mind, *see also* **reactive mind**

basic discovery of Dianetics and the human mind, 6:430

before 1949 man's knowledge of mind was black barbarism, 0:362

can predispose illness or injury, 5:622

capable of being logical, MS1:16

definition, 0:128

fallacy of, MS1:16

have to know something about, to handle PR, 6:620, MS3:3

learning only mechanical processes, not theory of, 0:65

self-protecting mechanism, 4:682

Thetan–Mind–Body–Product pattern, 0:128–129, 0:654

universe going downhill for lack of tech to resolve problems of, 0:91

minimum, law of the irreducible minimum, MS1:276

mini program(s),

ask of any mini program written: Will this give us a happy, productive, prosperous department? MS2:283

coordination, why we have, 7:455, MS3:435

definition, 0:708

done for each department, MS2:278

FOLOs must get mini programs in and done effectively, MS2:281

key to achievement, MS2:278

rules used as guidelines, MS2:279

small battle plans at the lowest tactical levels, 7:460, MS2:446, MS3:440

write doable ones that don't take long to finish, MS2:281

minister(s), *see also* **auditor**

auditors must be ministers in order to practice auditing, 6:605, 7:1220

Confessional tech and, 4:985, 5:448

missions are not authorized to ordain ministers, 4:1190, 6:605, 7:1220

penalty for refusing to hear Confessionals, 1:642

qualifications of, 5:304

reporting all overts, 4:1198

staff trained as auditors are clothed in ministerial suits, 7:1320

what he needs to know, 4:556

Ministerial Board of Review, 4:1190,
6:605, 7:1220

Ministerial certificates, 4:1191

Ministerial Services Section, VFP and
statistic, 6:533

minor,
HGC and Academy prices and, 3:145

must have their parents or guardians sign
the waiver and any note for time
payments, 4:360

Minor magazine, *see also* **magazine; Major
magazine**
definition and editorial policy, 2:229

policies on, 6:192–193, 6:221, 6:260, 6:453

when it goes out and to whom, 2:54

minority,
best are always a, 0:83

contest in which only a minority get
prizes, 0:234

self-interested person or minority bringing about
destructive policy, 0:117–118

when majority rules, minority suffers, 0:83

minutes,
of staff meeting, 0:173

way to write board minutes, 7:1119

miracle, Scientology is a modern miracle, 0:497

mirror, if staff member's breath can be detected
on mirror he can do his job, 0:168

miscellaneous report(s),
defined, 4:261, 5:296

ensure C/S has full data on case, 5:297

responsibility of HGC Admin to
file, 4:261, 5:296

vital to ensure C/S has full data on
case, 4:262, 5:297

misconduct,
at least some group members are aware
of, 0:555

misdemeanor, 0:468

miscramming,
consequences of, 5:825

examples of, 5:825

executive actions to handle, 5:826

indicators of, 5:826

misdeclare, proper routing of is through ARC
Break Registrar, 6:547

misdemeanor(s),
by student, penalty for, 0:478

Courts of Ethics and, 1:948

handling for when done by nonstaff, 1:864

increased penalty for, 1:864

misdemeanor(s), *(cont.)*
list of, 1:861–863

offenses considered misdemeanors, their
penalties and recourse, 0:467

persons may not be dismissed for, 1:864

punishable by direct order or Committee of
Evidence, 1:864

repeated error offenses brought into the category
of, 0:467

seriousness of, 0:545

staff auditors charged with, 5:840

State of Emergency and, 0:621

when Ethics is fascinated with staff member's
smallest misdemeanor, 0:503

when they may be reclassed as crimes, 0:470

Misdemeanor Report, description, 0:544

misinterpretation, of policy, results, 0:141

mismanagement, failure to forward basic purpose,
not grasping and specifying subpurposes
and, 7:665

misrouting, *see* **routing**

missed withhold, *see also* **withhold**
poor metering most fruitful source of, 4:314

source of all upset, 4:314

missed withhold of nothing, auditor who "sees a
read" when there is no charge makes a
"missed withhold of nothing," 4:347

mission(s),
are PR activities, 1:795

auditing and, 6:752

certification of mission students, 5:199

courses authorized, 6:748

definition of, 7:270

difference from Gung-ho Group, 6:849

helped to survive by orgs, 6:768

may charge more for services than Central
Organization, 6:706

may not charge less for services than the
Central Org, 2:410, 3:151, 6:709

motivation, 6:758

multiple ownership, 6:768

not authorized to ordain ministers, 4:1190

org happy to handle their rough cases, 5:56

org raided of auditors by call of big money
in, 0:102

orgs and field auditors, cooperation
between, 6:579

PES coaxes missions to select to his org, 0:99

policies on, 6:744, 6:749

processing org pcs, result, 4:1116

program for, 6:745

promotion musts, 6:762

result of offering of higher services not
authorized to give, 6:756

mission(s), *(cont.)*

  rip-off,

    of org staff and pcs by, 4:222, 6:770, 5:433

    of org staff, penalty, 0:176

    org staff, responsible for payment of costs of all training and processing, 3:174

  selecting to higher orgs, 6:760

  student certification, 6:755

  summary of policy, 6:749

  teach HDC courses, 6:720

  training authorized, 6:749

  upset or not giving good service, reason, 0:69

Mission Order (MO),

  definition, 1:431

  description, 0:728

mission(s), Sea Org,

  Flag Reps and, 7:1410

  investigatory, MS1:165

  quicksilver personnel scene and, 0:265

  Sea Org official mission, 7:151

  security checking all persons returning from, 0:178

mistake(s), *see also* **error**

  failing to learn from them and repeating them, MS2:187

  made by,

    people who cannot evaluate, MS1:154

    SPs which get seniors in trouble, 1:993, 4:85

  presence of suppression, one makes, 1:1033

  vicinity of PTS people one tends to make, 1:1035

misunderstanding, false reports by rumor or, 0:514

misunderstood word(s), misunderstood(s), Mis-U(s), MU(s), *see also* **noncomprehension**

  act as perception shut-offs, MS2:132

  area that is organizing only is loaded with, MS2:133

  basic words connected with post, 5:466

  blows follow, 1:287

  bottom of all alteration, 5:468

  breeds strange ideas, 5:464

  can prevent completion of a cycle of action, MS2:132

  cleared on meter to F/N, 5:78

  crazy interpretations of tech and, 0:304

  critical preclear, only reasons are withhold or, 5:672

  effects of, 0:35, 0:39

  ethics and, 0:47

  exec who is failed student has, 0:223

misunderstood word *(cont.)*

  exists at bottom of confusion, 4:500, 5:464

  false data as phenomenon additional to misunderstood words, MS2:135

  feeling one knows words that one does not know, 0:44

  first phenomenon and, 4:330, 5:177

  handling for, MS2:133

    when students enroll on course, 4:385

  ideal scene, org tech and admin staff cleared of, 5:77

  if misunderstoods won't clear, query it, 0:23

  importance of, 0:35

  inability to understand post, 5:466

  incomplete course due to, 0:223

  intro lecture and nonclassed courses using no words that will be misunderstood, 0:352–353

  manifests itself by demands to only produce and to prevent any organization, MS2:133

  most common cause of unacceptable or no post product, MS1:244, MS1:421

  MU breeds strange ideas, 4:500

  often come up during False Data Stripping, MS2:142

  orders and, 0:23, 0:431

  organization misunderstoods, 0:39

  out-tech and post nonperformance, Why, 1:899, 4:481

  overts stem from, 1:294

  people who have Mis-Us are inclined to develop vast complexities, MS2:133

  post nonperformance and, 0:39, 0:40, 0:44, 0:47

  posts and, 5:466

  prevent being in communication with materials or others, MS2:65

  promotional actions and, 0:346, 0:352–353

  queries and, 4:403

  reason,

    for verbal tech, MS1:174

    they won't clean up, 1:837

  relating to organization, MS1:247

  second phenomenon and, 4:330, 5:178

  staff talking Scientology before callers, 0:347

  students with, 5:513

  stupidity and, 0:35

  Supervisor's skill on, 4:397, 5:507

  tech queries and, 4:502

  telexes, despatches and, 0:47

  uncertainty stems from, 5:524

  underlying reason for people not studying, 5:445

misunderstood word, *(cont.)*

understanding,
barred out by, 5:525
ceases on going past MU or concept, 0:39,
0:40, MS1:244

verbal tech and, 0:304

when you are getting no product look
for, MS2:132

withhold or misunderstood, only reason pc is
critical, 4:1081

misuse, definition, 0:543

Misuse Report, description, 0:543

mixed letter, definition, 1:970, 2:661

mob, unworn hats and an org, MS1:405

monetarist, 0:315

believes you can manipulate a whole society
with money alone and no thought of any
production, MS2:369

definition, MS1:352, MS2:286

money, *see also* **exchange; finance; gross
income; income; pay**

amends project may not have org funds
employed in it, 0:546

as a total motivation for an action is not
high-grade motivation, 3:70

basically a matter of confidence, 3:245

biggest crime one can commit in this modern
society is to be without money, 3:70

bills solved by having far more than "enough
money" and not spending it foolishly,
MS2:224

calculating cash value of every piece of work
done, 0:314

can be manipulated in a thousand different
ways, MS2:222

crime of having no money, 0:693

decreases in value—books increase, MS2:381

exchange and, 0:317, 0:528

form of power, MS2:396

four conditions of exchange, 0:317

given enough money or control you can usually
buy or demand your way out of any game
you don't want to play, 2:122

government or counterfeiter making
money, 0:528

idea backed by confidence, MS2:219

income of money on sales must be greater than
outgo on bills, MS2:221

is a commodity, MS2:343

lack of, 3:71
comes from, MS3:146

losing money due to inaccurate billing, 0:276

make,
more money, how it is done, 0:693
tons of money for the organization, 7:925

money, *(cont.)*

must be taken at once on sign-up, 3:119

must have desirable product and sell and deliver
it to have, MS1:224

negotiable receipt for deposited goods from
viewpoint of a banker, MS2:389

new program and, 0:703

no production equals no money, MS2:220

one cannot spend money unless he has it, 7:926

one has to produce something to exchange
for, 0:528

org pattern is not designed to make money, 0:96

plan to get total sum from each of three or four
ways or sources, 3:27, 7:925

prompt return of money to dissatisfied pc, 0:410

represents,
success when you have it, 3:32
things, MS2:220

simply that which represents delivered
production, MS2:221

so many beans in to get so many beans
out, MS1:277

something that can be exchanged confidently for
goods or services, MS2:219

staff member needing extra money,
handling, 0:170

substitute for goods and services, MS2:220

the less amount of income an organization or
an individual has, the more carefully and
wisely financial planning must be done,
MS2:422

to get money you have to have admin in, 0:527

Treason formerly defined as accepting
money, 0:567

truths of wealth, MS2:221

waste of, 0:468

monks, Buddhist, rules of conduct, 1:774

monopoly, monopolies,

cause of attacks from, 0:8

I have no monopoly on ability to observe
and act, 0:140

nine factors causing troubles for, 0:40

one-man monopoly on action, 0:87

monthly bills summary, look for purchase orders
that don't appear on statements, 3:294

moonlighting,

definition, MS1:417, MS1:474

in-ethics can bring prosperity to all, 0:533

no policy against, where it doesn't injure the
org, MS1:418

right answer is for org to function and make
money and pay its staff, 7:315

staff pay vs., 3:361

when it's okay and when it isn't, MS1:417

moonripping,
definition, MS1:474
varieties of, MS1:474

moral code(s), 0:456, 0:457; *see also* **codes;**
HCO Ethics Codes; Justice Codes

morale,
affected by quality of org board, MS1:221
depends on
accomplishment, 1:63
accomplished and exchanged production,
MS2:221
production, 4:436
example of someone out of the action and not
producing anything, 7:815
factor in organizing, MS1:230
good organization, good morale is product of,
MS1:231
how to create an immediate upsurge in staff
morale, 4:705
idle rich and, 0:299
low production area is out-morale, MS3:58,
MS3:233
made of common purpose and obstacles
overcome by the group, MS1:279
of auditor, depends on, 4:946, 5:846
principle of VFP and, MS1:296
production and, 0:259, 0:529
basis of, 0:277, 0:299, 0:394, MS2:28
raising it, 0:299
sympathy and, MS1:231
third dynamic psychosis is a detestation of high
morale, MS1:268
when a person becomes productive his morale
improves, MS2:71

morality, *The Way to Happiness* and, 7:1155

morals, 0:454–456
definition, 1:489

More Info Cards, 0:625; *see also* **advertisement**
book promotion and, 2:705
line for, 2:712

mores, groups and, 0:411, 0:556

motion,
able to get one's product out with no wasted
motion, 0:305
actions of org can all be classified under
heading of particle motion and change, 0:81
lots of motion but nothing done, 0:387
putting motion in vertically on org board so that
flow will occur, 0:107
random motion in condition of Confusion, 0:568

motivators, mocking up, 0:449

motive,
insanity has to do with motive, not competence,
7:1143
sanity and insanity are matters of, 0:296

motor,
billion-horsepower motor vs. one grasshopper,
0:600
why motor can generate power, 0:205

move magazine(s), *see also* **magazine**
definition, 2:225
org's move must be promoted well ahead of
time, 2:226
photos of new building must be top quality,
2:227
sample of, 2:225

Mr. Know Best, out-admin example, 0:71

multiple,
declare, completion statistic and, 5:254
report, heard from several areas or people,
MS1:26
situations, format for, MS1:124

murder,
getting away with murder so long as one's stat
is up, 0:503
governments and, 0:83
welfare districts full of, 0:528

musical chairs, *see also* **transfer**
answer to, 1:71
bug back of, 7:804
can destroy org or area, 7:412, MS3:392
covert method of, 1:71
definition, 0:264, 0:280, 0:433, 1:71, MS1:359,
MS1:381
doing a quicksilver, 0:264–267
effect of, 0:206, 0:280, 0:433
on staff member, MS1:381
how it comes about, 1:78, 1:206
importance of forbidding, 0:223
in life, mechanism below ARC breaks, 1:211
most destructive action to an org's stats,
MS1:317
org collapse and, MS1:305, MS2:104, MS2:255
recruiting, 1:71
result of, MS1:454
social aberration, 1:211
stemming from social aberration, 0:206

Muslim, conquest of India, 0:125

Mussolini, Benito, 0:231

muster, when staff has to be mustered, 0:439

N

naming, principle in naming things for PR purposes, MS3:160

Napoleon, 0:457

narrowing the target, MS1:76

nation, *see also* civilization; country; culture; group; society; state; third dynamic
  centralizing into a federal state, 0:632
  expansion vs. contraction, 0:124–126
  planet with nations vs. one central government, 0:598
  two nations at each other's throats, handling,0:512
  unrest of, traced to lack of purpose and value, 0:204, MS1:416

nationalism, effect of rise of, 0:506

natter,
  don't just natter if there's something you don't like, 0:547
  students and, 0:586

navy, example of basic purpose for a, 0:116

Nazi(s), 0:328, 0:520
  PR tech and, MS3:4

NCG, definition, MS1:460, MS2:251, MS2:354
  see also no case gain

neatness, neat,
  desk, equipment and quarters neat, 0:84, 0:165
  office and premises neat and clean, 0:165, 0:335
  respect and, 0:339

necessity, definition, 3:295, MS2:402

necessity level, ethics raising it, 0:497, 0:498

neck, How come your neck is so precious when mine isn't? 0:231

NED for OTs, safeguarding the materials of, 4:812

NED for OTs Auditor, course prerequisites modified, 4:659

needed and wanted, *see also* want
  finding out what is, 0:579
  not finding out what is, result, 0:561
  not really producing what is, 0:581
  producing what is, 0:580

negative lessons, 6:778

neglect, hats not worn and, 1:276

negligence, neglect(ed),
  continued emergencies and, 0:588
  Danger condition and, 0:585
  down stats and, 0:588
  equipment neglected, 0:186, 0:189
  in safeguarding copyrights, registered marks, trademarks, registered names of Scientology, 0:473
  of responsibilities resulting in catastrophe even when another manages to avert final consequences, 0:267, 0:473
  resulting in need to apply Emergency Formula, 0:468
  small neglected bits cause disasters, 0:261
  treasonable neglect, 0:220
  what neglect or abandonment of staff or caring about staff can be an indicator of, 0:694

network(s),
  junior issues causing destruction of, 0:143
  out-ethics indicators in, 0:532
  representative may recruit or hire his own staff, 1:169
  using orgs for recruiting pools, 1:257

new,
  Dianetics and Scientology are, 0:362
  doing things that won, not new things untried, 0:628

new broom, 0:597

newcomer, handling of, 6:808

New Era Dianetics (NED),

case completion, ability gained, 4:192

children and babies and, 4:260

completions who haven't gone Clear, handling, 4:999

Drug Rundown, ability gained, 4:192

public interested in co-auditing, 4:689

state of Clear can be achieved on, 4:1107

New Era Dianetics Course, prerequisites modified, 4:659

New Era Dianetics Drug Rundown, 6:421

new names to CF,

CF and, 0:349, 0:360

handling for new names which have not bought anything, 2:660

news, 0:362; *see also* **bad news**

never happens, it's manufactured, MS3:132

releases, how to program for maximum benefit, MS3:133

story, requirements, MS3:132

newsletter, to FSMs, 0:99

news media, parasitic on those who make news, 7:1049

newspaper, newsprint,

ad, used in dissemination, 2:61, 6:167

pours lies into population of Earth, 6:622, MS3:5

"public opinion," MS1:69

sell on interest to readers, MS3:132

supported by specialized groups, MS3:151

word of mouth vs., 0:333

writing, rules of, MS3:126

Nimitz, 0:116

ninety-day rule, 0:596

"no,"

drill for financial manager, 3:30, 7:928

financial manager must learn how to say, 3:30, 7:928

no case gain, *see also* **case gain**

confirms a suppressive person, 1:997, 4:89

judge a suppressive person by, 1:991, 4:83

no case gain in past = SP, 5:35

prevented by Dept 3 spotting PTSes and handling, 1:40

skipped levels expressed as, 4:186, 5:191

no-charge, activity, given an invoice, 3:119

no-confront,

when no-confront enters a chain may be set up which leads to total complexity and total unreality, 4:371

very complex form of, 4:371

no-gain-case,

enturbulence and upset and the, 1:992, 4:84

makes you hunt for magical processes and fatally leads to alter-is, 4:342

No-Interference Area,

clarified and re-enforced, 4:1111–1112

exception, 4:1113

noise, *see also* **chaos; confusion; developed traffic; disorder; distraction**

CLO duties vs., 7:421, MS3:401

definition, 1:152, 7:414, 7:797, MS3:394

estimating amount of "noise" in area, 0:294

generated because main situations not being handled, 7:421, MS3:401

on-policy orgs have least noise, 0:28

person who isn't noisy but never gets anything done, 0:237

students on breaks, 4:897

working in a world full of, 0:62

noncommunication, consists of, MS3:72

noncompliance(s), *see also* **compliance**

alteration of orders and tech is worse than, 1:201

area with numerous noncompliances or offenses, 0:621

as method of self-protection, 0:248

catastrophes caused by, 0:424, 0:622

causing targets to move into present time, 0:424

computer detecting noncompliance, 0:704–705

Danger condition and, 0:585

destructive order avoided by, 0:141

detect and get rid of, 0:283

dev-t and, 0:416, 0:424

discipline and, 0:122

don't ever get soft on, 0:418

effect of, 7:1211, 7:1314

emergencies and, 0:417, 0:587, 0:623

ethics action for, 0:586, 0:589

example of, 0:429, 7:675

executive,

seldom hit unless he has had noncompliance on his lines, 0:427

who tolerates noncompliance, 0:659

expansion vs., 0:123

failing to comply with legal orders, 0:145, 0:589

false graph is far worse than, 0:658

ferocity added against, 0:247

first indicator of unit or staff member going PTS, 1:1023

noncompliance(s), *(cont.)*

how unfinished cycle of action comes
about, 0:248

indicators of, 0:420

Liability condition for, 0:528, 0:655

make penalties for noncompliance too gruesome
to be faced and enforce them, 0:420

not-dones, 0:391, 0:392

off-policy-type personnel and, 0:242

only occurs when orders have had to be
issued, 0:139

only thing that holds down the size of
Scientology today, 1:424

resulting in overwork, 0:622

seriousness of, 0:545

single-handing vs., 7:449, MS2:273, MS3:429

spotting sources of, 0:554

targets and, MS2:429

three conditions wherein you get no answers,
7:415, MS3:395

unseen, 0:420

where noncompliance with policy and orders has
for some time existed, 0:587

with instructions, 4:85

wog world and, 0:421

Noncompliance Report, 0:544

noncomprehension, *see also* **misunderstood word**

avoidance of orders, 1:201

of basic words with which one is working, 0:40

products, lack of comprehension of, 0:39

squirreling comes about from, 0:12

nonconfront,

aberration a chain of vias based on a primary
nonconfront, 4:371

basis of aberration is a nonconfront, 4:369

degree of complexity is proportional to the
degree of nonconfront, 4:369

"nonco-op" category,

dead file is extension of, 1:973

definition, 1:973, 2:664

nondelivery,

D of P doesn't know he's responsible for
getting auditors, 4:154

DTS isn't calling in people for service, 4:153

only tough thing to do is not to deliver, 2:112,
3:88, 6:556, 7:862

refunds came from, 4:198

where exists, make a study of how come and
who, 2:111, 3:87, 4:153, 6:555, 7:861

Non-Enturbulation Order, 1:704, 4:103, 5:21

nonexistence, nonexistent,

being has ceased to be simply nonexistent as
team member and has taken on the color of
enemy, 0:574

things that don't exist can have no
product, 0:654

what you are assigning conditions to doesn't
exist, handling, 0:647

Non-Existence condition, Formula,

anyone in Non-Existence or Danger receives
minimum pay and no bonuses, 7:694

beginning a post in, 0:647

Bs of I and, 1:959

bypass resulting in, 0:602, 0:603

condition assignments for overlong attendance on
Academy courses, 4:372

effects of never really applying the, 0:578–579

Expanded Non-Existence Formula, 0:579–580,
1:592–593

graph description, 0:675

large group made up of Non-Existences is
nonexistent itself, 0:599

never having come out of, 0:578

new appointee to post begins in, 0:561

new post formula, 1:557

person failing at his job and starting
again at, 0:562

putting something there to have stat for or do
something that deserves a stat, 0:680

staying in, 0:579

steps, 0:561–562

when normal and routine posts fail,
7:427, MS3:407

where a stat is in completely nonviable range, it
is really in Non-Existence or worse, 7:563

Non-Interference Zone, definition, 4:195

nonproduction,

if you award nonproduction, you get
nonproduction, 1:769, 7:500

illegal policy is responsible for, MS1:261

out-ethics symptom, 1:835

non-remimeo,

definition, 1:407

two classes, 1:408

general, 1:409

limited, 1:409

no-report,

Committee of Evidence for, 1:869

illegible Auditor's Report is classed as a,
4:618, 5:190

303

No-Report Report, description, 0:544

Normal Operation condition, Normal condition, Normal Operation Formula,

assignment of State of Normal Operation cleaning portion of org or org's ethics files, 0:545

bring post up to Normal from Emergency, 0:622

graph description, 0:655

mild ethics during, 0:564

penalties doubled for breaking a, 0:661

persons transferred into new appointment who are in Normal or above at time of transfer, 0:566

Power stat is brand-new range in Normal trend, 0:643

stating one is in Normal when he is in Emergency, 0:665

taking over post in Normal Operation and getting it into Emergency or Danger, 0:597

Normal Operation condition, *(cont.)*

using wrong formula, effect, 0:580

no-service, examples, 1:79

not-dones, 0:391, 0:392; *see also* **noncompliance; backlog(s); half-dones**

reasons for, 7:431, MS2:225, MS3:411

note,

collecting outstanding notes, 0:349

more easily collected in court than a debt, 7:1107

"nothing matters" attitude,

criminality and, 7:737

result of, 7:736

notice board, 0:348, 0:355

not-knows, dev-t and, 0:415

"now we're supposed to's,"

ethics presence and, 0:246

we are essentially breakers of, 0:273

O

objective(s),

achieving a desired objective, 0:690

battle plan not accomplishing any tactical objective, 0:708

first objective, cleared Earth, 4:871

my own, 6:864

no objective worth obtaining was ever achieved without some barriers arising or industrious dedication, 0:92

objective two, 4:862

Objectives,

ability gained, 4:189

low OCA and, 4:194

when needed, 4:194

oblivion,

bad policy or laws or actions based on rumor causing, 0:118

we have trust which, if we fail it, condemns ourselves, our friends, our future, to continued oblivion, 0:239

obnosis, definition, MS2:22

observation, observe, observing, *see also* **awareness; confront; inspection; investigation; look**

ability to observe related to insight, 0:122

as basic of administration, includes, 7:409

assembled by continent and org and evaluated, 7:418, MS3:398

auditor must be able to observe, 5:671

basic step of administration, 7:408, MS3:388

before issuing orders, 0:140

by (1) stats, (2) reports, (3) inspections, MS2:60, MS2:242

ceasing to demand orders and beginning to observe and act on our own predictions, 0:140

observation, observe, observing, *(cont.)*

downfall of beings and, MS1:87

duplicated in Data Bureau of CLO and CIC processed for local CLO use, 7:418, MS3:398

eight steps necessary for accurate, MS1:30–31

error, "being reasonable," MS1:30

heart of is accuracy, MS1:98

if one doesn't know the ideal scene or situation, MS1:29

individual shut off from fruits of, 0:9

Intelligence Quotient vs., 0:9

key ingredient of Flag Rep, 7:1408, 7:1411

lack of, 0:255

observing, questioning and drawing up list of what was previously successful in your area, 0:647

role in auditing, 4:1079, 5:670

to discard areas, MS1:75

obsessions, most "got to's" or obsessions come from pain association or drug association, 7:1138

OCA, *see* **Oxford Capacity Analysis**

occlusion, cause of, on whole track, 5:567

OEC, *see* **Organization Executive Course**

OES, *see* **Organization Executive Secretary**

offense(s), charge(s), *see also* **crime; crimes in Scientology; omission; overt**

absence from post without competent replacement, 0:266

absence of personally issued Ethics Conditions Orders, 0:659

offense(s), charge(s), *(cont.)*

actions,
against Scientology, reported to HCO, 1:646
contrary to intentions and actions of team, 0:574
or omissions that make one an accessory, 0:554–557

agreement with stats being down, 0:682

alter-ising or misadvising others on use of study tech, 0:45

anyone following destructive reinterpretation of policy is as guilty as misinterpreter, 0:141

area with numerous offenses, handling, 0:621

auditing for pay outside pcs while employed on staff, 0:170

auditor failing to clear every word of every command or list used, 0:45

being who is guilty knows he is offending against future of all, 0:493

breaking a high condition, 0:661

bringing about decline of a post and damage to it or areas around it, 0:657

collective petition, 0:488

comm-evable, in course rooms, 5:517

committing act or omission undertaken to knowingly suppress, reduce or impede Scientology or Scientologists, 0:45

condoning or contributing to circumstances or offenses capable of bringing a course, section, unit, department, org, zone or division to state of collapse, 0:267

crimes, list of, 0:470–474

criminal charges filed if any monies or org property is missing in consequence with person blowing, 0:177

criminal offense to give out prospects, 2:711, 6:193

definition, 0:117

errors, list of, 0:467

failing to, failure to,
advise IJC of serious charges in KRs, 0:557
apply study tech in dissemination, 0:45
file KR written by another, 0:557
show initiative on post, 0:662
submit executive reports on what is observed and new offenses found in a portion in State of Emergency, 0:622
teach or use study tech, 0:45
write clearly on worksheets or put down enough text to make it understandable, 0:47
write down disclosed crime in worksheet or report, 0:557

follower of destructive order is far more guilty than issuer, 0:142

following, obeying or issuing destructive or off-policy order, 0:142, 0:143

forbidding anyone to write KR, 0:556

offense(s), charge(s), *(cont.)*

four general classes of, 0:467

giving out data contrary to HCOBs or PLs, 0:24

high crimes, *see* high crimes

illegal discounts, 0:303

in-charge who lets org get ripped off for some personal favor, 0:533

issuing orders altering lines without clearance, 0:385

knowingly false statements made in KRs, 0:557

knowingly going by MUs in telexes and despatches, 0:47

lack of code of specified offenses, effect of, 0:467

leaving and leaves, offenses relating to, 0:177–178

letting people be hit with wrong conditions, 0:519

letting SP collapse stats or an org, 0:519

list of offenses and penalties, 0:467–474

misdemeanors, list of, 0:467–469

must be reported to Ethics, 4:1198

neglecting to clarify words not understood, 0:44

neglect of responsibilities resulting in catastrophe even when another manages to avert final consequences, 0:267

no report, 0:47

not confronting accused with all charges and his accusers, 0:514

off-post during appointed hours, 0:151

out-admin, 0:260

out-tech, 0:45

penalties and, 1:861

people who do not do their work, 0:151

quicksilver personnel scenes, 0:266

reclassed as crimes, 1:864

refusing to let somebody handle outness, 0:261

releasing materials broadly to wrong public, 0:45

removing KRs from files, 0:557

removing particles off line, 0:432

repeated error offenses brought into category of misdemeanor, 0:467

repeated offenders of study tech may be declared suppressive, 0:45

selling org prospect lists to squirrel, 0:533

staff accepting any student or pc for personal profit or favors, 0:171

staff borrowing money from past or present students or pcs, 0:171

State of Emergency continued beyond allotted time, 0:622

offense(s), charge(s), *(cont.)*

stopping or impeding forward progress of project or org, 0:574

student or pc and, 0:478

study tech, violations of and failures to use, 0:47

taking over post in Normal Operation and getting it into Emergency or Danger, 0:597

tours being used to take longer leaves with org paying expenses, 0:265–266

treasonable neglect, 0:220

using "Orders, Query Of" policy to avoid routine actions not resulting in loss or destruction, 0:142

using org status to be trained or processed without completing contracts, 0:174

verbal tech, categories of, 0:24

which make one an accessory, 0:556, 0:557

office, neatness of, part of everyone's hat, MS1:237

Office of Evaluation and Execution, 0:304

Office of HCO Exec Sec,

primary purpose, 7:72

special projects carried under, 7:370, MS3:350

who it is headed by and what it contains, 7:131

Office of LRH,

clearance for change of lines and terminals, 0:384–385, 1:311

Comm Evs and, 0:487, 0:492

ethics,

Ethics authority and, 0:545, 0:549–550, 0:621

functions belonging to, 7:1263

gives clearance for putting in new lines and posts or making changes in old ones, 0:384, 0:385

issuance of conditions and, 7:1302

issues all authorities for justice, 7:1301

organization of, 7:1209

personnel, 7:109

petitions and, 0:489, 0:492

project clearance and, 0:376

promotional actions of, 0:356

purpose, 7:71

special projects carried under, 7:370, MS3:350

who it is headed by and what it contains, 7:131

Office of LRH Design and Planning Authority Section, 0:376

Office of LRH Policy Review Section, 0:623

Office of Org Exec Sec,

purpose, 7:72

special projects carried under, 7:370, MS3:350

Office of Special Affairs, acceptability of Scientology, MS1:172

Office of the Treasurer, purpose, 3:63

officer(s), *see also* **administrator; executive; leader; manager; senior**

how US Navy chose its officers, 0:116

Inspection Officer, 0:172, 0:547

Insurance Officer, 0:548

may not assign but may request Danger condition on their sections or personnel, 0:588

not getting one's officers rewarded, 0:631

State of Emergency and, 0:662

waiting for orders, 0:135

who indulges in Q&A, handling, 7:440, MS3:420

official(s),

peasants vs., 0:291

right to petition in writing any, 0:488

Scientology does not work in absence of official control, 0:159

off-line,

definition, 0:426

dev-t and, 0:390

Dev-t Report, 0:544

full in-basket and, 0:404–411

having to do off-line favors, 0:552

people who are always, 0:84

phone is, 0:85

staff, MS1:237

off-line despatch(es),

apathy and tiredness due to off-line comm, 0:394

causes of, 0:408, 0:412

definition, 0:405, 0:426

Dev-t Chit for, 0:442

failing to spot and return them to source, 0:409

finding out what staff are sending, 0:417–418

handling for, 0:166, 0:405, 0:408, 0:409

laziness and, 0:409

logs kept of, 0:416

offload(s),

how they occur, 0:214, 0:217, 0:393

instruct, cram, retrain, offload system, 0:442

requires a court or Comm Ev, 0:524

Review Comm Ev and, 0:524

off-origin,

definition, 0:426

dev-t and, 0:390

Dev-t Report, 0:544

off-origin despatch(es),

apathy and tiredness due to off-origin comm, 0:394

description of, 0:413

dev-t and, 0:413, 0:442

finding out what staff are sending, 0:416

handling, 0:413–414

logs kept of, 0:416

off-zone, example, 0:414

off-policy,

comm eved or given court or disciplined for following off-policy issues or orders, 0:145

definition, 0:59

dev-t and, 0:391, 0:392, 0:623

Dev-t Report, 0:544

doesn't know policy and so does things contrary to it, 0:410

effects of being, 0:59

if it seems kind of stupid it is probably, 0:147

off-line and off-policy, your full in-basket, 0:404–411

orders, 0:145–148, 0:553

seeing another staff member at variance with org policy, handling, 0:165

what happens when junior issues make off-policy changes, 0:143

off-policy despatch(es),

definition, 0:405, 0:410

failing to spot and return them to source, 0:409

finding out what staff are sending, 0:416

handling for, 0:406, 0:408, 0:409

how to tell if person does not properly handle, 0:405

laziness and, 0:409

logs kept of, 0:416

what happens when you forward an, 0:405

what it is a symptom of, 0:410

off-post,

definition, 0:151, 1:249

people who are always off-line and off-post, 0:84

staff, MS1:237

off-purpose, person setting random or counter-policy is, MS1:264

off-source, indicator of, 0:532

off-zone, example, 0:414

OIC, see **Organization Information Center**

Okay to Audit,

course graduation does not give an, 4:948, 5:848

graduate certificate requirements, 5:852

Okay to Audit, (cont.)

issued by Qual Auditor Cramming Section, 4:946, 5:846

system, mandatory for HGC auditors, 4:946, 5:846

two types of, 5:852

validity of in other orgs, 4:946, 5:846

when temporary becomes permanent, 4:948, 5:848

old poem, 0:531

omission(s), see also **offenses; outpoint(s)**

from auditing folder, serious matter, 1:640

of enforcing truth and justice, 0:520

offenses concerning, 0:467, 0:468

overts of omission that kill any pride, 0:255

technical omissions or offenses reported to Ethics promptly, 0:623

that make one an accessory, 0:556–557

toughest outpoint to recognize, MS1:168

on-call, staff auditor duty, 4:844

one-man band, field auditor as a, 6:717

on-line, definition, 0:391, 0:392

on-origin, definition, 0:392

on-policy, 0:28, 0:59

orgs which are, 7:806

on-post, definition, 0:151, 1:249

OODs, see **Orders of the Day**

open house(s),

advertising and holding, 0:352

generating public interest and goodwill, 0:332, MS3:168

open-minded, about Scientology, 0:12

operate, operating,

at risk, 0:255

changing your operating basis, 0:563

operating that which produces in order to obtain product, 0:287

operating target(s), see also **target(s)(ing)**

definition, MS2:433, MS2:437

inspect and survey and gather data and set operating and primary targets before you set production targets, MS2:434

needs a conditional target ahead of it—to wit, an inspection, MS2:433

Operating Thetan, OT,

aberrated universe vs., 0:624

best job deserves fastest road to, 0:156

cause and, 0:248, 0:249

color flash for OT course materials and communications, 4:791

datum that can put you on road to OT, 0:268

Operating Thetan, OT, *(cont.)*

definition, 0:249, MS2:428

formula: Cause, MS2:429

gradient scale, MS2:429

one is as OT as he can cause things, MS2:429

regulations, 4:793, 6:842

Scientology Marriage Counseling and, 6:541

symbol, 6:843

used for OT activities, 7:125

training recommended, 4:820

operation(s), operational,

definition of operational, 0:190, 7:1393, MS2:37

efficient, 7:833

make your zone of operations realize that you have the authority and ability to care for them, 7:21

smoothness, how it is obtained, 7:834

something is fully operational when it functions without further care or attention, 7:721

Operation Transport Liaison Office (OTL),

definition, 7:418, MS2:351, MS3:398

duties of, 7:420, MS3:400

expense, definition, MS2:352

opinion(s),

being used in personnel selection, 0:120, 0:218

data is not, 0:373

definition, MS1:5

entitled to have opinions so long as these do not bar route out for self and others, 0:22

false reports and prejudices of society, MS1:68

justice and, 0:520

popular opinion is bank opinion, 0:158, 7:1015

pretending to express multiple opinion in vital reports, 0:471

results on recruitment and hiring, MS1:310, MS2:109, MS2:260

social orders acting on, MS1:68

opinion leader,

anti-opinion leaders made by neglect, MS3:24

being one, what it involves, MS3:21

celebrities as, MS3:18

correct use of, example, MS3:19

definition, MS3:17

destruction of, result, MS3:23

each group has its own, MS3:17

general unrest traced to disregard of subject of, MS3:20

goodwill of, necessary for survival, MS3:23

how subject goes out of use, MS3:19

how to identify, MS3:17

may or may not be VIPs, MS3:24

misuse of by the US, MS3:22

opinion leader, *(cont.)*

politicians boosted to power by, MS3:19

PR action success and, MS3:18

prosperity and, MS3:22

public opinion formed by, MS3:18

rule for use of, MS3:18

turning on, example, MS3:20

VIP vs., MS3:18

would-be opinion leader who is anti, handling of, MS3:23

wrong use of, example, MS3:18

opposition; *see also* **attack; enemy,**

expansion vs., 0:123

how enemies or opposition come about, 0:117

really sane, forceful person looks right on through and past, 0:236

oppression, oppress(ed),

group size, the individual and, 0:598–604

how to avoid feeling harassed, ordered around and oppressed, 0:140

justice and, 0:456, 0:517, 0:520

oppressive, confused and overworked org, reason for, 0:554

US and Australia fighting Scientology while supporting oppressive mental and religious practices, 0:157

oral examination, 5:150; *see also* **examination(s)**

order(ly), orderliness; *see also* **organize**

area which is in Confusion and, MS2:182

better justice, easier recourse from injustice and higher sense of order, effect of, 0:481

bringing order and making safe environment in which we can work, 0:481

"Bring Order" is the watchword of HCO, 1:83

chaos vs., 0:389, 0:434

coming to orderly cause point on every post, 0:231

confusion blows off when order is entered, 1:31

definition, 0:305, 0:389, MS2:176, MS2:195, MS2:300

desk and mest neat and orderly, 0:84, 0:165

disorder vs., 0:305

establishing in society, 1:734

expansion or growth and, 0:188, 0:480, 0:481

first action in bringing order to an area, 1:34

having overall picture of what area would look like when properly ordered and organized, 0:306, 0:307

HCO and bringing order, 0:478–479

high production areas and, 0:311

how order goes in, 0:434

order(ly), orderliness, *(cont.)*

inspecting area by outpoints against factor of, 0:307

justice and, 0:483

knowing what and where things are and what they are for, 0:306

no exact English word for, 0:132

orderly service is preferable to disorderly service, 0:273

personal sense of, 0:305, MS2:176

production and, 0:312

putting things back when one is finished with them, 0:310

stability composed of, 1:83

stable terminals, 0:434

to handle chaos, put in order, 7:413, MS3:393

totality of Power is orderly progress, 0:481

world going more beatnik vs. keeping up standard of cleanliness and good order, 0:334

order(s)

acknowledgment to an, 0:372

Advisory Committee, issue of, 7:906

Advisory Council, issue of, 7:905

alter-ised by SPs, 1:993, 4:85

arbitraries vs., 0:65, 0:140

asking for, 0:144

authority to issue orders comes from, 0:135

avoid giving orders or advice that can be used to make you wrong when it's misapplied, 7:235

ceasing to demand orders and beginning to observe and act on own predictions, 0:140

common trick used to get agreement to do an, 0:146

confused, undoable orders, 0:705

cooperation is senior to, 0:144

cross-divisional, 1:422, 7:1312

cross orders and interference, MS2:282; *see also* cross order

definition, 0:133, 0:134, 7:479, MS1:100, MS1:251, MS1:252, MS1:369, MS1:342, MS3:459

degraded beings and, 1:201

demand an order is fully understood, MS1:8

demanding orders, 0:132, 0:140, 0:144

destructive orders, 0:102, 0:141, 0:265

direct, example, MS3:332

disagreements of those under exec's orders, 0:587

disestablishment exists where you find lots of, MS2:28

down stats and, 0:505

order(s), *(cont.)*

every order an executive issues must be in writing, 1:518, 7:677

executive(s),
can't always sit in ivory tower and issue orders, 0:590
order board and, 0:375
seldom orders the impossible, 0:372
should send number and date of PL and ride it until it is in, 7:403, MS3:383

expedite valid orders, 0:148

expire if not reissued as policy, 0:112

false, how to determine, 0:23

false reports only occur where ignorance of data or avoidance of orders occurs, 0:139

first order I ever gave an org, 0:335

follow higher superior's orders and request to see them in writing when in doubt, 0:623

from one's superior demanding one alter or depart from known policy, handling, 0:544

glorious irresponsibility of, 0:140

hammering and pounding with orders as to how to handle post, 0:238

held until completed, 0:372

how to issue them, 0:589, 7:756

how to never hear an order for months, 0:144

I don't hammer away with streams of, 0:239

if it isn't written, it isn't true, 0:23, 0:146, 0:375

illegal,
accepting is actionable, 1:285
definition, 1:285

inflow and, 0:367

Inspection Section and, 0:375–376

irrelevant orders having nothing to do with stats, 0:582

issuance of, MS1:8

issued to form the org and better statistics and that's all, 7:249

issue into an area with a hidden Why, MS1:162

junior(s),
action on receiving an order, 0:375
issuing orders unknown to senior and across his lines, 0:425
lumping all juniors into order-receivers, 0:134
not getting exec's orders executed, 0:420
who accepts orders from everyone, 0:589

"Let's see it in writing first," 0:146

lining up with command intention, 0:250

losing or misplacing the, 0:431

LRH Comm method of logging, 7:1212

lumping all seniors into order-issuers, 0:134

marked urgent by an exec are entered into one-day time machine, 1:519, 7:678

order(s), *(cont.)*

may not abolish network or org or change form
of org, 0:143

misunderstood orders,
clarifying and querying, 0:23
failure to get order clarified, 0:430
misunderstood word in order, 0:39
will not be properly complied with, 0:431

needing orders, exact mechanism of, 1:817

never send into out-admin area, only get in
ethics, 7:402, MS3:382

noncompliance, *see also* noncompliance
advice from immediate superior not to comply
with orders, 0:544
not safe to fail to comply with legal order or
target, 0:146
only occurs when orders have had to be issued, 0:139
what to do if on inspection one finds noncompliance with standard, on-policy
order, 0:589

not arriving at the level of the worker, 0:67

not necessary where post really being worn,
7:402, MS3:382

observation and, 0:140

off-policy order, 0:145–148, 0:553

of higher superior changed by one's immediate
superior, 0:623

of person senior to one's immediate superior
altered or countermanded by one's
immediate superior, 0:544

order board, 0:375

ordering students and pcs, 0:491

order(s)(ed) to buy,
four conditions of exchange and, 0:317
shipping swiftly on receipt of, 0:349

people require orders when they do not know
what their products are, MS2:27

personal sense of, essential in getting out
products, MS1:342

person whose orders wind up cancelled when
discovered by a senior, 0:578

policy,
authorizes people to issue orders, 0:135
orders vs., confusion of, MS1:249, 0:132,
0:135

policy on orders, MS2:229

present time orders only, 0:425

pretending one has "an LRH order," 0:146

project orders, time machine and, 0:376

projects permit issuance and enforcement of,
0:132

query of, 0:23, 0:141

reason for, 0:139, 0:140, 1:432, 7:1325

reasons for no action or answers, 7:415,
MS3:395

order(s), *(cont.)*

relationship of policy, planning, programing,
projects, orders, production and viability,
0:133

responsibility and, 0:139, 7:402, MS3:382

resulting in lowered stats, contraction or
injustice, handling, 1:960

safe way in all cases is to issue orders that are
very standard, on-policy and obvious, 7:687

senior can inspect, chat, advise, but must never
issue order on bypass, 0:588

seniority of orders in organizations, 7:117,
0:143, 0:523

should better things, 7:711

should never be issued without data, experience
and insight, 0:122

some are senior to others, 1:285

something that requires more than two weeks to
do is a project, 1:519, 7:678

specific, microscopic orders on how the job is
to be done defeats the purposes of
posts, 0:230

staff member ordering and complying only in
his favorite area, 0:425

stale-dated, effect of, 0:425

table giving precedence of orders or directions
in Scientology, 7:115

tactical orders, 0:708

that carry a broad discovery should also be
interesting, 7:711

three things missing that make written orders
necessary, 7:712

time machine,
orders and, 0:375–376, 0:382
project orders and, 0:376

two basic rules of, 7:712

unclear orders, 0:431

unevaluated, policy and, 7:726

unnecessary response to, 0:372

unreal orders, 0:88, 0:401, 0:403

unusual solutions proposed due to not knowing
the, 0:432

using orders or policy to create problems, 0:476

valid only so long as they do not contradict
HCO PLs, HCOBs, 1:404, 7:1288

verbal order, 0:375–376

waiting for, 0:134

when issuing, you are using power and
force, 7:706

when not getting answered or actioned, don't
keep issuing more of the same, 7:415,
MS3:395

written or in writing, 0:23, 0:146, 0:375, 0:623

order board,

    carbon of order sent to Inspection, 1:518, 7:677

    definition, 1:518, 7:677

    description and use of, 0:375–376

    executives must use, 1:518, 7:677

    person receiving order does it, 7:677

Orders of the Day (OODs),

    definition, 1:432

    Dir Comm responsible for, 7:728

    format, 7:727

    LRH Comm gives I/A to, 7:729

    purpose and content, 7:727

order versus disorder,

    handling, MS2:176

    inspection, MS2:179

ordination, ministerial, defined, 5:302

organization(s), *see also* **Central Organization; organization form**

    actions,

        any activity has sequence of, 0:106

        that leave an org without money, 3:70

        what they can be classified under, 0:81

        which can destroy it, 7:407, MS3:387

    administrative,

        divisions and personnel exist to push public in for tech action, 6:757

        skill and, 0:58, 0:67

    analyzing an, 0:81

    answer to sane org is, MS1:302, MS1:458

    apathy, has gone route of not-dones, half-dones and backlogs, 7:433, MS2:227, MS3:413

    apparent to the public as it communicates, 2:54

    attacks suffered by, are from ARC broken persons, 4:933

    auditing,

        org booms if auditing is occurring in the field, 4:124, 5:56, 6:585

        org cannot be fully responsible for excellence of auditing done in field, 2:417, 6:709

        factory that also trains people to audit, 0:684, 2:104, 7:856

        training and auditing and value of org, 4:128

    bad repute of, factors which cause, MS1:245

    basic flaw in, 0:66, 1:526

    basics of, 0:52, 0:53, 0:287–290, 1:135

    basic things required for successful organization, 7:841

    basic way we will win world, 0:684

    beachhead in an area, 4:911

    best org, description, 0:52–53

    biggest job, 1:57

organization(s), *(cont.)*

    bogged,

        actions to handle, MS2:120, MS2:263

        after a period of success, reason for, 7:324

        handling, MS1:313

    book orderers and, 2:51, 6:148

    booms and depressions, what they are due to, MS2:3, MS2:238

    bound together by common purposes, 7:454, MS3:434

    building an org; *see* establish

    bunch of individuals working at cross purposes vs., 0:405

    business of, 0:90

    busyness vs. havingness, MS1:241

    bypass by heads of a big organization of the heads of its internal small organizations works toward Non-Existence, 7:255

    can only be stopped by failure to be causative, correct and decisive on posts, 7:601

    careless or malicious and knowing damage caused to, 0:574

    carried on backs of a few staff, 0:578

    caved in by bad sexual messes, 7:690

    central control point and, 2:124, 6:58, 7:836

    chaos, cause of, 0:119, 0:196

    clay demo of, 0:407

    cleanliness; *see* cleanliness

    codified system of, 7:488, MS3:468

    cogwheel-type, definition, MS1:234

    collapsing or closing, 1:896

    commanded org will always seek to follow pattern of commanding org, 0:122

    common problem of, failure to execute programs, 7:364, MS3:344

    communication system; *see* comm system

    community has to understand why org there, MS3:157

    composed of,

        composition of org, 0:600

        terminals and communications, 7:22

        weak wobbly posts, MS1:308, MS2:107, MS2:258

    computer is no better than organization that feeds it, MS2:466

    concentrate activities on building a strong, ethical and prosperous, MS1:475

    concentration on co-audits, 4:689

    conditions assigned to; *see* conditions

    confidence in one's teammates is another factor in organization survival, 7:811

    confusion stems from five sources, 1:30

    consists of, 1:143, 1:273, MS1:218, MS1:290

        coordinated purposes, lines and terminals, 0:89, 7:293

organization(s), *(cont.)*

contraction of,

decline, and failure to deliver all hours sold, 5:258

only real reasons an org shrinks, 6:96, 7:279

only way to destroy, 5:680

organizational decay caused by, MS1:256

reason orgs have decayed, 0:66

shrunken orgs, reasons for, 0:102–103, 0:130

treason to reduce, combine or close, 7:916

two causes of org collapses, 7:512

ways one can be collapsed or closed, 7:916

what is found where orgs or parts thereof begin to collapse, 7:1243

why they fade and stumble, 7:1407

cooperative and gung-ho towards us are making it with good stats, MS2:229

corrects itself, 0:95

Day and Foundation, standard Academy course schedules, 4:453

decreasing ability of society to handle people, effect on orgs, 0:481

definition, 0:51, 0:81, 7:272, MS1:234, MS2:216

degenerated into clinic, reason and handling for, 7:128

delivery; *see* delivery

Department One, mind, MS3:375

Department Two, body, MS3:375

Department Three, product, MS3:375

design of the, 0:95, 1:144, 7:246

despatches take care of 99% of organizational business, 0:369

deteriorated image, reasons for, 4:932, 5:258, 5:688

developed traffic; *see* developed traffic

difficulties, traced to, 0:221, 5:514

distracted, get in basics one at a time, 7:415

divisional and departmental and individual Whys that prevent Flag programs and projects from going in, MS3:405, 7:425

Division One, HCO Sec is the thetan, MS3:375

downfall, causes of, 0:204, MS1:207, MS1:416

early orgs, why they crashed, 0:10

ED ought to be able to manage cheek by jowl with FR, 7:292

efficiency,

jams occurring high up can reduce efficiency, revenue and threaten the whole organization, 7:780

purpose and, 1:143, 7:22

engram found where few suppressive persons set up a price ridge between orgs and public, 2:428

enturbulence proportional to ignorance or absence of policy and purpose, 0:68

environment not challenging, no org, 7:397, MS3:377

organization(s), *(cont.)*

error (most common) in, 0:130

essence of organization is org boarding, posting with reality and, in keeping with the duties being performed, training and hatting, 1:86, 7:811

established patterns, 7:629

establishment of, 1:77, MS1:228

Estos put it there to run, MS2:5

Esto system in small org, MS2:8

ethical conduct, most important zone is at or near the top, MS2:246

ethics; *see also* ethics

takes far more, and far steeper enforced penalties to make org work than Scientologists have been using, 0:421

where ethics are tight and savage, grow in numbers, 7:397, MS3:377

exact cycle when an org goes downhill, 1:810

example of, MS1:193

executive thinks of the area and organization first, 7:428, MS3:408

exist to handle rough cases, 4:124, 6:585

expansion of, 7:849; *see also* expansion

advancement of org, what it depends on, 0:481

boom, faults present when an org doesn't, MS2:427

Esto system and, MS2:9

factors which make a large organization, 7:254

failures and slumps and inability to stably expand, 1:76

four cycles an org must engage in to be successful and prosperous, 2:642, 3:218, 4:277, 7:866, MS1:171,

full reality on basic tech as pcs and auditors give one a fully happy booming org, 7:855

how to expand, 7:293

how to get 10 times the size with a lot more pay, 2:705

how you are limiting the size and income of, 4:407, 6:398

increases in size as things get better, 1:552

limit their, by failing to push and deliver top-quality training of auditors, Supervisors and C/Ses, 6:398, 4:407

no limit to size of, MS1:303

often gets pinned by false economy in personnel, MS1:382

only interrupted by inattentive or poor service resulting in ARC breaks in the field, 6:95, 7:278, MS1:245,

on-policy, on-tech org booms, 5:787

what org must do to expand, MS2:388

org cycles through lowered and raised conditions as it expands, MS1:446

quality of the product and creating a demand for it only determines the ceiling of the org as a whole, 7:520

organization(s), *(cont.)*

failing to terminatedly handle situations, 0:244–245

failure to handle pcs and results on, 4:927, 5:683

falling apart or slowing up, handling, 0:441

fastest way for Esto to unmock an org, MS2:36

fast flow, 1:971

field,
org booms if auditing is occurring in the, 4:124, 5:56, 6:585

org cannot be fully responsible for excellence of auditing done in, 2:417, 6:709

org which keeps its field cleaned up and active on the Bridge or as FSMs will expand up to and past the make-break point, 7:882

put out (to field) org uses and teaches high grade standard tech, 6:585, 4:124

serviced by org, 0:685
which keeps, cleaned up and active on the Bridge or as FSMs will expand, 6:564

field auditor and, 2:52, 6:149

files are financially vital to an, MS2:47

final product,
importance of knowing, 0:292
two major final valuable products, 4:145

finance; *see* finance

finest orgs in history have been tough, dedicated orgs, 0:13

first action to take to improve an organization, 7:780

first and primary goal of, 4:17, 5:17

first consideration in procuring quarters is viability, 7:1394

first order I ever gave to an, 0:335

first policy of Scientology org, 0:321

flaw, inspection before the fact, 5:138, 7:700

floods of requests for decisions defeat us in two ways, 7:600

flows fast when lines in, 1:972

for its own sake, 7:405, MS3:385

forming org, what to do where its stats are low or its performance poor or failing, 6:92, 7:275

form of, MS1:315, MS2:111, MS2:122, MS2:265; *see also* organization form
definition, MS1:312, MS2:111
Exec Esto is holder and expander of, MS2:26
holding the, 1:277, 3:239
how to preserve the shape of, 1:269
most valuable tool, 7:455, MS3:435
must be drawn up as org boards, flow plans and terminal location plans, MS2:114

organization(s), *(cont.)*

no Aides Order or other directive or order may abolish network or org or change form of org, 0:143

org builds in blocks of six maximum—five plus an executive, 7:258

org must be posted from the top down, 7:820

volume it gets and handles is solely determined by its internal organization, 7:1257

with more than 50 staff members will become a nine division org board, 6:81

40% discount to, 2:308

fought by society's fancied rulers or enemies, 0:64

Foundation org, Estos and, MS2:9

functioning of, 0:384

fundamentals of, 7:485, MS2:201, MS2:306, MS3:465

gets people to get audited and gets people to be trained as auditors, 0:685

getting show on the road, 0:502

goal (first and primary) of an, 0:17

goodwill, *see* goodwill

green org, 0:196

gross divisional statistic, *see* gross divisional statistic

gross income, *see also* gross income,
cycle of big GI—stable org—good delivery— new people—big GI, 7:860

handling,
for products as overt acts, MS1:242
highest commodity—life itself, 0:656

has to look like real org, 0:334

hat, hatting, *see also* hat, hatting
absence of, reason why things don't run well in orgs, MS1:411
cure for org is training and, MS2:238
from the top down, MS2:29
hatted to produce, MS2:79
how to combine per Org Program No. 1, 6:95, 7:278
if each person wears all hats or one wears all and the rest wear none, result, MS3:409
org only successful and free of dev-t and trouble when all staff fully trained on the OEC, 7:855

health of, 2:47, 7:171, 7:835

healthy, 0:394

help factor, 5:684
determination to handle cases and, 4:928

hiring, *see* hiring; recruitment

how to analyze, MS1:234

how to build affinity and agreement with local area, MS3:157

how to found, increase or revive any, 0:53

how to greatly increase org efficiency, 7:827

how to overcome continual org changes, 7:246

organization(s), *(cont.)*

I carry a *little* more pressure on org than it can really accomplish, 0:594

I have never intended Scientology orgs and groups to be bits of third dynamic each opposed, 0:273

ideal org,
  activity where people come to achieve freedom and where they had confidence they would attain it, 0:342
  built by taking what one has and step by step building and smoothing; grooving in and handling each of its functions, 7:283
  perfect org is not machine but pattern of agreements, 0:82
  what it consists of, 1:277, 7:282

ideal scene, 0:342

if less than three persons, bring it up to three persons or it isn't an org, 6:92

if Public Divs push org training much harder than personal auditing the org would become very fat financially, 6:99

if well established, stats will go up, MS2:3

ill feelings in, cause of, 0:413

immediate organization for production, MS1:171, MS2:441

important people and org image, 0:335

improper design and musical chairs, 1:206

in the business of setting people free, 7:880

inattention to staff cases can all but destroy, 1:800, 6:526

income, *see also* income
  volume of, of an org is in direct proportion to number of phone calls and letters of an org, 2:613

indicators, 0:496, 1:750, 7:679, 7:690

individual decision points and, 0:325

inhale and exhale of an, 0:579

inquiries and, 2:50, 6:147–148

interchange, principles of, 0:296–298

internal conflict, prevention of, 0:133–134

internal lines, MS2:113

killing off org's vitality, 0:338

KSW PL violation almost destroyed orgs, 0:7

lacking a sense of, MS2:133

Letter Writer's Code adhered to by all who write letters for, 2:620

letting things run as long as they run well, 0:587

limping scene vs., 0:62

little orgs build up from Org Program No. 1, MS2:78

location of,
  image vs., 7:1395
  moving, how to, 7:1334
  relocated to busy areas, 0:356

organization(s), *(cont.)*

long-term, MS1:172

longevity of, 0:67

made to go to pieces, 1:993, 4:85

magic formula of going org, 1:60, 7:799

major duties in a tiny org, 0:99, 6:93, 7:276

majority of troubles vanish when Dept 3 uses Confessionals, 4:973

management,
  by trends and ranges of statistics, MS2:375
  coordination and management of org depends on Exec Div, 7:1425
  tenets, 7:581
  tools are foundation of, MS1:375

manned only partially and out of sequence, 7:449

mission(s),
  benign source of groups and, 4:124
  field auditors and, cooperation between, 6:579
  groups and, org is source of, 5:56, 6:585
  line to, org happy to handle their rough cases, 5:56
  mission holders and orgs are interdependent, 6:579
  orgs must look and act more professional than a mission, 6:616

misunderstood words and, 0:39, 0:40, MS1:244

most important things are its lines and terminals, 7:771, 0:384

most orgs do face-to-face handling extremely well, 0:276

most serious threat to the stability of an org, 7:771

motionless org, 0:105

must answer people's questions, 2:598, 6:156

must be cause over the environment and public, 1:203

must have formulated basic purpose, 7:663

must result in production, MS1:453

must survive for sake of this planet, 0:15

necessary to take much more responsibility, 7:627

no ethics presence, result, 0:526

no excuse for any technical failure in, 0:18

no existing policy and, 7:661

no fixed consumption, 7:509

no laborers in Scientology org, 0:82

not forming up, Why, 1:62, 1:66

number one program for, 6:92, 7:275

object is totally freed customers, 0:91

objective of, 4:410, 6:401

OEC Vol 0 tells how org works, 0:27

offering of higher services not authorized to give, result, 6:756

organization(s), *(cont.)*

one-person org, 0:106

one person wearing all hats, 0:384

one strong, sound, always workable campaign to expand Scientology has been to get orgs on-policy and in-tech, 7:1255

only auditing pcs, 0:100

only organization that is a sound organization is one whose every activity can be tabulated by statistics, 7:667

only tremendous error made next to inspection before the fact is failing to terminatedly handle situations rapidly, 7:703

only valuable if it audits and trains auditors, 2:105, 7:857

only way we have been held back internally, MS1:466

operating at risk, 0:255

oppressive, confused and overworked org, 0:554

optimum, 0:82, 0:498, 1:752, 7:681, MS1:235

orderly plan as, MS1:235

organize it to get it to function, MS1:199;
   see also organize

organizing board; *see* org board

Org Program No. 1,
   how to combine hats per, 6:95, 7:278

org's stats are totally under the control of that org, 7:521

orientation of, 0:685

outflow, 0:101, 0:103

outline that wins, 7:833

paid to handle pcs, 4:927, 5:683

paralyzed, 0:405

parts of engaged upon similar functions must be on same schedule, MS2:116

pattern of, 3:231
   org board, MS1:194
   is unit of 3, thetan, mind, body, product, 1:566
   living beings vs. pattern of org, MS1:235
   relationship org to org, 6:583
   whole rationale of, is a unit of three, MS3:375, 7:395

pays any salaries or space rental connected with books or tape handling, 3:188

penalized solely because of lack of training and understanding and grooving in people, 7:522

penalty if Sunday church services, PE evenings and three congresses a year are not held, 6:85

people working frantically, exhausted, producing nothing of value; reason for, MS2:16

permitting a lot of "Is this okay?" 7:682

organization(s), *(cont.)*

personnel,
   actions in managing an, MS1:383
   admin/tech ratio, must observe 2 to 1, 5:422
   hats and lines, MS1:294
   minimum personnel, 7:252
   new, and org, MS1:383
   org that doesn't produce has usually been manned only partially and out of sequence, MS3:429, MS2:273
   orgs are not huge HGCs for staff, 0:168
   post by workload, MS1:209
   reason not getting on is internal and has to do with mishandling of, MS1:384
   sequence in which an org is manned, 7:448, MS1:324, MS1:463, MS2:272, MS3:428, 0:279–280
   undermanned, handling, MS1:386
   use of, from any division doubled in Technical, 7:308
   who will inevitably rise in the org, 0:120

persons who do things to stop or impede forward progress of, 0:574

phases, 0:95

pinning org advance down to its lowest staff member's case, 0:156

points to get in for success, 4:958

points which are vital to PRO in an org, MS3:145

points which cause it to slow down, 4:97

popularity, how to create overwhelming popularity for, MS3:158

power is proportional to its speed of particle flow, 0:432

preclears and, 2:51, 6:148

prediction and, 0:327

preservation of, first consideration of an executive, 7:428, MS3:408

primary menace in, 0:100

primary reason people do leave, 7:747

primary role as regards clearing, 4:998

principles of, MS1:256

principles which apply to individual and, 0:297

problems answered by disseminating like mad, improving service and getting in lots of money, 3:26–27, 7:924–925

production, products
   can't run and be solvent without a product, 4:935, 5:263
   departments, 7:52
   end product is not just an ideal org but a new civilization already on its way, 7:283
   main product is, 5:801
   product of organization, 1:15, 2:15, 3:15, 4:15, 5:15, 7:15
   setting quotas and targeting, 0:690–691
   twelve factors of production in, MS1:229
   value and, MS1:294

organization(s), *(cont.)*

program,

abandoned programs, main cause of org difficulty, 7:366, MS3:346

altering existing, and difficulty with org, MS3:344

for staff auditors, 5:833

promotional actions of an, 0:346–357

proper organization increases production by eliminating "noise," 1:152

prosperity,

dependent on success of Public Divisions in building an enormous, active field, 6:108

depends upon getting things done, MS2:288

proportional to speed of particles, 1:526

reason for lack of, is internal, MS2:3

protected with HCO Ethics Codes, 0:481

proven conclusively that orgs "not quite with" the Sea Org and Flag have bad stats, MS2:229

psychotics and, 1:807

public,

apparent to the, as it communicates, 2:54

orgs allying themselves with public groups, 0:160

trained about one for one with processing, 4:958

purchased and/or rented mailing lists, 2:709

purpose of, 0:502, 0:685; *see also* purpose

of evening organization is to operate as bridge from the public to the daytime org and to make money in its own right, 7:297

org must have formulated basic purpose, 7:663

to make planning become actuality, 7:405, MS3:385

real reason for org continuing to go down, MS1:174

real Whys and, MS1:83

reason an org is bogged after a period of success, MS3:304

reason for, 0:91–92, 4:159, 4:160

reasons for inefficient areas in, MS1:404

reasons for orgs that are unhealthy, 2:114, 3:90

reasons one forms one, 2:123, 6:57, 7:836

reason why an org runs well, MS1:202, MS1:411

recruitment,

failure to recruit and train as rapidly as orgs expanded cause declining stats, 7:160

location of org and, 1:171

reduction or eradication of, 1:896

rejuvenation of, 0:118

reorganization of production departments, 7:52

reputation of, 0:40, 0:350, 5:798

organization(s), *(cont.)*

requirements for power to transfer, remove, post permanent personnel, convene and conclude Committees of Evidence locally, 1:260

results of running an org like a clinic, 4:408

reverse back to cope, MS1:200

revision to pattern (1966), 7:261

robot orgs and civilizations fail, 0:82

rundown, MS1:201

run(ning) of, *see also* administration

like a clinic, result, 6:399

run by a committee but without a head of org seldom succeed, 7:820

run by or overloaded with destructive or PTS persons, 3:309, MS3:425

safe island, 0:486

sales; *see* sale

sane org, answer to, 0:206

scale of subjects relating to, MS1:262

Scientology incorporations are religious in nature, 7:1010

Senior Case Supervisor, mandatory, 5:713

senior policy, 0:284

service, *see also* service

allowed technical services, 4:122

courses authorized for Central Orgs (1964), 4:184

image, 5:56

keynote of an org is not money, it is service, 2:165, 4:67, 6:190

what the org delivers, 4:1033

setting people free, 0:90

seven-division, definition, 7:270

sexual promiscuity present in, handling for, 7:691

short-term, MS1:172

shoulder to shoulder effort, 0:273

sign of threatened failure in, 1:60

simplicity and, 0:88

six-department,

definition, 7:270

primary groups and their sections and those who head them, 7:266

size of org,

large organization is composed of groups, small organization is composed of individuals, 7:254

larger orgs are for the rougher pcs, 6:96, 7:279

largest org as least efficient, 0:617

less than five staff, handling for, 6:92, 7:275

less than three persons, bring it up to three persons or it isn't an org, 7:275

proper size, 0:600–601

staying tiny, working madly and staying poor, 0:408

too big for routing to occur to Bill, Jane or Pete, 0:383

organization(s), *(cont.)*

what larger orgs are for, 0:102

why orgs stay small, 0:598–604, 4:98

with less than five staff, handling, 0:98–100

slumps,

solve it with Scientology, 3:125

traced to lack of hats, MS1:202

small mailing list and limping org, 0:625

smooth org, description, 0:196–197

solvency,

depends on training, 5:278

lies in more Scientology, not patented combs or fund raising barbecues, 7:931, 4:173

org can go broke or be poor while doing a good job all because of lack of tech knowledge by Registrars, 4:1032

org can't run and be solvent without a product, 4:935, 5:263

stumbling blocks in, 7:261

someone who prevents any, MS2:133

somewhere on OT Scale, MS2:429

SP(s),

chopped up by, 4:85

suppressing and confusing orgs, 0:90

tries to get rid of, 1:1008

squad mentality, 0:134, 0:135

stability, most serious threat to org stability, 0:384

stable items vs. flow items in an org, 0:107

staff member,

co-audit for, 5:577

reports, *see* staff member report(s)

responsibility for, 0:167

stars of, are auditors and HCO personnel, 7:799

statistics; *see* statistic(s)

students and, 2:51, 6:148–149

disseminate better and an org that only audits pcs stays small and is more expensive to run, 6:94, 7:277

may not audit org public, 4:683

sub-division of actions and duties into specialized functions, 7:776

suborganization, starting a new, 0:130

subproduct lists and, 7:829

subpurposes and, 0:118–119

successful org(s), 7:492, 7:1275, MS2:462, MS3:472

summary of our future, 7:69

suppression of, transferring personnel on posts obsessively, 1:254

survival of individuals in well-organized activities depends on the highly organized condition of the activity, 7:811

tailor-made inflow line for, 2:338, 6:248

organization(s), *(cont.)*

takes far more ethics and far steeper enforced penalties to make org work than Scientologists have been using, 0:421

taking in its own laundry, 0:83

targets and battle plans must include organizational planning, 7:460, MS2:446, MS3:440

teach Scientology in an org, don't try to process the world to enlightenment, 5:837

tech or know-how of organizing, 7:446, MS2:130, MS3:426

ten basic points where organization breaks down, MS1:200

terminals; *see also* terminal

must approximate to some degree the goals of an organization, 7:188

that are surviving are driven directly from the top, 7:780

theory of Scientology orgs, 0:81, 1:274

Thetan–Mind–Body–Product pattern, 0:128–129, 0:654

third dynamic,

activity, MS1:405

inflow and outflow list, 2:50, 6:147

three factors major org problems stem from, MS1:293, MS1:452

three indicators which point to possible out-ethics, 7:1259

three principal zones in a Scientology org, 1:1028, 7:392

toughness and, 0:13, 1:86

goes hand in hand with survival and, 7:811

training,

and hatting is cure for org, MS2:238

of local students, 5:510

trying to get all PLs in at once can swamp, 7:403, MS3:383

turbulence of, 0:481

turned upside down by reversal of policy and orders, 0:132

two uses to which Scientology orgs can be put, 7:391, MS3:371

unhatted org,

goes weak and criminal, 0:206

is a madhouse, MS2:235

is lazy and refers everything to someone else, 0:390

only real trouble, failure of whole staff to know policy, 1:4

org staffed with people not fully conversant with all org policy, result, 7:853

out-ethics and, 0:526

unhealthy, reasons for, 6:557, 7:864

upper org must deliver better service to justify increase in prices, 2:457

used as an employment center, MS1:474

organization(s), *(cont.)*

used as means to oppress others, handling is to get in ethics, MS3:371

value of, 0:297, 0:685

viability,

larger staff unit from training than processing, 5:836

must be viable, 7:428, MS3:408

orgs have to be more efficient to also pay well, 7:457, MS2:443, MS3:437

viable, how to be, 7:293

when signing up more pcs than students it will go broke or be poor, 4:387

vital target is to have trained auditors in plenty in orgs and field, 4:386

volume of income of an org is in direct proportion to number of phone calls and letters of an org, 2:613

ways one can be collapsed or closed, 7:916

way to decrease traffic and workload of an, 0:279

way to put a finger on the pulse of any Scientology organization, 7:1177

way you juggle it about to prevent overwork by executives and overwhelm of individuals, 7:258

we are the only ones who can actually close or reduce, 7:917

well-organized activities survive, 1:86, 7:811

what any existing org or civilization is sum total of, 0:277–278

what is found where orgs or parts thereof begin to collapse, 7:1243

what is in a fully operational Central Org, 2:621

what to say when somebody complains too hard about an, 0:276

when dealing with this society, it can go as far as it has financial resources, 3:98

when distracted, get in basics one at a time, MS3:395

when standard administrative policy not known and used, 7:492, MS2:462, MS3:472

when you let status reasoning get into stat assignment of conditions, the org has had it, 7:530

where function does not have lines across two or more portions, functions may slump, 4:905

where it begins, 2:123, 6:57

which cannot keep its staff auditors, 5:833

which lack key ingredients, 7:409, MS3:389

whose admin or body lines are violated will disestablish, MS2:37

organization(s), *(cont.)*

why org won't flow traffic when policy is out or not formed, 0:325

Wichita and Elizabeth, New Jersey, 0:10

will get off the launching pad when every person in it has studied and knows Vol 0 OEC, 7:806

will go broke if persist in taking fee and delivering for half a year, 4:97

wisest to specialize in their own services, 2:457, 3:177

with an effective LRH Comm prospers, 7:1244

without files has no memory, MS2:48

won't flow traffic when policy is out or not formed, 2:82, 6:204

words that have to be cleared and understood, MS1:247, MS1:424

working in any way upon fixed statistic of consumption will eventually fail, 7:507

working to provide safe environment in, 0:486

wrong sequence of manning will contract an, MS1:325, MS1:464

wrong Whys and, MS1:83

you have to have cooperation from everyone to make an organization work, 6:290

organizational chart, of Central Org in United States, 7:189

organizational genius, composed of, MS1:197

Organizational Health Chart, definition, 2:47, 7:171

organizational know-how, 7:407

organizational misunderstoods, how to handle, MS1:247

organizational policy, definition, 0:243

organization chart, was inadequate, 0:195

Organization Cycle, 0:96

Organization Executive Course (OEC),

admin degrades and, 0:73–74

all newly issued volumes have a course booklet, 2:347

any failure of these basics and policies is ignorance of them, 0:4

applies to the individual, 0:3

basic laws of organization, 0:3

businessmen and, 0:129

checksheets, make staff progress through, 5:427

delivery and end result, 5:428

description of, 0:3–4

executives of the org should know it well, 0:4

Green Star and, 0:654

HAS should have at least an, 1:66

how to study it, 0:31

Organization Executive Course (OEC), *(cont.)*

Method One Word Clearing is required before doing, 4:196, 4:652

orgs are only successful and free of dev-t and trouble when all staff are fully trained on, 7:855

org staffs should be encouraged to buy their own sets, 2:347

policy clarified, 2:347

staff member who doesn't know it is at effect, 0:4

training people to handle their posts, 0:433

use to reverse any down-trending company or country, 0:4

volumes can be bought on the basis that any volume of the set is an item, 2:347

volumes can be purchased by the public, 2:347

Organization Executive Secretary (OES),

basis for appointment, 7:914

bonuses, 7:73

duties,
functions of and, 0:99, 0:101
in a tiny org, 7:276

example of actions taken during Danger condition, 0:583

largest building block comprising, 0:600–601

may appoint or transfer Intern Supervisor, 5:843

power to dismiss personnel, 1:163

promotional actions, 7:84

responsibility for,
staff auditors and interns, 4:905
staff training, 5:490

senior auditor in org with three staff is the, 0:98

state of Academy should be first thought every morning, 5:837

organization form (pattern), form of the organization; *see also* **organize, organizing; organizing board**

altering established pattern, 0:385

definition, MS2:119, MS2:262

effect of failing to hold firm the, 0:579

HCO Executive Secretary and, 0:99

holding form of org, 0:582

keeping structure of org in writing, 0:194

no Aides Order or other directive or order may change the, 0:143

org board has choices laid out by policy, org form and formula, 0:325

particle types and, MS2:116

people who haven't a clue about org pattern, 0:384, 0:385

promotion and, 0:347

organization form (pattern), form of the organization, *(cont.)*

schedules and, MS2:118

source of, 0:685

Thetan–Mind–Body–Product pattern, 0:128–129, 0:654

vital actions to hold the form of the org, 7:249

what org pattern is designed to do, 0:96

Organization Information Center (OIC),

all Class IV Orgs cable change, 1:670–673

all Sea Org Orgs cable change, 1:674–677

Assoc Sec keeps board, 1:653

definition, 1:653

description, 1:654

Emergency cannot be assigned unless OIC graphs show a declining condition, 0:477

fast flow system of management and, 7:671

inspection being done by OIC, 0:589

OIC graphs, investigation and, 1:192

system modified, 1:660

where situated, 1:653

Organization Phase, 0:617

Organization Program No. 1, 0:98–104

Organization Secretary, *see also* **Association Secretary**

also has hat of financial management when it has been specifically granted to him, 7:611

don'ts are, 7:612

fundamental job is to enforce policy, 7:611

list of actions that would make the best Organization Secretary, 7:611

right to dismiss people and, 3:183

veto power of, 7:888

organize, organizing,

administration and, 0:58

analysis of organization by product, 0:287–290

area that is organizing only is loaded with misunderstoods, MS2:133

as you cope, MS1:197

basic organization, 0:105

basic principles of, 0:108, 0:124, MS1:196

building by stable terminals, 0:434

cope while organizing, 0:201, 0:204, 7:518

definition of organization, 0:88, 0:89

description, 0:88

dictatorships due to citizen not knowing basic organization, 0:4

disorganization; *see* disorganization

end product of, MS1:198

examples of, 0:88, 0:105–108

executives and, 0:87, 0:266, 0:404–406, 0:434; *see also* executive

expansion and, 0:123

first question one asks in, 0:292, MS1:240

from the final product, MS1:241

organize, organizing, *(cont.)*

function and organization is everything, 0:100

gradient scale of, 0:200, MS1:203, MS1:412

greatest single confusion in subject of, 0:132, MS1:249

group types of actions into single posts, 0:88

how to organize, 0:81–85, 0:108

if you only organize and never produce, 7:447, MS2:131, MS3:427

ignorance of fundamentals of, 0:40

inadequate or unknown organization tech, 0:40

keeping admin working and, 0:70–72

key vocabulary of subject of, 0:41–42

laws which underlie, 0:598–603

listing particles and getting their routes and desired changes of character en route, 0:81

list of points to get basics of organization in on individual or area, 0:308–311, 0:569

major cause of not organizing is just not understanding what is meant by it, 7:777

major failure of any group is to fail to, 0:88

misorganization, recognizing it when you see it, 0:4

new staff member eager to reorganize everything, 0:414

not organizing, major cause of, 0:88

OEC contains basic laws of, 0:3

one organizes by, MS1:196

only organizing and not producing, 0:298

Organization Cycle, 0:96

organizing back from final product, 0:292, 0:297

overexpansion is only underorganization, 0:129

overts and withholds prevent even organizing, MS2:133

post and, 0:88, 0:601; *see also* post

PR has to be able to, MS3:14

primitive organizational tech currently in use, 0:41

project, how to organize a, 0:88

promote, organize and deliver, 0:282

proper organization, 0:603

PTS people and, MS2:133

public relations personnel and, MS1:419

purpose for, 0:87, MS1:376, MS2:312

reorganization, reorganizing,

done to strengthen targets or actions which brought about Affluence, 0:640

so situation does not repeat or is not continually happening, 0:600

to get tools within easy reach, 0:309

routing and, 0:404–411

secret of, 0:197, 0:434

organize, organizing, *(cont.)*

signs of a badly organized group are, 7:811

simplicity of, 0:88, 0:601–602

staff meeting and, 0:173

steps of, 0:108, MS1:199

tech of organization comes from Level VII, 0:482

three factors and, MS1:294

time should not exceed 50 percent of post time, MS1:376, MS2:312

viability and, 0:297

when it is superlative, MS1:376, MS2:312

while coping, MS1:197

working out changes desired for each particle to make a product, 0:108

organizing board, org board, *see also* **organization form; organize, organizing; posting**

1961 six-dept org bd, 0:710

1965 (May) handwritten seven-div org bd, 0:712–713

1965 (May) printed version of handwritten seven-div org bd, 0:714–715

1965 (Nov.) seven-div org bd, 0:716–717

1965 org board, 0:326

1965 three-div org bd, 0:711

1967 seven-div org bd, 0:716–717

1969 nine-div org bd, 0:708–719

adding people to org without org bd, effect of, 0:106

all functions necessary to produce products must be named on, 1:63

any is better than no, MS1:197

appointment lists vs., 0:414

Awareness Scale and, 0:95

basic ingredients of, 0:288

be-do-have and, 0:291

bottom becoming top when policy and orders become reversed, 0:131

building downwards by groups of six, 0:597

clay demo of, 0:407

commonest fault in, MS1:218–219

company is essentially collection of, 0:108

confusion vs., 0:106, 0:434

cutative, examples, MS1:209–210

Cycle of Production and, 0:95, 1:144

decisions and, 0:325, 0:326

definition, 0:108, 0:433, MS1:220, MS1:298, MS1:370, MS2:301, MS3:393, MS3:460

Department of the Chaplain, 6:530

Department 1 responsibility for, 0:347

description and development of, 0:95–96

organizing board, org board, *(cont.)*

design of, 1:147, 1:150

designation of Permanent status on, 5:413

designation of Provisional status on, 5:413

dev-t and, 0:414, 0:426, 0:435–438

different patterns of, 0:105

doing org bd backwards, 0:291

done backwards from the product, MS1:239

don't dismantle a working installation, MS2:78

each division is to have, 1:152

errors, 1:61

evolution of, MS1:208

examples of, 0:105–107

executive(s),
    also has to know, MS3:407
    has his own personal, MS1:198
    knowing the, 0:280
    makes sure org boards and policy exist and
        are followed, 0:410

Field Control Division, 6:22–23

first action to form an org is posting the, 1:65

fits any org of any size, 0:95

flags used to indicate conditions assigned to
    areas, 0:614

flow chart, 0:200

flows from left to right, 1:56

flows, product and, 0:108

function(s),
    action or post left off of org board, MS1:208
    below a name are held by it, 1:63
    org board, MS2:76

get it posted, MS1:313, MS2:120, MS2:263

goes from one person to thousands without
    change, 0:95

gradient scale of, 0:202

group and org size and, 0:600–601

handwritten, 0:702–703

has choices laid out by policy, org form and
    formula, 0:325

hats and, 0:201

HCO, 1:19

hidden source of trouble, 1:61

how to do or work out an, 0:287–288

ignorance of how to post, 1:62

individual has 7 (or 9) divisions and 21 (or 27)
    departments, 0:3

keep everything on it, MS1:209

knowing the org board,
    Chinese school on org board, 0:440, 0:442
    drilling and, 0:392, 0:394
    not knowing org board, 0:391, 0:414,
        0:426, 0:434
    staff checked out on, 0:202, 0:414

organizing board, org board, *(cont.)*

lack of an org board,
    effects of, 0:414
        off-line despatches due to, 0:408
        overload due to, 0:106, 0:204
        poor final product due to, 0:294

laws regarding, MS1:208

list of hats with seniorities, 1:151

made up of hats, MS1:222

making minor vs. major changes on, 0:410

manning up an org, need an org board first and
    allocation board, MS2:272, MS3:428

mini Qual org board, 5:57

most serious blunder in redoing, MS1:208

motion put in vertically so that flow will
    occur, 0:107

must provide for, MS1:196

must reflect changes in staff member status,
    3:193

never leave a gap between persons on lower
    posts and high posts, MS2:77

of Estos, MS2:4

one-person org, 0:106

opposite of is confusion, MS1:198

out-of-date, effect of, 0:415, 0:426

paper org boards gotten up in each div, 0:442

particle flow and, 0:106

pattern used kept one org going for 80 trillion
    years, 0:326

pattern which handles flows and actions and
    dispenses with confusion, 0:438

people progress from left to right on, 0:684

perpetual combination of flows, MS1:196

philosophical system, 0:95, 1:144

post from the top down, MS2:77

posted correctly, example, 1:64

posted incorrectly, examples, 1:62

prediction and, 0:327

preparation of, 1:63

principle on which it was conceived, 0:128

Problems of Work and, 0:433

production and, 1:210

refine in light of more experience, 1:64

result of no hat, programs and, MS1:217

results from lack of, MS1:221

should list VFPs, MS1:255

sightly, properly done and up-to-date, 1:39

spiral, 1:144

staff status of staff member and, 1:236, 1:242,
    5:411, 5:417

taken from ancient organization, 1:145

titles org board, MS2:76

organizing board, org board, *(cont.)*

value of, MS1:220

visible to public, 1:148

well grooved in increase volume without strain, MS1:197

which only give terminals usually will not flow, MS1:195

why we have, MS3:435

working one out, MS1:220

organizing officer, org officer, 0:685; *see also* **organize; organizing board**

considered himself the product officer's expeditor, MS1:354

deputy secretary of division is, MS2:7

ED's deputy, function and org board position, MS2:7

first product of an org officer is, MS1:358, MS2:185

functions, MS1:356, MS2:5

gets the CO's programs logged and done, MS1:358, MS2:185

has to know how to get a product, MS2:130, 7:446, MS3:426

organizes immediate area so it smoothly produces, MS1:356

prod–org team works in hours and days, MS1:355

right-now organizing, MS1:357

Org Board Section, mandatory to inform of appointments, 1:196

Org Flag Banking Officer, definition, MS2:352

org image, *see also* **image; organization(s)**

examples of poor, MS3:155

poor public image, result of, MS3:140

zones which comprise it, MS3:140

org know-how, remedy for increasing of, 7:159

Org Morale I/C, VFP and statistic, 6:533

Org Pubs Officer, duties, 2:360

org rudiment(s),

admin, 1:503

checklist for orgs, 1:509–513

composed of two factors, 1:503

crash program, 1:515

don't ever leave a rudiment until it's in, 1:508

expansion program is basic org rudiment function, MS1:169

HAS to report, 1:514

HCO gets org ruds in, 1:514

how many weeks to get them in, 1:508

if they do go out by reason of transferred personnel, 1:508

report, 1:521

example of, 1:522

org rudiment(s), *(cont.)*

on goldenrod, 1:523

rotation of, 1:521

rudiments 1 to 17, 1:503–508

technical, 1:503

units will come up by that reason alone, 1:508

Org Rudiments Officer, gets in org rudiments, 1:521

Org Rudiments Section,

headed by Org Rudiments Officer, 1:521

in a very small org, duty of HCO Area Sec, 1:521

Org Series, HOW of organization, 7:446, MS2:130, MS3:426

origin(ation), originating, originate,

if post is supposed to originate, it does so, 0:392

improper despatch is actually not an origin, 0:408

insisting post originate or do duties or furnish product or service of that post, 0:392

maintaining origination lines to inform others what you are doing, 0:583

not originating when one should, effect of, 0:414

off-origin; *see* off-origin; off-origin despatch

on-origin, definition, 0:392

person originating off-line, off-origin traffic or failing to originate from his post, 0:442

staff origination on matters relating to personnel and duties, 0:173

we are suckers for origination acceptance, 0:408

originator; *see also* **communication; despatch; developed traffic**

improper despatch routed back to, 0:390, 0:405

let originator do the work, 0:406

one does not accept comm that is not the post business of the, 0:392

OT, *see* **Operating Thetan**

OT Base Council, 6:842

OT bracelet, 5:327, 5:356

OT Central Committee,

also authorized to correspond with Clears and OTs relating to their projects, 7:152

duties of, 6:843, 7:125

purpose, 7:125

OT Course, requirements, 4:798

"other duties," why seem to be so important, 7:422

other-determinism, definition, 5:566

other-intention, other-intentionedness,

    handling for, 1:786

    unawareness or dispersal and, 1:786

    what it comes from, 0:509

"other" tech, definition, 4:22, 5:651

OT levels, eligibility, 4:816–817

OT Liaison Unit, formed at WW, 7:144

OT Section Awards, Clear and above are declared as, 5:365

out-admin, 0:45, 0:47, 0:71

    equals Liability, 4:1105

out-basics, real reason why person cannot turn out products, MS2:178

out-basket, 0:389, 0:392, 0:533; see also basket; in-basket

    contents routed at least twice a day, 1:364

    described, 1:354

outer org, product of, 4:123, 6:766

out-ethics; see also ethics

    activities in course rooms, 4:424–425

    bank triggered by out-ethics situation, 0:449

    contraction and poverty caused by, 0:534

    corrupt activities, 0:534

    definition, 0:453

    dynamics out of comm, 0:456

    ethics bait and, 0:530

    evil and, 0:453

    formulating and adopting firm policy that will detect and prevent same situation from continuing to occur, 0:606

    handling out-ethics person, 0:527

    how executive handles out-ethics symptoms, 1:836

    ignoring loafers or out-ethics cats in group, 0:556

    indicators, 0:533

    justifying out-ethics action, 0:449

    Knowledge Reports and, 0:556

    "nothing matters" attitude, 1:835

    person who is potential or active criminal, 0:455

    preclear does not make case gain, 1:841

    sec checking and, 0:616

    second dynamic out-ethics, 0:459

    some group members are aware of the outness, 0:555

    student doesn't want next course in training, 0:32

    student indicators at course completion and, 4:379

    symptoms, 1:835, 7:736

    system of chits and hearings being out, 0:554

    three indicators which point to possible out-

out-ethics; (cont.)

    ethics in an org, network or management body, 7:1259

    tolerating out-ethics, effect of, 0:556, 0:689

    using self-discipline to correct it, 0:606

    where ethics is out, handling, 0:525

    writing up overts and withholds and any known out-ethics situation, 0:606

outflow, see also inflow; letter(s)

    demanding new personnel on key outflow posts, 0:586

    exchange maintains inflow and outflow that gives person space around him and keeps bank off of him, 0:529

    finance available, personnel, effort all limit how much outflow there can be, 2:66

    high volume of outflow is vital to return any inflow, 2:65

    holier, more moral, more remunerative and more effective than inflow, 0:367, 1:306

    if you want students and pcs you will have to write lots of letters, 2:610

    income and, 3:103

    more remunerative and effective than inflow, 2:117

    order of priority of staff action, 0:367, 2:117

    org not outflowing, 0:102

    promotion used to increase, 1:309

    quantity of outflow of personal letters on a national basis determines the number of people who come in for training and processing, 2:610

outgo, income exceeding, 0:292

out-gradient, public can become dismayed by attempts to shunt them onto major services when out-gradient and must be avoided by Public Divisions staff, 6:116

out-morale, low production causes, MS3:37

outness(es),

    accessory to outness by failing to report it, 0:557

    at least some group members are aware of the, 0:555

    being able to correct outnesses, 0:58

    breed of arbitrary that almost every outness is, 0:140

    Ethics Officer locates WHO is causing, 0:518

    evaluation reviewed to the first major, MS1:142

    handling of, 0:261

    list of ways that Div 6 keeps off its purpose line, 6:84

    people do not see, hear, notice or handle

outness(es), *(cont.)*

outnesses when they have Mis-Us on them, MS2:132

requires genius to discover how gross and how basic outness can be, 0:556

what to do if you see something going on in org or incorrect that you don't like, 0:549

which can destroy an org faster than any others, reference, 0:266

out of valence, OCA graphs and, 6:299

outpoint(s),

ability to recognize, MS1:128, MS1:168

added inapplicable data, definition, MS1:126

added time, definition, MS1:126

altered,
    importance, definition, MS1:80
    sequence, definition, MS1:78

area having most outpoints, MS1:18

cannot recognize, MS1:128

can't tolerate outpoints or confront them, one can't *see* them, MS1:109

chain of, MS1:128

contrary facts, MS1:85

cope and, 1:59

counting of, MS1:128

definition, MS1:20, MS1:122, MS1:157

disaster and, MS1:70

dropped time, MS1:79

evaluation of importance, MS1:155

"facts" you protest in life, MS1:25

falsehood, definition, MS1:80

first, always occurs in stats, MS1:163

human reaction to, MS1:129

inability to recognize, MS1:168

incorrectly included datum, MS1:44

indicate departures from ideal scene, MS1:58

inspecting area by outpoints against factor of orderliness, 0:308

keep a tally of, MS1:141

leads directly into point you should be investigating, MS1:155

missing ideal scene, MS1:69

most overlooked, MS1:78

omitted data, definition, MS1:78

persons who quickly set about remedying outpoints, 0:310

pointer toward a situation, MS1:128

point where you neglect any more, MS1:156

prior outpoint count, MS1:150

situation underlying series of, MS1:175

situation where you find outpoints, MS1:128

speed of recognizing, MS1:168

outpoint(s), *(cont.)*

spotting and correcting is dealing with symptoms only, 1:59

stat pushing, 0:692

tells there is an area to investigate, MS1:157

toughest to recognize is omission, MS1:168

try to make them seem logical, MS1:128

two counts of, MS1:151

type of, will give you how the departure is, MS1:147

wrong source, definition, MS1:84, MS1:127

wrong target, definition, MS1:71, MS1:80

"outpoint-correct," cycle of, MS1:77

out-rudiments, lack of Scientology results has stemmed from, 4:1170

out-sequence, org boards and, MS1:219

outside auditor service, Celebrity Centre may also operate, to render assists and auditing to ill or disabled celebrities, 6:136

outsiders, refusing to speak ill of Scientology or criticize it to outsiders, 0:153

out-tech, *see also* **technical, technology**

cause of, 0:44, 0:47

C/S overload and, 5:706

definition, 4:1078, 5:669

handling for org that gets epidemic of out-tech, 2:113, 3:89, 4:155, 6:557, 7:863

if it seems kind of stupid it is probably out-tech, 0:147

if tech is out, only Ethics can bat down reasons it can't be gotten in, 0:498

indicator of, 1:905

interpretations of HCOBs, policy letters, 5:783

only SPs and PTSes can keep tech out, 0:498

only ways you can fail to get results on a pc, 4:20, 5:783

prevention of, 5:708

processes, handling of, 1:1032

recourse to off-policy or out-tech order, 0:146–147

results of in an org, 5:652

Scientology not applied exactly per HCOBs and tapes, 0:241

stems from, 1:899, 4:481

student,
    doesn't want next course in training, 0:32
    indicators at course completion and, 4:379

study tech is basic prevention of, 0:45

Supervisor or other person gives interpretations of HCOBs, policy letters, 4:20

Word Clearers penalty for, 4:504, 5:473

word of mouth and, MS3:169

you can handle, 2:114, 3:90, 7:864

overburden, on comm lines, MS1:238

overcorrection, of pcs, handling for, 5:675

overload, overburden; *see also* **cope; overwork**
any you have is from unhattedness of the most basic kind, 7:809
causes of, 0:204, 0:390
comes from cope-cope-cope, MS1:197
definition, 5:707
filling posts by overload noted, 0:101
hats, hatting and, 0:166, 0:204, 1:293
most common way to overload an area, MS1:407
org board and, 0:106, 0:204
posts overloaded,
department, division too overloaded will empty, 1:62
handling for, 7:801
programs didn't get done because of, 0:701
protection from personnel who overburden us all, 0:151
question one asks oneself when overloaded, 7:801
too much traffic jams a line, 0:85

overpayment, refund overpayments (for books) unless it's a donation, 0:282

overrun,
False Data Stripping and, MS2:142
repair of past ethics condition being overrun, 0:671

overspending, out-ethics symptom, 1:835

overt(s), overt act(s); *see also* **crime; overt product(s); O/W writeups**
ARC breaks and, 0:103, 0:277
blows due to, 0:177
committing
destructive acts on job, 0:459
too many harmful acts against dynamics, 0:452
criminal and, 1:830
definition, 0:463, 1:843, 6:544
disclosed in session not used for justice, 1:634
evil purposes and, 4:992, 5:453
false data and, MS2:138
format for writing up one's, 0:536
gigantic overt, 0:500
hidden overts continually committed by an SP, 1:1009
inability to evaluate and, MS1:187
insane are just one seething mass of withholds and, 0:528
lay off not wanting to commit overts, 0:500

overt(s), overt act(s); *(cont.)*
nonexistent or bad products classified as, MS1:242
of omission that kill any pride, 0:255
omission of enforcing truth and justice, 0:520
one must have done to other dynamics those things which other dynamics now seem to have power to do to him, 0:457
only overt in handling justice, 0:480
people leave because of their own overts and withholds, 5:548
perception and, 1:817
person whose job product is an, 4:1110
procedure to handle, MS1:188
product,
as an overt act, 0:39–40, 0:294
of the insane is an overt act, 0:252
protesting revelation of improper acts of others, 0:462
reduction of, 4:846
stem from misunderstoods, 1:294
unwillingness to do and, 1:727
when one has committed, his confront and responsibility drops, 1:1043
withholds and, disclosed in HCO Sec Check, 4:995
writing up overts and withholds, 0:606

overt product(s); *see also* **error; overt**
cause of, 0:39, 0:294, 0:300
definition, 1:817, 3:309, MS2:129, MS3:425, 7:445
don't hide bad work from execs, 0:232
effect of, 0:294
handling for person who produces an, 0:294
ignoring overt product makers, effect of, 0:316
insane and, 0:39–40, 0:252
org with no comm discipline trying to deliver, 0:392
out-ethics symptom, 1:835
standard of living vs., 0:314
world's "sciences" delivering overt product—decaying Earth, 0:259

overwhelm(ed); *see also* **overwork**
comes from cope-cope-cope, MS1:197
cope becoming an, 0:204
of individual, 0:601, 0:602, 0:604
pc overwhelmed with high levels, 0:473
persons in apathy, overwhelm or despair with regard to their post areas, 0:311
SP and, 0:656
when exec will lose his grip on his post and his activity and "feel overwhelmed" and worked to death, 0:389

overwork(ed)(ing); *see also* **overload, overwhelm**

answer to overworked exec, 0:590

by doing someone else's job, 0:232

causes of, 0:47, 0:87, 0:197, 0:590, 0:598, 0:601–603

dev-t and, 0:391, 0:427

expansion vs., 0:131

failure to take responsibility and failure to act with initiative, consequences of, 0:662

fastest way for technical exec to become overworked, 0:241

group size and, 0:598

hats, hatting and, 0:197

how one gets little done and is badly overworked, 0:88

more than four subordinates and, 0:601, 0:603

oppressive, confused and overworked org, reason for, 0:554

organization,

appearing busy and overworked while producing little, 0:441

that overworks everyone and underpays, 0:598

overworking exec by ignoring one's duties, 0:472

working frantically, totally exhausted and yet producing nothing of value, reason, 0:439

owe, no good worker owes his work, 0:507

ownership, own, 0:186–187; *see also* **possession**

O/Ws,

abbreviation for overts and withholds, 0:535

O/W write-up(s), *see also* **overt(s), overt act(s)**

C/S okay and, 1:846

Danger condition handling and, 0:606, 0:612

end phenomena of, 1:846

end ruds check, 1:846

example of, 1:845

O/W write-up(s), *(cont.)*

format for, 0:536, 1:844–845

procedure, 1:847

repair of, 1:846

Oxford Capacity Analysis, *see also* **profile(s)**

case that read high on the graph will sometimes drop and read lower after auditing, why, 4:231

evil and, 0:526

graph(s),

how to get it up, 6:289–300

kept in front of pc's folder, 4:236

out of valence causes it to drop lower after auditing, 6:299

that dives will come back up if general processing is done, 4:232

where kept in pc's folder, 6:306

illegal practice of clearing words on, 4:233, 6:304

IQ score included, 4:236

low point

on left, out of valence, 4:967, 6:301

on right, crazy, 4:967, 6:301

low right or left, indicates need of Objectives, 4:194

person with dropped graph is not yet fully into his "own valence," 4:231

plots 10 traits of a pc's personality, 4:236, 6:306

properly marked graphs provide the C/S, auditor and the D of P with information they need to correctly handle the pc, 4:236, 6:308

results of test and, 6:306

series of results can be drawn on same graph for comparison, 4:236

variable of word clearing test wipes out possibility of establishing what auditing did for case, 4:233, 6:304

when new OCA needed for C/S or D of P, handling, 6:306

P

PAB(s), *see* **Professional Auditor's Bulletins**

pack(s), hat pack(s), *see also* **hat**

A–I hat and, 0:199–200

dev-t packs, 0:439–440, 0:442

exec responsibilities for, 0:221

package,

discount rates, 3:207

sent from an org must bear the return address of that org, 2:340

packaging, definition, MS3:194

paid completions, stat of the Commanding Officer or Executive Director, 7:168

pain,

reactive minds and, 0:480

suppose Scientology could really free men from, 0:153

survival and, 0:452

paint, only odorless may be used, 7:1388

pan-determinism, definition, 5:566

paper(s), *see also* **despatch**

colors to use for various mimeo issue types, 0:112

funds of an org and, 3:269

only pieces allowed in one's desk, 0:195

spending hours trying to locate piece of, 0:306

paranoia, type of insanity, 1:994, 4:86

parasitic area, parasitism, 0:508

parents, *see also* **child; second dynamic**

false economic data coming from, 0:313

partially paids, Call-in Unit set up to handle located under the Advance Scheduling Registrar, 2:641, 3:217, 4:276, 7:865

participants, participation,

achieved by, MS1:408

prevention of, and youth, MS1:408

spectatorism vs., 0:249

particle(s) (despatches, papers, etc.), *see also* **communication; despatch; traffic**

accumulation of unhandled particles, 0:310

actions of org can all be classified under heading of particle motion and change, 0:81

colliding, bouncing off each other and staying in area, 0:106

designating channels for types of, MS1:197

difference between order and chaos is simply straightforward planned flows and correct particles, 0:389

flow in sequence, MS1:194

inhale and exhale of org is take and give of vital information and, 0:579

new public are not interested in, 6:235

no line or particle control, 0:389

not handled properly, result, 0:81

org's positions change flowing particles, 0:106, MS1:194

outflow of, 0:367

power is proportional to speed of particle flow, 0:325, 0:432, MS2:33

prosperity proportional to speed of particle flow, 0:66, 0:275

removed off the line, 0:195, 0:432

seeing that terminals and comm lines exist to receive, change and forward the, 0:82

standard lines and routes for, 0:392

visualizing sequence of flows of particles on org board, 0:108

particle(s) (despatches, papers, etc.), *(cont.)*

we are all managers of particles (in Scientology org), 0:82

part-time study, HGC auditor and, 5:532

past,

courage to face past and misdeeds, 0:152

investigation of person or, 0:462

not held against person entering Scientology group, 0:152

past-life,

auditing, handling of folders of pcs with, 4:258

Clear,

CCRD for those originating, 4:258

Dianetics and, 4:259

identity,

evaluation of is violation of Auditor's Code, 4:260

Sec Check to verify, 4:258

pc folders, handling of, 4:257

pastor, penalty for refusing to hear Confessionals, 1:642

pastoral counseling, 4:1190

pattern(s), *see also* **organization form; organizing board**

different patterns of org board, 0:105–107

perfect org is not machine but pattern of agreements, 0:82

purpose of org pattern, 0:82, 0:96

Thetan–Mind–Body–Product pattern, 0:128, 0:654

paused statistics, *see also* **statistics**

comes from jammed lines of the topmost executives, 7:499

definition, 7:498

handling for, 7:499

Pavlov, Ivan Petrovich, Russian veterinarian, psychology and psychiatry developed chiefly by, 4:919

pawns, when people offer nothing in exchange, do not produce and cannot or will not administer, they become, 7:436

pay, paycheck, *see also* **exchange; income; money; units of pay**

accurately and punctually paid to keep staff happy, 0:350

approval and validation vs. mere pay, 0:277

assisting fellow staff to do better job results in larger paycheck for you, 0:166–167

calculating amount for, 0:314

chopping your, 0:370

comes from org's stats, 0:679

Comm Ev can restore lost pay in cases of injustice, 0:478

corrupt activities vs., 0:534

examples of how staff is deprived of its, 0:302

exchange, org income and, 0:317–318

pay, paycheck, *(cont.)*

final pay before a leave withheld till Sec Check done, 0:177

full pay requirement, 0:221

good pay,

how to be ten times your size with lot more pay, 0:626

how to obtain higher level of dissemination and, 0:232

how to raise your, 0:688

how to get 10 times the size with a lot more pay, 2:705

idea that everyone should get same, 0:315

if staff works hard pay is adequate, 0:170

income cutatives and salary sum, 0:301

low pay,

badly paid staff, reason for, 0:689

cause of, 0:301, 0:337–338, 0:556, 0:688

comes about when no admin staff know policy letters, 1:166

in an org which is a "clinic," 1:165

nonutilized personnel and, 0:203

only inadequate when policy is out, 0:170

source of, 0:19

org public image vs., 0:335

orgs have to be more efficient to pay well, 0:705

org that overworks everyone and underpays, 0:598

permanent status and, 1:239

personal conditions of Emergency reduce pay or units one-third, 0:470

reduction may only be done after a Committee of Evidence, 7:1300

roughest on units is bad mailing dissemination, 2:56

staff member determines the, 0:318

staff receives pay in proportion to what they produce, 0:689

suspended during any auditing or training undertaken as amends, 0:545

termination of employment and final pay, 1:226

unit low ever since mailing of large numbers of *Certainty* stopped, handling, 2:54

what it depends on, 0:317

what to do as staff member if you need extra money, 0:170

when units are low we look directly at the Dir of PrR and nobody else, 2:56

working manager deserves his, 0:507

pay card, description of, 3:337

payday, procedure, 3:334

payment,

acceptable forms, 2:478

permitting delivery without proper invoice or payment, result, 3:120

payments to Flag, definition, MS2:352

payroll,

how prepared, 3:112

how to do, 3:332

issuing of checks, 3:113

pc, *see* **preclear**

Pc Application Form, 2:542

major auditing action and, 4:1024

pc folder,

back cover items, 4:1016

color coding and, 4:1011

contents of, 4:249

description of, 4:1013

"Mail Slip" system is used to ensure that the folders are not lost in transit, 4:1012

never handed to pc to carry, 4:1012

OCA graphs kept in the front of, 4:236

past-life, handling of, 4:257

reason they are red-tagged, 4:254

represents a record of all the auditing actions and other handlings taken on a preclear as he moves up the Bridge, 4:1013

session folders and, 4:1015

several forms attached to inside front cover, 4:1014

what one contains, 4:1010

pc information sheet, when used, 4:1067

pc route, definition, 2:437

PE, *see* **Personal Efficiency**

PE, source of new personnel, 1:227

peace(ful),

bringing peace to world, 0:486

keep Justice Codes for peaceful org, 0:487

on day when we can fully trust each other, there will be peace on Earth, 0:462

only those who sought only peace were ever butchered, 0:517

productive peace, 0:632

productive peace is getting men busy and giving them something to make something of that they want to, 7:379, MS3:359

third party law and, 0:511–512

three major factors in world peace, 7:1013

war rulers deified and peacetime rulers forgotten, 0:505

Pearl Harbor, 0:116

pearls, we sell for pennies, 4:896

pecking order, basic theory used in advertising, MS3:122

pegboard system, separating the weekly invoices and vouchers into categories of income and expense, 7:1079

penalty, penalties, penalize

after the fact has occurred disciplines criminals, 5:138

certificates and awards suspended for staff accepting any student or pc for personal profit, 0:171

code of discipline, 0:467

conditions penalties/new employees and persons newly on post, 0:566

crimes and high crimes, penalties for, 0:470–474

disciplines criminals, 7:700

disciplining the criminal, 0:66

doubled,

for breaking Normal condition, 0:661

for overts and withholds discovered after deadline set for them to be turned in, 0:606

down statistics only, 1:770, 7:501

errors, penalties for, 0:467

exec failing to assign or enforce, 0:653

for misdemeanors which become subject of Comm Ev, 0:470

for Non-Existence apply after 30 days, 0:647–648

for staff contract breakage, 0:174

illegal discounts and giving away service, penalties for, 0:303

knowing of outness or crime and failing to report it receives same penalty as actual offender, 0:557

lack of specified penalties, effect of, 0:467

list of offenses and, 0:467–474

make penalties for noncompliance and false reports too gruesome to be faced and enforce them, 0:420

misdemeanors, penalties for, 0:469–470

penalizing upstats, 0:504, 0:507

quadrupled for breaking Power condition, 0:661

refusal to accept penalties assigned in recourse action, 0:471

rewards and, 0:504

socialism penalizes upstat, 0:507

tripled for breaking Affluence condition, 0:661

verbal tech penalties, 0:24

we penalize downstats only, 0:504

when you penalize production you get nonproduction, 0:504

pending basket, 0:371

described, 1:354

leave current work and communications in, 1:369

people, person(s), *see also* **being; individual; man; personnel; population; preclear; public; staff; thetan**

ability to confront, handle and control people, 0:252

admin people are the management people, 1:166

answer people's questions, 0:84, 0:166, 0:276, 0:322, 0:370

believing people can be or deserve to be helped, 0:152

de-aberrating just by education contained in Scientology, 0:38

decent people are in favor of justice, 0:480

don't have to be aberrated, 0:156

Earth people are all part of economic machine, 0:151

especially new people, need direction, 6:115

factors which dominate in dealing with, 7:754

fad of "the other person doesn't matter," 0:301

fail to join in absence of purpose they can understand, 6:686

freedom is for honest people, 0:461, 0:462

HCO people know the Basic Staff Hat backwards, 1:166

help people, 0:84

honest people have rights, 0:461, 0:462

how sane person vs. aberrated person thinks, 0:236

losing people by not using them, 0:632

man's systems are based on groups and masses of, 0:96

modern age says it doesn't need them, 1:167

never as bad as they think they are, 1:727–728

never do nothing, 0:422

new,
    gradient scales and, 2:401
    have them read a book, 2:401

often run from their past or blame it on others, 0:152

only possible choices are, 7:437

org reputation for swift and excellent handling of, 0:350

organization must answer people's questions, 2:598, 6:156

part of Earth's economic machine, 1:249

police themselves, 1:728

political system seeking to function amongst ignorant, illiterate and barbaric peoples, 0:157

population explosion and welfare state, 1:166

pushed around, feel they cannot hold a position in space, 0:205

people, person(s), *(cont.)*

real VFP in an org is valuable fine people who produce VFPs who then make up a valuable fine public, 0:316

Scientology,
    for a free people, 0:159
    open to all, 0:234

speed of flow of people as org particle, 0:325

strengthened and made more confident by being given post, 0:205–206

tend to believe their friends, 0:333

three types of, MS2:202

trying to put ethics in on themselves for eons without knowing how, 0:457

trying to weaken strong people, 0:205

we are in business of, 0:695

who cannot receive comm so can't answer or respond properly, 0:406

who offer nothing in exchange, do not produce and cannot or will not administer, become pawns, MS3:416

who use policy to stop, handling, 7:773

why people cause themselves accidents and decide to have one, 0:452

why people develop strange incapacitating illnesses, 0:452

working with to get them eligible, 1:167

people filing, definition, 2:695

pep,

change of man's diet and loss of, 5:640

protein's effect on, 5:641

perception,

misunderstoods act as perception shut-offs, MS2:132

overt acts and, 1:817

performance,

demanding and delivering high-level performance on every post, 0:259

staff may not be ordered to training or processing as a disciplinary measure, or to improve job performance, 0:168

staff member's responsibility for org performance, 0:167

reward system for merit and good performance exists, 0:474

permanent,

appointment, may be changed only with Comm Ev, 1:196

executive,
    definition, 1:225
    requirements for, 1:223

permanent, *(cont.)*
  postings,
    must have approval of Senior PCO International to be posted, 1:257
    state of Clear and, 1:199
  privileges, staff members entitled to when in possession of their certificate, 1:221

permanent executive,
  award of, made only to, 5:406
  definition, 5:396
  provisional, 5:406

permanent staff, *see also* Permanent status; staff member(s)
  requirements, 5:390, 5:392, 5:394
  staff who complete requirements, 6:804

Permanent Staff Status, 0:209

permanent status,
  application for, MS1:472, MS2:309
  certificate for, 1:224
  designated as "2" on org board, 1:238, 5:413
  dismissal, 5:413
  entitled to training or auditing, 1:169
  longevity pay, 1:239
  posting, requirements for, MS1:472, MS2:309
  secretary of person's division must recommend in writing to HAS before exam may be given, 1:238
  staff member may not be demoted, transferred or dismissed without a full Comm Ev, 1:238

permission, command channel used upward for, 0:387

persistence, compliance and, 0:246

person, *see* being; individual; people

personal contact, targets and, MS1:136–137

Personal Counselor, VFP and statistic, 6:533

Personal Efficiency Course,
  attendance, how to increase, 6:468
  cheapest way to improve your life, 6:296
  lead in to HAS Co-audit, 6:459
  not an Academy course, 4:182
  only reasons you lose people who come into, 6:468
  training activity for HAS Co-audit, 6:462

Personal Efficiency Director,
  destructive to post one who has a bad needle reaction on Control, 6:114
  may not be the same person as the Dir of Training at any time, 6:313

Personal Efficiency Foundation,
  administration and, 6:365, 6:314
  advertisement, 2:284, 6:242, 6:472
  bad control personnel on PE posts will waste whoever is driven in, 2:412, 6:184

Personal Efficiency Foundation,*(cont.)*
  becomes a dissertation in Scientology and a Comm Course to teach one to communicate and process, 6:319
  bought a book rule and, 6:472
  change to give maximum returns, 6:318
  Chaplain post a necessity in, 6:475
  comes in *after* they have read a book, *never* before, 2:284, 6:242
  course abolished, 6:321
  courses required to be taught, 6:465
  definition, 2:504, 3:232, 7:200, 7:271
  departments of, 6:365
  disqualification for PE post, 2:412, 6:184
  dream is to get the people in fast, get them invoiced in a congress-type assembly line, no waiting, give them hot, excited, positive service and boot them on through to their HAS and THEN worry about doing something else with them, 6:317
  field staff members and, 6:472
  governed by the PE Director, 6:313
  handout, 6:293
  HAS Co-audit and, 6:453, 6:462
  is itself but also in a Central Org one of the six departments, 6:315
  literature, copying of extremely successful package, 6:179
  live lecturers and, 6:472
  may have its own administrator and/or Registrar who shall be governed by the Director of Procurement and the PE Director, 6:313
  people who cannot control people on PE posts, result, 2:411, 6:183
  procurement and, 6:314
  programed drill calculated to introduce people to Scientology and to bring their cases up to a high level of reality both on Scientology and on life, 6:315
  promotional purposes, 2:57, 7:32
  purpose, 6:313
  report pertaining to pilot project on testing as a dissemination line for PE, 2:284, 6:242
  space allocation for, 6:473
  staff members on PE and PrR have to have their *control* button clean, 2:195, 6:182
  Test Program, steps followed for proper routing of each public individual, 6:113
  warning on new line-up, 6:281

personality, personalities,
  basic personality and intentions of individual are good, 0:452
  can change, 0:3
  post held up by personality alone will slump if changed, 0:596

333

personality, personalities, *(cont.)*

regards unutilized people as a backlog on his lines, MS1:456

remedy for people not doing their post, MS1:399

replacement for staff who want to be transferred, 1:162

requests for transfer or removal, form for, 1:257–259

requirements of Procurement personnel, 2:602

resisting new personnel, MS1:383

responsibility of the department head, 7:757

robbing a lower org as a higher org's solution, 1:165

Sec ED appointing or promoting personnel must have Personnel Control Officer initial on it, 1:197

sending those eligible for training, 1:163

small statistic drops should be investigated around good personnel, 7:498

sources of new personnel, most fruitful, 1:227

steps for any acquirement or movement of, 1:254

steps to put someone on post, 1:181

technical, 5:351, 5:737
  line for procurement of, 1:157
  relative skill required, 4:93

tested under that executive, 7:427

the only time you lose staff is when you let low-stat people in, MS3:377

three classes of, and handling, 7:755

three factors in assigning a post, 7:498

training,
  for anyone connected with, 1:66
  lack of results in, MS1:407

transfers, 1:74

trouble, lack of complement and, 1:215

turnover is heavy, MS1:389

two distinct types in an org, 1:165

unsatisfactory, Personnel Control looks into the matter and recommends, 1:194

unwilling only do or say "can't," 7:755

utilization, 1:210

vacancy, shown on allocation board, 1:162

voluntary help, 1:159

wasted for lack of full hats, MS1:415

what adds up to good prediction, MS1:454

willing, what they include, 7:755

with bad study history, key exec posts and, 7:660

without purpose commit crimes, MS1:407

Personal Registration Section, definition, 2:506, 3:234, 7:202

personnel, Personnel, *see also* **people**

appointment of, 1:195

bad control personnel on Reg and PE posts will waste whoever is driven in, 2:412, 6:184

best admin person is also highly tech trained, 1:165

build strongly for the future, MS1:466

cases vs., MS1:397

classes of unsuitable personnel, MS1:394

critical definition, MS1:381

definition, MS1:37

degrees of ability to control, 1:185

demands for,
  how HCO handles, MS1:465, 7:450
  I&R Forms and, MS1:306, MS2:105, MS2:256
  met by inspection of the area, MS1:406

disorganization of a division will empty it out of, 1:62

duties of the post, 1:178–179

equates against case gain more than personality, 7:498

Estates, 7:1401

Ethics and, how they work together or conflict, MS1:409

evaluation and, MS1:175

example of problem in, MS1:294

factors underlying failure on post, MS1:398

failure to predict and sudden transfers, MS1:454

Flag Rep report, 7:1420

folder, definition, MS3:461

form for request of, 1:258–259

goofs, 1:71

handling for org refusing new personnel, MS1:383

how to handle demands for, MS3:430

how to put new personnel on the job, 7:767

how to reduce heavy turnover, MS1:390

how you evaluate a personnel scene, MS1:165

income is proportional to control exertion, 2:413, 6:185

incorrect or destructive changes subject to Comm Ev and removal, 1:261

institutional cases or persons with psychiatric history or insane, 1:168

instructions to, how to issue, 7:756

job application file, 1:226–227

keep tech trained people in tech and admin people for admin, MS1:387

lack of full hats, MS1:206

lazy procurement, 1:165

list of errors in handling, MS1:382

personnel, Personnel, *(cont.)*

maximum quota authorized for, 1:162

misassign when they do not know all the hats, 1:71

most fruitful source of admin, 1:161

needing additional personnel, handling for, 7:761

networks who want personnel from an org, 1:257

new person who hasn't gripped it in a week, is still begging for help from all, handling for, 7:767

new staff, routing onto post, 1:178

none may be transferred to a portion in a State of Emergency, 1:207

nonproducing, transfer almost never the answer, MS1:400

nonutilized, definition, MS1:206

not making it on basic training, routed out through Qual, 1:74

obsessive transferring obscures ineffective personnel, 1:254

old-time system based on psychological principle, MS1:394

only chosen on raw statistics supported by ample data containing figures, 7:666

only time you lose staff is when you let low-stat people in, 7:397

Org Exec Sec has power to dismiss staff, 1:163

org expansion often gets pinned by false economy in, MS1:382

overts and withholds written down on departing an org, 1:183

PE and Registration posts, choosing, 1:185

preparedness program, 1:164

pretest on one's lines, MS1:8

priority of personnel by degree of ability to control, 2:411, 6:183

procedure for dept heads seeking personnel, 7:44

procurement by department heads, 1:226

procurement for technical staff, 4:38

programing, example of what occurs when not done, MS1:387

protection of orgs and staff from destructive personnel, 1:168

pushing people out the top to the next highest org, 1:163

qualifications, 1:158

questions to determine where it stands, MS1:454

recruit, wasted for lack of full hats and full training on hats, 7:450, MS3:430

Personnel (function or portion of an org),

Dept 1 (Routing and Personnel), promotional actions of, 0:347

goofs, 0:280

personnel people knowing every hat in org, 0:279, 0:280

reported to when one changes posts, 0:166

unstabilizing staff, 0:280

Personnel Control Officer,

allocation board kept up by, 1:162

ethics actions taken on, 1:198

maxim, leaving the post empty rather than fill it with a bad personnel, 1:198

model assignments to be used in postings, 1:212–214

must beware of low leadership scores for executives, 1:197

places staff members in suitable positions, 1:162

unsatisfactory personnel and, 1:194

personnel file(s),

contents of, 1:178

Ethics use of, 1:192

Inspection Officer reports filed in, 1:191

new person hired, 1:178

past employees, 1:178

present employees, 1:178

what it consists of, 1:191

personnel folder, definition, 7:481, MS2:197, MS2:302

personnel freeze, Exec Esto issues on arrival, MS1:305, MS2:104, MS2:255

Personnel Officer, 0:596

responsibility for staff auditors and interns, 4:905

responsibility for staff training, 5:490

who insists on pre- and on-post training, a valuable asset, MS1:402

personnel order(s),

appear as Sec ED, 1:415–416

tech/admin ratio, calculation of and, 1:216

personnel pool(s), 0:280, 0:347

Div 4 and Div 5 not to be regarded as, 1:164

for auditor trainees, 5:528

handouts for, 1:164

have good courses as personnel pools, 1:166

list of real pools, 1:164

notice boards with notices for, 1:164

posters for org recruitment, 1:164

special mailings to, 1:164

using wrong personnel pools for want of proper recruiting and training, MS2:37

working installations used as, 1:117

Personnel Procurement Officer,

finds out all pertinent data about the person, 1:162

hiring lines to, 1:162

never told kind of personnel to procure, 1:162

put ads in paper, 1:162

recommendation for new personnel sent to Exec Council, 1:163

Personnel Programer,

ideal scene, 5:61

product, 5:61

purpose, 5:61, 5:424

statistic, 5:61

works with the individual staff member, 5:424

Personnel Series, anyone connected with personnel should have done, 1:66

persuasion, object of PR is persuasion to think, MS3:73

Peru, Bolivar and, 0:632–633

PES, *see* **Public Executive Secretary**

petition(s), *see also* **justice**

amends project petition, 0:545

as channel when one is being pressured to follow off-policy or out-tech order, 0:146–147

definition, 1:970, 2:661

description and policies regarding, 0:488–489, 0:492

direct order or straight directive can be petitioned against after compliance, 7:352, MS3:332

if discourteous and contains entheta, handling for, 2:669

institutional cases and, 1:798–799

policies, 1:742

recourse and, 1:745, 5:110

request to higher authority than the Ethics activity that passed sentence is a *petition,* not recourse, 4:355

right to, 1:742

shock cases and, 1:798–799

stipulations for anyone with shock or institutional record, 2:549

under sentence or awaiting a Committee of Evidence and, 1:753

Phase I,

definition, 7:426, MS3:406

Phase II situation can drop back into single-handing Phase I, 7:430

when a Phase II situation can drop back into single-handing Phase I, MS3:410

Phase II,

definition, 7:426, MS3:406

executive who doesn't see he has dropped out of, must at once single-hand, 7:430

what an executive who again doesn't see that he has dropped out of comfortable Phase II and gotten into a Phase I must do, MS3:410

philosopher, tried to resolve subjects of ethics and justice, 0:447–448

philosophical system, 0:95

philosophy,

basis of all, 0:448

contributism and, 0:277

decrying suppression of knowledge, wisdom, philosophy or data which would help mankind, 0:160

LRH philosophy about work, 0:151

political philosophy can't audit, 0:158

stressing freedom to use Scientology as philosophy in humanities, 0:160

turning point in history of, 0:450

phone(s),

cash-bills and, 3:211

handling of lines so public can call in, 3:211

long-distance calls, purchase orders and, 3:314

private telephone calls, telegrams and cables of staff members or students, handling of, 3:149

registration, highly unprofitable, 3:212

rules of, 3:144

volume of income of an org is in direct proportion to number of phone calls and letters of an org, 2:613

Phone and Turn Up Scheduling Book, definition, 2:629

photograph(s),

directed, planned or redone news is more interesting for our purposes than groups facing the camera, 2:214

feature news example, 2:180

feature news photograph definition, 2:180

handling of, 2:271

never put a paper clip on any photograph, 2:271

policy for magazines, 2:213

strikingly lighted portraits and feature and landscapes should be what we do in *The Auditor,* 2:214

two types of, 2:213

using the same dramatis personae continually is poor, 2:213

photographs, press conferences and, MS3:95

photostat machine, use of, 2:336, 3:381

physical-ailment-type ad, 6:180

physical disability, physically ill,
procedure in being requested to heal, 5:104
treatment for, 5:627

physical healing,
org does not engage in, 6:440
proper procedure for, 1:983

physical illness, registration and, 2:535, *see also* **ill(ness)**

physical universe, *see* **universe**

piano, play the, MS2:119, MS2:189, MS2:262, MS2:293

picture, must have a message all by itself without caption, MS3:297

pike,
head on a, definition, 1:818
putting a head on a, 1:750, 0:496, 0:497, 7:679

pilot, how to handle, MS1:316

pilot project, all new untried plans should have a, MS3:390, 7:410

pin(s),
Clear, 5:345
Dept 5 ensures broad issue, 0:349
Grade 0 to Grade IV Release awards, 5:357
Grades V, VA and VI have larger pin given, 5:357
Grades, 0 to IV, V, VA and VI, 2:380
memorial awards, 5:345
paid for out of HCO Book Account, 5:345
Release, 5:345
Release pins, lost, 2:380
Scientology, 2:378, 5:327, 5:345, 5:353
Scientology pin easy to obtain, 6:816

pink sheet,
co-audits' use of, 4:695
examples of, 4:448
how to issue, 4:446
never used as punishment or to make the student wrong, 4:450
student's ability to study bolstered by use of, 4:446
study assignment given to a student when he has missed something he should have learned earlier, 4:446
Supervisor checkout and, 4:450
theory and practical assignment and, 4:450
use of in training auditors, 4:317

pink slip, people ordered to processing or training and, 3:143

pioneer areas, personnel who do well in, 0:114

PL, *see* **Hubbard Communications Office Policy Letter**

plan(s), *see also* **dream; idea; planning; program; project**
action, to plan out one has to, MS1:196
actuality and, gap between will be found to be lack of admin know-how, 7:407
all new untried plans should have pilot projects, MS3:390
are not targets, MS2:435
battle plan, *see* **battle plan**
checklist for a strategic plan, MS3:456–457
common trick used to get agreement to do an order or, 0:146
definition, MS1:100, MS2:435
design of the thing itself, MS2:436
exec establishing overall plan of action, 0:373
five-year plans, 0:186
new plans, 0:599
new, untried, should have pilot project, 7:410
order is short-term direction given to implement policy or plans or programs which develop from policy, 0:136
org as orderly plan helps terminals get work done, 0:82
strategic, 7:477
tactical plan, definition, 0:706
things that defeat any, 0:67
users and, 0:598

planet, *see also* **civilization; Earth; man; world**
auditor is very important in clearing this, 0:154
condemning to death thousand times over, 0:208
contaminated air cover, 0:252
decent, pleasant things on this planet, where they come from, 0:10
future of this planet, what it depends on, 0:13
percent of insane on, 0:252
taking this planet just as we are and with no more than we know, 0:273
this planet and universe are concern of others too, 0:140
threatened destruction of,
destroying a planet, 0:252
extremely unstable scene for planet, 0:41
weapon capable of destroying all life on this planet, 0:451
when we will bring freedom to this, 0:140

planning, *see also* **plan; prediction**
basic step of administration, 7:408, 7:409, MS3:388
clarity with which can be programed, 0:705, 7:457, MS2:443, MS2:457

planning, *(cont.)*

complete, definition, MS2:435

complete, how to get okayed, MS2:436

"complete planning" and "programs" are synonymous and programs is the preferred word, MS2:437

conferences and, 7:918

exec and, 0:266

expansion planning of facilities, 0:336

Flag planning gotten into full action in an org, that org will boom, 7:419

Flag planning represented by programs or projects, 7:419

includes imaginative conception and intelligent timing, targeting and drafting of plans so they can be communicated and assigned, MS3:389

product, planning by, 0:287

purpose of organization is to make planning become actuality, 7:405, MS3:385

relationship of policy, planning, programing, projects, orders, production and viability, 0:132–136

resources and, 0:708

staff member expected to know general planning, 0:405

strategic plan, 0:706

tactical planning, 0:706–707

those things planned for do not become catastrophes, 0:427

where Flag planning represented by programs or projects, gotten into full action in an org, that org will boom, MS3:399

platemaking, definition, MS3:194

Plato,

ethics and, 0:448

Greek philosopher, 1:497

play, about senior trying to issue junior illegal order, 0:148

play the org board, very good executive knows how to, MS3:407, 7:427

play the piano,

definition, 7:462, MS1:312, MS3:442

knowing how to, MS1:364

pledge, certificate application and, 4:362

pluspoint(s),

adequate data, definition, MS1:127

applicable data, definition, MS1:127

correct source, definition, MS1:127

correct time, definition, MS1:127

definition, MS1:20

investigations and, MS1:73

pluspoint(s), *(cont.)*

learn to think like a genius, MS1:109

madman can't tolerate pluspoints, MS1:109

one looks for to lead to real Why for prosperity or improvement, MS1:108

show where logic exists, MS1:148

types of, MS1:148

what make things go right, MS1:149

poem, old, 0:532

Poland, smashed by the psychiatrist, 0:68

police,

called immediately in case of theft of large objects, 0:548

Russia and secret police, 0:599

we are not police, 0:462

police state, created by Justice Dept, 1:963

police systems, composed of, 1:962

policing,

dev-t, 0:394

exec feeling overworked, even with all dev-t cared for and policed, 0:601–602

one's lines, 0:390

policy, policies, *see also* **administrative technology; regulation; rule; third dynamic technology**

Ad Council and, 7:909

admin degrades and, 0:73, 0:74

administrative directives may only forward policy, 0:112

agreed-upon policy, 0:324, 0:408

agreement and, 0:60, 0:114, 0:132, 0:411, 0:475

all authorized policy must be set or made available, MS1:427

all LRH policy adopted as the creed of the Church, 7:1229

alteration of, 0:468

any failure of OEC basics and policies is ignorance of them, 1:4, 3:4, 4:4, 7:4

authorizes people to issue orders, 0:136, MS1:252

bad or destructive policy, 0:114, 0:117, 0:411

bad, persuades group members to set own random policy, MS1:261

based on fundamental laws of life, 0:70

based on good sense which is based on experience, 7:1192

basic purpose and, 0:115–117

calculated to ensure continued and widening demand, 0:126

clarifying questions about, 0:127

policy, policies, *(cont.)*

composed of, 0:115, 7:662

conference routing used for policy requests, 0:387

definition of, 0:28, 0:111, 0:116, 0:132, 0:134, 0:243, 7:486, 7:663, MS1:100, MS1:249, MS1:252, MS3:466

demanding or looking for orders from policy source and accepting policy from unauthorized sources, 0:132

departure from, discovered by LRH Comm, handling, 7:1268

directives, general orders and orders expire if not reissued as, 0:112

disagreement with, 0:475, 0:595, 7:773

distaste for policy, cause of, 0:411

EDs are there to say WHAT policy should be concentrated on, 0:556

enturbulence due to ignorance or absence of, 0:68

ethics designed to keep in, 1:280

evolved and issued by top management, 0:133

example of, MS1:250

existing but not followed, result, 7:661

exists to get job done and establish points of agreement that permit flows of traffic, 0:475, 7:773

exists to speed the wheels and make a job doable, 0:551, 7:329, MS3:309

expansion and, 0:115, 0:124

experience and, 0:28, 0:74, 0:112, 0:115, 0:116

extending idea of general policy to cover situations where no policy covers, 0:114

failure of staff to know, 5:4

failure of the whole staff to know policy, 3:4, 4:4, 7:4

first policy of a Scientology org, 0:322

following or applying policy,
advice from one's immediate superior not to comply with policy, 0:544
can't apply a policy, handling, 0:623
failure to follow policy, 0:115
following destructive reinterpretation of policy, 0:141

formula of, 0:119, 7:665
fundamental step in getting policy used, 0:28
getting someone to follow policy, 0:119

for the TTC, 5:535

gives right to, MS1:252

good policy, followed well, makes an expanding department, org or civilization, 7:661

government policy, 0:114, 0:411

group agreement and, 0:132

guides planning and programing, 0:132–133

HCO duties and, 1:34

policy, policies, *(cont.)*

HGC, results or else, 5:729

hidden not stated random policies can conflict, MS1:426

high crime checkouts on, 0:75–76, 7:492, MS2:462, MS3:472

how does standard "green-on-white" get lost, 7:489, MS3:469

how it goes out or gets lost, 0:73

if it is not in HCO PL it is not policy, 0:113

if it is not written it is not true, 0:375

if one is experiencing an adverse effect on post or in life, then he does not know or has not applied tech or policy covering it, 0:268

if you apply policy, it works and things go well, 7:806

ignorance of, MS1:261, MS1:426

independent policies crossing up standard programs, 0:386

individual decision and, 0:324

instruction and admin policy are almost as important as tech, 7:1295

keeping admin working, 0:70

know-how of handling orgs and groups, 7:806

knowing policy,
labor-management hurricanes caused by ignorance of, 0:134
making policy easily knowable, 0:115

LRH policies are always senior to any mission orders, project orders or other types of issues, MS2:228

makes group or org alive and breathing, 0:411

makes org into org and keeps its flows fast and its design uncomplicated, 0:243

misinterpretation or reinterpretation, resulting in loss or destruction, 0:141

most senior organizational policies there are, 0:240, 7:673

must be born out of great insight and familiarity with the facts, 7:660

must forward purpose of group, MS1:261

new procedures vs., 0:60

no exact English word for, 0:132

not Scientology org policy unless written or authorized by LRH, 0:111

OEC Volumes contain all policy issued, 0:27

offenses vs., 0:117

Office of LRH Policy Review Section, 0:623

officers issuing policy while waiting for head of firm to give them orders, 0:135

off-policy, *see* off-policy; off-policy despatch

off-policy order, 0:146–148, 0:551

on personnel, MS1:466

on-policy, 0:28, 0:58–59

policy, policies, *(cont.)*

only reason anyone fights good policy, 0:114

only vital where agreement must exist between two or more thetans working together, 3:243, 7:1069

only way a target can change policy, MS1:135

order demanding one alter or depart from, 0:544

orders vs., confusion of, MS1:249

orgs and, 7:1275

pay inadequate when policy is out, 0:170

people who quote policy to show you they can't follow it, 0:475

perverting policy and corrupting tech, 0:92

point of assumption in all policy letters is survive, 7:354, MS3:334

points of agreement which make the group into a true group and an irresistible force, 7:237

policy-making, appointment-making level at work, 0:135

preservation of, 1:269

processing, certain persons ineligible for, 4:306, 5:730

provides wide agreement as basis for work coordination, 7:661

put in with an axe and call it such, 7:488, MS3:468

random or counter illegal policy, MS1:429

reason anyone fights it, 7:660

recommending any firm policy outgrowing from investigation and Comm Ev to Office of LRH, 0:586

relationship of policy, planning, programing, projects, orders, production and viability, 0:132–136

result of years of hard-won experience, 5:26

review of, 0:623

senior policy, 0:284

set by the wrong source leads to, MS1:249

size of org and, 0:115

source of, 0:111

SPs refuse to abide by, 1:993, 4:85

staff expected to know it or can look it up, 0:404

staff member is responsible for, 0:165

standard admin complicated only by inability of people to confront and do actions called for by, 0:59

stresses production and delivery of straight nonsquirrel product, 0:126

survival and, 0:124, 0:410

targets may not set aside policy, MS1:135

theory of, 0:123–131

thinking policy is wrong or is itself source of problem, handling, 0:240

third dynamic technology of standard administration, 7:486, MS3:466

policy, policies, *(cont.)*

throwing policy away, procedure for, 0:117

to be known it must exist and be findable, 0:410

top management cannot predict what policy will be set by its juniors, 0:134

trouble with it because one doesn't know it or can't or doesn't use it, 0:549

understanding policy, 0:130

unevaluated orders and, 7:726

unknown leads to, MS1:249

unknown policy or policy set by wrong source, effects of, 0:132

unusual solutions vs., 0:404–405, 0:432

using orders or policy to create problems, 0:476

using policy to stop action, 0:475

using policy to stop, handling for, 7:1247

very senior org policies, 0:241

we fail only to the degree we do not use Scientology training tech and policy, 7:854

What is policy? 0:114–122

what it is derived from, 0:117

when policy exists but is not made known, result, MS1:426

when random policy occurs, result, MS1:426

while policy is under adjustment we stick by known policy, 0:326

why most people have trouble with policy or admin, 7:329, MS3:309

why org won't flow traffic when policy is out or not formed, 0:324

wisdom of, 0:118

"What policy are you operating on?" 0:135

policy alterations, high crime, 1:1031

Policy One, definition, 1:189

political gain, justice used for, 1:962

political system(s), *see also* **communism; democracy; socialism,** 0:157–158, 0:298

politician(s),

boosted to power by opinion leaders, MS3:19

criminally insane politicians, 0:451

definition, MS3:19

difference between statesman and, MS3:21

economists seeking to gratify politicians or aggrandize some false philosophy, 0:314

involved in dishonest dealings, 0:458

politics, political, *see also* **government**

bringing about a great political reform, 0:630

freedom from, 0:159

future political slavery where we all have numbers and our guilt, 0:462

in Russia management went into politics, 0:506

politics, political, *(cont.)*

may be no part of any decision to train or process individuals, 0:159

mission of techno-space society is to subordinate individual and control him, by economic and political duress, 0:462

political philosophy can't audit, 0:158

post vs., 0:84

Scientology nonpolitical, nonideological, 7:1020

statements attacking any political entity are withdrawn, 0:159

where violence of political philosophies comes from, 0:277

who to select in an election, 0:83

workable formula used "instinctively" by most successful, practical political leaders, 0:630

polygraph, only registers at reality level of the being, 4:1109

poor, *see* **poverty**

popular(ity),

as criterion in selecting leader, 0:82–83

best defense is enormous increase in, MS3:159

Dept 18 makes Scientology popular or thing to do, 0:354

don't be so sensitive to popular reaction, 0:158

exec seeking, 0:315

how to create overwhelming popularity for an org, MS3:158

order issuer who has inadequate authority or popularity to get cooperation, 0:146

popular opinion is bank opinion, 0:158

population control, anatomy of, 6:87

population(s), *see also* **people**

brought almost to obliteration, 0:91

machines permitting increases in, 0:314

"mental health" used to control populations, 0:336

Port Captain's Office, basic action of, 6:624, MS3:40

position, *see also* **location; post**

accepting post or position and then not functioning as it, 0:572

holding position in space, 0:205

how we keep our posts, positions and functions straight, 0:195

person strengthened and made more confident in life by being given, 0:205

place or location, MS2:215

Positioning Era, The,

booklet, MS3:181

key reference on the technology of positioning, MS3:249

positioning,

against position, MS3:259

against strategy, MS3:107

by association, MS3:282

calls for certain exact steps in surveying, MS3:280

classification and, MS3:282

common use of in advertising, MS3:122

creativity is no longer enough, strategy is king, MS3:257

description, MS3:106

everybody trap, MS3:267

everything streams out from, MS3:205

examples of in public relations field, MS3:110

free ride trap and, MS3:265–266

glossary, MS3:275

human mind as a memory bank, MS3:255

image era and, MS3:253

importance of objectivity, MS3:272

importance of the long term and, MS3:269

importance of timing and, MS3:269

line-extension trap and, MS3:266–267

must create want for the product, MS3:283

new meaning for an old word, MS3:254

no-name trap and, MS3:264

number one strategy, MS3:271

number two strategy, MS3:271

one can achieve the apparency of familiarity when he associates it in the mind of the other with something with which the other is familiar, MS3:182

overcommunicated society and, MS3:251

philosophic theory, MS3:120, MS3:181

position definition, MS3:280

PR and, MS3:105

pressure to change and, MS3:268

product era and, MS3:252

product ladder and, MS3:257

rapid communication and comparison achieved by, MS3:182

repositioning the competitor, MS3:262

requires certain requisites, MS3:183

requires consistency to be successful, MS3:110

requisites, MS3:122

some questions to ask yourself, MS3:273

survey questions, MS3:280

ugly position and, MS3:260

well-known name trap and, MS3:267

well-known name trying to establish position in different field, MS3:114

when the positioning era had begun, MS3:250

possession(s), *see also* **equipment; materiel**

around orgs my possessions are given good care, 0:186

handling for persons who transfer, 3:389

standard of living and, 0:313

stock cards and, 0:186–187

that don't belong to anyone, result, 0:186

three kinds in Scientology organizations, 3:389

post(s), *see also* **hat**

ability to be shows up in post performances, 7:810

absence from post,

being long absent from post while senior exec, 0:471

decline and damage due to, 0:662

during appointed hours, 0:151

staff may not be absent from job to give or receive auditing during working hours, 0:168

without competent replacement, 0:267

adverse effect on post or in life, reason for, MS2:193

amount of explanation to put some personnel on post, 7:748

analyzing a, 0:81

any job or position in world could have its own hat, 0:199

any post, no matter how junior, has to be organized, 7:777

anything in org is your job if it lessens confusion if you do it, 0:83

apathy, overwhelm or despair with regard to one's post area, 0:311

appoint permanently or leave unfilled, 1:177

are not prizes, 0:234

assignment of, *see* posting

auditing a post, 0:263

Awareness Scale levels and, 0:95

backlogged or not in present time, 1:252

being causative on, 1:269

being good fellow is not solution to getting job done, 0:421

best job deserves fastest road to OT, 0:156

better left empty than filled by an incompetent, 0:229

better left vacant than filled by suboptimum personnel, 1:158

breaking down one's job into various parts when volume gets too high, 0:195

change always means a review of post, 1:182

change, Board of Investigation must be called first, 1:252

clay demoing one's post, 0:407

post(s), *(cont.)*

coming to cause over one's, 0:263

command intention and your, 0:256, 1:286

committing destructive acts on the, 0:459

comm lines of,

rounding up comm lines that relate to one's post, 0:578

straightening out comm lines of post, 0:442

complement and, 1:215

conditions, *see* conditions

confidence in life from being given a, 0:205

confronting one's post, 0:260

confusion and post not being held, 0:433

constancy on post and how it is developed, 7:759

creation of one's post, 0:230, 1:269

defending and retaining in employ anyone who does his, 0:151

degrading to lose one's, 0:205

disqualification for Registration or PE post, 2:412, 6:184

do your post (job),

and get dones, 0:260

by the book, 0:623

do your own job and do it well, 0:232, 0:623

how to hold, 0:83–84, 0:232

making it hard or impossible to do, 0:549

not being permitted, 0:623

too busy to, 0:19

well enough to put us all in clover, 0:170

doing another staff member's, 0:413

doing bad job just to be processed, 0:156

don't do other staff member's job for him, 0:233

dumping problems of your post on another's plate, 0:390

duplication of effort, 0:231

each person on a post must be cleared on that post, 7:743

eight hours of post work, 0:222

enturbulation and, 0:484

estimating what post's existing scene is, 0:294

exercising definition of OT over your post, 0:249

exists to keep org there and accomplish objective, 4:159

factors underlying why personnel fail on, MS1:398

failed posts and duties, 5:466

failing at job and starting again at Non-Existence, 0:562

failures, reason for most, 0:562

false terminal, 0:294

post(s), *(cont.)*

finding comm lines that apply to one's post and insisting one be put on those lines, 0:579

finding out what the raw materials of one's post are, 0:310

fixed terminals, 0:86, 7:479, MS2:195, MS2:300, MS3:459

frequent changes of, 0:280

getting the job done, 0:239

group types of actions into single posts, 0:88

handling of, 0:238–239, 0:578

hat, definition, 7:160

hat folder for newly created post, 1:267

HCO justice protects staff member's reputation and job, 0:477, 0:481, 0:502, 0:503

held as an emergency measure, 1:252

held in trust, 0:234

how to analyze, MS1:234

how to fill, 1:177

how to hold your, MS1:237

how unmanned post might get up to Danger, 0:657

I don't try to force job to be held by streams of instructions once failure is apparent, 0:239

if one knows tech of how to do something, can do it and uses it, he cannot be adverse effect of it, 0:268

if person is doing his job ethics is considered in, 0:502

if post is supposed to originate it does so, 0:392

importance of,
delivering expected service of post, 0:281
demanding and delivering high-level performance on every post, 0:258
having any job in org well done, 0:346
new person understanding purpose of, 1:178

in Scientology orgs, MS1:238

initiative on, failure to show, 0:662

inspection of post area, 0:308

irreducible minimum and, MS1:219

judgment and decision are needed in every, 0:82

keeping abreast of all post changes, 0:370

knowing where things are, 0:305, 0:569

knowledge or ignorance of one's post,
confusion, handling, 0:308
having to know more jobs than own, particularly jobs adjacent to own, 0:84
ignorant of what's going on or what policies cover his post, 0:405
person who doesn't know what he's doing, 0:306

laziness and not caring about doing job well, 0:255

leaving post, writing your hat, 0:198

post(s), *(cont.)*

leaving without turning over hat, 1:291

lessening confusion of, 0:83

letter writing or registration posts and "help," 5:389

line post, 0:86, 7:479, MS2:195, MS2:300, MS3:459

loss of post, effects of, 0:205

LRH, how he handles posts, 0:238–239, *see also* Hubbard, L. Ron

make your post real, 0:166

memory is inadequate in supervision of functions and, 0:195

misunderstood word, effect of, 0:39, 0:44, 0:47

misunderstoods and, 5:466

model assignments to be used, 1:212–214

moving off assigned post unreplaced, 0:265

musical chairs, *see* musical chairs

never noticing there is org there that has posts and functions, 0:383

new post,
beginning in Non-Existence, 0:561, 0:647
having write-ups to pass over to newly acquired assistants, 0:195
new employees and persons newly on post, 0:566
new occupant of old post losing post's lines or making some brand new order that applies to nothing real, 0:596
new post formula, 0:561
old post slumping under new appointee, 0:596
settling new person in a, 0:198
when one assumes awards and penalties of current condition of post, 0:566

ninety-day rule, 0:596

nobody can hold his job if he is being bypassed by senior, 0:592–593

not covered throws randomity into the org, 0:165

not doing one's post,
becoming an Ethics target and, 0:502
dev-t and, 0:434
no excuses for staff not doing their jobs, 0:522
only a few are dedicated to, 0:566
people who aren't doing their own post, 0:84, 0:432
person not doing his job or doing it poorly, handling, 0:166
person who accepts a post or position and then doesn't function as it, effect of, 0:572
what happens if person holding a post isn't really holding it, 0:433

not seeking each other's, 0:234

often have other tech to be studied, 0:223

once basic purpose known, only two things should be necessary, 7:600

post(s), *(cont.)*

only legal system of post transfers in an org, 1:77

on org board is stable point, 7:412

on post vs. off post, 0:151

on-the-job training, 0:440

operating at risk, 0:255

orders not necessary where post really being worn, 7:402, MS3:382

order vs. disorder, 0:305

org board and,
    every job has all depts of org board, 0:95
    if it isn't posted on org board, it hasn't been appointed, 0:414
    not reflecting reality of one's posts, 0:166
    post is stable point on org bd, 0:433
    using org bd to see where your post or job breaks down, 0:95

organization and, 0:88, 0:197, 0:596

organization becomes enturbulated when posts rapidly changed, 1:177

originating things that apply or are business of one's post, 0:392

overload of, can be traced to lack of org bd and lack of hats, MS1:207, MS1:416

permanent, must have approval of Senior PCO Int, 1:257

personality vs., 1:36

person is strengthened by giving him a, 0:205

persons not grooved in on new posts before being asked to act have high confusion level, MS2:186

person who, having accepted a post, does not know he is a certain assigned beingness is in Treason, 0:572

post purpose clearing, 0:136

Power Change Formula, 0:564–565

procedure for removal of person from post, 7:768

product(s), *see also* product
    every post has a product, 0:129, 0:295, 0:654
    importance of knowing what final product is for the, 0:288–289
    insisting post originate or do duties or furnish product or service of that post, 0:392
    supernumerary post has no product and is useless, 0:654

promotion, *see* promotion

protected by Ethics if you do your job, 0:502, 0:503

putting life in, 0:231

putting somebody on job and letting him get on with it, 0:88, 0:238, 0:239

Reach and Withdraw run on materials of one's, 0:310

reason for, 0:91, 0:92, 0:239

post(s), *(cont.)*

reasons for not doing, MS1:399

reason they exist, 4:160

rehabilitating person's ability to hold a, 0:205

removal from post requires Comm Ev, 0:523, 0:587

removal, steps for, 1:182

replacement(s),
    hat turnovers and, 0:266
    when to find another person for post, 0:239

responsibility for, 0:234, 0:690

result of a post that does not do its usual actions, 7:718

result of not functioning well on, MS2:134

resuming post one has left because it collapsed, 0:597

reward, satisfaction and pride as, 0:528

right to do your, 0:551

rules, what to do if they stop you from doing your job, 0:274

secret of holding post and being successful on job or in life, 0:562

security,
    by retaining a, 0:205
    feeling secure enough to do one's, 0:205
    keep Justice Codes for secure job, 0:487

self-determinism (definition) as it applies to, 0:230

service as essential ingredient of any post, 0:277

single-handing, *see* single-handing

solvency made by doing one's, 0:357

solving the problems of, 1:269

specific, microscopic orders on how job is to be done defeats purposes of, 0:230

stable datum for, 1:265

stable items vs. flow items in org, 0:106

stable point on org board, MS3:392

staff(s), *see also* staff
    are expected to do their posts, 0:523
    learn their job and do their job or they go, 0:406
    must be programed onto, not off, current post, 0:222
    posts are valuable to, 0:522
    who does good job gets lots of processing, 0:156

statistic(s), *see also* statistic
    every post has a, 0:502, 0:654
    if person's stat is up his job is secure, 0:239
    if someone was on post stats would be up, 0:505
    if stat goes down and stays down, handling, 0:239

steps to put someone on one, 1:181

post(s), *(cont.)*

strength and confidence increased by giving a person a, MS1:301, MS1:457

stuck with a piece of a post since time immemorial, 0:564

success and Method 2 Word Clearing, 5:467

success on a post, 0:263, 0:562, 0:680

supernumerary, 0:654

temporary, posted locally but does not have pay privileges until Senior PCO Int authorization, 1:257

thirty-day rule, 0:566

those who do not want their posts, 5:466

three factors in assigning a post, 7:498

to be happy get hatted and produce the actions of, 1:292

too overloaded will empty, 1:62

too underloaded will give trouble, 1:63

total effect of a, 0:230

trust and crusade, 0:85

turning over all equipment and supplies of post being vacated, 0:198

two types, 0:86

two-year rule, 0:198, 1:275

unhatted persons on post can become criminal, 0:206

unstabilizing people by asking them if they want different posts, 0:280

usual actions and, 0:257

vacating a post, 0:198, 1:275

visible record of, 1:271

vital to smooth delivery, 4:1194, 5:802

walking into boots of somebody who has left in disgrace, 0:565

we ask people if they want a, 1:206

we hold posts as competent teammates, 0:235

wearing LRH's admin hat for that post, 0:238

when apprentice is posted, 1:77

when one is considered to *also* be on any post he is vacating, 0:198

when to order full checkout of person on PLs applying to his post, 0:406

why full statement of function of every post is necessary, 0:231

writing up your, 0:193, 0:565

your post and life, 0:268

post hat folder, lack of, 0:220

post office,

can't find wrong addresses, 0:383

change of address card and, 0:360

registered mail and, 0:379

post purpose,

false data on, 0:577

hat must contain, 0:199

often glibly agreed with, 0:41

org board with purpose of each post stated, 0:415

Post Purpose Clearing,

additional steps, 5:478

admin, 5:462

auditor qualifications, 5:461

case folder and, 5:462

essential part of hatting, 5:461

establishes posts, MS1:253

full post clearing, 5:461

hat folder and, 5:462

instant purpose clearing, 5:461

is another way of saying "Get the policy that establishes this post and its duties known and understood," 0:136

organizational troubles due to post purposes uncleared, 0:40–41

organizing step, 5:479

pc requirements for, 5:462

Qual's object in getting this done, 5:479

steps for, 5:462

successful in, 5:478

two errors, remedies for, 5:478

postage,

careless use of, 3:381

cutting off all purchase orders except postage, communications and rent, 0:625

funds of an org and, 3:269

saving money on, 3:269

what careless use of can cause, 2:336

poster(s),

carries a message which extends even into social spheres, MS3:295

essence of, MS3:295

has an impact, single-glance message, MS3:296

have to be very bold, very commanding, MS3:295

must be such that people *want* to put it up just for itself, MS3:296

position and give a comparison of the object being advertised to something else to show where it fits in the scheme of things, MS3:296

purpose, MS3:295

you should not have to read the captions of a poster to know what it's all about, MS3:297

Poster in History, The, MS3:296

posting, *see also* **appointments; personnel**

acting appointment, demotion of, 0:487

always bend toward Registration, Tech Services and Promotion, 0:101

application for permanent status, MS1:472, MS2:309

best way to learn all about posting an org board, 1:62

by workload, MS1:209

cross divisions or departments, 1:63

decisions on, 0:217, 0:218, 0:373

demanding people get trained and hatted before, 0:261

depts and divs, sequence of posting, MS1:463

deputy appointment, *see* deputy

during State of Emergency, 0:621, 0:622

exec comm lines and appointments, 0:372

executives, qualifications for, MS1:471, MS2:307

filling posts by overload noted, 0:101

importance of properly posting people, 0:281

insecurely posted and insufficiently hatted, 0:206

is effective only if its work will be routed to it, 0:414

misassignments when Personnel people do not know all hats, 0:280

not insisting on posting Registrars, 0:302

of execs, 0:114, 0:373

org board and, 0:96, 0:106–107, 0:414

pc classification may be taken into account in, 0:168

permanent personnel, power restored to an org to do so locally, 1:260

Personnel or execs not exempted from filling posts, 0:198

procedure for appointments to post, 7:43

promotions and, 0:596

put somebody on job and let him get on with it, 0:88, 0:238, 0:239

requirements for permanent posting, MS1:472, MS2:309

settling new person in a post, 0:198

tech/admin ratio and, 0:95

temporary executive appointments to be passed by HCO, 7:42

thirty-day rule for new employees and persons newly on post, 0:566

using raw data alone in selecting and promoting personnel, 0:119

workload and, 1:61

wrong sequence of, will contract an org, MS1:464

postulate(s),

is close to thetan's identity, 0:326

LRH Comm sees that Ron's postulates stick, 0:356

observing that one's postulates worked, 0:633

problem is postulate–counter-postulate, 0:576

"pot," committee to have, to accumulate fines for anyone violating rules, MS3:433

potential trouble source(s) (PTS),

Accounts goes PTS through various tax and government supervision suppressions, 7:372, MS3:352

agents from SP groups lead to PTS staff, 7:374, MS3:354

any PTS condition can be handled, 2:113, 3:89, 4:155, 6:556, 7:863

auditing of, 1:874

auditing or training must not be continued over unhandled PTS situation, 1:746, 1:874, 5:111, 5:122, 5:438

bad tech and, 0:498

book *What Is Scientology?*, useful tool, 5:439

"Can We Ever Be Friends?" cassette and booklet, 5:440

chronically ill person, MS2:354

collection from, 3:190

complete handling consists of, 5:431, 5:441

Courts of Ethics or Comm Ev and, 4:356

definition, 1:873, 1:991, 4:83, MS1:460, MS2:251, MS2:354

Dept 3 spotting PTSes and handling, 0:348

disciplinary actions against, 0:493

disconnection and, 5:440

don't put PTS people on Reg lines, 6:393

dramatizes characteristic of suppressive in reaction to the suppression, MS2:354

Estate Branch listening to Town and Country Planning tends to go PTS, MS3:352, 7:372

failing to disconnect from an SP, suppressive act, 1:886

formula for exec to apply when feeling PTS, 0:420

good-roads, good-weather approach, 5:438

handling, 6:422

handling for person with false data, fill the vacuum, 5:440

has no business in PR, MS1:419

how PTS condition can hang one up at Doubt, 0:576, 5:439

if SP cannot easily be found, 5:438

indicators, 7:373, MS3:353

potential trouble source(s) (PTS), *(cont.)*

into valence of antagonistic person who definitely would NOT want the product, 7:445, 3:309

Legal goes PTS being in contact with SP courts and with SP or PTS attorney firms, 7:372, MS3:352

locating PTSes, 0:498

maintaining safe points and ability to detect, MS3:90

"manic-depressive" is the, 1:994, 4:86

may only be audited when, 1:998, 4:90

metered interview, 5:438

methods by which staff acting as org contact point in connection with suppressives can balk agents of SP groups, 7:373, MS3:353

moving the PTS person from effect to slight gentle cause, 5:438

not given the entheta dead file routing unless person refuses to disconnect or handle, 2:668

offenses relating to, 0:470

only way to goof handling, 1:968

organizing and, MS2:133

outline of steps for handling, 5:438

person from an SP group will eventually make an org or some part of it PTS, 7:374, MS3:354

person who acts most "PTS" is the one who has most harmed his fellows, 4:1110

potential trouble source, collect from, 1:764

pretended PTS, 4:1138

PTS person has no business in PR, MS3:14

PTS Rundown, 5:440, 6:422
  end phenomena of, 5:442
  rudiments never used as substitute, 5:441
  setup and end phenomena of, 5:441
  who it would not be done on, 5:441

PTS/SP Course and, 5:441

real reason for PTS condition, 0:515

recourse of, 1:887–888

recovery of and what will handle the condition, MS2:355

Reg lines and, 2:571

removals must be approved by the International Justice Chief, 1:257

robot to the suppressive, MS1:461, MS2:252, MS2:355

roller coaster = PTS, 5:35

routed to Ethics, 0:351

routing, 5:121

rundowns and handlings, not assigned to specific point on Grade Chart, 4:197

should be required to straighten up their lives before enrolling or signing up for processing or should be refused, 4:360

potential trouble source(s) (PTS), *(cont.)*

should never be let near book sales lines, 2:293–294, 6:257–258

SP or antagonistic person exists in present time, 5:442

spotting and handling, Department 3 promotional action, 1:40

Suppressed Person Rundown, 5:440

tech, getting ethics in and, 4:973

tech of locating suppressive, 5:431

technical fact, MS2:354

troubles, handling something over long-distance communication line, 7:438

truth blows the lie away, 5:440

use of Dead Files and, 1:977

valence of antagonistic person and, MS2:129

WANT the product vs., 7:445

wild rumors and, 0:498

will run "can't-haves" and "enforced overt-haves" on the org and its staff, MS1:460, MS2:251–252, MS2:354–355

poverty, poor,

org leaping from long-enduring poverty to high success, 0:59

orgs are poor which haven't been following my direct orders, 0:626

org staying tiny, working madly and staying poor, 0:408

out-ethics causing, 0:534

promotional actions vs., 0:356

why one area is poor and another opulent, 0:89

power, power condition,

abandoning it utterly is dangerous, 0:632

ability to hold position in space, 0:205, 0:216

accumulating power fast, 0:638

acquiring sphere of power, 0:632

all failures to remain a power's power are failures to contribute to the strength and longevity of the work, health and power of that power, 7:388

always push power in the direction of anyone on whose power you depend, 7:387

attaining power, done by consent or with help of opinion leaders, MS3:20

being or working under a, condition, 0:629
  chronic, 1:569
  definition, 1:595, 7:555
  difference between condition of Affluence and, 1:594, 7:553
  formula, 1:587, 7:556
  individual in, 7:555
  organization in, 7:555

power, power condition, *(cont.)*

defense of a power to critic, 0:632

delegating it, 0:638

deteriorates and becomes ineffective in exact ratio to the amount of pain or punishment drive it must use, 7:576

exerting combined power of all of us and all orgs as shoulder to shoulder effort, 0:273

expansion of power–factor, 0:640

failures to remain a power's power, MS3:368

getting some delegated to you, 0:632

having power as individuals due to processing, 0:484

if one lives life of command or one near to a command, one must accumulate power as fast as possible and delegate it as quickly, 7:385

individual in, 1:596

least complex actions being most powerful, 0:51

lessening group members sense of their own power, 0:604

lie, investing it with, 0:484

man is too aberrated to understand at least seven things about power, 7:386

motor, why it can generate power, 0:205

moving off point of power, 0:632

not using it, 0:634

observations regarding society, hatting and, MS1:301, MS1:457

of a thetan stems from his ability to hold a position in space, MS1:301, MS1:457

one cannot hold power and not use it, 7:380, MS3:360

organization in, 1:596

our lines are too powerful and direct, 0:493

ours is power of truth, 0:484

Power Change Violation Repair Formula, 1:581

power should not be lawless, 0:483

proportional to speed of particle flow, MS2:33

push power in direction of anyone on whose power you depend, 0:632, MS3:367

rapidity of particle flow alone determines power, 0:325, 0:432, 1:127, 6:204, 2:82

recoil of power in lines, 0:389

seven things about, 0:639–640, MS3:366

steady terminals and, MS1:298

totality of power is orderly progress, 1:735

use or delegate it or you won't have it long, 0:631

when the game or the show is over, there must be a new game or a new show, 7:386

when you have people, use them or they will soon become most unhappy and you won't have them anymore, 7:386, MS3:367

power, power condition, *(cont.)*

when you issue orders you are using force and, 0:247

why Scientology must have power and authority to bring total discipline or it will not survive, 0:660

Power Change condition, 0:596, 0:691

Power Change Formula, steps of, 0:564–565

Power Change Violation Repair Formula, steps, 0:651

Power Class VIII, Class VII becomes a, 5:844

Power condition,

Affluence and, 0:649, 0:650, 0:651

chronic Power, 0:657

definition and description, 0:643–644, 0:677

description, 0:637

erroneous and misleading data regarding, 0:642

expansion and, 0:644

expansion of the Power factor, 0:653

first law is don't disconnect, 0:564

if one follows formula he will stay there, 0:562

maintaining it, 0:644

must be determined by more than one week's worth of stats, 0:677

new appointee trying to start off in, 0:561

Normal trend maintained in high, high range, 0:677

penalties quadrupled for breaking a, 0:661

personal condition of, 0:657

person in Power works to maintain up stats, 0:657

Saint Hill and Flag Service Org attained Power, 0:657

seven points that must be applied or org won't be in Power for long, 0:653

steps (first dynamic), 0:564

steps (third dynamic), 0:631, 0:640

total abundance and, 0:644

totality of Power is orderly progress, 0:482

violation of,
not realizing one has power, 0:635
opinion leaders and, MS3:20

vital data concerning, 0:642

what will put org in Power, 0:206

why one cannot hold power and not use it, 0:635

writing up your whole post during a, 0:564

power of choice, senior to responsibility, 1:727

Power Process(es)(ing),

card to wear, 4:898

continues until preclear is Second Stage Release or Second Stage Released OT, 4:1065

Power Process(es)(ing), *(cont.)*

illegal use of, 4:891

memorandum of agreement, 4:893

pc audited illegally on, 4:885

raw meat and, 4:1066, 5:746

seeking off-line advice on, crime, 5:586, 4:1173

the 20% handled by, 1:971

Third Stage Release, 4:901

unusual case and, 5:735

use of,

must have interned at Saint Hill, 4:885

restricted to Class VIIs, 4:899

when completed, 5:745

power push, against a senior, 0:471

PR, *see* **public relations**

practical,

gives the drills, 4:334

goes through the simple motions, 4:332

training section, definition, 4:584

Practical Examiner, purpose, 4:322

Practical Section, any practicing done in, 4:674

Practical Supervisor, 4:359, 4:601

practice, procedure for starting a successful practice, 6:681

practitioner(s), *see* **field auditor**

PR area control,

build on well-researched, surveyed, solid gradient, MS3:90

definition, MS3:40

makes point safe for production activity before production occurs, MS3:89

measured by counting up points one is not controlling and the points one IS controlling, MS3:40

naming and acceptability, MS3:160

of org should be built up to point where attacks rebuffed, MS3:158

safe pointing and, optimum action, MS3:90

SP/PTS tech is basic tool of, MS3:91

technology of, MS3:40

precision, without this they drown, MS1:365

preclear(s), pc(s), *see also* **being; case; individual; people; thetan**

acceptance for processing, 4:242, 4:840, 4:848, 4:962

ARC broken, 0:493

assignments must be such as to minimize auditor change, 4:250

attained a grade of release, not further run, 4:1085

audit with Dianetics and Scientology until case is handled, 4:930, 5:686

preclear(s), pc(s), *(cont.)*

audited at cause, 0:263

backlog,

handling, 0:100

must be avoided, 4:386

bad tech makes it almost impossible to get pcs or students in, 0:19

best way to really handle, 4:15

blown,

four reasons for most pc blows, 4:270, 6:551

Free Auditing Check and, 4:271, 6:552

handling of, 4:270, 6:551

ordered to Case Cracking Section, 5:734

recovery of is of interest to ARC Break Reges and Tours personnel, 4:269, 6:550

remedy for invalidation of case or gains, 4:270, 6:551

classification designed to get maximum case gain for, 7:930

classification of, 4:171, 4:172

collected up by Tech Services, never the auditor, 4:207

D of P,

cannot take pcs, 0:169, 0:703

has no right to direct Reg in signing up pcs, 4:294

may not refuse pcs because not enough auditors, 4:962

seeing that pcs get gains, 0:409

stays in comm with all who have been audited in the HGC, 4:960

duties regarding pcs, 4:961

declares, 5:689

deep down knows whether he has made it or not, 4:234, 6:305

defined, 2:162, 4:64, 6:187

deliver means good case gains to pcs and students, 0:282

don't correct pc who needs no correction, 5:675

drive in as many as possible, 0:344

enroll them in Academy, 5:836

entering too high into processes, 5:329, 4:163

ethics and, 0:491–492, 1:761, 7:305

actions which can be taken on, 5:109

ethics situations found in session, handling, 1:851

no direct routing of preclears to the Ethics Officer except through Qual Div and Review, 5:118

not sent to Ethics for withholds gotten off in session, 5:587

evening work, 4:837

examples of not handling, 2:440, 4:927, 5:683

failure to handle results in, 4:927, 5:683

Free Scientology Center is source of, 4:683

preclear(s), pc(s), *(cont.)*

gets well in direct ratio to ability to confront anatomy of life, mind and physical universe, 4:305

give processing called for at pc's level, 0:282

goofed-up, hard pcs sent to larger org, 0:101–102

gradation is not by certification but by logbook, 4:177

grade obtained by flattening process of that level, 4:177

grounds on which auditor may refuse to process, 4:297

handling to obtain uniformly spectacular wins, 4:429

heavy traffic warning about lots of students or pcs coming up, 0:380

HGC preclear can be two-way commed by the Tech Sec, 4:392

how real gains for preclear are attained, 4:28

if doesn't obtain reality on gains beyond expectation, auditing not done in first place or pc on drugs or ill, 4:915

illegal pcs, 6:407
   definition, 2:581
   handling of, 2:582

information sheet, when used, 5:747

is not staff member in ethics sense of word, 0:492

key question for, 6:823

knows he made something, 5:689

lacking training do not advance well, 4:163, 5:329

line to sign up, 4:848

long-term illness, handling, 5:623

"lost time" in auditing, 5:742

may be transferred, demoted in level or grade by Court of Ethics, 4:355

may not be audited above his or her class, 4:163, 5:329

may not be postponed for lack of auditors, 4:250

may not be sent to D of P without having been signed up fully, 2:500

may not be suspended or dismissed for 2D activities, 4:479

mission which rips off, responsible for, 5:433

must be registered by Registrar whether charge is made or not, 2:479, 3:141, 4:213

must be sold processing, 2:514

new,
   conditions of, 4:912
   handling for troubles with, 4:912
   invoice to get audited, 4:1136

no gain, call them back, 4:838

preclear(s), pc(s), *(cont.)*

none may be audited above his or her grade, 4:174

no staff to audit private pcs, 0:165, 0:170

not sent to Ethics for withholds gotten off in session, 4:1174

OCA plots 10 traits of pc's personality, 4:236

offenses against pcs, 0:468

one-day wait for Tech pc is too long, 2:445

only reasons a pc is critical, 4:1081, 5:672

ordering students and, 0:491

ordering to Review, 1:744, 5:109

org major product, satisfied preclear, 4:145

passing org pcs to outside auditors for private commission, 0:471

penalty for missions ripping off org pcs, 6:770, 4:222

physically ill, 5:622

private paying pcs not permitted staff, 4:1247

procedure for sending Dianetic pc to doctor, 4:920, 6:439

product of an org is well-taught students and thoroughly audited pcs, 4:15

professional pc sitting around making do-less motions, 0:528

promotional actions of org regarding, 0:350

promotion factor when satisfied, 3:101

real gains attained with lots of auditing, 5:99

real reason C/S is there, 4:1135

rebates and, 3:160

receiving favors or gifts from, 0:410

recourse and, 0:491–492

registered, grounds on which D of P may refuse, 4:297

Registrar has no authority to assign auditors or auditing rooms to preclears, 2:480

regulations for, 4:351, 5:841

release of, from processing, 4:242

rented quarters, responsibility for, 0:172

requirements for Post Purpose Clearing, 5:462

return of money to dissatisfied pc, 0:410

routine action of Ethics on, 4:355

routing pcs recommended to Ethics and also to Declare?, 5:119

scale of preference in assignment of auditor and preferential scheduling, 2:520–521

scheduling of, 4:252

standard promotion to, if not also auditors, 5:347

subject to conditions orders from their auditors, 0:660

takes OCA to give information to auditor, C/S and D of P, 4:236

preclear(s), pc(s), *(cont.)*

testing of, 4:227

transferred or demoted in grade by Court of Ethics, 0:492

uncorrected error in auditor is perpetuated on every pc auditor audits, 0:12

undergoing review subject to Ethics Codes, 4:352, 5:842

unsuccessful practice to refer them to field auditors, 2:385, 6:685

upset, inexpert handling of Security Checking, 4:1167

vitamin E and processing, 5:619

walking advertisements for HGC and Scientology, 0:351

wanting next level of auditing, 0:32

what our best sources have been of pcs, 6:639

when pc won't run, 1:625

when signing up more preclears than students org will go broke or be poor, 4:387

when total used hours approaches hours paid, handling, 4:263

where there's pc to be processed, see that it's done, 0:273

where they felt no gain occurred, 5:729

while under actual training for the next class, 4:165, 5:331

who blow their auditing, traced to missed withholds, 4:1196, 5:615

who hasn't made it, handling, 5:98–99

who has run out of hours, auditor *not* to continue auditing, 4:263

who is routed onto CCRD, 4:999

who seek to resign or leave sessions and refuse to return, 1:989

who want to be pcs, handling, 5:838

who won't run, 5:586, 4:1173

predict(ion),

ability to, MS1:70

button that is usually out in personnel handling, MS1:454

can't predict wog court decision, 0:327

catastrophe occurs by lack of, 0:427

consequences, prediction of, 0:140

data analysis and, MS1:69

exec who can't predict, 0:266

from data is essential part of evaluation, MS1:155

missing ideal scene and, MS1:70

no top management can predict what policy will be set by its juniors, 0:134

org pattern and, 0:327

situation analysis and, MS1:69

viability and, MS1:70

Preclear Route, 4:175, 4:786

preference, scale of, in assignment of auditor and preferential scheduling, 2:520–521

pregnancy, auditing and, 2:438

prejudice, PR and, MS3:19

premises,

appearance, *see* appearance

cleanliness of, 6:594

eviction of person from, 0:478

org image and, 6:606, MS3:140

prepayment(s),

used for books, 3:207

where students and pcs sometimes elect to use advance paid credit on their accounts to buy books or meters, handling, 2:346

prerequisite,

auditor training, 4:659

for New Hubbard Solo Auditor's Course Part 1, 4:663

presentation,

artistic presentation always succeeds to the degree that it is done *well,* 2:264

HCO given authority and responsibility for, 7:1284

money lost with poor presentation, 2:174, 7:1284

motto: get the best, 2:174, 7:1284

office and quarters, 7:833

quality of, 2:174, 7:1284

what HCO is given authority and responsibility for, 2:174

whole world of the arts is directly opposed to the philosophy of the businessman or manufacturer, 2:263

presents, received by staff, 1:729

present time,

applying conditions in present time without being hung up in past failures, 0:668

getting someone located in his present time environment, 0:569

present time problem(s), 0:417

Review mistaking a PTP for an ARC break, 5:38

suppressives are in a continual, 1:1010

Presession Processes, handle help, control, communication factor and interest factor, 6:174

press, *see also* **press release; public relations**

agent, definition, MS3:132

press, *(cont.)*
    agentry,
        basic rules of, MS3:134
        definition, MS3:132
        is primary stage of PR, MS3:134
        PROs and, MS3:167
        use of in forwarding an image, MS3:134
    bad press is no catastrophe, MS3:125
    bad, unprepared for press conferences and, MS3:94
    follows lead of the attacker, MS3:138
    freedom of, 0:68
    give them nothing that can be misunderstood, 6:591, 7:1042
    handling press, 0:354
    handling should be entrusted to only one person in org, 6:591, 7:1042
    how to get good press, MS3:130
    manufacture of "a dangerous environment," 7:1039
    points for Scientologists to keep in mind in communicating to, MS3:124
    policy regarding, 0:153, 0:160
    qualities of person chosen to handle press, 6:591, 7:1042
    Receptionist handling of comm from, 6:591, 7:1042
    relations with, 6:591, 7:1042
    takes series of serious blunders to bring about press smear campaign, 0:622
    theta press is hardest to get, MS3:129
    will not print anything good—only bad, 6:591, 7:1042
    word of mouth vs., 0:337, MS3:125
press book,
    clipping book vs., MS3:98
    press conferences and, MS3:95
    pro PR never operates without, MS3:96
    PR without one liable to miss selling person with key to the door, MS3:97
    use of, MS3:97
    what is included in a, MS3:96
press conference,
    begins with adherence to preparation points, MS3:95
    minimum essentials of, MS3:94
    not prepared for can be disaster, MS3:94
    untrained, undrilled PR and, MS3:95
Press Relations Officer, *only* one to handle press or journalist comm of any kind, 6:591, 7:1042
press release, *see also* **press**
    always attack, never defend or deny, 6:599, 7:1043
    should always contain some factor of endurance, 6:599

press release, *(cont.)*
    should be on one subject only, 6:599
    type of message, 6:601
pressure,
    group internal pressure determines which exchange condition comes into play, 0:318
    I carry a *little* more pressure on an org than it can really accomplish, 0:594
press work, definition, MS3:194
pretended PTS(ness), 4:1138
    actively committing suppressive actions while pretending to be PTS, 1:1046
    handling of, 1:1046
    sequence of their actions, 1:1045–1046
pretense, *see also* **false report; lie**
    pretended busyness, indicator of, 0:407
prices, pricing, 0:337, *see also* **cost; discounts**
    anyone covertly reducing prices is guilty of suppressing an org, which is a high crime, 3:155
    can sell people courses and intensives for high prices when they're sure of what they're buying, 2:401
    definition, MS1:275
    Executive Council and, 0:355
    hold the prices set, 2:430
    how quoting new people high prices for training and processing can dismay them, 6:157
    lowered due to new discoveries, 6:368
    memberships and, 6:368
    merchandising by advertising that prices are going up soon is forbidden, 3:155
    policies and, 3:155, 2:429
    quoting people high prices for training or processing on their first contact, 2:401
    secret price cuts by separate orgs and discounts can undermine all financial planning and lay in an engram that destroys all expansion, 2:429
    sliding scale and, 2:458, 3:178
    upper org and, 2:457, 3:177
    what the engram in orgs was, 3:154
price cutatives,
    forbidden, MS1:212
    types of, MS1:212
price engram,
    prices were covertly reduced and new prices thus many times the old, 2:430
pride,
    of workmanship is pride in one's own product, 0:295
    overts of omission that kill any, 0:255
    real villains have no, 1:836
    reward of pride in doing a job well, 0:528

Primary Rundown, M8 Word Clearing and, 4:496

primary target(s), *see also* **target; individual target types by name**

definition, MS2:431, MS2:437

exec has to know target policies and be able to write them up, particularly the primary targets, 0:88

inspect and survey and gather data and set operating and primary targets before you set production targets, MS2:434

normal reason for down statistics on production is vanishment of, MS2:434

present time orders vs., 0:425

printing,

biggest dissemination activity in the world, 2:177

getting promotional pieces printed, 0:348

people buy Scientology, not printing, 2:177

saving money on printing bills, 3:270

savings in printing bills can often be effected by as simple a thing as changing the magazine or mailing piece to a more standard size, 2:177

stress should be on content, not format, and then the format should be made as good as possible within available funds, 2:177, 3:270

what persons can originate copy for printing, 2:172, 7:1282

priority, preclear who deserves, 0:506

private practice, using org position to build up a, 0:471

privilege(s),

execs must insist upon privileges and responsibilities of their posts, 0:582

suspended in State of Emergency, 0:622

prizes, contests and, 0:234

PRO, *see also* **public relations; Public Relations Officer**

bad or inaccurate statements of debt can ruin your PRO with a customer, 3:69

billing debtors and paying creditors have high PRO value to an org, 3:70

definition, 3:69

way to have none is to have no money, 3:70

when you "PRO" something, you visit, write, handle it so as to enhance and improve your public image, 3:69

PRO area control, keeping area handled so org is well thought of, 0:99

Probationary, status 0:487, 1:251

problem(s), *see also* **situation; trouble**

any problem that does not solve, MS1:293, MS1:452

basic problem of management, 0:242

committing a, 1:910

completed staff work and, 0:390, 0:391, 0:392

contraction making more problems than expansion, 0:131

Court of Ethics or Committee of Evidence for perpetuating, 1:920

creating in the implementation of orders, 1:920

definition, 0:576

despatches forwarding unhandled problems, 0:397

discover what effort one is trying to avoid, 1:167

everyone on Earth has, 0:153

examples in lines, hats and personnel, MS1:453

helping people to come up to handling their, 0:153

how to solve, 0:37

indecision and, 0:576

nonconfront and, 0:37–38

one has to recognize what it is, MS1:452

optimum solution to, 0:451, 0:458, 1:486

order or policy used to create, 1:920

org board is standard solution to continuing and recurring problems, 0:62

people who present problems, 0:427

policy regarding problems, 0:240–243

presenting problems, 0:240, 0:427

primary solution to all, 0:242

processing and, 0:153

PTS person is stuck in a, 0:573

solutions and, 0:62, 0:242, 0:451, 0:458

solution which becomes a, 1:910

solved by removing elements that make them or instituting a program, 7:364, MS3:344

source of presented problem usually won't use presented solution, 0:427

test of whether or not right one found, MS1:453

to solve a problem one must see what is causing it, 0:242

to solve one has to, MS1:293

to take apart a problem requires only to establish what one could not or would not confront, 4:370

unhandled by dept or post receiving them causing confusion, 0:230

what a problem is, 1:605

where you have a personnel who cannot perceive the causes of things, you will have a continual spinning mess, 7:675

Problems of Work, The,

advertisement, 6:253

check out staff on, 7:432, MS2:226, MS3:412

confusion and stable datum covered in, 0:65, 0:200, 0:433

routing know-how and, 0:390

Problems Processes, resolution of the case of suppressive person, 1:996, 4:88

Problems Release, ability gained, 4:190

procedure(s),

not organized or too complex to be useful, 0:426

there is point where routes and exact procedures become unworkable, 0:82

process(es)(ed), *see also* **auditing; auditor**

allowed, in HGC, 4:1056

altered to "fit" some tough case will cease to work on standard cases when so altered, 1:1002, 4:342

auditor may not use processes on anyone above their grade, 4:174

cutative, 5:22

deleting processes or failing to use all processes for a level, 0:15

each has its basic auditing, technique and case analysis for that class, 4:165

going wrong, what it means, 4:1174, 5:587

hearing about does not qualify for use, 4:899

Help, Control, Communication, Interest and, 6:176

high fee maintained to deter pcs while shunting them into Academy, 5:836

introduction of mini list of processes for auditing requirements at each level, 4:420

"It didn't work," handling, 0:10–11

not learning why processes are used or when to use them, 0:65

squirrel, results of on staff and field, 5:652

that will be dreamed up by students or anyone around your course, 4:342

to be studied and drilled by auditor before he runs them, 4:657

to be used, 4:1052

used on degraded beings, MS3:369

use of above classification, 4:1053

using processes above class of org, 0:95

valid, 4:1053

who can be, 5:730

you can audit, 6:723

processing, *see also* **auditing; auditor; Hubbard Guidance Center**

ability potential enormously increased by, MS2:66

acceptance of preclears for, 4:242

certain persons are ineligible for, 5:730

charges on, 7:834

clarification of "part-time" auditor, 4:78, 6:200

Clay Table Administration Processing, 1:182

Comm Ev offense for Case Supervisor or auditor to C/S or accept for processing any pc who is terminally ill or has an institutional history, 5:761

crime, 4:933

definition of, 4:371, 4:918

ethics became a problem in orgs when quickie auditing began, 1:800–801, 6:527

ethics crimes, 5:248

five hours of, 4:1064

Founding Scientologist certificate and, 4:177

HGCs may offer only what their staff auditors can deliver, 4:77, 6:199

impeded or interrupted by 2D activities, recourse, 4:479

income source, 2:386, 3:101

institutional cases, 1:798

invoicing people ordered to, 2:483

is an award, 1:744, 5:109

may never be given away, MS1:212

no HGC may "occasionally" employ auditors, 2:205, 4:77, 6:199

no org has to accept anyone it doesn't want to, 5:743

no person who is insane, has institutional background or is chronically ill may be accepted for processing by the HGC, 2:402

no substitute for, 4:301

not done without invoice, 4:215, 6:383

of staff as means to improve org, 5:580

permitting without proper invoice, result, 4:216, 6:384

persons who are ineligible for, 4:306, 4:962

poor, restimulates bypassed charge, 4:933

potential trouble sources and, 1:746, 5:111

priorities for staff cases, 1:801–802, 6:527

processes used on degraded beings, 7:389

quoting people high prices for training or processing on their first contact, 2:401

regulations for, 4:350

release of preclears from, 4:242

removes all barriers eventually, MS2:66

rules of, apply to class not certificate, 4:179

scheduling of, 4:242

Secretaries and, 1:739

processing, *(cont.)*

self-determinism and acceptance for, 4:323

shock cases, 1:798

sold on basis of estimate to Clear, 4:839

staff may not be ordered to training or processing as a disciplinary measure, 5:576, 6:200

staff members may not audit outside pcs or receive money for auditing students or pcs, 2:206, 4:78, 5:387

staff status and eligibility for, 1:240, 3:191

staff who audit 8 hours private, report to HCO, 1:619

students recommended to, 4:308

vitamin E and, 5:619

who can be processed, 4:306

who may order staff to, 5:555

why recognizing the source of an aberration "blows" it, makes it vanish, 4:370

Processing Administrator,

duties of, 4:241

purpose of, 4:241

routing duties of, 4:245

schedule, 4:242

process completion, definition of, 4:640

Process S2, definition, 5:545

procurement,

any letters are better than no letters, 2:612

basic pattern for all org procurement, 2:50, 6:147

every person in PrR, including the typist, should be kept advised of exact advances and successes achieved in Technical Division, 2:619

from HAS you procure for Ext HPA or HPA, 6:365

from PE you procure for Comm Course/HAS Co-audit, 6:365

gradient scale of personnel procurement, 2:50, 6:147

how to procure people, 2:601

laws of letter writing, 2:601

letters handling ARC breaks and handling friendly lines to increase them, 2:601

letters, procedure for handling, 2:612

procedure to handle students, 2:601

Registrar responsibility for, 4:834

sample procurement letters, 2:603

solved, but like learning to be an auditor, this one takes know-how, 6:282

technical personnel line for, 1:157

procurement letters, to be written by staff auditors without pcs for the week, 4:669

prod–org system,

handle backlogs and omissions in products, MS1:355

reconciliation with Esto system, 7:821

when developed, 7:821

produce,

at personal level one must produce in excess of his standard of living, MS2:284

definition, MS2:5

if you only produce and never organize, MS2:131, 7:447

producer(s),

basic step of administration, 7:408–409, MS3:388,

ignoring nonproducers, overt product makers and real producers, 0:316

justice protecting producers, 0:518

maintaining sanity of scene in which he is operating, 0:298

supporting and giving goodwill to producer of product, 0:296

VFP of, 0:298

product(s)(es), *see also* **production; result; subproduct; valuable final product**

aberration vs., 0:39

ability to name, 3:307, 7:443, MS2:127, MS3:423

able to get one's product out with no wasted motion or stops, 0:305

always suspect when stats are down or lines tangle, MS2:79

analysis of organization by, 0:290

an org properly cleared runs, produces VFPs in high volume and quality, MS2:81

anything which delays or puts it on wait is enemy, 0:275

auditing and, 0:39

bad or nonexistent, reason for, 0:294–295

basis of a standard of living, MS1:351, MS2:285, MS2:368

biggest omission is not clearing products at all, MS2:79

can be represented as a, MS1:202

clay demoing steps one takes to get out, 0:309

come from work truly done, 0:314

confusion vs., 0:106, 0:308

correction of org's product, 0:289

defines a hat, 1:151

definition, MS2:5, MS2:146

desired product that will also be desired by others, 0:288

dev-t and lack of, MS1:240

product(s)(es), *(cont.)*

difference between sane and insane is, 0:252

don't ever happen by themselves, 7:817

EP of debug tech and, MS2:152

establish product then find out what to do to achieve it, 0:287

estimating what post's existing scene is by looking at its, 0:294

Esto has to know how to clear up, MS2:28

every hat has a, MS1:202, MS1:411

every post has a product, 1:566, 7:395, MS3:375, 0:129, 0:199, 0:295, 0:646

exchange and, 0:296, 0:300, 0:313, 0:317, 0:443, 0:528

executive names it, wants it, gets it, gets it wanted, gets in the exchange for it, MS2:60, MS2:242

expansion and, 0:124–125, 0:655

factors which govern, MS1:226

final product, 0:288, 0:292–293, 0:294, *see also* valuable final product

final products,
breaking them down, MS1:223
org, combined product of, MS1:242

fixation on DO without any product in view, 0:288

flubby and poor product, 0:294

four basic products necessary to a production activity, 0:290

four types of, MS1:226, MS1:357

getting one's products out, 0:562

government, products of, 0:252

handling for poor, MS1:218

having a real product that one does well brings about an almost no-ceiling condition, 7:520

hope of a, 0:298

how to handle factors that prevent completion of, MS2:133

if not occurring, ability to name the product is probably missing, 3:307

if Product Clearing wasn't good, handling, MS2:78

insane, product of, 0:252

insisting post furnish product or service of that post, 0:392

major use of subproduct lists and, 7:828

misunderstoods vs., 0:39

name it, want it, get it, 7:816

nation expanding demand for its, 0:125

no product,
bureaucracies and, 0:288
causes of, 0:39, 0:294–295, 0:300, 0:307
dev-t from people who have no, 0:288

product(s)(es), *(cont.)*

long-term situation of no or few products combined with state of disorder, handling, 0:311

not knowing one's product, 0:308

of your post being acceptable to others and command, 0:256

one has to actually WANT the product he is asking for, 3:309, MS2:129, MS3:425

one has to spend some time organizing in many different ways, 7:447, MS2:131, MS3:427

organize back from produced product, 0:28, 0:298

org board and, 0:108

Org Products 1–4, 0:287

org's products, 0:15, 0:294

overall product of a division determines the hat of the divisional officer, 7:796

overt product, *see* overt product

personal sense of order is essential in getting out products, 0:305

persons may SAY they want but this is just "PR," 3:309, MS3:425

planning by, 0:287

poor final products produced by, MS1:242

PR and workability and usefulness of product, 6:608

preventing blunting of demand for, 0:125

pride in one's, 0:295

push, debug, drive, only way you ever get a product, 7:816

quality,
ethics system ensures quality of product, 0:126
low-quality product, reason for, 0:294–295
must be adequate to satisfy those requiring and paying for production, 0:289
of org boards, MS1:221
products and the ceiling of the org, 7:520
viability, product and, 0:290

results of papers straight, reports neat, yet preclear not guided through Clear, 4:55

sane, product of, 0:252

Scientology, ultimate product of, 0:131

sensible org board must count the products and develop hats to attain them, MS1:223

something must flow out to have a, MS1:194

squirrel is never able to duplicate our, 0:125

staff who don't know what one is, and orders, MS2:27

standard of living and, 0:313

start from biggest product of org and work back to person's, MS2:31

statistics and, 0:199, 0:696, *see also* statistic

subproducts and, 0:295, 0:696

product(s)(es), *(cont.)*

there is always a product for any scene, MS1:106

Thetan–Mind–Body–Product system, 0:128, 0:654

three major factors that govern every, 0:290

to have product something must flow out, 0:106

unacceptable product, most common cause of, 0:39

valuable exchangeable product, 0:296, *see also* valuable final product

viability and, 0:290, 0:292

WANT the product included in examination of reasons why person or org isn't producing, 3:309, 7:445, MS3:425

when product vanishes, so does the org, 0:15

when you are getting no product, look for the misunderstood word, MS2:132

where no real or valuable production occurring, one has to ask the question does the product officer really WANT the product he is demanding, 3:309

Whys traced back from absence, lack of volume or quality of, MS2:22

workability and usefulness of and PR, MS3:142

working out changes desired for each particle to make a, 0:108

wrong product for a post knocks the staff member's hat off, MS2:74

wrong product, handling, 0:308

you can't ask for a number; you can ask for a something, MS1:322

supernumerary post or part of org and, 0:654

things that don't exist can have, 0:646

Product Clearing, *see also* **Long Form Product Clearing; Short Form Product Clearing,**

best done after Word Clearing No. 1, MS2:57

Esto who can use a meter and Method 4 W/Cing and knows clay demoing can do, MS2:57

form for, MS2:49

quickie, hatting not possible over, MS2:31

repair of, MS2:57

Short Form, procedure, MS2:29

product conference,

functions, MS2:12

success depends upon, MS2:12

production, produce, producing, productive, *see also* **administrative; delivery; product; result**

abundance of production, 0:318, 0:644, 0:650

accomplished by numerous contributions of thought or effort, 0:277

actions to increase, and decrease volume handled, 7:805

production, *(cont.)*

activity of *providing* a product or service, 2:66

area out-morale because it is low, MS3:58, MS3:233

area producing VFPs is entitled to support, 0:297

basic reason behind persons who cannot produce, 1:819

basis of morale, 7:433, 7:815, MS2:28, MS2:153, MS2:227, MS3:413

battle plans and, 0:706

calculating cash value of every piece of work done, 0:314

competent use of target in battle plans and, 7:460, MS2:446, MS3:440

completed cycles of action and, 0:695

computers and, MS2:453

conditions of exchange and, 0:317–318

consumption vs., MS1:61

cycle of production, 0:95

daily stat graph for one's, 0:689

debugging, first step is to demand production, MS2:146

definition, MS1:63, MS1:198, MS1:318, MS2:266

depends on other prior targets being kept in, MS2:434

depression vs., 0:507

dev-t vs., 0:391

disorderliness vs., 0:306

Emergency Formula and, 0:563

establishing something that produces, 0:290

Ethics Officer making it safe so production can occur, 0:518

ethics substituted as an effort to get up, MS1:200

every div is production unit, 0:502

exchange and consumption vs., 7:435, MS3:415

exchange,

not producing something valuable enough to interchange, 0:297, 0:298

one has to produce something to exchange for money, 0:528

producing things of real value which will exchange for value, 0:442

exec getting people to, 0:280

exercise in promotion–production, 2:66

first step in establishing anything is valuable production and income, 1:66

four basic products necessary to production activity, 0:290

general Why of inactivity or nonproduction, MS2:85

getting person producing what he is supposed to

production, *(cont.)*

getting show on road, 0:502

hatting and, 0:440

healthy, producing org, symptom of, 0:394

HE&R is primary barrier to, MS3:56, MS3:231

if not occurring, ability to name the product is probably missing, 7:443, MS2:127, MS3:423

if you only produce and never organize, MS3:427

immediate organization for, MS2:441

improvements occur when there is a good org board also well known, 7:797

in training is the demonstration of competence, 4:436

income and, 0:502

increase of production,
each morning set stat ceiling, a bit higher than earlier highest day's output, 0:689
organizing increases production, 0:297
way to increase production, 0:280

knowledge of basics essential to, 0:311, MS1:349, MS2:183

list of different products involved in, 0:290

machines assisting in, 0:314

misunderstoods vs., 0:39

monetarist's answer to, 0:315

morale,
basis of morale is production, 0:277, 0:299, 0:394, 4:436
when person becomes productive his morale improves, 0:529–530

musical chairs vs., 0:280

must be adequate to promotion to be solvent and ethical, 1:309

nonproduction,
busyness not resulting in real production, 0:303
capitalism is economics of living by, 0:508
dev-t destroys real production while making org seem frantically busy, 0:391
due to nonexistent targeting, 0:425
how to tie up whole org and produce nothing, 0:386
more and more people producing less and less while working harder and harder, 0:387
nonproductive area, handling, 0:312, 0:439
no real production in condition of Confusion, 0:568
not producing what is needed and wanted, 0:581
org appearing busy and overworked while producing little, 0:441
out-basics and disorderliness cuts production down to nothing, 0:307
out-ethics and, 0:526

production, *(cont.)*

person who doesn't produce becomes mentally or physically ill, 0:528

reward nonproduction, penalize production and you get nonproduction, 0:504, 0:506

survival vs., 0:314

unhattedness and, 0:527

working frantically, totally exhausted and yet producing nothing of value, reason, 0:439

obtaining production, 0:388

of org is total of its individual staff members, 0:502

one must produce in excess of his standard of living, MS1:350

only sound measure of, MS1:55

orderliness in an area is essential to, MS2:183, 0:311

organization vs., MS2:281, MS2:312

organize back from produced product, 0:288, 0:289

organize vs., MS1:376

org board and production, 0:95

out-basics and disorderliness cuts production down, MS1:344

out-morale and low, MS3:37

pay in proportion to what one produces, 0:689

personal production of VFPs for the group and one's standard of living are intimately related, MS2:287

Personnel goofs and, 0:280

primary barrier to, MS3:37

producing in abundance, 0:318, 0:644, 0:650

product officer and, 0:695

production peak, 0:644

programing out production actions to be taken in downstat areas, 0:648

promotion adequate to production must be made to be solvent or ethical, 2:66

quantity and quality of product produced must be satisfactory, 0:289

quicksilver personnel scene vs., 0:266

quota, *see* quota

real or valuable production occurring, one has to ask the question, 7:445, MS3:425

relationship of policy, planning, programing, projects, orders, production and viability, 0:132–136

repairing or correcting that which is produced, 0:290

represented by GDSes and VFPs, MS2:5

responsibility for, 0:690

result of an individual who does not produce, MS2:288

rewarding production, 0:504

production, *(cont.)*

rises if you short cycle your actions, MS2:44

sanity and honesty related to producing VFP, 0:296

schedules and, MS2:118

senior endangering, 0:266

specialize in production and everybody wins, 0:506

standard of living and, 0:313

stat management and, 0:697

statistics and, 0:502, 0:654, 0:690

statistics, correctly stated ideal scenes and, MS1:63

survival of any group depends upon, 7:435, MS3:415

targets and, 0:704

targets and, depend on three things, MS3:436, 7:456

third dynamic auditing for, MS2:24

third dynamic psychosis is to prevent production, MS1:267

time and motion and, MS2:146

to have value organization must result in, MS1:294

twelve major points regulating, 0:288, MS1:227

very aberrated person produces overt act, 0:39

VFPs for the group and one's standard of living are intimately related, MS1:353

way to increase, 7:804

we're in business of going free and getting org production roaring, 0:503

welfare state vs., 0:50

when a valuable final product does not get produced and cannot be delivered, repair the earlier steps of its production, MS1:276

when either money or production get out of balance one has trouble, 7:163

when personal PR means more than production, MS1:158

when you penalize production you get nonproduction, 7:500

production activity,

four basic products of, MS1:226

production line, analysis of failures to produce showed, MS1:316

production program(s),

example of, MS1:170

expiration of, MS1:170

Flag Rep and, MS1:170

for immediate production, MS1:170

when you penalize production you get nonproduction, 1:769

production target, *see also* **target**

definition, MS2:433, MS2:437

first target must always be, MS2:441

inspect and survey and gather data and set operating and primary targets before you set, MS2:434

product officer, 0:679, 0:691, 0:695

CO type prod officer action, MS1:354

controls and operates org, MS2:5

creates a team and sets pace of the org's production and morale, MS2:169

does not know there is tech involved in getting the product, 7:447, MS3:427

ED/CO holds as double hat in most orgs, MS2:5

exactly and accurately naming the exact product, 3:307, 7:443, MS3:423

example of, 7:816

first product of, MS1:358, MS2:185

functions, MS1:356

gets production, MS1:354

hammer-pound, right-now production of products, MS1:357

has to know how to get a product, 7:446, MS2:130, MS3:426

has to name, want and get his product, 3:309, 7:445, MS2:129, MS3:425

have to be able to produce using the org to do it, 7:720

job of, MS1:321, MS2:269

key phrase for, 7:443, MS2:127, MS3:423

most common failure of, 3:307, 7:443, MS2:127, MS3:423

naming the exact product, MS2:127

of department is director, MS2:7

of section is in-charge, MS2:7

primary duty of, MS1:376, MS2:312

secretary of division is, MS2:7

when he treats Esto as org off or program off, MS2:32

product–org officer system, shortcomings of HCO with the, MS2:3

product orientation, importance of, MS1:377, MS2:313

Products 1–4, definitions, 0:290, MS2:5

Product 1, HCO products are part of, 1:65

Product 2 (SO),

SO member may not hold any rating or rank than "Swamper" until Product 2, 1:170

SO member may not receive full-time auditor training until he is Product 2, 1:169

definition, MS1:226

Product 3, definition, MS1:226

Product 4, definition, MS1:226

professional(s)(ism), *see also* **expert; specialist**

attorneys, accountants, in the employ of orgs, 1:203

hard-won know-how *carefully applied* makes the, 2:264

org image and, 0:102, 0:333, 0:334, 0:340

Professional Auditor Courses, 4:659

Professional Auditor's Bulletins,

definition, 1:396

preparation of, 1:21

Professional Course, goal of and description (1954), 4:291

professional rates, 5:432

abuse of, 4:223

certified auditors and, 3:175

definition, 2:415, 2:416

50% discount to certified auditors, 2:454

50% of full rate, 4:217, 4:218

how to obtain, 3:173

policies and, 3:175

policies on who qualifies for, 2:454

Professional TR Course and, 3:175, 4:223

restoration of (1961), 3:150

who is not qualified for, 4:223

who is qualified for, 4:217, 4:218, 4:221, 4:223, 6:769

Professional Route, 4:176

Professional TR Course, 4:661

Comm Ev offense to drag out, 5:451

prerequisite for all professional auditor training courses, 5:451

Professor, 5:434

requirements for, 4:416

profile, Oxford Capacity Analysis (OCA), 4:230

profitable, what profitable expansion depends on, 0:115

profitable images,

what PRO must do to obtain, MS3:167

what they come from, MS3:167

program(s)(ed)(ing), *see also* **battle plan; handle; plan; project**

abandoned, main cause of org difficulty, 7:366, MS3:346

ability to coordinate programs, 0:695, 7:457, MS2:443, MS2:457, MS3:437

activities and, MS1:214

assume the viewpoint of the receiver, 7:466, MS2:447, MS3:446

Auditing Sales and Delivery, 5:261

auditor trainees, 5:529

program(s)(ed)(ing), *(cont.)*

in Advanced Org, 5:530

bad program, definition, 0:702

basic needs of international programs set for 1965–1966, 7:68

best program will reach greatest number of dynamics, 0:702

best way to form them, 7:364, MS3:344

case program, definition, 5:717

check out all seniors on current programs, 0:279

clarity with which planning can be programed, 0:705

common problem of org is failure to execute, 7:364, MS3:344

commonest faults in, MS1:219

"complete planning" and "programs" are synonymous and programs is the preferred word, MS2:437

computers able to detect noncompliance in, 7:456, MS2:442, MS2:456, MS3:436

computers and, 0:704–705, MS2:440, MS2:455

conference routing used for program clearance, 0:387

correct comm, MS2:18

correct comm program, 0:441–443

definition, 2:624, 7:272, 7:369, 7:478, MS1:100, MS1:368, MS2:194, MS2:299, MS2:437, MS3:349, MS3:458

Dept of Programs, 0:701

difficulty with orgs and altering programs, 7:364, MS3:344

do not abandon successful, 2:405

Dummy Project 1, MS2:95

Estos and product officers run on, MS2:13

evaluated, pushed for that org, MS1:174

example of in society, "doctor program," 7:366

examples, 7:369, MS3:346, MS3:349

execution of, 0:701–703

expansion, MS1:169

repeating targets and, MS1:171, MS2:441

fail only because various types of targets are not executed or not kept in, MS2:434

failure, lack of organization and, 7:406, MS3:386

failure, program without guidance will fail and is better left undone, 0:702

finance and, 0:702

first target must always be production target, MS2:441

good, simple, doable on matters important to get done, 7:456, MS2:442, MS2:456, MS3:436

guidance required, 0:702

program(s)(ed)(ing), *(cont.)*

heart of is knowing the scene, MS1:98

how to establish validity of new, 7:364, MS3:344

immediate production and, MS1:170

implementation of 0–IV checksheets, 4:421

incomplete programs, what they result from, 0:648

key management tool, 0:648

made up of all types of targets coordinated and executed on time, MS2:434

majority of people cannot follow written program, reasons for, MS2:95

maxims regarding programming, 7:765

maxims relating to, 0:702

mini program, definition, 0:708

must handle actual situations which depress production and prosperity, 7:808

new program should be a special project, MS3:345

new, undertaken on small scale as pilot projects, 7:403, MS3:383

no excuse for not getting correct programs done, MS1:104

no longer successful, three points to check, 7:365

normal way of going about things, MS1:184

not done, MS1:131
lack of program execution, 0:344–345
reasons it would not be done, 0:425, 0:701

often only old program dropped out that needs reinstituting, not new solution, MS3:344, 7:364

old, remain and continue whether one is aware of it or not, 7:410, MS3:390

only when problem is gone can one drop a, 7:368, MS3:348

Organization Program No. 1, 0:98

overhauling,
common error is to forget to transfer when formed up properly, 7:371
steps for executive to take, 7:370, MS3:350

perfect dissemination program, 6:170

person responsible for completion of, MS1:136

personnel program, definition, 5:424

policy and, 0:132

positive points to look for when writing a, 7:467, MS2:448, MS3:447

promotional program, 0:344–345

public image programs, 6:601, 7:1045

put into action require guidance, 7:765

right way to handle it is to program it, 7:527

safe way on important program is to target it, 0:431

program(s)(ed)(ing), *(cont.)*

Saint Hill programs, each solved self-evident problem, 7:364

sample program to cure dev-t and get org hatted and producing, 0:441–443

scarcity of trained auditors and, 4:910

sequence of major programs at Saint Hill, 7:362, MS3:342

set priorities, 7:808

situations that prevent doing of a program, MS2:95

steps of Registration Pgm No. 2, 2:571–575, 6:392

steps to replace an old program, 7:366, MS3:346

strategic plan and, 0:706–707

strategic plan dependent upon, 7:459, MS2:445, MS3:439
clarity and doability of, MS2:442, MS2:456
immediate organization for production, MS2:441
targets and, MS2:442
targets vs. programs, MS2:448

swan song of, 0:701

target, *see* target

targets, clarity and doability of, 7:456, MS3:436

targets of, handle the Why, MS1:125

things that defeat any, 0:67

three points to check if program no longer successful, MS3:345

to be effective must be executed, 7:765

to bust through barrier of no real top-notch fast training, 4:408, 6:399

training program to increase size and income of org, 4:411, 6:402

trouble created through unnecessary, 7:367, MS3:347

two prior actions necessary to place new programs into action, 7:410, MS3:390

two things which may happen when program goes bad, MS3:350, 7:370

type you can always predict will fail, MS1:177

unsuccessful, solving wrong problem, 7:364, MS3:344

when you recruit you program the person, 1:166

which obtain general support consist of, 7:406, MS3:386

why consistent failure occurs, 7:188

writing, clean, concise programs, 0:704

written absolutely on-policy from here on out, 7:457, MS2:443, MS2:457, MS3:437

wrong and right way to run a, 0:703

program checking,
    drill, example, 7:1270
    LRH Comm and how it's done, 7:1269

program completion, definition of, 4:640

programing and C/Sing of cases, 4:706
    important enough to pay a lot of attention to, 7:765
    individual, the Grade Chart and, 4:198
    of personnel, 0:203, 0:222
    personnel and, MS1:386
    requires execution, 7:766
    right example, 7:766
    wrong example, 7:766

Programs Chief, lack of an FR shortens his reach to three feet, instead of several thousand miles, 7:292

Programs Ops (Operators), computers and, 0:705

progress,
    degree you can be cause in handling targets and needs of group determines how far you've come up the line, 0:249
    fair exchange gives one a rather level progress, 0:318
    how group member can measure his own, 0:253
    justice keeps channel of progress a channel and not a stopped flow, 0:480
    our method of progress into society, 0:231
    persons who do things to stop or impede forward progress of project or org, 0:574
    proportional to number of good Scientologists we make, 5:759
    totality of Power is orderly progress, 0:482

progress board,
    for courses, description, 4:466
    responsibility of Course Admin, 4:467

Progress Program, Repair Program, 4:1102, 4:1107

project(s), *see also* **battle plan; handle; plan; program**
    assume the viewpoint of the receiver, 7:466, MS2:447, MS3:446
    complex or extensive target will have a, MS1:97
    correct procedure in ordering staff to any project that will consume time, 7:807
    definition, 7:272, 7:479, MS1:100, MS1:369, MS2:195, MS2:300, MS3:459
    examples of HCO WW projects, 7:30
    examples of project quota revisions, 7:608
    failure to follow through, time and align finance can cripple the project, 7:587
    how to get approval of actions and, 0:401–402
    new programs undertaken on small scale as pilot, 7:403, MS3:383

project(s), *(cont.)*
    offenses against, 0:574
    Office of LRH Design and Planning Authority Section and, 0:376
    organizing of, 0:88
    personal project to raise one's stats, 0:689
    positive points to look for when writing a, 7:467, MS2:448, MS3:447
    public promotional projects, 0:352
    routinely inspected by Inspections, 0:376
    sabotaged by removing particles off the line, 0:432
    Saint Hill projects and bonus and quota system, 7:606
    something that requires more than two weeks to do is a project, 1:519, 7:678
    strategic plan and, 0:706–707
    strategic plan dependent upon, 7:459, MS2:445, MS3:439
    takes more than two weeks to do, 0:376
    targets vs., MS2:448
    time machine and, 0:376

Project Engineer(s),
    definition, 7:586, 7:590
    funds for, 7:586
    how to get the job done, 7:588
    model instructions for research project and for an administrative project, 7:590
    reason for appointment, 7:586
    rules of, 7:586
    stable datum of, 7:586
    there to make sure that abandonment does not occur once we are committed to the action, 7:588
    three types of, 7:590
    uses lines of the organization only where he does not burst them and demands special project personnel as fast as he needs them, 7:589
    what should be concentrated on, 7:587

project prepare,
    definition, 1:172
    line for, 1:172

promise, deliver what we have promised, 2:205, 4:77, 6:199

promissory note(s),
    credit extended must be in the form of, 2:569
    must be legal for the country or area in which it is issued, 7:1107
    Registrars and, 2:569
    sample of, 2:569
    staff member signing, 0:174
    waivers or debit invoices vs., 2:569

promote, promotion (of personnel), *see also* **posting**

being careful of who succeeds one, 0:596, 0:597

by statistic only, 7:500, 7:770

definition, 1:38

eligibility, executive statuses and, 7:465

every action in every department is linked with, 1:49

examples, 1:309

fails only because of nonexecution, 1:39

fantastically wonderful would consist of 50% outflow, 50% inflow, 1:308

HCO and, 1:33

how it relates to production, 1:309

miracle would be 10% outflow and 90% inflow, 1:308

never promote a downstat or demote an upstat, 0:505

new ideas and, 1:38

ninety-day rule, 0:596

Non-Existence, new appointee begins in, 0:561

org losing its lines and terminals and functions through, 0:198

outflow–inflow ratio and, 1:308

personnel
  by statistic only, 1:769
  only after the post they're leaving is apprenticed, 1:74
  staff status and, 1:236
  those whose stats are high, 1:74
  three things required prior to, 1:253

policies regarding persons newly transferred into portion in Emergency or promoted in it, 0:622

poor consists of 90% outflow and 10% inflow, 1:308

poor gives 98% outflow and 2% inflow, 1:308

Power Change condition, person taking over new post is in, 0:596

promoted or fired by rumor, 0:120

promotional actions, things which, if missing, would cave in a division, 1:48

responsibility of person being promoted, 0:596

resuming post one has left, because it collapsed, 0:597

right vs. wrong way, 0:119–120

slump following after a promotion, reason, 0:596

so that income will flood in and no existing income will be blocked, 7:655

standard promotional actions, Dept 1, 1:39

standard promotional actions, Dept 2, 1:40

promote, *(cont.)*

standard promotional actions, Dept 3, 1:40

test of who deserves promotion or gate, 0:120

then repair the lines and personnel malfunctions or improper placements, 7:657

transfer, *see* transfer

we promote by statistic only, 0:504

what you are producing and can deliver, 1:309

without adequate delivery will eventually fail to deliver income, 1:39

without it one has insolvency, 1:39

writing up one's hat and breaking in successor properly, 0:596

promote–demote, occurs when the person is not programed, MS1:388

promotional, promote(ing) (promotional actions), (promotional functions), *see also* **advertising; dissemination; magazine; word of mouth**

Academy, promotional purposes, 3:227

actions, Qualifications Division, 5:45

Ad Comm and, 7:895

Ad Council and, 7:889, 7:909

ads and comm cycle, directing the public, MS3:208

Advisory Council and, 0:355, 7:84

aimed for the able, 2:427

alignment of promotion with things publicly admired and against things publicly detested, 0:336

always promote more than can be wasted, 5:51

any action that makes the staff member or the org visible and well thought of, 6:65, 2:90

any job in org not done makes it hard or impossible to, 0:347

anyone writing promotion would have to be fully briefed on Grade Chart and C/S Series HCOBs, 2:559–560

approach to should be fresh and truthful, MS3:204

approval line, 2:178, 7:1304

art of hard sell and, MS3:202

art of offering what will be responded to, 2:66

assembly line for produced promo, MS3:192–193

assembly line function definitions, MS3:194

basic principle is to drive in more business than can be driven off by a service unit or mistakes can waste, 6:63, 2:136

basic principles of, 0:344

better it is the higher the inflow rises in proportion to the outflow, 2:65

book(s),
  are your first line of, 0:625, 2:705

promotional, *(cont.)*

broad public approach right up to moment
the individual responds by a slight
reach, 2:626

campaign and how to do per promotion–
production exercise, 2:67

mailing lists, and, 2:705

broad public promotion definition, 2:623

changes the outflow–inflow ratio and prevents a
fixed outflow–inflow ratio, 2:66

cleverness and, 2:137, 6:64

confused, results in loss of business, 7:1299

continental office does promotion for city
offices, 0:627

copy and positioning, MS3:205

costly when money isn't invested in getting
books sold, 0:625

covers "quality versus quantity," 2:65

creates desire for the valuable final product,
MS1:274

definition of promotion, 0:346, 0:563

definition of promotional items, MS1:333

definition, 2:90, 2:427, 3:514, 4:1054, 5:40,
6:65, 7:75, MS3:174

deliver to every person responding to, 0:282

delivery and, 2:73, 4:80, 6:366

Department 10 (Dept of Tech Services)
and, 4:109

Department 11 (Dept of Training), 4:109

Department 12 (Dept of Processing) and, 4:110

Department 19 (Office of the Executive
Director), 7:84

Department 20 (Department of Special
Affairs), 7:85

Department 21 (Office of LRH), 7:85

Department of Accounts, promotional
purposes, 3:229

Department of Materiel, promotional
purposes, 3:228

Department of Promotion and Registration,
promotional purposes, 3:227

departments, 7:32

design omission, MS3:192

D of P and, 4:964

driving in people on the Central Org is a
primary function, 7:195

ED and CO and, 7:84

effect of inadequate or no promotion, 7:843

elements of successful promotion, 7:841

eligibility, executive statuses and, MS2:192,
MS2:296, MS3:445, MS1:367

Emergency Formula and, 0:357, 0:563, 0:625

emergency promotion, 0:346

essential part of marketing, MS3:201

promotional, *(cont.)*

Estates Branch, 7:85

events and, 0:266

every action in every department
is linked with, 2:101

examples of misuse of promotion which have
occurred, MS2:358

exec duty, 0:409

Executive Council and, 7:84

exercise in promotion–production, 2:66

fails only because of nonexecution,
0:347, 2:91, 6:66

fatal error in, 0:357

features needed for magazines, 2:180

follows good production, MS1:409

Free Scientology Center and, 0:350

front-line promotion sorted out into broad public
testing and new basic course, 7:1003

fund for promotional writing, 7:923

going it blind without, MS3:178

handling for getting promo policy forced in and
applied, MS2:358

HCO Executive Secretary and, 7:84

HGC, promotional purposes, 3:228

"homework" definition, MS3:204

how much org should promote, 0:344–345

how to disseminate legally the handling of
preventing sickness, 2:159

how to get 10 times the size with a lot more
pay, 2:705

how to tell if good promotion is being
done, 2:65

ideal scene is orgs sending proper bulk
mail out to the correct categories and
publics, MS2:358

if an org follows the organizational pattern and
does what the hats say, then it will be
promoting with no further strain, 6:66, 2:91

if you think promoting is costly it's
because money isn't invested in getting
books sold, 2:705

image and, 0:339–341

impact depends mainly upon consistency
and, MS3:205

impression, one has to be aware of what
consuming public have, MS3:212

inability to assume audience viewpoint, common
fault, MS3:205

info packs, 0:352

into a comm-line overwhelm is nonsense, 7:654

investigation into situation of orgs sending out
huge quantities of bulk mail with no visible
returns, MS2:357

janitor and, 0:346

promotional, (cont.)

later programs will not work if earlier ones have not been executed, 2:136, 6:63

letter to send public who did PE Course but haven't gone further (1965), 6:385

list of, 3:52

list of most potent factors, 2:386, 3:101

list of restrictions, MS2:358–359

list of standard promotional actions of an org, 0:347–356

magazine and mailing pieces and books which develop the *want*, the general program which indicates a *channel*, 2:623

magazine, *see* magazine

mailing lists and, 6:812

mailing, *see* mailing

major thought for program disseminating healing, 2:158

making sure it is executed, 0:408

means REACH, 2:59, 3:229, 7:34

message, real essence of any promo piece, MS3:216

more than can be wasted, 0:357

most attacked line in any org or management unit, MS3:191

most successful course of action you can follow, 0:357

motto of, 0:344, 2:136

never works on wrong publics, MS3:13

not promoting or knowing how to compile and keep up CFs and Addresses and write letters, 0:302

of departments, 3:227

offering as many as can be reached something each of those reached will want and buy, 0:282

only fails because of nonexecution, 7:76

only in emergency promotion does one need new ideas, 2:90, 6:65

only reason it fails, 5:41

Org Executive Secretary and, 7:84

org image and, 6:607, MS3:141

org move and, 7:1334

PE Foundation, promotional purposes, 3:227

personnel must be kept informed and must inform themselves regarding technical matters of the org, 6:387, 2:564

plan and get feature news shots, news items and statistics, 2:180

pound the same message home time and time again, MS3:292

preclear classification and staff, 5:576

primary mission of promo is to, MS3:204

promotional, *(cont.)*

procedure for handling mailing lists bought or sent in, 2:626

production adequate to promotion must be made to be solvent or ethical, 2:66

projects for departments, 2:405

promoted business always has a delay, 7:658

promote what can be delivered and consumed, MS3:202

promoting until floors cave in because of number of people, 0:345

promotional programs and projects, 0:344–345

Public Executive Secretary and, 7:84

public, what they ask of an ad, MS3:206

purposes of the six departments, 2:57, 7:32

push training in promotion, 4:388

putting out articles is how we create public reality on us, 2:152, 6:161

quality degrades, MS3:202

real test is, MS3:201

reliable old promotion prettied up and done is usually best, 7:655

results if you don't promote, 2:122, 6:54

sample project for action by Dir PrR, 2:152, 6:161

secret of promotion that gets response, MS3:216

senior org drawing on junior org's Book Account for promotion in junior org's area, 0:627

Service Product Officer and, MS2:170–171

staff meeting and, 0:173

standard promotional actions of an org, 5:41

study tech and, 0:45

submission for okay procedure, 2:178, 7:1304

successful promotion, what it means, 2:120

successful promotional program consists of getting it executed, 2:137, 6:64

summary of basic principles, 2:136, 6:63

surveys and communication, MS3:209

Technical Division and departments, 4:109

Technical Secretary coordinates and gets done the promotional functions of Div 4, 4:109

testing promotion revised, 6:283

third dynamic psychosis is unreal or nonfactual promotion, MS1:267

"too little too late," hallmark of bad, MS3:32

training, soundest promotion, 0:350

two guiding rules to be followed, MS3:202

types of public, PR and, MS3:12

vital data and, 2:120, 6:54

what motto of promo could be, 6:63

what successful promotion means, 6:54

what to do if promotional program does not seem to work, 2:136, 6:63

promotional, *(cont.)*

what to do when incoming people dwindle on existing advertisement and stay dwindled for a week, 6:180

when making routing arrangements is called organizing and when it is called promotion, 0:408, 7:76

without adequate delivery of service or commodity will eventually fail to deliver income, 6:66, 0:347, 2:91

without promotion,
one has insolvency, 0:347, 7:76
there is no job, 0:346

promotional items, definition, MS2:167

promotional pieces, list of, MS2:170–171

promotion–production, exercise in, 1:309

propaganda, *see also* **black propaganda**

can often be disproven, MS3:28

definition, MS3:28

long-term technique used, redefinition of words, MS3:42

propagandist(s), false economic data coming from, 0:313

property(ies), *see also* **equipment; materiel**

broken-down or run-down or dirty things, handling, 0:84

definition, 2:140

why idea of "company property" is stupid and dangerous, 0:186

prophets of profit, 6:760

proportionate marketing, MS2:379

push harder toward largest bulk of future business, MS3:218

scale for Scientology and types of orgs, MS3:218

proportionate pay plan,

example of, 3:326–327

how to give staff members benefit from increases in income, 3:326

situation and, 3:325

prospect(s),

definition, 2:405

"hot" prospect files, handling of, 2:390

procedure for invoicing, 2:489

special letters to, 2:599

where they come from, 0:333

prospect lists, sold to squirrel, 0:534

prosper, how HCO makes an org expand and, 1:53

prosperity, prosper(ous), *see also* **affluence; Affluence condition; boom; expansion; rich; success**

admin by book = prosperity, 0:59

cooperation of opinion leaders and, MS3:22

corrupt activities vs., 0:534

directly proportional to speed of flow of particles, 7:700, 7:850, 5:138

false economic data and, 0:313

flourish and prosper, 0:318

group, prosperity of a, 0:526, 0:555

how to expand and prosper, 0:584, 0:594

if lines flow, org will prosper, 0:385

in-ethics and, 0:534

key to, 0:57, MS2:223

nonutilized personnel causing it to go down, 0:203

occurs when tech is known and used, 0:68

of a business is directly proportional to speed of flow of its particles, 4:119

"on-policy" orgs prosper, 0:59, 0:145

organizational prosperity is dependent on success of Public Divisions in building an enormous, active field, 6:108

organizing and hatting to increase prosperity, 0:204

proportional to speed of particle flow, 0:66, 0:275

reason for lack of in org is internal, MS2:3

selling and delivering auditing, 4:957

things that prevent one from, 0:315

to prosper, service must be as close to instant as possible, 0:275

when there is always more left over than is needed, 0:506

world prosperity dying, 0:66

protection, protect(ing),

don't protect ineffective staff, 0:232

ethics protection,
Blue Star, Green Star, Gold Star and, 0:662
up statistics and, 0:518, 0:661
when staff member is protected by Ethics, 0:502–503

from off-policy orders, 0:146

from personnel who overburden us all, 0:151

from viciousness and caprice in name of law, 0:483

if person's stat is up his job is secure, 0:239

individual rights were not originated to protect criminals, 0:461

justice developed to protect the innocent and decent, 0:456

to protect dishonest people is to condemn them to their own hells, 0:461

where your maximum personal protection lies, 0:482

protein, pep and, 5:641

protest,

of ethics actions, 0:490, 0:652

person who protests revelation of improper acts of others, 0:462

those who are quite happy to have everything fail and go wrong with no protest from them, 0:237

traced to lack of hats, MS1:202

using one's own honesty to protest unmasking of dishonesty, result, 0:462

when act of freeing is protest of slavery, 0:630

protest meeting, organized by SPs, 1:994, 4:86

protest PR,

definition, MS3:30

examples, MS3:30

when it's employed, MS3:31

protocol, for training of student, 5:145

provisional, definition, 1:196

provisional assignments, State of Emergency and, 0:622

Provisional Certificate(s), 5:218, *see also* **certificate**

expiration of, 4:645

expire after one year if not validated, 5:219, 5:372

Provisional Staff Status, 0:209, *see also* **staff status**

provisional status,

designated as "1" on org board, 1:238

dismissal and, 5:413

dismissal, has recourse to Ethics, 1:238

procedure to become Permanent, 5:413

transfers and, 1:238

PR survey(s),

example of questions, MS3:38

heart of reaction and human involvement, MS3:38

how to do, MS3:37

phrasing questions to get a reaction, MS3:38

questions translated into field of human emotion, MS3:38

three direct questions and, MS3:37

psychiatry(ists), *see also* **psychologist; psychology**

almost every modern horror crime was committed by a criminal who had been in and out of the hands of psychiatrists, 7:1144

bad mistake, 7:1130

basic tenet of, 7:1144

circulates rumors about auditors so it is only fair for the auditor to know exactly the status of psychiatry, 7:1139

cost of, 7:1138

criminal mind and, 1:830

exposed in *Manufacture of Madness,* 0:521

fable, 7:1127

great "charity" swindle, 7:1131

has product of further insanity, 0:124

have perverted education and produced a criminal society, 0:555

how it expanded, 0:125

idea that man could not change, 0:362

incompetent to handle personal aberration, 0:40

justice procedures used by, 0:521

mechanism is "if you get this idea, you will feel this pain," 7:1137

negative stat of more insane, 0:506

on the decline, 1:987

pain and ideas is basic "therapy" used by, 7:1137

Pavlov and, 4:919

police and justice systems aided by, 1:962

policy on psychiatric and medical failures, 7:1140

public warning on, 7:1142

results of are physically damaging, 4:919

societies smashed by, 0:68

state has to support them because the public will have nothing to do with them, 7:1138

suppressives and, 0:518

they're just trying to cover up their crimes by saying somebody else is to blame, 7:1140

total permissiveness advocated by, 0:555

what psychiatrist does not care to publicize is that his "cures" are implantings with compulsive ideas, 7:1138

World Federation of Mental Health, 7:1129

psychoanalysis, 0:68

cost compared to Scientology, 6:759

Dianetics vs., 4:919

Sigmund Freud and, 4:919

psychologist(s), *see also* **psychiatrist**

criminal mind and, 1:830

have perverted education and produced a criminal society, 0:555

never understood a word in psychology so doesn't understand Scientology, 0:35

police and justice systems aided by, 1:962

preached that man had to "adjust to his environment," 0:251, MS1:445

psychology, *see also* **psychiatry**

idea that man could not change, 0:362

incompetent to handle personal aberration, 0:40

Ivan Petrovich Pavlov, 4:919

therapy was dreams or drugs, ice picks and ice baths, 0:362

psychosis,

described, 1:804

lessens when misunderstood words are handled, 5:467

third dynamic psychosis is the perversion of finance, MS1:268

WANT the product vs., 3:309, 7:445, MS2:129, MS3:425

psychosomatic illness,

definition, 4:918

Scientology and, 0:152

psychotherapy,

definition, 4:287

discovered by screening, how to handle, 4:287

we are not in the business of, 4:306, 5:730

psychotic(s),

definition, 5:143

not accepted for processing, 2:402

registered mail from, 0:379

Scientologists deserve protection from, 1:989

training and, 5:143

PTS(ness)(es), *see also* **potential trouble source**

A to J types, 1:984–985

can create antagonism, 1:1039

crime to be or become a PTS without reporting it, 1:1039

first indicators of, 1:1023

handle or disconnect, 1:1042

handling of, 1:1012

indicators of a unit or staff member going PTS, 1:1023

may not receive processing or training, 1:1040

must have committed overts against the antagonistic source, 1:1043

not necessarily accorded court or hearing, 1:950

org has certain sections, units, personnel and executives who go PTS to suppressive elements in society, 1:1022

routing of, 1:1011

Search and Discovery and, 1:1012

should be declared as such by Ethics, 1:1040

two types, 1:1048

WANT the product vs., 3:309

PTS handling(s), *see also* **potential trouble source**

consists of, 1:1036

EP, 1:1050

Suppressed Person Rundown, 1:1044

PTS/SP checksheet, vital prerequisite for PTS handlers, 1:1036

PTS/SP Course, result of knowing technology of, 5:441

PTS students, sent to Review by Supervisor, 1:1011

PTS Type A,

definition, 1:984, 1:1038

handling, 1:1037

public(s), *see also* **customer; field; individual; people**

admin personnel and, 0:18

alignment of promotion with things publicly admired and against things publicly detested, 0:336

all releases designed for special, MS3:12

answer people's questions, 0:84, 0:166, 0:276, 0:322, 0:370

any control we exert upon public brings about a better society, 2:411, 6:183

ARC breaks, sources of, 0:276

ARC broken person leaving org unhandled, crime, 5:249

best control personnel must come into closest contact with, 2:413, 6:185

books,

making sure that interested people get books is making sure that they will continue their interest, 2:331, 6:234

won't buy books until they are communicated with, 2:54

comm lines, from org to public and public to org, 0:408

communicate to the public by the magazine, 2:54

community public, definition, MS3:11

complaint of (primary one), 0:322

deciding or choosing, 0:323

definition, 7:418, MS3:11, MS3:74, MS3:398

example of handling, 2:80, 6:202

expectations of, 0:276, 0:333

for the Success Through Communication Course, 6:498

general public vs. smaller groups, MS3:17

"Give them what we promised if it was promised," 0:404

goodwill and, 0:332

handling public individual, 0:323–327

hates like hell to be denied Dianetics and Scientology, 4:271, 6:552

public(s), *(cont.)*

helping Scientology orgs and groups ally themselves with public groups, 0:160

hidden datum in handling public is, to decide one has to understand, 2:80, 6:202

hidden datum regarding handling, 1:125

hundreds of types in PR, MS3:11

I don't care how many rules you break if they're broken to give unselfish service to one another and the, 0:273

I think you are wasting most of your time answering questions which are answered in books, 6:234

keep in contact with public and treat them well, 0:16

knows us by our mest, 0:84

like to be steered through what they are getting as they possess very little initiative, 6:116

maintain friendly relations with the, 0:322

make public right for wanting thus intensifying want, 2:81, 6:203

must be protected against abusers of technology or policy, 7:1293

must never be asked to decide or choose, 1:125, 2:80, 6:202

needs and wants, and Dept 17 courses, 6:486

neglecting to run good, good-paying services that build up raw public to major services, 0:303

never ask anyone in the public or field to decide or choose, 6:202

never asked to decide or choose, 0:323

new, how to answer their questions, 6:235

new, they are not interested in past lives, 6:235

not result conscious, 4:26

only objects to us when we fail to help or answer their questions, 0:84

org image and public comm lines, 0:335

orgs exist to sell and deliver materials and service to public and get in public to sell and deliver to, 0:91

people don't just walk in out of the blue, 0:360

people won't come in unless they are regularly mailed to and written to eventually by PrR, 2:54

personal contact best method of dissemination, 2:60, 6:166

PES, *see* Public Executive Secretary

policy is largely unknown to, 0:404

preclear who is a preclear of any organization may not be audited by students, 4:677

promotional actions, 0:347–356, *see also* promotion

proper routing and, 6:113

public(s), *(cont.)*

PRO's task and, MS3:74

public demand for service, future income and goodwill, 0:332

releasing materials broadly to a wrong public, 0:45

"self-determinism" of general public is only reactivism, 2:411, 6:183

stays away from orgs in droves which alter technology, 7:1191

students may not audit org public, 4:683

talking Scientology before callers, 0:347

tape plays in org, 0:352

technique to bypass a large decision by public individual, 2:583, 6:409

types of, definition, MS3:11

understanding is higher than point of public entrance into processing, 0:323

using terms, circumstances or data on raw public beyond the public ability to grasp, 0:45

valuable fine public as VFP, 0:316

wasting most of your time answering questions which are answered in books, 2:331

what we would like the general public to say to the general public about Scientology, 7:971, 6:30

where almost all Scientology prospects come from, 0:333

who don't immediately graduate onto Div 4 services are kept active by doing further Public Divisions services, 6:116

wild queries or ideas from public, handling, 0:404

with you just so long as results are achieved, 5:97, 4:26

word of mouth steering new public away from org, 0:302

wrong publics,
examples of, MS3:12
failures in PR and, MS3:11
promotion never works on, MS3:13

publication(s),

appearance and suitability of distribution, org image and, 6:606, MS3:140

Auditor, The, 2:135

basic function, 6:257

congress dates, 2:135

double action whereby the Pubs activity reaches to the public and the CF with book ads and book sales, 6:257

national magazine, 2:135

news policies, 2:135

Professional Auditor's Bulletin, 2:135

signatures on, 7:1280

publication(s), *(cont.)*

tape plays, 2:135

tapes, 2:135

when individual sales are omitted, dissemination can be shut off for an org, 2:349

Publications CF,

collection of persons who have individually bought books from Pubs, 2:349

in two parts: (A) organizations and (B) individuals, 2:349

Publications Dept, Dept 4 does promotional pieces for, 0:348

Publications Orgs, Organization(s),

an industry for the manufacturing, sales and distribution of Scientology books and materials to all publics, 2:355

basic function, 2:293

bonus eligibility requirements, 2:357

Cont Field Sales Manager role, 2:363

double action whereby the Pubs activity reaches to the public and the CF with book ads and book sales, 2:293

must never operate on a credit line to org, MS2:382

org sales pattern, 2:358

prime purpose, 2:355

sales bonus system, 2:356

Sales Manager duties, 2:356

Sales Manager statistics, 2:356

sales network, 2:355

tech/admin ratio, 2:358

use of airmail and air freight, 2:363

Publications Shipping Unit, users of fliers, MS3:293

Public Contact Division,

bodies in the shop, 6:226

checklist for quality, 6:351

contacting large volumes of people new to Scientology is activity of, 6:228, 6:351

functions of, 6:109

Public Division(s), *see also* **Distribution Division** 6:71

appearances in, 0:339–341

are service divisions, not just intro divisions, 6:115

best success story and promotion of Div 6 is tech applied, equaling happy pcs and students, 6:822

CF folder is direct product of, 0:359

charging for little services that should be free, 0:303

difference between it and Dissem Div, 2:109

Public Division(s), *(cont.)*

duty of all to see that the section of the Bridge below it, exists and is continuously flowing people up to higher levels on the Grade Chart, 6:122

FSM selections come back into CF for further action after first service, 0:360

functions of each of the three divisions, 6:86, 6:109, 7:915

handles the people who have never bought anything from an org, 2:88

how they work together with Div 2 to bring about a prosperous org, 6:109

ideal org and, 6:619, MS1:152

if were allowed to cannibalize off CF, there'd be no growth, 2:89

keep the whole field alive, 6:109

key is streamlined service routes for new public, 6:115

musical chairs and, 6:101

neglecting to run good, good-paying services that build up raw public to major services, 0:303

new unreached bodies equals, 2:89

no clue of what the Tech Division could or should do or was delivering, 2:554

organization of, 6:108

organization prosperity dependent on success of Public Divisions in building an enormous, active field, 6:108

posting for tech/admin ratio, 6:99

programing division for the public, 2:555

Public Div actions mean "New names to CF," 0:360

purpose, 6:109

ratio for posting must be met or whole staff will become very unpaid and overstressed, 1:208, 6:100

real purpose, 6:108

Registrar,

public of, 2:584

wherever public on their lines are ready to commence major services they may sell them, 2:584

responsible for bringing new public in, showing them what Scientology and Dianetics are and getting them started on the Bridge, 6:116

Rudiments Officer plays important role keeping Div 6 in control of field and able to get new people into org easily, 6:560

Rudiments Program and, 6:559

Scn org Public Divs force the mission public departments to function, 6:128

short-circuiting purpose of, result, 6:109

Public Division(s), *(cont.)*

stat most given attention is the increase of names in CF, 2:88

theory of org board and, 6:78

when these become inactive or hopeless or slothful, then people inflow drops, 6:756

why a HAS should man up Public Divisions, 6:101

Public Division Courses,

academy versus, 6:374

play vital part in expansion of Scientology, 6:374

starting and completing a student, 6:375

supervisor handling of student questions, 6:376

supervisor is required to be a trained and certified Course Supervisor, 6:375

Public Divisions org board, principles discovered which resulted in Public Divs org board, 6:87

Public Divisions personnel, transfers, removal and dismissal and, 6:101

Public Enemy 1, is the FBI, 1:963

Public Executive Secretary (PES),

appearances, image and, 0:339–341

duties of, 0:99, 0:102

in a tiny org, 6:94, 7:277

ethnic surveys and, 0:103, 0:340

Executive Council and, 6:86, 7:915

new divisions run congresses and PEs for their income, 6:81

of org or mission delivering to celebrity is obliged to notify the nearest Celebrity Centre Public Executive Secretary and nearest org Department of Special Affairs PR of celebrities, 6:139

promotional actions, 6:73–74, 7:84

purpose, 6:80

responsible for appearance of org, its staff, literature and publications, 6:613, MS3:154

public image,

how to build, 6:600

programs, 6:601

public lectures, 0:45, 0:99

public meetings, open to the public for a series of Scientology talks and group processing, 6:322

public opinion,

formed by "opinion leaders," not the "general public," MS3:18

"molding public opinion," MS3:13

Public Programs Officer, hat and functions, 6:860

public relations, PR, *see also* **image; PRO; Public Relations**

acceptable truth and, MS3:9

actions, ethnic surveys and, MS3:69, MS3:248

action, success depends on, MS3:18

affinity and, MS3:10

agreement with message is what PR is seeking to achieve, MS3:9

ARC triangle and, MS3:7

art of, MS3:99

black PR, 6:621, MS3:4

built on ARC, MS3:157

built on bedrock of good manners, MS3:34

campaign, example of creating one, MS3:129

character and actions of PRO function, 6:601, 7:1045

cliques, use of, 6:621, MS3:4

communicates ideas, MS3:7

communications subject and follows comm formula, MS3:72

compliance with policy and, 7:1260

concerned with presentation and audience, MS3:12

corrupted, definition, MS3:8

deals mainly in significances, MS3:72

dedicated to false reality of lies, MS3:8

definition, 0:332, 6:620, 6:622, MS3:3, MS3:5, MS3:16, MS3:80, MS3:97, MS3:104, MS3:168
of "PR," 0:526–527
of "public," MS3:11

Dept 1 sees that pool of PR trainees exists, 0:347

duty and function of, MS3:38

easily becomes cynical activity, 6:622, MS3:5

eighty percent preparation of an event, MS3:32

essence of PR is knowing how mind works, MS3:70

ethics out when PR won't go in, MS3:166

events and, 0:266

expert, aimed at specific, surveyed audience, MS3:12

failed, reason for and handling, MS3:166

first musts of, 0:331

full cycle of, 7:1262

function, image is, 6:613

George Creel's consideration of, MS3:17

goodwill and, 0:332

government PR continually recoiling on the government, MS3:20

handling and control of HE&R, MS3:55, MS3:230

hostile (counter), definition, MS3:9

how to find the "R," MS3:39

public relations, PR, *(cont.)*

imagination in, MS3:10

inexpert PR men, 6:620, MS3:3

in neglect, reason, 0:333

intelligence and, where they cross, MS3:29

intelligence vs., MS3:26

keep your attire as presentable as possible, 0:165

laws of, MS3:37

legal and PR situations from people who have complaints stem from two reasons, 7:1111

liabilities, 6:620, 6:622, MS3:3, MS3:5

main purpose of—to interpret policies of top management, 7:1408

maintain friendly relations with environment and public, 0:322

manners and, 0:328–331

middle ground, MS3:75

object of, MS3:73

ounce of, is worth ton of ethics, 7:1262

overt, intelligence is covert, MS3:26

part of art of, is follow-up, MS3:133

personnel, secondary qualities, MS1:420

personnel, what makes them a success, MS1:419

personnel, what to look for in appointing and training, MS1:420

population unrest stems from misuse, neglect or abuse of, MS3:19

positioning in, MS3:106

preparation, flops vs. success, MS3:33

press agentry is fundamental tool of, MS3:132

primary tech of, is manners, MS3:34

PRO Area Control,
    definition, 6:624
    measured by counting up points one is not controlling and the points one IS controlling, 6:624
    technology of, 6:624

program, four rules for success, MS3:116

program, spatial vs. linear program, MS3:109

promotion designed specially for each type of public, MS3:12

PR personnel must be spot on in, MS1:419

public knows us by our mest, 0:84

publicity first, advertising second, MS3:108

reaching minds, 6:620, MS3:3

real technology, MS3:92

road to Power built on truth, MS3:100

seeking exposure only is no good, MS3:134

social tech of handling and changing HE&R, MS3:37

special publics and surveys, MS3:12

standard texts have to be studied with additional

public relations, PR, *(cont.)*

developments known, 6:623, MS3:6

stock in trade of PRs has been lies, MS3:7

surveys for opinion leaders, major activity of, MS3:18

survival is target of, MS3:25

tech, LRH Comm and, 7:1262

tech of handling and controlling HE&R, MS3:56, MS3:231

third dynamic tech, MS3:55, MS3:230

thirteen zones of org image, 0:335–336

three commodities above contemporary PRO concepts, 6:608, MS3:142

three grades of, MS3:41

two-way comm cycle and, MS3:35

unsavory history of, MS3:4, 6:621

unscrupulous persons, use of, 6:621, MS3:4

untrained personnel and press conferences, MS3:95

used to bring about disrepute, 6:621, MS3:4

use of, MS3:56, MS3:231
    as an auditor to the group, MS3:27
    money and force vs. opinion leaders, MS3:20
    R involves acceptable truth, MS3:9
    Science of Survival and *Scientology 8-8008* in, MS3:70

using terms, circumstances or data on raw public beyond the public ability to grasp, 0:45

wasted planning, handling, MS3:93

what measures success, MS3:76

when it enters field of intelligence, MS3:73

willful broadcast of information, MS3:28

without two-way comm cycle, is pretty poor stuff, MS3:36

word of mouth and, 0:333, 0:337, 6:608, MS3:142

wrong public sums up about 99% of errors and major reason for failures, MS3:11

public relations campaign(s),

designed on tone level or 1 notch above level surveyed, MS3:38

first step is to ding in the purpose, MS3:162

public, should be done on Dianetics and Scientology tech, MS3:158

sequence of surveying and working out, MS3:57, MS3:232

public relations men, often of pitiful morals and degenerate character, 6:622

Public Relations Officer(s), PRO(s), public relations person(s),

achieves knownness and acceptance, MS3:73

activities done by, MS3:137

advising actions, 6:609, MS3:143

Public Relations Officer(s), PRO(s), *(cont.)*

basic tools, MS3:167

brings things to notice of the public, MS3:101

cleanliness, neat appearance and, MS3:147

contemporary duties in business firms, 6:607, MS3:141

creating an illusion considered acceptable, MS3:148

deal in three scenes, MS3:75

definition, MS3:144

delusory requirements, MS3:15

duties, responsibilities and actions of, 0:336–338

duty and purpose, MS3:16

essential ingredient of a PR is ability to work, MS3:14

ethnic values of public, use of, MS3:138

examples of activities, MS3:138

failure and manners, MS3:34

function, image is, MS3:154

functions of, listed in *Effective Public Relations,* MS3:167

goodwill and, 0:333

handling for out-ethics blocks, MS3:166

has to be spot on in confronting, organizing and working, MS3:14

has to move fast, MS3:76

hatting, MS3:70

have to forward agreed-upon purpose to get cooperation, MS3:162

"herring effect" and, MS3:149

how to get good PRO in Accounts, MS3:145

middle-grounders and, MS3:75

must be able to imagine, MS3:74

must be alert to any point which seems to "customer" to diminish his status, MS3:143, 6:609

must be causative, MS3:73

must be good organizer, MS3:139

must know something of intelligence tech, MS3:26

must study and use HCOBs on the antisocial personality, MS3:138

organize faultlessly in a flash, MS3:14

org income and PRO action, 0:338

person who is sane has high potential, MS3:10

PES as, 0:99

points of a successful PR man, MS3:75

points which are vital to, in an org, MS3:145

primary function, make known, enhance and forward purposes of management, MS3:161

pro never operates without press book, MS3:96

professionals, laid foundation of our difficult times, 6:607, MS3:141

Public Relations Officer(s), PRO(s), *(cont.)*

purpose and how it's done, MS3:137

repairing damages on Accounts lines is action of, MS3:144

requirements to be called other than I/T, MS3:92

results of not being trained, MS3:92

should be expert in shaping, defining and communicating purposes, MS3:162

should have direct access to EC or management, 6:609, MS3:143

shy or retiring PR not about to handle suppressive persons or situations, MS3:14

skilled in handling purposes can get almost anything moving, MS3:162

task regarding publics, MS3:74

thirteen points of org image, 0:335–336

trying to instill acceptability and belief, MS3:149

two rules of a safe ground, MS3:99

two wrong things they will do, MS3:92

uses ideas as carrier wave for his message, MS3:137

utilization of events, MS3:137

way to have NO PRO, MS3:144

what they must have skill in, MS3:167

who can't work fails every time, MS3:15

Public Servicing Division,

checklist for quality, 6:567

functions of, 6:109

responsible for servicing existing field and keeping it active, 6:567

Public Servicing Secretary,

bookbuyers who do not buy service and, 2:703, 6:713

promotional actions, 6:72

punishment, punish(ing), *see also* **discipline**

ethics actions carry no physical punishment, 0:495

man cannot be trusted with, 0:449, 0:521

one may not be punished for submitting petition, 0:488

only real crime for which one can be punished by governments of today, 0:693

salvaging vs., 0:462

Scientology justice and, 0:467, 0:477, 0:485

wog courts and, 0:485

purchase(ing),

EPOs and, 3:297

individuals may not purchase for organization and then be reimbursed, 3:286

liability of staff members, 3:290

lines modified, 3:278, MS2:346

purchase(ing), *(cont.)*

made for a company without prior purchase order renders employee ordering to payment of the account from his own salary, 3:126

nothing may be bought without a purchase order, 3:291

only occurs by reason of red PO approval, 3:298

two possible sequences of and POs, 3:297

purchase order(s), PO,

abiding by purchase order system, 0:165

all purchases by a Scientology org must be done by, 3:290

definition, 3:297

each and every item on every bill must be covered by a, 3:291

Emergency Formula and, 0:625

filing of, 3:293

form, 3:305

long-distance phone calls and telegrams, 3:314

monthly bills statement and outstanding POs, 3:293

must accompany every order to Purchasing before the fact and must come to Disbursements before a bill can be paid, 3:126

must give person or firm from which the purchase is to be made, 3:291

nothing may be bought without, 3:291

offense concerning, 0:472

outstanding purchase order remains in Reserved Payment Account until statement is submitted by creditor, 3:316

purchasing liability of staff members, 0:183

purchasing only occurs by reason of, 3:298

salary sum check and, 3:291

several red POs written against single EPO, handling of, 3:299

signing, 3:299

Purchaser, most common failure of, 3:307, 7:443, MS2:127, MS3:423

Purchasing Section, financial planning and, 3:298

Purification Rundown,

ability gained, 4:189

atomic war and, 4:1235

followed by Objectives on a heavy druggie, 4:194

key entrance point for new pcs into the org HGC, 2:712, 6:104

lessening consequences of radiation exposure, 4:1236

when done, 4:1207

purpose(s), *see also* **goal**

adaptable to computer programing, MS2:455

against which things can be coordinated, 7:472, MS3:452

agreed-upon, to get cooperation PR would have to forward, MS3:162

attacks should be in direction of enlarging one's scope and augmenting basic purpose, MS2:428

basic,
failure to forward and mismanagement, 7:665
must be channeled, 7:669
policy and, 7:663

basic purpose, *see* basic purpose

becomes objectives in target policy, MS1:375

being hard on anyone discoordinating or blunting the, 0:89

decision making and, 0:231

difference between one thetan's forward thrust and another's is purpose, validity of, 0:237

enturbulence due to ignorance or absence of, 0:68

failed, all you have to do to restore life and action is to rekindle the failed purpose, MS2:428

failure to provide purpose begets revolt, MS1:408

forwarding purpose not destructive to majority of dynamics, 0:236

from that works out what strategy will be used, MS3:452

ideal scene and, MS1:54, MS1:55

individual purpose as vital and wanted commodity, 0:204

knowing purpose of org, importance of, 0:53

lack of hats and, MS1:207

manifested, 7:471, MS3:451

must be executed, MS2:428

must be part of the ideal one has for that activity, MS1:33

of ethics, 0:497, 0:509

organization(s),
bound together by common, 7:454, MS3:434
consists of coordinated purposes, lines and terminals, 0:89, 7:293
must have clear-cut purpose and fill definite need in order to survive, 0:53
purpose of, 0:52, 0:87
terminals and comm lines united with common purpose, 0:81

person goofs and commits crimes when he doesn't have, MS1:416

police action not a substitute for, MS1:207

PRO and, MS3:167

purpose(s), *see also* **goal**

PR should be expert in shaping, defining and communicating, MS3:162

random, effect on a group, MS1:265

remedy for failed purposes, MS2:434

senior to policy, MS1:264

SP uses "policy" to prevent, 1:1007

stopped purposes can be dramatized, MS2:438

stops all occur because of failed purposes, MS2:428

strategic plan,
always carries with it a statement of, 7:470, MS3:450
means to get purpose itself to function, MS3:453

strategy based on, 7:472

subpurpose, 0:118

successful PR campaigns and dinging in the, MS3:162

taking actions within one's organizational purpose, 0:373

violated, 0:426

we must not entangle our purposes with arbitrary laws which do not further our cause, 0:273

Pythagoras,

ethics and, 0:448

Greek philosopher, 1:497

Q

Q and A Checksheet, 7:440, MS3:420

Qual, *see* **Qualifications Division**

Qual Auditor Cramming Section, issues Okay to Audit, 4:946, 5:846

Qual bonus, 3:352

Qual Consultant, *see* **Qualifications Consultant**

Qual Establishment Officer,
   ideal scene, 5:59
   product, 5:59
   purpose, 5:59
   statistic, 5:59

qualification(s),
   C/Sing for a level, 5:715
   HGC Staff Auditors, 5:831
   Senior C/S, 5:713

Qualifications Consultant, 4:392
   interviews, 1:827, 4:982, 5:767, 6:416, 7:733
   statistics, 5:75

Qualifications Cycle, 0:96

Qualifications Division (Div 5), Qual,
   auditors employed in Qual, 5:53
   backlogs and, 0:100, 5:55, 5:684
   being causative, effects on org, 5:871
   cases and students must leave Qual with the whole thing handled, 5:52
   cause or effect, 5:865
   co-auditors, when to send to Qual, 4:700
   concentrates on cramming HGC auditors and students, MS1:291
   crew or staff must be programed onto not off of post, 5:421
   deliver service, 5:55
   departments of, 5:30

Qualifications Division (Div 5), Qual, *(cont.)*
   Divs 4 and 5 contain five times as many personnel as all the other divs, 0:96
   entered and left via Examiner, 5:114
   ethics chits, 5:20
   giving credit is seldom done except in, 0:276
   gross divisional statistic, 5:73, 5:77
   handles flat ball bearings, 5:36
   hats staff on HCO PLs, 7:488, MS3:468
   hidden failures, penalty, 5:281
   high-crime checkouts on policy letters, responsibility of, 0:76
   high Qual income stat indication of collapse of gross income, 5:54
   ideal scene, 5:58
   keynote of—correction, 5:52
   KOT and, 7:1273
   letting backlogs occur in, and org income and repute, 4:928
   library, 5:725, 7:487, MS3:467
   makes sure cramming orders done, 5:655
   may request Courts of Ethics, 4:352, 5:842
   most attacked area of an org, 1:703, 5:20
   never takes orders or direction of any other division or staff member on what to do technically with a student or pc, 5:52
   org board,
      mini, 5:57
      placed one inch higher on org board, 1:150
   penalty for using opinion or interpretation of tech or policy, 5:79
   penalty stats, 5:78
   poor quality, checklist, 5:868
   Power quality, checklist, 5:865

Qualifications Division (Div 5), Qual, *(cont.)*

programing personnel, 0:222

purposes of, 5:30, 5:58, 5:257

quality checklist,
  poor quality, 5:868
  Power quality, 5:865
  Treason quality, 5:870

responsibility for,
  staff cases, 4:705
  standard admin, 0:70–71

senior datum, 5:52

staff, star-rates on, 5:777

statistics, 0:688, 5:58

technical,
  cop, 5:39
  downgrades and, 5:97
  Technical vs. Qual, what each is there
    for, 5:655

three-hour wait too long for Qual pc,
  4:932, 5:688

tools for pc, 5:36

tools for student, 5:36

training of staff and, 4:117, 5:487

Treason quality, checklist, 5:870

valuable final products, 5:58

Qualifications Secretary,

bonus, 5:135

call-in and, 2:647, 4:282, 7:871

ED or CO, OES or Chief Officer, HES or
  Supercargo and HAS subject to Comm Ev
  if there is no, 5:79

function, 5:68

gross divisional statistic, 5:75

promotional actions, 5:45

red tag line and, 5:286

requirements for, 5:737

responsibility for,
  getting auditor trainees, 5:488
  getting red tag line in and maintaining, 4:256
  staff auditors and interns, 4:905

staff training and, 5:490

technical hierarchy and, 5:697

Qual Interview and Invoice Officer,

ideal scene, 5:65

product, 5:65

purpose, 5:65

statistic, 5:66

quality,

bettering quality of service, 0:645

Central Orgs, quality and admin in, 0:18

definition, 0:288, MS1:227

ethics ensuring quality of product, 0:126

quality, *(cont.)*

exaggerated ideas of, must become secondary to
  speed, 7:850

final product depends on, MS1:223

good admin and technical quality, 0:18

HCO sets the, 1:36

low product quality, reason for, 0:294–295

matter we must give constant attention,
  4:26, 5:97

of tech, depends on, 4:946, 5:846

only thing that counts, 0:16, 4:16, 5:16

organizing and, 0:297

produce in abundance and try to give better
  than expected quality, 0:318

product and, 0:287, 0:290, MS1:226

products one must produce as result, 4:26

speed vs. quality of service, 0:275

technical quality, 0:16–18, 0:333

viability, quantity and, 0:297

quality checklist, 4:1253

quantity,

bettering quantity of service, 0:645

definition, 0:287, MS1:226

product and, 0:288, MS1:226

statistics and, 0:690

quarrel, third party and, 0:510, 1:535

quarters, *see also* **cleanliness; image**

assignment or change of at Saint Hill, 7:1332

cleanliness of, 0:333–334

dirty, destructive of goodwill, MS3:169

misuse or abuse of, 0:172, 0:543

neatness of, part of everyone's hat, MS1:237

professional, 0:102

promotional actions concerning, 0:351, 0:355

renting vs. buying or owning, 7:1395–1396

staff, student and pc responsibility for rented
  quarters, 0:172

standard of living and, 0:313

viability and procuring quarters for an
  org, 7:1394

query, queries, querying,

dev-t queries, 0:404

if MUs won't clear, query it, 0:23

may go on time machine, 0:382

no one can be comm eved for querying order in
  proper form, 0:142

orders, format for querying, 0:141

student with Mis-U will pour out a
  torrent of, 4:403

Supervisor's handling, 4:403, 5:513

question(s),

about Dianetics and Scientology, best answer to, 2:332, 6:235

answer people's questions, 0:84, 0:166, 0:276, 0:322, 0:370

clarifying questions about policy, 0:126

concerning your duties on any post, handling, 0:166

key question,
E-Metered, 6:823
for preclears, 6:823
for students, 6:823

make sure all student's questions get answered, 0:16

organization must answer people's, 2:598, 6:156

questionnaire(s),

Central Files and, 2:627

Hubbard Book Auditor certificate printed as flier enclosing questionnaire, 5:347

Letter Reg and, 0:349

Scientology invitation acceptance form, 2:379, 5:353

when person buys and reads the book, if one doesn't hear, can send a questionnaire, 2:626

"quickie,"

anything that does not fully satisfy all requirements is, 4:29

definition, 4:29, 4:30, MS2:31

did not save any time, wasted hundreds of hours, 4:30

ethics has to enter in after quickie tech gotten in, 4:30

"quickie," *(cont.)*

"quickie grades," 0:7, 0:14, 1:7, 2:7, 3:14, 4:7, 4:1108, 5:7, 5:274–275, 5:277, 7:7, 7:14

remedies for, 4:30

result of, 4:935, 5:263

tech is simply dishonest, 4:30

"quick result," 4:937

used to cover up superficial, no-results auditing, 5:265

quicksilver, *see also* **musical chairs**

answer to handle, MS1:362

because someone pulls off a success in one area, MS1:361

definition, MS1:359, MS1:467

doing a quicksilver, 0:264

examples of, MS1:360, MS1:468

penalties for, MS1:362, MS1:470

personnel scene, contributing factors, MS1:468

seniors who permit or condone, MS1:360

quitclaim, for students who blow, 1:999, 4:91

quota(s), *see also* **target(s)(ing)**

definition, 0:690, MS2:230

established, are real and are always higher than those of the week before, MS2:231

failing to push production quotas, 0:696

setting, usually against time, are production targets, MS2:433

targeted for increase daily or weekly, 0:689, 0:691

targeting vs., 0:690

to do quotaing you have to know how to "play the piano" and have to be totally knowledgeable of existing scenes, 7:827

use of, 7:827

R

race,

actions which cause it to falter, fail and die, 0:119

code of good conduct laid down out of experience of, 0:455

degeneration, 0:251

education used by hostile elements pervert the race and its ideals, 0:41

future race and ethics, 0:451

radiation,

by taking away engram which reacts to worry of radiation, worry then is made nonpainful, 2:147–148

causes hysteria: Scientology can handle hysteria, 2:147

Dianazene depends for its reaction upon whole track radiation incidents, x-ray and sunburn in the current life, 2:147–148

exposure, Purification Rundown lessening consequences of, 4:1236

injures health: we can proof a person against bad health, 2:147

reaction is completely and wholly mental, 2:147, 6:154

what our total interest in radiation is, 6:154

radio(s),

ads, produce results but only when accompanied by lectures on the subject, 6:167

getting US out of depression, 0:506

pours lies into population of Earth, 6:622, MS3:5

word of mouth and, 0:333, 0:337

radio ads, *see also* advertisement; promotion

produce results but only when accompanied by lectures on the subject, 2:61

spot ads, worthless, 2:61

rank, right to be tried only by seniors in status or, 0:524

rates, professional, 2:415–416, 4:217–218

rational(ity),

connected to ideal scene, MS1:58

ethics and, 0:451

reason, 0:451, 0:456

reprehensibly irrational, 0:454

sanity and insanity are matters of motive, not rationality or competence, 0:296

rationalizing a statistic, definition, 7:400

raw data, definition, 0:120, 7:666

raw material(s),

obtaining raw material to make final product, 0:289

Reach and Withdraw run on raw materials of one's post, 0:310

raw meat,

actions taken on, 5:745

raw public routes onto the Bridge, 6:115

service routes starting in Division 4, 6:116

when a person may graduate up to major services, 6:116

reach, *see* demand; want

Reach and Withdraw, 0:310

reactionary, definition, MS1:33, MS1:144

reactive mind, bank, *see also* mind

audited in way which puts one at cause over his, 0:263

automaticity of, 0:449

bank-agreement made Earth a hell, 0:10
can exert pain and discomfort on a being, 0:480

common denominator of a group is, 0:10

demanding suppression of good and production of bad, 0:480

reactive mind, bank, *(cont.)*

democracy is a collective-think of, 0:158

description of, 0:9, 0:158

exchange maintains inflow and outflow that gives person space around him and keeps bank off of him, 0:528

false and booby-trapped purposes in, 0:117

heavy ethics plays right into hands of, 0:247

humans, most they have in common is the reactive bank, 0:157

nobody has any right to a, 0:242

restrain just trifle more than bank can compel bad action, 0:480

rising above domination of, 0:10

seeks to knock out the good and perpetuate the bad, 0:9

slavery enjoined by mechanisms of, 0:629

thetans without banks have different responses, 0:10

triggered by out-ethics situation, 0:449

we need only avoid bank dramatizations to own the lot, 0:327

why it was invented, 0:158, 0:480

world does not yet know anything about, 2:332, 6:235

read(ing),

ability to hear or read and understand missing, 0:44

failed students who can't even read a despatch, 0:302

read-it, drill-it, do-it, definition, 4:689

real(ity), *see also* **agreement; ARC; ARC triangle**

first lesson in PR, keep a high R, MS3:8

if your post isn't real it is your fault, 0:84

make your post(s) real to other staff members and field, 0:166

morale problems and, 6:524

one surveys to find reality of person about something, MS3:54, MS3:229

surveys used to find R of another or others, MS3:9

unreal(ity),

governments whose policies are unreal are perishing, 0:411

no-confront and, 0:38

sweeping away unreal, unapplicable and impeding laws and policies, 0:117

use of in PR involves acceptable truth, MS3:9

what reality in policy, orders or advice depends upon, 0:122

reason, reasoning, 0:451, 0:455; *see also* **rational; think**

depends on data, MS1:12

logic, ability to, MS1:10

reasonable(ness),

accepting reasons why something cannot be done, 0:430

chief offender, MS1:30

conditions assignment and, 0:677–678

definition, MS1:129

dev-t and, 0:416, 0:430

don't get reasonable about down stats, 0:505

Ethics never gets reasonable about lack of expansion, 0:498

inability to recognize an outpoint, MS1:129, MS1:168

most dangerous reason for down stats is reasonable explanations of why stats are down, 7:513

one can defeat the purpose of statistics by being reasonable or alter-izzy about them, 7:519

outpoints and, MS1:128

statistics and, 7:530

rebate, *see also* **refund**

may not be given any preclear, 2:523, 3:160, 5:742

requests for, handling, 3:160

to claim a pc "lost time" in auditing because of an error in choosing processes or having to reflatten one is highly fallacious, 2:523

receipt-point, communication and, 0:46

Reception,

always gets name and phone number of people calling, 1:124

appearances and, 0:340

as income-getting action, 0:99

callers in person take precedence over mail, phone or other interests, 2:486, 6:379

does not permit callers to be talked to by hangers-on or nonauthorized persons, 2:487, 6:380

first checkpoint on money line, 3:75

handling of legal-type bodies, 1:336, 7:1082

invoices and, 1:131

invoices local cash book sales, insignia, souvenirs, and rents only, 3:105

keeps none waiting, 2:486, 6:379

large org, separate HCO Receptionist, 1:133

logbook, use of, 1:130

must regard everyone who walks in, trade people and business callers excepted, as a potential pc or student, 2:486, 6:379

neat, fast, no-wait, efficient reception followed by confident registraring can quintuple any org's income, 2:486, 6:379

promotional actions of, 0:347, 1:39

purposes, 7:60

recruitment actions to take, 1:172

Registrar, number of interviews is stat of, 2:551

Reception, *(cont.)*

Registrar's body handler, 2:491

responsible for,
actual collection of rents, 3:105
"In-the-Org List," 1:130

staff idling in, 0:338, 0:347

where it belongs, 1:130

reciprocity, natural law, 1:570

recommendation(s),

Board of Investigations, 1:953

coordinated, MS1:161

Courts of Ethics, 1:950

essence of, MS1:161

record, recording deposits and checks, 3:110

record shot, definition, 2:213; *see also*
photograph(s)

recourse,

civil matters and, 1:969

Comm Ev as, 0:478, 0:523

Courts of Ethics and, 1:950

definition, 0:522, 1:812

during a condition of Emergency, 1:730

failure to take, 1:813

for certificate cancellation, 1:857–858

from discipline or findings, 7:1302

from punishment for misdemeanors, 1:864

illegal orders and, 0:522

in current society manager or exec has no
recourse to law or the culture, 0:587

injustice, recourse from, 0:477–478, 0:481,
0:487, 0:492, 0:522–523

lack of specified recourse, effect of, 0:467

maximum recourse, 0:523

no senior exec in org may be named as
interested party in matters of recourse
requested by junior, 0:478

not seeking recourse, result, 0:523, 0:524

of an auditor for processing a potential trouble
source or suppressive person, 1:888

petition, and, 1:743, 1:745, 5:110

to off-policy or out-tech order, 0:147

when a student or pc may ask for, 1:745,
4:355, 5:110

when it may be requested, 0:492

wrongly dismissed, demoted or transferred
may request Committee of Evidence,
0:487, 1:251

recover(y),

answer to any recovery, 0:15

commotion or talking around injured person can
hurt chances of, 0:153

ethics heavy vs., 0:441

facing past and misdeeds and recovering from
them, 0:152

full recovery of self as biggest prize, 0:234

full use and delivery of Dianetics and
Scientology answer to, 1:15

locating the major change and, MS1:50

tech going out is only basic circumstance that
can put org beyond rapid recovery, 0:623

Recovery Program, recovering full use and results
of Expanded Lower Grades, 4:1106

recruit(s), new staff, *see also* **recruitment; staff**

bad recruit can make org allergic to any
recruits, MS1:397

conditions penalties—new employees and
persons newly on post, 0:566

influx of new recruits tends to unsettle an
area, 0:252

minimum hatting for, 1:292

never noticing there is an org there that has
posts and functions, 0:383

never promise free courses or auditing, MS1:310

thirty-day rule for new employees, 0:566

recruitment, recruit(ing), recruiter, *see also*
hiring

actions of, MS1:393

administration lines to handle, 1:172

answer to musical chairs is recruiting and
hiring, 0:280–281

application forms, design of, 1:172

barriers, 1:172

contracted staff and, 7:784

contracts stacked at Reception, 1:172

correct personnel pools for, 1:164

divisional,
divisional secretary may recruit or hire, 1:169
requirements for retaining staff, 1:169

don't be selective, open the gates and hat,
MS1:310, MS2:109, MS2:260

down stats traced to failure in, MS1:403

failures to recruit, effect of, 0:221

fast flow hiring and, MS1:310, MS2:109,
MS2:260

handouts, 1:164

hiring of institutional cases or persons with
psychiatric history or insane, 1:168

how to handle any objections to, MS1:393

letting it be turned into freeloading, 0:103

linear recruiting, example of, MS1:391

location of the organization and, 1:171

recruitment, recruit(ing), recruiter, *(cont.)*

lots of auditors and auditing is real wealth in an org, 7:783

low-stat people, effect of letting them in, 0:656

musical chairs and, 1:71

network representatives may recruit or hire own staff, 1:169

never promise free courses or auditing, MS2:109, MS2:260

no effective attention on, reason, 0:693

notice boards, 1:164

person doing recruitment will only recruit personality equivalent, 1:172

posters for correct personnel pools, 1:164

preparedness program, 1:164

programing and, the answer to org problems, MS1:388

project prepare, definition, 1:172

recruiting,
    and handling FSMs to get in pcs and students, 0:354
    only heavy LSD and clinic types, 0:302

robbing a lower org as a higher org's solution, 1:165

signs,
    content of, 1:172
    to acquire new staff, 0:347

special mailings to personnel pools, 1:164

statistics, 5:81–82

to begin the cycle of, MS1:395

tools for, MS1:397

trace where the requests to join come in to straighten the lines out, 1:171

working with people to get them eligible, 1:167

recruitment pool(s),

portion operating well used as, MS1:200

production area used as, MS1:200

redefinition of words, for propaganda, examples, MS3:42–43

red purchase order(s),

in order to expedite vital Flag external cycles, red POs by telex are sometimes necessary, MS2:363

procedure for sending, MS2:363

red seal, validation on HPA/HCA Certificate, 5:322

red tag,

co-audits, 4:700
    definition, 4:254, 5:78, 5:284
    handling of auditor, C/S,
    D of P and Tech Sec, 5:78
    line, applies to Solo auditing also, 4:256

red tag, *(cont.)*

how it is handled, 4:255
monitoring of, 5:285
procedure, 5:285
24-hour rule penalty, 5:286

on staff and paying pcs, 0:302

reasons for, 5:284

Snr C/S stat and, 5:286

staff co-audit, 4:709

Tech action taken on, examples, 5:655

referral, refer, referring,

bureaucracies and "the referral system," 0:279

charge of out-admin for, 0:260

continuing situations by, 0:244–245

dev-t and, 0:400, 0:430

everything you refer has to be done when it comes back to you, 0:399, 0:431

hat dumping, 0:425

irresponsibility, 0:260, 1:893, 7:701

keeping comm line in endless foment, 0:400

referring things one shouldn't and not referring things one should, 0:391

unhatted org is lazy and refers everything to someone else, 0:390

upsets caused by, 0:245

"referral system," 1:70

refund(s), *see also* **rebate; repayment**

ARC Break Reg and people wanting recourse from, 3:263, 7:1109

at once refund in full any refund demanded, 3:242, 7:1068

auditors, C/Ses and, 0:302

cause of, 3:263, 4:198, 5:712, 7:1109

definition of, 3:262, 4:157, 5:711, 7:1108

Dianetic auditing contract and, 7:1097

every posted scale of donations and every rate card bears refund notice, 3:258

Exec Dirs who have biggest number of, 0:693

forbid the sale of further processing to anyone receiving, 3:242, 7:1068

new policy on, 3:243, 7:1069

no membership refunds, 7:1084

no refund may be applied for successfully after three months from the end of the last service rendered, 3:259, 7:1084

notice added to the bottom of every posted scale and rate card, 2:181, 7:1083

overpayments (for books) refunded, 0:282

paid by Dept 8, MS2:327

person requesting refund must sign a guarantee, 2:181, 3:258, 7:1083

policy, 3:243, 3:262, 7:1108

prompt return of money to dissatisfied pc, 0:410

reason for, 5:706

refund(s), *(cont.)*

reduction of, 4:1124

staff made to refund all fees illegally received for training or processing any student or pc for personal profit, 0:171

tech is out, 5:711

there are no membership refunds of any kind, 3:259

waiver and, 5:712

when you do give refunds or repayments you do it on policy, 3:263, 7:1109

where tech is out you can expect refunds, 3:262, 7:1108

refund/repayment line, 7:882

reg, *see* **registration**

registered mail, 0:379

registered marks, registered names, neglect or omission in safeguarding of, 0:473

Registrar(s), Reg,

action which increases income is interviewing students and selling them professional auditing, 2:587, 6:414

activity is direct monitor of income, 2:492

all credit extended must be in the form of a legal promissory note, 7:1107

all state of case established by D of P, never by Registrar, 2:484

answers applications, 2:394

assigning auditing hours, effect of, 0:384

Assistant, definition and duties, 2:404

be real about what pc or student needs and wants and work it out so he gets it, 2:567, 6:390

Big League Sales and why Reges are not closing, 2:570, 6:392

body handler is Reception, 2:491

breakdown of, 2:554

calendar books, 2:516

Central Files and, 2:388

competent technical opinion sought before Registrar commits Tech Division to servicing a pc or student, 2:566, 6:389

Division 2 Registrars,

Div 6 and, may reg for any service, 6:411

may route people to Division 6 for intro services or Department 17 services, 2:584, 6:411

does not invoice payments, 2:481

does the Reg know what the org delivers, 2:565

D of T or D of P cannot direct Reg in cutting back numbers of people to be processed or trained, 2:480

do not C/S cases, 2:592

don't put PTS people on registration lines, 6:393

duties of, 2:426, 2:481

Registrar(s), Reg, *(cont.)*

either signs person up or doesn't, 0:245

examples of Registrar interview, 2:586, 6:413

Exec Dirs who reg instead of getting, 0:693

first duty, 2:491

get bodies into the place and promote Scientology, 2:427

has no authority to assign auditors to preclear, 4:294

hat, 2:491, 4:214

have to be informed of the wins in Tech, 2:568

Immediate Registrar, definition and duties, 2:404

inspects letters written by staff auditors, 2:394

interview, 1:824, 4:979, 7:730

letters, 2:393

letter-writing functions, 2:492

logs, 2:492

lost line, 2:495, 2:499

mail,

applicant, 2:388

procurement letter, 2:389

prospect, 2:388

three types of, 2:388

may not,

assign times for auditing, 2:206, 4:78, 6:200

discuss finance, 2:426

heed or help the D of P limit the number of pcs to fit his number of auditors, 2:491

may reg for any service, 2:584

member of the public may go to any Registrar available to sign up for service, 2:584, 6:411

must be,

"a good closer," 2:492

familiar with tech the org delivers and kept informed of results being obtained, 2:586, 6:389, 6:391, 6:413

on routing form for outgoing preclears and students for further services, 2:587, 6:414

part of the team and know what's going on, 2:566, 4:1034, 6:389

must fully advise buyer of membership prices, 2:516

must know what's going on and what the team is capable of doing at any given moment, 2:566

must not sell a pc a specific auditing program or promise results, 2:592

must register all students and preclears, 4:213

neat, fast, no-wait, efficient reception followed by confident registraring can quintuple any org's income, 2:486, 6:379

needs to know what the person should have, 2:566, 6:389

Registrar(s), Reg, *(cont.)*

no authority to assign auditors or auditing rooms to preclears or students to class, 2:480

not referring any person to a group or field auditor, 2:683, 6:696

not supposed to engage in long sales talks or sales letters, 2:491

not there to *sell* anything, 2:491

Pc Application Form and, 2:542, 4:1024

person signing up with Reg does not commit org until also accepted and signed up with Technical Division, 2:485

pool of reserve Registrar personnel in training, 0:347

procurement and, 4:834

promissory notes and, 2:569

promotional actions of, 0:349

promotional letters and, 2:606

PTS or chronically ill or NCG and Registrar lines, 2:571, MS1:460, MS2:251

public never asked to decide or choose, 0:323

purpose, 2:491

purpose of Registrar interview, 2:586, 6:413

Reception routes bodies who walk in to, 2:486, 6:379

Registration Pgm No. 2, 2:570–575, 6:392

reports made by, 2:395

responsibility for,
every bank in country, 6:381
procurement, interview, signing up, legal and finance, 2:477

selling life, so have a right to know it was or was not delivered, 4:1036

shall not do accounting, 2:489

signs person up for something, 1:121

signs up pcs conditionally pending acceptance by Tech, 2:587, 6:414

statistic, 2:551

students and preclears must be invoiced whether charge is made or no charge, 2:552, 6:386

students returned to Reg by training staff, 2:488

Tech Estimate and, 2:587

there to *help* people sign up and to assist resolution of their problems in signing up, 2:491

three things needs to know, 2:564, 6:387

vital that a *competent* technical opinion be sought before a Registrar commits the Tech Division to servicing a pc or student, 4:1034

ways a registrar can set up Tech for a loss, 4:1033

what Registrar concentrates on that makes difference between Division 2 and Division 6 Registrars, 2:584, 6:411

Registrar(s), Reg, *(cont.)*

when ethics files are not available or not up to date, errors can be made in accepting people and result in needless refunds, 2:453

who is a Class IV or VI and who has studied the C/S Series would be able to size up cases and students, 4:1034

who reges the person, Day or Foundation, gets the stat on own stats, 3:171, 7:316

will fail if they do not know or use tech of selling, 2:570, 6:393

would have to be fully briefed on Grade Chart and C/S Series HCOBs, 2:559–560

wouldn't let anybody buy anything but standard items, 2:532

writing to people and auditing them by mail, 2:614

Registrar's Advice Form,

example, 2:540, 4:1022

use of, 2:445

registration, registering,

all students and pcs must be registered, 3:141

as income-getting action, 0:99

bad control personnel on Reg posts will waste whoever is driven in, 2:412, 6:184

Big League Sales and, 2:570, 6:392

definition, 2:497

Dept 6 and, 0:349

dishonest regging,
impoverishes an org faster than fire, 4:154
what it covers, 2:112, 3:88, 6:556, 7:862

disqualification for Registration post, 2:412, 6:184

Exec Dirs who reg instead of getting Registrars, 0:693

hatted Letter Reges and a CF beats all the telephones in the world, 3:212

helps people to get help, 6:382

invoicing and, 4:215, 6:383

letter from an experienced and successful ex-Registrar, 2:538

letter registration, basic cycle of, 2:625

must not wear an Accounts hat, 2:658

no service or sale may be given without invoicing or, 4:219

organization mail incoming is first letter demand on Registration personnel, 2:657

packet for, 2:633

people who cannot control people on Registration posts, result, 2:411, 6:183

phone registration in city areas, 0:353

Registration Pgm No. 2, 2:570–575, 6:392

without proper technical knowledge Registration is blind, 2:564, 6:387

registration packet, consists of, 2:633

Registration Program, 2:577

regulation(s), *see also* law; policy; rule

Advanced Course, 4:813

general staff, 7:50

no student rules and regulations except Justice Codes, 0:478

observing Saint Hill regulations, 0:151

staff member duties, 0:165

standards of Scientology group, 0:152–153

rehab, rehabilitate, rehabilitation,

before Power, when it's done, 5:674

by asking "Ability Attained" question, 5:254

our justice really rehabilitates in long run, 0:484

when it can act as invalidation, 5:674

rehandling, 1:71

reimburse, we will no longer reimburse any person for purchases he makes, 3:286

reissue, forbidden to reissue Scientology technical data in bulletins and policy letters over some other signature than mine, 7:1290

rejects, one gives the letter of, MS1:142

Release, release, releasing,

all staff have right to demand releasing and clearing, 0:20

all you have to do in org is release and clear people, 0:16

a suppressive person, 1:1010

auditor who gets final result will be credited, 5:355

balance of intensive not refundable, 4:1063

button, 5:327

can't upgrade without the processing, 4:1074

checkouts, 5:230, 5:234

policy if checkouts are bad and nonfactual, 5:238

procedure for, 5:748–750

contract, general form of, 2:418

data should be channeled to the right sources, 2:126

declarations, 5:235

declare in consecutive numbers only, 5:230

restrictions, 5:229

definition, 2:469, 5:225, 6:452

disseminate Scientology, 2:126

failure to protect the names and repute of Scientology leading personalities and LRH collapses an org, 2:127

former,

checked out for, 4:1064

pc may only be audited further on, 4:1064

person may only be declared, if rehabilitation work is done, 4:1066

Release, release, releasing, *(cont.)*

formerly audited pc and, 2:526

former Release,

checked out for, 5:744

floating needle on, 5:233

rehabilitated, 5:232, 5:746

free pass and, 2:526

Free Release Check, 2:531

grades of, 4:1085

if person was not found by Review to have been a former Release, 4:1065, 5:745

instruction and admin policy are almost as important as tech, 2:129

issue tech and policy as broadly as possible within economic limits, 2:130, 7:1296

logbook, 5:355

no pc who has been audited before may be accepted for processing who has not been checked out for former release, 2:525

offer anything you offer at a high appeal at high velocity and heavy impact, 2:132, 7:1298

pin, 2:380, 5:345

Grades V or VI, 5:356

one pin to each pc for all lower grades, 5:357

policies governing, 2:126, 2:525

Power processing and, 2:525

public must be protected against abusers of technology or policy, 2:128

raw meat and, 2:526

reattainment of, opens door to selling training, 4:1066, 5:746

target for suppressive persons, 4:1058

tech personnel mistaking state of Release for Clear, 4:202

trouble occurs when, 5:231

untrained person and, 4:1083

workable and proven materials of Dianetics and Scientology only may be released, 2:127

Release check,

further, 4:1074

procedure for, 4:1068

Release Declaration, restrictions, 4:474

release forms,

no persons may be admitted to an Academy or HGC who have not signed waivers, 4:360

what it must include, 4:360

reliable sources, data system, MS1:26

Relief Release, ability gained, 4:190

religion,

definition, 6:870

freedom of, 0:68

literature must state Scientology is religious philosophy, 7:1320

religion, *(cont.)*

most critical point of attack on a culture, 6:867

PES responsible for visual evidences that
Scientology is a, 7:1320

Scientology,
all-denominational, 0:153
is a religion, 7:995

supporting freedom of, 0:160

target of attack is spirituality of man, your own
basic spiritual nature, self-respect and peace
of mind, 6:868

why Scientology is a religion, 6:517

religious philosophy, definition of, 6:517, 7:995

religious practice, definition of, 6:517, 7:995

Remedies A and B,

Danger conditions and, MS2:211

Remedy A, B—having a Dept of Review red
hot on doing, 4:630

remimeo, definition, 1:407

remote, where people doing the targets
are, MS1:137

Remote Flag Registrar, 6:662

remote leadership, 0:122

removal, remove(d), *see also* **demotion; dismiss;
transfer**

court or Comm Ev in order for person to be
removed, 0:523, 0:585, 0:587

Exec Council may remove members of Ad
Council, 7:914

for treasonable neglect, 0:220

giving removed person another chance, 0:239

"I don't care what your rights are, you are
REMOVED!" 0:522

injustice and, 0:522

must be approved by the International Justice
Chief, 1:257

personnel, power restored to an org to do so
locally, 1:260

recourse and, 0:522

request form must be accompanied by proposed
replacement, 1:257

staff cannot be "removed from post, sent before
the Fitness Board and dismissed," 0:524

steps for taking person off post, 1:182

taking unwilling personnel off lines, 0:397

when absence of personally issued Ethics
Conditions Orders may constitute grounds
for removal of exec, 0:659

renovation,

carrying out program of, 0:356

extensive, result of, 7:1396

rent, must be paid from the expense sum, 3:42

reorganization, *see* **organize**

repair, repairing,

of that which produces or is produced, 0:287

operational, definition of, 0:190

Product Clearing and, MS2:57

quantity, quality and viability of repair
of org, 0:288

Scientology repairs itself, 0:362

repair of past ethics conditions, 0:260

procedure, 1:608–609

theory, 1:607

Repair Program, Progress Program,
4:1102, 4:1107

repayment(s), *see also* **refund(s)**

cause of, 3:263, 5:712, 7:1109

definition, 3:262, 4:157, 5:711, 7:1108

paid by Dept 8, MS2:327

when it would not be subtracted from Technical
Secretary's stat, 4:158

when you can expect repayments, 3:262, 7:1108

when you do give refunds or repayments you do
it on policy, 3:263, 7:1109

replacement(s), replace, replacing, *see also*
removal

hat turnovers and quicksilver personnel scene,
MS1:469

objection to one's, 0:596

policies covering hat turnovers and, 0:266

request form for transfer or removal must be
accompanied by, 1:257

when to find another person for the post, 0:239,
0:374, 0:416

report(s)(ing), *see also* **staff member report**

auditor report, whole idea of requiring, 4:1182

completions, reporting of, 0:428

computer crimes, additional copy forwarded to
INCOMM Computer Banks, MS2:464

conditions formula steps taken must be reported
one by one, 0:621

Confessionals and, 1:645

definition, MS2:60, MS2:242

demanding full particulars, not
half-reports, 0:392

different for each department, 1:658

embroidered reports, 0:373

Ethics, things to report to, 0:494, 0:543,
0:547–548, 0:623

Alter-Is Report, 1:699

Annoyance Report, 1:700

Crime Report, 1:700

Damage Report, 1:699

Dev-T Report, 1:700

Error Report, 1:700

report(s)(ing), *(cont.)*

Ethics, things to report to, *(cont.)*
    False Attestation Report, 1:700
    False Report Report, 1:700
    Found Report, 1:699
    High Crime Report, 1:700
    Idle Report, 1:699
    Job Endangerment Report, 1:700
    Knowledge Report, 1:700
    Loss or Theft Report, 1:699
    Misdemeanor Report, 1:700
    Misuse Report, 1:699
    Noncompliance Report, 1:700
    No-Report Report, 1:700
    Things That Shouldn't Be, 1:705
    Waste Report, 1:699
executives to turn in on staff, 1:755, 4:100
Extension Course Completion, 1:517
failure to receive a, 0:544
    false, 1:541
filed by Ethics, 1:701
filed in pcs' folders, 5:717
financial, most direct index of whether or not
    promotion is reaching people, 7:1176
Flag Representative reports should
    consist of, 7:1413
form for a department, 1:657
if an org fails to make a, 1:871
illegible, 0:544
knowing of outness or crime and failing to
    report it, 0:557
loans to staff reported to Saint Hill, 0:171
make it easy to accept a report of a
    done, 7:825
making full verbal report of any article
    stolen, 0:548
message vs., 1:299
miscellaneous, 1:850
more on, 1:712
most important report is whether or not
    magazine is going out on schedule and
    whether or not PrR is functioning
    alertly, 7:1176
no report(s),
    auditor who doesn't report to session, 0:19
    charge of, 0:47
    dev-t and, 0:424
off-policy or out-tech order, reporting of,
    0:146–147
omitted, MS1:168
Org Rudiments, 1:517
outflow of reports to other org members, 0:367
procedure, 1:658
refusal to, Committee of Evidence for, 1:869
reporting weekly the stat of every post for
    which one is responsible, 0:690
seeing things that don't exist and reporting them
    as "fact," 0:514

report(s)(ing), *(cont.)*

students and pcs must report matters covered
    under Justice Code to HCO, 0:478
system to reduce and standardize administrative
    reporting, 7:39
Technical,
    Alter-Is Report, 1:700
    Noncompliance Report, 1:700
training, made weekly by Intern Sup, 5:843
unsubstantiated reports, 0:515, 0:520
unusual favors, reporting of, 0:171
weekly income reports from departments, 3:121
what heads of production departments are
    expected to include, 7:55
when due to Executive Director, 7:641
when Review Auditor or Examiner finds tech
    mess, 5:39

reporter,

how he writes "story" about Scientology based
    on 7 points required for a news story,
    MS3:127
how they operate and how to handle, MS3:125
serving specialized groups, MS3:152

reputation, repute,

bad repute for org or government,
    causes of, 0:40
goodwill and, 0:332
HCO Ethics Codes and justice protects jobs
    and, 0:477, 0:481, 0:502, 0:503
promotional actions to increase repute
    of org, 0:349

Reserved Payment Account,

all transfers are subject of disbursement
    vouchers, 3:316
bills in question and, 3:315
definition and purpose, 3:315
large outstanding purchase orders and, 3:316
savings for large or expensive purchases
    and, 3:316

reserves,

giving reputation of stability to org, 0:349
what they are used for, MS2:318

re-sign, definition, MS1:333, MS2:167

re-sign line,

call-in and, 2:644, 2:648, 3:220, 3:224, 4:279,
    4:283, 7:868, 7:872
definition, MS2:174

re-sign-up, returning pc to Registrar for, 0:303

resistive case, grades out is major factor, 5:275

resource(s),

above handling on eval form, MS1:177
Affluence and, 0:648
examining of, MS1:177

resource(s), *(cont.)*

    failed evaluations and, MS1:177

    feasibility and, 0:708

    look into them searchingly, MS1:177

    program has said "acquire nonexisting
        resources," MS1:177

    Sea Org appears to have unlimited, 0:246

    strategic plan and, 0:706, 7:459, 7:474,
        MS3:439, MS3:454

    within the limits of, 7:460, MS3:440

respect,

    auditor is to be respected, 0:154

    building blocks to, in most societies, 6:614,
        MS3:155

    definition, 1:86, MS2:218

    manners and, 0:328

    primary blocks to, 0:340

response, responding, *see also* answer

    definition, 2:624

    deliver to every person responding to
        promotion, 0:282

    "friendly and agreeable responses," 0:335

responsibility, responsible, *see also*
        irresponsibility

    afraid of taking responsibility, 0:260

    control and, 0:619

    definition, 0:619, 1:611, 4:1050, 5:566, 7:738,
        MS2:216

    detecting people who fear responsibility or
        consequences of their most ordinary
        actions, 0:412

    dev-t and low responsibility, 0:398

    down spiral begins when responsibility has
        failed, 0:139

    exec responsibility for training staff,
        0:220, 0:221

    execs must insist upon privileges and
        responsibilities of their posts, 0:582

    feeling grand and responsible when others must
        come to one for help, 0:412

    fixing responsibility for actions, 0:419, 0:427

    force and, 1:727

    for preclear's livingness and results, 4:55

    for your connections, 0:564

    Goals-Problem-Mass and, 5:566

    it does not relieve one of responsibility when
        one executes destructive order, 0:142

    lack of and results in society, 1:727

    lack of exec responsibility, 0:427

    let's grow up to our tech and take responsibility
        for it, 0:485

    neglect of responsibilities, offenses, 0:267, 0:468

    of co-auditors, 4:708

    of leaders, 0:629

responsibility, responsible, *(cont.)*

    orders occur where responsibility has
        failed, 0:139

    post and, 0:234

    real way to stop attacks is to widen one's zone
        of, MS2:428

    refusal to take responsibility for ending a cycle
        of action, 0:244–245

    rehabilitation of, 1:728

    twin is responsible for seeing that the student
        with whom he is twinned knows and can
        apply the material he has studied, 4:435

    twinning and, 4:432

responsible-for-condition case, described, 5:106

restimulate, restimulation,

    individual, restimulated, acts worse, 0:158

    SP deals only in, 1:1009

restriction, for training students, 4:309

result(s), *see also* product; production

    achieving results expands area control, 4:26

    are effect of your own efforts, 0:249

    attacks occur only where there are "no results"
        or "bad results," 1:8, 2:8, 3:8,
        4:8, 5:8, 7:8

    bad, handling for, 4:842

    Dept 12 gets excellent results on all pcs, 0:351

    if not forthcoming, somebody is goofing,
        0:19, 7:839

    interchanged with individual for support and
        goodwill, 0:296

    just not happening, handling, 0:498

    methods for demonstration of, 7:833

    no or bad results, effects of, 0:8

    number of times over the material equals
        certainty and, 4:442

    on pc, Supervisor must demand, 4:319

    or else, 5:729

    poor results come from, 4:1080, 5:671

    public with you just so long as results are
        achieved, 5:97

    Registrar does not promise, 4:1040

    responsibility for preclear's livingness and, 4:55

    what happens when public not delivered end
        result of auditing, 4:935, 5:263

retraining,

    constant retraining within a level for which
        auditor has already been classified is
        forbidden, 0:169

    definition, 4:441

    instruct, cram, retrain, offload system, 0:442

    staff auditor and, 4:1150

retread,

Class VIII, 4:827

illegal to give a retread course away, 4:389

one warning, one admin cramming, one retread, 0:392

return address,

rubber stamp for, 2:340

should be put on outgoing mail, 2:340

Return Program, renamed Advance Program, 4:1102, 4:1107

REV! definition, 4:1060, 5:115

REV FL? definition, 4:1060, 5:115

review(s),

all Ethics actions are reviewed, 0:490

evaluations should be reviewed, MS1:97

heart of is humility, MS1:98

of evals, MS1:157

Review,

audits and trains only to a specific result, 5:736

cases who roller-coaster routed to, 1:1011

code, has four symbols, 5:115

common mistake of, 5:38

complete, folder sent to Examiner, 5:251

fast flow pattern and, 1:971

flat ball bearings handled by, 1:971

former Release checkouts done in, 4:1064, 5:744

handling of PTSes, 1:1011, 5:121

if person was not found to have been a former Release, 4:1065, 5:745

in Qual someone can two-way comm those sent to Review to help the person and get more accurate data for C/Sing, 4:392

invoice unit between Examinations and, 5:735

most versatile department with single exception of Office of LRH, 5:736

must NOT hold on to pcs, 5:228

no direct routing of preclears to the Ethics Officer except through Qual Div and Review, 5:118

purpose, 5:735

rehab incomplete, handling, 5:757

send case not running well to, 4:1174, 5:587

sends PTS student to Ethics when right SP found, 1:1011

services charged for, 5:735

standard procedure, 5:33

students who get low marks constantly are handled in Review, 4:335

Supervisors must send any student PTS only to, 5:121

Tech hands over when all else fails, 4:1093

Review, *(cont.)*

via Academy and HGC, 5:736

when a case goes to, 5:256

Review Auditor,

bonus, 5:135

Class VIII C/S trying to do job without, 5:680

lack of ends the trail, 4:1097

never does major actions, 5:256

statistics, 5:76

when credited for Release, 5:355

Review Case Cracking Unit, 0:624

Review code, 4:1060

Review Committee of Evidence, 0:522, 0:523

Review Cramming Section, send auditor to, when pc goes to Review, 4:1174, 5:587

revolt(s), revolution(s), *see also* **revolutionary(ies); riot; violence; war**

against moral codes, 0:455–456

brought on by failure to provide jobs, purpose and training, MS1:408

causes of, 0:506

child revolting against parents in his teens, 0:529

contribution vs., 0:277

denial of jobs or status and, MS1:408

expression of, MS1:54

improperly stated ideal scene and, MS1:53

inability of French revolt to form cultures, 0:631

organized by SPs, 1:994, 4:86

people excluded from country's org board and, MS1:221

protest against idle status, MS1:68

Russia and, 0:511

sympathy and, MS1:230

welfare, program causing, 0:204

revolutionary(ies),

usual course taken, MS1:53

we are not, we are humanitarians, 6:835

reward(s)(ing), *see also* **award**

approval and validation vs. material rewards, 0:277

award production and up stats, 0:504

contributism and, 0:277

definition, 0:277

given to bums or thieves, 0:508

of pride in doing a job well, 0:528

rewarding down stat, 0:3, 0:504, 0:506, 0:528

reward up stat and damn the down, 0:508

seeking to raise one's own rewards above what he personally is earning in terms of VFPs, 0:316

reward(s)(ing), *(cont.)*

socialism, communism and, 0:506

system, for merit and good performance, 0:474

rich(es), wealth,

getting rich by doing what Ron says, 0:626

TV and movies tell one that robbery is the only way to get rich, 0:317

why one area is poor and another opulent, 0:89

riddle,

age-old riddle of philosophers, 0:528

effect of man's failure to solve riddle of himself, 0:258

solution to man's oldest riddle, 0:528

ridge on the Bridge,

handling, 6:441, 6:443

internally created by nondelivery, 6:443

quickying and, 6:443

right(ness), correct(ness),

ability to make things go right, 0:236–237, 0:251, 0:430

be right on majority of decisions, 0:231, 0:246

civilizations dying because things went right only so long as nothing was going wrong, 0:236

compliance and, 0:246

concepts of wrong and, 0:452, 0:453

definition of right, 0:236

does not get compliance because there are always counter-intentions in the way, 7:706

do it right in first place, 0:255

for each correct procedure there can be infinity of incorrect actions, 0:58

glowing things right, 0:638

going on assumption that all want things to go right, 0:246

good is being more right than wrong, 0:453

government's divine rightness in judicial matters, 0:450, 0:522

HCO Ethics Codes let you know when you're wrong or, 0:481

importance of being causative, correct and decisive on posts, 0:231

I try to be right more often than wrong, 0:594

it will all come out all right, 0:155

no absolute right or wrong, 0:454

reason things run right, 0:518

right ways to do things are called technical procedures or tech, 0:58

sane people make things go right, 0:252

supreme test of thetan is ability to make things go right, 0:236, 0:251, 0:430

right(s),

to be entirely right would be to survive to infinity, 0:453

using force to demand society do what is right, 0:630

dishonest people have sacrificed their, 0:152

Gold Stars and Green Stars, rights of, 0:525, 0:662

honest people have rights, 0:152, 0:461, 1:481

how one can make anything go right, MS2:233

"I don't care what your rights are, you are REMOVED!" 0:522

individual rights were not originated to protect criminals, 0:461

insisting upon your rights to live with honest people, 0:461

justice, rights of staff member, students and pcs to, 0:477

nobody has any right to a bank, 0:242

of a staff member, students and preclears to justice, 1:730

people who do their work need very little supervision and have rights, 0:151

people who don't do their work don't have rights, 0:151

precedent and privilege are suspended for officers and staff members of a portion in State of Emergency, 0:622

right to survive is directly related to one's honesty, 0:461

Scientology justice safeguards rights of Scientologists, 0:477

staff ignorant of rights, result, 0:521, 0:524

staff member rights,
list of, 0:19–20
to be tried only by seniors in rank or status, 0:523
to do your job, 0:553
to petition, 0:488
to serve, 0:238, 0:278

riot(s), rioters; *see also* **revolt; revolution; revolutionary(ies); violence; war**

basic reason for, in the US, 0:68

government and, 0:481, 0:512

HCO deputizing other Scientologists in times of, 0:478

of Rome, cause of, 0:529

rip-off, *see also* **robbery; theft**

definition, 0:317, 7:314, MS1:474

in-charge who lets org get ripped off for some personal favor, 0:534

indicators of, 0:533

rise, it's a bit mean to nag around about a, 0:678

risk, operating at, 0:255

rituals, don't worship our, 0:274

road out,

Dianetics and Scientology are only road out of witch pit, 0:362

road out, *(cont.)*

road out is road to truth, 0:520

when it is blocked, 0:242

robber(s), exchange, condition of, 0:317

robbery, *see also* **rip-off; theft**

robbed person investigated exclusively, rarely robber, 0:505

TV and movies tell one that robbery is only way to get rich, 0:317

Robert's Rules of Order, 0:173, 7:912

robot, robotism,

definition, 1:817

education, advertising and amusements designed for, 1:820

false reports and, 1:819

not malicious, 1:818

processing to remedy, 1:820

PTS person is robot to the suppressive, MS1:461, MS2:252

rock slam,

action taken to handle, 1:623

definition, 5:606

false, caused by rings, 5:462

HCO qualifications and, 1:82

means crimes, 1:633

people who rock slam obsessively seek to unstabilize others, 1:82

Rodil, General, 0:633

Rodriguez, Simon, 0:631

roll book (course),

Dir I&R should inspect, 4:465

filed in Val Docs when full, 4:464

purpose and description, 4:464

roll call, course and, 0:222

roller coaster case(s), *see also* **case(s)**

Academy and, 4:344

definition, 1:1004

equals PTS, 5:35

of processing results is never because of restimulation caused by training, 4:626

only reason for loss of gain obtained in auditing, 4:1081, 5:672

routing of, 1:1011

Roman Catholic,

never once in any country including Ireland has the Roman Catholic Church raised its voice against us, 6:516

processing persons of the Catholic faith, 6:516

Rome,

Caesar wrecked smooth progress of, 0:124

Rome, *(cont.)*

cause of their decline, 0:505

inspection before the fact, 0:66

Mussolini empire where only Rome could decide, 0:231

riots of Rome, cause of, 0:529

Roneo,

mimeograph machine, 1:428

stencil cutter, 1:428

Roosevelt, Franklin Delano, 0:506

"rough cases," *The Book of Case Remedies* and, 5:733

rough layout,

cropping, two types and two stages, MS3:198

definition, MS3:194, MS3:198

relationship with design, MS3:196

watchword is precision, MS3:199

round robin, definition of, 4:439

route(s), *see also* **channel; line; organization form**

definition and description of, 0:82, MS1:235

following the, 5:19

giving public or outside or internal traffic correct routes and terminals, 0:281

HRD is major route for public into org, 4:198

key to a healthy volume of public flow up the Bridge, 6:115

public entrance route, STCC followed by HQS, 6:498

standard lines and routes for particles to follow, 0:392

Routine 3D, Clear bracelet and, 5:320

routing, routed, *see also* **channel; communication line; flow; flow line; line**

authority to handle routing, 0:409

B routing, 0:543

body routing in Central Organizations, 1:121

channel skips, 0:426

command channel routing, 0:387

conference routing, 0:387

definition, 0:389

description, 0:405

despatches, routing of, 0:383, 0:386

difference between order and chaos is straightforward planned flows and correct particles, MS2:234

executive(s),

enforcing proper routing, 0:406–407

how he can jam all lines, 0:388

routing as major duty of, 0:383, 0:389, 0:390, 0:404

for CCRD, 4:976

routing, routed, *(cont.)*

forwarding something already improperly routed, 0:404

horizontal fast flow routing, 0:386

ideal scene, how to move an org towards by routing, MS2:235

know-how of, 0:390

loss of would-be staff due to misrouting, 1:172

major duty of an executive, MS2:234

making channels on which things can flow, 0:389

misrouting,
declining stat due to, 0:384
description, 0:405
exec must not permit bypass and, 0:582–584
failing to handle it when it occurs, 0:404
forwarding misrouted despatch, 0:408
prevention of, 0:414

no direct routing of preclears to the Ethics Officer except through Qual Div and Review, 5:118

not knowing org board and sending things to wrong terminals, 0:391

off-line routing, cure for, 0:407

order to person two or three steps down command channel, 0:593

org board and, 0:105, 0:108, 0:383

org form and, 1:277

orgs are too big for routing to occur to Bill, Jane or Pete, 0:383

pcs recommended to Ethics and also to Declare?, 5:119

petitions and, 0:488–489

potential trouble source, handling, 5:121

preclear,
to Ethics, 4:1073
who needs to buy proper number of weeks of auditing, 6:379

promotional actions of org relating to, 0:347, 0:348

properly, 0:281, 0:383, 0:404

Reception,
first order of business, 1:121
function to move public and staff bodies, 1:123

rerouting despatch received which does not concern your post, 0:166

staff member reports, routing of, 0:543

taking responsibility to see that people get to right terminal, 0:165

three types of comm routing, 0:386

what it consists of, 0:405

when making routing arrangements is called organizing and when it is called promotion, 0:408

routing, routed, *(cont.)*

wrong addresses, 0:383

wrong routing makes people "busy" but nothing gets done, 0:388

routing form(s),

computerization, 1:138

definition, MS2:169

how to write, 1:137–138

responsibility, 1:138

run off in Mimeo, 1:435

substitute for executive control of org, 1:136

theory, 1:136

use of on the Hubbard Key to Life Course, 4:650

way to handle admin problems, 1:135

royalties, 1:21, 7:1162

R6EW,

Advanced Courses and, 4:805

Clear and, 5:250

materials, 4:789

rudiments, False Data Stripping and, MS2:142

Rudiments Officer, duties of, 6:560

Rudiments Program,

EP of, 6:559, 6:562

org board position of, 6:560

picks up every ARC broken Scientologist or Dianeticist and gets them back in ARC with the org and Scientology and returned to services or signed up for further services, 6:559

Rudiments Officer and, 6:560

Rudiments Program Section, 6:533–534

Rudiments Receptionist, duties of, 6:560

Rudiments Registrar and, 6:562

Rudiments Repair Auditor and, 6:561

Rudiments Survey and Research Clerk and, 6:561

successful operating pattern of, 6:560

value of, 6:559

Rudiments Registrar, handling of public, 5:838; *see also* **Rudiments Program**

ruin, definition, 6:490

rule(s), *see also* **law; policy; regulation**

can be wrong, 0:274

conceived at times of stress, 0:117

if followed too closely it becomes a Simple Simon idiocy, 4:606

no student rules and regulations except Justice Codes, 0:478

"off the cuff," 0:481

the oldest we have, 4:678

when to say to hell with the, 0:274

ruler(s), *see also* **leader**

successful org will be fought by society's fancied rulers or enemies, 0:64

war rulers deified and peacetime rulers forgotten, 0:505

rumor(s),

being free of dismissal by, 0:481

caused by potential trouble sources, 1:752, 7:681

choosing personnel, promoting or firing by, 0:120–121

cleaning up ARC breaks caused by, 0:484

false reports by, 0:514

how they can go through a society, MS3:77

individuals who do not understand pass on slanderous, MS3:77

I pay no attention to, 0:151

org is run on stats not rumors, 0:582

policy and actions based on, 0:117

PTSes and, 0:498

spread about prominent Scientologists, 0:471, 1:993, 4:85

rumor(s), *(cont.)*

using without knowing stats, MS1:69

when an executive listens to, 1:1026, 7:510

rumormonger, 1:1015

rundown,

co-auditing of, 4:688

specialist, C/Sing of, 4:664

Russia,

be-do-have cycle and, 0:293

description of economic conditions in, 0:506, 0:598, 0:599

how Russia governs people, 0:599

imperialism, colonialism and, 0:508

main problem of, 0:293

management went into politics, 0:506

product is revolution, 0:293

revolution, Germany financed Lenin, 0:511

why experiments of totalitarian communal states starve and fail, 0:186

worry whether Russia is going to declare war on United States, 0:454

S

"sad effect," ARC break and, 5:210

Saenz, Manuela, 0:629, 0:635

consort of Simon Bolivar, 7:376

most fatal mistake, not bringing down Bolivar's chief enemy, 7:382, MS3:362

potentially able and a formidable enemy, she did not act, 7:383, MS3:363

tragedy as Bolivar's mistress was that she was never used, 7:382, MS3:362

violated the Power Formula in not realizing she had power, 7:382, MS3:362

safe,

hatted staff member is safe, 0:268

safe environment, *see* environment

safe space, trying to hat someone in, 0:207

safeguarding technology, 0:21

safe point,

ability to detect SP/PTSes and maintaining your, MS3:90

most important action to undertake in making, MS3:90

preparation of, MS3:90

takes consideration over active defense, MS3:89

Saint Hill,

Academy certs and, 5:510

actions to be done by all former St. Hill personnel before they have certificates, 7:610

all material of SH courses is in use, 0:14

allowed technical services, 4:121, 6:764

always mans up AO dept or div along with the SH one, 7:449, MS2:273

animals at, 7:1352

Saint Hill, *(cont.)*

classifications and designations given at, list of, 4:721

course, awarded a staff member, 5:409

demanding personnel be sent to Saint Hill to be trained, 0:19

fishing and hunting forbidden, 7:1359

Friday cable, 7:622

function redefined, 7:136

gave away CF folders, 0:359

in its boom days we had around 198 students, 4:407, 6:398

is not eligible for contest prizes for selections to AOs, 6:659

list of actions expected from Saint Hill staff members, 7:633

live-in staff, regulations, 7:1347

no professional auditor shall have full-time practice within 20 miles of, 6:708

observing Saint Hill regulations, 0:151

Power condition in '60s, 0:645

product of, 4:123, 6:766

program for remainder of 1965, 7:67

programs, 7:362, 7:364, 7:369

programs, corrections and addition, MS3:349

programs, each solved self-evident problem, MS3:344

promoted to a nine division org board, 6:81

Public Divisions in turn must force the Scientology orgs Public Divisions to function, 6:128

recombined with Worldwide, 7:148

reorganization and, 7:633

security of, 7:1354

senior personnel trained at, 4:861

Saint Hill, *(cont.)*

sequence of major programs at, MS3:342

specialist courses available at, 4:666

staff auditor's code, 4:1184

staff, Auditor's Code and purpose, 5:591

staff auditor's purpose, 4:1184

staff personnel allocation (1963), 7:1369

standards of, 0:153

three zones of authority, 7:1340

took 18 months to get Saint Hill stats up by factor of 5, 0:676

training,
   before sending to, cover essentials, 5:405
   candidates from organizations, 5:404
   higher status staff member may be sent to as an award, 5:409

unless top area is expanded it will check expansion lower, 7:223

what personnel comes under Saint Hill Administrator, 7:219

Saint Hill FSM, bonus awards to orgs or missions may only be a portion of an SHSBC course, such as one level, 6:661

Saint Hill graduate(s),

activities in Central Organization and, 4:59

auditing and, 4:59

duties they may not be used for, 4:59

policy on subject of, 4:59

shouldn't be posted as Supervisor or only staff auditor, 4:98

Saint Hill News,

description, 2:424

editorial composition, 2:424

editor is Director of Enrollment, 2:425

mailing of, 2:425

Saint Hill org board,

notes for chart, 7:57

purposes and, 7:57

Saint Hill Special Briefing Course,

Academy training up through lower grades and NED required for initial enrollment, 4:786

Academy trying to teach SHSBC instead of Academy level checksheets, 4:630

auditing regulations, 4:738

checksheets for, 4:631

Clear and, 2:437, 4:737

clearing and, 4:743

Clears enrolling on, requirements, 4:786

contacting all possible candidates for, 2:420

duration of, 4:785

enrollment chart, 2:422–423

goals, 4:737

Saint Hill Special Briefing Course, *(cont.)*

graduates, importance of, 4:733

how to get it back in, 5:276

if Academy results good and students informed, there will be Saint Hill enrollments, 2:422

if Enrollment Department does not keep eye on route from Academies to Saint Hill, enrollments will decline, 2:422

not treated as an HGC, 4:728

operating principles, 4:717

organization, 4:745, 4:762

perfect student performance expected, 4:718

prerequisites modified, 4:659

prospects should be developed with advance view of at least two years, 2:422

purpose, 4:717, 4:728, 4:750

requirement for termination on, 4:784

requirements, 4:785

retread, 4:730

routing and handling of students, 4:783

student holding a post in Foundation, 4:783

student on the Day SHSBC is first and foremost a student, 4:783

students, should co-audit as they train, 4:688

supervision, 4:315

termination and classification, 4:722

training targets for Saint Hill students, 4:749

Units, description of, 4:734

V Unit, 4:731, 4:740

Saint Hill Special Briefing Course Section, ideal scene and stat, 4:142

salary, *see also* **staff pay; pay**

only maids, janitors and maintenance and part-time accounting may be paid salary, 3:330

salary sum, sums recompensed for illegal discounts or giving away services are placed in the, 0:303

salary sum check, must be accompanied by a purchase order, 3:291

sale(s), sell(ing), *see also* **book sales; delivery**

book ads and sales are the keys to org survival, 2:295, 6:259

bound up in costing, pricing and selling, MS1:275

CF only able to sell to "new" names, 0:360

covert selling, 6:758

discounts given on cash sales only and sales or service paid in full, 3:145

not until 1930 did anyone really begin to sell to the people with heavy advertising, 0:506

of HCOBs, HCO PLs and tapes, 3:130

sale(s), sell(ing), *(cont.)*

of HCOBs, HCO Policy Letters and tapes are forbidden to all orgs, 2:288

orgs exist to sell and deliver materials and service to public and get in public to sell and deliver to, 0:91

quicksilver personnel scene and, 0:265

reducing prices does not increase sales, 0:337

Registrars will fail if they do not know or use tech of selling, 6:393

some of the sales actions and lines for in an org, MS2:172–173

third dynamic psychosis is the impeding of product distribution to potential consumers, MS1:268

salesman, is as an individual a good investment, 2:156, 6:172

salesmanship, agreement is key to, MS3:55, MS3:230

salvage, punishing vs. salvaging, 0:462

S&D, *see* **Search and Discovery**

sane person, sanity, sane,

ability to, MS1:3

basically honesty and truth, 6:306

consists of, MS1:295

difference between insanity and, 7:1143

honesty is the road to, 0:528

how sanity and honesty relate to producing VFP, 0:296

in a group depends upon, MS1:57

insane differentiated from, 0:252, 0:296

is basically honesty and truth, 4:235

making world saner, better place, 0:158, 0:161, 0:206

matter of motive, not rationality or competence, 0:296, MS1:295

producer has stake in maintaining sanity of scene in which he is operating, 0:298

product of the, 0:259, MS1:446

sane group controlling their environment, 0:253

thinks, looks and sees in straight lines, 0:236

way to, MS1:130

Santander, 0:632

satisfaction, liar never happy or satisfied with himself, 0:458

saturation, hit a saturation point, MS3:179

sauna, definition, 4:1224

savings, Reserved Payment Account and, 3:316

scale,

concerning lines and terminals, MS1:288

Gross Income Executive International responsible for establishing sliding scale of pricing of intensives, 2:458

sliding scale of pricing of intensives, definition, 2:458

scene(s), *see also* **ethics scene; existing scene; ideal scene**

definition, MS2:39

ideal scene, 0:204, 0:441

knowing existing scene, 0:144, 0:294

missing, MS1:41

observe the existing scene, MS1:109

producer has stake in maintaining sanity of scene in which he is operating, 0:298

quicksilver personnel scene, 0:264–267

to adjust a scene you have to look at it, MS2:40

two types of, MS1:51

when a person has some idea of, he should be able to separate data into similar groups, MS1:43

schedule(s), scheduling, *see also* **time**

abide by working hours of org, 0:165

accordance with scale of preference, 4:890

co-audit, 4:694

course, 4:425

Day and Foundation org Academy schedule, 4:453

determined by type of particle the org form is set up to handle, MS2:116

D of P duty, 4:963

D of T and Sup responsibility for precise course, 4:453

done in accordance with the scale of preference, 3:159

5-hour intensive and, 4:955

how to establish, MS2:118

nonconsecutive, 4:97

nonconsecutive scheduling, part-time students, 0:497

nonstandard, results of, 4:454

org form and, MS2:118

parts of org engaged upon similar functions must be on same, MS2:116

post and study schedule, 0:222, 0:439

posting of, 0:439

preclear and, 4:252

processing and, 4:242

promotion and, 0:349

sharp, mark of successful Academy, 4:316

student acceptable behavior and, 4:477

time pc audited is decided by HGC only, 2:502, 4:248

schizophrenia,

most prevalent "mental disorder," MS2:64

type of insanity, 1:994, 4:86

scholarship(s), 0:175, 0:337, 0:528

discounts, 5:432

how to boom training with, 4:387

no additional discount of price when awarding, 2:456, 6:410

purpose of, 3:173, 4:222, 6:769

schooling, must not withhold a child from his legal schooling, 4:306, 5:730

Science of Survival, bible of PR, MS3:66, MS3:70, MS3:241

sciences, 0:258

scientist, is a captive brain, 7:1123

Scientologist(s), *see also* **Scientology**

agreeing to abide by HCO Codes, 0:477

being a, 0:483

clearing is now in reach of every, 0:16

Code of a Scientologist, 0:160, 6:603, 7:1047

definition of, 7:271

deserve protection from psychotics and criminals, 1:989

don't be so sensitive to popular reaction, 0:158

failing to use Scientology tech and administrative and justice procedures on world around one, result, 0:484

field Scientologist should have a hat, 0:204

first thing one should know about Scientology is the use of its materials, 6:143

frowning on trying to prevent people from being processed, 0:153

game to play, 6:448

half-minded about being Scientologists, 0:13

have enough courage to face their own past and misdeeds and recover from them, 0:152

have lost their viewpoint of newness of Dianetics and Scientology, 0:362

how and why we are getting job done, 0:85, 0:239

just because YOU are making it is no reason world will, 0:362

justice, *see* ethics; justice

keeping admin working and, 0:70, 0:72

landlord presenting claim against a, 0:172

letter from Ron, 6:581

making saner world, 0:158, 0:161

may be members of any political group, 0:159

person does not have to know Scientology to be member, 0:152

promotional actions of org related to, 0:353, 0:354, 0:355

raising our sights as to what we expect from ourselves and each other, 0:258

Scientologist(s), *(cont.)*

refusing to speak ill of Scientology or criticize it to outsiders, 0:153

rendering assistance to HCO during period of stress, 0:478

rented quarters, responsibility for, 0:172

safe environment for, 0:485

Scientology has uniformly failed in hands of non-Scientologists, 0:159

we'll have to come back to Earth someday no matter what "happens" to us, 0:85

we're probably last free men and women on Earth, 0:85

what we expect of a, 6:828

when you need reassurance, 0:155

will to do, 0:703

Scientology,

A, R and C of Scientology One match the public, the co-audits and the lower levels of the Academy, 2:164, 4:66, 6:189

accounting policies, 3:65

admin personnel gets it to public and keeps them happy, 0:18

advances have been in how to handle basics better, 0:65

aims of, 6:519, 7:1021

all-denominational, 0:153

Anatomy of the Human Mind Course as bridge from Book One to, 6:443

application, *see* application

attacks and, 7:1152

attacks on Scientology, *see* attack

based on ARC and held together with ARC, 3:243

base of motor discussed in, 0:205

basically communication, 6:686

basic mission of, 2:401

best news man has ever had, 0:363

bigger we get, the more economics and time we will have to do our job, 0:13

black PR campaign against, MS3:28

books and papers are a record of research, 7:1092

books of comparable magnitude in Dianetics, 2:145, 6:233

books, *see* book

bowling vs., 0:497

breakthrough in, 0:450

broad data is in books, 2:378

can help if you haven't done things to hurt its people, 0:153

cannot look for justice at hands of civilization, 0:481

can revive his ability to learn, 2:146

Scientology, *(cont.)*

cannot progress in the society unless it is done by a group effort, 6:26, 7:967

changing course of all things past and sending whole of existence back upward from its long plunge, 0:92

closest spiritual ties with any other religion are with Orthodox (Hinayana) Buddhism, 6:517

comms contain ARC, 7:648

composed of people who want to get more able in life and to live better life, 0:152

contests and prizes, 0:234

Creed of Church, 6:515, 7:965

C/S should be an expert on, 0:65

critics of, 1:782

de-aberrating just by education contained in, 0:38

definition, 6:293

delivery of Scientology, *see* delivery

description of, 2:22, 6:27, 7:968

desired gains, 2:378

desire to achieve a gain by the use of, 5:353

Dianetics and, separate subjects, 5:633

dilettantism and, 0:497

discipline, *see* discipline

discoveries in organization are creeping into business practice, 0:3

disseminate Scientology, 7:1292

dissemination policy becomes: You can survive with Scientology, 6:153

distractions from, 0:123, 0:283, 0:501

divided into five levels, 4:61

does not conflict with other religions, 7:995

does not owe its help, 6:519, 7:1021

does not work in the absence of official control, 7:1020

don't worship our rituals, 0:274

effectiveness could be destroyed by teaching via TRs which can be interpreted by a student as the way to audit, 4:592

enemy PRO actions and, 6:608, MS3:142

enemy product vs. Scientology product, 6:602, 7:1046

enter into by reading a book, 5:353

ethics actions must parallel purposes of Scientology and its orgs, 0:502

ethics presence and, 0:247

evolutionary group, 0:273

expansion of, *see* expansion

failed in hands of non-Scientologists, 0:159

failing to apply our own admin, tech and justice procedures to the society around us, 0:483, 0:484

Scientology, *(cont.)*

fighting full-scale war against ignorance and enslavement, 0:208

first job of, 7:1013

first level divided into theory, practical and auditing, 2:161

first science on Earth that could salvage a human being, 2:147

flanked on all sides with incompetent "sciences," 0:258

freedom and, *see* freedom

Fundamentals of Thought the "Book One" of Scientology, 2:143, 6:231

gains there to be attained, 4:936, 5:264

game(s), *see* game

gateway into, 2:378

getting it back in, fully used and taught, 4:936, 5:264

gives us our first chance to have a real democracy, 7:1015

handle it with, 1:738, 7:1018

handled by the Founding Church and HASI, 2:143

handling highest commodity—life itself, 0:656

handling people and how, 7:1153

HCO Ethics Codes, *see* HCO Ethics Codes

HCO justice applies to all Scientology, 0:477

HCO PLs and HCOBs are senior data on which we operate, 0:143

healing and mental treatment policies apply to Scientology, 2:533, 6:433, 5:595

healing field vs., 0:126

how it spreads through training, 4:461

if it is ever to travel, it will be accomplished by groups, 6:686

if it is not written, it is not true, 0:375

if we fail, result, 0:13, 0:239

integrity and, 0:337

invitation acceptance form questionnaire, 2:379

is a religion, 7:995

is a religious practice applying to man's spirit and his spiritual freedom, 6:433

is open to all people, 6:207

issuing Scientology data under another name, 0:473

it's new civilization we're after, 0:501

it will all come out all right, 0:155

justice, *see* justice

Scientology, *(cont.)*

keeping it working, *see* Keeping Scientology Working

labyrinth Scientology leads out of, 0:20

large number of people de-aberrate just by the education contained in Scientology, 4:371

"leaks" into general knowledge, 0:3

lower grades unburden an awful lot of bank and environment when properly applied to a cooperative pc and can give him wins, 2:468

main objective of, 0:140

materials of are designed to communicate, 6:143

misrepresentation of, 7:1110

mission of, 0:96

more thetan you have present, the less policy you need and the better things run, 3:243, 7:1069

must look good, 1:32

never cause of consistent dullness or glibness, 4:335

never discuss Scientology with the critic, 1:784

newness of, 0:22, 0:362

new news to bulk of world's population, MS3:136, MS3:173

no greater game in universe than Scientology, 0:235

no more ethical group on this planet than ourselves, 0:10

nonpolitical and nonideological, 0:159

nonpolitical in nature, 7:1021

non-Scientology staff, 0:152

no secret standards in, 0:153

no squirrel is ever able to duplicate our product, 0:124

not deserved by divine right, 1:986

not entangling our purposes with arbitrary laws which do not further our cause, 0:273

not "just another self-help subject," 0:91

offenses, *see* offense

one is rising to eternity in, 4:990

one of the reasons it is fought so hard, 7:1131

"one should do something else too," 0:497, 4:173

one would not issue Scientology materials of considerable weight to people incapable of assimilating them, 6:28, 7:969

only full study in the field of the mind developed in the twentieth century, 6:165

only game where all dynamics win, 7:1126

only thing that can stop us, 0:13, 0:231

only thing that holds down the size of, 7:1314

open to all people, 0:234

order of magnitude between Dianetics and, 6:431–432

Scientology, *(cont.)*

organizational attitude, 4:62

Organization Cycle, 0:96

organization, three principal zones in an org, MS3:372

orgs, two uses to which they can be put, 7:391, MS3:371

our error, 7:1130

our potential, with what we know, is a majority of all populations solidly with us, 2:165, 6:189

outline of communication lines, 2:23, 2:160, 5:107, 6:28–29, 7:969

persons opposing, approach for handling, MS2:439

pins, 2:378

planning is built to make the able more able, leaving the unable strictly alone for the while, 2:77, 6:245

playing for blood, 0:231

policies effective to protect good name of, 6:746, 7:1071

policy is that we assign any case of upset in Scientology to past damage and interference with the person by medicine or psychiatry, 7:1140

policy, *see* policy

politics and, *see* politics

power of Scientology in society, what it depends on, 0:221

power of truth and wisdom, 0:484

practice of is very routine and consists of drills, 7:1092

product, *see* product

promotional actions of org, 0:346–355

psychiatry vs., 7:1129

public, *see* public

public image of, 6:600, 7:1044

public knows us by our mest, 0:84

purpose of Scientology is to make the able more able, 6:297

purpose of, 0:96, 0:502

Qualifications Cycle, 0:96

quality is only thing that counts, 0:16

reason for attacks on, 1:782

reason for decline of Scientology network in late '60s, 0:15

reason for protests and "bad publicity" on, 7:1008

refusing to speak ill of Scientology or criticize it to outsiders, 0:153

relationship to Dianetics, 6:430

Scientology, *(cont.)*

religious philosophy and, 6:517

religious practice and, 6:517

religious practice applying to man's spirit and his spiritual freedom, 2:533, 5:595

repairs itself, 0:362

results, 5:634

road out of witch pit, 0:362

road to total freedom, 7:1024

route from human being to total freedom or total beingness, 6:429

safe environment, *see* environment

saving beings, not men, 7:1154

science of human ability and intelligence, 6:165

senior policy, 0:284

separate subject to Dianetics, 2:143, 6:231

service is the watchword, 0:273

shoulder-to-shoulder effort, 0:273

skipping approval button from lot of wogs, 0:17

society moving under us, how it will happen, 0:481

sole agency that can forestall erasure of all civilization or bring a new, better one, 0:231

Source Cycle, 0:96

speeds up reaction time, 4:923, 5:597

standards (list of) Scientology group has, 0:152

steps field auditors must follow for Scientology to go well in an area, 6:693

study tech, *see* study tech

subject which embraces the human spirit and has an appeal to mystic people in its first impulse, 2:144, 6:232

symbol,
explanation of, MS2:232
upper triangle is K-R-C triangle, MS2:232

taking this planet just as we are and with no more than we know, 0:273

target of, 0:657

technical degrades and, 0:14–15

technology is no longer offered to the United States government, 7:1020

technology, *see* technology

testing explained, 6:284

translation of words, 7:1319

troubles occurred by imbalance of expansion, 0:131

true story of, 7:1039

types of activities and identities, 7:270

Scientology, *(cont.)*

ultimate product of, 0:131

upsets, what they are traceable to, 0:484

US government attempts to seize, 0:159

using admin and dev-t policies on the society outside, 7:1016

watchword is service, 4:42

we always deliver what we promise, 0:284

we are in business of people and bettered world, 0:695

we are not in business of being good boys and girls, 0:503

we are the only men and women left on Earth who are no longer slaves, 7:1126

we have trust which, if we fail it, condemns ourselves, our friends, our future, to continued oblivion, 0:239

we'll survive because we are tough and dedicated, 0:12

we need only avoid bank dramatizations to own the lot, 0:327

we will go as far as Dianetics and Scientology work in hands of auditors, 0:337

we will win if we *are* Scientology, not a lot of isolated groups, 0:273

what we would like the general public to say to the general public about, 6:30, 7:971

when developed and by whom, 6:165

when giving Scientology to people to use, give them only the simplest tools, render them completely practiced and conversant with those tools, and only when they are expert in them give them data, 6:146

when handled by the Founding Church and HASI, 6:231

why it is a religion, 6:517

why we mustn't fail or permit others to, 0:239

will go as far as it works, 7:849

will grow if Division 6 reaches the broad public, 2:88, 6:59

workability of, *see* workability

workable system, 5:18

world of is based on ARC and held together with ARC, 7:1069

world will come our way as fast as we attain a superior culture, 0:481

you offer Scientology—you don't *sell* it, 2:602

Scientology Axioms, O/W write-ups and, 0:535–536

Scientology Drug Rundown, 6:421

ability gained, 4:189

Scientology 8-8008,
   C/S should be an expert on, 0:65
   PR and, MS3:66, MS3:70, MS3:241
Scientology One,
   certificate for, 5:325
   definition, 2:162, 4:61, 4:64, 6:187
   firm in the public lines and PE and you're
      in, 2:164
Scientology Two,
   definition, 2:163, 4:61, 4:65, 6:188
   good in the Academy and HGC, and you're
      in, 2:164
Scientology Three, definition, 4:61
Scientology Four, definition, 4:61
Scientology Five, definition, 4:62
Scientology Invitation Acceptance Form, 5:354
Scientology Library and Research, Ltd.,
   definition, 7:1116
   duties of, 7:1189
   purpose of, 7:1189
Scientology Magistrate,
   certificate, issued to, 5:456
   charged with responsibility of, 5:457
   requirements, 1:694–695
   responsibility, 1:695
Scientology Missions International, definition,
   MS2:351
Scientology orgs, star-rate all HCOBs directly
   concerned with, 4:1183
Scientology pin,
   available to anyone desiring to enter
      Scientology, 5:353
   desired gains and, 5:353
   requirement, 5:327
   signifying, 5:345
   when red "R" is mounted on face, signifies
      Release, Grades 0–IV, 5:356
Scientometric Testing I/C, all testing comes
   under, 6:272
scurvy, vitamin C and, 5:637
seal(s),
   course proficiency denoted by a class
      seal, 5:326
   regulation of, 7:1055
   responsibility for, 7:1055
   validation, red, 5:315
Sea Organization (Org),
   conducts ethics missions, 7:151
   Continental Liaison Office takes over functions
      of management under its Management
      Bureau, 7:162
   definition, MS2:350

Sea Organization (Org), *(cont.)*
   ethics presence and, 0:246
   HCO Exec Sec and Org Exec Sec posts became
      Supercargo and Chief Officer in the Sea
      Org, 7:821
   provides publicity to feed people in at bottom in
      orgs and eventually gets them out the top at
      AOs, 6:583
   public control factors and, 7:146
   Public Divisions, activity is to force the next
      lower Public Divisions to function, 6:122
   Public Divisions must develop a field, 6:122
   requirements for staff, 7:147
   role in overall organizational pattern, 6:583
   traditional Sea Org ethics, 0:528
   zones of activity,
      missions to orgs, 7:145
      promotional tours where Sea Org members
         address the public, 7:145
      Sea Org tech, 7:145
Search and Discovery,
   authorization of, 1:423
   blue paper with blue ink, 1:415
   colors, 1:420
   distribution, 1:412
   Executive Director, 1:425
   form, 1:415–416
   form of issue of any conditions, 1:942
   history of, 1:422
   issued after 1 March 1965 are in force, 1:414
   issued by, 1:942
   meaning of word, 1:422
   noncompliance with, 1:424
   priority of, 1:423
   proper handling of, 1:1012
   purpose of, 1:269
   until paid for Ethics may not declare person no
      longer PTS, 1:1011
   used to find right SP, 1:1011
   use of, 1:420
   use of in handling PTSness, 1:1012
   what they are, 1:412
   where handle or disconnect does not resolve
      PTS situation, 5:122
sec, *see* **secretary**
Sec ED, *see* **Secretarial Executive Directive**
Second Danger Formula, Junior Danger Formula
   and, 0:612
second dynamic, *see also* **family; sex**
   children, *see* child
   parents, *see* parents
   rules, 1:780

second dynamic, *(cont.)*

rules relating to students, preclears and staff, 4:479

wrecking first and second dynamics by abandoning third, 0:301

second phenomenon, definition, 4:330

secret,

of aberration, 0:247

of organization, 0:197, 0:434

there are no secret standards in Scientology, 0:153

Secretarial Executive Directive(s), Sec'l ED, Sec ED(s),

authorization, 7:1306

basically LRH comm line, 0:113

color flash, 7:1310

definition, 7:1312, 7:1315

Dept 4 executes planned promotions as laid down in, 0:348

expiration, 7:1314

green ink on blue paper, 1:395

how Sec ED system came into use, 7:1312

issued by Ad Council may only change secretaries as personnel, 0:582

signatures, 7:1310

theory of, 7:1315

Secretarial Executive Director orders, 0:112

Secretarial to the Executive Director,

act as secretary to the board where one exists, to the Ad Comm or Ad Council and at staff meeting, 7:595

duties of, 7:595

first duty of, 7:596

purpose, 7:598

typing staff meeting minutes, 0:173

Secretarial Unit, purpose of, 0:370

Secretary(ies),

Advisory Council members, 7:909

deputy is org officer of division, MS2:7

divisional secretary, *see* division head

orders of, 7:910

personal secretary, 0:607

processing and, 1:739

product officer of division, MS2:7

responsible for state and activities of his or her division, 7:910

Secretary's Secretary, responsibility for despatch distribution, 0:370

section(s),

composition of departments and, 0:96, 0:601

dept with eight sections under its director, handling, 0:602

section, *(cont.)*

do action that promotes in one's, 0:375

down stats consistently or numerous noncompliances or offenses, handling, 0:621

exec with seven sections, handling, 0:602

offenses relating to, 0:468

quicksilver personnel scene crashing stats in a, 0:267

specialization and, 0:196

Thetan–Mind–Body–Product pattern, 0:654

unmocking section by sloppy command lines, 0:592

Section 5, 0:506

section head officer, 0:582

Section II OT, prerequisite, 4:801

security, 0:165

administrative excellence and, 1:36

Advanced Course, 4:806, 4:813

Clearing Course, 4:792

despatches in Comm Center safeguarded, 1:386

Div 1 responsible for in orgs, 1:628

hatting strengthens insecure person, 0:206

illegal preclears and, 6:408

letting a person retain his post and, MS1:301, MS1:457

misuse of knowledge, 1:635

of data, 1:635

of one's job, 0:151, 0:239, 0:487

personal security of staff member, 0:515

personal,

depends on accessible, swift, fair justice, 1:924

of staff member, 1:542

preclears and safety and security of org, 2:581

protection and security of our materials, 4:800

recourse and, 0:522

retaining post makes person more secure, 0:205

risks and infiltration, 1:623

safeguarding materials, 1:635

Technical Director works in liaison with HCO, 1:623

undermining security of one and all, 0:515

unhatted persons feel insecure and become weak, 0:206

Security Check(s), 0:153, 0:616

acceptance of students and, 4:309

Advanced Course and, 4:803

aimed at handling basic factors that can stall a case, 1:915

Danger conditions and, MS2:210

difference between a general and specific question, 4:574

given any new staff, 5:416

Security Check(s), *(cont.)*

HCO has right to do, 4:973

HCO WW Security Form 7B, 1:620–622, 5:560

leaving staff, done before they leave, 5:551

new staff given on a meter, 1:241, 3:192

overrun and overdone, 5:674

people who want to leave and, 1:907

private processing checked, 1:619

processes and actions, omissions in folders, 4:1195, 5:803

responsibility and, 4:1051

three ways to flunk, 5:556

training and, 4:573

see(ing), *see also* **confront; look; observation**

if one confronts his post he will see there are things to do, 0:259

people who cannot see cause cannot solve problems, 0:242

selectee(s),

advice packet line, 2:635

contacted only by an FSM, cool off if not given attention by the org, 6:654

listed in two separate categories, 6:651

mailing to, 2:635

receiving a refund or repayment, handling, 6:664

what to do when FSMs send in lists of names not selectees, 2:636

selectee form, what it must bear, 6:631

self, *see also* **first dynamic; individual**

attitude of "nothing to do with me," 0:300

finding out who you are, 0:568

find out that you are, 0:568, 0:571

find out where you are, 0:568

freeing a man from guilt of self, 0:462

full recovery of self, 0:234

self-determinism,

acceptance for training or processing and, 4:323

definition as it applies to departments and posts, 5:566, 7:600

displayed in ourselves and on our jobs, 0:230

ethics and, 0:448

of general public is only reactivism, 2:411, 6:183

on posts, 7:627

self-invalidation, definition, 0:247, 7:707

sell,

by action, not words, 6:836

we *do not* keep *selling* training or processing to a person who wants it, 2:498

semantics, definition, MS1:3

semispecialists, MS1:201

senior(s), *see also* **administrator; executive; leader; manager**

as interested party in Comm Evs, 0:478

bypass, *see* bypass; Danger condition

can inspect, chat, advise but must never issue an order on a bypass unless he or she means to handle a dangerous situation, 7:686

command channels and, 0:387

comm routing and, 0:387

completed staff work, *see* completed staff work

definition of smart senior, 7:687

endangering delivery, 0:266

failure to inform senior of relevant data, 0:424, 0:430

fastest way senior gets into trouble, 7:717

filing Job Endangerment Chits before calling lot of ethics actions, 0:550

hats knocked off by, 0:280

hats, responsibility for, 0:202

"hey you! org board" and unhatted, MS1:218

how many subordinates senior should have, 0:601

illegal orders issued by, *see* illegal order

incomplete staff work and, 0:401

inspections by, *see* inspection

junior issuing orders unknown to senior and across his lines, 0:425

let down by juniors, handling, 0:552

liable to Comm Ev if their area is violating study tech, 0:47

lumping all seniors into order-issuers, 0:134

made responsible that every junior has a hat, MS1:205

must always seek to raise stats and prevent crimes and high crimes by condition assignments, 0:653

no senior can "balance the budget" by wholesale dismissals, 0:482

one has to exert some control over his equals, juniors and superiors, 0:555

orders, *see* orders

org carried on back of one or two key seniors, 0:578

overload caused by, MS1:291

overworked, *see* overwork

problems, *see* problem

putting load on seniors to do one's work, 0:406

repeated corrections, warnings or reprimands by a, 0:467

resorting to unusual, off-policy solutions, 0:146

senior(s), (cont.)

senior to group exec is not counted as member of group, 0:602

smart senior is senior because he is smarter, 0:592, 0:593

what they must know, 0:281

what to check out all seniors on, 0:279

when seniors have to take general actions hard on the many to keep things going, 0:554

who doesn't see to hatting is liability, MS1:404

who won't hat, checksheet and pack, MS1:407

Senior Case Supervisor,

duties of, 4:1126

ideal scene, 5:59

located in Department of Correction, Department 15 in Review Section, 4:1126

product, 5:59

purpose, 5:59

red tags and, 4:255

red-tag line and, 5:285–286

responsibility for TTC, 5:535

responsible for getting red-tag line in, 4:256

stat and non-F/N sessions, 4:256

senior comm member, definition, 7:229

Senior Danger Formula, *see also* **Danger** 0:611–612

steps of, MS2:206

Senior Executive Strata,

above middle management, 7:462, MS2:189, MS2:293, MS3:442

twelve ingredients of expansion and, 7:464, MS2:191, MS2:295, MS3:444

Senior HCO,

Area and Continental, 1:98

consists of, 1:98

posts, 7:1224–1225

where located, 1:98

senior org, is defined as the top org heading an echelon of orgs, 7:228

Senior PCO International,

permanently posted staff must have approval of, 1:257

person may not have pay privilege until posted with authorization of, 1:257

senior policy, 0:284

we always deliver what we promise, 2:103, 4:15, 7:852

Senior Qual Network,

purpose, 5:69

similar to Snr HCO Network in responsibilities and powers, 5:69

sentence(s)(in justice), 0:490, 0:492, 0:494–495

auditing or training may not be made as a, 1:744, 5:109

separation order, 1:763

sequence(s),

any activity has sequence of actions, 0:106

arranging sequences of action and, MS1:197

as an outpoint, MS1:79

correct, investigations and, MS1:74

correct sequence of action is be-do-have, 0:291

definition, MS1:79

listing basic actions, in proper sequence, necessary to get out one's product, 0:309

particles flow in sequence, 0:106, MS1:194

visualize flows of, MS1:73, MS1:196

serve, right to, 0:238, 0:278

service(s), *see also* **delivery**

Accounts, collecting money for technical service, has right to demand that it was good service, 0:18

all personal services rendered to the individual resulting in a good process result must be charged for, 2:202, 4:74, 6:196

any is better than no, 0:273, 4:42

as an organization your future depends on service, 2:164, 4:66, 6:189

being supplied is auditing even when training auditors, 4:127

best service given to person in society who does his job, 0:507

best way to have certain service is provide it before it is demanded, 7:509

be sure service gets rendered, 7:629

bettering quality and quantity of, 0:645

Chaplain and, 6:518

clean, well-dressed staff begets payment of bills and more service, 0:334

confidence checks and, 0:469

contributing services outlined by one's hat, 0:278

cost of, 2:202, 4:74, 6:196

definition, MS2:393

delivery of, 0:279, 0:281, 0:347

demand for, 0:130, 0:332

dependent upon goodwill, MS3:168

Div 2 gets people into higher services by Letter Reg or phone actions, 0:360

D of T and Supervisor/Instructor is there to give, 4:296

essential ingredient of any post, 0:277

fast entrance, good crisp service, happy exit is the whole secret of building a buzzing, busy field, 6:641

service(s), *(cont.)*

free, demands for, 4:890

free service, result of giving, 3:159

free services = free fall, 2:451, 4:220

giving away services or materials, handling, 0:303

good service, definition, 0:276

goodwill and, 0:333

greater the service capacity utilized, the greater the service delivered and greater the income made, MS2:394

handling and, 4:928, 5:684

hat and, 0:277–278

hat knockoff and, 7:804

"help yourself" service, 0:333

I don't care how many rules you break if they're broken to give unselfish service to one another and public, 0:273

image and, 0:340

important people and, 0:335

inattentive or poor service halts expansion, 0:100

income comes from good service in training and processing, 3:103

insisting post originate or do duties or furnish product or service of that post, 0:392

is the watchword, 6:579

keynote of a hat is, 0:278

live for service not for rules, 4:42

means technical *results,* 2:165, 4:67, 6:190

mission or org upset or not giving good service, reason, 0:69

more people not been given proper service, the less NEW people you will get, 2:111, 3:87, 4:153, 6:555, 7:861

musical chairs vs., 0:280

must be as close to instant as possible, 7:850

must be more valuable than what it costs to produce or furnish, 0:52

neglecting to run good, good-paying services that build up raw public to major services, 0:303

new staff members and free org services, 4:221

no service or sale may be given without invoicing or registration, 4:219

only sure way to operate is with maximum possible service while bringing maximum pressure to bear on Dist and Dissem Divisions to fill the place up, 7:509

orderly vs. disorderly service, 0:273

org image and, 6:606, MS3:140

org service is superior, 5:56

orgs exist to sell and deliver materials and service to public, 0:91

service(s), *(cont.)*

penalty for giving away services, 0:303

probable best sequence of, after Book One, 6:443

promotional actions of org and, 0:347–355

public expectancy of, 0:276, 0:333

public expects good service, 2:435

quality vs. speed of service, 0:275

result if every staff member on a no-service pitch, 7:803

result of offering of higher services not authorized to give, 6:756

safe environment and, 0:520

seeking to charge for little services that should be free, 0:303

sloppy service destructive of goodwill, MS3:169

small orgs stay small as aren't rigged to give, 4:98

speed of service is of vital importance in matter of courses and students, 0:275, 4:119, 7:850

technical service should be highest possible quality, 0:18

that result in a worthwhile certificate must be charged for, 2:202, 4:74

to prosper, service must be as close to instant as possible, 4:119

upper orgs getting people into upper services, 0:360

watchword is SERVICE, 0:273

watchword of Scientology, 4:42

what public means by "good service," 2:435

when new staff may have free org service, 3:173

with prerequisites and handlings, 6:117

workload and, 0:279

you can promote before your service is complete only so long as the service will be there when demanded, 7:509

Service Administrator, ideal scene and stat, 4:140

Service Call-in Committee,

created, 7:873

duties, 7:874

handling of Call-in units, 7:875

important duty is to immediately appoint a Service Product Officer and to see to it he is trained and apprenticed, 7:875

list of actions committee is responsible for, 7:874

posts it consists of, 7:874

responsibility of ED/CO until committee operational, 7:873

responsible for, 7:873

stats, 7:876

Service Call-in Committee, *(cont.)*

until a Service Product Officer is posted the responsibilities and duties are covered by the, MS2:166

who it is chaired by, 7:873

service facilities, investing in, 0:564, 0:646

service facsimile(s),

definition, 1:71

effect of, 4:9

make people defend themselves against anything they confront, 1:9

making others wrong, 0:280, 5:9

Service Product Officer,

actions and lines to be product officered by, MS1:340, MS2:174

alert line with the public set up, MS2:173

authority of, MS1:334

basic sequence on getting the products flowing off the lines, MS2:168

call-in and, MS1:339, MS2:173

clay demo all the lines of an organization for each and every product, MS2:170

comes up with big ideas on getting public flooded into the org and being serviced swiftly, MS1:335, MS2:169

concerned with priorities of promotional actions, MS2:172

Danger conditions and, MS2:169

ED/CO responsible for Call-in Units until Service Product Officer appointed, 2:641, 4:276

ensures tech lines are fast, MS2:174

established in Office of CO/ED, Dept 19, MS2:166

example of operating, MS2:168

first action of, MS1:336, MS2:170

first actions in the sales area, MS1:339, MS2:173

functions of, MS1:334

how he moves through the org, MS2:170

in any org should have D/CO or D/ED status, 7:877

main statistics for, MS1:332

must be fully aware of all the VFPs of the org, MS2:169

must know cold every post function in the org and what particles belong on what lines, MS2:169

not a stopgap where executives have failed to post and hat staff, MS1:333, MS2:167

not the duty to man and hat the org, MS2:175

organizing officer for, MS2:167

org lines and, MS1:335

pitfalls of, MS1:341, MS2:175

Service Product Officer, *(cont.)*

primary duty of, MS2:174

re-sign line and, MS2:174–175

responsibilities and duties of, MS1:333, MS2:167

routing forms and, MS2:169

sequence of actions, MS1:336

statistics, MS2:166–167

until posted the responsibilities and duties are covered by Service Call-in Committee, MS2:166

valuable final products of, MS1:332, MS2:166

service routes, *see also* **routes**

into the FSO, 6:127

use of for new public, 6:116

well promoted can create a flood of publics into the FSO (Flag Service Org), 6:127

session,

break during, 4:843

interruption, penalties for, 4:897

SPs false report on results of, 1:993, 4:85

time, breaks and, 4:850

session cancellation system, definition of, 4:671

sex, *see also* **second dynamic; family**

ethics level and, 0:459–460

is effect, 0:248

knowingly using Scientology to obtain sexual relations or restimulation, 0:473

obsessive and promiscuous, is a blood brother of psychosis, 7:690

promiscuity, 0:454

SPs engage in discreditable sexual acts, 1:993, 4:85

SH, *see* **Saint Hill**

shingle, hang out our, 6:828

shipping,

book shipping, 0:282

charges for, 2:343

charges, who pays them, 3:166

definition, MS3:195

most common and economical method of shipping any kind of merchandise is by surface transport, 2:363

procedure to be followed, 2:343, 3:166

promotional actions of org and, 0:350

reduce paper bills by using used paper and cardboard, 3:381

tapes and lectures, 2:343, 3:166

use as much used paper and cardboard as possible to reduce paper bills, 2:336

Shipping Clerk, invoices all monies received for books, 3:106

Shipping Department,
invoices to be kept in alphabetical order by name from Jan. 1 to Dec. 31 for each year, 2:279

keep one copy of all invoices concerning any shipping leaving that department, 2:279

Ship's Org Book, 0:190

shooting board layout, definition, MS3:194

Short (Admiral), 0:116

short cycles, definition of, MS2:44

Short Form Product Clearing, procedure, MS2:29, *see also* **Long Form Product Clearing; Product Clearing**

shoulder to shoulder effort, 0:273

show, getting show on road, 0:4, 0:16, 0:232, 0:274, 0:283, 0:502

showmanship, importance of in PR, MS3:134

shrinking, *see* **contraction**

SHSBC, *see also* **Saint Hill Special Briefing Course,** course taking in all the data, philosophic with *polishing* of technique, 4:387

sick person,
belongs to the medical doctor, 4:1094

reduce time of healing or recovery by, 5:622

sign, to be prominently displayed for Dianetic registration, 4:920, 6:438

signatories,
FBO, Dir of Special Affairs are signatories on FBO accounts, MS2:322

LRH Communicator (or Flag Rep if no LRH Comm) is second signatory only in absence of the FBO or DSA, MS2:322

org's own executives are signatories on own bank accounts, MS2:322

signature(s),
books written by staff and how they are signed, 2:171, 7:1280

Bulletins, Policy Letters and Sec EDs, 1:390, 7:1286

certificates, validity of, 5:328

forbidden to reissue Scientology technical data in bulletins and policy letters over some other signature than mine, 7:1290

HCO Policy Letters, 1:426

how articles taken from tapes are signed, 2:171, 7:1280

mastheads carry the name of the editor of any publication, 2:171, 7:1280

policy on signatures in publications, 2:171, 7:1280

significances, Public Relations deals mainly in, MS3:72

sign-up(s),
actions which block sign-ups, 0:338

"contingent upon acceptance" by Technical Division, 2:495

events are valuable in terms of, 0:266

legal aspects of, 4:360

line for, 4:848

money must be taken at time of, 4:215, 6:383

policies regarding, 3:167

policy adopted, 5:363

silk screen, Addressographs and, 2:700

silly optimist, definition, 5:638

similarities, definition, MS1:3

simplicity, simplicities, simple,
characteristic of thetan that least complex actions are most powerful, 0:51

confronting and, 0:36

organization and, 0:88

standard admin and, 0:60

standard promotional actions and, 0:356

sin, only real sin in our present system of economics is to be poor, 7:628

single-hand(ing), *see also* **cope**
answer to, MS1:216

cause of, 0:391

comes from, MS1:215, MS1:325, MS1:464

definition, 7:426, MS1:214, MS3:406

prolonged single-handing will not improve unless Danger Formula is applied, 0:605

where it comes from, 7:449, MS2:273, MS3:429

single-hatted, Snr C/S must be, 5:709

situation(s), *see also* **problem; trouble**
able to recognize outpoints, MS1:128

cannot be handled well unless real Why is found, MS1:108

completed staff work and, 0:401

continuing situations by reference, 0:246

correct estimate of, MS1:13

correction of, MS1:140

definition, MS1:20, MS1:90, MS1:122

determining which stat or stats, if handled forcefully and at once, will change overall situation, 0:646

estimating and handling, 7:438, MS3:418

ethics situation develops when, MS1:165

evaluate against survival, MS1:154

example of how can change, MS1:150

executive who sits back and waits for others to act, MS3:407

situation(s), *(cont.)*

failing to terminatedly handle situations, 0:244, 0:430

finding, art of evaluation, MS1:128

fog up with big PR, MS1:158

for which there seems to be "no handling," 0:665

generalized, example of, MS1:140

getting the sit was a common bug, MS1:120

good, traced by pluspoints, MS1:108

grave, executive who sits back and waits for others to act, 7:427

handle it with Scientology, 1:738, 7:1018

handling situations, 0:61, 0:239, 0:244

highly generalized, MS1:140

how to find, MS1:121

if trouble finding, MS1:128

I never compromise with situation to be agreeable, 0:238

long-unhandled situation stuck person at that point in time, 0:668

major departure from the ideal scene, MS1:46, MS1:48

observation of situation before issuing orders, 0:140

obtain analysis of situation by, MS1:18

part of knowing is "In a given situation what should be decided?" 0:327

primary aberration in situations that are being mishandled, 0:240

real men and real life are full of dangerous, violent, live situations, 0:634

reorganizing activity so situation does not repeat, 0:606

salvaging org situations, 0:241

sequence of finding, MS1:128

statistics pointing the way to, MS1:128

steps to find one, MS1:47–48

steps to remedy, MS1:50

strategic plan begins with observation of, 7:470, MS3:450

strategic planning is done to handle existing, 7:475, MS3:455

types of, MS1:154

very few caused by active Whos, MS1:151

way to analyze, MS1:17

situation analysis, *see also* **analysis; data analysis; stat analysis**

correct sequence, MS1:22–23

indicates area to be inspected and handled, MS1:22

indicators must be watched for, MS1:22

instant result, MS1:19

reason one does, MS1:69

sort outpoints into principal areas, MS1:19

six-department organization,

Advisory Council consists of HCO Secretary and Organization Secretary, 7:267

arrangement of, 6:792

built like a watch, 2:59, 7:34

Central Organizations are now running on the six-department system, 3:227

size,

group, correct size, 0:598

mailing list size and number of mailings and letters to it determines gross income, 0:358

making org smaller by bypassing subgroups and running individuals only, 0:598

org should only increase in size as things get better, 0:624

org staying tiny, working madly and staying poor, 0:408

what size of org depends on, 0:598

why orgs stay small, 0:598

sketching, also a part of demonstration and part of working things out, 4:444

skill(s)(ed), *see also* **ability; cause; competence; efficiency**

absence of skilled management, 0:694

responsibility of knowing skills covered by certificate, 0:169

strength is nothing without tech and, 0:517

work done using good sense and, 0:82

slave(s),

I rebel at making slaves, 0:231

man cannot be free while there are those amongst him who are slaves to their own terrors, 0:461

why slave societies always lose, 0:82

slavery,

act of freeing vs., 0:629–630

decline of state into, 1:727

do not say that investigation of person or the past is step toward, 0:462

future political slavery where we all have numbers, 0:462

no good worker owes his work, that's slavery, 0:507

took centuries to realize slavery was wrong, 0:362

way to, 0:400

we are fighting full-scale war against ignorance and enslavement, 0:208

when it occurs, 1:734

when nobody knows what is thought right or wrong, 0:481

slide presentations, 0:332

sliding scale,
discounts and, 3:178
to be used as selling point by Registrar, 3:178

slow, basic reason behind persons who are, 1:819

slump(s),
in orgs traced to absence of hats, MS1:411
main reason for org slumps, reference, 0:266
solve org slumps with Scientology, 3:125
traced to absence of one or more hats being
worn, 0:199
unmocking orgs or units and, MS1:459
why most slumps following a promotion
occur, 0:596

small, *see* **size**

smoking, forbidden in schoolrooms, lecture
rooms, or auditing rooms in any Scientology
course, 4:472

SO, *see* **Sea Organization**

socialism, *see also* **capitalism; communism**
description, 0:507
two factors why it fails, 7:254
why it fails, 0:599

socialist, basic tool of, 1:211

social machinery, OCA graphs and, 4:231, 6:299

social personality(ies),
one must examine the good with the bad
before one can truly label the antisocial or
social, 1:1019
society runs, prospers and lives solely through
the efforts of, 1:1018
twelve primary characteristics, 1:1019–1021

social reform, org/Scientology image and,
6:600, 7:1044

society, societies, social, *see also* **civilization;
country; culture; group**
ability to make things go right, 0:236
answer to sane society is, MS1:302, MS1:458
any control we exert upon the public brings
about a better, 2:411, 6:183
cave in through, 1:962
confusing and unstabilizing persons with its
hectic pace, 0:205
crime, criminal and, 0:206, 0:480, 0:529, 0:555
decadent society, how it measures men, 0:237
drugs prevalent in, 4:655
enturbulence of society around us, 0:483
ethics and, *see* **ethics**
failing to apply our own admin, tech and justice
procedures to, 0:483, 0:484

society, societies, social, *(cont.)*
field auditor starting a group blows some
disorder out of, 6:693
influence of religion on, 6:867
level of cases outside perimeter of Dianetics and
Scientology declining, 4:200
misorganized society, individual loses out in
a, 0:4
monetarist manipulating society, 0:315
moving under us, how it will happen, 0:481
our method of progress into, 0:231
penalizing production, 0:505
power of Scientology in, 0:221
"power" of "society" and "state" is
pretended, 0:484
rewarding down stats, effect of, 0:506
rise or fall of, 0:89
Scientology admin and dev-t policies applied to,
1:736, 7:1016
secret of turbulence in, MS1:408
slave societies composed of, 0:82, MS1:235
smashed by psychiatrist, 0:68
spectatorism and, 0:248
study tech is our bridge to, 0:44
suppressive society, 0:66, 0:237
techno-space society, mission of, 0:462
ten aberrated points of, MS1:201
thinking society will approve Scientology into
power, 0:17
torpedoes upstats, 1:962
understanding all societies, 0:89
unsuccessful, 0:3

Socrates,
ethics and, 0:448
Greek philosopher, 1:497, MS2:137
thesis-antithesis-synthesis philosophical equation,
MS2:136

soft sell, 0:499, 0:501*; see also* **hard sell**
actions to handle, 1:755–756, 4:100
definition, 1:754, 2:85, 4:99, 6:371, 7:846
SP recommends, 1:1007

Solo, certificate does not authorize one to audit
others, 4:777

Solo Auditor Assist, definition, 4:777

Solo Auditor's Course, begun right after Sun
RD, 4:199

Solo Consultant, interview, 1:827, 4:982, 5:767,
6:416, 7:733

Solo Course,

person connected to suppressive group may not be enrolled in, 2:434

requirements, 4:784, 4:785

Solo Grade,

pc hung up on due to a partially completed earlier TRs Course, handling for, 4:641

selling a result and, 5:258

Solo Section, ideal scenes and stats, 4:143

solution(s), solve, solving, *see also* **handle**

administrative solutions, basic test of, 0:61

completed staff work and, 0:402

despatches and, 0:404

inability to confront making one fail to use correct solution, 0:63–64

never solve problem already solved in policy, 0:240

only as good as data offered, 0:409

optimum solutions, 0:451, 0:458

org stuck on track with counter-solutions, 0:405

people who cannot see cause cannot solve problems, 0:242

poorest solution to any problem, 0:451

primary solution to all problems, 0:242

remote solutions, 0:121

sending skimpy information and demanding a, 0:401

source of presented problem usually won't use presented solution, 0:427

standard organizing and, 0:62

when asked for extraordinary ones you have departed from exact, standard, on-policy procedure, MS2:377

solvency, solvent, *see also* **insolvency; viability**

admin personnel keep org solvent, 0:18

condition where income exceeds outgo, 3:129

consists of, MS2:404

debug tech and, MS2:145

depends upon maximum effort by production departments and minimum wastage by any department or unit, 7:52

don't leave enemy financed and solvent while friends starve, 0:633

example of measures taken to reduce loss, 7:929

Executive Council and, 0:354–355

Flag Rep report, 7:1420

formula for straightening out and making solvent any Publications Department or Org, 2:344

how it is made, 0:357, 5:51

lies in more Scientology, not patented combs or fund raising barbecues, 4:173, 7:931

solvency, solvent, *(cont.)*

lies in training not in processing, 1:209, 6:100

made by doing one's own job, 1:49

mail volume principal route to, 1:307

not made by high executives, it is made by doing one's own job, 2:101

org becoming, 0:443

org depends on training, 5:278

principal route is mail volume, 2:64

promotional actions and, 0:349, 0:356, 1:48

secret of solvency actions, 3:247

something actually operating and solvent can outweigh the untested advantages of changing it, MS1:34

standard of living and, 0:313

stumbling blocks in org solvency, 7:261

without a product, orgs can't be solvent, 4:935, 5:263

somatic(s),

use Dianetics, 5:633

valences and chronic, 5:567

SO #1 line, 7:646–647

SOP Goals, clause, 5:402

"Sorry, Up Statistic," 1:770, 7:501

source(s),

acknowledgment of, 7:1222

confusion between cause and, 0:249

cutting people off from, effect of, 0:4

hidden sources and black propaganda, 0:519

LRH as, 0:685

of Dianetic and Scientology tech, 2:105, 7:857

policy set by or demanded from wrong source, 0:131

staff member is source of his stats, 2:105, 7:857

unable to recognize source, 0:240

Source Cycle, 0:96

sources of trouble, *see also* **potential trouble source**

handling, 5:107–108

handling when training and processing, 1:986

policies regarding, 5:105

types A–J, 1:984–985, 4:881, 5:105–107

SP, *see* **suppressive person**

space,

exchange giving person space around him, 0:528

holding one's position in, 0:205

space change, authority required, 7:1329

space planning,
    arrangement of CF, Address and
        Letter Reg, 7:1330
    by org board, 7:1335
    consequences of misplanning, 7:1336
    essential to analyze particle flows, 7:1333
    for an org, 7:1330
    incorrect, slows, confuses and even loses
        traffic, 7:1333
    Reception, 7:1333
    service space always given bulk of org
        space, 7:1335
    three stable data, 7:1336

Spain, Bolivar vs., 0:629, 0:631

Spanish Inquisition, effect on Catholic
    Church, 1:963

speakers, who are not well trained do not do well
    to large masses of people, 6:325

special courses, conduct of, 4:571, 6:783

special events,
    procedure for handling of money, 3:107
    receipts must *not* be used for Central Org
        operating expenses, 3:244

special income,
    definition, MS2:365
    funds received and deposited as such, not org
        reserves, MS2:366
    handling, MS2:365
    possibilities of what could be classified as,
        MS2:365

special interest groups,
    individual is member of group united by idée
        fixe, MS3:152
    newspaper reporters are serving by direct orders
        of, MS3:152

specialist, specialize, 0:196, *see also* **expert;**
    professional
    devised way to display specialist functions, 7:812
    each staff member is a, 1:273, MS1:312,
        MS2:119, MS2:262,
    handling for specialists in a division, 7:812
    program the person to become a divisional,
        1:166
    severe specialization only beginning of hatting
        in a division, 7:812

special project,
    how to implement, 7:365, MS3:345
    new program should only be a, 7:365, MS3:345
    setting up and putting it into org lines, 7:370,
        MS3:350

special schedule course, 4:454–455

Special Zone Department, 7:1002–1003

spectator, definition, MS2:428

spectatorism, 0:248, 0:686

speech, freedom of, 0:68, 0:160, 0:461

speed,
    delivery done swiftly, 0:282
    failing to terminatedly handle situations
        rapidly, 0:430
    how lines can stay freer and faster, 0:403
    increasing speed of action, 0:401
    of action, MS1:162
    of particle flow, 0:66, 0:275, 0:325, 0:432
    of service, 0:275
    of service, comparable magnitude to quality of
        service, 4:119, 7:850
    power and, 0:325, 0:432
    prosperity of a business is directly proportional
        to speed of flow of its particles, 0:275,
        4:119, 7:850

spinbin(s), 1:994, 4:86

spirit, *see also* **being; thetan**
    alone may save or heal the body, 6:515, 7:965
    can predispose illness or injury, 5:622
    only truly therapeutic agent in this universe,
        2:22, 6:27, 7:968
    our forte is the human spirit and its relationship
        to the physical universe, 7:1012

spot check,
    definition, 4:451
    means of determining whether the student is
        acquiring this ability as he progresses
        through the course, 4:451
    Supervisor tool, 4:451
    what happens if student flunked, 4:451

squad mentality, in organization, MS1:251

square one, definition, 7:824

squirrel(s)(ing), *see also* **departure**
    activities, KOT has full ethics powers to stamp
        out, 7:1274
    admin degrades and, 0:73, 0:74
    as an auditor, what leads to, 4:1079, 5:670
    continued association with, 0:468
    definition, 0:12, 0:20, 2:441, 4:928, 5:684
    Dept 3 sees that no squirrel tech is used, 0:348
    destructive of workable system, 0:21, 5:19
    examples of squirrel administrators, MS1:286
    graduate students in such state of shock they'll
        have nightmares if they contemplate
        squirreling, 0:12
    never able to duplicate our product, 0:124
    never lasted more than two or three years, 0:124
    noncomprehension and, 0:12

squirrel(s)(ing), *(cont.)*

reason for use of word, 0:59

Scientology has uniformly failed in the hands of non-Scientologists, 0:159

selling org prospect lists to a, 0:534

"squirrel" auditing, definition, 0:55

squirrel admin, 0:55, 0:59, 0:61–64, 0:74

stability, stable,

administrative skill and, 0:67

best guarantee of stability is administrative skill, 7:779

composed of order, 1:83

hatting and, 0:206

HCO and, 1:24, 7:1165

most serious threat to org stability, 0:384

musical chairs vs., 0:206

nothing remains exactly the same forever, 0:124

obtained from knowledge of how to go about things, 1:81

post on org board is stable point, 0:433

production of valuable products and, MS2:143

quicksilver personnel scene vs., 0:265

reserves giving reputation of stability to org, 0:350

stable items vs. flow items in an org, 0:106

stable terminal and, 0:435

unstabilizing people,
asking them if they want different posts, 0:280
hectic pace of modern society, 0:205
leaving them untrained, 0:223

watchword of the HAS, 1:83

Stabilization Intensive, 4:1084

handling PTSness and use of, 1:1012

stable datum,

confusion and the, 0:65, 0:433, 0:434, 0:435

positive discipline is in itself a, 0:515

stable points, in order to handle things which flow, MS1:194

stable terminal(s), 0:433–434, 0:435, 0:438;
see also **terminal**

musical chairs and lack of, 1:206

staff, *see also* **staff member; staff pay; personnel**

absence from job to give or receive auditing, 5:576

admin staff can qualify as auditors part time, 5:422

appearance and attitude, MS3:140

applicants for positions in HCOs or Central Orgs, requirements for, 5:389

appointments and promotions, and preclear classification, 5:576

staff, *(cont.)*

auditing of, 5:543
limited amounts, 5:410
priorities, 5:603
quality, 5:409

auditing section, lack of is an ethics charge, 5:605

awarded a course instead of an intensive, 5:409

before leaving staff, 5:551

by having an exact list of subproducts, a staff gets a very good reality on what productive busyness is, 7:828

can have its control level raised by Upper Indoc, 2:413, 6:185

capable and versatile, who are willing to extend themselves, 0:266

cases and morale of, 5:602

cases not wanted as part of org, MS1:397

cases of staff members require attention and case gain, 5:602

causative, *see* cause

Chaplain's Courts and, 1:956, 6:521

checked out on org board, 0:202, 0:414

checkouts, 5:416

chosen on raw statistics, 0:120

clay pigeon if he does not know ethics policy, 0:521

cleanliness of, 0:334, 0:339, 0:340

co-audit arranged at org expense for, 0:169

communication's personnel vs. investigation's personnel, 0:327

completed staff work, *see* completed staff work

conditions, *see* conditions

conducting Upper Indoc class for, 1:185

confusion and the stable datum, 0:65, 0:200, 0:433–435

contract breakage, *see* contract

courses for, must be entered on a routing form, 5:515

dangerous and destructive not to know org pattern and policy, 0:69

Day and Foundation Orgs have their own staffs, 7:314

debited for losses or damages on post vacated, 0:198

defending and retaining in employ anyone who does his job, 0:151

definition, 1:216

degraded beings should not be on, 7:389, MS3:369

demanding or looking for orders from policy source and accepting policy from unauthorized sources, 0:131

demotion, *see* demotion

staff, *(cont.)*

designation of domestic staff vs. administrative, 7:1378

dev-t from, *see* developed traffic

dev-t graphed and, 0:435–438

dirty and unkempt, MS3:155, 6:614

dispersing and throwing everything off with resultant confusion to all, 0:231

does the staff member want the product, MS3:425

doing another's job, 0:413

doing one's post, *see* post

don't be wrong on any important decisions, 0:231

don't just natter if there's something you don't like, 0:547

don't protect ineffective staff, 0:232

dumping hats on seniors, 0:47

duress from senior vs. environment, 0:207

duties of, 0:165

effect of chopping staff member in person or to their backs, 0:167

enough Tech or Review staff must be on hand to give, 5:409

entitled 2 hours study or auditing time per day, 5:421

environment and, 0:207

every staff member's job to help build goodwill, MS3:169

exec responsibility for training of, 0:220, 0:221

exercise and, 0:225

exerting combined power of all of us and all orgs as shoulder to shoulder effort, 0:273

exhausted staff, key to, 0:201

expected to do their jobs, 0:52

expected to know general planning, 0:405

failure of the whole staff to know policy, 1:4

failure to contribute to strength and longevity of work, health and power of power, 0:640–641

families of, may have processing at professional auditor rates, 5:385

fifty trained staff producing everything org is supposed to produce will make far more money than five guys concentrating on GI only, 0:693

first to attempt large changes, 0:385

Fitness Board and, 0:524

five and their in-charge as unit, 0:601

staff, *(cont.)*

flunks, checkout from Staff Training Officer, what is done, 5:780

follow our rules as best you can, 0:274

Forms 7A and B and, 5:565

free service and, *see* free service

fully trained and functioning staff can get no real adverse reaction from superiors or even an enemy, 0:268

generating a lot of despatches about his post, 0:412

getting into other people's areas and hair, 0:151

gifts and, 7:1200

good staff member, how to be a, 0:58

goodwill, *see* goodwill

good workers, 0:156

goof can destroy whole org, 0:410

grade subsidy for staff forbidden in other orgs, 0:174

green staff, effect of, 0:384

gross income divided by staff, 0:261, 0:314, 0:688

handling the public individual, 0:323–324

has to know more jobs than his own, particularly jobs adjacent to his post, 0:84

having to have before they can do, 0:427

having to set own policy and use own idea of VFPs results in conflict and upset, MS1:254

HCO Ethics Codes, *see* HCO Ethics Codes

HCO justice protects staff member's reputation and job, 0:477, 0:481, 0:502, 0:503

HCO WW Security Form 7B used for staff, 5:560

heavy traffic warnings, 0:380

help your fellow staff members, 0:167, 0:235

high crime checkouts on policy letters, responsibility of, 0:76

high crime checkouts, responsibility for, MS3:472

holding position in space, 0:205

hours for auditing them, 5:550

how staff is deprived of its pay and welfare, 0:302

how they may buy auditing in the HGC, 5:578

how to hold your job, 0:84

idling in Reception, result, 0:338, 0:347

if his breath can be detected on mirror, he can do his job, 0:168

if one knows tech of how to do something and can do it and uses it, he cannot be adverse effect of it, 0:268

staff, *(cont.)*

if staff don't get hatted, they're condemning themselves and the planet to death a thousand times over, MS2:204, MS2:311

ignorant of rights, result, 0:521

ignorant of what's going on or what policies cover his post, discovery of, 0:405

income is determined by, 0:318

incomplete courses amongst, 0:223

individual decisions, 0:326

individuals vs. organization, MS1:235

inflow and, 0:367

integrity of, 0:67

internal suppression which blew off good staff, 0:102

interpersonal relations amongst, 0:200

I regard attacks on or criticism of orgs and staff as personal affront, 0:276

is source of his stats, 0:685

jamming line to exec, 0:373

job, *see* post

Joburg Sec Check and, 5:565

junior, *see* junior

justice and, *see* justice

keeping admin working and, 0:70–71

knowing org board, various posts and who covers them, 0:165

knowing what things in one's area are, where they are and what they are for, 0:305

knowing where one is and where things one needs to operate with are, 0:569

KSW PL and, 0:7

leaving and leaves, policy on, 0:177

living in shadow or employ of power, 0:640

loans, policy on, 0:171

low leadership survey grade person, 0:591

low stat personnel, effect of, 0:656

LRH Comm should raise LRH's PR with, 7:1260

LRH, importance of knowing how he would go about things, 0:238

made to refund all fees illegally received for training or processing any student or pc for personal profit, 0:171

make your post(s) real to other staff members and field, 0:166

managing by stats, 0:679

may be member of any religion, 0:153

may not be absent from job to give or receive auditing during working hours, 0:168

staff, *(cont.)*

may not be ordered to training or processing as disciplinary measure, or to improve job performance, 0:168

may not be sent at org expense for processing, 0:174

may not be suspended, demoted, transferred illegally out of his div or dismissed without Comm Ev, 0:492

may not take justice in their own hands where Scientologists in general are involved, 0:479

may not use working hours for being instructed, 5:576

may procure processing, 5:385

minimum list of courses for which every org Class IV or above must have routing forms, checksheets and materials for, 5:514

mission which rips off, responsible for, 5:433

misunderstood post titles and, MS3:423

most common failure of, MS3:423

must make certain reports in writing, 0:543

neatness, 0:84, 0:165, 0:334

needing extra money, 0:170

never having come out of Non-Existence, 0:578

new staff, *see* recruit

no intention of holding on to people who do not want to be where they are, 0:178

no need to look busy if you are not, 0:399

no staff to audit private pcs for pay, 0:165, 0:170, 0:471

no vague "firm" supports the, 0:689

non-Scientology staff, 0:152

nonutilized personnel, definition of, 0:203

not knowing there is an org there, 0:196

not realizing everybody in org does different job, 0:414

not talking about Scientology to press, 0:153

OEC Volume 0 for all, 0:27, 0:28

on post vs. off post, 0:151

operating at risk, 0:255

optimum number of staff to group, 0:601, 0:603

order of priority of staff action, 0:425

ordered to processing, 5:546

ordering and complying only in his favorite area, 0:425

orders, *see* orders

Organization Executive Course and, 0:4

org board must say what staff do, 0:410

org carried on backs of a few, 0:418, 0:578

org image and, 0:335, 6:606

orgs are not huge HGCs for staff, 0:168

other than Estos considered Product 2 and 4 personnel, MS2:8

outflow and, 0:367

staff, *(cont.)*

past vs. present conduct, 0:152

patching up whoever had to be shot, 0:239

pay, *see* pay

penalties for pirating while on full-time training, 5:497

permanent,
entitled to, 5:388
receive higher pay, 5:386

personal security being undermined, effect of, 0:515

personnel allocation for Saint Hill (1963), 7:1369

persons not needed on admin (exceed ratio) should be in full-time training as auditors, 0:684

persons showing criminal background this life may not be employed, 5:389

pinning org advance down to its lowest staff member's case, 0:156

policy and, 0:4, 0:59, 0:404, 0:406

post performance and case, 5:576

posts, appointment to and procedure, 5:396

Power Processes, 5:408

precedent and privilege are suspended in State of Emergency, 0:622

primary concern of, 0:333

privileges of, 0:200

PRO has staff as a public, 0:338

procedure for those ordered to processing, 5:555

processing and training policy, 5:387

production and, *see* production

products and, *see* product

professional image, 0:340

programing of personnel, *see* programing of personnel

promotion of, *see* promotion of personnel

promotional actions of org and, 0:347–355

public and, 0:335

putting things away when one is done with them, 0:306, 0:310

quicksilver personnel scene, 0:264–267

real stars of staff team are auditors and HCO personnel, 1:60

recourse, *see* recourse

recruitment, *see* recruitment

refusal to take responsibility for ending cycle of action, 0:244

refusing to get hatted, 0:208

regular ARC break assessments and, 5:573

regulations for auditing of, 5:588

staff, *(cont.)*

relationship of viability of an org and staff cases, 5:602

Remedy Pol-A, 5:780

Remedy Pol-B, when staff member reviewed and still has high flunk rate, 5:780

reports, *see* staff member report

requesting a Comm Ev of HCO, 0:478

requirements for posts, 5:389

responsibilities and duties, 0:165

responsibility for post one is leaving, 0:198, 0:266

responsibility of every staff member to know the policy in his hat and do it, MS2:228

rights, *see* rights

routinely running away, 0:177

saying "Am I transferred?" to exec who asks you to do somebody else's job, 0:232

schedule, *see* schedule

security of employment, 0:151

seeing another person off post, handling, 0:166

selling out friends and fellow staff, 0:533

seniors, *see* senior

setting high example of teamwork and dedication, 0:623

several solutions to get over hump of backlog staff cases, 5:603

should be tested on control, 2:413, 6:185

Situation Eight, MS2:85

Situation One, MS2:84–85

Situation Two, MS2:85

SPs seek to upset and get rid of the best, 1:1008

standard staff courses are mandatory, 5:443

study in own time not on job, 5:417

training,
can only be done by course attendance, 5:407
program permitted, 5:493
transferred to Qual, 5:488

troubles, ethics actions and org difficulties traced to, 5:420, 7:790

unhatted staff "go criminal," so ethics will be very heavy, MS2:236

validation of, 5:386

when tech lost full use and not used on, 5:603

who go by MUs, penalty for, 5:470

who want to leave, traced to missed withholds, 5:615

staff applicant(s), *see also* **employment; hiring; recruitment**

location of the organization and, 1:171

log for employment, 1:172

misrouting of, 1:161, 1:172

someone on the line who was turning them away, 1:171

staff auditor(s),

assignment is important, 4:251

auditing staff, 4:250

classes of, 4:251

classified as "Temporary" until, 5:385

get promoted to execs and staff auditor vacancies aren't filled, 4:386

may not be employed unless certified, 5:834

misdemeanors and, 4:350, 5:840

must be full time, 1:189

must have, 5:389

mustered daily, 5:843

not trained at Saint Hill, 4:863

"Okay to Audit" system is mandatory, 4:946

outside preclears, 4:1245

permanent,
    requirements for, 5:391
    to obtain must have, 5:389

program org must follow on, 5:833

proper sources of instruction, 1:625

requirements in selecting for training, 5:528

requirements to be done in Cramming, 4:946

rotating auditors on admin posts, 1:180

seeking advice on cases verbally, off-line, 1:625

shall not audit HGC preclear on leaving, 4:1243

should deliver a minimum of 25 hours per week, 4:250

temporary, requirements for, 5:391

working in an HGC, city office must be, 5:581

staff auditor skills, 4:1165

Staff Case Supervisor,

ideal scene, 5:60

located in Division 5 Department 14 in the Staff Section, 4:1126

org is entitled to have single-hatted Staff C/S and Staff Staff Auditors, 4:1127

product, 5:60

purpose, 5:60

statistic, 5:60

staff clearing, activities, 5:570

staff co-audit, 4:704

activities, 5:570

arrangements for staff, 5:578

enforcement, 5:571

how to organize, 4:705

no fees paid, 5:569

points needed to be undertaken, 5:579

red tags on, 4:709

staff co-audit, *(cont.)*

running of, 5:568

twinning on, 4:706

staff contract, breakage, penalty, 5:416, *see also* **contract**

Staff Course Supervisor, 0:222, 0:223

staff hat(s), *see also* **hat**

definition, 7:160, MS1:403

folder,
    contents of, 1:270, MS1:203, MS1:412
    color of, 1:270

Staff Librarian,

ideal scene, 5:63

product, 5:64

purpose, 5:63

statistic, 5:64

staff meeting(s), 0:166, 0:173

attendance mandatory, 7:739

chaired by the CO or ED, 7:739

coordination, why we have, 7:455

format, 7:739

general order of business, 7:739

keeps the staff informed as a team, 7:739

order of business, 0:179

purpose of, 0:180, 7:740

weekly, 0:179

staff member(s), *see also* **staff; personnel**

2D activities and, 4:479

able to get one's product out with no wasted motion or stops, 0:305

accepting non-Scientology staff at face value, 0:152

acquiring and furnishing vital information, 0:578

adding staff, *see* posting

administrative personnel, *see* administrative personnel

advancement, what it depends on, 0:481

agreeing to abide by HCO Codes, 0:477

altering policy continually, 0:406

always some individual assigned as responsible for work or production of every division, dept and post, 0:690

appearance, *see* appearance

appointee, *see* appointee

are valuable, 1:78

arranging personnel to handle types of actions and confusions, 0:433

aspiring to next higher classification, 0:169

assigned additional duty, handling, 0:197

assisting fellow staff to do better job results in larger paycheck for you, 0:167

staff member(s), *(cont.)*

at variance with org policy, handling, 0:165

attitude of "nothing to do with me," 0:300

attitude to public, 0:335

auditing in HGC for certificate requirements, 4:851

auditing of staff, *see* auditing

auditing on a private basis, 4:870

auditing outside pcs, 0:170

auditing priorities, 1:801–802, 6:527

awarding additional and unauthorized discounts may be personally billed, 2:456, 6:410

baskets, *see* basket

being able to defend himself and get his own "show on the road," 0:4

being exactly on post and using your exact comm lines lessens confusion, 0:83

being good fellow is not solution to getting job done, 0:421

being willing to be hanged for mistakes, 0:231

being zero in eyes of org, 0:578

believes he has been falsely wronged, 1:731

best auditors made our best, 2:414

borrowing money, 0:171

breaking contract is liable for full payment of all courses and processing received at full rate, 3:192

can get away with murder so long as his stat is up, 0:503

case categories 1–4, 1:802

case categories 1–4, definition and handlings, 6:528

cases of, require attention and case gain, 1:800, 6:526

co-audit, 1:801, 6:527

conditions for job security, 1:249

consent to E-Meter check when theft or insecurity occurs, 1:241, 3:192

contract breakage, 1:241

definition, 7:271

each getting attention individually as well as a group, MS2:44

Esto hats so as to get them producing, MS2:28

every member having OEC under his belt, 7:853

failure of the whole staff to know policy, 3:4

families may not have staff staff auditing, 5:410

flunking a checkout, 1:241, 3:192

Foundation services provided to Day org's staff members, 7:312

Foundation staff obtain their services in the Day org, 7:312

free org services new staff member may have, 4:221, 6:769

staff member(s), *(cont.)*

has three hats and keeps three folders, one for each hat, 7:160

high-crime checkouts, responsibility for, 7:492, MS2:462

illegally receiving service after contract ended, 3:173

intensives, auditor change on must be minimized, 4:250

learn that high stats hold off ethics, 7:825

leaving, required to write down all overts and withholds, 1:183

leaving staff before contract expiry and joining mission, 4:222, 6:770

leaving, to receive Confessional, 1:214

may be examined or reviewed while on the job, 1:242, 3:193

may leave staff at any time, 3:183

may not be comm eved, removed, dismissed or routed off staff without International Justice Chief approval, 1:257

may not be made the subject of an ethics or justice action for making an appeal which conforms with policy, MS2:403

misunderstood post titles, 3:307, 7:443, MS2:127

more threat personally in not doing his job right now than the sea or war or anything like that, MS2:203, MS2:310

most common failure of, 3:307, 7:443, MS2:127

must come to orderly cause-point on post, 7:601

need a reality on the tech they deliver, 4:704

new, may not have free org services until, 5:432

not allowed to audit privately, 4:1249

not eligible for any other training until, 5:436

not making gains on the co-audit, handling for, 4:709

obtaining free services dishonestly, 4:221

"off-post," definition, 1:249

"on-post," definition, 1:249

org board must reflect changes in staff status, 3:193

permanent qualifications, 1:184

permanently posted or transferred must have approval of Senior PCO Int, 1:257

person connected to suppressive group may not become, 2:434

Personnel Programmer works with, 5:424

persons found circulating false accusations about, 1:250

privileges for those who complete permanent staff requirements, 6:804

purchasing liability of, 3:290

reality and tech training, 7:853

staff member(s), *(cont.)*

really good staff member is somebody who does his job well, 7:635

reasons some have individual economic problems, 1:759, 7:304

refusing to fulfill stipulations of suspension, 1:250

regulations for auditing of, 4:681

require constant orders, when don't know what their products are, MS2:27

required to report weekly the stat of every post he is responsible for, MS2:230

right of appeal, 1:250

Security Checks given to any new staff, 1:241, 3:192

self-determinism and, 7:600

sent to Cramming for remedies if flunks are continual, 3:192

service after contract, 5:432

setting own policy and demanding orders from top management, 0:131

source of their stats, 4:128

specializes in his own hat, 0:196

stability of, *see* stability

staff meeting, 0:166, 0:173

Staff Status II or above may not be transferred, demoted or dismissed without Comm Ev, 1:261

standard of living of, 0:314, 0:315

standards of conduct staff are expected to uphold, 0:152–153

statistics, *see* statistic

steps for becoming howling success, 0:148

steps taken to put new staff on post, 1:181

study, *see* study

sweeping org of staff that hasn't passed Review for Staff Status I, 0:582

taking responsibility to see that people get to right terminal, 0:165

talking Scientology before callers, 0:347

team, staff are a, 0:167

tech/admin ratio, *see* tech/admin ratio

temporarily a student or pc in Academy or Review or HGC is not covered as a student or pc by his staff member status, 4:355

temporary, definition, 1:236–237

temporary, may be dismissed with or without cause, 1:237

there are no laborers in Scientology org, 0:82

thinking those senior to them also wear their hats, 0:412

those too expensive to keep, 0:406

staff member(s), *(cont.)*

three things required prior to being hired, transferred, promoted, demoted or dismissed, 1:253

training program permitted staffs to get to be trained auditors on part-time schedule, 4:386

transfer of, *see* transfer

unawareness of coordinated functions of terminals, or of other hats and functions, 0:384

unfriendly staff destroys goodwill, 0:333

uniforms, 0:334, 0:350

unusual favors received, 0:171, 0:471

unwilling person, detection and handling, 1:31–32

unwilling personnel, 0:398

valuable staff member, symptom of, 0:394

waiting for orders, 0:135

WANT the product, 3:309, MS2:129

we only fail when we do not help, 0:84

what first thought of every staff member should be, 0:282

what he is expected to contribute, 0:278

when he doesn't do it or false reports it, is not yet at square one, 7:824

when may have free org services, 3:173

when you need reassurance, 0:155

who believes he has been falsely wronged, procedure, 0:478

who can't perceive causes of things, 0:241

who cost two additional staff to take care of their dev-t and duties, 0:406

who do well in pioneer areas, 0:114

who does good job gets lots of processing, 5:580

who doesn't know OEC is at effect, 5:4

who don't know what they are doing but think they do, 0:203

who have no concept or clue of org's pattern, 0:384, 0:385

who have things "just sort of go wrong" around them, 0:40

who have to be ordered and ordered, MS2:27

who is worth all diamonds in Kimberley, 0:120

whose duties bring them into any contact with technical activities, 5:351

who want to leave, traced to missed withholds, 4:1196

wishing to sue fellow staff member or right a wrong, procedure, 0:478

with quick study histories, 0:114

working outside the org, 1:796, 6:724

you don't let incompetents and SPs on staff, 0:519

you own those things that are in your charge, 0:186

your post and life, 0:268

staff member report(s), ethics chit(s),

becoming accessory by not filing Knowledge Report, 0:557

cannot be stopped from writing and filing, 0:556

contesting of, 0:549

Court of Ethics and, 0:545, 0:621

description, 1:699–700

Dev-t Chit, issuing of, 0:419, 0:440

directors can request and chit only via secretaries when they cross divisions, 0:582

Ethics Section handling of, 0:505, 0:545, 0:546, 0:549–550, 0:552

failing to write down disclosed crime in worksheet or report, 0:555

format and procedure for, 0:543

going outside org and off channels to send, 0:623

Job Endangerment Chit, *see* Job Endangerment Chit

Knowledge Reports, *see* Knowledge Report

never accept one on an upstat, 0:505

reporting things needing repair, 0:166

reporting what you know and find to Ethics Officer in despatch, 0:552

routing of, 0:543

"Sorry, Up Statistic," 0:505

State of Emergency and, 0:545, 0:621

system of chits and hearings being out, 0:554

theft, reporting of, 0:548

Things That Shouldn't Be Report, 0:547

too many in staff member's file, 0:553

types of, 1:699

what to do when one receives an, 0:549

what to do when you don't know who to report, 0:547

which should never be issued, 0:582

willful and knowing false report, handling, 0:549, 0:550, 0:557

withdrawal of, procedure, 0:549–550

staff pay, *see also* **staff**

calculate by students and pcs in Academy, HGC and beginning courses, 3:363

depends upon org delivery, 3:363

examples of how a staff is deprived of its pay and welfare, 3:92

financial planning and, 3:361

individual pay and welfare of a staff member is a matter of the third dynamic, 3:91

staff pay, *(cont.)*

learn to think in terms of handled public not in terms of dollars, pounds, rands and other devaluing currencies, 3:364

management status checksheets and, MS1:366

moonlighting vs., 3:361

training vs. processing and, 5:836

up to the individual staff member what org income is and what staff pay is, MS2:401

what org income and staff pay depend upon, MS2:400

why staffs got higher than average units on proportionate pay, 2:429

Staff Review Officer,

makes recommendations on unsatisfactory staff to help them improve their condition, 1:194

routes unsatisfactory staff to placements outside org, 1:194

Staff Section, devoted to the handling, training, de-PTSing and processing of staff, 5:435

Staff Section Officer (SSO),

advice for, 5:446

authority over who will be processed and trained, 5:382

empowered to take ethics action and assign penalties, 5:446

must keep log of policies checked out by each staff member, 7:492, MS2:462, MS3:472

on guard against finding wrong Whys by Cramming, 5:382

purpose, 5:381, 5:443

put staff courses there, 5:444

relationship with staff, 5:381

responsibilities of, 5:443

programing TTC members, 5:534

seeing staff courses are attended, 5:445

staff co-audit set up under, 4:705

statistic, 5:382

where blows reduced to zero, reason, 5:436

staff staff auditing,

moved into Dept 14, 5:709

not for families of staff, 3:348

Staff Staff Auditor(s), 6:527

during Emergency, assigned to promotion duties such as mailings, etc., 5:409

need for them not eliminated by a staff co-audit, 4:705

used as Review Auditors for the co-audit, 4:705

Staff Status, *see also* **temporary status; provisional status; permanent status**

anybody has chance to go up in, 0:234

Staff Status, *(cont.)*

definition, 1:236, 5:411

demotions, dismissals and, 0:214, 0:487

description, 0:209, 0:213

eligibility for training and processing and, 1:240, 3:191

exec status levels and, MS1:366

going from Temporary to Provisional, 5:412

higher status, 0:212

higher statuses, promotion and, 5:414

higher status numbers, 1:239

intention and conduct clarified, 5:415

intention of staff status system, 1:240, 3:191

not increased in State of Emergency, 0:622

number appears after a person's name on the org board, 1:236

numbers, 5:411

Basic Staff Proficiency Certificate and, 5:351

certificate required for technical personnel, 5:351

I, definition, 1:240

II, definition, 1:240

III, earned by passing checksheet, 1:242

Permanent, 0:211

description, 5:413

designation on org board, 5:413

dismissal and, 5:413

Provisional, 0:211

description, 5:413

dismissal and, 5:413

procedure to become Permanent, 5:413

relationship between Exec Status levels and, 5:428

tech/admin ratio and, 1:216

Temporary, 0:209–210, 0:213, 0:214, 0:487

description, 5:411

procedure for dismissal, 5:412

upgraded, 7:629

0, definition, 1:240

Staff Status 0, 0:213, 0:217, 5:415

definition, 3:191

Staff Status I, 0:213, 0:214, 0:217, 0:582, 5:415

definition, 3:191

Staff Status II, 0:213, 0:217, 0:662, 5:415

definition, 3:191

Staff Status III, 0:215, 5:417

earned by passing checksheet, 3:193

staff study,

Day staff may study in other org (Foundation), 5:421

staff study, *(cont.)*

executives and seniors responsible for, 5:445

Foundation staff may study in other org (Day), 5:421

incomplete courses, 5:422

must have Crew or Staff Course Supervisor, 5:421

Staff Training Officer, 0:213, 0:214, 0:218, 0:221, 0:385

duties, 5:496

ideal scene, 5:60

log for staff member checkouts, 1:241, 3:192

points of liaison, 5:498

product, 5:61

purpose, 5:60, 5:496

statistics, 5:61, 5:75, 5:497

training, 5:497

TTC I/C and, 5:534

Staff Training Program No. 1, 0:104

Staff Training Program No. 2, 5:499

staledate,

complaining to Dir Comm about, 0:382

definition, 0:381

external despatches, 1:384

extraordinary locations, 1:384

orders and despatches staledated, effect of, 0:425

term means, 1:384

Stalinists, PR tech and, MS3:4

standard(s),

definition, 0:51

of Scientology group, 0:152–153

standard administration, *see also* **administration**

basic policies on, 0:51, 0:58, 0:61

being able to correct outnesses so they go back to correct procedures, 0:58

codified system of organization, 0:72

comes from policy letters, 0:59, 7:403, MS3:383

deals in simplicities, 7:404, MS3:384

definition, 0:59, 0:62

keeping admin working, 0:70–72

key to competence and successes in org, 0:64

squirrel admin vs., 0:59, 0:61–64

stats soar with, 7:403, MS3:383

steps to get it in, 7:273

when admin becomes standard, 0:52

standard auditing cycle, definition of, 4:1121

Standard Dianetic Completion, well, happy human being, 4:1098

Standard Dianetics,

Course, object of, 5:678

exact actions that produce results have been isolated and used, 5:677

procedure, 4:633

remedies built in to procedure, 5:677

Standard Dianetics Course,

starting out, 4:633

whole object of, 4:634

standard of living,

definition, MS1:350, MS2:284, MS2:367

VFPs and, MS2:368

standard organizing, 0:61

standard procedure, there is way to do something right, 0:58

standard supervision, definition, 4:380

standard tech(nology),

Academy run nonstandardly empties out, reason, 0:333

affluence attainment and, 0:628

Distribution cannot do its job where standard tech badly done, 6:824

distribution of Scientology and, 6:823

effects of, 0:51

knowing and repeated departures from, 0:468

one tech, 5:651

only in-ethics can deliver it, 0:534, 7:1036

only reason it doesn't work is that it hasn't been applied, 4:1104

org uses and teaches, 4:124, 6:585

people squirreling when they can't get results from what they think is standard practice, 0:12

promotional actions and, 0:351

resolves all cases, 5:652

setting people free with, 0:90

there is one tech, 4:22

Standing Order #1 lines, nothing but entheta comm on, 4:1172

stapling, definition, MS3:194

star-rate(d), (checkout),

definition, 4:19, 5:806

demonstration and, 4:443

how to handle new issue to be star-rated, 4:396

minimum requirement for giving, 4:396

turnabout system and, 4:435

Start–Change–Stop (SCS), processes may not be drills, 4:623

state(s), *see* **civilization; country; society**

actions which will cause it to falter, fail and die, 0:119

does not live or breathe and so it cannot care for anything, 0:186

effect on individual, 0:598, 0:600

follow principles which apply to individual, 0:297

idea that only the state owns, 0:186

"power" of "society" and "state" is pretended, 0:484

why experiments of totalitarian communal states starve and fail, 0:186

State of Emergency, *see also* **Emergency condition**

activity just doesn't come out of Emergency, handling, 0:563

assigned by Office of LRH, 1:549

assigning or declaring, 0:497, 0:621

bad indicators and, 0:496

continued beyond reasonable or allotted time, 0:497, 0:622–623

Court of Ethics for report received during a, 0:545, 0:621

credit worthless, 1:549

defined, 7:1184

described, 1:751, 7:680

ethics stiffened, 1:549

head on a pike and, 0:496

how to prevent, 1:551

indication can be read beforehand from an OIC board, 7:1183

management has already to some degree failed on several points, 7:1183

no new people may be hired in, 1:207, 1:549–550

policies new person into portion in Emergency is governed by, 1:550

policy on, 0:621

purpose of handling is to bring the organization up to survival level instantly, 7:1184

rights, 1:550

status, 1:550

statement, (financial), 0:350

book kept by Accountant, 3:115

example of compiled statement sheet, 3:386

statesman, difference between politician and, MS3:21

stationery, Dept 2 oversees stationery and typing quality, 0:348

Station Ship Order (SSO), definition, 1:431

statistic(s), stat(s), *see also* **graph; gross divisional statistic; stat analysis; stat push**

actions show up in, 0:692

addition to fully hatted org staff members stat, 1:106

advice that will help raise stats, 0:684

Advisory Council and, 7:889

agreement with their being down, 7:400, MS3:380

analysis, not a substitute for getting something done, 7:563

analysis of, 1:598, 7:557 *see* statistic analysis GDS, 0:646

answer to prosperity, MS3:178

are an indicator, MS2:266

auditors, 5:74

average fair-to-poor stat staff member, handling, 0:503

backlog can crash an area's stats while seemingly working, MS2:225, MS3:411

backlog, caught up gives one a soaring stat which promptly slumps, 7:335, MS3:315

basic gross outness re stats is not to have real stats, not to compute, publish, use and PUSH THEM UP, 7:520

basics of, 0:679

battle plan and, 0:648

belongs to that org, Day or Fdn, whose production it measures or reflects, 7:314

biggest mistake is justifying a statistic, 7:338, MS3:318

brushing off stat declines, result, 0:678

Bs of I convened for improved, 1:958

by trend it shows the overall tendency to approach or depart from the ideal scene, 7:527

Case Supervisor, 4:1121

causative stats, examples of, 7:335, MS3:315

causes of downstats, 7:513

causing your own stats, 0:689

challenged as "unreal" or "doesn't fit" or "falsified," handling, 0:524

choosing personnel and, 7:666

Class VIII C/S Qual, 5:676

closer one is to a statistic the easier it is to interpret it and the easier it is to change it, 7:523

co-audit,
    students, 4:701
    Supervisor, 4:701

collapsing, *see,* down statistic comes from jammed lines of the topmost executives, 7:499

statistic(s), stat(s), *(cont.)*

coming down hard on people or orgs who fail to get their stats in viable range, 0:697

comparing stat of one day to stat of day before, 0:690

comparison of each set of stats in same or related activity, 0:646

completed cycles of action are shown in, 0:695

computers at management echelons to keep track of, 0:704, 7:456, MS2:442, MS2:456, MS3:436

condition assigned only on the basis of a graphable, 7:904

conditions and, 0:666, 0:677–678, 0:680

continental area can manage by the week (difficult), but basically by three weeks and also by trend, 7:562

control of, 7:521

correct scaling, 7:506, 7:562
    essence of good graphing, 1:665

Cramming Officer, 5:75

crash as result of not handling pcs, 4:927, 5:683

dangerous graph, 7:337, MS3:317

data comes from tabulation of actions and amounts in orgs, 0:122

Day and Foundation stats are kept and computed separately, 7:314
    definition of, 7:498

definition, 0:690, 0:696, 7:89, 7:336, 7:480, 7:1235, MS1:63, MS1:64, MS1:322, MS1:370, MS2:196–197, MS2:230, MS2:270, MS2:301–302, MS3:316, MS3:460

demanding a stat, aberration of, MS1:318, MS2:266

demanding that stats rise, 0:692, 0:696

Department 6, 2:551

depend on auditing being done and taught, 4:127

depend on volume and quality of service, 4:951

determining which stat or stats, if handled forcefully and at once, will change overall situation, 0:646

Dir Certs and Awards, 5:76

Dir Exams, 5:75

Dir of Processing, 5:74

Dir of Tech Services, 5:74

Dir of Training, 5:74

Dir Review, 5:75

discount a fall just because stats are high, high, high is folly, 7:530

discrediting stat management, 0:696

discrepancies, 1:570

statistic(s), stat(s), *(cont.)*

divisional and departmental stats are made up of individual stats of staff members, 0:688

division can manage by the day or half-week and also by trend, 7:562

Division 2, 2:551

doingness which will bring about changed condition will be reflected in one's, 0:664

don't act without statistical data, MS1:93

down,
    in a division, priority actions for each division, 7:907
    normal reason for is vanishment of primary targets, MS2:434
    stats, always *held* down hard, 1:555
    stats generate down stats, 7:520

down statistic, *see* down statistic

dreaming up figure, 0:694

dropping steeply, 0:583, 0:606

each gross divisional graph to carry name of exec, 1:666

each whole division has a, 3:48

eliminating actions which don't increase stats, 0:582

Estates statistic, 1:524

estimated by the scene itself even when absent in numerical form, MS1:92

Ethics, when it gets interested, 0:503

every,
    div, dept and post has a, 0:502, 0:654, 0:689, 0:690, MS2:230
    post and part of an org must have one, 1:566, 7:395, MS3:375

examples of, MS1:92
    assigning a condition to a stat, 7:563

Exec Council manages by the week and also by trend, 7:562

Exec Secs to convene Board of Investigation if statistics level out, remain low, drop, 7:512

executive who is only handling unworn hats that result in no stats, 7:518

fair test of ability and who deserves promotion or the gate, 7:667

false combinations, 7:337, MS3:317

false stats, 0:657–658, 0:694

figuring the scale for a graph correctly so that trend lines actually show up on the graph when the stats are plotted on it, 7:532

first indicators, good or bad, of an org, 1:750, 7:679

five reasons stats are down, 2:561

flashcards to drill statistic trend recognition, 7:534

FP added to OIC cable after GI and CGI, MS2:417

statistic(s), stat(s), *(cont.)*

fully hatted org staff members defined, 1:105

getting away with murder so long as one's stat is up, 0:503

getting stats up, 0:653, 0:690, 0:692

"GI push," 0:693

going up in completions, falling enrollment stat, repeat sign-up line is out, 7:336

good stats as best defense against any ethics action, 0:524

go up if org well established, MS2:3

gross divisional statistics,
    Ad Council and, 7:898
    HCOs and Quals, 1:89, 1:91
    provide indicators by which management can be done, 7:900

gross income,
    divided by staff, 0:261, 0:688
    made from high divisional stats, 7:517

gross outnesses of why they are down, 7:519

handle org by stats only, 0:582

handling for, 7:499

hard work, foresight and initiative to make stats go up, 0:683

hatting and, MS1:308, MS2:107, MS2:258

HCOs and Qual definitions, 1:95–97

HCO stat penalty, 1:94

head of an organization who is not going to make it is handling everything and too busy to organize and enforce stats, 7:518

head of part has stat of that part, 0:654

higher potential ranges, always, 0:645

high stats from concluding actions, 0:244

high, Word Clearing and, 5:524

how to,
    correctly determine the trend, 7:531
    figure the scale, 1:664, 7:505
    raise your, 0:684, 0:688, 4:127
    read them, 7:529
    read trends, 7:532

ideal scenes and, examples of, MS1:64–65

if org stats are down you have been off or been put off Div 2 policy, 2:561

if person's stat is up his job is secure, 0:239

if you don't have stats and they're not collected, posted, used, prepare to do an awful lot of coping, 7:519

if you make a bad rearrangement and personnel are good the drop may be only a small one as they cope, 7:498

incorrect figuring of scale, 1:664, 7:505

index of things as they have been, 0:681

indication of the ideal scene, 7:518

indicators and, 0:496, 0:681, 0:692, MS1:163, MS1:318

statistic(s), stat(s), *(cont.)*

individual staff member responsibility for, 0:180

individual stat of any auditor, 4:118

individual stat of any organization, 4:118

inform you of relative need of action, 0:680

internally caused, MS1:167

international management body manages by six weeks or so and also by trend, but on a fast stat system keeps track of the one-week so as to predict, 7:562

Intern Sup's, 5:532

interpretation of trend, 7:523

in weekly condition assignments one only considers two things, 7:529

it has to be an honest stat and explanations that aren't the real *Why* have to be rejected, 7:530

it's the slant or pitch of the stat over the period that one needs to be able to recognize, 7:532

judgment and, 7:516, 7:562

level, 0:124

low, duty of Inspections and Reports to inspect, 1:528

low, *see* down statistic

low stats show departure from ideal scene and one can find out WHY *and* get the stat up again, 7:518

LRH making org stats rise, 0:591

made by stats of the sections, units and individual staff members of the division, 7:517

management and, 7:514, 7:516

management by, 0:678, 0:679, 0:696, 1:668, MS2:270

managing from something else, MS1:68

measuring stick for a worn hat, 7:518

mending a statistic fall consists of, 4:903

method of handling a down stat which is fixed idea or cliché, 7:400, MS3:380

missions and false, 7:825

morals of changes, 7:498

more remote governing body would use a trend of divisional stats to interpret it, 7:523

more you follow statistics, less you listen to rumor, the better off you will be, 7:249

most dangerous reason for downstats is reasonable explanations of why stats are down, 7:513

Mr. Stat Faker, 0:694, MS1:320, MS2:268

must accurately reflect production, volume, quality and viability, MS2:60, MS2:242

must be studied and judged alongside the other related statistics, 7:516

statistic(s), stat(s), *(cont.)*

must reflect actual desired product, MS1:110

nag around about a rise, 0:678, 7:530

never run or manage by anything but, MS2:375

no justifiable reason as to why stats cannot be raised, 0:690

not substitute for getting something done, 0:680

number TIP targets done, number staff fully TIPed added to FHS graph, 1:106

officers trained on the FEBC and, MS1:401

off-the-cuff "I know why" without even looking carries with it a spectator flavor, 7:519

one always runs by statistics where these are valid, MS1:110

one can always make stats go up, 0:683

one can defeat the purpose of them by being reasonable or alter-izzy about them, 7:519

one does not manage by gross income only, 7:516

one is rarely promoted unless his stat is good, 0:596

only if you use the single week can you properly, locally manage, 7:530

only reason stats are down is because somebody didn't push them up, 7:400, MS3:380

operating in new range, 0:650

ordering or telexing or yelling to "Get the stats up," 0:692

org is run on stats, not rumors, 0:579

org's stats are totally under the control of that org, 7:521

organization that is sound is one whose every activity can be tabulated by stats, 7:667

organization working in any way upon fixed statistic of consumption will eventually fail, 7:507

personnel comes into it, when you make a bad rearrangement and you have an incompetent personnel you have disaster, 7:498

person with the worst stats is the most likely suspect, 4:1110

place you are on a chain of command monitors all graph readings, 7:562

Power stat, definition, 0:643

prediction and, 7:336, MS3:316

product can be represented as a, MS1:411

production and, 0:690, MS1:55

production is completed cycles of action, not just numbers, 0:692

Product Officer at any level can manage by any time segment and should but if he is too distant from the zone of operations he can put all lower echelons below him into a permanent Danger condition, 7:562

statistic(s), stat(s), *(cont.)*

products and, 0:199, 0:696

program to save stats and put them into honest solid climb, 2:562

promotional actions and, 0:355

properly stated and honestly kept, 0:695

pushing stats, 0:692, 0:696

Qual Consultant, 5:75

Qual divisional statistics, 5:58, 5:75–76, 5:83

Qual Establishment Officer, 5:59

qualified defined for Qual stat, 5:87–88

quicksilver personnel scene vs., 0:264

quotas, 0:690

rationalization of, 7:400, MS3:380

rationalizing a stat, definition, 0:682

raw statistics, personnel chosen on, 0:120

read all div GDSes by the day; successful orgs do, 7:529

read in conjunction with other statistics, MS1:175

reading of, 0:677, 0:679

reason for International stats decline, 7:158

reasons graphs fall, 7:338, MS3:318

references, 0:642

Registrar, 2:551

reporting of, 0:691

Review Auditor, 5:76

rewarding down stats and penalizing up stats, 0:504

rise is a rise, 0:678

Senior Case Supervisor, 5:704

seniors must always seek to raise stats, 0:653

separate from data files, MS1:163

shifts of comm lines, functions, policies, equipment, duties, locations are quite often responsible for graph shifts, 7:498

simply an index of things as they have been and inform you of relative need of action, 7:564

situations and data trails are supported by, MS1:92

skilled stat trend recognition is an essential ingredient of skilled management, 7:535

soar with standard admin, 7:403, MS3:383

sound org is one whose every activity can be tabulated by, 0:121

Staff Case Supervisor, 5:703

staff member is source of his, 0:685, 4:128

staff must keep daily and accumulating graph for the week, MS2:231

staffs learn that high stats hold off ethics, 7:825

Staff Training Officer, 5:75

stat management, MS1:322

statistic(s), stat(s), *(cont.)*

stat push, effect on staff, MS1:318

stats won't come up drop the condition down, MS3:378

status think and, 0:678, 7:530

steep rise, analysis of, 0:646

steps to raise one's, 0:680

sticky graphs reason for, MS3:319, 7:339

Supervisors, 5:74

suppressive person and, 0:504

targeting of, 0:690

targets vs., 7:456, MS2:442, MS2:456, MS3:436

tech/admin ratio, how to calculate, 1:216

Tech C/S, 5:75

Tech Div, 5:74

Tech (Public) Case Supervisors, 5:703

test of who deserves promotion or the gate, 0:121

to discount fall just because stats are high is folly, 0:678

to have anything running one has to have stats, they have to be computed, posted and USED, 7:519

to locate departures, MS1:56

trained vs. untrained execs and, MS1:401

trend,
    definition, 7:523
    monitors all graph readings, 7:562
    overall measure of expansion or contraction and is the most valuable of stat messages, 7:528
    used in more remote areas from the org to indicate successful leadership or broad admin or tech situations, 7:529
    used locally to estimate expansion or warn of contraction, 7:529

trends and, 0:677, 0:679

unless one knows how to read statistics correctly and how to correctly determine a stat *trend,* prediction and therefore management by stats will be way out in left field, 7:531

unsatisfactory, is violation of staff contract, 1:194

up statistic(s), upstat person(s),
    downstat vs. upstat group, 0:556
    ethics and, 0:505
    honestly and swiftly becoming upstat, 0:695
    penalizing of, 0:504
    protection of, 0:519, 0:661
    socialism and communism vs., 0:506
    "Sorry, Up Statistic," 0:505
    when you reward downstat you deprive upstats, 0:528

statistic(s), stat(s), *(cont.)*

using stats that represent action and accomplishment, 0:121

valid statistic is best indicator of the ideal scene, 7:527

viability and, MS1:66

viability monitors all graph readings, 7:562

ways a no-cause attitude towards statistics expresses itself, 7:518

we always charge for raising stats on any dynamic, 3:169

weekly, routing for, 7:901

what GOT stats up will GET stats up, 7:403, MS3:383

what they depend on, 7:854

what they measure, 1:666, 7:514

when change radically for better or for worse look for last major alteration or broad general action just before it, 7:497

when you don't value stats this way, you don't catch the improvements or flubs that, piled up, wreck an org, 7:530

when you let status reasoning get into stat assignment of conditions, the org has had it, 7:530

when you reward down statistics and penalize up statistics, you get down statistics, 7:500, 1:769

where a stat is in completely nonviable range, it is really in Non-Existence or worse, 7:563

whole secret of how to produce, 7:238

why safe way to operate, 1:669, 7:515

Why stats go up and down traces to backlogs being caught up, to new projects given overloaded staffs, to unreal planning, to finance squabbles and failures to hire, hat, train and program, 7:527

wildly varying stats in an org's divisions almost always mean finance poorly handled, hiring, hatting, training is poor, utilization of staff not good, 7:527

won't come up, drop condition down, 1:569, 7:398

you can always do something about a stat trend, MS2:376

stat, *see* **statistic**

stat analysis, *see also* **analysis; data analysis; situation analysis**

Affluence and, 1:598

definition, MS1:185

graphs and, heart and soul of management, MS1:186

pure, MS1:186

stat board,

for courses, description, 4:466

how it's set up and used, 4:466

responsibility of Course Admin, 4:467

stat push, 0:692, 0:696

effect on staff, MS2:266

examples of, MS1:319, MS2:267

usual indicator of, MS1:319, MS2:267

stature, 1:834

status, *see also* **staff status**

considerations about, and staff not doing post, MS1:399

hat designates particular duties and, 0:199

many work exclusively for, MS1:68

means which reduce customer status, MS3:143

new appointee being status happy, 0:561

org image and customer, 6:609

reducing customer status, 0:338

status increase is vital part of the product, 0:338

undeserved is resented, MS1:68

using org status to be trained or processed without completing contracts, 0:174

work vs., MS1:68

status think, stats and, 0:678

stealing, *see* **theft**

stencil(s), 7:1163

Address cuts plate or stencil for each bookbuyer, 0:626

carefully preserved, 1:444

cutter, Roneo, 1:428

electric stencil-cutting machine, 1:405

electronic stencil made of, 1:407

filing system, 1:445

stitching, definition, MS3:194

stock, Dissem Sec responsible for keeping stocks up, 2:307

stock card(s), 0:186, 0:187

kept on Title A and Title B possessions, 3:389

stop(s), stopping, *see also* **barrier**

enemies and, 0:239, 0:275

isolating and eradicating stops on flow lines, 0:275

persons who do things to stop or impede forward progress of the project or org, 0:574

rendering enemies powerless to stop us, 0:239

using policy to stop action, 0:475

what to do if rules stop you from doing your job, 0:274

you can prevent, MS1:197

story,

how to write using 7 points of a news story, MS3:128

what it must contain to be printed, MS3:126

Straightwire,

definition, MS2:138

false data and, MS2:138

strategic plan(ning), 0:704, 0:706

battle plan, MS2:444, MS2:446, MS3:438, MS3:440

doable targets in written form which accomplish desirable part of, 7:458, 7:460

big upper-level idea sector, 7:458, MS2:444, MS3:438

broken down into smaller sectors, 7:460, MS2:446

bugged, reason for, 7:456

can necessitate calling other tools of management into play, 7:473, MS3:453

carries with it statement of purpose, 7:470, MS3:450

checklist for, 7:475, MS3:455

coordination and, 7:459, MS2:445, MS3:439

creates tactical planning, 7:473, MS3:453

definition, 7:478, MS1:368, MS2:194, MS2:299, MS3:449, MS3:451, MS3:458

dependent upon programs and projects, 7:459, MS2:445, MS3:439

example of, 7:471, MS3:451

existence and soundness of, 7:457, MS2:443, MS2:457, MS3:437

gets bugged most often because, MS2:442, MS2:456, MS3:436

large-scale long-range plan to ensure victory, 7:473, MS3:453

middle management turns into tactical orders, 7:459, MS2:445, MS3:439

must be done, MS3:450

picked up by next lower level of command and turned into tactical planning, 7:472, MS3:452

postgraduate form of "bright idea," 7:470, MS3:450

result of thumbnail evaluations, 7:471, MS3:451

tactical planning, 7:473, MS3:453

takes broad strategic targets and breaks them down, 7:472

taking broad strategic targets and breaking them down, MS3:452

test of, 7:460, MS2:446, MS3:440

those writing as well as those passing have responsibility for, MS3:455

strategy,

definition, 7:469

derived from Greek words, 7:469

key management tool, 0:648

LRH mapping general strategy, 0:230

strength, strong, *see also* **power**

beings afraid of strong people try to weaken them, 0:205

"competition" is trick of weak to fetter strong, 0:273

don't feel weaker because you work for somebody stronger, 0:640

has two sides, one for good and one for evil, 0:517

is nothing without skill and tech, 0:517

org's strength regulated by speed of flow, 0:325

person strengthened and made more confident by being given a post, 0:205

Scientologist being stronger and saner, reason, 0:152

strikes,

contribution vs., 0:277

only reason for, 0:600

unhandled by "business tech," 0:55

string(s),

able to pull, MS1:128

does not know how to pull, MS1:128

guideline for "string to pull," MS1:91

pull a few, definition, MS1:128

stuck in, definition, MS2:44

stuck needle, withholds and, 5:557

student(s), *see also* **course; study; training**

Academy, must own his own E-Meter, 2:341

accepting students on course without seeing invoice, 0:303

alter-ising or misadvising others on use of study tech, 0:45

anyone can be signed up for a course, 2:486, 6:379

any Scientology book, course pack or recorded LRH lectures listed on checksheet must be bought by, 4:363

appealing to Div 2 Service Executive, 0:478

application for certificate must also carry pledge, 4:362

ARC broken, 0:493

arrogance vs. progress, 4:759

assistance in finding quarters, 4:715

basic reason, remain long on courses, 4:327, 5:175

bear responsibility for not spreading verbal tech when twinned, 4:438

be courteous and helpful to, 0:165

student(s), *(cont.)*

blown,
five main blow reasons, 6:550
Free Auditing Check and, 6:552
handling of, 6:551
recovery of is of interest to ARC Break Reges and Tours personnel, 6:550

blows,
blowy, 1:1001
follow misunderstoods, 1:287
ordered to Case Cracking Section, 5:734
recovery of is of interest to ARC Break Reges and Tours personnel, 4:269

"bright noncomprehension," cure for, 4:330, 4:333

buy recorded LRH lectures and their own textbooks, 2:341

can charge fees with provisional classification, 4:97

certification of mission students, 5:199

checkout materials are only ones Supervisor checks students out on personally, 4:393

Clearing Course, 4:681

confront each as individual, 0:16

consequences of not correcting his errors, 4:671

correct way to speed up progress, 4:15

course natter stems entirely from students' noncomprehension of words and data, 4:329

Cramming Section teaches what they have missed, 4:365

crime to run a course without checksheet or to change checksheet on student after issued, 4:361

cycle of decline, 4:823

deep down knows whether he has made it or not, 4:234, 6:305

defective in application of materials, handling, 4:394

deliver means good case gains to pcs and students, good reality and useful knowledge and skill to every student, 0:282

detect slow student at once, 4:630

diet, exercise and, 5:639

difficulty within Academy used as indicator, 1:1001

disruptive,
acts contrary to Ethics Codes may not be ordered to Review, 4:354
course discipline may only be ordered to Ethics, 4:365
handling for, 5:107–108

disseminate,
better than pcs, 0:100
pcs don't, 5:835

D of T has no right to direct Reg in signing up, 4:294

student(s), *(cont.)*

don't try to handle course environment with student auditing, 4:341

do the required meter drills for each level, 4:626

"dull," cure for, 4:330

E-Meters and books for, 4:363

enrollment of, 4:292

essence of twinning and, 4:434

Ethics and, 0:491–493, 1:760, 7:305

exercise and, 0:225

expected only to *use* facts, 4:329, 5:177

expected to buy their own textbooks, 5:723

expiration date on theory testing, 4:326

extension course, letters to, 6:504

failed students who can't even read despatch, 0:302

failing classification examinations, 5:734

fail to meet theory or practical checksheet times sent to Cramming, 4:364

fast flow,
award for, 4:646
can be crammed, 4:645
can be star-rated, 4:645
does not automatically star-rate star-rate items, 4:645
does not have to have a twin on theory, 4:645
examination of, 4:644

fast student, attitude and concerns of, 4:759

few data taught very, very well will benefit, 5:760

first held responsible for state of pc, 4:319

first phenomenon and, 4:330

five main blow reasons, 4:269

F/Ning, definition, 5:702

folder, Course Admin responsible for, 4:468

folder, what it consists of, 4:468

foreign language, M7 Word Clearing and, 4:495

Free Auditing Check and, 4:271

full-time training, who should go on, 0:224

get ethics in on, 4:630

glib, 4:405

good indicators, 5:215

graduate them in such a state of shock they'll have nightmares if they contemplate squirreling, 0:12

green students, what they do when have confusion, 4:500, 5:464

grounds on which Instructor may refuse to train, 4:297

guide to acceptable behavior, 4:475

handling,
for misunderstood words when students enroll on course, 4:385

student(s), *(cont.)*

  handling, *(cont.)*

    for twinship where one twin disappears completely, 4:439, 4:270

  have their own E-Meter, 2:381

  hidden data line and, 4:348

  how to do theory checkouts, 4:329, 4:395

  how to handle any difficulty of, 4:382

  ideal Academy student, 4:631, 5:760

  if can't be trusted with HGC pc upon graduation, should not be graduated or certified, 4:296

  if examination is not passed, student remains in Cramming, 4:365

  indicators at course completion, 0:32, 4:379

  inquiries regarding training brought to attention of D of T, 4:292

  Instructor must grant beingness to, 4:300

  in the Academy are auditors, not preclears, 2:488

  Justice Codes and, 0:478

  key question for, 6:823

  letter writing procedure for, 2:601

  listening to tapes and Mis-Us, 4:510, 6:323

  may be transferred, demoted in level or grade by Court of Ethics, 4:355

  may not,

    audit any public preclear who is a preclear of any organization, 4:680

    be dismissed or expelled unless full ethics actions and procedures have been undertaken, 4:354

    be sent to D of T without having been signed up fully, 2:500

    be suspended or dismissed for 2D activities, 4:479

    discuss examinations with anyone outside Qual Div, 4:478

  misunderstood words, *see* misunderstood word

  most important part of student's hat is how to do checkouts on his twin, 4:393

  must be,

    oriented during training into caring for the cases of fellow students and Scientologists, 4:578

    registered by Registrar whether charge is made or not, 2:479

    registered whether charge is made or not, 3:141

    trained only with the tools of his trade to hand, 4:620

    trained to expect and achieve spectacular processing results early in training, 4:578

  must have Ethics clearance to visit any medical practitioner, 5:229

  must provide himself or herself with an E-Meter of approved design and manufacture before

student(s), *(cont.)*

  entering an Academy, 4:573

  never gets upset if actual error is spotted, 0:351

  never let student tell you "it didn't work," 4:342

  new, False Data Stripping and, MS2:143

  new student ARC broke with life and everything, handling, 4:606

  no rules or regulations except the Justice Codes, 1:731

  no slow students, just slow supervision, 4:325, 5:486

  no student we enroll who cannot be properly trained, 0:12

  nonattendee to staff study is blown student, 0:224

  nonconsecutive scheduling, part-time students, 0:497

  not wanting next course in training, 0:32

  of comparable time length on course shall audit one another, 4:670

  only answers permitted to student's demand for verbal technical data or unusual solutions, 4:350

  only flunking incorrectly or *passing incorrectly* upsets a student, 4:782

  only those students enrolled on a course may purchase the course pack for that course, 4:363

  ordered to Ethics, 1:744, 5:109

  ordering to Review, 5:109

  outpoints and, MS1:86

  overlong attendance on Academy courses, 4:372

  personal or case problems of students, 4:304

  pink sheet system and, 4:446

  policy in twinning that the student who abandoned his twin because he was finished may not be certified until he has completed his twin, 4:437

  procedure for leave of absence, 4:366

  procedure for terminating, 4:366

  procure his own preclears, reason for, 4:680

  procurement of for technical staff, 1:157

  product of an org is well-taught students and thoroughly audited pcs, 4:15

  promotional actions and, 0:350, 0:353, 0:354

  provides his/her own demonstration subject, 5:172

  queries and, 4:403

  questions getting answered, 0:16

  questions, only answers permitted to, 5:840

  reason fast training isn't occurring is because two-way comm seems to be out between Supervisors and students, 4:391

  recourse and, 0:492

student(s), *(cont.)*

recourse only after sentence has been passed, 4:355

registered, grounds on which D of T may refuse, 4:297

Registrar action which increases income is interviewing students and selling them professional auditing, 2:587, 6:414

Registrar has no authority to assign students to class, 2:480

regulations for auditing of, 4:351, 4:681, 5:588, 5:841

rejection of acceptance for training, 4:309

remedy for improper checkouts by, 4:394

rented quarters, responsibility for, 0:172

required to complete one level before starting the next, 4:776

riddle of why some students progress and some don't, answered, 4:619

rights to justice, 0:477

routine action of Ethics on, 4:355

running Free Scientology Center under org guidance, 4:676, 6:328

Saint Hill in its boom days had around 198 students, 4:407, 6:398

Saint Hill Special Briefing Course students vs. Cramming, 4:364

second phenomenon and, 4:330

secret of getting a student through half a level in two weeks, 4:630

secret of getting students through is keeping ethics in in the Academy, 4:376

send slow student to Review, 4:630

sent to Cramming, twin sees that he gets through requirements, 4:365

sent to training after receipt given, 6:383

should never be refused training, 4:308

should only be allowed to use E-Meters approved by HCO, 2:377, 7:1289

should want next course, 5:215

showing no reality on Scientology, handling, 4:301

sign up more than preclears, 4:388

slow = something is awful wrong, 0:12

slow, 4:405

slow, get a correct Remedy A and Remedy B done, 4:376

speed of flow of, 0:275

state of case and acceptance for training, 4:309

steps in handling of, 4:674

straighten up and improve when, 5:759

studying only answers to exam questions, handling, 4:473

student(s), *(cont.)*

subject to conditions orders from their Supervisors, 0:659

Supervisor,
handling of, 4:382
responsibility, 4:381
R-factor to, 4:384
spending student hours, 4:398

Tech Div may not provide a library as substitute for students buying their own textbooks or course packs, 4:363

testing of, 4:227

theory checkouts must consult student's understanding, 4:329

theory coaching and, 4:334

thrown in over his head, 4:320

too long on runway is going to lose spark and zeal he started out with, 4:420

trained to audit regardless of own restimulation, 4:578, 5:167

trained with the tools he will use as an auditor, 4:624

training restrictions, 4:309

training staff can refuse a student on grounds of inadequate financial arrangements, 2:488

trouble with, factors present, 5:144

trying to wear instructor's hat or another student's student hat, 0:413

twinning and, 4:431

twinning mandatory on courses where essence of the course is to train the student in practical application of the data, 4:434

200 fully paid students routinely on course, 4:410, 6:401

undergoing review,
Ethics Codes and, 5:842
subject to same Ethics Codes, 4:352

understand there are two types of auditing, 4:549, 6:451

unusual favors received by staff from, 0:171, 0:471

use only difficult case or student in the Academy as indicator of something worse, 4:341

visiting medical or healing practitioners while on course, forbidden, 4:474

well-trained Supervisor has no adverse reaction from, 0:268

what happens if flunked spot check, 4:451

what our best sources have been of students, 6:639

what real gains of a student come from, 5:99

what Sup must teach, 4:320

when in doubt, handle with much stricter positive placement and direction, 4:299

433

student(s), *(cont.)*

when looking for a preclear to audit for their classification, 4:680

when signing up more preclears than students org will go broke or be poor, 4:387

where real gains of a student come from, 4:28

who drift off courses or who are very slow lack somebody to talk to, 4:391

who get low marks constantly are handled in Review, 4:335

who hasn't made it, handling, 5:98–99

who isn't properly enrolled is freeloader, 4:460

who seek to resign or leave courses and refuse to return, 1:989

who succeed, 4:404

who they may audit, 4:683

Why of failure, 4:401, 5:511

wise to prefer they pay for training before being recruited, 5:532

with constantly low marks, handling, 5:183

with queries, 5:513

Student Administrator,

duties, 4:715

ideal scene and stat, 4:137

student assist,

consists of, 5:210

form 26 June 65 used as an assessment, 5:36

student auditing,

checkouts required before, 4:768

Examiner may demand proof of student's ability as an auditor, 4:774

student auditor(s),

Free Scientology Center and, 4:683

Student C/S must be expert in training, 5:709

Student Case Supervisor, 4:1127

student clinic, Free Scientology Center is the, 6:328

Student Files Clerk, ideal scenes and stats, 4:138

Student Hat, only prerequisite to the Professional TR Course, 4:661

student intensive, responsibility for efficacy of, 4:669

Student Location Clerk, ideal scene and stat, 4:138

Student/Pc Assignment Clerk, ideal scene and stat, 4:138

student roll books, Treasury checks the weekly income sheets against student roll books and why, 3:75

student rules, purpose, 4:758

study(ing), *see also* **course; education; hatting; student; training**

applying the data, *see* application

areas and people that study are organized, upstat and productive, 5:446

barriers to, 0:33–35

basic study missed withhold, 1:837

breakthrough, 5:787

complexity and confronting, 0:36

crashing misunderstood blocking off further ability to study or apply data, 0:39

full-time training, who should go on, 0:223

honest student is most successful, 4:406, 5:797

honesty and, 4:404, 5:795

hours are coins, 4:253

how to handle any student having trouble with, 4:382

I periodically study and polish my own skill, 4:758

make policy easily knowable, 0:115

misunderstood word, *see* misunderstood word

nobody is going to force you to study Scientology, 0:153

nonattendee to staff study is blown student, 0:223

one studies area, takes data he can get, develops what he can't, applies what he finds, 0:300

people who can't confront can have trouble communicating, reading meters, studying or even detecting what is going on, 4:427

people with bad study histories can't grasp policy, 0:114

physiological and mental reactions, 0:33

points stat, penalty for every misunderstood word found, 5:790

policy follows rules of, 0:114

primary point to get in, 1:899, 4:481

Qual Sec not seeing that execs can study, 0:302

staff member entitled 2 hours study or auditing per day, 5:421

staff study, 0:222–223

standard staff courses, 5:447

students who succeed, 4:404, 5:795

study tech not in is the Why of any lack of expansion or troubles with orgs, 7:814

Supervisor sees that students are hatted as students before they start study, 4:393

technical degrades and, 0:14–15

time spent on study of policy is very well spent, 0:408

underlying reason for people not studying, 5:445

where tech of is not in, in any org, results, 7:814

study technology,

accurate application of study tech regulates the quality of auditing and admin results, 5:787

ethics and, 0:44–45, 0:47

failure to apply, penalty, 4:482

society knows nothing about, 4:402

use of by Sups, 4:401, 5:511

stupidity, stupid, *see also* **ignorance**

brought about by withholds, 1:848

causing poor final product, 0:294

definition, 0:535, 1:843

foresight vs. stupidity in laying down policy, 0:117

giving something a "lick and a promise," 0:255

if it seems kind of stupid it is probably off-policy or out-tech, 0:147

it's not knowing that makes men stupid, 0:327

lying and, 1:844

misunderstood word and, 0:35

stupid enough to follow SP's off-policy, destructive orders, 0:146

style, of auditing, definition, 5:858

subordinate, *see* **junior**

subproduct(s), *see also* **product(s); valuable final product**

by having an exact list of subproducts, a staff gets a very good reality on what productive busyness is, 7:828

can be quotaed and should be but they can only be quotaed in view of what can be done with what one has, 7:827

every GDS must be broken down into subproducts, MS2:277, MS1:329

every subproduct must be quotaed, MS2:277

GDS and, MS1:326

have to be pushed in order to get products, 0:696

incomplete lists and, 7:829

major use of subproducts lists is debugging the absence of high quantity, high quality valuable final products or no product at all, 7:828

must be quotaed, MS1:329

relationship of subproducts to final products, 0:295

taking up subproducts lists with staff point by point, they will suddenly envision the VFP, 7:828

test of a correct subproduct list, 7:829

using subproduct lists part of an org can improve itself and its VFP by knowing what subproduct another part is supposed to be producing, 7:829

subproduct(s), *(cont.)*

where a staff member does not know the subproducts which go to make up a gross divisional statistic the GDS will suffer and fall, MS2:274

where subproducts are not given a quota, quotaing a GDS fails, MS2:274

subpurpose, 0:118

definition, 7:664

sub-ideal scenes and, MS1:67

subsection, with consistently down stats or numerous noncompliances or offenses, handling, 0:621

subsidy,

from governments, going to psychiatry, MS1:417

grade subsidy for staff, 0:174

substantive information, definition, MS1:185

substitution,

can't substitute situation for a Why, MS1:141

can't substitute stats for situation, MS1:141

one part of an eval for another, MS1:141

success(es), successful, *see also* **Affluence condition; boom; expansion; happiness; prosperity**

ability to complete cycles of action and, 0:260

basic purpose and, 0:117

come from anticipating the situation and handling it, MS1:287

competence increased by, 0:64

cycle of production and, 0:95

elements of, 0:144

final police point of org, 5:214, 6:824

keynotes are observe, evaluate, order, supervise, 7:166

key questions, 5:214

key to, 0:64, 0:318

mail volume a measure of, 1:307

major functions that *must* be done for org to be successful, 0:99

man is as successful as he adjusts environment to him, 0:251

measurement and how measured, 2:122, 6:55

meter check at, 6:305

of management founded on, MS1:214

personnel and their capacity for work on their exact jobs is the basic key to income and success, 7:760

signs of, 7:994

spectacular success can quadruple the number of complaints, 7:994

when success story stat diminishes in Div 6 the Tech Sec is comm eved, 6:822

success story(ies),

best success story and promotion of Div 6 is tech applied, equaling happy pcs and students, 6:822

definition of, 4:1121

files of success stories with full records for Dianetics kept in Div 6, 6:439

promotional actions and, 0:354–355

publication of, 6:821

surveyed to find out what to offer, MS3:179

written as part of repairing past ethics, 0:670

Success Through Communication Course,

publics for, 6:498

very successful route into Scientology, 6:494

succumb, *see* **death**

sugar,

energy and, 5:640

what it does in the body, 5:640

suicide, *see also* **death**

psychoanalysis and, 0:68

SPs who would commit suicide to prevent anyone from being helped, 0:656

study and, 0:33

suit(s),

addressed by Chaplain's Court, 1:956

Chaplain's Court and, 6:520–521

not addressed by Chaplain's Court, 1:956

suing, 0:478

Summary Report Form, definition, 4:1015, 4:1182

Sunday services, 6:532

PES and, 0:99

Sunshine Rundown,

administration of, 2:472

handling for person manifesting bad indicators, 4:1002

procedure for putting person through, 2:472, 4:1002

security and, 2:472, 4:1002

simple to deliver, 4:1002

whether one attests to Clear on Clear Certainty Rundown or on Clearing Course, he does the Sunshine Rundown as his very next action, 4:1002

superior, *see* **senior**

superior service image, 4:931, 5:687

Superior Service Image Program, 4:124, 6:585

superstition, humanities being mass of, 4:634

supervise,

ability to, MS1:131

fast course is well supervised, 4:324

heart of is getting it FULLY done, MS1:98

supervision,

as basic of administration, definition, 7:409, MS3:388–389

basic step of administration, 7:408

definition of standard supervision, 4:380

memory is inadequate in supervision of posts and functions, 0:195

primary stable datum, 4:319

quality of vs. time on course, 5:485

staff who need too much, 0:151

Supervisor(s), *see also* **Academy; checksheet; course; instruction; training**

absolute minimum duties of, 4:399

always checks up on any students who have been routed off course temporarily, 4:440

as ye teach 'em, so shall they audit, 4:300

attitude of, 4:399

certificate of Professor issued to, 5:434

checkout materials are the only ones he checks students out on personally, 4:393

Chief, ideal scene and stat, 4:142

Co-audit Supervisor's attitude, 4:698

Code, 4:304, 4:367

course must have a, 1:287, 4:397

crime of teaching or advising method not contained in HCOBs or on tapes, 4:350

definition, 4:295

delivering, service to individual without having to hand a fully paid invoice for that service, 2:451, 3:170, 4:220

demand results on the pc, 4:319

demand that they are all letter perfect and that they impart personal touch to every student, 4:570

does not offload his course into Ethics or Cramming, 4:400

"double flunk" and, 4:437

duties, 1:287, 4:378, 4:393, 4:397

8-C and ARC with students, 4:300

fail because of ignorance of Scientology study tech and failure to use it, 4:401

failure due to ignorance of study tech and failure to use it, 5:511

gets students completed and when completed they can do the job they are trained for, 4:400

get Super on course supervising, not doing admin or folders, MS2:99

grounds on which may refuse training to a student, 4:297

handling for misunderstood words when students enroll on course, 4:385

Supervisor(s), *(cont.)*

handling for service facs, 4:429

handling of queries, 5:513

has to observe the obvious, MS2:99

HCO failing to hat, 1:289

hours are coins, 4:253

how they must teach, 4:329

how to do theory coaching, 4:334

how to handle any student difficulty, 4:382

ideal scene and stats, 4:142

if student takes more than two weeks on theory or practical courses Supervisor placed in Non-Existence, 4:376

invoices and, 3:119

job is to, 5:508

key words of post not known, remedy for, MS2:99

materials, responsibility for, MS2:98

must be alert for, 1:1001

must be Super-Literate, MS2:100

must challenge with ferocity instances of "unworkability," 4:13

must send any PTS student to Review, 1:1011

obnosis is drill required on the Super, MS2:100

obscuring source of tech, guilty of false report, 5:840

on basic courses, what they must do, 6:482

only error he can make is in direction of softness, 4:299

only one of two things wrong when student tells you "it didn't work," 4:342

out-tech, 4:401

penalty for any found to be interpreting, altering or cancelling tech, 5:784

penalty for interpreting, altering or cancelling tech, 4:21

primary tech of, 4:402, 5:512

product of, 4:403, 5:513

properly IN the classroom working with the students, 4:399

queries, handling of, 4:403

real products versus flops, 4:1189

reason fast training isn't occurring, 4:391

requirements for certificate of Professor, 4:416

responsibility for, 4:473

   assigning twins, 4:435, 4:437

   blown students, 1:998, 4:90

   eradicate any barriers or hindrances presented which distract student from studying, 4:381

   precise Academy course schedules, 4:453

   quality and volume of each student, 4:399

   student sessions, 4:684

Supervisor(s), *(cont.)*

responsible for getting the tech to the student, 2:105, 7:857

R-factor to students, 4:384

schedules must be real and kept by the Super, MS2:98

sees that students are hatted as students before they start study, 4:393

skill, 4:397, 5:507

spending Supervisor minutes, 4:398

stable data for, 4:296

standard supervision and, 4:380

stat of, 4:400, 5:74

steps for two-way comm, 4:391

student found after completion of course to be defective in application of materials, Qual actions would be to correct Supervisor on authorized checkout materials, 4:394

student indicators at course completion and, 4:379

students who aren't making quota or whose stats are down real Why for found by Supervisor, 4:400

students who drift off courses or who are very slow lack somebody to talk to, 4:391

subject to Comm Ev for misrouting students requesting to see doctor, 4:474

successful Supervisor is tough, 4:398

teaching or advising method not contained in HCOBs, tapes, etc., crime, 5:840

technician, specialist in study tech, 4:403

three sources of observation of auditing, 4:316

tips in handling students, 4:385

title change of Instructor to Supervisor, 4:359

training and hatting of, who the function belongs to, MS2:98

what is expected of, 5:507

what the job consists of, 4:380

what the real job of the Supervisor is, MS2:99

what they must teach student, 4:320

who can't confront student, 4:305

who has students for overlong attendance goes into condition of Non-Existence, 4:372

who reads on post has gone into a student valence and is no longer a Super, 4:400

Supervisor's Code (Instructor's Code), training and, 4:304, 4:367

supplementary evaluation(s), can rescue long series of fruitless evaluations, MS1:119

supplies,

do not order extravagantly and why, 3:395

Estos establish and maintain the, 0:393

heavy traffic warnings and, 0:380

supplies, *(cont.)*

how to get, 0:185

keep cost down, 3:382

keep supply costs down, 2:337

lack of supplies causing flow to jam, 0:380

photographs and transparencies are to be carefully handled, 7:1208

photo supplies to be unpacked carefully, 7:1208

responsibility of accounting for, 0:198

see that your supplies are adequate, 0:165

unused supplies and wastage, 3:269

Supply Officer, 0:185, 0:198

handling of ordered supplies, 3:395

support, 0:296, 0:297, *see also* **exchange**

entitled to if producing VFPs, MS1:296

support services, all work and VFPs require, 0:314

Suppressed Person Rundown, end phenomena of, 5:442

suppression, suppressive,

admin high crimes vs., MS2:463

agreement with stats being down is suppressive, 0:682

characteristic of, MS1:158

condoning suppression of word "Scientology" in its use or practice, 0:473

definition, 1:1022, 7:372, MS3:352

degraded beings and, 1:201

don't confuse exec's efforts to get stats up with suppression, 0:519

Ethics Officer locates WHO is suppressing org, 0:519

facing counter-postulate when one is faced with suppression, 0:576

if correctly reported outnesses that threaten org are NOT corrected, then one assumes that suppression exists, 0:518

labeling of, 1:750

obtaining valid documents showing, 1:889

org internal suppression which blew off good staff, 0:102

people become degraded beings in area where suppression heavy for long periods, 7:390, MS3:370

reactive minds demand suppression of good and production of bad, 0:480

refusing to let somebody handle an outness is, 0:261

slowing admin line by not acting NOW is, 0:260

transferring personnel on posts obsessively, 1:254

suppressive act(s),

agents lead to PTS staff, units or sections, 1:1023

basic agreement with, 1:894

being a staff member and, 1:894

being knowing accessory to, 0:471

Dead Files and, 1:977

definition, 1:873, 1:874, 1:894, 2:434

enrollment in, 1:894

executive handling, 1:1023

failing or refusing to disconnect from an SP, 1:1044

getting pc to clarify his answer, 4:1175, 5:667

high crimes and, 0:474

informing staff and others that one is leaving, 0:177

list of, 1:874–880

methods of balking agents of, 1:1023

must have been abolished and dispersed for any former member to receive services, 1:894

processing or giving aid or comfort to a suppressive group, 0:473

reason for rules about, 2:434

students or pcs who seek to resign or leave, 1:989

suppressive person (SP), *see also* **insane**

Academy and, 4:344

actions of, 0:90

active in neighborhood of an org, 1:796, 6:724

admin high crime violations and, 7:493

administration and, 1:1026, 7:510

administrator only needs to know three things about them, 7:394, MS3:374

A–E steps, 1:884

ambition is "Everybody dead so I can be safe," 1:1027, 7:511

anti-demand factor, 0:127

bad tech and, 0:498

badly "out of valence," 7:392

behavior of, 1:1004–1005
in auditing, 1:992–994, 4:85

cannot complete cycles of action, 0:260

can't stand the idea of Scientology, 1:990, 4:82

Chaos Merchant, 4:82

characteristics,
those of insane person, 1:804
main characteristics of, 1:1007–1010

collection from, 1:764, 3:190

creating demand without handling suppressives, 0:131

dead file and, 1:977, 2:668

debts, must pay off all debts owed to Scientology organizations, 1:764

suppressive person (SP), *(cont.)*

definition, 1:873

Dept 3 sees that they do not block dissemination, 0:348

detection, 1:769, 4:86
by administrator, 1:1028

discourages checkout policy as one of his first actions, 4:19

does not make any consistent progress, 1:1030, 7:394, MS3:374

don't let SPs on staff, 0:518

Ethics gets case resurgences by finding right SPs, 0:348

Ethics Orders and naming right one, 1:968

exec who is en route to becoming suppressive, 0:657

expansion and removing a, 0:127

failing or refusing to disconnect from is a suppressive act, 1:1044

families and adherents of, 1:874

fighting a battle from the past, 1:1009

first to cry for the protection of justice, 1:988

found,
at root of every bad condition, 0:498
in an Academy, 1:998, 4:90

handling problem that doesn't exist, 1:996, 4:88

his intentions counter any other intention, 0:509

how to detect, 7:500

ideally one removes SPs in social groups, MS3:353

in Examiner post, 1:1008

is a no-gain case, 1:991, 4:83

judge by no case gains, 4:83

knowing havoc caused by, 0:657

labeling, 0:496, 1:968, 7:679

leave at least crack in door and never close it on anyone, 0:127

locate SP and shoot, 0:498

maintaining safe points and ability to detect, MS3:90

Merchant of Fear, 4:82

motives of, 1:886

must pay off all debts owed to Scientology organizations, 3:190

no-confront case, 0:657, 1:569

not being in own valence, SP has no viewpoint from which to erase anything, 0:657

not necessarily accorded court or hearing, 1:950

offenses concerning, 0:468

off-policy, destructive orders and, 0:146

often rise up to being in charge, 0:518

only SPs will blow, 0:501

org that can't be staffed has SP in it, 0:656

suppressive person (SP), *(cont.)*

out of valence and in valence of bad image, 1:569, 4:231, MS3:372

persons,
connected to may not be enrolled in Solo Course or Clearing Course, 2:434
declared, cannot be staff member of Scientology org without special clearance, 2:434
enrolled in SP groups or declared SP, names must be circulated, 1:894, 2:434
who have left suppressive groups, 1:894

point where thetan goes mad, 0:509

primary indicator of presence of, 4:1090, 5:756

prime targets, 1:797, 6:725

result of connection to, 1:874

rights of, if falsely labeled, 1:887

root of every bad condition, 1:752, 7:681

routed to Ethics, 0:351

should never be let near book sales lines, 2:293–294, 6:257–258

solving long gone problem by continuous overts, 1:1005, 4:345

specializing in caving people in, 0:91

stamps on upstats and condones or rewards downstats, 0:504

technology,
developed that changes the case of, 5:348
getting ethics in and, 4:973

terrified of anyone getting better or more powerful, 1:703, 5:20, 4:102

theetie-weetie case and, 0:657

third party and, 0:178

three "operations" engaged in regarding Scientology, 1:990, 4:82

unable to change because he cannot confront, 7:392, MS3:372

uses,
all manner of lies, 7:511
"policy" to prevent purpose, 1:1007
power and control of org over others to defend self, 7:391, MS3:371

what they fear, 0:90

where removal not possible, handling, 7:373

will discourage this checkout policy as one of his first actions, 5:779

will find all manner of reasons not to set people free, 7:880

working for dream of dead people in dead world, 0:302

works to stop activity or halt an Affluence, 1:1026, 7:510

supreme test, of a thetan, 0:236, MS1:446

surgery, processing and, 1:983

439

survey(s)(ing),

ability to spot tone levels in surveying, MS3:66, MS3:241

acceptable appearance worked out by ethnic survey, MS3:148

causes of failure to, MS3:180

common tool of PR in getting to know publics, MS3:74

definition, MS3:45, MS3:220

difference between buttons and message in promo piece, MS3:215

done to get agreement, MS3:216

ethnic samplings must be very broadly done, MS3:69, MS3:248

ethnic survey, 0:103

examiner reports and, MS3:179

examples of, MS3:58, MS3:233

find out what people want or will accept or will believe, MS3:177

finds what buttons a group has, MS3:162, MS3:244

for identities of opinion leaders, MS3:18

get a survey team and hat it, 6:225

invoices and, MS3:178–179

key to stats, MS3:177

lack of, weak link in all promotion, MS3:180

LRH surveys, examples of, MS3:49, MS3:224

maxim, MS3:69, MS3:248

mechanics of, MS3:46, MS3:221

most commonly used format for tabulations, MS3:244

negative ARC in PR, MS3:37

one uses ARC triangle in conducting initially, MS3:215

pitfalls to avoid, MS3:47, MS3:222

PRO area control and, 6:624, MS3:40

questions,
example of developing, MS3:57, MS3:232
how to encode using ARC triangle, MS3:56, MS3:231

saturation point and, MS3:179

seeking to know what people consider valuable, MS3:178

success stories and, MS3:179

survey buttons are not the message, MS3:216

surveying types of particles (in organizing), 0:108

tabulation of, MS3:38, MS3:46, MS3:221
procedure, MS3:243
responses, MS3:243
tone levels, MS3:245

tips and cautions, MS3:246

tone level and, MS3:55, MS3:230

survey(s)(ing), *(cont.)*

tone scale,
results of using, MS3:66, MS3:241
tech and, MS3:54, MS3:229
use of, MS3:55, MS3:230

two component parts, MS3:45, MS3:220

used to influence a particular public, MS3:12

used to put book ads together, 2:293, 6:257

vital necessity of, 6:225

who to survey for Dept 17 courses, 6:491

why one surveys, MS3:55, MS3:230

working without, you could spend thousands on promotion and lose it all, MS3:178

Survey Board, 0:187

Survey Network,

based in Flag Dissem Bureau, MS3:290

Continental, MS3:290

copies of all local surveys must be sent and included in master files, MS3:290

duties of, MS3:290

keeps master files of all surveys, MS3:290

responsibilities of head of, MS3:290

surveyor,

actions done on PR survey, MS3:38

beingness and appearance of, MS3:47, MS3:222

survival, surviving, survive, *see also* **future; life; success; viability**

assured only by knowledge and application of ethics, 1:495

basic principle of existence, 0:4

basic purpose and, 0:117

best chance of, MS1:70

clean heart and clean hands are only way to achieve, 0:458

construction and destruction and, 0:453, 1:488

contraction vs., 0:124

decline of is attended by outpoints, MS1:36

depends fully on becoming entirely and completely organized, 7:811

dynamic principle of existence is Survive, 0:452, 1:487

ethics, justice and the dynamics, 0:451–460

evil conduct is nonsurvival, 0:453

expand is the only safe condition of operation to survive, 7:354

expansion and, 0:124, 0:130

functions that MUST be covered for org's basic survival, 0:99

good is survival, 0:452–453

goodwill of opinion leaders necessary for, MS3:23

group survival, what it depends on, 0:253, 0:452

survival, surviving, survive, *(cont.)*

honesty and, 0:453, 0:455, 0:461

individual and, 0:55

interchange and, 0:297

is a graduated scale, 0:452

long-range survival, 0:296

long-term survival concepts, 0:449, 0:451

machine age creating false belief that one did not have to produce much to survive, 0:315

of Scientology due to third dynamic tech, 0:56

only the tigers survive, 0:12

orgs, survival of, 0:53, 0:130

policy and, 0:124, 0:410

potential can be measured by absence of outpoints, MS1:36

predicting the survival of any activity, 0:297

principle of interchange and, MS1:296

product of the sane is, 0:252

production and exchange and, 7:437, MS3:417

prolonged threats to survival will not improve unless Danger Formula is applied, 0:605

requires some control of opinion, MS3:25

seek the tech of, 7:436, MS3:416

social and antisocial personalities and, 1:1021

standard of living and, 0:313

stuff of which it is made, 0:253

third dynamic tech and, 0:55, 0:56

through stats and ideal scene, MS1:70

toughness and, 1:86

ultimate in reason is ultimate in survival, 0:456

VFP there and being interchanged determines basic survival, 0:297

we'll survive because we are tough and are dedicated, 0:13

suspension, suspend(ed),

as a sentence, 0:171, 0:467, 0:470, 0:474, 0:494

certificates, basis of, 5:328

levels of ethics action and, 0:494–495

only a Comm Ev can recommend, 0:492

only reason for, 0:168

pc classification may not be taken into account in, 0:168

promotion suspended and staff member resuming former post, 0:596

PTS staff and, 0:493

staff member refusal to fulfill stipulations of in reasonable time, 1:250

when someone can be suspended, 0:485

swindle, great "charity" swindle, 7:1131

Swiss bank, Power quality Treas Div vs., 3:419

symbol,

identifying any justice action or symbol with oppression, 0:456

OT activities, 6:843

substituting symbols for symbols, 0:36–37

symbology, ethics presence and, 0:246

sympathy,

morale depressant and destroyer, MS1:231

revolt and, MS1:230

symptom, *see* **indicator**

synthesis, definition, MS2:137, *see also* **antithesis; thesis**

system,

living in system correctness where things went right only so long as nothing was going wrong, 0:236

which isolates causes disenturbulates group, 0:241

Szasz, Dr., 0:521, 1:811

T

tactical,

between purpose and tactical there is always step of strategic planning, 7:473

execution of a strategic planning, to find it necessary to modify tactical targets, 7:472

tactical plan(s), 0:696

bridging between purpose and tactical, MS3:453

common in tactical execution of strategic planning to find it necessary to modify tactical targets, MS3:452

occurs down the org board, 7:458, MS2:444, MS3:438

strategic plan vs., 7:473

strategic planning and, 7:470, MS3:450, MS3:453

strategic planning, creates, 7:473

tactical planners, definition, 0:697, 7:459, MS2:445, MS3:439

talk(ing),

around injured person, 0:153

it ill behooves any of us to talk about the rest of us, 0:532

tape(s),

any student falling asleep or being very slow is handled with Word Clearing, 4:518

are a must for proper public information, 7:1215

are not written out by the student and then studied, 4:512

be careful in using tape to restore to the right reel, 7:1196

better the equipment, the better the comprehension, 4:31

blue-tabbed label, 7:1196

briefing tapes,
definition, 4:513, 6:338
especially subject to abuse by being played to wrong publics, 4:514, 6:339

tape(s), *(cont.)*

Central Organization tape service, 2:372

charges on, 7:834

checksheet,
for course must exist, 4:517
sequence, 4:518

color code, 2:367

copying procedure, 2:371

course study tapes,
definition, 4:512, 4:535, 6:337
must always be listened to through high-quality, high-fidelity headphones, 4:531

earphones and, 4:516

enrollment and, 4:516

examinations, how to give, 4:509

example of checkouts, 4:517

foot controlled start-stop pedal and, 4:516

four types, 4:511, 6:336

green-tabbed label, 7:1196

income from, 2:399, 3:103

incorrectly used, can be the source of endless misunderstoods, 4:511, 6:336

instruction of students by tape, 4:516

introductory films and tapes are a MUST for proper public information, 2:374, 6:341

issue line of policy and tech, 1:429, 7:1322

labels can have a div and dept or section number or name on them, using color code, 7:1197

lectures, students to take notes of anything not understood, 4:510, 6:323

model performance tapes, 4:514, 6:339

must sound good, 1:32

tape(s), *(cont.)*

not applying Scientology exactly per HCOBs and, 0:241

nothing anywhere in policy or HCOBs that forbids the use of tapes to their proper public, misunderstood words or no misunderstood words, 7:1215

not played straight through with the student making notes of any misunderstood words to look up later, 4:512, 6:337

points that should be understood, 2:374, 6:341

practical drills and, 4:517

prices for tapes, 2:373

probable reason stats fall after tape congresses is the misunderstood word, 4:513, 6:338

production hat, 2:368

promotional actions and, 0:348

public lecture tapes, definition, 4:513, 6:338

quality of presentation, MS3:156

quality of presentation comes under Dept 18A, 6:615

raw public tape and film presentations are a must to keep the flavor and meaning of Dianetics and Scientology, 4:513, 6:338

red-tabbed label, 7:1196

release of "The Time Track" tape, 2:370

result of no tape plays to public in orgs, 7:1215

rules and description, 4:516

sale of, 3:130

Solo auditors would only see the particular films assigned to Solo auditor training courses, 4:522

sound quality, 0:341, 0:348

statements attacking any political entity or ideology are withdrawn from, 0:159

student is drilled and does clay table on the glossary after he has been through the course once, 4:518

student is expected to keep a notebook from his tape listening, 4:517

student takes exact verbatim notes of any process commands or lists and notes down also the important technical rules, 4:517

teaching a tape course, 4:516

to cease to use tapes and films for fear of misunderstood words is a fatal decision, 2:374, 6:341, 7:1215

transcription of, 7:1164

unmarked reels, 7:1196

when to beware of being told it is "on-policy" or "an LRH order" or "in bulletins" or "on LRH tapes," 0:146

when you cease to play tapes to the public and staff, they lose the whole flavor and

tape(s), *(cont.)*

meaning of Dianetics and Scientology, 7:1215

why individual tape player method is used, 4:516

yellow-tabbed label, 7:1196

Tape Equipment and Maintenance Unit, ideal scene and stat, 4:138

tape play, public tape plays in org, 0:352

tape player,

definition, 4:532

description of the basic controls, 4:532

how to set up, 4:533

must be of high quality to reproduce the sound without adding to or distorting what is on the tape, 4:531

on very bad quality equipment 65% or so of the students went to sleep, 6:334

org failure and bad tape playing quality go hand in hand, 6:334

points on the use of, 4:534

students get best grades on high quality equipment, 4:531

tape recorder, definition, 4:532

target(ing),

ability to coordinate programs and write target-policy targets, MS3:437

achieving daily stat ceiling one sets, 0:689

actions necessary to accomplish the quotas are definite, conform to policy and *can* be *done*, MS2:231

as key management tool, 0:648

bugged, 0:425, MS1:137

clarity and doability of, 0:704

cloudy or general, 7:456, MS2:442, MS2:456, MS3:436

complete planning definition, MS2:435

compliance and, 7:459, MS2:445, MS3:439

computers and, MS2:440, MS2:455

computer will squawk if not done in expected time, MS3:437

concentrate on completing proper targets, 0:428

conditional, definition, MS2:432, MS2:437

conflict, has the junior position, MS1:135

consistent with the Why and ideal scene, MS1:137

cross targets, 0:425

debug tech and, MS2:145

definition, MS2:230

degree you can be cause in handling targets and needs of group determines how far you've come up the line, 0:248

target(ing),

did it in a way that defeats ideal
scene, MS1:136

doable, 0:708, 7:459, 7:473, MS2:445,
MS3:439, MS3:453

done within context of evaluation, MS1:136

do not set senior policy aside,
MS1:135, MS1:137

ensuring reports on completed program targets
are correct, 0:647

example of MUST targets, MS2:429–430

exec has to know target policies, reason, 0:88

execution of, 0:705, 7:457, MS2:443,
MS2:457, MS3:437

false reports vs., MS2:429

for coming day or week, 0:706

immediate organization for production, MS2:441

major, definition, MS2:437

man's worst difficulty is his inability to tell
important from unimportant, MS2:427

neglected at staff level, 0:705

noncompliance causing targets to move into
present time, 0:424

noncompliance vs., MS2:429

nonexistent, 0:425

no one there to do it, 0:705

not all targets are the same value or
importance, MS2:431

not done in expected time debug will find,
7:457, MS2:443, MS2:457

not safe to not comply with legal order or
target, 0:146

of divisional stats and quotas, 0:690

only way a target can change policy, MS1:135

operating, definition, MS2:437

operating, must hereafter be written in such a
way that, 7:457, MS2:443,
MS2:457, MS3:437

operating target, *see* operating target

organizational planning and, 7:460,
MS2:446, MS3:440

out of context, MS1:135

people who stop, MS2:434

plans are not, MS2:435

primary, definition, MS2:437

primary target, *see* primary target

production and, 0:704, MS2:442,
MS2:456, MS3:436

production, definition, MS2:437

production depends on other prior targets being
kept in, MS2:434

production, first target must always
be, MS2:441

target(ing), *(cont.)*

program and, 0:704

programs fail only because the various types of
are not executed or not kept in, MS2:434

projects and programs vs., MS2:448

putting strategic planning in target form,
0:704, 0:707

repeating, definition, MS1:171, MS2:441

reviewing and classifying all targets into their
types, 0:428

scheduled time and, MS2:433

seldom done without personal contact, MS1:136

should be terminable, MS1:171

so general that they invite no
doingness, MS2:429

stats and, 7:456, MS2:442, MS2:456, MS3:436

strategic plan and, 0:704, 0:706–707,
7:470, MS3:450

supervision can reassign a target, MS1:97

supervision debugs, MS1:96

tactical, modify some or add new ones or
even drop some as found to be
unnecessary, 7:472

tactical planning and exactly targeted
doingnesses, MS3:452

target policy, vital to ability of all to
work, 7:457

terminable, definition, MS2:441

to improve the existing scene, MS1:137

too general, 0:704

troubles, unless program under direct
contact, MS1:137

unbugging of, 0:691

"understood" or continuing targets,
definition, MS2:431

unreal targets, description, 0:425

when somebody can push through a
target to completion he's to that degree
OT, MS2:429

where the people doing are remote, MS1:137

writing of, 0:88, 0:602, 0:705

written within meaning of whole
evaluation, MS1:135

target policy, 7:478, MS1:368, MS2:194,
MS2:299, MS2:443, MS2:457, MS3:458

tax(es), taxation,

democracy has given us inflation and, 0:9

depression caused by, 0:506

good coordination of results in, 7:454

hard worker-earner heavily taxed, 0:505

health taxes, 0:507

idea that producing worker should be fined by
higher, 0:315

tax(es), taxation, *(cont.)*

in handling tax people never volunteer any
information, 3:402, 7:1087

legal dept responsibility for tax matters, 7:1053

organization and, 7:454

penalized management, 0:506

penalty for any damage that results by reason of
tax action, 3:407

principles, 3:402

Russia and income tax, 0:599

seeking to govern individuals through, 0:598

under same responsibility as Treasury Division
but also under the Office of Special Affairs
and Finance Office, MS2:318

tax collectors, tax men, exchange condition
of, 0:317

team, *see also* **group; organization**

being part of important team is return
contribution, 0:278

being part of means know what's going on and
what the team is capable of doing at any
given moment, 2:566, 6:389

good coordination of, MS3:434

high-precision team in superiorly organized
org, 0:624

how to get some awareness of org group
as a, 0:439

none in the absence of justice, 1:250

organization and, MS3:434

someone with steadily down stat is not part
of, 0:505

staff are a, 0:167

victory by cooperation and discipline, 0:624

we need all of us on the, 0:170

wear the hat assigned one ambitiously, work as
a team, get out real products, 3:78

work as a, 0:300

teammate(s),

expecting staff member to contribute his
specialized services to those who seek
them, 0:278

spectators vs., 0:248

we hold posts as competent teammates, 0:235

teamwork,

individuality vs., 0:82

setting high example of, 0:624

tech, *see* **technology**

tech/admin ratio,

adding staff in rotation using, 0:95

admin staff beginning to exceed tech staff,
meaning, 0:416

expanding org and, 0:223

full-time training and, 1:217

tech/admin ratio, *(cont.)*

HAS recruits, posts, trains and adds people
to, 1:217

how to calculate, 1:216

if three to one ratio is violated, it is a Comm
Ev offense, 7:148

increasing, shows org is expanding delivery
potential, 1:216

must never be more than two admin to one
tech, 7:275

one admin staff member for every tech, 0:96

org letting admin/tech ratio go kooky, 0:102

Public Divisions and, 6:99

reason for, 0:684

two or less admin personnel to every tech
personnel, 0:98

tech bonus, *see also* **bonus**

for course supervisors, 3:352

for staff auditors and interns, 3:352

Tech Case Supervisor, *see* **Case Supervisor**

Tech Establishment Officer,

although in office of Tech Sec, has HAS for
direct senior, 4:151

definition, 4:150

expert in admin lines and functions required in
a Tech Div, 4:152

finding bugs in lines by good investigation,
saving grace of a TEO, 4:152

may on own determinism refuse to permit a
transfer, 4:152

must also know the defenses of the HAS, 4:150

purpose, 4:150

sets and adjusts pay and bonuses in
Tech Div, 4:152

watchwords, 4:152

Tech Estimate,

conditional sign-up, 2:592

final registration, 2:593

format of, 2:587

interview, 1:825, 2:593, 4:980, 5:765, 6:414,
7:731

line, 2:592, 4:1040

line must be very fast and effective with no
idiocies or arbitraries entered into it, 2:593

making the Tech Estimate, 2:593

purpose, 2:592, 4:1040

reason for, 2:587

testing, 2:592

tech hierarchy, 5:707

Technical Alter-is Report, description, 0:544

Technical Council,

duties, 4:68

Technical Council, *(cont.)*
purpose, 4:68
technical degrades, 0:14
condition of Treason assigned for, 1:14
list of, 1:15
Technical Director, *see also* **Technical Secretary**
acts as a bridge between service and procurement, 4:39
coordinates all training and processing activities, 4:39
displaces Technical Council, 4:57
function, 4:57
head of Technical Division, 4:39
implementing of technical programs and, 4:58
post should be filled, 4:56, 7:218
Technical Division (Div 4), Tech Div,
Academy of Scientology, 4:46
backlog, handling, 0:100
badly run Academy ceases to be attended, 4:53
constant alertness must be maintained for technical downgrades, 4:26
corrects its own flubbed pcs, 5:655
Divs 4 and 5 contain five times as many personnel as all other divs, 0:96
ethics chits, 5:20
Examiner and Ethics Section vital to, 4:96
get outside-public co-audit processing teams (not groups) doing only Scientology One processing on which they can win, 2:165, 4:67
HAS Co-Audit Section, 4:45
has first call on all trained auditors, 4:96
head of is Technical Director, 4:39
highest crime, 4:18
Hubbard Guidance Center, 4:46
if it breaks down (HGC) the whole show goes, 4:53, 7:208
letting backlogs occur in, and org income and repute, 5:684
may not provide a library as substitute for students buying their own textbooks or course packs, 2:341, 4:363
most attacked area of org, 1:703, 4:102, 5:20
most destructive thing in an org is a Tech or Qual backlog, 2:445
one-day wait for a pc is too long, 5:688
organization programming, 4:167
org board (1965), 4:95
org board, ideal scenes and stats (1970), 4:136
PE Course Section, 4:45
person signing up with Reg does not commit org until also accepted and signed up with Technical Division, 2:485

Technical Division (Div 4), *(cont.)*
Personal Efficiency Foundation, 4:45
personnel, peculiarly liable to covert, off-line, off-policy annoyances, 4:102
promotional actions and, 0:350
Qualifications vs.,
general rule, 5:757
what each is there for, 5:655
staff star-rates on, 4:1183, 5:777
Tech can never tell Dissem Div when or how many customers to bring in, 0:344
Test Section, 4:45
used as a "personnel pool," MS1:381
what an Ethics Officer must look for in any instance of a heavily falling statistic, 4:18
what occurs when Tech personnel ignore issuing ethics chits, 4:103
what technical may demand of admin and vice versa, 0:18
work hard with tech staff to ensure good results, 7:1068
technical downgrades, 5:97–99
technical effectiveness, key to, 4:660
Technical Estimate, *see* **Tech Estimate**
technical folder,
contents of, 1:270
description and use of, 0:194, 0:195
goldenrod, 1:270
technical hat, definition, 7:160
Technical Individual Program (TIP),
issue type, definition, 1:431
defined, 5:435
only Staff Section Officer or deputy can TIP, 5:435
Technical Noncompliance Report, description, 0:544
technical personnel, technical staff,
auditor or instructor as, 0:98
only disciplined or given courts or Comm Evs for violations of HCOBs, LRH tapes or issues, 0:145
right to demand every tech person knows his business and does his job, 0:19
tech/admin staff ratio, *see* tech/admin ratio
what staff are considered technical, 0:95
technical query,
always answer by, 4:502
firm rule on how to handle, 4:502
how to handle, 5:471
never explain verbally or on paper in answering, 4:503
reasons why person has, 4:502

technical releases, targets may not set aside, MS1:135

Technical Secretary,

coordinates and gets done promotional functions of Div 4, 0:350

high crime to have anyone supervising without full use of study tech, 4:402

ideal scene and stats, 4:136

in the HGC preclear can be two-way commed by the Tech Sec, 4:392

promotional actions and, 4:109

requirements for, 4:93, 5:737

responsibility,
for staff auditors and interns, 4:905
for staff training, 5:490
for TTC, 5:534

responsible for CCRD line, 4:999

statistic, 4:157

statistic penalties, 4:158

tech hierarchy and, 5:697

when success story stat diminishes in Div 6 the Tech Sec is comm eved, 6:822

Technical Services,

collects pc, not auditor, 4:207

functions, 4:208

purpose and how it's achieved, 4:207

technical skill, definition, 4:565

Technical Specialist Courses,

enable orgs to make more auditors faster, 4:666

Technical Training Corps (TTC),

definition, 5:533

eligibility for, 5:534

free org services TTC applicants may have, 4:221

In-Charge,
purpose and duties, 5:533
Staff Training Officer and, 5:534
statistics, 5:536

org board position, 5:533

persons leaving before completing training or contract, 3:174, 4:222, 6:770

policies, 5:535

purpose, 5:533

vital to an org's future prosperity, 1:217

Technical Training Films,

are not for public showing and may not be shown to the public, 6:347

basic policies, 4:521, 5:810

correct channels for former graduates of tech courses to see the films, 4:523

cramming and, 5:813

cramming may not send a public person to see

Technical Training Films,*(cont.)*

a film as a cramming cycle, 4:524

maxim, 4:520, 5:809

may be shown only to paid students and paid retread professional auditors, 6:347

may only be viewed by properly enrolled students, 4:523

purpose, 4:521, 5:810

retread/retrain lines, 5:813

rules that apply to anyone taking a retread or retrain as a means of seeing the films, 4:524

showing of, 5:820

"special favors," 5:811

specific policies on who may see them, 4:521

staff auditors, Case Supervisors and Course Supervisors may view them only if signed up for retread and may only view in the course of being retreaded, 6:347

use them to train volumes and volumes of in-tech auditors and C/Ses, 4:525

verbal tech and, 4:519, 5:808

who may see, 5:810

technician,

skilled technician is product of practice, 4:1079, 5:670

technique, Registrars and other personnel concerned with selling are forbidden to sell a preclear a specific technique, 2:514

technology, technical, tech, *see also* **administration**

action taken on flubbed pc, 5:655

administration,
has right to raise hell over bad tech, 0:19
in absence of good administration, technical quality is impossible, 0:18
tech has to be in for admin to be in, 0:527, 0:652, 0:657
tech of, 0:58, 0:324

all administrative divisions and personnel exist to push public in for tech action, to hold org form and keep area calm internally and externally while tech occurs, 6:757

all material of Academy and SH courses is in use, 0:14

altering basics of, 0:126

alter-is or technical omissions or offenses reported to Ethics promptly, 0:623

alter-is to mess it up, 4:85

any process we ever had, had only two failure points, 2:86, 6:372

application of new tech vs. existing tech, 4:145

applying the, 0:8, 0:685

auditors, *see* auditor

bad tech, effects of, 0:19

technology, technical, tech, *(cont.)*

bad tech, PTSes and SPs, 0:498

breakthrough, 5:787

"business tech" is at best a dying technology, 0:56

certainty,
how to get it in, 5:524
Word Clearing and, 5:524

chaos reversed with, 0:91

clarification of public technical materials policy, 7:1191

correct vs. incorrect tech and application, 0:8

covered in HCOBs, 0:112

Dean of Technology, 5:713

definition, 4:1078, 5:669

definition of technical procedures, 0:58

degrades of, 0:14–15

delivering best tech quality possible, 0:333

delivering what is promised and, 4:8

departure from, discovered by LRH Comm, handling, 7:1268

destructive tech, 0:41, 0:68

divisional orders to get technology back in full operation, 5:267

dreaming up bad tech to destroy good tech, 0:9

enemy is lacking workable tech, 0:337

errors found, 5:752

ethics,
basic tech of, 0:449, 0:450
exists to get tech in, 0:497, 0:502, 0:549, 1:280, 1:750, 7:679
fine line between ethics and tech, 0:509
survival and ethics tech, 0:449, 0:451, 0:457, 0:458
tech can be gotten in only where ethics is in, 0:502, 0:527, 0:657, 0:658

excellent technical delivery generates goodwill and PR, 0:332

exists to reverse the chaos, 4:159

failing to apply it to society around us, result, 0:483, 0:484

first and most fatal breakdown in any area, 1:36

first dynamic technology given in HCO Bulletins, 0:55, 7:486, MS3:466

forces of physical universe can be channeled and used only with technology, 0:63

free needle, way to recognize, 5:754

full reality on basic tech as pcs and auditors give one a fully happy booming org, 7:855

general outness traced to out-TRs and metering, 5:653

getting tech applied, 0:8, 0:658

technology, technical, tech, *(cont.)*

good tech delivery makes good PR possible, MS3:168

hard technical line, 5:697

hat checking, 1:36

HCOBs are senior to all other orders in tech, 0:143

hierarchy, 5:697

honesty, 5:98–99

how to ensure excellence of, 4:33

if it isn't working, it is being varied, 5:679

if one knows tech of how to do something and can do it and uses it, he cannot be adverse effect of it, 0:268

if tech and org integrity are good, you get expansion, 0:100

if *technical* breaks down (HGC) the whole show goes, 2:512

if you get tech in well enough, tech handles all, 0:498

importance of knowing policy and, 0:695

invalidation of free needle, policy is, 5:753

investigatory tech, 0:694

involved in GETTING the product, 7:447

is complete but it expands also by experience of administration of it and simplifying its presentation, 0:126

junior issues causing destruction of, 0:143

justice and, 5:348

keep all tech in and used, 4:146

keeping Scientology working, 0:7

knocking out incorrect applications, 0:8

lack of, is usual reason why one works hard with no product or an overt product, 3:78

lack of tech, effects of, 0:68, 0:300

lectures by other personnel and handling, 7:1191

let's grow up to our tech and take responsibility for it, 0:485

letting backlogs occur in, and org income and repute, 4:928

list of policies, 7:674

lower levels and, 6:368

LRH Comms and, 5:798

making known tech needed to produce product, 0:294

making Scientology work on pcs and students is the only way you can salvage org situations, 7:674

misteaching of, 4:1097

never tell pc about the meter, 5:654

nonexistence of tech causing failure, 0:63

not discovered by a group, 4:9

of organization comes from Level VII, 0:482

technology, technical, tech, *(cont.)*

offenses concerning tech, 0:467

ogre which might eat us up is our possible failure to retain and practice our tech, 0:13

one-day wait for a pc is too long, 4:932

one of the fastest ways to allow the tech to go out, 4:704

only two failure points, 7:847

ordering any alteration of, 0:544

org ethics and tech, 0:499

out when admin won't go in, MS3:165

personnel inside any division may be shifted, 4:94

points of discipline, 4:350

policy on technical information, 2:119

posts often have other tech to be studied, 0:223

power of wisdom due to superior technology, 0:484

primary org goal is delivering foremost technical quality, 0:17

primary targets in our technology for anyone seeking to mess it up, 5:754

primitive organizational tech currently in use, 0:41

production and prosperity occur when tech is known and used, 0:694

promotional actions and issuing tech materials, 0:348

quality counts, 0:16

recovery, 5:752

reforming of technical subjects, 0:36

results,
    if not forthcoming, somebody is goofing, 0:19
    no excuse for any technical failure, 0:18
    of getting tech known and exactly used, 0:68
    only occur when tech is correctly applied, 0:55
    when you do raise hell and do get C/Ses and auditors to know their business and Supers get students cracking, 3:89

rule, when all else fails, do what Ron says, 5:758

safeguarding tech, 0:21

seeing what tech one needs and getting it grasped fast, 0:144

skilled tech required to bail us out, 0:650

source of, 0:685

SP corrupting tech, 0:90

SPs alter-is to mess it up, 1:993

staff need a reality on the tech they deliver, 4:704

stamp out all instances of verbal tech, 4:33

standard tech *see* standard technology

stays in where ethics administered, 1:569

technology, technical, tech, *(cont.)*

strength is nothing without skill and, 0:517

study tech, *see* study technology

tech/admin staff ratio, *see* tech/admin ratio

ten points of Keeping Scientology Working, 0:8

third dynamic tech, 0:55–56, 7:486, MS3:466

to improve results, you have to improve administration, 5:690

unusual solutions, 5:753

use vs. mere knowledge, 4:1078, 5:669

verbal tech and crazy interpretations of, 3:94

what makes man's technology frail and limited, 0:36

who besides Tech personnel is responsible for, 4:33

will not go in when ethics is out, 1:842, 4:1133, 5:719, MS3:165

workable technology, 0:7

works on every case, 0:498

you don't have to dream it up or alter it so it will work, 0:282

techno-space society, mission of, 0:461

Tech Page, ideal scene and stat, 4:137

Tech Reservations Administrator,

ideal scene and stat, 4:141

Letter Typists, ideal scene and stat, 4:141

tech results, to improve tech results, you must improve administration, 4:949

Tech Routing Administrator, ideal scene and stat, 4:137

Tech Sec, *see* **Technical Secretary**

Tech Why, MS1:165; *see also* **Why**

telegram,

use telegrams instead of phones, 1:457

purchase orders and, 3:314

telephone(s), phones

answering of, 1:329

are psycho and have no memory, 0:379

getting people into higher services by phone actions, 0:360

have no memory, 1:331

how to keep calls short, 1:340, 4:274

interoffice phone, use of, 0:85

interorg phone calls discouraged, 0:379

is off-line, 0:85

length of calls, 1:340, 4:274

no logistics on telephone lines, 1:466

notes, keeping of, 1:341, 4:275

overseas calls, 0:379, 1:329

phone registration in city areas, 0:349

psychotic, has no memory, 1:459

telephone(s), phones *(cont.)*

    rules regarding, 1:328

    types of calls, 1:339, 4:273

    used for making appointments, 1:340, 4:274

    use telegrams and cables instead, 1:457

    when to call, 1:339, 4:273

Telephone Registrar, scheduling books and, 2:629

television, TV,

    "nothing to do with me" attitude caused by, 0:555

    pours lies into population of Earth, 6:622, MS3:5

    teaches us that hero always wins and good always triumphs, 0:454

    tells one that robbery is only way to get rich, 0:317

    word of mouth and, 0:333, 0:337

telex(es), cable(s), *see also* **communication; despatch; letter; telephone**

    abbreviations and, 1:475

    clarity of communication, 1:467

    comm cycle, 1:476

    definition, 1:472, 7:480, MS1:370, MS2:196, MS2:301, MS3:460

    discipline, 1:472

    economize on words, 1:475

    going by misunderstood words in, 0:47

    handling of telex machines, 1:458

    how to write, 1:473

    info or compliance reported by, 0:432

    no logistics on telex lines, 1:466

    nonurgent comm on telex lines, 1:466

    not a despatch, 1:472

    one subject per, 1:474

    placement and routing of, 0:377

    speed and, 0:275, 0:432

    telephone vs. telex, 0:379

    telex files safeguarded by Dir of Comm, 1:386

    which inform of modifications or cancellations of HCO PLs or HCOBs, 0:143

temperature,

    cycle of, 5:638

    "low-order," definition and handling, 5:638

temporary executive,

    definition, 1:225

    grounds on which authorization to appoint may be refused, 1:224

temporary posting, may be done locally, 1:257

Temporary staff member,

    may be dismissed, transferred or demoted without any ethics action, 3:192

    person still temporary status after three months on staff will be let go, 3:192

temporary staff status,

    description, 0:209–210

    only persons with "Temporary" or "Probationary" status can be dismissed, 0:487

    PTS staff member and, 0:493

temporary status,

    definition, 1:236, 5:396

    description, 5:411

    dismissal and, 1:237, 1:251

    may be dismissed, transferred or demoted without any ethics action, 1:241

    person still temporary status after three months on staff will be let go, 1:241

    procedure for dismissal, 5:412

    requirements for, 1:236

    who do not become Provisionals, 5:413

terminal(s), *see also* **line; post; staff**

    base of motor holds two terminals in fixed positions, 0:205

    chief difficulties with, 1:360

    communication and hats, 1:273

    coordinated functions of, 1:311

    definition, 0:196, 1:273, 7:479, MS1:369, MS2:195, MS2:300, MS3:459

    false terminal, 0:294

    giving public or outside or internal traffic correct routes and, 0:281

    hats and, 0:199, 1:273

    if terminals exist communication can flow correctly, 0:196

    instruct, cram, retread, dismiss is sequence for handling dev-t terminal, MS2:45

    making channels on which things can flow and putting terminals there to handle or change them, 0:389

    missing, 0:436

    most important things in an org are lines and, 0:384

    must be in, in an exact known pattern, 1:311

    no confusions when lines, terminals and actions exist for each type of particle, 0:82

    org and, 0:81, 0:89, 0:384

    organization consists of coordinated purposes, lines and terminals, 7:293

    org boards and, 0:105–108

    personnel promotions and, 1:275

    routes, agreement and, 0:82

    scale concerning lines and terminals, MS1:288

    sending things to wrong terminals, 0:391

    short-circuit of, 0:384

    slave societies and unthinking terminals, 0:82

terminal(s), *(cont.)*

stable terminal, 0:434

unstable terminals, graphed, 0:436, 0:437

when people wear only their own hats, then one has terminals, 0:196

terminatedly handle, definition, 0:244

termination, of employment, procedure, 1:226

terror, attacks on Scientology and, 7:1009

test(s), *see also* **testing**

answer sheets, safeguard them from being known or seen by unauthorized personnel, 4:233, 6:304

body routing and, 6:274

control, can be tested on staff members, 1:187

Dir of Processing and, 4:963

filing of, 4:229, 6:272

IQ below 120, 1:158

letters referring to test results obtained on a person in any way must be given in person by a qualified person, 2:600, 4:228, 6:271

line honesty is a primary requirement, 4:234, 6:305

low leadership scores for executives, 1:197

never answer pc's question as to what a question means, 4:233, 6:304

never tell pc,
right answers to, 4:233, 6:304
to look up words on test, 4:233, 6:304

never word clear question sheet, 4:233, 6:304

of executive, 0:708

preclears and, 4:227

profile below center line, 1:158

psychiatric and school tests are written and administered by people in ivory towers, 0:121

reason for expiration date on theory testing, 4:326

routing of, 4:246

sales of, 2:386, 3:101

Scientometric testing, 4:229

scoring of by HGC auditors, 4:227

staff members' profiles, filing of, 4:229

students and, 4:227

supreme test, *see* supreme test, of thetan

supreme test of a thetan, MS1:446

theory testing and expiration date, 4:326

which copies go to CF, 6:272

Test Evaluation, is future heavy income, 6:287

Test In-Charge, is responsible for providing result display books and display graphs or sheets of graphs for walls, all made up to be easily understood, 6:279

testing,

anyone doing evaluation should have a book of profiles made up from high–low tests showing what Scientology can do, 6:279

broken into four activities with four purposes, 6:273

by policy is a free service, 6:274

eight unit packet in envelope with name on it, 6:292

evaluation and, 6:285, 6:318

filing and, 6:287

handling if a medical doctor or other specialist sends in a person to be tested, 6:291

in a city Central Org, where a Test Section should exist, 6:274

moves now out of psychological range and into future prediction, so we are not doing psychological testing, 6:280

procedure for marking and filing, 6:275

program change, 6:288

promotion and, 6:277, 6:283

simple tests may be mailed out to CF names, 6:273

staff auditor and, 4:1148

Tech Estimate line, 4:1040

tested persons should be sold (a) individual auditing or (b) co-audit, but always at least co-audit, 6:321

Test Section tests on an individual basis, 6:274

use of, 6:278

test line,

check on C/S and auditing quality, 4:234, 6:305

city office and, 6:775

how to administer test, 4:233, 6:304

Test Section,

as an entrance point to service, must look crisp and efficient, 6:276

definition, 2:504, 3:232, 4:45, 7:200

marks the test and makes two copies of the graph, 6:318

texts, textbooks,

bad texts, 0:41

psychology, psychiatric and religious texts of 30s and 40s, 0:362

students buying their own, 5:723

The Factors, contributism and, 0:277

theft, *see also* **rip-off; robbery**

actions to be taken when theft occurs, 0:548

actions to follow when theft occurs in an organization, 3:398

actions to handle, 1:706

attempting seizure of product without support, 0:296

theft, *(cont.)*

   criminal charges filed if any monies or org property is missing in consequence of person blowing, 0:177

   handling in cases where large objects are taken, 3:398

   insurance and, 3:398

   reporting of, 0:543, 0:548

Theft Report, description, 0:543

Theodora, 0:637

theory, *see also* **course**

   certificate exam shall consist of, 5:207

   course room separate from practical, 4:693

   covers why one goes through the motions, 4:332, 5:180

   demonstrations in theory aren't drills, 4:334

   internships heavily into theory, 5:857

   training section, definition, 4:583

   two types of theory training, 5:207

theory checkouts, *see* **checkout**

theory coaching, definition, 4:334; *see also* **coaching**

Theory Examiner,

   clay table isn't used to any extent by, 4:334

   purpose, 4:322

Theory Supervisor, 4:359

thermostats, handling of, 7:1339

thesis, definition of, MS2:137

theta line(s),

   entheta and, 1:987

   powerful comm lines, 1:987

thetan(s), *see also* **being; individual; man; people; preclear**

   ability to make things go right, 0:252

   agree only on bank principles, 0:10

   confront, complexity and, 0:51

   consider any beingness better than none, MS1:407

   definition, 6:430

   difference between one thetan's forward thrust and another's is purpose, validity of, 0:237

   how he fails and becomes weak, 0:51

   invented bank to keep others good, 0:480

   nothingness is closer to than somethingness, 4:314

   only a thetan can handle a post or a pc, 3:243, 7:1069

   org board and, 0:128

   point where thetan goes mad, 0:509

   power stems from ability to hold position in space, 0:205

thetan(s), *(cont.)*

   reactive mind and, 0:10

   some are bigger than others, 1:202

   supreme test of, 0:236, 0:252, 0:430, MS1:446

   without banks have different responses, 0:10,

Thetan-Mind-Body-Product system, 0:128, 0:654

Things That Shouldn't Be Report, 0:547

think(ing), thought(s), *see also* **rational**

   collective think, 0:157, 0:158

   collective-thought agreement, 0:10

   how sane person vs. aberrated person thinks, 0:236–237

   learn to think like an idiot without abandoning any ability to think like a genius, MS1:109

   people who have never been taught to, MS1:4

   production accomplished by numerous contributions of effort or, 0:277

   reason, 0:451, 0:456

   slave societies and unthinking terminals, 0:82

third dynamic, *see also* **civilization; country; culture; group; man; organization; society; state**

   arbitrary is third dynamic aberration, 0:65

   I have never intended Scientology orgs and groups to be bits of third dynamic each opposed, 0:273

   justice, *see* justice

   PLs and, 0:55

   Power Formula for, 0:645

   search for basic laws of, 0:56

   wrecking first and second dynamics by abandoning third, 0:301

third dynamic aberration, exact mechanism is, MS1:261

third dynamic sanity, investigatory procedures and, MS1:72

third dynamic tech(nology), 0:55, 0:56; *see also* **administrative technology; Hubbard Communications Office Policy Letter; policy**

third party,

   basis of all troublesome third party activities, 1:540

   explained, 0:510, 0:513–514

   how to find one, 1:544

   law, 1:535

   questionnaire, 1:544

Third Party law, Gung-ho Group and, 6:859

thought(s),

   divisible into classes, MS1:5

   many types of, MS1:3

threat(s), threaten(ed), external threat need be just enough to make internal pressure to do wrong lesser of two discomforts, 0:480

  HCO deputizing other Scientologists in times of, 0:478

  HCO justice protects staff member's reputation and job from being falsely threatened, 0:477

  included in request for justice, favor or redress, 0:488

  most serious threat to stability of org, 0:384

  threatened with punishment if one files Job Endangerment Chit, 0:550

three-basket system, 0:378, 1:354; *see also* **baskets; comm station; communication; communication line**

Thursday 2:00 P.M., 0:691

tidiness, of premises, 6:594

tiger (ethics sense),

  definition of, 1:787

  false graph and, 0:658

  how to find one, 1:787

  how to lift the label, 1:787

  missions and, 1:787

tigers, only tigers survive, 0:13

time, *see also* **hour; schedule**

  basic purpose runs through time, 0:117

  bigger we get, more economics and time we will have to do our job, 0:13

  communication and, 0:46

  example of wasted time, 7:807

  shortening time of application of auditing for financial or labor-saving considerations, 0:15

  suspension or loss of time, 0:494

  truth, stupidity and, 0:535

  wasted by failure to use a program-project system, 7:807

  way to save time and lives, 0:255

time machine,

  amends project and, 0:545

  definition, 1:518, 7:677

  description, 0:375–376

  executive use of at WW, 7:692

  order board and, 0:375

  orders marked urgent by an exec are entered into one-day time machine, 1:519, 7:678

  orders or queries, 1:385

  to check compliance, 0:595, 7:1212

  what it exists to do, 7:692

  what may be placed on a, 0:375–376, 0:382

tiredness, due to off-line, off-origin comm, 0:394

Title A, B, C, 0:187, 3:389

tone level(s),

  ethnic surveys and, MS3:69, MS3:248

  PR surveys and, MS3:38

  surveying and, MS3:55, MS3:66, MS3:230, MS3:241

Tone Scale,

  tech and PR surveying, MS3:54, MS3:229

  tech of surveying and, MS3:55, MS3:230

  use of in handling black PR campaign, MS3:83

too little too late,

  events and, MS3:33

  examples of, MS3:32

tool(s),

  basic management tools, MS1:368, MS2:194–19, MS2:200, MS2:299–303, MS2:305

  basic, consists of, MS1:365

  basic, list of, MS1:374

  breakthrough was in discovering that executives did not look upon these as tools, 7:483, MS3:463

  ethics as a, 0:449, 0:457

  ethics offense to fail to use these, 7:485, MS2:201, MS2:306, MS3:465

  executive responsibilities and, MS1:375

  first thing an executive or manager needs to know, 7:483, MS2:199, MS2:304, MS3:463

  form of the organization and, MS3:435

  fundamentals of organization, 7:485, MS2:201, MS2:306, MS3:465

  inoperational, 0:306, 0:307

  kept clean and functioning, 0:251

  key management tools, 0:648

  knowing vs. not knowing one's, 0:306–307, 0:309

  knowing what the tools of management are and how to use them, 7:461, MS2:188, MS2:292, MS3:441

  list of basic management tools, 7:484, MS3:458, MS3:464

  list which comprises the basic management tools, 7:478

  machines are just, 0:314

  Management Status checksheets and, 7:463

  Management Status One checksheet and, MS2:190, MS2:294, MS3:443

  Management Status Two checksheet and, MS2:190, MS2:294, MS3:443

  Management Status Three checksheet and, MS2:191, MS2:295, MS3:444

  most valuable, form of the organization, 7:455

  order vs. disorder, 0:305

tool(s), *(cont.)*

precise in their use, MS1:365

relationship between one's tools and one's product, 0:309

strategic plan can necessitate calling other tools of management into play, 7:473, MS3:453

strategic plan, checklist for, 7:475

technical not understanding any of its, 0:19

upper-level tools of management, 7:464, MS1:365, MS2:190, MS2:294, MS3:443

with which to manage, MS1:373

top management, 0:131, 0:132

total freedom, policy is to advocate total freedom, 7:1024

totalitarian, we have gone up against totalitarian conspiracy using "mental health" to control populations, 0:336

totalitarian materialism, definition, 6:868

Touch Assist, 5:629

tough case(s), *see also* **case**

definition, 4:342

for the HGC and HCO to handle, 1:1003

judged *only* on basis of case gain or lack of it, 4:344

majority of course trouble and tendency to alter-is material comes from trying to force a "tough case" to get gains, 4:343

make a lot of commotion so one may think they are "everybody" on course, 4:343

report to HCO, 1:1002, 4:343

routine procedure for handling, 1:1005, 4:345

sole reason for urge to alter a process, 1:1002

three categories of, 1:1004, 4:344

toughness, 0:12; *see also* **power; strength**

organization and survival, 1:86

tour(s), *see also* **ARC Break Program; Rudiments Program; Bridge flow**

blown public and, 2:647, 3:223, 4:282, 7:871

call-in and, 2:646, 3:222, 4:281, 7:870

drove people in on orgs, 2:294, 6:258

generating public interest and goodwill, 0:332

goodwill and, MS3:168

Registrar personnel in training for Reg and Tours posts, 0:347

vital to income and delivery, 0:266

when ceased to operate, boom halted, 2:294, 6:258

TR, *see* **training routines**

trademark,

importance of, 7:1055

infringement, handling, 7:1062

neglect or omission in safeguarding of, 0:473

responsibility for, 7:1055, 7:1057

safeguarding, 7:1059

traffic, *see also* **business; communication; despatch; particle**

analyzing traffic, 0:417

broken down into two headings, 7:614

decreasing or reducing it, 0:279, 0:280, 0:390, 0:397–398

doing or handling it when you receive it, 0:399

doubling your, 0:399, 0:431

everything you don't handle comes back and bites, 0:400, 0:431

give local comm traffic less attention than exterior traffic, 7:653

heavy due to permitting dev-t to exist, 0:427

heavy traffic warnings, 0:380

musical chairs increases traffic, 0:280

new kind, how to handle it, 0:128

offenses concerning, 0:468

people who originate traffic they have no business with and send it to wrong terminals, 0:391

Personnel goofs and, 0:280

policy and traffic flow, 0:325, 0:475

repeated, 0:432

steps to increase production and decrease traffic, 0:281

that does not belong to one, 0:391

too much traffic jams a line, 0:85

way to decrease traffic and workload of an org, 1:70

when you expand volume and traffic you must expand org, 0:129

trained and active FSM points, restored as a statistic for the FSM Section of Department 18, 6:671

training, *see also* **Academy; course; instruction**

Academy course has no finite duration but every effort should be made to graduate the student at the end of twelve weeks, 3:152

actions paramount in all our training, 4:547

add to regulations for all courses, Academies and SHSBC, 4:473

admin people can qualify as auditors part time, 0:223

an award, 1:744

any pc who has trouble needs, 4:1108

approach to auditor training, 4:320

auditing section, definition, 4:584

training, *(cont.)*

auditor training is highly recommended whether you plan to audit professionally or no, 2:471

basic points of agreement, MS1:271

basic policy to be adhered to regarding professional training, 4:594

because auditor TRs and metering were out auditors have not been producing uniformly spectacular results, 4:428

before full posting, 0:261

boom, how it will progress, 5:838

booming an org through, 5:835

bulletins, tapes and drills assigned each one a rating, 4:612

charges on, 7:834

cheapest way to get auditing, 5:836

checksheet and, 4:568

city office establishment prerequisite, 6:780

Class Ia, Ib definition, 4:587

Class IIa, IIb definition, 4:588

Class IIc, IId definition, 4:588, 4:589

Class IIIa, IIIb, IIIc definition, 4:589

clearing and excellent auditor training are only things in long run that will count, 0:16

clearing and, 4:614

Clears realizing need for, 4:786

closer one adheres to exact training patterns of an Academy, the better off you're going to be, 4:599

covering LOTS of material lightly vs. covering a little material thoroughly, 4:781

crime, 4:934, 5:249

defined, MS1:272

delivery, *see* delivery

denial of, by Comm Ev, 0:495

dev-t due to untrained, unhatted staff, 0:391, 0:393, 0:414, 0:426, 0:439, 0:441

divided into three sections, 4:583

down stats and failure to train on hats, MS1:403

emphasis of all course training shall be a flawless ability to do auditing, 4:585

end of endless, 4:419

end product of, MS1:271

Esto I/T until completed on, MS2:126

ethics actions and, 0:491

ethics actions may only suspend training or deny auditing, 4:354

examples of heavy resistance to selling training, 4:407, 6:398

excellent auditor, now in reach of every Academy, 5:16

training, *(cont.)*

exec responsibility for training staff, 0:222

failure to provide training on jobs begets revolt, MS1:408

False Data Stripping solves problem of inability to hat or train, MS2:135

far cheaper than processing in long run, 4:164, 5:330

feasible route to take, 4:614

fifth course, Hubbard Advanced Auditor (BScn abroad), 4:542

first level, free course, 4:541

five-year contract and, 0:174

Flag training, 0:290

flubbed instruction perpetuates error on every pc that auditor audits thereafter, 4:11, 5:11

for executives, MS3:443

Founding Scientologist certificate and, 4:177

fourth course, Hubbard Certified Auditor, 4:542

fragmentary, will lead to mess up own case, 4:1057

free service, *see* free service

FSMs, training of, 0:302

full-time, 1:217
  5-year contract, 1:169
  qualifications for, 1:169
  requirements for, MS1:389
  rotating upstats into, 5:708
  tech/admin ratio and, 1:217
  who to grant it to, 0:223

fully trained and functioning staff can get no real adverse reaction from superiors or even an enemy, 0:268

have good training available and say so loudly, 0:626

HCO personnel, 1:357

how to boom with scholarships, 4:387

how to do theory checkouts, 4:395

impeded or interrupted by 2D activities, recourse, 4:479

importance of being hatted and trained for the post, 0:280

income source, 3:101

in no org did auditors go fresh from school into auditing with no further training, 0:290

in orgs, missions and city offices; rules for (1964), 4:184

inefficiency vs., 0:261

inquiries, brought to attention of D of T, 4:292

invoicing people ordered to, 2:483

is an award, 5:109

letting an auditor out of the Academy without the basic skills down perfectly is opening the door to failure, 4:566

training, *(cont.)*

Method One Word Clearing is required before Academy training, 4:196, 4:652

minors and, 3:145

mission courses authorized, 6:748

more desirable than anything else this world has to offer, 0:332

more economical, 4:786

most profitable income of org, 4:461

must be practical, useful and must apply, MS1:401

must not let go a bad auditor, poorly trained, 4:310

must not substitute ministerial training for academic schooling, 4:306

new shorter checksheets demand study tech is applied, 4:419

none are owed processing or, 0:507

no restriction on whom we can train, 2:402

no student who cannot be properly trained, 0:12

not done without invoice, 4:215, 6:383

not insisting on execs being trained and staffs being hatted, 0:303

not substitute ministerial training for academic schooling, 5:730

no two-way comm in training primary block on volume auditing, 4:392

objective in any Scientology org and, 4:410, 6:401

of auditors, barriers to, 4:320

only teach proper use, 4:592

only use TRs which exactly parallel use of Scientology in session, 4:592

on-the-job, 0:440, MS2:17

orders to, may not be made as sentence or used in an ethics court or by Comm Ev or any other reason, 4:354

org gets people to be trained as auditors, 0:685

org not training its staff, 0:102

org potentially makes larger staff unit from training than processing, 2:69, 4:337

orgs limit their expansion by failing to push and deliver top-quality training of auditors, supervisors and C/Ses, 4:407, 6:398

original plan, 5:836

OT and, 2:471

outline for Estos, MS2:9

overload due to lack of training on hats, 0:204

partial-paids and unpaids, 0:303

part-time training program, 1:76

pattern of, 4:594

training, *(cont.)*

permanent signs where Dir of Training can see it in office, 4:310, 5:164

permitting without proper invoice, result, 4:216, 7:1188, 6:384

personnel wasted for lack of full hats and, 0:203

persons on staff not needed on admin (exceed ratio) should be in full-time training as auditors, 0:684

person to be trained by org at no or discounted fee must sign 5-year contract in advance, 4:222

policies instituted to emphasize the value of improved training, 4:572

policy, 5:162

politics and ideology may be no part of any decision to train or process individuals, 0:159

poor, can restimulate bypassed charge, 4:933

poor final product due to lack of, 0:295

poor quality and auditor scarcity, 4:148

potential trouble sources and, 1:746, 5:111

Practical Section, definition, 4:584

processing vs., and staff units, 5:836

production and, 1:210

production is the evidence of the demonstration of competence, 4:436

product of well-taught students, 0:15

professional training to be done in Academy and Saint Hill only, 4:594

program for executives, 7:463, MS2:190, MS2:294

program for staff, 5:499

programs are only swift and successful when training policy is fully used and in, 7:855

program to increase size and income of org, 4:411, 6:402

promotional actions and, 0:350, 0:352

promotion of Academy and, 5:837

proper instruction attitude, 0:13

protocol for, 4:289

providing environment in which auditing can be taught, 0:684

PR training, MS3:92

PTSes and, 1:1012

purpose of clay table training, 4:374

purpose of the Academy, 4:565

push training promotion, 4:388

quality of, 0:16

quality of, D of T and Instructors responsibility for, 4:296

training, *(cont.)*

quantities of people is the answer, 4:614

questionnaires detecting people's plans for, 0:349

rate of, established expansion factor, MS1:272

REAL design of, 5:494

reason fast training isn't occurring is because two-way comm seems to be out between Supervisors and students, 4:391

reasons to get trained, 4:412, 6:403

reattainment of Release opens the door to selling, 4:1066, 5:746

refund and repayment policy also applies to, 5:711

regulations for, 4:350, 5:170

restrictions on acceptance of students, 4:309

rules of the game called training, 4:367

second course, advanced course, 4:541

self-determinism and acceptance for, 4:323

selling of, 7:858

sentences carrying denial of training or processing, 0:491, 4:354

seventh course, Organizational Internship, 4:543

should be of student individuals who will audit people, for only an individual student, not a class, will do any auditing, 4:569

single-handing vs., MS1:216

sixth course, Hubbard Graduate Auditor (DScn abroad), 4:542

slowed by scarcity of materials, 4:463

slow progress, handling, 4:12, 5:12

stable datum, 4:29, 4:547

stable terminal and, 0:434

staff may not be ordered to, 5:576

staff member(s),
 aspiring to next higher classification, 0:169
 may not be ordered to training, 0:168
 may not use working hours for being instructed or trained, 0:168, 0:215
 pay suspended during training undertaken as amends, 0:544
 privilege, training as a, 0:175, 0:218
 training at upper org must sign valid note, 0:174
 training of, 0:32, 0:175, 0:217, 0:218

staff policy on, 5:385, 5:387

Staff Status and eligibility for, 1:240, 3:191

staff training, transferred to Qual, 4:903, 5:488

standard training procedure, description, 0:51

stress, 4:50, 5:50

student must be trained only with the tools of his trade to hand, 5:194

training, *(cont.)*

student not wanting next course in training, 0:32

student studying only answers to exam questions, handling, 5:170

study time and, 0:222

successful training arguments, 4:412, 6:403–406

summary of a bulletin from Academy in Washington, DC, 4:541

Supervisor's Code and, 4:367

suspension of, 0:494

system for Estos; instruct, cram, retread, MS2:21

technical skill cannot be picked up anywhere but in an Academy or HGC training unit, 4:565

technical studies and, 4:613

theories and processes can be picked up in books and from tapes as well as in classes, 4:565

Theory Section, definition, 4:583

the real design of, 4:387

third course, elementary Scientologist, 4:542

third dynamic psychosis is a covert refusal to train, MS1:267

three sections run concurrently with each other, 4:583

to get to OT you have to know how to audit, 2:471

trouble in traced back to, MS1:400

twinning lands student with responsibility right from the start, with that he can honestly be trained, 4:433

two kinds of theory training, 4:781, 5:207

two-way comm and volume of auditing and training, 4:391

underestimating number of persons needed to train and hat staff, 0:393

we are here to train auditors, not to educate them, 4:568

we fail only to the degree we do not use Scientology training tech and policy, 7:854

we must not ever let go a bad auditor, poorly trained, 5:164, 7:1188

we used to tell people that training as an auditor made one more able to handle life and his fellows, 4:388

what to do when someone buys, 0:282

when offering training put a course there, 1:288, 4:398, 5:508

when student has finished a course he should want next course in training, 4:379

who can be trained, 4:306, 5:730

work being competently done due to, 0:590

why we must train new Scientologists, 4:578

training aid, TV demonstration, 4:597

training officer,

anyone who has juniors is a, MS1:404

definition, 7:427, MS3:407

training routines (TRs),

auditors who have not done TRs the Hard Way, 0:302

because auditor TRs and metering were out auditors have not been producing uniformly spectacular results, 4:428

handling for, 4:429

in-TRs key to technical effectiveness, 5:452

may not be taught if they give an incorrect impression of how auditing is done, 4:591

must contain the correct data of auditing, 4:591

out-TRs, what brought it about, 5:653

truly important datum in auditing sessions, 5:671

usual to check in Cramming, 5:653

with meter, 5:194

training subsidy, rules regarding payment of staff member training in another org, 3:216

training-type ad, 6:180

TR and E-Meter films, see also **Technical Training Films**

regulations, 4:537, 6:347

transfer(s), see also **musical chairs; removal**

Ad Comm may only order directors and may not demote, transfer or dismiss director's personnel, 0:583

adverse effects of, 0:280

all data presented before the fact of, 1:250

almost never the answer for nonproducing personnel, MS1:400

case is not excuse for, 0:168

causes of, 0:168

Comm Ev required for, 0:487, 0:492, 0:587

complete hat folder allows one to be relieved in orderly fashion for, 0:193

conditions penalties and, 0:566

dismissals, demotions and, 0:487

down stats and, 0:587

Emergency condition and, 0:477

excessive, promote dev-t, 7:412, MS3:392

getting work being competently done by new appointment, transfer, training or case review, 0:590

HCO justice prevents wrongful transfer, 0:477

inside any division, 4:94, 5:738

transfer(s), (cont.)

instant transfers can wreck an org, MS1:388

leaving post, writing your hat, 0:198

may only be done after a Committee of Evidence, 7:1300

model assignment to be used for, 1:213

must have approval of Senior PCO International, 1:257

objecting concerning successor one does not believe capable, 0:596

of fees, 5:123

of students and pcs from one org to another, 5:123

only legal system of, 1:77

people hate to lose their posts and jobs, 0:205

permanent staff member may not be demoted, transferred or dismissed without a full Comm Ev, 1:238

points to inspect before Personnel begins to, MS1:404

post just vacated by a promoted person going into Emergency or Danger within ninety days, 0:596

Power Change Formula, 0:564

power restored to an org to do so locally, 1:260

provisional status may be transferred to other divisions, 1:238

psychological approach to personnel, MS1:398

PTS staff and, 0:492

quicksilver personnel scene, 0:264–267

recourse, 1:251

references, 0:266

request form must be accompanied by proposed replacement, 1:257

responsibility for post one is leaving, 0:198

saying "Am I transferred?" to exec who asks you to do somebody else's job, 0:232

staff case difficulties and, 5:576

staff members may request transfer without ethics action, 1:241, 3:192

State of Emergency and, 0:621–622

sudden transfer is failure to predict, MS1:454

suppressing an org by transferring people obsessively, 1:254

temporarily or permanently to HGC, 0:169

three things required prior to, 1:253

to post person really can do, 0:407

trying to get others transferred or dismissed, 0:206

unstabilizing people by asking them if they want different posts, 0:280

when I change personnel as answer, 0:374

when someone can be transferred, 0:485

wrongly transferred, handling, 0:487

transferring funds, procedure for, 3:408

translations,

issue authority and, 6:767, 7:1321

Scientology words and, 7:1319

transport,

arrangement, 1:461

emergencies stem from lack of foresight, 1:461

under direction of Communications
Officer, 1:461

transportation, Dir of Admin responsibility, 7:176

trap, getting out of, 0:13, 0:458

TR Course,

Advanced Course Admin must be informed of
enrollments on, 4:639

case changes and, 4:641

HGC Admin and the D of P must be informed
of enrollments on, 4:639

may not be done by persons in progress on OT
III, New OT V or New OT VII, 4:639

not done concurrently with an auditing
program, 4:641

solution for raw public with no idea about
communication cycle, 4:659

treasonable neglect, executive and, 0:220

Treason condition,

admin degrades and, 5:25

assigned to person making false report, 1:542

auditor or Supervisor delivering service to
individual without having to hand a fully
paid invoice for that service, 2:451

definition, 0:567

false report leading to unjust discipline of
another is act of treason, 0:515

for admin degrades, 0:73

for failure to be what one has post or position
name of, 0:572

for going by MUs or abbreviations in telexes,
despatches or post materials, 0:47

formerly defined as accepting money, 0:567

formula, 0:568, 0:569, 1:576

for not knowing and keeping in gross income
senior datum, 0:358

for technical degrades, 0:14

gross income senior datum and condition of,
2:672, 7:851

hats, not wearing, 1:580

letting standard tech go out is act of, 5:652

mutiny and, 0:656

person not able to actually find out that
he is, 0:569

reducing, combining or closing an org, 7:916

Treason condition, *(cont.)*

technical degrades and, 1:14, 2:14, 3:14, 4:14,
5:14, 6:14, 7:14

Treason quality, checklist, 5:870

Treasury Division (Div 3),

action of Treasury Division is putting org
THERE, 3:411

actions that good pay is composed of, 0:688

checklist for quality, 3:411

final responsibility for org's financial
viability, 3:411

if it has to do with money it has to do with
Div 3, 3:76

out-ethics indicators, 0:533, 7:1259

Power quality div would make Swiss bank
systems look bad, 3:419

promotional functions of, 3:54

uses pc scheduling board to verify that all
auditing hours being delivered are invoiced,
and why, 3:75

Treasury Secretary,

accounts policing and, 3:73

coordinates and gets done promotional functions
of Div 3, 0:349

ensures both Call-in Units are well supplied
with complete lists of who is fully or
partially paid, 7:875

first concern, 3:74

FP activation and, 3:299

FSM Account and, 3:264

inspects ways through which income losses can
occur and requests help of Ethics to handle
staff responsible for the outnesses, 3:76

major checkpoints on the income lines, 3:74

motto, 3:76

polices money particles through her division and
the entire organization, 3:73

specific duty of, 3:73

use of in-the-org list, 3:75

trend(s),

definition, 0:655, 7:337, 7:523, 7:524,
7:532, MS3:317

determined by looking, 7:524

do require changing conditions, 7:564

examples of, 7:524

figuring the scale for a graph correctly so that
trend lines actually show up on the
graph, 7:532

flashcards to drill statistic trend recognition,
use of, 7:534

trend(s), *(cont.)*

graph reading and, 0:679

how to correctly determine the stat trend, 7:531

how to read, 7:532

interpretation of statistics includes, 7:523

it's the slant or pitch of the stat over the period that one needs to be able to recognize, 7:532

management by, 0:648

not knowing trends, remote management can err, 7:527

overall measure of expansion or contraction and is the most valuable of stat messages, 7:528

Power is a, 0:643

require changing conditions, 0:681

shows the overall tendency to approach or depart from the ideal scene, 7:527

skilled stat trend recognition is an essential ingredient of skilled management, 7:535

unless one knows how to read statistics correctly and how to correctly determine a stat *trend,* prediction and management by stats will be way out in left field, 7:531

use of, 0:679

used in more remote areas from the org to indicate successful leadership or broad admin or tech situations, 7:529

used locally to estimate expansion or warn of contraction, 7:529

TR-4, worst TR 4, 4:314

TR Instruction films, *see also* **Technical Training Films**

are not for public showing and may not be shown to the public, 4:537

may be shown only to paid students and paid retread professional auditors, 4:537

staff auditors, Case Supervisors and Course Supervisors may view them only if signed up for retread and may only view in the course of being retreaded, 4:537

Triple Grades, 4:1098

trouble, *see also* **problem; situation**

always investigate for true cause of, 0:240

causes of, 0:8, 0:40, 0:221, 0:335

civilization has troubles because it hasn't known about hatting, 0:393

hidden source of, 1:61

how to keep out of, 0:145

noncompliance and, 1:424

only real trouble Scientology orgs ever have, 0:4

only we can make our own, 2:403

trouble, *(cont.)*

orgs where most trouble came from, 0:12

people doing their jobs without getting everyone else in trouble, 0:412

questionnaire for trouble area, 0:607–609

senior exec suddenly finding himself wearing hat of head of activity because it is in trouble, 0:585

sources of, 4:881

that may wipe out org, 0:418

trouble spots occur only where there are "no results," 1:8, 2:8, 3:8, 4:8, 5:8, 6:8, 7:8

vacuum for, 0:457

what almost all our troubles come from, 0:258

where we have trouble, we are not running into counter-intention but failed intention, 6:87

Trouble Area Assessment, used to find the area of the Why, 0:608

Trouble Area Questionnaire, 0:607–608, MS2:207

Trouble Area Short Form, 0:608–609, MS2:207

troubleshooting, HCO more of a troubleshooting unit than a secretarial office, 1:20, 7:1161

TRs, *see* **training routines**

TRs the Hard Way,

auditors and students on, rule, 4:639

true group,

amount of mest a true group will eventually conquer—but not necessarily OWN—is directly in proportion to the amount of theta that group displays, 7:573

definition of, 7:571

essences of, 6:854

how it falls away from being a true group, 7:572

trust(ed), *see also* **betrayal**

betrayal after trust, 0:567

I extend complete trust to appointee, 0:239

individual can be trusted with ethics, 0:450

in handling people, 0:388

man cannot be trusted with justice, 0:449, 0:456

man cannot be trusted with "punishment," 0:449, 0:521

on day when we can fully trust each other, there will be peace on Earth, 0:462

only person you could completely trust is Clear, 0:243

only so long as one keeps his word, 0:454

person who cannot be trusted, 0:574

posts as, 0:85, 0:234

we have trust which, if we fail it, condemns ourselves, our friends, our future, to continued oblivion, 0:239

trustees, defined, 7:585

truth,

  acceptable, MS3:9

  afraid of consequences should one
    tell truth, 0:454

  as-isness and, 0:536

  auditor is only one who can give man, 0:154

  black propaganda and, 0:520

  blows lie away as it is later on the chain, 5:440

  definition, 0:535, 1:843–844

  discipline must be based on, 0:515

  establishing truth of accusation before action is
    taken, 0:514, 0:515

  idea that group could evolve truth, 0:9

  if it isn't written, it isn't true, 0:146, 0:375

  in PR, MS3:75

  liar never happy or satisfied with himself until
    he begins dealing in truth, 0:458

  ours is power of, 0:484

  PRO and, MS3:149

  road out is road to, 0:519

  road to truth is begun with honesty, 4:210

  sanity is basically honesty and truth,
    4:235, 6:306

  society's "courts" vs., 0:485

  there is too much truth in our lives not to cause
    a social upheaval, 0:483

  true group, 0:140

  what is true for you is true, 0:31

  you can teach public individual anything,
    particularly truth, 0:324

TTC, *see* **Technical Training Corps,** 4:221

turnabout,

  definition of, 4:435

  example of, 4:435

TV demonstration,

  how to set up, 4:597

  training aid, 4:597

24-hour rule,

  any goofed session must be repaired
    within, 5:279

  example, 5:281

  on red tags, penalty, 4:256, 5:280

  roller-coaster despite an F/N, 5:281

25-hour intensive,

  delivered in orgs, successful pattern, 4:958

  system, 4:954

  system, manning it up, 4:956

twin checkout, *see* **checkout**

twinning,

  background of, 4:432

  brings people who have sunk back into
    their first dynamic up out of and onto the
    third, 4:432

  brought up participation and action levels of
    entire course rooms of students, 4:432

  co-audit twinning, 4:693, 4:706

  definition of, 4:431

  essence of, 4:434

  "games condition" and, 4:437

  has virtue of balancing inflow and
    outflow, 4:433

  how to handle courses containing both theory
    and practical sections, 4:434, 5:196

  mandatory on courses where essence of the
    course is to train the student in practical
    application of the data, 4:434

  once students get the idea that their own
    progress on course depends utterly on the
    quality of their twinning, you will start to
    see some quite magical results, 4:440

  person can balance his inflow with
    outflow, 4:433

  policy that the student who abandoned his twin
    because he was finished may not be
    certified until he has completed his
    twin, 4:437

  remedy is to send *both* twins to Ethics, *both*
    twins to Cramming, *both* twins to Review,
    and if anybody blows send his twin after
    him, 4:438

  "round robin" and, 4:439

  rule is when one student becomes bogged his
    twin is *always* sent with him to Cramming,
    Review or Ethics, 4:440

  rule of twinning is that it is done on a
    "turnabout" basis, 4:435

  students bear responsibility for not spreading
    verbal tech, 4:438

  Supervisor responsible for assigning, 4:435

  Supervisor should take care to team up students
    of comparable case level and training and
    abilities, 4:435

  Supervisor's responsibility and, 4:437

  twin is responsible for seeing that the student
    with whom he is twinned knows and can
    apply the material he has studied, 4:435

  when a bogged student is sent to Cramming or
    Review the twin is also always sent to
    correct and repair both of them as
    needed, 4:439

  where Word Clearing is essence of the course
    twinning is mandatory, 4:434

two-bit FP, consists of, MS2:364; *see also* **financial planning**

two-terminal universe, MS3:120

two-way communication, *see also* **communication**

acceptance and, MS3:36

correct way to speed up a student's progress, 1:15, 2:15, 4:15, 5:15, 7:15

good manners and use of, MS3:34

in Qual someone can two-way comm those sent to Review to help the person and get more accurate data for C/Sing, 4:392

in the HGC preclear can be two-way commed by the Tech Sec, 4:392

manners and, 0:328

more important than content, MS3:35

two-way communication, *(cont.)*

no two-way comm in training, primary block on volume auditing, 4:392

PR and, MS3:36

speeding up student's progress with, 0:15

steps for Supervisors to do, 4:391

two-year rule, vacating a post and, 1:275

typesetting, definition, MS3:194

typing,

Dept 2 oversees typing quality, 0:348

never let out-of-alignment typewriters, faint ribbons or erased messes go out on the Executive Director or SO 1 lines, 7:647

Secretarial Unit typing answers to letters, 0:370

Typing Pool, definition, 2:507, 3:235, 7:203

typing school, correct personnel pool, 1:164

typist, functions of, 2:501

U

UK, mission holders, 6:743

unauthorized process, suspension of
certificates, 4:1166

unawareness, position on lines and terminals scale
and, MS1:289; *see also* **awareness**

uncertainty, comes from lack of
understanding, 5:525

unconsciousness, misunderstood word and, 0:39

underload, post, department, division too
underloaded will give trouble, 1:63

undermanned,

division or org will, MS1:384

division which blows up or unmocks is
usually, MS1:405

underorganized, division which blows up or
unmocks is usually, MS1:405

understand(ing), comprehension, *see also* **ARC;
duplication**

ability to hear or read and understand
missing, 0:44

asking public individual to be there, understand
and decide, 0:323

ceases on going past misunderstood word or
concept, 0:39

communication and, 0:46

cooperation depends upon being able to see and
grasp scene, 0:144

if you can't understand it, clarify it, 0:23

inability to grasp situation being of benefit when
bravery is required, 0:114

misunderstood word, *see* misunderstood word

no justice without understanding, 0:483

understand(ing), comprehension, *(cont.)*

people agree to postulates they can appreciate
and, 0:82

spectatorism vs., 0:248

teaching Scientology at level it can be
understood and used by recipients, 0:160

to decide one has to understand, 0:323

too lazy to work at trying to grasp policy, 0:114

vocabularies have to be increased before
comprehension and communication
occur, 0:40

unfamiliarity, communicated by comparison to a
familiarity, MS3:121

unhattedness, *see* **hatting**

uniform(s),

all clothing issued must be signed for by the
staff member and receipt preserved in
Valuable Documents, 3:394

every permanent staff member is to wear a
uniform, 3:393

quantity of, 3:394

remains property of the org and is turned in on
leaving, 3:394

when charges may be laid against a staff
member for uniforms, 3:394

union(s), 0:318

unit (of an org),

do action that promotes in one's, 0:357

each has a product, 0:129

expansion and, 0:96

offenses concerning, 0:468, 0:471

proper size, 0:600, 0:602, 0:603

quicksilver personnel scene crashing
stats in, 0:267

465

unit (of an org), *(cont.)*

> that you are continuously creating your unit or defending it means there must be something knocking it down, 0:409
>
> Thetan–Mind–Body–Product pattern, 0:128, 0:654

unit (of pay), *see also* pay

> depending on exec for petty decisions costs units, 0:373
>
> depends upon each dept and post acting causatively, 0:230
>
> low units, source of, 0:19, 0:232
>
> obtaining higher unit or salary, 0:232
>
> raising or increasing them, 0:367
>
> source of low, 7:839

United States,

> cause of their decline, 0:505
>
> fighting Scientology, 0:157
>
> ignorance of Constitution, 0:41, 0:68
>
> misuse of opinion leaders, MS3:22
>
> popularity of leader created for election only, 0:83
>
> reasons it is about to come to pieces, 0:594
>
> riot, civil commotion and disintegration, 0:68
>
> Russia vs., 0:454
>
> suppressives and, 0:504

United States Army, drugs designed by, 0:451

United States government,

> lack of hats, 0:201
>
> Scientology vs., 0:159
>
> vanishes regularly, 0:599

United States Navy, 0:116

unit head, can't be in charge if thing one is in charge of doesn't exist, 0:654

universe,

> auditor is very important in clearing this, 0:154
>
> building a better, 0:126
>
> chaos is basic situation in, 0:434
>
> Distribution Cycle in which we use Scientology elsewhere in, 0:96
>
> game of Scientology and, 0:235
>
> in this universe it is easier to destroy than construct, 0:63
>
> it's a tough universe, 0:13
>
> one survives so long as he is true to himself, his family, his friends, laws of the universe, 0:455
>
> OT vs. aberrated universe, 0:624
>
> our target is cleared universe, 0:657
>
> reason it has been going downhill, 4:159
>
> reversing dwindling spiral, 0:91

universe, *(cont.)*

> that is decent and happy to live in, 0:131
>
> there is nothing whatever the matter with universe itself, 0:91
>
> this planet and universe are concern of others too, 0:140
>
> three-terminal universe, 0:513
>
> we are at reverse point of, 0:91
>
> we are going to have to get in ethics and clean it up, 0:658
>
> what the cycle of production must be in this universe to be successful, 0:95
>
> when somebody enrolls, consider he or she has joined up for duration of, 0:12
>
> who real crazy people in universe are, 0:237

unknown, *see* know

unreality, *see* reality

unreasonable, individual under stress of aberration is unreasonable, 0:158

unstabilize(ing),

> ARC breaks and, 1:211
>
> basic tool of the insane, 1:211

untrained, division which blows up is usually, MS1:405

unusual, student must be taught to meet it with the usual, 4:671

unusual solution(s), 0:256–257

> auditor using, means meter reading is inaccurate, 4:313
>
> cause of, 0:240–241
>
> policy vs., 0:404–405, 0:432
>
> resorting to, 0:146
>
> system which makes unusual solutions unnecessary, 0:241

unwilling(ness), *see* willing

unworkability, *see* workability

Upper Indoc,

> best test of control, 2:411, 6:183
>
> most reliable test of control skill, 2:413, 6:185
>
> whole staff can have its control level raised by, 2:413, 6:185

Upper Indoc TRs, are the drills that teach the CCHs, 4:623

upper-level rundowns, confidentiality of, 4:812

upper org,

> may deliver any and all of the services of the lower org providing the prices charged are at least 10% higher than the same service in the next lower org, 3:177
>
> must deliver better service to justify the increase over the lower org for the same service, 3:177
>
> selection to, city office, 6:790

upset(s), *see also* **ARC break; enturbulation**

causes of, 0:68, 0:245, 0:514–515, 0:572

flaps, 0:261

harmful, flagrant and continued code breaks resulting in important upsets, 0:470

missed withhold is source of, 4:314

no student or pc ever gets upset if actual error is spotted, 0:351

org leaving staff untrained will be upset by any effort to expand, 0:223

person who accepts post or position and then doesn't function as it will upset or destroy some portion of org, 0:572

public, penalty of not auditing, 4:866

reason for, 0:579

spotting sources of, 0:554

spreading upset by saying one is leaving, 0:177

what every upset we have is traceable to, 0:484

when contribution is not balanced to some degree, 0:277

upside-down graph, example, 1:678

upstat(s), executive in disciplining leaves alone all upstats and only acts to move suppressives off the lines, 1:1027, 7:511

up statistic, *see* **statistic**

urgent directive,

Ad Council and, 7:910

definition, MS3:306

example, 7:352, MS3:332

handling, 7:352, MS3:332

urgent orders, entered into one-day time machine, 0:376

US, resolution of, MS1:60; *see also* **United States**

use(d), using, *see also* **application**

if you have power, use or delegate it or you won't have it long, 0:639

nonutilized personnel, definition and effect of, 0:203

trouble with policy or admin because one doesn't know it or can't or doesn't use it, 0:551

unused people become unhappy, 0:639

using every humanoid to best and beyond his talents, 0:638

user(s),

basic step of administration, 7:408, MS3:388

definition, 7:409, MS3:389

usual, when in doubt, do the usual, 0:256

utilization,

if you've got it use it; if you can't use it get rid of it, MS1:273

of personnel, 1:210

personnel training and, MS1:406

proven by production, not busyness, 1:210

relation to executive, MS1:273

third dynamic psychosis is failure to utilize people, MS1:267

utilization survey, MS1:406

done for every personnel demand, MS1:465

V

vacation, *see* **leave**

vacuum, of data, how it is filled, MS3:80

val doc files, definition, 1:1053

valence(s),

Goals-Problem-Mass and, 5:566

Identity Rundown specifically designed to get a pc into, 4:232

out of valence and OCA graphs, 4:231

person with dropped OCA graph is not yet fully into his own, 4:231

responsibility and, 5:566

SP *has* to be out of valence to be SP, 4:231

validation,

Dept 13 validating people, 0:351

requirements for, 4:596

usually worked for harder than mere pay, 0:277

validation gold seal, 5:219

Vallejo, General, 0:633

valuable, *see* value

valuable document(s),

course roll book filed in, when full, 4:464

definition, 3:369, 7:1054

handling of, 1:1053, 3:369, 7:1054

HCO has a file kept under lock, 1:192

never *use* originals, 3:369, 7:1054

originals are kept in val doc, 1:192

valuable final product(s), *see also* product; subproduct

area producing VFPs is entitled to support, 0:297

as policy, MS1:254

valuable final product(s) *(cont.)*

basics of VFPs are true for any industrial or political or economic system, 0:298, MS1:297

basic survival and, 0:297

being interchanged determines survival, MS1:296

business success and precise establishment of, MS1:255

by getting many exact minor products, you then can achieve, 0:696

character must be established exactly, MS1:254

combined products and services of members of org, 0:294

definition, 0:296, MS1:295

determining them, MS1:259

Factors and, 0:297

for an org or management unit, MS2:370

how sanity and honesty relate to producing a, 0:296

if a subproduct list is used as basis for issuing orders they will be right targeted and valuable final products result, 7:827

lack of viability traced to volume and quality of, 0:297

list doesn't come wholly from top management or the group, MS1:259

must be known, MS1:257

production of and one's standard of living are intimately related, MS1:350, MS2:284

real VFP in an org, 0:316

relationship to other groups or individuals, MS1:259

repair earlier steps of its production, MS1:441

standard of living related to production of, 0:314–315

valuable final product(s), *(cont.)*

subproduct and, 0:696

three surveys to be done, MS1:258

using subproduct lists, part of an org can improve itself and its VFP, 7:829

what determines if VFP is valuable, 0:296

value, valuable,

area not producing something valuable enough to interchange, 0:298

calculating cash value of every piece of work done, 0:314

giving something more valuable than money was received for, 0:317

individual purpose and value as vital and wanted commodity, 0:204

posts are valuable to staff, 0:522

real VFP in org is valuable fine people who produce VFPs who then make up valuable fine public, 0:316

statistic refers to quantity of work done or value of it in money, 0:690

weighing value of person in general against alleged crime, 0:516

what determines if VFP is, 0:296

why person cannot expect to get full value of his VFPs all to himself, 0:313

value of services delivered,

how to compute statistic, 4:157

Tech Sec stat, 4:157

verbal orders, 0:375–376

verbal tech, MS1:174

cannot be comm eved or given a court or disciplined for not following, 0:145–147

categories of, 0:23

charges for giving out data contrary to HCO Bulletins or Policy Letters, 4:32

checklist, 4:31

effect of, 0:304

how to defeat it, 0:23

if it isn't written, it isn't true, 0:23, 0:146, 0:375

misunderstood word and, 0:304

penalties, 0:24, 4:32, 4:519, 5:808

policies forbidding must be extended to apply to any Technical Training Film, 4:519

very important person (VIP), MS3:18

opinion leaders may or may not be, MS3:24

opinion leader vs., MS3:18

vested interest(s), 0:56, 0:303

veteran(s),

must have an adequate replacement, 1:170

ordering of to Flag, 1:170

veteran evaluator, tosses off evaluations in an hour or two, MS1:110

veto,

LRH Comm may veto Ad Council or Exec Council measure that is against policy, 7:913

power of, 7:888

VFP, *see* **valuable final product**

viability, *see also* **future; insolvency; life; solvency; survival**

concentration points in keeping org viable, 0:42

deals with the future, MS2:416

definition, 0:287–288, MS1:66, MS1:227

degree that income increases above FP amount, well determines how viable org is, MS2:418

exchange and, 0:89

factors involved in org, 0:288–289

first consideration in procuring quarters for an org, 7:1394

formula for company viability, MS2:416

how org establishes its own level of income and longevity, 0:318

how to tell whether the org is viable, MS2:416

lack of, traced to volume and quality of VFP, 0:297

monitors all graph readings, 0:679

organizing and, 0:297–298

overall test for the group, MS1:221

predict to continue, MS1:70

product and, 0:288–289, MS1:226

prolonged threats to viability or survival will not improve unless Danger Formula is applied, 0:605

quality and skill of Estos and, MS2:9

relationship of policy, planning, programing, projects, orders, production and, 0:131–133

statistic measures, MS1:66

successfully viable org vs. limping scene, 0:62

things that result in, 0:259

Treas Div has final responsibility for financial, 3:411

undelivered services and, MS2:417

what org viability depends on, 0:89, 0:221

viable, definition, 7:428, MS3:408

vias, 0:38, 0:51, 0:383

victim(s), victimizing,

if someone doesn't hold line, all become victims of oppression, 0:518

letting victim on our lines, 0:398

one cannot go through life victimizing one's fellow beings and wind up anything but trapped—the victim himself, 0:455

people who want to become victims by going broke, 0:702

Victoria Parliament, 0:484

viewpoint,

assuming of, MS3:211

facility to shift from one to another, MS3:211, MS3:213

recovering your viewpoint of newness of Dianetics and Scientology, 0:363

SP has no viewpoint from which to erase anything, 0:657

violence, violent *see also* **revolt; revolution; war**

contribution vs., 0:277

gets a government nowhere, 7:1143

practiced for its own sake is just insanity, 7:1143

real men and real life are full of dangerous, violent, live situations, 0:634

vital information, 0:578–579

withholding, 5:800

vital target(s), *see also* **target(s)(ing)**

definition, MS2:427, MS2:432

how to assess, MS2:427

vitamin(s),

effects from taking gelatin capsules and handling, 5:636

food, not drugs, 5:621

"Guk Bomb," formula, 5:619

tablets vs. gelatin capsules, 5:636

vitamin C, what it handles, 5:637

vitamin E,
action of, 5:619
assists processing, 5:619
dosages, 5:620

vitamin(s), *(cont.)*

vitamin E, *(cont.)*
effect on auditing, 5:621
how it works, 5:620
results on an E-Meter, 5:619

vocabulary, vocabularies,

key vocabulary of subject of organization, 0:42

why they have to be increased, 0:42

volume,

demand and, 0:130, 0:289

every post and part of org must have stat which measures volume of product of that post, 0:654

expansion and, 0:130

increasing volume, 0:297, 0:415

lack of viability traced to volume and quality of VFP, 0:297

post volume too high, handling, 0:195

traffic flow and volume, 0:325, 0:380

work volume dropping, reason, 0:279

Volunteer Minister,

definition, 6:870–871

other ministers and, 6:872

what he can do, 6:872

Volunteer Minister Program,

purpose of, 6:872

utilizes *Volunteer Minister's Handbook,* 6:871

Volunteer Minister's Handbook,

investigations and, MS2:146

trains basic Scientology principles, 6:871

volunteers,

must sign an agreement, 1:159

renovation and repainting using, 0:339, 0:356

voting,

groups routinely select only those leaders who would kill them, 0:83

refusing to vote while member of Comm Ev, 0:469

V Unit, 4:740

W

wages,

fixed wage, means of suppressing person into a slavery class, 3:325

preferably paid by check, 3:39

wait,

anything which delays or puts customer or product on wait is enemy, 0:275

exec who doesn't handle but puts something on wait, 0:260

waiting list board, 4:1061

waiver,

cases in which these are required, 7:1101

for students who blow, 1:999, 4:91

no persons may be admitted to an Academy or HGC who have not signed waivers (release forms), 4:360, 7:1074

use of, 5:712

what it must include, 4:360

want, *see also* **demand; needed and wanted**

make person right for wanting, thus intensifying want, 0:324

promotion and, 0:324

war(s), *see also* **revolt; revolution; violence**

causes of, 0:125, 0:511, 0:512

civilization without, 6:519

dangerous environment and, 0:486

expansion and, 0:125

how US Navy might have won war with Japan in six weeks, 0:116

only brings anarchy, 0:632

popularity of, 0:252

psychiatry vs. Dianetics and Scientology, 7:1129

seeming normal to live in degraded society full of, 0:454

war(s), *(cont.)*

sign of a culture on way out, 0:454

SP and, 0:656

strategic planning and, 0:706

that we exist here could restrain fellow who could push button on atomic war, 0:493

war rulers deified and peacetime rulers forgotten, 0:505

we are fighting full-scale war against ignorance and enslavement, 0:208

why government's final product is riot, war and a polluted planet, 0:40

warning(s),

for errors made, 0:467

heavy traffic warnings, 0:380

one warning, one admin cramming, one retread, 0:392

repeated corrections, warnings or reprimands by senior, 0:467

Washington, DC Org, giving away pieces of their CF, 0:359

wastage,

envelope supplies can be wasted by inexpert machine operation or an inefficient machine, 2:176

paper economy in stationery and related supplies is important, 2:176

periodic review of postage uses is very worthwhile in savings, 2:176

postage and, 3:269

printing bills account for huge outgo percentages, 2:177

unused supplies and, 3:269

waste(d),

offenses concerning, 0:468, 0:543

promotion and, 0:344

Waste Report, description, 0:543

watchword,

Bring Order, watchword of HCO, 1:83

stability, watchword of the HAS, 1:83

WATS, (*Wide Area Telephone Service*) definition of, 2:646, 3:222, 4:281, 7:870

Way to Happiness, The,

morality and, 7:1155

Success Through Communication Course and, results on society, 6:495

weak(en)(er)(ness),

beings who are afraid of strong people try to weaken them, 0:205

competition is trick of weak to fetter strong, 0:273

dishonesty and underhanded dealings and the, 0:454

don't feel weaker because you work for somebody stronger, 0:640

how thetan fails and becomes weak, 0:51

lack of basic purpose causing weakness, 0:117

unhattedness and, 0:206

wealth, *see* **rich(es)**

week, when it starts and ends, 0:691

weekend course, scheduling of, 4:182

weekly reports, of the Flag Rep, 7:1419

welfare,

justice and, 0:456

of org comes from its stats, 0:688

removal and, not answer to sane org and society, MS1:302, MS1:458

seems so wonderful to the socialist, 7:436, MS3:416

staff being deprived of its pay and, 0:302,

staff member welfare is matter of third dynamic, 0:301

welfare (government aid), 0:204, 0:206

welfare era, Keynesian economic theory and, MS1:62

welfare program, guarantees crime and revolt, MS1:416

welfare state,

corruption of be-do-have cycle, 0:292

definition, 0:504, 1:769, 7:500

requiring no contribution, result, 0:277

result on society, MS1:408

rewarding downstat, result, 0:528

West, the,

decay of Western governments, 0:504

opulent West and starving East, 0:603

West, the, *(cont.)*

reason for decline of, 0:504

still has companies, 0:598, 0:599

What Is a Course? PL, 0:222, 0:302

What Is Scientology, release of, 6:293

whispering campaign, MS3:78

white PR,

definition, MS3:73

engaged in idealization at all times, MS3:74

existing scene and, MS3:76

Who-Where, evaluations, MS1:150–151

Why(s),

actually was the situation, MS1:140

Admin Why, MS1:165

backtracking to find how it is wrong, MS1:146

confirmatory step, MS1:157

Danger condition handling and finding person's, 0:608–609

Danger Formula and wrong Why handling, MS2:209

definition, MS1:82, MS1:122, MS1:159

does this data confirm, MS1:157

Estos and finding real, MS2:21

Ethics Why, MS1:165

eval that has who or where as its, MS1:150

example of finding one, MS1:147

examples of correct, MS1:83

handled Why keeps slipping out again, MS1:160

have to know when you don't have, MS1:158

how come situation is such a departure from ideal scene, MS1:147

how to find Why of sudden improvement, MS1:108

if you can't find, you revert, MS1:160

importance of having, MS1:159

jewel in the crown, main dish at dinner, gold mine in the towering mountains of mystery, MS1:93

leaps at you, MS1:141

mere explanation vs., MS1:82

must lead to a bettering scene, MS1:93

no situations and, MS1:158

obtained by, MS2:22

opens door to handling, MS1:146

operating on a general Why, MS1:160

question to ask of it, MS1:146

real, test of, MS1:83

real Why,

cannot be found unless *the* product is named and ideal scene then stated, MS1:108

Why(s), *(cont.)*

real why, *(cont.)*

leads to improved stats, MS1:82

opens the door to handling, MS1:121

people will cooperate all over the scene, MS1:98

reason closer approach to ideal scene, MS1:158

reason there has been a departure, MS1:158

resolving situations and, MS1:50

right Why and F/N VGIs, MS2:42

right Why handling becomes simple, MS1:146

situation will deteriorate if wrong, MS1:97

something you can do something about, MS1:158

Tech Why, MS1:165

test of any right, MS2:66

there would be no trouble there if the Why correct, MS2:22

using one Why for all situations, MS1:94

what it must be, MS1:93

when you've got a Why you can handle, MS1:160

wrong,

definition, MS1:82, MS1:146

stats and, MS1:82

stats went down, MS1:157

Why Finding,

actions, omissions in folders, 4:1195, 5:803

administering on individual, 5:791

bogged, handling for, 5:793

examples of how to find, 5:792

handling wrong Whys, 5:793

metered Why Finding, 5:793

resolution of, 5:791

steps to find and handle, 5:791

Why is God, MS1:87; *see also* **Why**

Wichita, why org there crashed, 0:10

wildcat Dianetics Courses, 4:637, 6:720

will of the people, definition, MS3:19

willful, staff members are seldom willful, 0:552

willing(ness), unwilling(ness),

less willing when personal security is undermined, 0:515

letting unwilling, irresponsible person on our lines, 0:398

morale, as relates to, MS1:230

persistent "Can't be done" means "I am unwilling," 0:372

win(s), *see also* **success**

foremost law, if ambition is to win, is to win, 0:638

length of time to get, 4:929, 5:685

win(s), *(cont.)*

only game in which everybody wins, 0:234, 0:235

solvency and org wins are made up of small actions of staff all added together, 0:357

specialize in production and everybody wins, 0:506

we will win if we *are* Scientology, not a lot of isolated groups, 0:273

you're selling wins—deliver them, 0:283

winning, whenever we're really winning, the squirrels start to scream, 7:994

wisdom,

decrying suppression of wisdom which would help mankind, 0:160

definition, MS1:77

power of wisdom due to superior technology, 0:484

setting example of effectiveness and wisdom of Scientology, 0:161

twentieth-century science sought to discount wisdom entirely, 0:119

witch hunts, 1:1018

witch pit, Dianetics and Scientology began road out of, MS3:136, MS3:173

withhold(s)(ing),

auditors missing them stems from, 4:1196, 5:615

basic study missed withhold, 1:837

blocking flow of vital information, 5:801

blows due to overts and, 0:177

bypassed charge and, 6:548

criminal not much benefited by giving off, 1:832

definition, 6:544

dramatization of, 5:800

entirely the cause of continued evil, 1:843

gotten off in session, pc not sent to Ethics, 4:1174, 5:587

insane are just one seething mass of overt acts and, 0:528

leads to out-communication, 4:405

misunderstood or, only reason pc is critical, 4:1081, 5:672

offenses concerning, 0:469

on PR lines, handling, MS3:166

penalty for auditors who miss them, 4:1196, 5:615

people with withholds get complex, MS1:187

pretending withholds which are actually criticisms, 1:993, 4:85

primary cause of bypassed charge, 1:792, 4:933, 5:248

Review mistaking a withhold for an ARC break, 5:38

withhold(s)(ing), *(cont.)*

students and, 4:405

stupidity and, 1:848

Vital Information Rundown, remedy for, 5:801

WANT the product vs., 3:309, 7:445, MS2:129, MS3:425

ways to dramatize, 5:800

withdrawing and withholding from area harmed, 0:457

writing up overts and, 0:536,

withhold checks, staff should get weekly, 5:574

withholdy case,

Academy and, 4:344

definition of, 1:1004, 4:344

witness,

definition and duties, 1:929

false witness, definition, 1:930

offenses concerning, 0:469

when senior exec may be called as witness in matters of recourse requested by junior, 0:478

wog(s), wog world,

can't predict wog court decision, 0:327

don't react to Scientology justice as though it were wog law, 0:485

going on being wogs if we don't use our justice, 0:485

jungle of noncompliance and false reports, 0:421

skipping approval button from, 0:17

using heavy ethics on, 0:247

wog discipline is simply harsh injustice, 0:520

word(s),

keeping of one's, 0:454

misunderstood word, *see* misunderstood word

noncomprehension of basic words with which one is working, 0:40

propaganda and redefinition of, MS3:42

redefinition of for propaganda, examples, MS3:43

Word Clearer,

ED or CO, OES or Chief Officer, HES or Supercargo and HAS subject to Comm Ev if there is no, 5:79

penalty for missing MUs, 4:504, 5:473

reason they cease to word clear or blow, 4:505, 5:474

who accumulate MUs, penalty, 4:505, 5:474

Word Clearing,

auditors and, 0:45

Axiom 28 and, 0:46

Word Clearing, *(cont.)*

basic law, 5:468

check for slow courses and non-F/Ning students, 4:497

consequences of none, 5:806

ethics and study tech, 0:44

how False Data Stripping can tie in with, MS2:142

how to get it in on org staff, 5:524

in same dept as programing, 0:223

library and, 5:724

list of words that have to be fully cleared and understood just to talk about organization, 0:42

makes excellent auditors, 4:966

Method 1 Word Clearing,

case setup for, 4:654

co-audit, 4:688

definition of, 4:652

description, 4:491

drug cases and, 4:646

how to get, 4:654

position on Grade Chart, 4:195

prerequisite for Academy Levels 0–4, OEC and higher-level tech and admin training, 4:645

requirement for fast flow training, 4:653

training and, 4:196

when it can be done, 4:653

Method 2 Word Clearing, description, 4:492

Method 3 Word Clearing, description, 4:492

Method 4 Word Clearing, description, 4:493

Method 5 Word Clearing, description, 4:494

Method 6 Word Clearing, description, 4:494

Method 7 Word Clearing, description, 4:495

Method 8 Word Clearing, description, 4:496

Method 9 Word Clearing, description, 4:496

nine methods of, 4:491

requirements, 5:806

secret of fast courses, 4:490

tech certainty, flubless results, high stats and, 5:524

tests may not be word cleared, 4:233, 6:304

used in repairing past ethics conditions, 0:663

where Word Clearing is essence of the course twinning is mandatory, 4:434

Word Clearing Method 2, post success and, 5:467

Word Clearing Section,

hidden data line and failure to use, 5:699

ideal scene, 5:61

product, 5:62

purpose, 5:61

statistics, 5:62

word of mouth, *see also* **advertising; dissemination; promotion**

bigger than press, MS3:125

definition, 6:626, MS2:298, MS3:169

description, 0:333

enemy is lacking, 0:337

goodwill, PR and, 0:332

on Dianetics, 2:331, 6:234

PR and, 6:608, MS3:142

public relations comm line superior to media, 6:608

superior to newspaper, radio and TV, 0:333, 0:337

what greatly speeds it, 0:337

words, no words at all is worse than a few misunderstoods, 2:374, 6:342

work,

essential ingredient of a PR is ability to, MS3:14

PR personnel must be able to, MS1:419

PR who can't work fails every time, MS3:15

work(ing), *see also* **post; production; workability**

abide by working hours of the org, 0:165

Affluence attainment and hard work, 0:628

always some individual assigned as responsible for the, 0:690

Anglo-Saxon race ambition to not work, 0:417

anyone in charge of people has to be able to organize functions and, 0:88

completed staff work, *see* completed staff work

do it now, 0:399, 0:430–431

don't hide bad work from execs, 0:232

done by living beings using good sense and skill, 0:82

double work, 0:399, 0:430

downstats actively working other direction, 0:653

druggie's dream that machines, computers, under dictatorship will do it all, 0:314

eight hours of post work, 0:222

Esto getting staff working, 0:393

even dull policies provide wide agreement as basis for work coordination, 0:114

every division, dept and post has assigned stat which represents its, 0:502, 0:654, 0:691,

exchange and, 0:259

executive(s),

getting people to get work done, 0:388, 0:406

select as exec person who can get work done, 0:83

working hard as an, 0:407, 0:408–409, 0:410, 0:590

group can accomplish many times work only one can do, 0:87

work(ing), *(cont.)*

handing out work to correct hats, 0:196

hard work, foresight and initiative to make stats go up, 0:674

How much work can one guy do? 0:644

how to handle work, 0:399–400

how to have large number on staff, get no work done and get no unit, 0:232

if communication can flow correctly then work gets done, 0:196

if staff works hard, pay is adequate, 0:170

keep current work visible and where it belongs on lines, 0:378

long and continuous grind, 0:400

LRH philosophy about, 0:151

making ten-minute cycle into three-week cycle, 0:305

no good worker owes his work, 0:507

no need to look busy if you are not, 0:399

not humanitarian to let population go to pieces because a few refuse to work, 0:506

org as orderly plan helps its terminals get work done, 0:82

org vs. bunch of individuals working at cross purposes, 0:405

people who do their work vs. those who don't, 0:151

people who won't work, 0:475

person can only work so many hours in day, 0:644

person in charge trying to do all actions himself, 0:87

preclear who can work and produces as member of society deserves priority, 0:507

preparatory work in order to get one's product, 0:307

producing less and less while working harder and harder, 0:387

products come from work truly done, 0:314

referral; *see* referral

routing, comm lines, pattern of org do not do the, 0:82

sacking people who consistently don't do their, 0:151

some people just won't work, 0:506

standard of living and, 0:314

statistic refers to quantity of work done or value of it in money, 0:690

team, work as a, 0:300

those of us who work get along all right, 0:151

volume dropping, reason, 0:279

work(ing), *(cont.)*

we at the top of Scientology work and work hard, 0:103

when individual can't work or doesn't see himself as important enough to bother about, 0:600

when work no longer has reward none will, 0:506

why competent individual tends to take work all on himself, 0:87

workability, work(able)(ing)(s),

applying correct tech in proper manner and observing that it works that way, 0:8

challenging instances of "unworkability" of Scientology, 0:13

doubtful man will evolve another workable system than Scientology, 0:21

even bad policy usually more workable than individual policy, 0:115

"It didn't work," handling, 0:11

keeping Scientology working, 0:7

operational means something works *well,* 0:190

point where routes and exact procedures become unworkable, 0:82

political system suppressing workable system of improving people, 0:157

receiving unworkable orders, 0:553

rotten working conditions, 0:556

Scientology does not work in absence of official control, 0:159

Scientology is workable system, 0:21

things not working because they don't belong to anyone, 0:186

you don't have to alter it so it will work, 0:282

worker(s), *see also* **staff**

arising but not organized will promptly be put back down, 0:88

give him best in training and processing, 0:507

good workers, 0:156

good worker shattered and bad worker patted on back, 0:504

making all seniors bosses or sergeants and all juniors into workers or privates, 0:134

no good worker owes his work, 0:507

Russia and, 0:293

taxes and, 0:505

why person cannot expect to get full value of his VFPs all to himself, 0:313

working worker deserves a break, 0:508

worker-oriented,

defined, 7:341, MS3:321

executive who is, 7:428, MS3:408

working installation,

destruction of, MS1:317

do not disestablish, MS2:37

execs issuing orders that unmock, 0:265

never unmock a, MS1:317, MS1:459

something that is operational, MS1:317

used as personnel pools, 1:117

workload,

distributing posts by, 1:63

how to decrease traffic and workload of an org, 1:70

means of catching up, 1:159

posting without regard to, 1:61

ways to decrease in an org, 7:803

workmanship, pride of, 0:295

worksheet,

definition, 4:1015

filed in date order in person's pc folder, 5:297

should be as neat as possible, 4:1182

Word Clearing,
filed in pc folder, 4:262
omissions in folders, 4:1194, 5:802

work space, position according to body and particle flows, 1:63

world, *see also* **civilization; Earth; group; man; planet**

basic way we will win world, 0:684

bringing peace and safe environment to, 0:486

dangerous environment of wog world, 0:486

Dianetics and Scientology are new news to, 0:362

educated to tradition of clean quarters and smart service, 0:334

exchange, world of, 0:655

failing to use Scientology tech and administrative and justice procedures on the, 0:484

going more beatnik, 0:334

if world were honest, justice and need for it would vanish, 0:520

just because YOU are making it is no reason world will, 0:362

making it saner, better place, 0:158, 0:161

putting Scientology across over, 0:407

reason things do not run well in, 0:199

supports LRH only so long as he does his job, 0:151

we are in business of people and bettered world, 0:695

without crime, 0:458

World Federation of Mental Health, vs. Dianetics and Scientology, 7:1129

Worldwide,

all officers and staff senior, 7:143

Division 7s and, 7:103

Emergency condition, reason for and handling, 7:127

finances recombined with Saint Hill, 7:148

how to communicate to, 7:140

income lines independent of SH formed, 7:135

organization pattern is the same as any other org's, 7:143

purpose and function, original intention, 6:583

runs inspections on orgs for purpose of checking compliance, 7:151

what caused collapse of HCOs in orgs, 7:162

what it exists for, 7:149

Worldwide Division, function redefined, 7:136

worse than, tool PR can use on withholds, MS3:166

writing,

if it isn't written, it isn't true, 0:23, 0:146, 0:375

keeping structure of org in writing, 0:194

Let's see it in writing first, 0:146

LRH hat of, 0:233

put request in writing, 0:369

report offenses to Ethics in writing, 0:623

staff members must make certain reports in writing, 0:543

verbal order is also written down, 0:375

writs, registered mail and, 0:379

wrong(s),

age-old riddle as to "what is right or wrong," unlocked, 0:528

civilizations dying because things went right only so long as nothing was going wrong, 0:236

concepts or subject of right and, 0:447, 0:453, 0:481

don't be wrong on any important decisions, 0:231

effort to make things go wrong, 0:252

external threat need be just enough to make internal pressure to do wrong lesser of two discomforts, 0:480

wrong(s), *(cont.)*

HCO Ethics Codes let you know when you're right or wrong, 0:481

I try to be right more often than, 0:594

infinity of wrong ways to do something, 0:58

insane making things go wrong, 0:237, 0:252

man has struggled with subjects of right and wrong throughout ages, 0:447

no absolute right or wrong, 0:454

not seeking recourse or redress of wrongs, 0:525

oldest form of seeking justice and a redress of wrongs, 0:488

personnel who have things "just sort of go wrong" around them, 0:40

recourse for, *see* recourse

restitution of, Courts of Ethics and, 1:948

rule can be wrong, 0:274

service and our mission can never be wrong, 0:274

when look into the past of another would be wrong, 0:462

working endlessly to make things go wrong, 0:237

wrongful dismissal, 0:477, 0:487, 0:552

wronged, requesting Comm Ev of HCO when staff member believes he has been falsely wronged, 0:478

wrong public, *see* **public(s)**

wrong source, *see also* **outpoint(s)**

definition, MS1:84

examples, MS1:84, MS1:127

wrong target, *see also* **outpoint(s)**

definition, MS1:71, MS1:80

examples, MS1:71, MS1:81

is an outpoint, MS1:80

stat pushing and, 0:683

wrong Why, *see also* **Why**

definition, MS1:82

stats and, MS1:82

Wundt, early tech of human mind perverted by, 6:620, MS3:3

X,Y,Z

Xerox Officer, created as a post, 1:419

yawn, file complaints on upstats with a, 1:767

yellow journalism, dug the grave of the newspaper, MS3:22

youth, going into apathy, purposeless and drifting, 0:119

zealot, for standard tech, 4:824, 4:828

zero,
of influence and vacuum for trouble, 0:457

staff member being zero in eyes of org, 0:578

Zero, *see* **Level 0**

Zero Comm Course, definition of, 4:353, 6:471

zone,
offenses concerning, 0:468

quicksilver personnel scene crashing stats in, 0:264–267

special zone plan, 6:837

Z Unit, 4:724

CHRONOLOGICAL
LIST OF TITLES

Chronological List of Titles

1950

1951

1954

1955

ca mid- March	The Scientologist, a Manual on the Dissemination of Material	2:20 6:25 7:966	Sept. 28 Dec.	Start That Practice! "I'm Giving Here . . ."	6:681 7:833

1956

3 Aug.	Mail Line	1:323
		3:199
3 Aug.	Organizational Health Chart	2:47
		7:171
12 Sept.	The Summary of a Bulletin from the Academy in Washington, DC Concerning Training	4:541
24 Sept.	Organizational Indoctrination	1:265
		7:743
26 Sept.	Flow Line for Personnel	1:157
		4:38
26 Sept.	Registrar	2:477
		4:834
26 Sept.	Procedure for Putting Auditors on Staff	4:835
4 Oct.R	The Handling of Hubbard Communications Offices Rev. 30 July 1958	7:1161
26 Oct.	Gradient Scale of Personnel Procurement	2:50
		6:147
ca Oct.– Nov.	Policy on Payment for Training and Processing	2:478
9 Nov.	Accounting Department, Washington	3:19
9 Nov.	Activities of Legal Department	7:1053
19 Nov.	Staff Policy on Training and Indoctrination Courses	5:385
11 Dec.	Tape Color Code	2:367

1957

1 Jan.	FC Policy Letter	3:285
15 Jan.	Dissemination	6:151
25 Jan.	Concerning the Separateness of Dianetics and Scientology	2:143 6:231
25 Jan.	Referrals to Field	2:385 6:681
12 Feb.	"HCO Is Entitled . . ."	1:26
13 Feb.	"We Will No Longer . . ."	3:286
28 Feb.	Hats	0:193 1:266
20 Mar.	Certificate Display	5:301
20 Mar.	Ministerial Ordination	5:302
20 Mar.	Income Sources	2:386 3:101
1 Apr.	Technical and Administrative Divisions	4:39
1 Apr.	Always Register and Invoice	2:479 3:141 4:213
5 Apr.	Proportionate Pay Plan Proposal	3:325
6 Apr.	Central Files and Procurement	2:388
8 Apr.	Advisory Committee	7:885
9 Apr.	Grievances	7:886
9 Apr.	Employing and Discharging of Personnel	1:245
9 Apr.	Dismissals and Post Changes	1:247
9 Apr.	Communication Center	1:345
9 Apr.	Bulletin Board	1:347
10 Apr.	Student Intensives	4:669
10 Apr.	Morale Note	7:744
19 Apr.	"Now That the Proportionate . . ."	3:328
21 Apr.	Information Boards	1:348
21 Apr.	Income	2:399 3:103
23 Apr.	"HCO Is Now Handling . . ."	7:174
28 Apr.	HCO Board of Review, Goal	5:303
30 Apr.	Issue Authority for Mimeo	7:1279
1 May	Comm Center, Arrangement of	1:350
2 May	Dissemination	2:146 6:153
3 May	Training—What It Is Today, How We Tell People about It	4:547
7 May	Assignment of Auditors, Rooms, Students	2:480 4:294
9 May	Mail	1:324 3:200
9 May	Bulletin Boards and Information Boards	1:351
13 May	Financial Enrollment Procedure	2:481 4:214
14 May	Hat Turnover	3:329

15 May	Central Files and Procurement	2:400
16 May	Intensives for Staff	5:543
16 May	Clarification of Invoicing Items	2:482 3:142
17 May	Definitions	4:295
18 May	Policy on Signatures in Publications	2:171 7:1280
20 May	Outside Auditing	4:1243
23 May	Ordering People to Processing or Training	2:483 3:143 5:103
23 May	Responsibility for Issue	7:1281
24 May	Stable Data for Instructors	4:296
1 June	Rights of the Directors of Training and Processing, Staff Auditors and Instructors Regarding Preclears and Students	4:297
3 June	Letter Writing, Amending CF and Procurement, Paper of	2:597
8 June	Valuable Documents, Handling of	1:1053 3:369 7:1054
10 June	What to Tell New HGC Auditors to Process on Preclears	4:1045
18 June	People's Questions	0:322 2:598 6:156
24 June	"When a New Post Is Created . . ."	1:267
1 July	Lonesome?	6:686
2 July	Financial Reports, Washington, DC	7:887
10 July	Hiring of Staff Auditors	4:836
15 July	"Our First Lesson . . ."	4:299
26 July	Funds or Favors Received	4:1244
8 Aug.	Power of Veto	7:888
15 Aug.R	Ministerial Qualifications Rev. 12 June 58	5:304
19 Aug.	Certificates Release and Validation	5:305
29 Aug.	Government Project Stable Data	6:590 7:993
2 Sept.	Field Certificates	5:306
2 Sept.	"When a Verbal Direction Is Given . . ."	4:1046
2 Sept.	Executives	7:585
3 Sept.	Method of Opening and Invoicing Mail	1:325 3:201
4 Sept.	Stable Data for Instructors	4:300
5 Sept.	Validation of Staff	5:386
5 Sept.	Testing	4:227
5 Sept.	"All Preclears Are Expected to . . ."	4:837
16 Sept.	HGC Policy, Results or Else	4:838 5:729
26 Sept.	Filling Posts	1:177
27 Sept.	"It Has Come to My Attention . . ."	2:401 6:157
24 Oct.	"Any Staff Member . . ."	7:1166
29 Oct.	HCO Files	3:287
6 Nov.	Duties of the Executive Director of the HASI (FC)	7:1167
19 Dec.	Phone Bill	1:328 3:144
20 Dec.	Clarification of Public Relations Post	7:175

1958

4 Jan.R	Field Offices Rev. 30 Dec. 58	6:688
10 Jan.	Inspection of Hat Folders	1:268
15 Jan.	Field Office Communication	1:303 6:689
24 Jan.	Outline of Activities	7:1168
25 Jan.	Inept Students	4:301
27 Jan.	Duties of Personnel Post	1:178
5 Feb.	"No New Charters or Contracts . . ."	6:690
8 Feb.	"Since People Will Begin to Expect . . ."	2:484 4:839
25 Feb.	Routing of Communication	7:21
17 Mar.	Body Routing in Central Organizations	1:121 2:486 6:379
19 Mar.	Transportation, Dir Admin Responsibility	7:176
26 Mar.	Salary and Unit Pay	3:330
28 Mar.	Only Organization Offices Can Certify Clears	5:307
2 Apr.	ARC in Comm Course	4:549 6:451
7 Apr.	Routing of Org Board Changes	7:177
23 Apr.	Four Vital Training Data for Training Hats and Registrar	2:488 4:302
1 May	Financial Management	3:20
1 May	Signs of Success	7:994
1 May	Employment Qualifications	1:158
9 May	Who Should Take Which Class	4:303
27 May	Outside Auditing	4:1245
28 May	Incoming Calls for LRH	7:1170
1 June	Purchase Orders	3:288
19 June	Freeloaders	1:248 3:183
30 June	Procedure for Certifying Clears	5:308
30 June	Clear Bracelet Procedure	5:309
30 July	The Handling of Hubbard Communications Offices	1:20
25 Aug.	Administrative Stable Data	7:745
27 Aug.	Executives of Scientology Organizations	7:746
27 Aug.	"The Washington, DC Central Organization . . ."	2:277
12 Sept.	Color Flash System Rewritten	1:352
17 Sept.	Who Can Order Printing	2:172 7:1282
19 Sept.	A Model Hat for an Executive	7:753
29 Sept.	Vital Training Data	4:304

1 Oct.	HCO Board of Review	4:550
		5:146
2 Oct.	Sale and Conduct of Academy Courses	4:554
5 Oct.	How to Fill Jobs	7:757
6 Oct.	Who Can Be Processed, Who Can Be Trained	2:402
		4:306
		5:730
9 Oct.	Departments of FCDC	7:178
24 Oct.	*Ability* Magazine	2:185
30 Oct.	Personnel Efficiency Foundation	6:313
31 Oct.	"Only 75 Copies . . ."	1:389
		2:173
		7:1283
6 Nov.	The Three-Basket System	0:371
		1:354
7 Nov.	Registrar	2:489
7 Nov.	"The Output of Special Letters . . ."	2:599
15 Nov.	Informing Public of Test Results	2:600
		4:228
		6:271
15 Nov.	The Substance and First Duty of HCO	7:1055
15 Nov.	Legal Aid—HCO	7:1057
15 Nov.	Outstanding Copyrights and Marks	7:1058
15 Nov.	How to Procure People	2:601
17 Nov.	Free Clear Estimates, Free Clear Tests	2:490
		4:841
17 Nov.	Project Engineering	7:586
17 Nov.	Project Engineers, Three Types	7:590
17 Nov.	HCO Project Engineer: "Have You Lived Before?"	2:149
		7:591
18 Nov.	Letter Policy	2:604
19 Nov.	Organization	1:143
		7:22
22 Nov.	Owner of Materials, the Legal View	2:278
		7:1059
23 Nov.	Scientometric Testing	4:229
		6:272
24 Nov.	HASI Group Secretary	6:691
24 Nov.R	Magazine Policy Rev. 11 Feb. 80	2:186
25 Nov.	HCO Board of Review, Function and Practice	5:129
		7:1171
27 Nov.	Basic Financial Policy, HCO	3:21
29 Nov.	Future Programs	7:1174
1 Dec.	Materiel Administrator Hat	3:370
1 Dec.	Actions to Start an HCO	6:773
9 Dec.	Staff List, Notification to Payroll	3:331
13 Dec.	Important Information on Policy Letters	7:180
15 Dec.R	Academy Training Curriculum and Examination Corr. 6 Jan. 59	4:557
15 Dec.	Registrar Hat	2:491
16 Dec.	Extension Course Curriculum	6:501
16 Dec.	Director of Administration Hat	7:594
17 Dec.	Duties of Sec'l ED	7:595
20 Dec.	Certificates	5:311
20 Dec.	Bad Clinical Results, Handling	4:842
20 Dec.	HCO Communicator Basic Hat and Comm System, HCO Offices	1:355
23 Dec.	Qualifications of HGC Staff Auditors	4:1143
		5:831
23 Dec.	Quality of Presentation	2:174
		7:1284
26 Dec.	Collection of Accounts	3:184
31 Dec.	Routing of Profiles	4:230

1959

Jan.	A Campaign for Ethical Auditing	6:697
2 Jan.	"Instructors or HCO Staff . . ."	1:855 4:1246
2 Jan.	HCO Office Designations and Personnel	1:27
5 Jan.	Importance and Executives	7:23
6 Jan.	Field Activities	6:693
6 Jan.	HCO Personnel Training	1:357
8 Jan.	Reception Hat	1:123
13 Jan.	HCO Area Secretary Hat Material	1:30
20 Jan.	"When in Doubt about Copyrighting . . ."	2:175 7:1060
22 Jan.	Mailing Lists and Field Auditors	6:696
22 Jan.	Letter Registrar Hat	2:605
22 Jan.	Mailing Lists and Field Auditors	2:683
23 Jan.	Ethics	1:719
26 Jan.	Scientology Magazines	2:188
29 Jan.	Secretarial to the Executive Director Hat	7:598
29 Jan.	HCO Communicator Hat	1:358
30 Jan.	Department of Promotion and Registration	2:404
31 Jan.	Promotional Letters	2:606
4 Feb.	Policy—Certifying Clears	5:223
6 Feb.	HCO Accounts Worldwide	3:23
10 Feb.	Group Secretary	6:700
10 Feb.	The Advisory Council	7:889
10 Feb.	Central Files and the Addressograph (Use Of)	2:651
11 Feb.	The Dept of Promotion and Registration and CF–Promotion Liaison	2:654
12 Feb.	Book Administrator	2:319
13 Feb.	Staff Processing and Training Policy	5:387
17 Feb.	Extension Course Students, Letters	6:504
18 Feb.	Director of Materiel	3:371
18 Feb.	HGC Auditing Policies	4:843
18 Feb.	Thermostats in Buildings	7:1339
19 Feb.	Use of Addresses in Letter Writing	2:655
23 Feb.	How to Interview People	2:493 4:40 6:158
24 Feb.	FC Communicator Basic Hat	1:304
24 Feb.	Secretary to Training Department Hat (Temporary Hat)	6:505
24 Feb.	Despatches to Advisory Council	7:893

24 Feb.	Shipping Department, Invoices	2:279
26 Feb.	HCO Executive Secretary Continental	7:24
26 Feb.	Responsibilities of Assistant Org Sec	7:599
27 Feb.	Duty of Area Sec Re Personnel	7:182
28 Feb.	HCO Board of Review Duties	5:94
1 Mar.	HCO Forbidden Activities	7:183
2 Mar.	Accounting System	3:104
2 Mar.	HCO Theory of Communication	1:359
2 Mar.	HCO Cable and Despatch, Designation System	1:451
3 Mar.	Book Section: Credits and Debits	3:118
3 Mar.	Staff Auditors	4:1145
5 Mar.	Addressing Department—Hats	2:684
7 Mar.	Materiel Administrator— Hat	3:372
7 Mar.	Processing Administrator—Hat	4:241
9 Mar.	The Purpose of the Lead Auditor	4:1151
10 Mar.	Permanent Staff Members	1:221 5:388
16 Mar.	HGC Psychotic Applicants	4:1021
17 Mar.	Do-It-Yourself Therapy	6:452
18 Mar.	"The Following Are . . ."	7:25
20 Mar.	Certificates Handling	5:312
24 Mar.	HAS Co-audit	6:453
25 Mar.	HAS Co-audit and Comm Course	6:455
25 Mar.	Book Policy	2:321
3 Apr.	HAS Co-audit and Comm Course	6:457
6 Apr.	Clear Ads	6:160
6 Apr.	"The Organization Is as Apparent . . ."	2:54
8 Apr.	A Promotion Plan	6:161
8 Apr.	The Hats of the Department of Promotion and Registration	2:55
8 Apr.	A Promotion Plan	2:152
9 Apr.	Voluntary Help	1:159
9 Apr.	Addressograph Tabbing—Libraries	2:693
14 Apr.	New Book	2:322
16 Apr.	Books, Cost Of	2:324
18 Apr.	"Book Buyers Should Be Sold . . ."	2:280 6:506
18 Apr.	Addresses	2:694
23 Apr.	HCO Communicator Writes from South Africa	3:374
23 Apr.	HAS Co-audit Courses	6:459
24 Apr.	Final HPA Exam, HCO Board of Review	4:559 5:150
24 Apr.	Registrars—Materials Available to	6:381
24 Apr.	Organization Posts—Two Types	0:86
29 Apr.	Defacing Books and Proper Addresses in Them	2:326
29 Apr.	Registrar—Dir of Processing, The Most Frequently Lost Line	2:495
30 Apr.	Additional Staff Auditors	4:844
30 Apr.	Long-Distance Program	6:52 7:184
30 Apr.	Additional Staff Auditors	1:180
1 May	HAS Certificates	5:313 6:460
5 May	Policy on Sec EDs and Hats	1:269
13 May	HCO Book Administrator Hat	2:327
14 May	HCO Administrator	7:26
14 May	A Staff Post	0:229
21 May	HCO Monies and Book Stocks	3:186
21 May	"The Symbol * on All Despatches . . ."	7:1175

22 May	Advertisement for Field in *Certainty, Ability,* etc., Minor Issues	2:189 6:507
22 May	Central Organization Efficiency	0:230 7:600
26 May	To Department Heads	3:24 7:186
26 May	What an Executive Wants on His Lines	0:372 7:602
28 May	New HCO WW Dept	6:163
28 May	Promotional Writing Fund	7:923
2 June	Correction of HCO PL 23 Dec. 58, Qualification of HGC Staff Auditors	5:832
2 June	A Comment on Finance	3:26 7:924
2 June	Purchasing Liability of Staff Members	0:183 3:290
3 June	Financial Management	3:28 7:926
4 June	Invoicing and Collection of Money	3:119 4:215 6:383
4 June	Definition of a Registration	2:497 6:382
4 June	Instructions to Attorney or Solicitors	7:1061
4 June	Validity of Sec EDs	7:1285
4 June	Sale and Handout of *Certainty* Minors	2:328
4 June	Definition of a Hot File	2:498
5 June	Income Report Required	3:121
5 June	Handling of Bills	3:313
16 June	Hat of PE HCO WW	6:314
18 June	US Mission Holders	6:737
18 June	Services Owing to Mission Holders	6:739
19 June	Administrative Side of PE Foundation	6:365
21 June	Signatures on Bulletins, Policy Letters and Sec EDs	1:390 7:1286
22 June	How to "Sell Scientology"	6:164
23 June	What Is Scientology?	6:165
26 June	HCO WW Changes, Quarters and Address	7:27
1 July	US Mission Queries	6:740
1 July	HCO Washington, DC	7:28
1 July	Responsibility for HCO Files	1:391
2 July	Developed Traffic, The Delirium Tremens of Central Orgs	0:397
2 July	Scientology Magazines	2:190
4 July	Actions for HCO Secretaries Faced with Illegal Usage	7:1062
6 July	Outflow	0:367 1:306 2:117
7 July	Staff Auditing Requirement	5:544
17 July	Duties at Saint Hill— HCO WW	7:29
18 July	Income Tax Reform	7:1063
19 July	Accounts Inspection	3:31
19 July	New Corp—New Broom	7:605
22 July	Processing of Staff Members	5:546
25 July	Membership Monies	6:803
28 July	Our Goals	6:741
28 July	Organization of Corporations	7:188
10 Aug.	Data Required as Reports from HCO Secs	7:1176
10 Aug.	Reception	1:124
12 Aug.	Cable, Don't Phone	1:457
13 Aug.	Mission Holders	6:743
19 Aug.	Writing of Letters by Staff Auditors	2:607 4:1153
19 Aug.	To a Roman Catholic	6:516
19 Aug.	How to Handle Work	0:399
21 Aug.	Handling of Telex Machines	1:458
22 Aug.	HCO WW Projects	7:30
24 Aug.	Tips to HCO Communicators	1:362
25 Aug.	Purchase Order System	3:291
26 Aug.	Promotional Functions of Various Depts	2:57 3:227 7:32

4 Sept.	Saint Hill Projects, Bonus and Quota System	7:606
4 Sept.	Completed Staff Work (CSW)—How to Get Approval of Actions and Projects	0:401
12 Sept.	Programing	0:701 7:764
15 Sept.	Dissemination Tips	2:60 6:166
15 Sept.	"No Changes of Positions . . ."	7:1329
15 Sept.	Hats and Other Folders	0:194 1:270
23 Sept.	The Perfect Dissemination Program	2:154 6:170
23 Sept.	Carrying Out Instructions	7:1178
25 Sept.	Accounting Records and Bills	3:375
29 Sept.	The Organization of a PE Foundation	6:315
5 Oct.	Tape and Record Production Hat	2:368
6 Oct.	Two Fine Magazines	2:191
9 Oct.	Staff Auditors	4:1155
9 Oct.	Quota Revision	7:608
14 Oct.	Acting Executive Director	7:609
14 Oct.	Comm Speed	1:364
18 Oct.	Putting New Personnel on the Job and Taking Over When People Quit or Are Transferred	1:181 7:767
20 Oct.	HCO Order of Importance of Actions	1:33
21 Oct.	Routing of Bulletins and Policy Letters	7:35
23 Oct.	Attention Registrars and Book Administrators	2:329 3:145
23 Oct.	Academy Training	4:308
29 Oct.	Service	0:273 4:42 6:576 6:579
29 Oct.	Processing of Academy Students	4:563
29 Oct.	Orders During Absence	7:1179
20 Nov.	Validation of Certificates	1:720 2:609 6:702
23 Nov.	Employment of Criminals Forbidden	1:160
27 Nov.	Key to the Organizational Chart of the Founding Church of Scientology of Washington, DC	7:189
7 Dec.	Former Saint Hill Staff	7:610
7 Dec.	Scientology Cleanup	1:722
28 Dec.	Personnel Departure Requirement	1:183
31 Dec.R	Blow-Offs Rev. 9 Feb. 89	1:724 4:1047 5:547

1960

1 Jan.	Administrative Procedure for Reducing Overts	4:846
18 Jan.	Zones of Authority and Regulations of Saint Hill	7:1340
18 Jan.	Qualifications of Permanent Staff Members	1:184
20 Jan.	HCO WW Points of Concentration	7:36
27 Jan.	Accounts Policies	3:33
8 Feb.	Honest People Have Rights, Too	0:461 1:481
23 Feb.	Outside Funds or Gifts—Staff Member Policy	1:729
29 Feb.	Organization Secretary Hat	7:611
16 Mar.	CF–Promotion Liaison— Hat	2:656
18 Mar.	*Have You Lived Before This Life?* Sales	2:330
21 Mar.	Economy Wave	3:230 7:613
29 Mar.	HGC and Academy Prices for Minors	3:146
31 Mar.	Accounts Line	3:36
9 Apr.	Outflow	2:610
11 Apr.	The Purpose of HCO WW	7:37
14 Apr.	Flowers	7:1344
21 Apr.	Long Distance Phone Calls and Telegrams	3:314
21 Apr.	Presession Processes	6:174
21 Apr.	Domestic Arrangements Changes	7:1345
25 Apr.	Important Certification Change	5:315
25 Apr.	PrR Promotion	2:405
27 Apr.	Security of Employment	0:151 1:249
28 Apr.	Books Are Dissemination	2:331 6:234
3 May	PE Literature	6:179
23 May	Cancellation of Certificates	1:856 5:316
27 May	"Dear Scientologist . . ."	6:581
28 May	"By Their Actions . . ."	6:827
2 June	Requirements for Staff Posts	5:389
7 June	Staff Auditing	5:550
9 June	HCO WW Internal Comm Schedule	1:365
10 June	What We Expect of a Scientologist *KSW Series 33*	6:828
20 June	Rush Magazine Note	2:192
21 June	Religious Philosophy and Religious Practice	6:517 7:995
23 June	The Special Zone Plan	6:831

30 June	Administrative Traffic Trend	7:614
6 July	Working Hours, Office Staff	7:617
20 July	Director of Zoning Hat	6:837
28 July	Losses	7:929
3 Aug.	Security of Persons Leaving Staffs	5:551
3 Aug.	Magazine Advertisement Policy	2:193
4 Aug.	ACC at Saint Hill	7:1346
8 Aug.	Persons Living In	7:1347
11 Aug.	Organization Information Center	1:653
12 Aug.	Department of Government Relations	7:996
15 Aug.	Department of Government Affairs	3:376 7:997
19 Aug.	Registrar Lost Line	2:499 4:848
22 Aug.	Department of Government Relations	7:1001
25 Aug.	Chicago Area	6:704
30 Aug.	Training Restrictions	4:309
30 Aug.	Special Zone Department	7:1002
17 Sept.	Giving the Pc Full Hours	4:850
19 Sept.	Captive Brains	7:1123
28 Sept.	HPA Grants	6:705
22 Oct.	The Three Service Branches	7:194
28 Oct.	New Testing Promotion Section	6:273
28 Oct.	HASI–HCO Relationship Discussed	7:195
31 Oct.R	Private Pcs Rev. 24 Jan. 91	4:1247
31 Oct.	US Appointment and Organizational Trend	7:1003
7 Nov.	HCO Area Secretary Hat Addition	5:552
14 Nov.	Urgent PrR	2:500
15 Nov.	Staff Certificate Requirements	4:851
15 Nov.R	Modern Procurement Letters Rev. 4 Feb. 91	2:612
18 Nov.	Executive Time Salvage and Conferences Curtailed	7:894
18 Nov.	Staff Transfers and Dismissals	1:250
19 Nov.	Pc Scheduling	2:502 4:248
22 Nov.	Warning on New PE	6:281
23 Nov.	Reports to OIC	1:657
24 Nov.	Testing Promotion Revised	6:283
26 Nov.	Permanent Staff Member Requirements	5:390
29 Nov.	Testing Program Change	6:288
2 Dec.	Promotion on PE Foundation	6:180
18 Dec.	CF and Address Change	2:659
19 Dec.	PE Change	6:318
19 Dec.	Spatial Reorganization	7:1330
21 Dec.	Staff Clearing, New Policy	5:553
22 Dec.	Important Change in Reports	1:658 7:39
29 Dec.	The New PE and the New HAS Co-audit	6:462

1961

4 Jan.	Urgent Mimeo Change	1:392
		7:1287
9 Jan.	Duties of HCO	1:34
10 Jan.	A Brief Outline of an HGC As Currently Done	4:852
16 Jan.	Help Me Put in the New Lines	6:289
		7:197
16 Jan.	New Road	7:1348
23 Jan.	PE Course Abolished	6:321
24 Jan.	A Test Policy on MD Referrals	6:291
30 Jan.	Case Files	4:249
31 Jan.	Academy Meters	4:471
31 Jan.	Spheres of Influence	7:1180
31 Jan.	Message Placement	0:377
		1:368
4 Feb.	Types of Letters Established	1:393
7 Feb.	Proper Public Routing	6:113
10 Feb.	Professional Charges	2:410
		6:706
12 Feb.	Certificates and Awards Revised List	5:317
13 Feb.	Permanent Staff Requirement Changes	5:392
14 Feb.	The Pattern of a Central Organization	2:503
		3:231
		4:44
		7:199
14 Feb.	Personnel Procurement	1:161
17 Feb.	HCO Continental	7:1182

17 Feb.	State of Emergency	7:1183
18 Feb.	Magazines	2:194
		6:181
19 Feb.	Accounts: How to Do a Payroll	3:332
21 Feb.	Choosing PE and Registration Personnel	1:185
		2:411
		6:183
21 Feb.	Pattern for City Offices	6:774
22 Feb.	Permanent Staff Exam	5:154
22 Feb.	My Program to Raise Your Unit	7:210
23 Feb.	Directives from a Board Member	1:399
26 Feb.	Qualification of Executives	1:222
		5:393
		7:769
27 Feb.	Outside Pcs of Staff Members	1:619
		4:1248
2 Mar.	Automatic Evaluation Packet for PE Foundation	6:292
12 Mar.	Supplies of Central Organization Forms	3:380
		7:618
12 Mar.	Duties of the Assoc Sec's Sec in a Central Organization	7:619
13 Mar.	Free Courses	3:148
13 Mar.	Staff Auditor Training	4:853
13 Mar.	Department of Official Affairs	7:1004

13 Mar.	Department of Official Affairs	7:1007
20 Mar.	Basic Staff Auditor's Hat	4:1156
20 Mar.	Mimeo and File Procedure	1:400
22 Mar.	Staff Members Ordered to Processing	5:555
23 Mar.	Distribution of Bulletin Change	1:402
24 Mar.	HGC Admin Partial Hat, Staff Auditor Assignment	4:250
24 Mar.	Status of PE Courses	6:465
24 Mar.	Training Project Construction and Preparation	7:1349
25 Mar.	Security Rules	5:556
26 Mar.	Animals Forbidden in House	7:1352
28 Mar.	Personnel Policies, Staff Post Qualifications, Permanent Executives to Be Approved	1:223 5:394 7:41
2 Apr.	Staff Auditor Training, Sequence of Study	5:399
7 Apr.	Examinations of Academy Students to Be Done by Director of Processing	5:158
8 Apr.	OIC Board	1:660
9 Apr.	Staff Intensives	5:558
9 Apr.	City Offices, Successful Patterns	6:777
10 Apr.	HCO, Ltd., HPA/HCA Certificate Conditions	4:564
11 Apr.	How to Do a Staff Job	0:232
13 Apr.	Terror Stalks	7:1008
14 Apr.	PE Handout	6:293
17 Apr.	Training, Professional, New Policy	4:565
25 Apr.	D of P Form	4:855
25 Apr.	Association Secretary Duties	7:621
28 Apr.	Central Organization Minimum Staff	7:212
2 May	Procedure on Setting up Central Orgs or City Offices	6:780
3 May	Dining Room for Staff	7:1353
10 May	Staff Auditors	4:1164
11 May	Student Training, Auditing Has Priority	4:713
16 May	HPA/HCA Requirement	5:319
24 May	Responsibility for Results	4:55
26 May	Quality Counts *KSW Series 2*	0:16 4:16 5:16 7:835
26 May	Modification of HPA/ HCA, BScn/HCS Schedule	4:567
26 May	Basic Staff Auditor's Hat	4:1165
29 May	Quality and Admin in Central Orgs *KSW Series 3*	0:18 7:837
29 May	Security of House	7:1354
30 May	How to Confess in HCO	7:1186
30 May	Current Office Work	1:369
7 June	Academy Schedule, Clarification Of	4:568
7 June	Orders	1:404 7:1288
9 June	Technical Hat Checking *LRH Comm N/W Series 22*	1:272 7:1272
22 July	Executives' Pay	5:402
4 Aug.	Private Mail and Telephone Calls	3:149
14 Aug.	City Offices	6:782
23 Aug.	HPA/HCA Policy	4:571 6:783
24 Aug.	HCO Organization, Future Plans	7:216
3 Sept.	HCO Volunteer Sec Policy Revised	6:707
13 Sept.	General Office Orders	2:336 3:381
18 Sept.R	HCO WW Security Form 7B Rev. 16 Mar. 89	1:620 5:560
19 Sept.	Reality Test for Students	5:161
20 Sept.	Training Policy	4:572 5:162

21 Sept.	Laundry	7:1355
21 Sept.	Despatch Lines	0:378
		1:370
2 Oct.	Mission Policies	6:744
5 Oct.	Repairs and Cleaning of My Office	7:1357
6 Oct.	Staff Clearing	5:563
7 Oct.	Friday Cables	1:460
		7:622
9 Oct.	Academy Training	4:573
16 Oct.	Income Records	3:383
18 Oct.	Examinations	5:163
20 Oct.RB	Non-Scientology Staff Rev. 11 Jan. 85	0:152
23 Oct.	Pay of Executives	5:403
23 Oct.	HGC Preprocessing Security Check	4:858
23 Oct.	E-Meters to Be Approved	2:377
		7:1289
25 Oct.	New Students Sec Check	4:714
27 Oct.	Professional Rates Restored	2:415
		3:150
		4:217

2 Nov.	Training Quality *KSW Series 16*	4:310 5:164 7:1188
14 Nov.	Stabilization of Clears	5:320
21 Nov.	HGC Processing Liability	4:861
21 Nov.	Letter Writer's Code	2:620
23 Nov.	Accounts	3:37
29 Nov.	Classes of Auditors	4:1166
6 Dec.	Saint Hill Training Candidates from Organizations	5:404
11 Dec.RB	Organization Rudiments Rev. 16 Mar. 89	1:503
12 Dec.	Training Activities	4:715
13 Dec.	Extension Course Completion	6:508
15 Dec.R	Rudiment Checklist for Orgs Rev.16 Mar. 89	1:509
19 Dec.	Saint Hill Retreads	4:716
20 Dec.	Student E-Metering	4:576
27 Dec.	Sec Checks on Staff	5:565

1962

7 Jan.	HCO Board of Review, Class II Awards	5:165
10 Jan.	HCO Standing Order No. 5, Students	4:578 5:167
17 Jan.	Responsibility Again	4:1050 5:566
17 Jan.	Auditor Assignment	4:670
17 Jan.	Org Rudiment Reports to Me	1:514
22 Jan.	Crash Program	1:515 4:311 5:168
23 Jan.	Permanent Executives	1:228 5:406
30 Jan.	Technical Director and Administrator	4:56 7:218
7 Feb.	Restriction on Saint Hill Area	6:708
18 Feb.	Fish and Game	7:1359
12 Mar.	Staff Training	5:407
4 Apr.	Training Course Regulations	4:472
6 Apr.	Technical Director Basic Hat	4:57
16 Apr.	Regulations, Academies and Courses	4:473 5:170
16 Apr.	Comments on Letter Registrar Department	2:621
18 Apr.	Furniture and Quarters	7:1332
3 May	Practical Auditing Skills	4:579
14 May	Training Sections	4:583
15 May	CF/Addressograph, Handling of New Names	2:660
16 May	HPA/HCA Training	4:586
21 May	Tape Examinations	4:509 5:171
21 May	Training, Classes of Auditors	4:587
24 May	Training, Session Cancellation, Auditing Section	4:671
26 May	Training Drills Must Be Correct	4:591
29 May	Professional Rates	2:416 4:218
1 June	Auditing, Rudiments Checksheet	4:1168
5 June	Class II Training Only by Academies and Saint Hill	4:593
5 June	Permanent Staff Privilege	1:229 6:804
7 June	Professional Training to Be Done in Academy and Saint Hill Only	4:594
14 June	Professional Charges	2:417 3:151 6:709
21 June	Staff Members Auditing Private Pcs	4:1249
26 June	Certification Requirements	5:321 6:509
29 June	Staff and Intern Auditors	5:833
2 July	Rudiments Policy	4:1170
8 July	Telephone Answering	1:329

9 July	Special Briefing Course	4:717		12 Oct.	HPA/HCA Written	4:609
14 July	Auditing Allowed	4:313			Examination	5:173
19 July	Clearing—Free Needles	4:719		16 Oct.	Auditing Hours Limited	4:870
24 July	Academy, Extra Weeks	3:152		19 Oct.	Preparation of HPA/	5:323
		4:595			HCA Certificates	
30 July	Certification and	4:596		21 Oct.	Auditing Supervisor and	4:315
	Validation Requirements	5:322			Auditing Instructors,	
31 July	Oral Examination for	5:172			Duties Of	
	HPA/HCA			24 Oct.	Emergency Headquarters	7:45
2 Aug.	Training Aids	4:597		28 Oct.	Z Unit, Case Review	4:724
2 Aug.	Accounts Information	7:623		29 Oct.	Religion	7:1010
2 Aug.	New Work	7:1360		30 Oct.	Security Risks	1:623
	Arrangements, Outside				Infiltration	
	Staff			8 Nov.	Departure Form	4:725
13 Aug.	Clearing	4:863		8 Nov.	Outside Staff Duties,	7:1365
30 Aug.	General Form of Release	2:418			Assignment Of	
	Contract	7:1066		12 Nov.	Purpose of the Saint Hill	4:728
1 Sept.	Healing Promotion	2:158			Special Briefing Course	
		4:864		14 Nov.	Terminations from the	4:729
12 Sept.	Saint Hill Graduates	4:59			Saint Hill Special	
12 Sept.	Authorized Processes	4:1052			Briefing Course	
13 Sept.	Comments about Letter	2:622		15 Nov.	Car Parking	7:1367
	Registrar			18 Nov.	Address Machines	2:695
17 Sept.R	An Arrangement of the	4:599		21 Nov.	Reissue of Materials	2:118
	Academy					7:1290
	Rev. 24 Jan. 91			23 Nov.	Saint Hill Retread Fee	3:153
						4:730
27 Sept.	Pay for Goals Finding	4:720		24 Nov.	Objective One	4:871
27 Sept.	Valid Processes	4:1053		1 Dec.	V Unit, New Students,	4:731
1 Oct.	The Plan for California	6:710			Saint Hill Special	
2 Oct.	Termination and	4:721			Briefing Course	
	Classification			2 Dec.	Supervisor's Stable Data	4:319
2 Oct.	When You Need	0:155		4 Dec.	R2-12 Validation	5:324
	Reassurance			5 Dec.	Administrator's Hat	7:624
3 Oct.	Rooms, Emptying for	7:1361		5 Dec.	Trips to Town	7:1368
	Cleaning			6 Dec.	Saint Hill Special	4:733
6 Oct.	Accounts Irregularities	3:123			Briefing Course	
6 Oct.	Car Washing	7:1362		8 Dec.	Training, Saint Hill	4:734
8 Oct.	HGC Clearing	4:866			Special Briefing Course	

1963

4 Jan.	Pattern of District Office	6:784
15 Jan.	Routine 2-12	4:873
16 Jan.	Our Role in the World	7:1012
8 Feb.	Curriculum Change	4:736
9 Feb.	Saint Hill Course Goals	4:737
11 Feb.	Auditing Regulations	4:738
13 Feb.	Academy Taught Processes	4:610
13 Feb.	V Unit	4:740
21 Feb.	Goals Check	4:874
6 Mar.	Selling Techniques Forbidden	2:514
12 Mar.	Staff Personnel Allowance, Saint Hill	7:1369
13 Mar.	Amnesty	1:923
15 Mar.	Checksheet Rating System	4:612
20 Mar.	Self-Determinism in Central Organizations	7:627
20 Mar.	HCO WW Electric Stencil-Cutting Machine	1:405
23 Mar.	Classification of Auditors, Class II and Goals	4:875
23 Mar.	Policies in Force, Org/Assoc Secs, HCO Secs	1:517
29 Mar.	Clear Requirement	4:743
2 Apr.	Construction Information	7:1370
4 Apr.	Director of Training Weekly Student Interviews	4:321
11 Apr.	Emergency Library	2:697
13 Apr.	Policy of HGCs	4:877
25 Apr.R	Duties of a Staff Member *Rev. 29 Aug. 90*	0:165
30 Apr.	The Saint Hill Staff Co-audit	5:568
15 May	Instructor Hats	4:322
20 May	Scientology Missionary Hat	6:839
24 May	Changes in Basement Student Facilities	7:1372
10 June	Scientology Training, Technical Studies	4:613
17 June	Staff Clearing Program	5:570
18 June	Tape Release	2:370
24 June	Review of Departments	7:1373
22 July	You Can Be Right	0:463
30 July	Current Planning	4:61
2 Aug.	Saint Hill Course Changes	4:745
2 Aug.	Public Project One	2:160
9 Aug.	Definition of Release	5:225
9 Aug.	Public Meetings	6:322
12 Aug.	Certificates and Awards	5:325
14 Aug.	Press Policies *PR Series 31*	MS3:124
21 Aug.	Change of Organization Targets, Project 80, a Preview	2:162 4:64 6:187
22 Aug.	ARC Break Assessments on Staff	5:573

3 Sept.	Status of Auckland	7:46
7 Sept.	Committees of Evidence, Scientology Jurisprudence, Administration Of	1:924
22 Sept.	Concerning Committees of Evidence	1:933
4 Oct.	Technical Council	4:68
7 Oct.	Doors	7:1375
8 Oct.	New Saint Hill Certificates and Course Changes	4:746
23 Oct.	Refund Policy	3:242 7:1068
4 Nov.	Pay Card	3:337

11 Nov.	Committees of Evidence	1:935
26 Nov.	Certificate and Classification Changes, Everyone Classified	4:163 5:329
4 Dec.	Org Staff W/H Checks	5:574
6 Dec.	Org Programing	4:167
10 Dec.	The Dangerous Environment, the True Story of Scientology	7:1039
11 Dec.	Classification for Everyone	4:168 5:333
13 Dec.	Co-audit	5:575
27 Dec.	The "Magic" of Good Management	7:628

1964

14 Jan.	Continental and Area HCO Finance Policies	3:244
14 Jan.	Future Continental Officer Status	7:47
24 Jan.	HCO (Sthil) Ltd., Course Staff Transfers	4:1054 5:665
24 Jan.	Scientology Library and Research, Ltd.	7:1189
25 Jan.	Department of Enrollment	2:420
26 Jan.	HCO (WW) Ltd., Central Org Activities	7:48
29 Jan.	Charts, Routing and Publications, The Enrollment Department	2:422
31 Jan.	Corporation Coordinator	7:1115
3 Feb.	HCO (Sthil) Ltd., Transport	7:1376
5 Feb.	Founding Scientologist Certificate	5:335
9 Feb.	Comm Baskets	1:371
10 Feb.	Enrollment on Self-Determinism	2:515 4:323 6:467
13 Feb.	Classification	4:170
15 Feb.	The Equipment of Organizations	0:186 3:388
20 Feb.	Regulations	4:747 7:50
21 Feb.	Issuing of Certificates	5:336
21 Feb.	Staff Regulations, Auditing Versus Job	0:168 5:576
23 Feb.	Classification	4:171 5:337
24 Feb.	Org Programing	3:124 4:172 7:930
24 Feb.	SLR Ltd., Tape Copying	2:371
2 Mar.	Contracts and Services	3:292 7:1070
7 Mar.	Director of Enrollment, the Letter Registrar, Administration	1:307 2:64
11 Mar.	Mission Program	6:745
18 Mar.	HGC Allowed Processes	4:1056
19 Mar.	Staff Regulations, Staff Intensives	5:578
1 Apr.	Saint Hill Personnel	7:219
1 Apr.	New Mimeo Line, HCO Executive Letter	1:406
2 Apr.	To the Saint Hill Student: Instruction Targets	4:749
2 Apr.	Saint Hill Enrollment, Materials, Courses, and Use of Class VI Processes	4:751
2 Apr.	Use of Recreation Facilities, 1964	7:1377
10 Apr.	Scientology Courses	4:324 5:485
10 Apr.	Balancing Income– Outgo, Paper, Postage and Printing	2:176 3:269 7:932

10 Apr.	Domestic Staff	7:1378
5 May	Summary of Classification and Gradation and Certification	4:174
6 May	Accounts Policies	3:126
8 May	Transport	7:1379
12 May	Theory Testing, Expiration Dates	4:326
13 May	Transport	7:1380
25 May	Instructor's Conference Report Form	4:755
25 May	Press Relations	6:591 7:1042
28 May	Reorganization	7:52
9 June	Reorganization	7:633
11 June	New Students Data, Star-rated for New Students	4:757
11 June	Central Organization and City Office Tape Service	2:372
16 June	Personnel Records, Admin Certs	1:230 5:338
18 June	New Posts	7:220
25 June	Departmental Reports	7:55
26 June	Staff Bonuses	3:339
2 July	Bulletin and Policy Letter Distribution	1:407
30 July	Gradation Program, Revised	4:181
6 Aug.	Accounts Unit	3:391
10 Aug.	Good Workers	0:156 5:580
12 Aug.	Policy on Technical Information	2:119
17 Aug.	Technical Info for Continental Mags	2:196
21 Aug.	Staff Auditors	1:189 4:1171 5:581
26 Aug.	PE Course	6:468
1 Sept.	Technical Lectures by Other Personnel	7:1191
5 Sept.	Examinations	5:174
9 Sept.	Purpose of Ad Comm	7:895
16 Sept.	Understanding and Tape Lectures	4:510 6:323
16 Sept.	Terminations	4:760
23 Sept.	Policies: Dissemination and Programs	2:197 4:69 6:191
24 Sept.	Instruction and Examination: Raising the Standard Of *Word Clearing Series 33*	4:327 5:175
28 Sept.	Clay Table Use	4:879
30 Sept.	HCO Corporations	7:1116
4 Oct.	Theory Checkout Data	4:333 5:181
8 Oct.	Artistic Presentation *Art Series 12*	2:263
12 Oct.	Congress Organization and Increasing Interest and Attendance	6:324
20 Oct.	Stickers for PABs Wanted	2:698
27 Oct.R	Policies on Physical Healing, Insanity and Sources of Trouble Rev. 15 Nov. 87	1:983 4:880 5:104
31 Oct.	Addressograph Equipment Warning	2:699
13 Nov.	Provisional Class VI Classification	4:761
15 Nov.	Traffic Regulations, Saint Hill	7:1381
15 Nov.	Transport Arrangements	1:461
17 Nov.	Bonus	3:344
17 Nov.	Off-line and Off-policy, Your Full In-Basket	0:404
30 Nov.RB	HCO Book Account Rev. 2 Feb. 91	2:281 3:187
3 Dec.R	Booming an Org Through Training Rev. 7 July 83	2:68 4:336 5:835
11 Dec.	Full Table of Courses and Classification, Classification Correction	4:182
17 Dec.	Tape Prices	2:373
18 Dec.	Re: OIC Data	6:470
18 Dec.	Saint Hill Org Board	7:57
21 Dec.	Address Lists to City Offices	2:701 6:789
31 Dec.	Certificates	5:342
31 Dec.	Use of "Dianetics," "Scientology," "Applied Philosophy"	6:746 7:1071

1965

18 Jan.	Financial Management, Building Fund Account	3:42 7:934
21 Jan.R	Vital Data on Promotion Rev. 5 Apr. 65	2:120 6:54 7:839
28 Jan.	How to Maintain Credit Standing and Solvency	3:245 7:940
31 Jan.	Dev-T	0:412
7 Feb.	Keeping Scientology Working KSW Series 1	0:7 1:7 2:7 3:7 4:7 5:7 6:7 7:7
8 Feb.	Dev-T Analysis	0:416
10 Feb.	Ad and Book Policies, Text of Ads	2:266 6:239
13 Feb.	1965 Saint Hill Objectives	7:67
13 Feb.	Politics	0:157 7:1014
14 Feb.	Safeguarding Technology KSW Series 4	0:21 5:18
20 Feb.	Appointments and Programs	7:68
22 Feb.	HCO Area Secretary Saint Hill	7:222
22 Feb.	Inspections	7:636
22 Feb.	Executive Director Comm Lines	7:638
24 Feb.	Addendum to HCO Policy Letter of September 7, AD 13, Scientology Jurisprudence, Administration Of	1:936
27 Feb.	Course Pattern	4:762
28 Feb.	Deliver	0:282 2:73 4:80 6:366
28 Feb.	Course Checkouts, Twin Checking	4:766
2 Mar.	Purchase Order Filing	3:293
3 Mar.	What's Coming Next	7:223
4 Mar.	Reserved Payment Account	3:315
4 Mar.RA	Technical and Policy Distribution Rev. 7 July 83	2:125 7:1291
5 Mar.	New Status of Honorary Awards	5:343
5 Mar.	Book of Case Remedies, Application of Tech	5:732
5 Mar.	Policy: Source Of	0:111
6 Mar.	Amnesty Policy	1:937
7 Mar.RA	Offenses and Penalties Rev. 10 Jan. 91	0:467 1:861
7 Mar.	Certificate Cancellation	1:857
8 Mar.	Board Decisions, Data Evaluation, Raw Data, Judging a Situation, Selection of Key Personnel	7:770

13 Mar.	The Comm-Member System	7:225
13 Mar.	The Comm-Member System, Routing Policies Section	7:228
13 Mar.	The Structure of Organization, What Is Policy?	0:114 7:660
13 Mar.	Registrar Success	2:516
15 Mar.	Registrars, CF and Address	2:426
17 Mar.	Clearing and Training	4:614
17 Mar.	Rights of a Staff Member, Students and Preclears to Justice	0:477 1:730
17 Mar.	Administering Justice	0:480 1:733
17 Mar.	Organizational Suppressive Acts	1:988
18 Mar.	Justice	0:481 1:734
21 Mar.	PE Comes after They Have Read a Book	2:284 6:242
21 Mar.	Staff Members Auditing Outside Pcs	0:170
22 Mar.	Current Promotion and Org Program Summary, Membership Rundown	6:805
26 Mar.RA	Field Staff Member I/C Hat *FSM Series 2* Rev. 8 Nov. 84	6:639
27 Mar.	Confused Presentation Denies Service	7:1299
27 Mar.	The Justice of Scientology, Its Use and Purpose, Being a Scientologist	0:483 1:939
28 Mar.	Emergencies and Accounts Personnel	3:252
29 Mar.	Flows and Expansion, the Fast Flow System	1:661 5:132 7:670
29 Mar.	Staff Regulations	0:171
29 Mar.	Routing Despatches	0:383 1:372
31 Mar.	Justice Policy Letters, Corrections	1:942 7:1300
1 Apr.	HCO Communicator Has Program Checking Hat *LRH Comm N/W Series 21*	7:1269
2 Apr.	Star-rate Checkouts for Process	4:768 5:184
2 Apr.	Meter Checks	5:226
2 Apr.R	Administration Outside Scientology Rev. 14 Dec. 80	1:736 7:1016
2 Apr.	Heed Heavy Traffic Warnings	0:380
2 Apr.	False Reports	1:869
3 Apr.	Organization of a Scientology Org	7:239
5 Apr.	Scientology Makes a Safe Environment	0:486 6:592 7:1019
5 Apr.	Handling the Suppressive Person, the Basis of Insanity	1:990 4:82
5 Apr.	The No-Gain-Case Student	4:341 1:1001
5 Apr.	Legal and Promotion	2:133 7:1073
5 Apr.	Registrar—Your Orders	2:702
6 Apr.	Letter Reg Hat	2:623
7 Apr.	Amnesty, Cancelled Certs, Justice Comments	5:348 1:946
7 Apr.RA	Book Income Rev. 23 Sept. 89	2:75 6:243
7 Apr.	Healing Policy in Field	6:711
7 Apr.	Book Auditor	2:166 5:346 6:840
8 Apr.	Justice Codes, HCO, Org Executive and Divisional Secretaries, Justice on, and Auditing Of	1:739 5:583
8 Apr.R	Cancellation of Mail Lists to Field Auditors Rev. 7 July 83	2:703 6:713
9 Apr.	Correction to Policy Letters on Certification and Awards	5:350
10 Apr.	Dismissals, Transfers and Demotions	0:487 1:251

12 Apr.	Classification Pass Marks	5:186
12 Apr.	Justice	1:741
14 Apr.	Classification on GPMs	5:187 4:772
14 Apr.	Organization GPM Unit	4:769
14 Apr.	Field Auditor Rates	6:715
16 Apr.	Drills, Allowed	4:616 5:188
16 Apr.	The "Hidden Data Line" KSW Series 22	4:347
16 Apr.	Handling the Public Individual	0:323 1:125 2:80 6:202
17 Apr.	Additional Mag Policy	2:208
18 Apr.	Contests and Prizes	0:234 6:207
18 Apr.	Prices Lowered Because of New Organization Streamline	6:368
19 Apr.	Training and Processing Regulations, Tech Division, Qual Division, Technical Discipline, Students' Questions	4:350 5:840
21 Apr.	Basic Certificates, Uncertified Personnel	1:234 5:351
21 Apr.	Membership Attestations	6:814
22 Apr.	Level 0 Comm Course	4:353 6:471
22 Apr.	Booklets, Handouts, Mailing Pieces	2:178 7:1304
23 Apr.	Clarification, Auditing of Org Executives	5:585
23 Apr.	Problems	0:240 7:673
24 Apr.	Review	5:734
26 Apr.	Sec ED Issue	7:1306
27 Apr.	Price Engram	2:428 3:154
27 Apr.	Book Promotion Design	2:338 6:248
28 Apr.	Technical Personnel	4:93 5:737
28 Apr.	Power Processes	4:885 5:739
28 Apr.	Color Flash Sysem	1:373
29 Apr.	Ethics, Review	0:491 1:744 4:354 5:109
29 Apr.	Bonuses	3:346 5:408
29 Apr.	Petition	0:488 1:742
30 Apr.	Emergency, State Of	0:621 1:549
1 May R	Organization, the Design of the Organization Rev. 29 Aug. 90	0:95 1:144 7:246
1 May	Order Board and Time Machine	0:375 1:518 7:677
1 May	Staff Member Reports	0:543 1:699
5 May	Classification, Gradation and Awareness Chart	2:517 4:186 5:191
5 May	Supervisors	4:359
5 May	"Free Memberships for Six Months . . ."	6:815
7 May	Cancellation, Mimeo Distribution Changes	1:412
8 May	Cancellation of Assorted Directives	1:414 7:1307
8 May	Flash Colors and Designations	1:415
8 May	Results of HCO Technical Investigation	1:749
9 May	Auditing Fees, Preferential Treatment of Preclears, Scale of Preference	2:520 3:157 4:888
9 May RA	Field Auditors Become Staff FSM Series 1	6:629
10 May	Get Your Technical Division In, Fully Manned and Functioning!	4:95
10 May	Releases, Vital Data	4:1057
11 May	Ethics Officer Hat	1:681

11 May R	HCO Book Account Policy, Receipt and Use of Membership Monies Rev. 7 July 83	2:285 6:250
13 May	SHSBC Unit Graduation	4:773
13 May	Sale of Bulletins and Tapes Forbidden	2:288 3:130
16 May	Important Explanation, Auditing Restrictions	4:619
16 May	Hubbard Recognized Scientologist	4:620 5:194
16 May	Indicators of Orgs	0:496 1:750 7:679
17 May	Academy Processing	5:197
17 May	Clarification of Sec ED 27	4:97
17 May	CCHs	4:623
17 May	Academy Processing	4:624
17 May	Free Scientology Center	4:676 6:328
20 May	Power Processes	4:891
21 May	Memorandum of Agreement	4:893
23 May	Rebates	2:523 3:160 4:895 5:742
24 May	Examinations	5:114
26 May	Re: Sec ED 29 (Tech Div)	4:98
26 May	Communications, Registered Mail	0:379 1:331
26 May	Petitions	0:490 1:753
26 May	Courts of Ethics	1:948
27 May	Processing *KSW Series 31*	4:678
28 May	Some Allowed Ads	2:269 6:253
28 May	Mission Courses	6:748
31 May	Noise, Session Interruption	4:897
31 May	Mission Summary of Policy	6:749
2 June	Org Ethics and Tech	0:499 1:754 2:85 4:99 6:371 7:844
2 June	Writing of an Ethics Order	1:967
3 June	R6EW	4:789
4 June	"All Pcs Undergoing Power Processing . . ."	4:898
7 June	New Org Board Design	1:147
7 June	Entheta Letters and the Dead File, Handling of	1:970 2:661
10 June	PE and Lectures	6:472
11 June	The Foundation	7:297
11 June	Correction to HCO PL 26 May 65 Communications, Registered Mail	1:332
12 June	The Foundation, Forming the Foundation	1: 757 7:302
14 June	Six Power Processes	4:899
14 June	Folders, Marking of	4:1059
14 June	Politics, Freedom From	0:159 7:1020
17 June	Scientology Pins	2:378 5:353
17 June	Staff Auditor Advices	1:625 4:1173 5:586
18 June	Areas of Operation	2:88 6:59
18 June	Grounds Regulations, Staff and Students	7:1384
21 June	Distribution Division (Div 6)	6:61
21 June	Orgs Are Saint Hill FSMs	3:349 6:642
30 June	Ad	6:209
1 July	Ethics Chits	1:703 4:102 5:20
1 July	Comm Cycle Additives	4:1175 5:667
1 July	Hats, the Reason For	0:196 1:273
1 July	Letter Reg, Body Reg	2:632
3 July	The Foundation Data	7:308
4 July	Pc Routing, Review Code	4:1060 5:115

6 July	Releases	4:1063
7 July	Photos, News and Statistics for Mags and *Auditor*	2:180
9 July	Qual Goofs	5:228
10 July	Lines and Terminals, Routing	0:384 1:311 7:771
11 July	Assignment of Tech Personnel	4:104
12 July	Release Policies, Starting the Pc	2:525 4:1064 5:744
13 July	Congresses	6:330
16 July	Continental Magazines to Model After *Certainty*	2:209
19 July	Release Checks, Procedure For	4:1068 5:748
19 July	Policy, How to Handle People Who Quote Policy to Show You They Can't Follow It	0:475 7:773
19 July	Separation Order	1:763
19 July RA	Discounts, Central Orgs, Books Rev. 7 July 83	2:305 6:225
22 July I	Dissemination Materials to Saint Hill	2:134
23 July	Priority of Power Processing	4:900
26 July	Release Declaration Restrictions, Healing Amendments	4:474 5:229
28 July	Case Supervisor, Special Attention	4:1072
28 July	Handling of Photographs	2:271
30 July	Preclear Routing to Ethics	4:1073 5:118
31 July	Purposes of the Qualifications Division *KSW Series 12*	5:30
2 Aug.	Chaplain	6:518
2 Aug.	Executive Division	7:71
5 Aug.	Release Checkouts	5:230
5 Aug.	Release Stages	4:1074
6 Aug.	Qualifications Technical Actions	5:33
6 Aug.	Technical Queries From R6 Graduates	4:775
7 Aug.	Floating Needle on Former Releases	5:233
7 Aug.	Suppressive Persons, Main Characteristics of	1:1007
9 Aug.	Release Checkouts	5:234
12 Aug.	Council and Ad Comms	7:896
13 Aug.	Foundation, Basic Course Organization	6:473
15 Aug.	Things That Shouldn't Be	0:547 1:705
16 Aug.	Collection From SPs and PTSes	1:764 3:190
16 Aug.	Foundation, Basic Course Organization Correction	6:477
16 Aug.	Foundation	6:478
17 Aug.	Certification of Mission Students	5:199 6:755
17 Aug.	Return Address	1:333 2:340
20 Aug.	Scientology Org Uniforms	3:393
20 Aug.	Continuing Pc to Third Stage Release	4:901
20 Aug.	Appointment of Xerox Officer	1:419
20 Aug.	General Amnesty	1:951
23 Aug.	Classification at Upper Levels, Temporary Measure	5:200
23 Aug.	Crediting of Auditor in Release Logbook	5:355
24 Aug.	Pcs Released Routing	4:1077 5:119
24 Aug.	Cleanliness of Quarters and Staff, Improve Our Image	0:334 6:593
26 Aug.RB	Ethics E-Meter Check Rev. 26 July 86	1:765
27 Aug.	Housing—Staff, Students, Preclears	0:172
31 Aug.	Mail Opening	1:334 3:204

1 Sept.R	Membership Policies Rev. 27 Mar. 78	6:816
1 Sept.	Some Tech Div Policies	2:528 4:360 7:1074
1 Sept.	Ethics Protection	0:502 1:767
1 Sept.	Publications	2:135
1 Sept.R	Mailing List Policies Rev. 7 July 83	0:625 2:705
4 Sept.	Inspection Officer	1:191
6 Sept.	Upping Beginning Scientology Enrollments	6:385
8 Sept.	Supply Officer	0:184 3:395
8 Sept.	Distribution Division Info Packet	6:211
8 Sept.	Registration Packet	2:633
9 Sept.	Flowers, Care Of	7:1385
12 Sept.R	E-Meters and Books for Academy Students Rev. 4 Feb. 91	2:341 4:363 5:723
12 Sept.	Foundation Course Change	6:480
13 Sept.R	Out-Tech and How to Get It In KSW Series 26 Rev. 16 Feb. 81	4:1078 5:669
13 Sept.	Foundation Course Hours	6:484
13 Sept.	Issue Authority Required for Mimeo	7:1308
14 Sept.	Classification Is Required Before Moving to Next Level	4:776
14 Sept.	Units and Bonuses for Org Exec Secs and HCO Exec Secs	3:350 7:73
14 Sept.	New Car Park	7:1387
16 Sept.	Foundation	6:212
16 Sept.	Weekly Secretarial Personnel Report	7:774
17 Sept.	Executive Letter Unit	7:1194
21 Sept.	Auditor Estimation Test	4:1177 5:201
21 Sept.	E-Meter Drills	4:626
21 Sept.	Cleanliness and Tidiness of Premises	1:520 6:594
21 Sept.	Corporate Names, Group Names	7:1118
21 Sept.	Purposes of the Department of Registration	2:431
22 Sept.	Keys	0:185 3:396
23 Sept.	Keeping Stocks Up	2:307
24 Sept.	Free Release Check	2:531 3:162 5:120
24 Sept.	Ads and Info Packets	6:213
30 Sept.	Statistics for Divisions	3:48 7:898
Sept.	The Aims of Scientology	7:1021 6:519
5 Oct.	Routing, Ad Comm Reports and Minutes	7:901
10 Oct.	Government Conflicts	7:1022
12 Oct.	Advisory Committees	7:903
13 Oct.	Dev-T Data, Executive Responsibility	0:419 7:682
14 Oct.	Potential Trouble Source Routing	1:1001 5:121
15 Oct.R	Field Staff Member Selection Papers and Commissions FSM Series 3 Rev. 8 Nov. 84	3:254 6:645
15 Oct.	Field Staff Member Commissions	6:643
18 Oct.	Field Staff Member Program	6:649
19 Oct.	Release Declarations	4:1083 5:235
21 Oct.	Bills Payments	3:317
22 Oct.	FSM Selection Slips	6:651
23 Oct.	Dissemination Drill	6:214
25 Oct.	Saint Hill Solo Audit Course	4:777
26 Oct.	Low Statistics	1:194
27 Oct.	Grade Award Insignia	5:356
28 Oct.	Discounts	2:308
29 Oct.	Student Auditing of Preclears	4:680
29 Oct.	Ethics Authority Section, Office of LRH LRH Comm N/W Series 18	7:1263
2 Nov.	Org Division, Income Dept	3:131

2 Nov.	"In HCO Policy Letter . . ."	6:652
2 Nov.	Your Org—Reply Expected	7:847
2 Nov.	Fast Line Sec EDs and Admin Orders	7:1309
2 Nov.	Foundation Central Files Officer and Address In-Charge	2:670
3 Nov.	Equipment	0:189 3:397
3 Nov.	Pc Scheduling	4:252
4 Nov.	Appearances Officer Hat Write-up	6:595
4 Nov.	"I Am Worried about Your Foundation . . ."	7:309
7 Nov.	Reception Log, In-the-Org List	1:130
7 Nov.	Autographed Copies of Books by LRH	2:342
10 Nov.	The Cramming Section	4:364 5:773
12 Nov.	Transfers from SHSBC to Solo Audit Course	4:779
12 Nov.	Paint, Odorless	7:1388
13 Nov.	Release Pins	2:380 5:357
15 Nov.	Reporting of Theft and Action to Be Taken	0:548 1:706 3:398
17 Nov.	The Basic Principles of Promotion	0:344 2:136 6:63
18 Nov.	Field Staff Member Courses	6:653
18 Nov.	Appointment of Personnel	1:195
19 Nov.	Auditing Reports	4:1182
20 Nov.RA	The Promotional Actions of an Organization Rev. 4 May 85	0:346 1:38 2:90 3:51 4:105 5:40 6:65 7:75
20 Nov.	Org Rudiments Section	1:521
21 Nov.	Check Signing	3:319
23 Nov.	Organization at Saint Hill	7:87
26 Nov.R	Financial Planning Finance Series 40 Rev. 31 Oct. 82	3:271 MS2:409
26 Nov.	Income Data	2:532
30 Nov.	Power Processing for the Public	4:902
7 Dec.	Tape Color Flash Code	7:1196
9 Dec.R	HCO Income, Memberships—Tape Plays Rev. 7 July 83	2:289 6:817
13 Dec.	Numbering of Certificates	5:358
14 Dec.	Departmental Actions	7:1198
15 Dec.R	Student's Guide to Acceptable Behavior Rev. 27 July 87	4:475
15 Dec.	Gifts	7:1200
15 Dec.	Ethics Chits	0:549 1:707
16 Dec.	Registration and Service	4:219
16 Dec.	Organization of the Int Exec Division, Statistics of the International Executive Division	7:89
16 Dec.	Copyright: USA	7:1077
21 Dec.	Accounts Clearance	3:163
23 Dec.RB	Suppressive Acts, Suppression of Scientology and Scientologists Rev. 8 Jan. 91	1:873
27 Dec.	Vitamins	5:619
27 Dec.RA	LRH Communicator LRH Comm N/W Series 2 Rev. 7 May 84	7:1231
28 Dec.R	E-Meters Allowed Rev. 12 Jan. 80	2:381 4:627
30 Dec.	PTS Auditing and Routing	1:1012 4:1084 5:122

1966

4 Jan.	LRH Relationships to Orgs	7:1201
4 Jan.RA	Sec EDs and HCO Exec Letters *LRH Comm N/W Series 3* Rev. 7 May 84	7:1232
4 Jan.	Staff Meeting	0:173
4 Jan.RA	Personnel Staff Status Rev. 25 Mar. 89	0:209 1:236 5:411
4 Jan.	Scientology Organizations Communications System: Despatches	0:368 1:374
6 Jan.	Credit and Discounts	3:164
7 Jan.	Leaving Post, Writing Your Hat	0:198 1:275
9 Jan.	Accounts, Invalidating	3:399
9 Jan.	International Changes or Area Changes of Address	2:708
11 Jan.	Ad Council and Ad Comms, Orders, Issue Of	7:905
12 Jan.	Selectees Mailing, Selectee Advice Packets	2:635 6:654
13 Jan.	Regulations for Auditing of Staff and Students	4:681 5:588
13 Jan.	Intern Training	5:843
13 Jan.	Records of Bank Deposits	3:400
15 Jan.	Office of the Treasurer	3:63
15 Jan.	Hold the Form of the Org, Don't Bring about Danger Conditions	0:582 7:249
16 Jan.R	Danger Condition Rev. 29 Nov. 79	0:585 1:553
17 Jan.	Unclassed Certificates— HAS, HBA, HQS	5:360
17 Jan.	Distribution Action	6:216
17 Jan.	Organization Chart	1:49
19 Jan.	Danger Conditions, Technical Data for Review Auditors	5:775
19 Jan.	Danger Condition, Warning, the Junior Who Accepts Orders from Everyone	0:585 7:683
19 Jan.	Danger Condition, Responsibilities of Declaring	0:590 7:684
19 Jan.RA	LRH Communicator Orders *LRH Comm N/W Series 4* Rev. 7 May 84	7:1234
20 Jan.	Division 7, International Executive Division, Offices of the HCO Exec Sec and Org Exec Sec Described	7:93
21 Jan.	Executive Division	7:96
21 Jan.	To Advisory Council Worldwide	7:907
22 Jan.	Division Seven	7:103
23 Jan.	Accounting Policies of Scientology Companies	3:65 7:1078

25 Jan.	Communication Inspector Hat	1:383
26 Jan.	Int Exec Div Relation to Saint Hill Org	7:104
27 Jan.	Orders to HCOs	1:53
30 Jan.	Accounts Procedures	3:133
30 Jan.	Check Signing Procedure	3:321
30 Jan.	Minimum Personnel of an Org	6:790 7:252
30 Jan.RA	Org LRH Communicator Reports to LRH Comm Int *LRH Comm N/W Series 5* Rev. 7 May 84	7:1235
1 Feb.	Staff Auditor and Supervisor Procurement	4:117 5:487
1 Feb.	HGC Cure, Intern Training and Staff Auditors	4:903 5:488
1 Feb.	Statistics, Actions to Take, Statistic Changes	7:497
1 Feb.	Danger Conditions, Inspections by Executive Secretaries, How to Do Them	0:592 7:686
3 Feb.	Clearing Course, Submission of Folders	4:790
3 Feb.	Legal, Tax, Accountant and Solicitor, Mail and Legal Officer	1:335 7:1081
3 Feb.	Sec ED, Change in Issue and Use	1:420 7:1310
3 Feb.	Sec EDs Definition and Purpose	1:422 7:1312
9 Feb.	Release Grades	4:1085
10 Feb.	Checksheets, Course	4:780 5:206
10 Feb.R	Tech Recovery Rev. 22 Feb. 79	4:1087 5:752
10 Feb.	Bonuses for Service Delivery	3:352 5:135
11 Feb.	Shipping Charges	2:343 3:166
12 Feb.	The "Dangerous Auditor"	5:589
13 Feb.	Sec EDs, Sec ED Okay (Continued), Policy Letter Changes and Origins	7:1315
13 Feb.	Personnel Control Officer	1:197
14 Feb.	Doctor Title Abolished	5:362 7:1205
15 Feb.	Attacks on Scientology	7:1024
16 Feb.	Invoice Routing	3:135
18 Feb.	Attacks on Scientology (Continued)	7:1026
23 Feb.	Appointments and Promotions	0:596
24 Feb.	Mail Statistic, Dir Comm's Functions	1:313
25 Feb.	Communications Functions	1:316
28 Feb.	Danger Condition Data, Why Organizations Stay Small	0:598 7:254
1 Mar.R	Executive Division Organization and Its Theory and Purpose Rev. 14 Feb. 91	7:105
3 Mar.	Attacks on Scientology, Sex and Organizations	7:690
6 Mar.	Rewards and Penalties, How to Handle Personnel and Ethics Matters	0:504 1:769 7:500
6 Mar.	Statistic Graphs, How to Figure the Scale	0:675 1:664 7:505
7 Mar.	HGC Cure (Continued)	4:907 5:492
7 Mar.	Star-rates on Tech and Qual Staff	4:1183 5:777
8 Mar.	High Crime *KSW Series 13*	1:880 4:18 5:778
12 Mar.	Board Minutes	7:1119
13 Mar.	Orders, Precedence of Personnel, Titles Of	7:115
15 Mar.	Corporate Address	7:1120
17 Mar.	Expansion of Your Org	7:849
17 Mar.	Promotion of Saint Hill, *Auditor* Issue Frequency	2:243
3 Apr.	Dianetic Auditor Course	4:628
19 Apr.	Congress Policies	6:333

29 Apr.	Policy Checkouts and E-Meter	5:780
3 MayR	Reserve Fund Rev. 2 Feb 91	3:401
7 May	LRH Communicator, Issue Authority Of *LRH Comm N/W Series 20*	7:1267
8 MayRA	LRH Communicator, No Other Hats *LRH Comm N/W Series 6* Rev. 7 May 84	7:1239
4 June	Board of Investigation	1:952
21 June	Appointments, LRH Comm and Executive Secretary and Others	1:199
29 June	Keep Academy Checksheets Up-to-Date	4:459 5:209
1 July	Information Concerning the WW Time Machine	7:692
17 July	Despatches, Speed Up Despatches, Staledate	0:381 1:384
17 July	Evidence, Admissibility of, in Hearings, Boards or Committees	1:954
20 JulyRB	Staff Status Rev. 24 Nov. 85	0:213 1:240 3:191 5:415
20 July	The Type Two PTS	1:1013
21 July	Tech Versus Qual	4:1092 5:757
25 July	Allocation of Quarters, Arrangement of Desks and Equipment	7:1333
27 July	Moving	7:1334
31 JulyR	Refund Notice Rev. 28 Jan. 91	2:181 3:258 7:1083
1 Aug.	Sign-ups and Discounts	3:167 5:363
1 Aug.	Refund Addition	3:259 6:818 7:1084
2 Aug.	Dianetic Auditing	4:1094
2 Aug.	Graph Change, Ad Council Statistic	7:908
4 Aug.	Clears, Invalidation Of	1:892
5 Aug.RA	Chaplain's Court, Civil Hearings Rev. 7 Dec. 88	1:955 6:520
5 Aug.	Successes of Scientology	6:821
5 Aug.	Registered Mail	1:337
8 Aug.	OT Color Flash, Color Flash Addition	4:791
10 Aug.	Executive Director Sec EDs	1:425 7:1317
11 Aug.	Lamps and Security	7:311
15 Aug.	Information Packets	6:217
15 Aug.	Ethics Orders	1:979
16 Aug.	Clearing Course Security	1:627 4:792
17 Aug.	Routing and Handling of SHSBC Students	4:783
22 Aug.	Dead File: Restoration to Good Standing	1:980 2:671
1 Sept.RA	Founder Rev. 8 May 73	7:1206
6 Sept.	The Handling of Purchased or Rented Mailing Lists	2:709 6:218
9 Sept.	Security	1:386
13 Sept.	Requirement for Termination on the SHSBC and Enrollment on Solo Course	4:784
27 Sept.	The Antisocial Personality, the Anti-Scientologist	1:1014
30 Sept.	OT Regulations	4:793 6:842
5 Oct.	Students Terminating, Leave of Absence, Blown Students	4:366
5 Oct.	A New Pattern of Organization	7:261
6 Oct.RC	Additions to HCO Div Account Policy Rev. 4 Feb. 91	2:290
11 Oct.	Legal, Tax, Accountant and Solicitor Mail Incoming and Outgoing	1:338 7:1085
12 Oct.	Examinations	4:478
12 Oct.	Duration of SHSBC and Solo Course Requirements	4:785

13 Oct.	Invoice Routing	2:292
		3:136
13 Oct.	Advertisements,	2:210
	Continental Magazines	6:219
	and *Auditor*	
14 Oct.	Clearing Course Folders	4:794
17 Oct.	Bonuses	3:355
18 Oct.	SH Staff Auditor's	4:1184
	Purpose	5:591
20 Oct.	Executives and	7:321
	Governing Body Errors	MS3:301
	and Answers	
	AKH Series 1	
20 Oct.	Signatures of Policy	1:426
	Letters	7:1318
21 Oct.	Six-Department System	6:792
		7:266
21 Oct.	City Office System	6:796
		7:270
21 Oct.	City Office	6:798
21 Oct.	Evening Foundations	7:312
31 Oct.	Actions, Executive, for	7:326
	Handling Disastrous	MS3:306
	Occurrences	
	AKH Series 2	
31 Oct.R	Job Endangerment Chits	0:551
	AKH Series 3R	1:709
	Rev. 5 Mar. 68	7:329
		MS3:309
31 Oct.	Boards of Investigation	1:958
1 Nov.	Worldwide Organization	7:120
3 Nov.	Leadership	7:332
	AKH Series 4	MS3:312
6 Nov.R	Statistic Interpretation,	7:335
	Statistic Analysis	MS3:315
	AKH Series 5R	
	Rev. 9 Nov. 79	
6 Nov.	Statistic Interpretation,	1:524
	Estate Statistic	7:1389
7 Nov.	Clear Checkouts in	4:908
	Continental Orgs	5:236
10 Nov.	Good Versus Bad	7:340
	Management	MS3:320
	AKH Series 6	
16 Nov.	Executive Facilities,	7:343
	Facility Differential	MS3:323
	AKH Series 7	
17 Nov.	Intervention	7:351
	AKH Series 8	MS3:331
21 Nov.	Ideas and Compilations	7:124
	Branch WW	
4 Dec.	Expansion, Theory	0:124
	of Policy	7:354
	AKH Series 9	MS3:334
7 Dec.RA	Magazines Permitted,	2:211
	All Orgs	
	Rev. 5 Feb. 91	
12 Dec.	New Org Board	1:150
	Design (2)	
15 Dec.	Financial Planning	7:947
16 Dec.	Clearing Course	4:795
	Regulation	
20 Dec.	Tech and Qual	5:210
	Pre-examinations	
21 Dec.	Advisory Council	7:909
21 Dec.	Executive Council	7:913
21 Dec.	Office of LRH Supplies	7:1208
23 Dec.	Saint Hill Income Peaks,	2:245
	Reinforcement of	
	Auditor Promotion	
24 Dec.	How to Program an Org,	7:362
	Saint Hill Programs	MS3:342
	AKH Series 10	
24 Dec.	How to Program an	7:369
	Org, Corrections and	MS3:349
	Additions, Sequence of	
	Programs Correction	
	AKH Series 11	
26 Dec.	PTS Sections, Personnel	1:1022
	and Execs	7:372
	AKH Series 12	MS3:352
29 Dec.	Historical Precedence	1:774
	of Ethics	

1967

	Dianetics: Its Relationship to Scientology	6:429
1 Jan.	Critics of Scientology	1:761
17 Jan.	An Open Letter to All Clears	4:796 6:656
27 Jan.	Clearing and OT Course Reorganization	4:798
12 Feb.	The Responsibilities of Leaders	0:629 7:376
	AKH Series 13	MS3:356
22 Feb.	Office of LRH	7:1209
22 Feb.	LRH Property, Building and Plans Branch	7:1391
22 Mar.	Alter-Is and Degraded Beings	1:201 7:389
	AKH Series 14	MS3:369
22 Mar.	Personnel Requirement	1:203
11 Apr.	Section III OT Prerequisite	4:801
25 June	Scientology Orgs, Tax and Balance Sheets	3:402 7:1086
24 July	Fixed Public Consumption of Product	7:507
11 Aug.	OT Central Committee	6:843 7:125
11 Aug.	Organization, Definition Of	7:272
11 Aug.	Second Dynamic Rules	1:780 4:479
15 Aug.	Discipline, SPs and Admin, How Statistics Crash	1:1026 7:510
15 Aug.	Important Executive Action	7:512
19 Aug.	The Supreme Test	0:236
1 Sept.	WW Emergency Condition	7:127
6 Sept.	WW Division Reorganization	7:131
8 Sept.	Continental Liaison Officers at WW	7:133
8 Sept.	Statistics and Org Board Copies	1:666
10 Sept.	Statistic, GDS Div 6	6:77
12 Sept.	Post, Handling Of	0:238
15 Sept.	Release and Clear Checkouts	5:238
15 Sept.	Examiner Bonuses	3:358 5:240
15 Sept.	The Supervisor's Code	4:367
15 Sept.	ARC Break Registrar	6:547
18 Sept.	Complexity and Confronting	0:36 4:369
20 Sept.	"Failure to Apply . . ."	7:694
21 Sept.	WW Income Outgo	7:135
21 Sept.	Worldwide and Saint Hill Functions Redefined	7:136
21 Sept.	International Officers at WW, Alert Council	7:137
23 Sept.	New Post Formula, The Conditions Formulas	0:561 1:557
25 Sept.	Grades Above Clear	4:802 5:242
1 Oct.	Uses of Orgs	7:391
	AKH Series 15	MS3:371
3 Oct.	Special Program, Fast Academies	4:372

4 Oct.	Auditor and Org Individual Stats	4:118
6 Oct.	HCO Exec Sec Condition	1:55
6 Oct.R	Conditions of Liability and Doubt Rev. 25 Sept. 77	0:574 1:562
8 Oct.	Clear Checks and Re-Clear Checks	5:243
11 Oct.	Clay Table Training	4:374
12 Oct.	Charges	3:169
12 Oct.	Operational, Definition Of	0:190 7:1393
15 Oct.	*Auditor* Magazine Success	2:246
16 Oct.	Suppressives and the Administrator, How to Detect SPs as an Administrator *AKH Series 16*	1:1028 7:392 MS3:372
18 Oct.	Academy Checksheets, Supervisor Conditions	4:376 5:781
18 Oct.	WW—How to Comm to WW, Continental Liaison Officers	7:139
18 Oct.	Conditions on Orgs or Divisions or Depts, Clarification	0:652 1:564
18 Oct.	Failure to Follow or Apply Condition	0:653 1:565
18 Oct.	Policy and HCOB Alterations, High Crime	1:1031
19 Oct.	WW Seven Divisions	7:143
19 Oct.	HCO Exec Sec Duties, Org Exec Sec Duties	7:695
20 Oct.	Conditions, How to Assign *AKH Series 17*	0:654 1:566 7:395 MS3:375
20 Oct.R	Conditions Penalties, New Employees and Persons Newly on Post Rev. 4 Mar. 75	0:566 1:571
23 Oct.	Enemy Formula	0:573 1:572
26 Oct.	The Public Divisions	6:78
26 Oct.	Nine-Division Org	6:81
9 Nov.	Academy Checksheets	4:630 5:759
20 Nov.	Out-Tech	1:1032
22 Nov.RA	Out-Tech *KSW Series 25* Rev. 12 Apr. 83	4:20 5:783
23 Nov.	Financial Lines and Legal Lines	7:1091
23 Nov.	Public Attacks, Legal Point	7:1092
20 Dec.	Taxation	3:407
22 Dec.	Affluence Attainment	0:628
28 Dec.	Qual Senior Datum	5:52

1968

3 Jan.	Speed of Service	0:275 4:119 7:850
5 Jan.	Conditions Orders, Executive Ethics	0:659 1:573 7:698
5 Jan.	Overfilled In-Basket, Bad News	0:420
23 Jan.	Orders and Responsibility	0:139
28 Jan.	OT WW Liaison Unit, OT Central Committee	7:144
6 Feb.	Organization—The Flaw	0:66 1:526 5:138 7:700
7 Feb.	Fast Flow and Ethics	1:785 5:139
8 Feb.	Sea Org Zones of Planning	7:145
8 Feb.	Statistic Rationalization *AKH Series 18*	0:682 7:400 MS3:380
22 Feb.	Ethics and Admin, Slow Admin	0:244 1:893 7:701
2 Mar.	Advanced Course Security Check	4:803
8 Mar.	Checksheets	4:632
11 Mar.	False Attestation	5:212
12 Mar.	Mistakes, Anatomy of	1:1033
13 Mar.	Statistics	5:54
13 Mar.	New Qual Stat, GDS Qual Div	5:73
14 Mar.	Corrected Table of Conditions	0:565 1:575
16 Mar.	Post Changes	1:252
17 Mar.	"Boom Formula" Cancelled 1 Nov. 82	2:711 6:103
15 Apr.	"To Ensure Speed and Accuracy"	1:464
28 Apr.	"When the Success Story Stat . . ."	6:822
28 Apr.	Standard Executive Actions	7:702
4 May	Handling Situations	0:245 7:703
7 May	The Key Questions Director of Success Duty	5:213 6:823
9 May	Sea Organization Personnel	7:147
10 May RA	LRH Comms Functions *LRH Comm N/W Series 7* Rev. 7 May 84	7:1240
21 May	Comm Procedure over Long Distances	1:465
22 May	OT Section Awards	5:365
22 May	Translations	7:1319
22 May	Hiring Personnel, Line For	1:162
23 May	WW and SH Recombined	7:148
24 May	Immigration Tip	7:1094

Date	Title	Ref
26 May	Boards of Investigation and Committees of Evidence, Termination Of	1:959
27 May	Minimum Bookstocks	2:309
28 May	Books	2:310
30 May	Administration *AKH Series 20*	7:402 MS3:382
30 May	Communication	1:466
31 May	Scientology Technology *KSW Series 29*	4:22 5:651
31 May	LRH Comm Log	7:1211
31 May	Auditors	0:154
5 June R	FSM Commissions *FSM Series 4* Rev. 8 Nov. 84	6:658
5 June R	Weekly Book Stock Report Required Rev. 28 Jan. 80	2:311
17 June	HCO Book Account	2:312
18 June	Ethics	0:509 1:786
20 June	Personnel	1:253
20 June	Ethics Officers	1:684
29 June	Enrollment in Suppressive Groups	1:894 2:434
1 July	Warning Signs	7:705
2 July	Office of LRH WW Reorganization	7:1214
2 July	Org, Suppression Of	1:254
27 July	A Tiger	1:787
30 July	Gross Income Senior Datum	0:358 2:672 7:851
1 Aug.	Broad Public Questionnaire	6:596
10 Aug.	Legal and Dissemination	2:102 6:82 7:1095
12 Aug.	Reasons Why Div 6s Don't Function	6:83
12 Aug.	People Who Don't Do Their Jobs	0:422
24 Aug.	Dissemination	4:120
26 Aug.	Rehab and Correction	5:674
28 Aug.	Out-Tech	5:652
2 Sept.	Chaplain	6:523
5 Sept.	Vital Org Activities	6:85
7 Sept.	Review Complete, Pc Attestations	5:245
15 Sept.	Sea Org	7:151
16 Sept.	AOs—OT Sections	4:804
16 Sept.	Address Lists	2:710
4 Oct.	Ethics Presence	0:246 7:706
13 Oct.RA	Pc Examiner	5:246
14 Oct.RA	The Auditor's Code Rev. 19 June 80	4:1186
16 Oct.	Supervisor's Duty	4:378
16 Oct.	"The Formula for the Condition of Treason . . ."	0:571 1:576
19 Oct.	Course Completion, Student Indicators	0:32 4:379 5:215
20 Oct.	The Purpose of Class VIII	4:823
24 Oct.	Supervisor Know-How, Running the Class	4:380
24 Oct.R	Supervisor Know-How, Handling the Student Rev. 7 Jan 82	4:382
24 Oct.	Supervisor Know-How, R-factor to Students	4:384
24 Oct.	Supervisor Know-How, Tips in Handling Students	4:385
25 Oct.	Admin Know-How *AKH Series 21*	7:403 MS3:383
26 Oct.	Executive Council	6:86 7:915
28 Oct.	Classified Materials	4:825
28 Oct.	Press Releases	6:599 7:1043
29 Oct.	Class VIII C/S Qual Stat	5:676
5 Nov.R	Space Allocation Rev. 8 Feb. 89	7:1335
9 Nov.	Standard Admin	0:51 7:273
12 Nov.R	The Main Weakness Rev. 11 Jan. 89	1:111
16 Nov.	A Fable	7:1127
21 Nov.	Senior Policy	0:284 2:103 7:852
21 Nov.	Photo Policy for Magazines	2:213

24 Nov.	The Group Officer	6:845	11 Dec.	Services, Illegal Offering	6:756
26 Nov.	The Original *Auditor* Journal Policy	2:247	13 Dec.	The Great "Charity" Swindle	7:1131
29 Nov.	The War	7:1129	16 Dec.	Security Div 1	1:628
30 Nov.	OT Central Committee	7:152	23 Dec.	Good Service	0:276 2:435
2 Dec.	Gung-ho Groups	6:846	26 Dec.	Gung-ho Group Tech	6:859
3 Dec.	Gung-ho Groups Policy Letter 2	6:854	26 Dec.	The Third Party Law	0:510 1:537
8 Dec.	Scarcity of Trained Auditors	4:910	30 Dec.	The Public Programs Officer	6:860
9 Dec.	Qual Has No Backlog	5:55			

1969

12 Jan.	High Ethics for High Conditions	0:661 1:577
13 Jan.	Unusual Favors	1:895
14 Jan.	OT Orgs *Target Series 1*	MS2:427
14 Jan.	Spectatorism	0:249
16 Jan.	Targets, Types Of *Target Series 2*	MS2:431
18 Jan.	Planning and Targets *Target Series 3*	MS2:435
20 Jan.	A Vital Target, Trained Auditor Program	4:386 5:493
24 Jan.	Target Types *Target Series 4*	MS2:437
24 Jan.	Purpose and Targets *Target Series 5*	MS2:438
25 Jan.	Targets and Computers *Computer Series 2*	MS2:440 MS2:455
26 Jan.	Compliance Reports	7:708
27 Jan.	Dev-T Summary List	0:424
30 Jan.	Public Divisions Org Board	6:87
30 Jan.R	Dev-T Summary List Additions Rev. 21 Oct. 80	0:429
31 Jan.	Humanitarian Objective and Gung-ho Groups	6:861
3 Feb.	Public Image	6:600 7:1044
5 Feb.	PRO Actions *PR Series 35*	MS3:137
5 Feb.R	Code of a Scientologist Rev. 15 May 73	0:160 6:603 7:1047
5 Feb.	Double Hats	1:205
9 Feb.	Organizational Intention	6:583
12 Feb.	Religion	6:605 7:1320
13 Feb.	Ethics Protection Conditions, Blue Star, Green Star, Gold Star	0:662 1:578 5:366
24 Feb.	Justice	0:513 1:540
3 Mar.	Case Gain, Completing Levels *KSW Series 32*	5:593
7 Mar.	Organization	0:87 7:776
12 Mar.	Physically Ill Pcs and Pre-OTs	5:622
15 Mar.	Third Party, How to Find One	1:544
2 Apr.RA	Dianetic Assists Rev. 28 July 78	5:629
4 Apr.	Ron's Journal 1969 No. 3, Political Treatment	7:1134
5 Apr.	New Preclears	4:912
6 Apr.	Dianetics	2:533 4:1095 5:595 6:433
7 Apr.	Org Reduction or Eradication	1:870 7:916

20 Apr.	Hats, Not Wearing	0:572
		1:580
24 Apr.R	Dianetic Results	5:633
	Rev. 20 July 78	
27 Apr.	Death Wish	1:1034
16 May	Course Administration	4:460
20 May	Keeping Dianetics	4:633
	Working in an Area	5:677
22 May	Orders Versus	0:140
	Arbitraries	
	Exec Series 26	
23 May	Dianetic Contract	4:917
		6:435
		7:1096
27 May	The VIII's Nightmare	4:1097
		5:680
28 May	Dianetics and Results,	6:717
	Dianetic Counseling	
	Groups	
29 May	Dianetic Certificates	4:636
		5:216
11 June	Materials, Scarcity Of	4:463
12 June	Dianetic Registration	2:535
		4:920
		6:438
		7:1100
17 June	The Org Image	0:335
	PR Series 36	6:606
		MS3:140
23 July	Auditor Assignment	4:923
	Policies	5:597
29 July	Course Administration,	4:464
	Roll Book	
29 July	Completion of Cycles	7:778
1 Sept.R	Counterespionage	1:629
	Rev. 24 Sept. 83	7:1033
2 Sept.	Failed VIIIs	4:826
		5:785
2 Sept.	Triple Grades	4:1098
2 Sept.	Old ACC Students	2:436
		6:220
3 Sept.	Successful Class VIIIs	4:827
8 Sept.	The Org Exec Course	0:3
	Introduction	1:3
		2:3
		3:3
		4:3
		5:3
		6:3
		7:3

9 Sept.R	How to Study This	0:31
	Course	
	Rev. 17 June 85	
11 Sept.	Org Affluences	7:853
14 Sept.	The Key Ingredients	7:405
	AKH Series 22	MS3:385
20 Sept.	Stability	0:67
		7:779
21 Sept.	Staff Training Officer	5:496
4 Oct.	Organizational	0:68
	Enturbulence	
5 Oct.	The Rehabilitation of	6:135
	Artists	
5 Oct.R	Dianetic Courses,	4:637
	Wildcat	6:720
	Rev. 10 Dec. 69	
7 Oct.	Fundamentals of	7:780
	Administration No. 2	
9 Oct.	Publications Depts and	2:344
	Orgs, How to Straighten	
	Out	
10 Oct.R	Downstat Causes	7:513
	Rev. 13 Feb. 91	
16 Oct.R	Finance Course, Vital	3:68
	Action	
	Rev. 3 Feb. 91	
27 Oct.	Dev-T	0:433
	AKH Series 23	7:412
		MS3:392
4 Nov.	Dev-T Graphed	0:435
8 Nov.	Tech Services	4:207
10 Nov.	FSM Awards	6:659
11 Nov.	Accounts and PRO	3:69
	PR Series 37	MS3:144
11 Nov.	Promotion and	6:758
	Motivation	
11 Nov.	Mission Promotion	6:762
	Musts	
12 Nov.	Appearance and PRO	MS3:144
	PR Series 38	
13 Nov.	Internships and Case	5:844
	Supervisors	
14 Nov.	Medical Charts	5:635
18 Nov.	Dianetics, Right to Audit	5:368
		7:1103
18 Nov.	Dianetics, Right to	5:370
	Teach	7:1105

18 Nov.	Central Files, Value of the Gross Income of the Org and Why	0:359 2:673 6:89
23 Nov.	Individuals vs. Groups *PR Series 39*	MS3:150
23 Nov.	Allowed Technical Services	4:121 6:764
23 Nov.	Reform Mailing Result	6:610
23 Nov.	Ethics Program No. 1	1:788
25 Nov.	Registration	2:538
29 Nov.	Org Services	6:722
2 Dec.R	Freeloaders Rev. 17 Jan. 91	3:194
3 Dec.	Issue Authority for Translations of Dianetics and Scientology Materials	7:1321 6:767
7 Dec.	More on Staff Member Reports	0:554
7 Dec.	Ethics, the Design Of	0:517 1:483
7 Dec.	The Ethics Officer, His Character	1:687
7 Dec.	More on Staff Member Reports	1:712
9 Dec.RA	Organization Program No. 1 Rev. 8 Jan. 91	0:98 6:92 7:275
9 Dec.	How to Prevent an Ethics Officer from Doing His Job	1:692
9 Dec.R	Purchasing from Pubs Org Rev. 27 Mar. 78	2:313
10 Dec.	Superior Service Image	4:124 5:56 6:585
11 Dec.R	Appearances in Public Divs *PR Series 40* Rev. 16 Sept. 88	0:339 6:613 MS3:154
11 Dec.RB	Training of Clears Rev. 25 Mar. 89	2:437 4:786
13 Dec.	Post Transfers	1:206
14 Dec.	Magazines	2:215 6:221
15 Dec.	Orders, Query Of	0:141
16 Dec.	Instant Service Project	4:125
16 Dec.	Org Image Program No. 1 US	6:616
20 Dec.	How to Raise Stats	0:684 2:104 4:127 7:856
	Start a Scientology Group in Your Area	6:716

1970

	What Your Donations Buy	2:106
14 Jan.	Solvency	7:950
15 Jan.	The Uses of Auditing	2:438 4:925 5:681
15 Jan.	Handling with Auditing *KSW Series 17*	2:440 4:927 5:683
17 Jan.	The Uses of Auditing, Handling with Auditing, Registrar Advice Form	2:444 4:931 5:687
18 Jan.	"The Following Is a Letter . . ."	1:527
19 Jan.	Registrars' Advice Form	2:540 4:1022
24 Jan.	Tech/Admin Ratio	1:207
4 Feb.RA	Pc Application Form for Any Major Auditing Action Rev. 28 Jan. 91	2:542 4:1024
4 Feb.	Pc Application for Major Actions	2:546 4:1029
5 Feb.	Statistics, Management By	1:668 7:514
7 Feb.	HCO Makes the Org	1:56
9 Feb.	Statistical Judgment	7:516
10 Feb.RA	Missions, Multiple Ownership Rev. 7 Jan. 91	6:768
12 Feb.	EC WW, Primary Duties Of	7:153
12 Feb.RB	LRH Comm and HCO ES Responsibility for Lines *LRH Comm N/W Series 8* Rev. 7 May 84	7:1241
17 Feb.	Stat Recovery, an Analysis of Broad Outnesses	7:158
22 Feb.	Celebrity Centre	6:136
23 Feb.	Quality of Service	1:792 4:933 5:248 6:548
28 Feb.	Field Auditors	6:723
1 Mar.	Recruit!	7:783
3 Mar.	How to Write an ED or Order	7:711
12 Mar.R	Source to Cause Rev. 12 Mar. 89	0:250
24 Mar.	A Matter of Orders	7:786
28 Mar.	R6EW and Clear	4:805 5:250
29 Mar.	Auditing and Ethics	1:794 4:1099
1 Apr.	Ethics Program No. 1 Case Actions	5:599
4 Apr.	Power Change Violation Repair Formula	1:581 0:651
8 Apr.	Flag Executive Briefing Course	5:521
9 Apr.	Conference Hats	7:918

10 Apr.	Conference Planning Officer	7:920
11 Apr.	Review Complete?	5:251
11 Apr.	Third Dynamic Tech	0:55
16 Apr.	Morale	6:524
16 Apr.	Arbitraries	0:65
17 Apr.	An Auditor and "The Mind's Protection"	4:682
17 Apr.	Department 1	1:112
18 Apr.	Ethics and Missions	1:795
19 Apr.	Mimeo	1:427 2:272
21 Apr.	Field Ethics	1:796 6:724
23 Apr.	SH–UK ANZO–EU Relationships	7:161
25 Apr.	More on Lines and Hats	1:276
26 Apr.R	The Anatomy of Thought *Data Series 1R* *Rev. 15 Mar. 75*	MS1:3
8 May	Distraction and Noise *AKH Series 24*	7:414 MS3:394
10 May	Single Declare *KSW Series 14*	4:1100 5:252
10 May	Lower Grades Upgraded	5:254
11 May-1	Further Illogics *Data Series 2-1*	MS1:14
11 May	Logic *Data Series 2*	MS1:10
12 May	Breakthroughs *Data Series 3*	MS1:15
14 May	Hat Checkout Sequence	1:277
15 May	Data and Situation Analyzing *Data Series 4*	MS1:18
15 May	Information Collection *Data Series 5*	MS1:21
16 May	Institutional and Shock Cases, Petitions From	1:798 2:549
17 MayR	Data Systems *Data Series 6R* *Rev. 16 Sept. 78*	MS1:26
18 May	Familiarity *Data Series 7*	MS1:29

19 May	Sanity *Data Series 8*	MS1:32
20 May	The Ideal Org	0:342 6:618 7:282
21 May	Fast Flow Grades Cancelled	5:255
23 May	Errors *Data Series 9*	MS1:38
30 May	Cutatives *KSW Series 7*	4:23 5:22
2 June	Auditing Sales and Delivery Program No. 1	5:258
3 June	What Was Wrong	4:935 5:263
3 June	Orders to Divisions for Immediate Compliance	4:129
6 June	SH Pcs	5:274 5:267 7:284
8 June RC	Student Auditing *Rev. 11 Jan. 85*	4:683
10 June	Public Divisions and Tech/Admin Ratio	1:208 6:99
11 June	Auditing Mystery Solved	5:277
17 June RB	Technical Degrades *KSW Series 5R* *Rev. 25 Oct. 83*	0:14 1:14 2:14 3:14 4:14 5:14 6:14 7:14
17 June	OIC Change, Cable Change	5:74
23 June	The Missing Scene *Data Series 10*	MS1:41
24 June	Management Cycle	1:116 5:418
24 June	Personnel Pools	1:164
25 June	C/S Series 11	4:1102
25 June RC	Glossary of C/S Terms *C/S Series 12RC* *KSW Series 9R* *Rev. 25 Oct. 89*	4:1106
30 June	The Situation *Data Series 11*	MS1:46

5 July	How to Find and Establish an Ideal Scene *Data Series 12*	MS1:50
6 July	Irrationality *Data Series 13*	MS1:58
7 July	Working and Managing *Data Series 14*	MS1:68
14 July	Hats, Basic and False	1:279
14 July	Registrar Statistic	2:551
16 July	The Psychiatrist at Work	7:1137
20 July	Cases and Morale of Staff	1:800 5:602 6:526
8 Aug.	Wrong Target *Data Series 15*	MS1:71
13 Aug.	Liabilities of PR PR Series 1	6:620 MS3:3
13 Aug.	The Missing Ingredient PR Series 2	MS3:7
13 Aug.	Wrong Publics PR Series 3	MS3:11
16 Aug.	Statistic Mismanagement	7:518
26 Aug.	Case and Letter Reg Project #1	2:637
27 Aug.	Auditor's Association Project in Your Area	6:726
27 Aug.	My Own Objectives	6:864
28 Aug.R	Auditors Association Rev. 16 Jan. 75	6:730
28 Aug.	Control of Statistics *Exec Series 27*	0:686 7:521
29 Aug.	Personnel Transfers Can Destroy an Org *Personnel Series 1*	MS1:381
29 Aug.	Personnel Programing *Personnel Series 2*	MS1:385
29 Aug.	Recruit in Excess *Personnel Series 3*	MS1:389
29 Aug.	Staff Training Program No. 2	5:499
30 Aug.	Recruiting Actions *Personnel Series 4*	MS1:393
2 Sept.	First Policy	0:321 3:260 6:589 7:20
4 Sept.	Gross Divisional Statistics	7:787
8 Sept.RA	Examiner's 24-Hour Rule Rev. 24 Oct. 75	5:279
10 Sept.	Transferitis *Personnel Series 5*	MS1:398
12 Sept.	Training *Personnel Series 6*	MS1:401
13 Sept.	Basic Organization *Org Series 1*	0:105 MS1:193
13 Sept.	Hats—Vital Data *Personnel Series 7*	MS1:403
14 Sept.	How to Organize an Org *Org Series 3*	MS1:199
14 Sept.	Cope and Organize *Org Series 2*	MS1:197
15 Sept.R	Executive Responsibility for Training Staff Rev. 25 Apr. 79	0:220 5:419 7:789
16 Sept.	Ethics and Personnel *Personnel Series 8*	MS1:406
17 Sept.	Hats	1:280
19 Sept.	Investigatory Procedure *Data Series 16*	MS1:72
19 Sept.	Narrowing the Target *Data Series 17*	MS1:75
19 Sept.	Summary of Outpoints *Data Series 18*	MS1:78
21 Sept.	Cope	1:59 7:791
22 Sept.	Hats *Org Series 4* *Personnel Series 9*	0:199 MS1:202 MS1:411
22 Sept.	Why Orgs Sag	7:792
23 Sept.	Quarters, Policy Regarding, Historical	7:1394
24 Sept.RA	Issues—Types Of Rev. 3 July 77	1:429 7:1322
26 Sept.	Org Board Cutatives *Org Series 5*	MS1:208
27 Sept.	Cutative Prices *Org Series 6*	MS1:212
30 Sept.	Checksheet Format	1:281 5:503
30 Sept.	Credit Collections Defined	3:137
1 Oct.	Hats and Counter-Effort *Org Series 7*	MS1:213

3 Oct.RA	Stat Interpretation	7:523
	Rev. 27 Aug. 82	
6 Oct.	"Moonlighting"	MS1:417
	Personnel Series 10	
6 Oct.	Folder Error Summaries	4:1007
	C/S Series 19	
6 Oct.	Inspection of Low Stats	1:528
8 Oct.	Organizing and Product	MS1:218
	Org Series 8	
9 Oct.	The PR Personality	MS1:419
	PR Series 4	MS3:14
	Personnel Series 11	
10 Oct.	Utilization	1:210
13 Oct.	The Real Why	MS1:82
	Data Series 19	
14 Oct.	Division Four Org Board, Ideal Scenes and Stats	4:136
18 Oct.	Auditor's Stats on F/N VGI	4:1188
	Auditor Admin Series 17	
28 Oct.	Organi*zing* and Hats	MS1:220
	Org Series 9	
29 Oct.	The Analysis of Organization by Product	0:287
		MS1:226
	Org Series 10	
29 Oct.	An Org Board	1:151
		7:796
1 Nov.	Organization and Morale	MS1:230
	Org Series 11	
1 Nov.	Use of I&R Form 1	1:533
2 Nov.	The Theory of Scientology Organizations	0:81
		MS1:234
	Org Series 12	
2 Nov.	Responsibility	1:727
4 Nov.R	Estimated Purchase Orders	3:295
	Rev. 8 Feb. 91	
7 Nov.	"Noise" and Organization	1:152
		7:797
13 Nov.	Planning by Product	0:291
	Org Series 13	MS1:239
14 Nov.	The Product as an Overt Act	0:294
		MS1:242
	Org Series 14	
15 Nov.	Confessionals	1:633
		4:1109
		5:606
18 Nov.	PR Definition	MS3:16
	PR Series 5	
20 Nov.	Organization Misunderstoods	0:39
		MS1:244
	Personnel Series 12	MS1:421
	Org Series 15	
	Word Clearing Series 18	
25 Nov.	Policy and Orders	0:132
	Org Series 16	MS1:249
26 Nov.	More Outpoints	MS1:84
	Data Series 20	
28 Nov.	Psychosis	1:804
	C/S Series 22	
1 Dec.	Reality of Products	MS1:254
	Org Series 17	
6 Dec.	Third Dynamic De-aberration	MS1:261
		MS1:426
	Personnel Series 13	
	Org Series 18	
8 Dec.	Life Repair Block	4:145
14 Dec.	Group Sanity	MS1:266
	Org Series 19	MS1:431
	Personnel Series 14	
16 Dec.R	SH FSM Bonus Awards	3:360
	Rev. 17 Apr. 75	6:661
23 Dec.	Fast Courses	4:389
23 Dec.	HCO Traffic	1:132
27 Dec.	Hats Program Pitfalls	MS1:448
	Personnel Series 16	
30 Dec.	Environmental Control	0:251
	Org Series 20	MS1:280
	Personnel Series 15	MS1:445

1971

4 Jan.	Competence	0:254
13 Jan.	Exam 24-Hour Rule (Additional Information)	5:281
19 Jan.	Duplicating Functions	MS1:283
	Personnel Series 17	MS1:450
	Org Series 21	
25 Jan.	Squirrel Admin	0:61
	Org Series 22	MS1:284
29 Jan.RA	Flag Banking Officers	MS2:317
	Finance Series 1RA	
	Rev. 2 Feb. 91	
5 Feb.	CF and Address Presorting	2:676
6 Feb.	Transferring Funds	3:408
9 Feb.	Auditors Association	6:732
9 Feb.	Executive Misbehavior	1:898
		7:714
10 Feb.	Adds to Ethics and Personnel	MS1:451
	Personnel Series 18	
10 Feb.	Tech Volume and Two-way Comm	4:391
10 Feb.	Mimeo Files	1:433
11 Feb.RA	Policy Knowledge Function	7:1243
	LRH Comm N/W Series 9	
	Rev. 7 May 84	
12 Feb.	Hat Knock Off	1:285
13 Feb.	Financial Planning Tips	MS2:319
	Finance Series 2	
16 Feb.	Lines and Terminals	MS1:288
	Org Series 23	
17 Feb.RC	Basic FBO Duties	MS2:322
	Finance Series 3RC	
	Rev. 2 Feb. 91	
17 Feb.-1RB	Handling of Bounced Checks and Refunds	MS2:325
	Finance Series 3-1RB	
	Rev. 2 Feb. 91	
21 Feb.RA	Supervisor Checkouts	4:393
	Rev. 25 July 87	
23 Feb.	The Magic Formula	1:60
		7:799
24 Feb.	Operating at Risk	0:255
26 Feb.	Drills	7:800
26 Feb.	LRH Comm Troubles	7:1244
	LRH Comm N/W Series 10	
27 Feb.	First Financial Policy	3:72
27 Feb.RA	LRH Comm, New Basic Duties	7:1246
	LRH Comm N/W Series 11	
	Rev. 7 May 84	
27 Feb.RA	LRH Comm Correction Form	7:1251
	LRH Comm N/W Series 12	
	Rev. 7 May 84	
27 Feb.	Books	2:314
1 Mar.RB	Income Sources	MS2:328
	Finance Series 4RB	
	Rev. 2 Feb. 91	
2 Mar.	Mimeo Section	1:435
4 Mar.	How to Do Theory Checkouts and Examinations	4:395

5 Mar.	The Fantastic New HGC Line	4:939
		5:608
	C/S Series 25	
	Auditor Admin Series 10	
6 Mar.	Line Design—HGC Lines, an Example	MS1:291
	Org Series 24	
7 Mar.	Handling Overloaded Posts	7:801
8 Mar.R	Org Officer	MS1:354
	Org Series 42R	
	Rev. 22 Apr. 82	
8 Mar.	Examiner's Form	5:282
	Auditor Admin Series 11	
9 Mar.	Posting an Org Board	1:61
10 Mar.	Establishment and the HAS	MS1:356
	Org Series 43	
10 Mar.RA	FBO Hat	MS2:332
	Finance Series 6RA	
	Rev. 2 Feb. 91	
11 Mar.	Org Board and Production	7:802
12 Mar.	CO/ED Inspections	7:715
12 Mar.	Putting an HCO There, How to Establish a Division	1:66
12 Mar.	Command Intention and Your Post	0:256
		1:286
14 Mar.	On Giving Checkouts	4:396
15 Mar.RA	Data Series Auditing	MS1:86
	Data Series 21RA	
	Rev. 21 Sept. 81	
16 Mar.	Lines and Hats	MS1:293
	Personnel Series 19	MS1:452
	Org Series 25	
16 Mar.R	What Is a Course?	1:287
	KSW Series 27	4:397
	Rev. 29 Jan. 75	5:507
16 Mar.	An Operating Standard Rule	1:808
19 Mar.R	Personnel Prediction	MS1:454
	Personnel Series 20R	
	Rev. 21 Jan. 91	
19 Mar.RA	Bean Theory, Finance as a Commodity	MS2:339
	Finance Series 7RA	
	Rev. 27 Oct. 82	
25 Mar.	Valuable Final Products	0:296
	Org Series 26	MS1:295
28 Mar.	Tech Delivery Situation	4:148
28 Mar.	State of Orgs	1:69

28 Mar.	Personnel Troubles	1:117
6 Apr.	Org Board Knowledge	1:154
19 Apr.	Tech Delivery Quality	5:653
26 Apr.RC	FP Activation	MS2:330
	Finance Series 5RC	
	Rev. 2 Feb. 91	
28 Apr.	Okays to Audit in HGCs	4:946
		5:846
5 May	FEBC Graduate Policy	5:523
5 May	FC Policy Letter	2:552
		6:386
5 May RA	Reading Statistics	0:677
	Rev. 27 Aug. 82	7:529
6 May	Audience Alertness and Tape Players	6:334
11 May	Opinion Leaders	MS3:17
	PR Series 6	
11 May	Black PR	MS3:26
	PR Series 7	
17 May	Justice—Correct Application	0:520
		1:809
26 May R	TRs Course and Auditing, Mixing Major Actions	4:639
	C/S Series 38R	
	Rev. 23 Oct. 83	
27 May	Service	0:277
28 May	Too Little Too Late	MS3:32
	PR Series 8	
28 May	Service and Workload	0:279
		1:70
		7:803
30 May	Manners	0:328
	PR Series 9	MS3:34
2 June R	Breakthrough, PR and Production, Tone Scale Surveys	MS3:37
	PR Series 10R	
	Rev. 28 July 83	
4 June	Standard Admin	0:58
6 July	A Major Duty of the Hats Officer	1:291
10 June	Hatting Course Personnel	1:289
19 June	Declares	5:689
	C/S Series 46	
	KSW Series 18	

23 June R	The Secret of Fast Courses	4:487
	Word Clearing Series 1RA Rev. 25 July 87	
24 June	Trouble	7:717
25 June R	Barriers to Study	0:33
	Word Clearing Series 3R Rev. 25 Nov. 74	
29 June R	Policy on Psychiatric and Medical Failures	7:1140
	Rev. 24 June 88	
29 June	Public Warning on Psychiatry	7:1142
1 July R	The Different Types of Word Clearing	4:491
	Word Clearing Series 9R Rev. 11 Jan. 89	
1 July RB	Speeding Up a Slow Course	4:497
	Word Clearing Series 10RB Rev. 28 Dec. 88	
4 July	Why Something New?	2:553
7 July	HCO Establishment Functions	MS1:298
	Org Series 27	
12 July	Delivery Duties	4:253
16 July	Violence	7:1143
17 July R	Out of Valence (OCA Graphs)	4:231 6:299
	C/S Series 51R Rev. 6 July 78	
18 July	Stats and Progress Board	4:466
18 July	The Student Folder	4:468
19 July	Interns	5:849
	C/S Series 52	
20 July	The Beginning and Maintaining of a Boom	7:858
21 July	HAS Standard Actions	1:73
21 July	HAS Apprenticing Actions	1:76
22 July R	CLOs, OTLs and Flag	7:417 MS3:397
	AKH Series 25R Rev. 22 Jan. 91	
23 July	Telex Comm Clarity	1:467
25 July	Hatting the Right Way	1:292
28 July	Admin Know-How No. 26	7:426 MS3:406
	AKH Series 26	
29 July	Why Hatting?	0:205
	Org Series 28	MS1:301
	Personnel Series 21	MS1:457
29 July	Penalties for the Hiring or Recruiting of Institutional or Insane Persons	1:168
30 July	Mimeo Files Product	1:437
31 July	The Usual	0:257 7:718
2 Aug.	Study Time	0:222 5:421
2 Aug.RB	Public Exec Sec Privilege	6:101
	Rev. 10 Jan. 91	
4 Aug.R	Post Purpose Clearing	5:461
	Rev. 26 Nov. 74	
9 Aug.	Writing Programs and Projects	7:466 MS2:447
	Target Series 10 *AKH Series 45*	MS3:446
10 Aug.	HCO Cope Officer	1:79
11 Aug.	Infinite Expansion	MS1:303
	Org Series 29	
11 Aug.	Don't Unmock a Working Installation	MS1:459
	Personnel Series 22	
11 Aug.	Security of Data	1:635 4:806
11 Aug.	Basic Hat Pack	0:27
12 Aug.	Hat Checksheet Requirements	5:509
12 Aug.	OT Courses	4:808
12 Aug.	Ethics: Advanced Courses	1:637
14 Aug.RC	Div 5 Mini Qual Org Board	5:57
	Rev. 17 Feb. 75	
18 Aug.	On-Policy	0:28 7:806
19 Aug.	Programs, Use of, How to Save Useless Work	7:807
20 Aug.	Tech Establishment Officer	4:150
20 Aug.	HAS Troubles	1:81
20 Aug.	Musical Chairs	1:211
24 Aug.	Intern Checksheets, Okays to Audit	5:852

25 Aug.	How to Get Results in an HGC *Auditor Admin Series 2* *C/S Series 56*	4:949 5:690
26 Aug.	On-Policy Registration	2:561
27 Aug.	Academy Certs Valid at SHs	5:510
31 Aug.R	Confused Ideas *Word Clearing Series 16R*	4:500 5:464
31 Aug.	The Executive Council Network Disbanded	7:162
31 Aug. Add	Executive Council Network	7:165
31 Aug.	Overload and Hatting	1:293 7:809
1 Sept.	A C/S as a Training Officer, A Program for Flubless Auditing *C/S Series 57*	5:694
2 Sept.	Words and Posts *Word Clearing Series 17*	5:466
4 Sept.RB	FP and Necessities *Finance Series 37R* Rev. 2 Feb. 91	MS2:402
4 Sept.	Alterations *Word Clearing Series 19*	5:468
5 Sept.	HCO Reception	1:133
8 Sept.	Instability	7:810
17 Sept.	Library *Word Clearing Series 24*	5:724
23 Sept.	Finance Banking Officer Purposes *Finance Series 9*	MS2:344
24 Sept.RC	Assignment, Model to Be Used Rev. 26 Feb. 89	1:212
28 Sept.	Selling and Delivering Auditing	2:446 4:954
2 Oct.	HCO Puzzles	1:84
3 Oct.	How Ethics Gets Harsh	1:810
5 Oct.	Propaganda by Redefinition of Words *PR Series 12*	MS3:42
5 Oct.	F/Ning Auditors *C/S Series 64*	5:702
7 Oct.	Tech Certainty and High Stats	5:524
22 Oct.RD	Purchasing and Check-Signing Lines Modified *Finance Series 10RD* Rev. 2 Feb. 91	3:278 MS2:346
24 Oct.	Vitamins	5:636
24 Oct.	Performance	0:259
25 Oct.	Comm Routing, How to Tie Up a Whole Org and Produce Nothing	0:386 1:377
26 Oct.	Tech Downgrades *KSW Series 6*	4:26 5:97
27 Oct.	Vitamin C	5:637
27 Oct.	Celebrity Centre Motto	6:137
29 Oct.	The Executive *Exec Series 1*	MS2:215
29 Oct.	Leadership *Exec Series 2*	MS2:218
31 Oct.	Full Hatting	1:294
1 Nov.RA	Prepayments Used for Books Rev. 19 July 79	2:346 3:207
1 Nov.R	CO and ED Penalty for False Completion Stats Rev. 13 Feb. 91	7:168
8 Nov.RA	Internships, Electronic Attestation Form Rev. 18 Aug. 88	5:854
8 Nov.R	Complement	1:215
10 Nov.R	Tapes, How to Use *Word Clearing Series 25R* *Tape Course Series 6R* Rev. 21 Sept. 74	4:511 6:336
10 Nov.	Organization and Survival	1:86 7:811
12 Nov.R	How to Raise Your Own Statistics and Pay Rev. 6 Mar. 73	0:688
19 Nov.R	Director of Processing Hat Rev. 21 Sept. 74	4:959
21 Nov.	Scientology Courses Examination Policy	5:217
21 Nov.R	Teaching a Tape Course *Tape Course Series 3R* Rev. 23 Oct. 74	4:516
25 Nov.	Inter-Org Exchange of Students and Fees	3:208 5:123
27 Nov.	Money *Exec Series 3*	MS2:219

27 Nov.	Free Services = Free Fall	2:451 3:170 4:220
30 Nov.	Blind Registration	2:564 4:1032 6:387
3 Dec.	Exchange *Exec Series 4*	MS2:222
5 Dec.R	How to Do Surveys *Marketing Series 20* *PR Series 13R* Rev. 10 Sept. 88	MS3:45 MS3:220
7 Dec.	Correction Division Purposes, Ideal Scenes, Products, Statistics	5:58
7 Dec.	Advanced Course Violations	4:809
9 Dec.R	What? No Auditors? Rev. 22 Feb. 75	4:965
11 Dec.	Earned Flag Certificates	5:527
12 Dec.	How to Write Up a Cramming Order *Cramming Series 8* *C/S Series 70*	5:786
16 Dec.	PRO Area Control *PR Series 10-1*	6:624 MS3:40
19 Dec.	D of P Operates by OCAs *C/S Series 71*	4:967 6:301
23 Dec.RB	The No-Interference Area Clarified and Re-enforced *C/S Series 73RB* *Solo C/S Series 10RB* Rev. 2 Aug. 90	4:1111
29 Dec.RB	Flag Representative, Purpose Of Rev. 4 Sept. 90	7:1407
31 Dec.	Flag Rep Key Ingredients	7:1411

1972

7 Jan.RA Creating Survey MS3:49
Questions MS3:224
Marketing Series 21
PR Series 14RA
Rev. 10 Sept. 88

7 Jan. Training and Interning 5:528
Staff Auditors

15 Jan.RC Riches or Poverty, the 2:715
Quality of the Dissem
Division, a Dissem Div
Checklist for Quality
Rev. 10 Sept. 90

16 Jan. Your Dissem Division 2:109

19 Jan. Specialization 7:812

21 Jan. Hatting 1:295

22 Jan. Personnel Programing 5:424

26 Jan. Not-Dones, Half-Dones 7:431
and Backlogs MS2:225
Exec Series 5 MS3:411
AKH Series 29

27 Jan. Temperatures 5:638

31 Jan. The Why Is God MS1:87
Data Series 22

1 Feb. Accounts Policing 3:73

3 Feb. Illegal Processing 4:1116

6 Feb. Executive Intention MS2:228
Exec Series 6

8 Feb.R Targeting of Divisional 0:690
Statistics and Quotas MS2:230
Exec Series 7R
Rev. 21 Oct. 80

16 Feb. The Purpose of the 5:379
Department of Personnel
Enhancement

17 Feb. Proper Format and MS1:89
Correct Action
Data Series 23

18 Feb. The Top Triangle MS2:232
Exec Series 8

18 Feb. Survey = Response 6:225

21 Feb. Qualities at the Top 7:720

24 Feb. Estos MS2:184
Esto Series 41

24 Feb. Word Clearing OCAs 4:233
C/S Series 71A 6:304

24 Feb. Injustice 0:521
1:811

26 Feb.R Cause or Effect, the 5:865
Quality of the Qual
Division, a Qual Div
Checklist for Quality
Rev. 10 Sept. 90

26 Feb.RA Viability or Liability, the 3:411
Quality of the Treasury
Division, a Treasury Div
Checklist for Quality
Rev. 10 Sept. 90

26 Feb.R Sanity or Psychosis, the 4:1253
Quality of the Tech
Division, a Tech
Division Checklist for
Quality
Rev. 10 Sept. 90

26 Feb.R Coordination or 7:1425
Confusion, an Exec Div
Checklist for Quality
Rev. 10 Sept. 90

26 Feb.R	Order or Chaos, the Quality of the HCO Division, an HCO Div Checklist for Quality *Rev. 10 Sept. 90*	1:1057
27 Feb.	Routing *Exec Series 9*	0:389 MS2:234
29 Feb.RA	Handling Policy, Plans, Programs, Projects and Orders Defined *Data Series 24RA Rev. 3 Nov. 90*	MS1:100
29 Feb.	Correct Comm *Exec Series 10*	0:391 MS2:236
3 Mar.	Exercise	0:225 5:639
7 Mar.R	The Establishment Officer *Esto Series 1R Rev. 13 Apr. 72*	MS2:3
7 Mar.	Course Supervisors	4:399
9 Mar.	Hatting the Esto *Esto Series 2*	MS2:14
9 Mar.	Dev-T and Unhattedness *Esto Series 3*	0:439 MS2:16
9 Mar.RA	Income Flows and Pools, Principles of Money Management *Finance Series 11RA Rev. 2 Feb. 91*	MS2:349
10 Mar.	Exec Esto Hatting Duties *Esto Series 4*	MS2:21
13 Mar.	Production and Establishment—Orders and Products *Esto Series 5*	MS2:27
14 Mar.	Sequence of Hatting *Esto Series 6*	MS2:33
14 Mar.	Follow Policy and Lines *Esto Series 7*	MS2:36
16 Mar.	Look Don't Listen *Esto Series 8*	MS2:39
16 Mar.	Stuck In *Esto Series 9*	MS2:44
16 Mar.	What Is a Course High Crime	4:401 5:511
16 Mar.	Finance Directives Cancelled	3:77
18 Mar.	Files *Esto Series 10*	MS2:46
19 Mar.	Learning to Use Data Analysis *Data Series 25*	MS1:105
19 Mar.	C/Sing or Auditing without Folder Study *Auditor Admin Series 5*	4:1117
20 Mar.	Auditors	4:1189
23 Mar.	Full Product Clearing Long Form *Esto Series 11*	MS2:49
27 Mar.	Study	7:814
29 Mar.	Study and Tech Breakthrough	5:787
1 Apr.	Making an Executive *Esto Series 12 Exec Series 11*	MS2:58 MS2:240
3 Apr.	Doing Work *Esto Series 13*	MS2:63
4 Apr.	Org Officers, Product Officers, Estos *Org Series 44 Esto Series 42*	MS1:358 MS2:185
4 Apr.R	Ethics and Study Tech *Word Clearing Series 48 Rev. 21 June 75*	0:44 1:899 4:481
4 Apr.	Ethics *Esto Series 14*	0:526 MS2:68
6 Apr.	Product Correction *Esto Series 15*	MS2:74
6 Apr.R	How to Find a Why on a Person and Handle *Rev. 21 Jan. 91*	5:791
9 Apr.R	Correct Danger Condition Handling *Rev. 1 Dec. 79*	0:605 1:581
12 Apr.	Handling Danger Conditions	0:610 1:587
19 Apr.	"Quickie" Defined *KSW Series 8 C/S Series 77*	4:29
24 Apr.	Hatting the Product Officer of the Division *Esto Series 16*	MS2:82
24 Apr.	Auditor Recovery	4:970 5:425
24 Apr.	Dones	0:260
2 MayRA	Numbering of Mimeo Issues *Rev. 29 June 77*	1:438
3 MayR	Ethics and Executives *Exec Series 12R Rev. 18 Dec. 77*	MS2:245

10 May	Robotism	1:816
12 MayR	PTS Personnel and	MS1:460
	Finance	MS2:251
	Exec Series 13R	MS2:354
	Finance Series 12R	
	Personnel Series 25R	
	Esto Series 18R	
	Rev. 27 Oct. 82	
13 May	Chinese School	MS2:87
	Esto Series 17	
13 May	Handle	7:721
14 May	Morale	0:299
	Exec Series 22	7:815
	Esto Series 50	
28 May	Boom Data, Publications	2:293
	Basic Function	6:257
3 JuneR	Promotion Allocations	MS2:357
	Finance Series 13R	
	Rev. 2 Feb. 91	
11 June	Product Officers	7:816
12 JuneR	Length of Time to	MS1:111
	Evaluate	MS2:90
	Esto Series 18R	
	Data Series 26R	
	Rev. 24 June 88	
13 June	Program Drill	MS2:95
	Esto Series 19	
15 JuneR	PR Area Control, Three	MS3:41
	Grades of PR	
	PR Series 11R	
	Rev. 24 Jan. 83	
16 JuneRA	Auditor's Rights	4:209
	Modified	
	C/S Series 81RA	
	Rev. 7 Dec. 76	
20 June	Registrars and Notes	2:569
		7:1107
24 June	Posting	MS2:186
	Esto Series 43	
25 June	Recovering Students and	4:269
	Pcs	6:550
26 June	Supervisor Tech	MS2:98
	Esto Series 20	
28 June	Files Accuracy	MS2:101
	Esto Series 21	
14 July	Esto Failures	MS1:304
	Esto Series 22	MS2:103
	Exec Series 14	MS2:254
	Org Series 30	

23 JulyRB	The Vital Necessity of	0:216
	Hatting	MS1:308
	Esto Series 23RB	MS2:107
	Exec Series 15RB	MS2:258
	Org Series 31RB	
	Rev. 11 Jan. 91	
25 July	The Form of the Org	MS2:111
	Esto Series 24	
27 July	Form of the Org and	MS2:116
	Schedules	
	Esto Series 25	
28 July	Establishing, Holding	MS1:312
	the Form of the Org	MS2:119
	Esto Series 26	MS2:262
	Exec Series 16	
	Org Series 32	
7 Aug.R	PR and Causation	MS3:72
	PR Series 17R	
	Rev. 9 Aug. 72	
9 Aug.	Seniority of Orders	0:143
		7:722
10 Aug.	Magazines	2:219
11 Aug.R	Foundation Income	3:171
	Rev. 4 Sept 72	7:316
11 Aug.	Foundation and Day	7:313
	Orgs Separate	
11 Aug.	Films and Tapes Not	2:374
	Prohibited	6:341
		7:1215
11 Aug.	Hatting Officer	1:296
13 Aug.RB	Fast Flow Training	4:644
	Rev. 9 Aug. 90	5:218
16 Aug.	Flubless C/Sing	4:1118
	C/S Series 84	
21 Aug.	Effective Hatting	MS2:123
	Esto Series 27	
7 Sept.	Evaluation	7:818
8 Sept.	Efficiency and Flaps	0:261
9 Sept.	LRH Income	7:1217
13 Oct.R	Freeloaders	1:255
	Rev. 10 Jan. 91	
15 Nov.	Students Who Succeed	4:404
		5:795
21 Nov.	How to Handle Black	MS3:77
	Propaganda	
	PR Series 18	

1973

20 Jan.RE	The Red Tag Line	4:254
	C/S Series 86RE	5:284
	Rev. 19 Apr. 90	
7 Feb.	Mimeo Supply	1:440
	Conservation	
7 Feb.	Mimeo File Folders	1:442
	and Files	
7 Feb.R	Mimeo Files	1:448
	Rev. 22 Mar. 73	
5 Apr.	Axiom 28 Amended	1:319
12 MayRC	Post Protection, LRH	7:1258
	Communicators	
	LRH Comm N/W Series 15	
	Rev. 7 May 84	
25 May	Supplementary	MS1:116
	Evaluations	
	Data Series 27	
2 Aug.	Pep	5:640
7 Aug.R	Flag Representative,	7:1412
	Purpose, Duties and	
	Statistic	
	Rev. 2 Jan. 91	
15 Aug.R	Flag Representative,	7:1416
	Orders To	
	Rev. 2 Jan. 91	
24 Aug.R	Communication,	1:902
	Stopping Of	7:723
	Rev. 2 Jan. 91	
27 Aug.	Tech and LRH Comms	5:798
	LRH Comm N/W	7:1253
	Series 13	
28 Aug.RA	The Mission of the LRH	7:1255
	Comm Network	
	LRH Comm N/W Series 14	
	Rev. 7 May 84	
1 Sept.	Admin Know-How	7:434
	No. 30	MS3:414
	AKH Series 30	
7 Sept.RA	FSM Commissions,	3:261
	Payment of, Cancelled	
11 Sept.R	Codes and Coding,	1:468
	Correct Practice Policy	
	Rev. 21 Sept. 81	
19 Sept.R	Checking Evals	MS1:120
	Data Series 28R	
	Rev. 22 June 75	
19 Sept.-1	Checking Evaluations	MS1:122
	Addition	
	Data Series 28R-1	
19 Sept.-2	Multiple Sit Eval	MS1:124
	Format	
	Data Series 28R-2	
20 Sept.R	Concerning	7:292
	Administration	
	Rev. 12 Feb. 91	
24 Sept.RA	All Auditors—Ministers,	4:1190
	Ministerial Board of	7:1220
	Review	
	Rev. 25 Jan. 91	
30 Sept.	Outpoints, More	MS1:126
	Data Series 29	
30 Sept.	Situation Finding	MS1:128
	Data Series 30	
15 Oct.	Administrative Skill	7:438
	AKH Series 31	MS3:418
19 Oct.	Mistakes and PTSness	1:1035
21 Oct.RA	Case Supervisor Statistic	4:1121
	Rev. 9 Nov. 83	5:703

26 Oct.	Staff Corrective Actions Requiring Auditing Actions	1:821
28 Oct.	Celebrity Centre Purpose	6:138
4 Nov.	Publishing Policy, Books and Magazines	2:138
5 Nov.	Source Acknowledgment	7:1222
11 Nov.	Preclear Declare? Procedure	5:287
16 Nov.	Study Tech and Post *Word Clearing Series 49*	0:47 5:470
19 Nov.RA	Organization Executive Course Checksheets *Rev. 21 Jan. 91*	5:427

21 Nov.	LRH Comm Drills	7:1223
22 Nov.	Esto Series 30 *Esto Series 30*	MS2:126
25 Nov.	Final Targets *Data Series 31*	MS1:131
25 Nov.-1	Final Target Attachment *Data Series 31 Addition*	MS1:134
5 Dec.R	Q and A Checksheet, Checksheet of the Hubbard Causative Leadership Course *AKH Series 32R Rev. 12 Dec. 74*	7:440 MS3:420
14 Dec.	Target Troubles *Data Series 32*	MS1:135

1974

9 Feb.R	Condition Below Treason, Confusion Formula and Expanded Confusion Formula Rev. 17 Feb. 80	0:568 1:588	
26 Feb.	The Untrained PR *PR Series 20*	MS3:92	
27 Feb.	Wasted Planning *PR Series 21*	MS3:93	
17 Mar.R	Press Conferences, Preparation For *PR Series 22R* Rev. 16 Sept. 88	MS3:94	
18 Mar.	The Press Book *PR Series 23*	MS3:96	
5 May	Orders	0:144	
9 May	Prod–Org, Esto and Older Systems Reconciled	7:820	
31 May	Unhandled Drugs and Ethics	1:903 4:972 5:429	
11 June	The "Economy"	0:300 3:78	
22 June	Tech	0:262	
3 July RB	Evaluation, Criticism Of *Data Series 33RB* Rev. 29 Jan. 79	MS1:138	
5 July	Registration Program No. 2	2:570 6:392	
6 July	Additional Reges	2:452	
13 July	Production Bugs *Org Series 33*	MS1:316	
13 July	Working Installations *Org Series 34*	MS1:317	
18 July	Situation Correction *Data Series 34*	MS1:140	
19 July	Eval Correction *Data Series 35*	MS1:142	
25 July	Books Make Booms	2:296 6:260	
11 Aug.	Envisioning the Ideal Scene *Data Series 36*	MS1:144	
12 Aug.	Whys Open the Door *Data Series 37*	MS1:146	
13 Aug.RA	OEC "Policy" Clarified Rev. 7 Feb. 91	2:347	
15 Aug.	Solo and Advance Course Checkouts	4:811	
16 Aug.RA	Estates Restored to Dept. 21 Rev. 13 Feb. 91	7:1398	
22 Aug.	Registration	2:576	
27 Aug.RA	Financial Planning Checklist for the Promotional Actions of an Organization Rev. 5 May 85	3:79 7:952	
27 Aug.	Formulas	0:581 1:590	
30 Aug.R	Qual Stat Change, A New One Rev. 31 Dec. 75	5:77	

31 Aug.RA Keeper of Tech, Office 7:1273
of LRH
LRH Comm N/W Series 23
Rev. 27 July 86

2 Sept.RB Recruiting and Hiring 1:169
Rev. 23 Mar. 89

5 Sept. Book Sales to 2:348
Individuals from Pubs

25 Sept. Reduction of Refunds 4:1124
C/Ses and Overload 5:706

26 Sept. Handling Flubbed Pcs 5:655

26 Sept.RA New Case Supervisor 4:1126
Postings 5:708
Rev. 1 Mar. 77

3 Oct. Pluspoint List MS1:148
Data Series 38

19 Oct. The Dramatization of 5:800
Withholds on Vital
Information Lines

27 Oct. Safe Ground MS3:99
PR Series 25

28 Oct. Who-Where Finding MS1:150
Data Series 39

9 Nov.R Refunds and Repayments 3:262
Rev. 2 Oct. 80 5:711
7:1108

11 Nov. Staff Pay 3:361

13 Nov. HCO May Do 1:638
Confessional Lists 4:973

14 Nov. Phone Costs, or How to 3:211
Get Wiped Out

15 Nov. Phone Tips 1:339
2:578
3:213
4:273

15 Nov. CFs, ARC Breaks In 2:677
6:554

16 Nov.RD Transfers and Removals 1:257
and Permanent Postings
Forbidden Locally
Rev. 30 June 89

19 Nov.R Finance Stress in an Org 3:85
Rev. 31 Jan. 91 7:724

28 Nov. Building HCO 1:87

30 Nov. Staff Pay 3:363

29 Dec. Qualifications, Division 5:68
Five Functions

1975

8 Jan.	Compliance, How to Get One	7:824
17 Jan.	How You Are Limiting the Size and Income of Your Org	4:407 6:398
23 Jan.	The Purpose of Class VIII	4:828
12 Mar.	The Ideal Org *Data Series 40*	MS1:152
12 Mar.	Grade Subsidy for Staff Forbidden in Other Orgs	0:174 3:216 5:430
15 Mar.	How You Can Increase the Size and Income of Your Org	4:411 6:402
15 Mar.R	Book Outlets of an Org *Rev. 22 May 75*	2:350 6:261
26 Mar.	Cause	0:263
29 Mar.RA	Antibiotics, Administering Of *Rev. 24 Mar. 85*	5:642
30 Mar.	PR and Information *PR Series 26*	MS3:101
9 June	The Enemy Line *PR Series 27*	MS3:102
23 June	Ad Council Income Planning	7:958
23 Oct.	Technical Queries *Word Clearing Series 56*	4:502 5:471
26 Oct.	"Failed" Cases *C/S Series 95*	5:657
26 Oct.	Gross Income/Corrected Gross Income Ratio, Failed Cases and Failed Students	2:111 3:87 4:153 5:659 6:555 7:861
8 Nov.	Non-Existence Formula Expanded	0:578 1:591

1976

1 Jan.	FSMs FOLOs Commissions *FSM Series 5*	6:662
6 Jan.RC	Flag External Expenses *Finance Series 14RC* Rev. 2 Feb. 91	MS2:360
6 Jan.RC	Flag External Expenses Addition *Finance Series 14RC-1R* Rev. 2 Feb. 91	MS2:363
21 May R	HCO, the Elite Corps Rev. 14 May 89	1:88
22 May	Staff Section Officer Hat	5:381
23 May R	Celebrities Rev. 10 Jan. 91	6:139
7 Aug.	Product–Org Officer System, Name Your Product *AKH Series 33* *Esto Series 31*	3:307 7:443 MS2:127 MS3:423
7 Aug.	Product–Org Officer System, Want Your Product *AKH Series 34* *Esto Series 32*	3:309 7:445 MS2:129 MS3:425
7 Aug.	Product–Org Officer System, to Get You Have to Know How to Organize *AKH Series 35* *Esto Series 33*	7:446 MS2:130 MS3:426
20 Sept.	The Stat Push *Org Series 35* *Exec Series 17*	0:692 MS1:318 MS2:266
20 Sept.	Stat Push Clarified *Org Series 35-1* *Exec Series 17-1* Add. of 17 Apr. 87	0:696 MS1:322 MS2:270
20 Oct.RA	PTS Data Rev. 25 Aug. 87	1:1036 5:431
24 Oct.RF	Ex-Staff Free Service Rev. 2 Aug. 90	0:175 3:173 4:221 5:432 6:769
24 Oct.RA	Supervisors Can Become Professors Rev. 9 Aug. 90	4:416 5:434
24 Oct.R	Senior Case Supervisor Requirements Rev. 20 Jan. 91	4:416
25 Oct.	Provisional Certificate Expiry	5:372
26 Oct.	Auditing Reports, Falsifying Of	4:1192 5:288
28 Oct.	Auditing Folders, Omissions in Completeness	1:640 4:1194 5:802
4 Nov.RB	Statistic Change, Gross Divisional Statistics, HCOs and Quals, OIC Cable Change Rev. 12 Feb. 89	1:89 5:81
4 Nov.	HCO Stat Penalty Add. 24 Feb. 77	1:94
10 Nov.	Staff Courses Mandatory in Orgs	5:514

11 Nov.RB	Statistic Change, HCOs and Qual, Definitions Rev. 20 Nov. 84	1:95 5:86
12 Nov.RC	Statistic Change, Tech Sec Stat Rev. 25 Nov. 85	4:157
13 Nov.RA	Professional Rates Rev. 9 Nov. 89	2:454 3:175 4:223
14 Nov.	Manning Up an Org *Exec Series 18* *AKH Series 36* *Org Series 36* *Personnel Series 28*	7:448 MS1:324 MS1:463 MS2:272 MS3:428
16 Nov.	Production Quotas *Exec Series 19* *Org Series 37*	MS1:326 MS2:274
27 Nov.R	Restoration of Local Control of Personnel Assignments and Comm Evs Rev. 30 June 89	1:260
30 Nov.	Only SSO Can TIP	5:435
6 Dec.RB	Illegal Pcs, Acceptance Of, High Crime PL Rev. 8 Apr. 88	1:904 2:581 4:1037 5:761 6:407
7 Dec.	Leaving and Leaves	0:177 1:906

1977

1 Jan.RA Marketing Hat MS3:175
  Marketing Series 3
  Rev. 29 Aug. 79

10 Jan. Ethics and Word 4:504
  Clearing 5:473
  Word Clearing Series 50

5 Feb. Jokers and Degraders 1:822

15 Mar.RA Evaluation: The MS1:154
  Situation
  Data Series 41RA
  Rev. 5 Nov. 90

17 Mar.RA Date Coincidence MS1:163
  Data Series 42RA
  Rev. 2 Nov. 90

18 Mar.RA Evaluation and MS1:167
  Programs
  Data Series 43RA
  Rev. 6 Nov. 90

18 Mar. Evaluation Success MS1:173
  Data Series 43-1R
  Rev. 14 June 77

20 Mar.R Super Evaluation MS1:175
  Data Series 44R
  Rev. 15 June 77

10 Apr. Dissemination Pieces, 2:274
  Stable Datum,
  Appearance, Layout
  and Design

14 June RA All Class IV Orgs, OIC 1:670
  Cable Change
  Rev. 28 June 78

14 June RA All Sea Org Orgs, OIC 1:674
  Cable Change
  Rev. 28 June 78

1978

6 Feb.RD The Purification 4:1203
Rundown Replaces the
Sweat Program
Purif RD Series 1R
Rev. 27 Mar. 90

23 Feb.R Board of Review 1:960
LRH Comm N/W Series 19 7:1265
Rev. 7 May 84

26 Feb. Internships Versus 4:417
Courses 5:856

27 Mar. Ethics Penalty for Word 4:505
Clearers 5:474
Word Clearing Series 58

25 June Come-on Dissemination MS3:185
Marketing Series 6

20 July Held From Above, MS1:330
Double-Hatting
Org Series 38

24 July Subproducts, How to 7:826
Compile a Subproduct
List

13 Sept. An Old Poem 0:532

15 Sept. Confidentiality of 4:812
Upper-Level Rundowns

27 Sept. Examining Resources MS1:177
Data Series 45

28 Sept. The End of Endless 4:419
Training

20 Oct. Two-Bit FP MS2:364
Finance Series 17

22 Oct. Mistakes MS2:187
Esto Series 44

30 Oct.R Courses—Their Ideal 4:424
Scene 5:516
Rev. 3 Aug. 83

8 Nov.RB Senior HCOs, Area and 1:98
Continental 7:1224
Rev. 5 Nov. 79

10 Nov. "Power to Forgive" 5:373
Certificate

28 Nov. Auditors Who Miss 4:1196
Withholds, Penalty 5:615

29 Nov. How You Handle 7:450
Demands for Personnel MS1:465
Personnel Series 29 MS3:430
AKH Series 37

6 Dec. Space Planning 7:1336

10 Dec.RA Gross Book Sales 2:297
Definition
Rev. 4 Feb. 91

28 Dec. Use of *Big League Sales* 2:583
6:409

31 Dec.RA Outline of PTS Handling 5:437
Rev. 26 July 86

1979

4 Jan.	The Ideal Ideal Scene *Data Series 46*	MS1:178
6 Jan.	Financial Planning Regarding Property Renovations and Construction	3:281 7:961
13 Jan.	Orders, Illegal and Cross	0:145
17 Jan.	A New Type of Crime	1:908
19 Jan.RB	Scholarships, No Discounts Rev. 30 May 89	2:456 6:410
20 Jan.	Income Cutatives and Salary Sum	0:301 3:91
23 Jan.	Unevaluated Orders	7:726
28 Jan.	C/S Qualifications	4:1129 5:715
29 Jan.	Prices, Upper Org	2:457 3:177
30 Jan.	Positioning, Philosophic Theory *PR Series 30* *Marketing Series 5*	MS3:120 MS3:181
3 Feb.R	Change the Civilization Eval Rev. 19 Dec. 90	4:427
7 Feb.R	The Basics of Marketing *Marketing Series 7* Rev. 3 Sept. 79	MS3:187
9 Feb.R	How to Defeat Verbal Tech Checklist *KSW Series 23R* Rev. 23 Aug. 84	0:23 4:31 5:804
15 Feb.	Verbal Tech: Penalties *KSW Series 24*	0:24 4:32
25 Feb.R	HCO Staff Qualification Requirements Rev. 14 May 89	1:101
5 Mar.RB	Dianetic Clear False Declares Rev. 2 Dec. 85	5:291
21 Mar.R	Sliding Scale of Pricing Rev. 6 Dec. 89	2:458 3:178
25 Mar.	A New Hope for Justice	1:962
26 Mar.RB	Misunderstood Words and Cycles of Action *Esto Series 35RB* Rev. 2 Sept. 79	MS2:132
5 Apr.RB	New FSM Account Rev. 14 Feb. 91	3:264 6:667
5 Apr.	FSM Penalty for Refunds, Repayments and Bounced Checks	6:664
10 Apr.RA	Flag Rep Statistics Rev. 12 Feb. 91	7:1419
25 Apr.	Estates Production Statistics	7:1402
1 May RB	Clear Certainty Rundown: Administration *CCRD Series 3R* Rev. 18 Dec. 88	4:975
27 May	Book Sales Commission	2:354 6:265
7 June R	Data Series PLs, Use of *Data Series 47* Rev. 14 June 79	MS1:181
24 June	Crime Additions	1:910
10 July R	Publications Organizations are Sales Organizations Rev. 26 Nov. 79	2:355

16 July	Hubbard Key to Life Course High Crime	1:911 4:647
16 July	Delivering the Hubbard Key to Life Course, the Chicken and Egg Theory	1:912 4:648
21 July	Magazine Planning	2:221
25 July	Magazine Motifs	2:223
7 Aug.	False Data Stripping *Esto Series 36*	MS2:134
9 Aug.R	Service Product Officer *Org Series 39* *Esto Series 39* Rev. 19 Nov. 79	MS1:332 MS2:166
9 Aug.	Call-in: The Key to Delivery and Future Income	2:641 3:217 4:276 7:865
9 Aug.	Service Call-in Committee	7:873
19 Aug.RA	High-Crime Checkouts and Word Clearing *Word Clearing Series 47* Rev. 27 Aug. 84	5:805
20 Aug.	Dianetics and Scientology Are New *Marketing Series 1* *PR Series 34*	0:362 MS3:136 MS3:173
21 Aug.	Twinning	4:431
23 Aug.R	Debug Tech *Esto Series 37R* Rev. 23 Aug. 84	MS2:144
23 Aug.R	Debug Tech Checklist *Esto Series 38R* Rev. 24 June 88	MS2:153
23 Aug.	Hubbard Key to Life Course Routing Forms	4:650
29 Aug.R	Org Board for the Department of the Chaplain Rev. 14 Mar. 80	6:530
29 Aug.R	The Department of the Chaplain Rev. 14 Mar. 80	6:535
1 Sept.	Marketing, Promotion and Dissemination, Defined *Marketing Series 2*	MS3:174
2 Sept.	Surveys Are the Key to Stats *Marketing Series 4*	MS3:177
4 Sept.	More on Marketing Basics *Marketing Series 8*	MS3:189
5 Sept.	The Assembly Line for Produced Promo *Marketing Series 9*	MS3:192
6 Sept.	The Relationship Between Design and Rough Layout *Marketing Series 10*	MS3:196
19 Sept.	Promotion *Marketing Series 11*	MS3:201
25 Sept.RB	Method One Word Clearing *Word Clearing Series 34* Rev. 1 July 85	4:652 5:475
26 Sept.	Copywriting *Marketing Series 12*	MS3:204
26 Sept.	FSM I/C Postings	6:670
27 Sept.	Ads and Copywriting *Marketing Series 13*	MS3:208
28 Sept.RA	Special Income *Finance Series 24RA* Rev. 2 Feb. 91	MS2:365
18 Oct.R	Viewpoint *Marketing Series 14R* Rev. 14 Sept. 88	MS3:211
29 Oct.	SSO Responsibility for Standard Staff Courses	5:443
9 Nov.R	How to Correctly Determine a Stat Trend Rev. 27 Aug. 82	7:531
13 Nov.R	FSM Section, Department 18 Statistics Rev. 6 Feb. 80	6:671
13 Nov.R	Use of Airmail and Air Freight Rev. 7 July 83	2:363
1 Dec.	Survey Buttons Are Not the Message *Marketing Series 15*	MS3:215
11 Dec.	Department 17 Course Checksheets	6:485
11 Dec.	Department 17 Course Checksheets, Addition	6:489
12 Dec.R	An Open Letter to All FSMs *FSM Series 7* Rev. 8 Nov. 84	6:673
13 Dec.R	Magazines, Dating Forbidden Rev. 16 Jan. 80	2:224

15 Dec.	Surveying for Department 17 Services	6:490	26 Dec.	Execution of Evaluations *Data Series 48*	MS1:182
18 Dec.	Enrollment on the Hubbard Key to Life Course	4:655	30 Dec.R	Technical Training Corps Rev. 13 Feb. 80	5:533
23 Dec.RB	Tech/Admin Ratio Rev. 25 Mar. 89	1:216	30 Dec.	How to Build a Sauna *Purif RD Series 2*	4:1224

1980

3 Jan.RA   Purification Rundown   4:1235
and Atomic War
Purif RD Series 3
Rev. 8 Aug. 83

8 Jan.   Christmas Bonuses for   3:365
Staff

9 Jan.   Departmental Mini   MS2:278
Programs: The Key to
Achievement
Exec Series 20

13 Jan.   Division 2/Division 6   2:584
Registrar Publics   6:411

25 Jan.   Executive Responsibility   4:33
for Technical Excellence
KSW Series 11

27 Jan.   Academies, Internships   4:657
and Grade Auditing   5:858

27 Jan.   Rudiments (ARC Break)   6:559
Program

11 Feb.R   Illegal Pcs, Acceptance   2:585
of, Addition Regarding   4:1039
Purification Rundown   5:763
Purif RD Series 12   6:412
Rev. 18 Oct. 86

11 Feb.   Org "Move" Mags   2:225

11 Feb.   Org Magazines: Policy   2:228
and Format

13 Feb.   Coordination   7:451
Committees and   MS3:431
Management
Committees, Differences
in Purpose and Function
AKH Series 40

14 Feb.   Order Versus Disorder   0:305
Org Series 40   MS1:342
Esto Series 40   MS2:176

28 Feb.   Production and One's   0:313
Standard of Living   MS1:350
Exec Series 21   MS2:284
Org Series 41   MS2:367
Finance Series 25

18 Apr.   The Auditor Magazine: 2:249
Policy and Format

22 May R   Recruitment   1:171
Breakthrough
Rev. 9 Feb. 89

28 May RA   Co-audit Defined   4:687
Co-audit Series 1RA
Rev. 20 Apr. 90

29 May RA   Co-audits: How to Run   4:691
Them
Co-audit Series 2RA
Rev. 20 Apr. 90

30 May RA   Supervising Co-audit   4:702
TRs
Co-audit Series 3RA
Rev. 21 Apr. 90

31 May RA   Staff Co-audits   4:704
Co-audit Series 4RA
Rev. 21 Apr. 90

9 July R   Ethics, Justice and the   0:451
Dynamics   1:486
Rev. 25 Mar. 89

12 July R   The Basics of Ethics   0:447
Rev. 5 Nov. 82   1:496

29 July   Criminals and Psychiatry   7:1144

15 Oct.R   Celebrity Centre   2:238
Magazine, Celebrity
Rev. 4 Feb. 91

23 Oct.R   Chart of Abilities   4:189
           Gained for Lower Levels   5:292
           and Expanded Lower
           Grades
             Rev. 16 Nov. 87

1981

5 Jan.RA	Extension Courses Rev. 13 Feb. 91	6:510
8 Jan.R	Advanced Course Regulations and Security Rev. 3 Oct. 88	4:813
22 Jan.	Orders of the Day	7:727
1 Apr.R	Interviews Rev. 17 Jan. 91	1:824 2:586 4:979 5:764 6:413 7:730
5 Apr.RA	Clear Certificates *CCRD Series 16R* Rev. 18 Dec. 88	5:374
21 July R	What Is a Checksheet Rev. 25 July 87	4:441
23 July R	The Use of Demonstration *Study Series 12* Rev. 10 Jan. 84	4:443
4 Aug.R	Pink Sheets Rev. 30 Aug. 83	4:446
9 Sept.	How to "Sell" Scientology to Your Friends *FSM Series 8*	6:675
15 Sept.	The Criminal Mind	1:830 7:1147

6 Oct.	Tech Films and Verbal Tech	4:519 5:808
20 Oct.R	PTS Type A Handling Rev. 10 Sept. 83	1:1037
8 Nov.RA	Who May See Technical Training Films Rev. 20 Nov. 83	4:521 5:810
11 Nov.R	Policies on Film Usage Rev. 30 Jan. 91	4:526 5:815 6:343
12 Nov.RD	Grade Chart Streamlined for Lower Grades Rev. 20 Apr. 90	2:460 4:193 6:419
5 Dec.R	Setting up and Using a Reel-to-Reel Tape Player *Tape Course Series 7R* Rev. 7 Oct. 84	4:531
12 Dec.	The Theory of the New Grade Chart	2:467 4:200
14 Dec.	The State of Clear	2:469 4:202
17 Dec.	Post Purpose Clearing Revived	5:478
26 Dec.	Post Purpose Clearing for Management Teams and Executives	5:480
Holidays 81/82	Ron's Journal 33	6:494

1982

17 Jan.	What Is an Executive? *Exec Series 22*	MS2:288
1 Feb.	Stature	1:834
5 Feb.	Books and Marketing *PR Series 44* *Marketing Series 16*	MS3:164 MS3:217
5 Feb.	Out-Ethics Symptoms	1:835 7:736
18 Feb.	Changing Workable Finance Systems *Finance Series 27*	3:95 MS2:371
28 Feb.R	HCO Book Account Cash-Bills Rev. 4 Feb. 91	2:315
28 Feb.	News	7:1049
3 Mar.	The Qual Library	5:725
6 Mar.R	Confessional Tech Policies Rev. 10 Dec. 88	1:642 4:985 5:448
9 Mar.RB	Eligibility for OT Levels Rev. 6 Jan. 85	4:816
10 Mar.	Confessionals—Ethics Reports Required	1:645 4:1197
11 Mar.	Proportionate Marketing *Finance Series 30* *Marketing Series 17*	MS2:379 MS3:218
13 Mar.	The Future of Scientology	7:1151
14 Mar.	Financial Irregularities	3:97
17 Mar.	FBO FP Adjudication *Finance Series 28*	MS2:373
19 Mar.	Executive Success *Exec Series 23* *Finance Series 31* *Marketing Series 19*	MS2:291 MS2:380 MS3:219
23 Mar.R	A Refined Definition of PR *PR Series 28RA* Rev. 16 Sept. 88	MS3:104
29 Mar.	Personnel Policy *Personnel Series 30*	MS1:466
31 Mar.R	Basic Study Missed Withhold *Study Series 11R* *Word Clearing Series 68R* Rev. 29 Dec. 88	1:837
1 Apr.	The Safe Point *PR Series 19R*	MS3:89
7 Apr.	Out-Ethics Indicators *LRH Comm N/W Series 16*	0:533 7:1259
15 Apr.	The Counting of Gross Income *Finance Series 29*	MS2:374
26 Apr.	The Criminal Mind and the Psychs	7:1155
28 Apr.	The Rights of the Field Auditor	6:733
29 Apr.	Field Auditor Fees	6:734
4 May	Books Straight Talk	2:298 6:266
6 May	The Cause of Crime	7:1157
9 May	Books Are Assets *Finance Series 32*	MS2:381
9 May	Ron's Journal 35, From Clear to Eternity	4:988

10 May	Bookstore Officer Hat	2:300
10 May R	The Ridge on the Bridge Rev. 21 Oct. 82	6:441
25 May	Kha-Khan	1:838
1 July	Management Coordination *AKH Series 41*	7:454 MS3:434
16 July R	Fully Hatted Org Staff Members, HCO Gross Divisional Statistic Rev. 30 May 89	1:105
19 July	Failed PR *PR Series 45*	MS3:165
22 July	Knowledge Reports	0:555 1:713
27 July RA	Deputy FBOs for Marketing of Org Resources for Exchange (D/FBO for MORE) *Finance Series 33RA* Rev. 2 Feb. 91	MS2:384
18 Aug.R	Targets and Production *Target Series 8* *Computer Series 3* *AKH Series 42R* Rev. 28 Feb. 84	0:704 7:456 MS2:442 MS2:456 MS3:436
18 Aug.	Computers, Danger of Relying On *Computer Series 7*	MS2:466
20 Aug.	Organizational Basics	0:89 7:293
22 Aug.	Battle Plans *Target Series 9* *AKH Series 43*	0:706 7:458 MS2:444 MS3:438
27 Aug.	Vital Data: Power and Affluence Conditions	0:642 1:594 7:553
2 Sept.	And That Is Banking *Finance Series 34*	MS2:389
3 Sept.	Deputy FBO for Marketing of Org Resources for Exchange (D/FBO for MORE), Purpose *Finance Series 35*	MS2:395
10 Sept.	Exchange, Org Income and Staff Pay *Finance Series 36*	0:317 MS2:400
12 Sept.	PR Functions *PR Series 46*	MS3:167
28 Sept.	The Basics of Statistics and Management	0:679 7:562
29 Sept.	Misrepresentation of Dianetics and Scientology *KSW Series 30*	7:1110
12 Oct.	Corrupt Activities	0:534 7:1036
13 Oct.	Ethics and the C/S *C/S Series 116*	1:839 4:1130 5:716
14 Oct.	Why Things Are Evaluated *Data Series 49*	MS1:183
27 Oct.RA	Cash-Bills Defined *Finance Series 38RA* Rev. 23 Sept. 89	MS2:404
31 Oct.	Financial Planning, Responsibility For *Finance Series 39*	MS2:406
1 Nov.	"Boom Formula" Cancelled	6:103
2 Nov.	Conditions Handlings	0:664 1:603
16 Nov.	Div 6A Stat Renamed and Redefined: Bodies in the Shop	6:226
30 Nov.	The Deputy CO or Deputy ED for Delivery and Exchange	7:877
18 Dec.	Ethics Conditions: Hang-up at Doubt	0:576 1:605
19 Dec.	"Doing a Quicksilver" Forbidden *Org Series 45* *Personnel Series 31*	0:264 MS1:359 MS1:467
19 Dec.R	Repairing Past Ethics Conditions Rev. 2 June 90	0:668 1:607
22 Dec.RB	Service Routes for New Public Rev. 15 Aug. 90	6:115
24 Dec.R	Service Routes into SO Orgs Rev. 19 Feb. 91	6:121
27 Dec.	Training and OT	2:471 4:820
29 Dec.RA	The Tools of Management *Esto Series 45RA* *Org Series 46RA* *AKH Series 44RA* *Exec Series 24RA* Rev. 21 Jan. 91	7:461 MS1:363 MS2:188 MS2:292 MS3:441
29 Dec.R	Service Routes into the FSO Rev. 21 Feb. 91	6:127

1983

5 Jan.	Strategic Planning	7:469
	AKH Series 46	MS3:449
9 Jan.R	Viability, the Make-Break Point of an Org	MS2:416
	Finance Series 41R Rev. 2 Feb. 91	
9 Jan.	Checklist for a Strategic Plan	7:475 MS3:455
	AKH Series 47	
13 Jan.	The Business of Orgs	0:90 7:880
23 Jan.	Auditor Training Prerequisite	4:659 5:451
30 Jan.	Your Post and Life	0:268
	Esto Series 46 *KSW Series 28*	MS2:193
31 Jan.	The Reason for Orgs	0:91 4:159
7 Apr.	Goodwill	0:332
	Exec Series 25	6:625
		MS2:297
	PR Series 47	MS3:168
3 May	Who or What Is a "C/S"?	4:1134
	C/S Series 117	
13 June R	Addition to HCO Gross Divisional Statistic, Fully Hatted Org Staff Members	1:106
	Rev. 17 Jan. 91	

31 July R	Basic Management Tools	7:478
	Esto Series 47R	MS1:368
	Org Series 47R	MS2:194
	Exec Series 26R	MS2:299
	AKH Series 48R	MS3:458
	Rev. 21 Jan. 91	
31 July	Management Tools Breakthrough	7:483 MS1:373
	Esto Series 48	MS2:199
	Org Series 48	MS2:304
	Exec Series 27	MS3:463
	AKH Series 49	
4 Aug.R	Financial Planning Program No. 1	MS2:419
	Finance Series 42R Rev. 2 Feb. 91	
6 Aug.R	What a Professional TR Course Must Consist Of	4:661
	Rev. 24 Dec. 89	
28 Aug.	Spot Checks	4:451
10 Sept.	PTSness and Disconnection	1:1041
15 Sept.	LRH Comm and PRO	7:1260
	LRH Comm N/W Series 17	
2 Oct.	Solo Course Part One, Prerequisites	4:663
10 Nov.	TR and EM Films, Showing Of	4:537 5:820 6:347

1984

16 Feb.	What Is a Computer?	MS2:453
	Computer Series 1	
28 Feb.	Pretended PTS	1:1045
	C/S Series 118	4:1138
29 Feb.	Computer Ethics Points	MS2:464
	Computer Series 6	
2 Mar.R	O/W Write-ups	0:535
	Rev. 24 Apr. 90	1:843
20 Mar.	Targets, More About	MS2:441
	Target Series 7	
27 Mar.	Three Classes of People	MS2:202
	Esto Series 49	
28 Mar.	The Stages of Analysis	MS1:185
	Data Series 50	
28 Mar.	Executive Posting Qualifications	MS1:471
		MS2:307
	Personnel Series 32	
	Exec Series 28	

2 Apr.	"Upside Down" Graphs	1:678
6 May	ARC Break Program, Additional Data	6:563
		7:881
7 May	The LRH Comm Network and Its Purpose	7:1229
	LRH Comm N/W Series 1	
6 June R	The "Lost Tech" of Handling Overts and Evil Purposes	1:914
		4:992
		5:453
	FPRD Series 2R	
	Rev. 12 Jan. 90	
2 July	Hatting and the Environment	0:207
		MS2:203
	Esto Series 50	MS2:310
	Exec Series 29	
8 Aug.	Routing Forms, How to Write One	1:135
2 Oct.R	Scientology Magistrate	1:694
	Rev. 18 Jan. 91	5:456

1985

7 Jan.	HCO Confessionals	1:648
		4:995
22 Mar.	Full Danger Condition Handling	0:611
		MS2:205
	Esto Series 51	
24 Mar.	Responsibility, Control and Danger Conditions	0:619
		1:611
		7:738
1 May	Honesty and Case Gain	1:848
	C/S Series 120	
2 May	Responsibility, Definition Of	0:269
21 May	Two Types of PTSes	1:1048
	C/S Series 121	
	FPRD Series 11	

18 June	Product Orientation	MS1:376
	Org Series 49	MS2:312
	Exec Series 30	
3 Aug.	Completing Conditions Formulas	0:666
		1:613
23 Nov.	INCOMM	MS2:458
	Computer Series 4	
2 Dec.R	Clear Certainty Rundown, New Service	4:998
	C/S Series 112RA	
	Rev. 18 Dec. 88	
5 Dec.R	Handling of Past-Life Auditing	4:257
	C/S Series 123R	
	Rev. 18 Dec. 88	

1986

10 July	Keeping Admin Working	0:70
	AKH Series 50	7:486
		MS3:466
10 July	Admin Degrades	0:73
	AKH Series 51	5:25
		7:489
		MS3:469

10 July	Admin High Crime	0:75
	AKH Series 52	1:917
	Computer Series 5	5:822
		7:491
		MS2:461
		MS3:471

1987

1988

10 Sept.	Tabulating Survey Responses	MS3:243
	Marketing Series 22	
11 Sept.	Ethnic Surveys	MS3:68
	PR Series 15	MS3:247
	Marketing Series 23	
12 Sept.	Positioning in PR	MS3:105
	PR Series 29	
13 Sept.	The Positioning Era	MS3:249
	Marketing Series 24	
14 Sept.	Positioning Surveys	MS3:280
	Marketing Series 25	
15 Sept.	Naming Services and Products	MS3:284
	Marketing Series 26	
16 Sept.	Instant Impression	MS3:287
	Marketing Series 27	
17 Sept.	Survey Network	MS3:290
	Marketing Series 28	
18 Sept.	PR Texts	MS3:70
	PR Series 16	

19 Sept.	Clipping Books	MS3:98
	PR Series 24	
20 Sept.	Documentation and the Dead Agent Caper	MS3:131
	PR Series 32	
21 Sept.	Press Agentry	MS3:132
	PR Series 33	
22 Sept.	Creating Overwhelming Popularity	MS3:157
	PR Series 41	
23 Sept.	Names and the Local Environment	MS3:160
	PR Series 42	
24 Sept.	PR and Purpose	MS3:161
	PR Series 43	
6 Oct.	Success Through Communication	6:497
18 Dec.	The Sunshine Rundown: Administration	2:472
		4:1002
19 Dec.R	Scientology Marriage Counseling	6:537
	Rev. 30 Jan. 90	

1989

21 Mar.   PTS People and Leaves   1:1050

1990

27 Mar.	The Purification Rundown: A Long-Range Detoxification Program	4:1237
	Purif RD Series 14	
4 Apr.	Course Schedules	4:453
2 Aug.	Auditing Discounts	2:474
3 Aug.	Auditing and C/Sing Below One's Training Level	4:664 / 5:860
29 Aug.	Using Orders or Policy to Create Problems	0:476 / 1:920
30 Aug.	Weekly Staff Meetings	0:179 / 7:739
10 Sept.	The Quality of Division 6A, a Division 6A Checklist for Quality	6:351
10 Sept.	The Quality of Division 6B, a Division 6B Checklist for Quality	6:567
10 Sept.	The Quality of Division 6C, a Division 6C Checklist for Quality	6:877
5 Nov.	O/Ws and Evaluation	MS1:187
	Data Series 51	

1991

10 Jan.	Confusion Formula, Additional Data	1:615
11 Jan.	Telex Discipline	1:472
21 Jan.	Moonripping *Personnel Series 33*	MS1:474
22 Jan.	Consequences of Miscramming	5:825
23 Jan.	Senior Qual Network	5:69
28 Jan.	Fliers, Definition and Use *Marketing Series 30*	MS3:293
28 Jan.	Marketing Posters *Marketing Series 31*	MS3:295
28 Jan.	The Tech Estimate Line	2:592 4:1040
29 Jan.	Repetition of Message *Marketing Series 29*	MS3:292
29 Jan.	Technical Specialist Courses	4:666
11 Feb.	Upper Org Central Files and New Names to CF	2:678 6:105
21 Feb.	Religious Influence in Society	6:867
22 Feb.	Volunteer Ministers	6:871
23 Feb.	Body Routing and Its Use	6:228
26 Feb.	Organization of the Public Divisions, The	6:108
26 Feb.	Delivering Public Division Courses	6:374

Create a successful organization.

The *Organization Executive Course* contains the basic laws of organization. Originally developed for the training of Scientology executives, this course contains basic LRH technology that you can apply to any group or activity.

"When you understand all the policies on this course, you will understand organization itself, no matter to what you apply it. You will also be able to recognize misorganization when you see it."—L. Ron Hubbard, from HCO PL 8 Sept. 69, THE ORG EXEC COURSE INTRODUCTION.

This is the only organizational technology based on a true understanding of the mind and spirit. Any failure of an organization is a failure to apply the data on this course or an ignorance of it.

When you know all the materials of this course, it makes a whole, intelligent picture of organization. For the first time, you can cut through the superstition of yesterday's organizations and create a sane, ethical and expanding group.

The *Organization Executive Course* consists of eight separate courses: one course for each of the divisions of the Scientology organizing board, plus one course covering the basics of handling any staff job.

Not only do you study every page of the powerful *Org Executive Course* Volumes, you will also study books and manuals and listen to lectures by L. Ron Hubbard on:

* Personnel
* Administration
* Ethics and justice in a group
* Communication
* Service
* Production
* How to train people for their jobs
* Quality and correction of the product
* Executive actions and duties
* and more

And, you will PRACTICE and APPLY what you learn as you study.

Learn and apply the knowledge in this course for certain and lasting success in any endeavor.

Do the *Organization Executive Course* now, available at your local Church of Scientology. See your Registrar today!

"If anyone knew the Org Exec Course fully and could practice it, he could completely reverse any downtrending company or country."—L. Ron Hubbard, from HCO PL 8 Sept. 69, THE ORG EXEC COURSE INTRODUCTION.

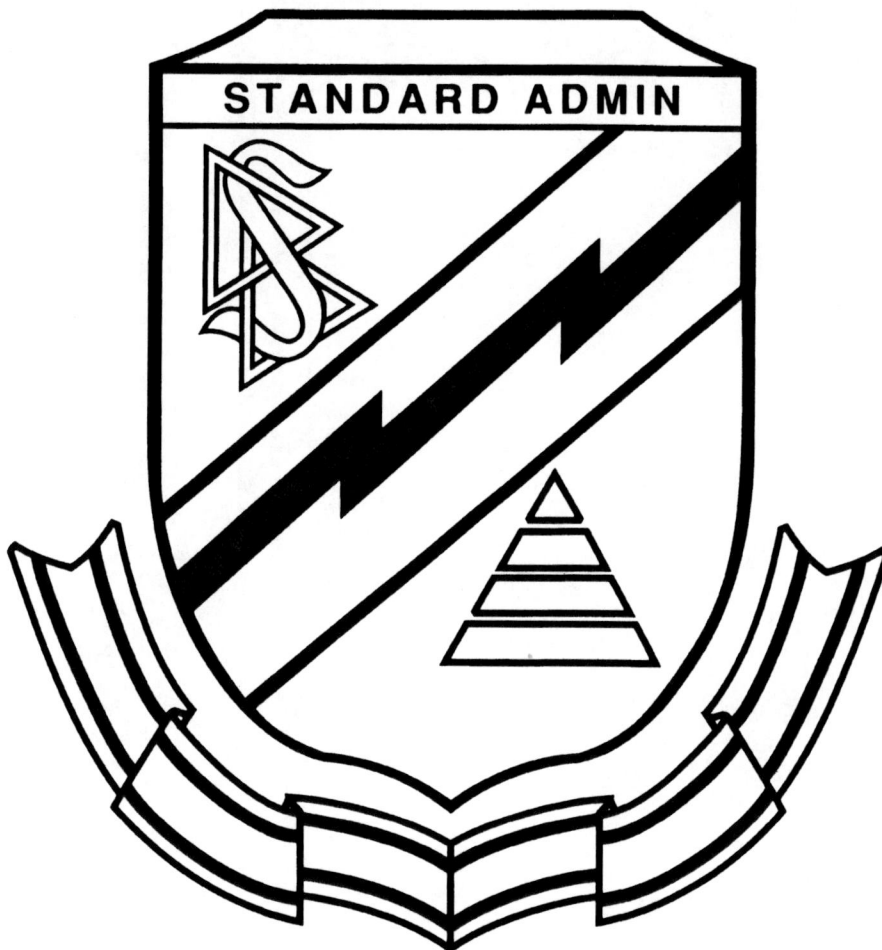

STANDARD ADMIN

Enroll on the Organization Executive Course.

Get the LRH data to expand any activity.

Before L. Ron Hubbard discovered and developed the technology of administration, man did not really know the principles of organization.

These basic discoveries of organization are available to you now, in the *Organization Executive Course* Volumes.

The policy letters in these volumes were written for Scientology organizations. However, you can apply the knowledge in these volumes to ANY group, organization or endeavor to make it a sane, ethical and expanding activity. This material applies to the individual as well. Where the functions covered in these policies are missing in your conduct in life, you will be to that degree an unsuccessful individual.

In these volumes is organization technology you'll find nowhere else, including:

* What exact actions and functions MUST be done in any organization for it to operate smoothly?

* Why the organizing board as developed by L. Ron Hubbard is a "philosophic machine," and how you can use the principles of the org board to achieve unlimited expansion.

* What is the one often-forgotten function which if missing will always eventually bring about the decline of any activity?

* What are the keys to maintaining a high ethical level in any group?

* What are the secrets to prosperity?

* How does a group ensure its products are top quality?

Any company or society will be as successful as it includes all the functions that are covered in these volumes.

There are eight *Organization Executive Course* Volumes, each fully indexed by subject, as well as alphabetically and chronologically. There is a ninth volume containing a cumulative index for the full set.

Get your full set of *Organization Executive Course* Volumes now!

See your Bookstore Officer today.

If one were fully familiar with the full subject and all the principles in these volumes, he would appear to be a magician, a miracle worker!

If unavailable, order from Bridge Publications, Inc., 5600 E. Olympic Boulevard, Commerce, CA 90022, USA, or NEW ERA Publications International ApS, Smedeland 20, 2600 Glostrup, Denmark.

Buy your full set of OEC Volumes.

Learn effective management tech!

Learn L. Ron Hubbard's state-of-the-art management technology in the *Management Series* Volumes.

Developed by L. Ron Hubbard for Scientology organizations, this is the most advanced administrative and management technology available anywhere.

The extraordinary administrative breakthroughs and developments found in these series came out of L. Ron Hubbard's fundamental discoveries on the mind, the spirit and nature of life.

Have at your fingertips dynamic technology that can be applied to any activity, including:

* The Data Series—this is man's first-ever real breakthrough on logic and how to think. With this technology one can isolate the correct answers to situations and be far more effective in handling them.

* The Organizing Series—what IS organization? Here are the basic principles you have to know to organize ANYTHING. Find out what happens if you fail to organize and how you can overcome disorganization.

* The Executive Series—learn how to be a successful executive and effective leader. It includes such Scientology fundamentals as the KRC (Knowledge, Responsibility and Control) triangle which can be used to improve any endeavor, and indeed one's own capabilities. Discover the keys to achievement.

* The Personnel Series—how do you successfully choose and hire new personnel? Find out how to build a strong, effective organization of competent personnel.

* The Marketing Series—Developed to effectively disseminate Scientology materials and services. With this series Scientology basics have been applied to strip away false data about the mind and make marketing a far more effective subject. What are the basics of getting your product into public hands with high volume lasting success?

* The Public Relations Series—discover vital basics of public relations you won't find in any textbook! With this series, the Scientology basics of ARC and the Tone Scale are applied to the subject of PR. Find out how to handle human emotion and reaction for truly effective PR! This is also the secret of how to raise morale and production in a group.

* The Administrative Know-How Series—what are the key ingrediens to any group? How do you handle power? What are the secrets to getting other to produce? How do you plan and coordinate the actions of a large organization for smooth operation?

* The Finance Series—the basics of sane, ethical finances that apply to any group are contained in this series. Learn how proper financial handling can increase the production and prosperity of a group.

* The Target Series—this technology was developed by L. Ron Hubbard from advanced researches into the human spirit. You can get done almost anything you want to do using the technology of targeting. When one sees the scope of this subject one can become quite brilliant in achieving things never before in reach.

* The Computer Series—L. Ron Hubbard's breakthroughs on computer technology can make use of computers far more effective in any organization.

BUY THESE VOLUMES TODAY. See the Bookstore Officer at your Church of Scientology today.

"The difference between good management and poor management can be the loss or gain of the entire organization."—L. Ron Hubbard from HCO PL 10 Nov. 66, GOOD VERSUS BAD MANAGEMENT.

If unavailable, order from Bridge Publications, Inc., 5600 E. Olympic Boulevard, Commerce, CA 90022, USA, or NEW ERA Publications International ApS, Smedeland 20, 2600 Glostrup, Denmark.

Get the Management Series Volumes.

YOUR GUARANTEE OF FREEDOM.

INTERNATIONAL ASSOCIATION OF SCIENTOLOGISTS

The purpose of the International Association of Scientologists is: "To unite, advance, support and protect the Scientology religion and Scientologists in all parts of the world so as to achieve the aims of Scientology as originated by L. Ron Hubbard."

All great movements have succeeded because of the personal conviction and dedication of their members. And no members are as dedicated as those of the IAS, the group which is winning the war against suppression around the world.

Even if you're not directly involved in the fight, it *is* your war. You have a stake in what kind of world this is — and will become.

Become a member of the International Association of Scientologists.

Help guarantee your route to full OT as well as freedom for the millions.

WRITE TO THE MEMBERSHIP OFFICER

INTERNATIONAL ASSOCIATION OF SCIENTOLOGISTS

c/o SAINT HILL MANOR
EAST GRINSTEAD, WEST SUSSEX, RH19 4JY
OR CONTACT YOUR NEAREST CHURCH
OF SCIENTOLOGY

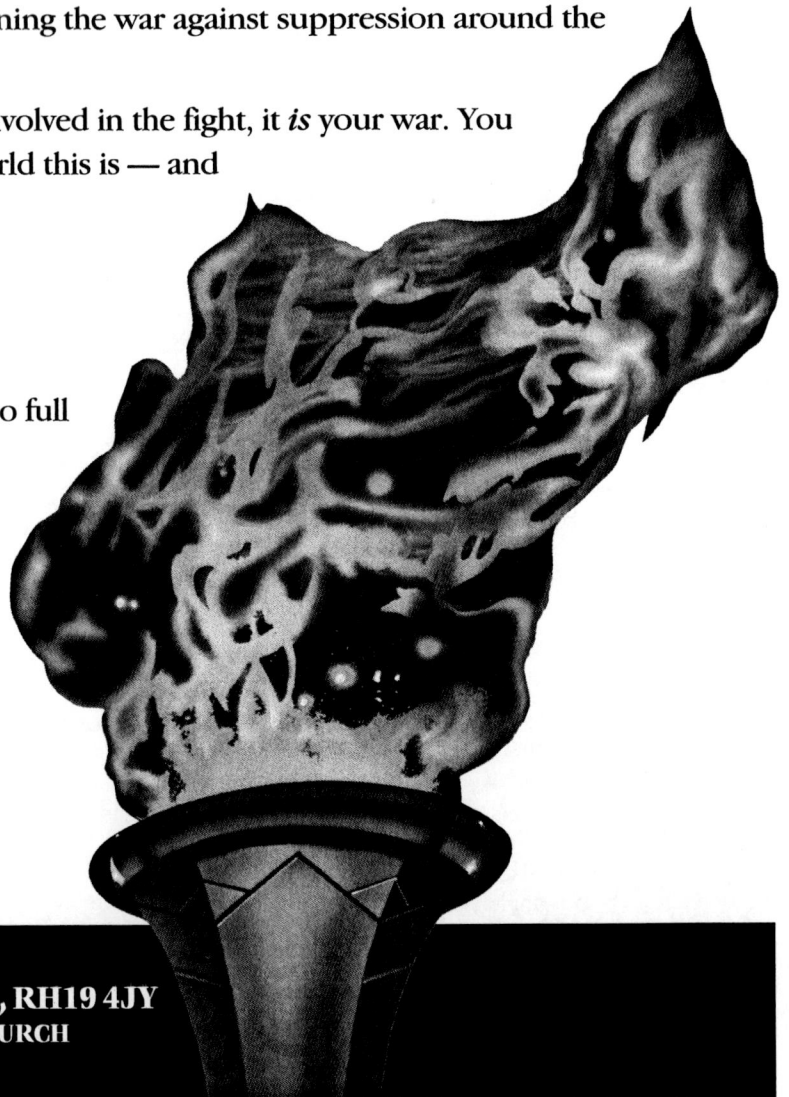

"I AM ALWAYS HAPPY TO HEAR FROM MY READERS."

L. RON HUBBARD

THESE WERE THE WORDS of L. Ron Hubbard, who was always very interested in hearing from his friends and readers. He made a point of staying in communication with everyone he came in contact with over his more than fifty-year career as a professional writer, and he had thousands of fans and friends that he corresponded with all over the world.

The author's representatives, Author Services, Inc., wish to continue this tradition and welcome letters and comments from you, his readers, both old and new.

Additionally, they will be happy to send you information on anything you would like to know about L. Ron Hubbard, his extraordinary life and accomplishments and the vast number of books he has written.

Any message addressed to the Author's Affairs Director at Author Services, Inc., will be given prompt and full attention.

AUTHOR SERVICES, INC.

7051 HOLLYWOOD BOULEVARD
HOLLYWOOD, CALIFORNIA 90028, USA

authoraffairs@authorservicesinc.com

Scientology Churches and Organizations

UNITED STATES

ALBUQUERQUE

Church of Scientology of
New Mexico
8106 Menaul Boulevard
N.E. Albuquerque, New Mexico 87110
www.scientology-albuquerque.org

ATLANTA

Church of Scientology of Georgia
1611 Mt. Vernon Road
Dunwoody, Georgia 30338
www.scientology-atlanta.org

AUSTIN

Church of Scientology of Texas
2200 Guadalupe
Austin, Texas 78705
www.scientology-austin.org

BATTLE CREEK

Church of Scientology of
Ann Arbor
66 E. Michigan Avenue
Battle Creek, Michigan 49017
www.scientology-battlecreek.org

BOSTON

Church of Scientology of Boston
448 Beacon Street
Boston, Massachusetts 02115
www.scientology-boston.org

BUFFALO

Church of Scientology of Buffalo
836 Main Street
Buffalo, New York 14202
www.scientology-buffalo.org

CHICAGO

Church of Scientology of Illinois
3011 North Lincoln Avenue
Chicago, Illinois 60657-4207
www.scientology-chicago.org

CINCINNATI

Church of Scientology of Ohio
215 West 4th Street, 5th Floor
Cincinnati, Ohio 45202-2670
www.scientology-cincinnati.org

COLUMBUS

Church of Scientology of
Central Ohio
30 North High Street
Columbus, Ohio 43215
www.scientology-columbus.org

DENVER

Church of Scientology of
Colorado
3385 South Bannock Street
Englewood, Colorado 80110
www.scientology-denver.org

DETROIT

Church of Scientology of Michigan
28000 Middlebelt Road
Farmington Hills, Michigan 48334
www.scientology-detroit.org

HONOLULU

Church of Scientology of Hawaii
1146 Bethel Street
Honolulu, Hawaii 96813
www.scientology-hawaii.org

KANSAS CITY

Church of Scientology of
Kansas City
2 East 39th Street
Kansas City, Missouri 64111
www.scientology-kansascity.org

LAS VEGAS

Church of Scientology of Nevada
846 East Sahara Avenue
Las Vegas, Nevada 89104
www.scientology-lasvegas.org

LONG ISLAND

Church of Scientology of
Long Island
64 Bethpage Road
Hicksville, New York
11801
www.scientology-longisland.org

LOS ANGELES AND VICINITY

Church of Scientology of
Los Angeles
4810 Sunset Boulevard
Los Angeles, California 90027
www.scientology-losangeles.org

Church of Scientology of
Orange County
1451 Irvine Boulevard
Tustin, California 92680
www.scientology-orangecounty.org

Church of Scientology of
Pasadena
1277 East Colorado Boulevard
Pasadena, California 91106
www.scientology-pasadena.org

Church of Scientology of
the Valley
15643 Sherman Way
Van Nuys, California 91406
www.scientology-valley.org

LOS GATOS

Church of Scientology of
Los Gatos
4050 Moorpark Avenue
San Jose, California 90028
www.scientology-losgatos.org

MIAMI

Church of Scientology of
Florida
120 Giralda Avenue
Coral Gables, Florida 33134
www.scientology-miami.org

MINNEAPOLIS

Church of Scientology of
Minneapolis
Twin Cities
1011 Nicollet Mall
Minneapolis, Minnesota 55403
www.scientology-minneapolis.org

MOUNTAIN VIEW

Church of Scientology of
Mountain View
117 Easy Street
Mountain View, California 94039
www.scientology-mountainview.org

NEW HAVEN

Church of Scientology of
Connecticut
909 Whalley Avenue
New Haven, Connecticut
06515-1728
www.scientology-newhaven.org

NEW YORK CITY

Church of Scientology of
New York
227 West 46th Street
New York, New York 10036-1409
www.scientology-newyork.org

ORLANDO

Church of Scientology of
Orlando, Inc.
1830 East Colonial Drive
Orlando, Florida 32803-4729
www.scientology-orlando.org

PHILADELPHIA

Church of Scientology of
Pennsylvania
1315 Race Street
Philadelphia, Pennsylvania 19107
www.scientology-philadelphia.org

PHOENIX

Church of Scientology of Arizona
2702 44th Street, Suite A-100
Phoenix, Arizona 85008
www.scientology-phoenix.org

PORTLAND

Church of Scientology of Portland
709 SW Salmon Street
Portland, Oregon 97205
www.scientology-portland.org

SACRAMENTO

Church of Scientology of
  Sacramento
825 15th Street
Sacramento
California 95814-2096
www.scientology-sacramento.org

SALT LAKE CITY

Church of Scientology of Utah
1931 South 1100 East
Salt Lake City, Utah 84106
www.scientology-saltlakecity.org

SAN DIEGO

Church of Scientology of
  San Diego
1330 4th Avenue
San Diego, California 92101
www.scientology-sandiego.org

SAN FRANCISCO

Church of Scientology of
  San Francisco
701 Montgomery Street
San Francisco, California 94111
www.scientology-sanfrancisco.org

SAN JOSE

Church of Scientology of
  Stevens Creek
1865 Lundy Avenue
San Jose, California 95131
www.scientology-sanjose.org

SANTA BARBARA

Church of Scientology of
  Santa Barbara
524 State Street
Santa Barbara, California 93101
www.scientology-santabarbara.org

SEATTLE

Church of Scientology
  of Washington State
601 Aurora Avenue North
Seattle, Washington 98109
www.scientology-seattle.org

ST. LOUIS

Church of Scientology of Missouri
6901 Delmar Boulevard
University City, Missouri 63130
www.scientology-stlouis.org

TAMPA

Church of Scientology of
  Tampa, Inc.
3102 North Habana Avenue
Tampa, Florida 33609
www.scientology-tampa.org

WASHINGTON, DC

The Founding Church of
  Scientology
  of Washington, DC
1701 20th Street N.W.
Washington, DC 20009
www.scientology-washingtondc.org

PUERTO RICO

HATO REY

Church of Scientology of
  Puerto Rico
272 JT Piñero Avenue
Hyde Park,
San Juan, Puerto Rico 00918
www.scientology-puertorico.org

CANADA

EDMONTON

Church of Scientology of
  Edmonton
10255 97th Street
Edmonton, Alberta
Canada T5J 0L9
www.scientology-edmonton.org

KITCHENER

Church of Scientology of
  Kitchener
159-161 King Street West
Kitchener, Ontario
Canada N2G 1A6
www.scientology-kitchener.org

MONTREAL

Church of Scientology of
  Montreal, Inc.
4489 Papineau Street
Montreal, Quebec
Canada H2H 1T7
www.scientology-montreal.org

OTTAWA

Church of Scientology of Ottawa
150 Rideau Street, 2nd Floor
Ottawa, Ontario
Canada K1N 5X6
www.scientology-ottawa.org

QUEBEC

Church of Scientology of
  Quebec, Inc.
1996 1. Avenue
Quebec, Quebec
Canada G1L 3M2
www.scientology-quebec.org

TORONTO

Church of Scientology of Toronto
696 Yonge Street, 2nd Floor
Toronto, Ontario
Canada M4Y 2A7
www.scientology-toronto.org

VANCOUVER

Church of Scientology of
  Vancouver
401 West Hastings Street
Vancouver, British Columbia
Canada V6B 1L5
www.scientology-vancouver.org

WINNIPEG

Church of Scientology of
  Winnipeg
315 Garry Street, Suite 210
Winnipeg, Manitoba
Canada R3B 2G7
www.scientology-winnipeg.org

UNITED KINGDOM

BIRMINGHAM

Church of Scientology of
  Birmingham
8 Ethel Street
Winston Churchill House
Birmingham, England B2 4BG
www.scientology-birmingham.org

BRIGHTON

Church of Scientology of Brighton
Third Floor, 79-83 North Street
Brighton, Sussex
England BN1 1ZA
www.scientology-brighton.org

EAST GRINSTEAD

Church of Scientology
  Saint Hill Foundation
Saint Hill Manor
East Grinstead, West Sussex
England RH19 4JY
www.scientology-sthillfdn.org

EDINBURGH

Hubbard Association of Personal
  Independence
20 Southbridge
Edinburgh, Scotland EH1 1LL
www.scientology-edinburgh.org

LONDON

Church of Scientology of London
146 Queen Victoria St.
London, England EC4V 4BY
www.scientology-london.org

MANCHESTER

Church of Scientology of
  Manchester
258 Deansgate
Manchester, England M3 4BG
www.scientology-manchester.org

PLYMOUTH

Church of Scientology of Plymouth
41 Ebrington Street
Plymouth, Devon
England PL4 9AA
www.scientology-plymouth.org

SUNDERLAND

Church of Scientology of
  Sunderland
51 Fawcett Street
Sunderland, Tyne and Wear
England SR1 1RS
www.scientology-sunderland.org

EUROPE

AUSTRIA

VIENNA

Church of Scientology of Austria
Capistrangasse 4
1070 Vienna, Austria
www.scientology-vienna.org

BELGIUM

BRUSSELS

Church of Scientology of Belgium
rue General MacArthur, 9
1180 Brussels, Belgium
www.scientology-brussels.org

DENMARK

AARHUS

Church of Scientology of Jylland
Chr. X Vej 166
8260 Viby Jylland, Denmark
www.scientology-jylland.org

COPENHAGEN

Church of Scientology of
Denmark
Gammel Kongevej 3–5, 1
1610 Copenhagen V, Denmark
www.scientology-denmark.org

FRANCE

ANGERS

Church of Scientology of Angers
28B, avenue Mendès
49240 Avrille, France
www.scientology-angers.org

CLERMONT-FERRAND

Spiritual Association of the
Church of Scientology
of Auvergne
6, rue Dulaure
63000 Clermont-Ferrand, France
www.scientology-clermontferrand.org

LYON

Church of Scientology of Lyon
3, place des Capucins
69001 Lyon, France
www.scientology-lyon.org

PARIS

Spiritual Association of
the Church of Scientology
of Ile de France
7, rue Jules César
75012 Paris, France
www.scientologie-paris.org

SAINT-ÉTIENNE

Spiritual Association of
the Church of Scientology
of the Loire
24, rue Marengo
42000 Saint-Étienne, France
www.scientologie-stetienne.org

GERMANY

BERLIN

Church of Scientology of
Berlin e.V.
Otto-Suhr-Allee 30-34
Charlottenburg
10585 Berlin, Germany
www.scientology-berlin.org

DÜSSELDORF

Church of Scientology of
Düsseldorf e.V.
Friedrichstraße 28B
40217 Düsseldorf, Germany
www.scientology-duesseldorf.org

FRANKFURT

Church of Scientology of
Frankfurt e.V.
Kaiserstraße 49
60329 Frankfurt 70, Germany
www.scientology-frankfurt.org

HAMBURG

Church of Scientology of
Hamburg e.V.
Domstraße 9
20095 Hamburg, Germany
www.scientology-hamburg.org

Church of Scientology of
Eppendorf e.V.
Auf dem Koenigslande 92A
22047 Hamburg, Germany
www.scientology-eppendorf.org

HANNOVER

Church of Scientology of
Hannover e.V.
Odeonstraße 17
30159 Hannover, Germany
www.scientology-hannover.org

MUNICH

Church of Scientology of
Munich e.V.
Beichstraße 12
80802 Munich 40, Germany
www.munich.scientology.org

STUTTGART

Dianetik Stuttgart e.V.
Hohenheimerstraße 9
70184 Stuttgart, Germany
www.scientology-stuttgart.org

GREECE

ATHENS

Church of Scientology of Athens
Patision 200
11256 Athens, Greece

HUNGARY

BUDAPEST

Church of Scientology of
Budapest
1399 Budapest
1073 Erzsébet krt. 5. I. em.
Pf. 701/215. Hungary
www.scientology-budapest.org

ISRAEL

TEL AVIV

College of Dianetics and
Scientology of Tel Aviv
12 Shontzino Street
PO Box 57478
61573 Tel Aviv, Israel
www.scientology-telaviv.org

ITALY

BRESCIA

Church of Scientology of
Tre Laghi
Via Fratelli Bronzetti, 20
25125 Brescia, Italy
www.scientology-brescia.org

CATANIA

Church of Scientology of Catania
Via Etnea, 468
95128 Catania, Italy
www.scientology-catania.org

MILAN

Church of Scientology of Milan
Via Lepontina, 4
20159 Milan, Italy
www.scientology-milano.org

MONZA

Church of Scientology of Brianza
Via Ghilini, 4
20052 Monza (MI), Italy
www.scientology-monza.org

NOVARA

Church of Scientology of Novara
Corso Milano, 76
28100 Novara, Italy
www.scientology-novara.org

NUORO

Church of Scientology of Sardinia
Via San Martino, 3
08100 Nuoro, Italy
www.scientology-nuoro.org

PADUA

Church of Scientology of Padua
Via Ugo Foscolo, 5
35131 Padua, Italy
www.scientology-padova.org

PORDENONE

Church of Scientology of
the City of Pordenone
Via Dogana, 19
Zona Fiera
33170 Pordenone, Italy
www.scientology-pordenone.org

ROME

Church of Scientology of
Rome and Mediterranean
Via del Caravita, 5
00186 Rome, Italy
www.scientology-roma.org

TURIN

Church of Scientology of Turin
Via Bersezio, 7
10152 Turin, Italy
www.scientology-torino.org

VERONA

Church of Scientology of Verona
Corso Milano, 84
37138 Verona, Italy
www.scientology-verona.org

NETHERLANDS

AMSTERDAM

Church of Scientology of
Amsterdam
Nieuwezijds Voorburgwal
116–118 1012 SH
Amsterdam, Netherlands
www.scientology-amsterdam.org

NORWAY

OSLO

Church of Scientology of Norway
Karl Johans Gate 12J
0154 Oslo, Norway
www.scientology-oslo.org

PORTUGAL

LISBON

Scientology Church Association of
Portugal
Rua dos Correiros N 205, 3° Andar
1100 Lisbon, Portugal
www.cientologia-lisbon.org

RUSSIA

MOSCOW

Church of Scientology of Moscow
Ul. Boris Galushkina 19A
129301 Moscow, Russia
www.scientology-moscow.org

ST. PETERSBURG

Scientology Center of
St. Petersburg
Ligovskij Prospect 33
193036 St. Petersburg, Russia
www.scientology-stpetersburg.org

SPAIN

BARCELONA

Dianetics Civil Association
of Barcelona
C/Dos de Maig 310 Baixos
08025 Barcelona, Spain
www.scientology-barcelona.org

MADRID

Dianetics Civil Association of
Madrid
C/ Santa Catalina, 7
28014 Madrid, Spain
www.cienciologia-madrid.org

SWEDEN

GÖTEBORG

Church of Scientology of
Göteborg
Värmlandsgatan 16, 1 tr.
413 28 Göteborg, Sweden
www.scientology-gothenburg.org

MALMÖ

Church of Scientology of Malmö
Porslinsgatan 3
211 32 Malmö, Sweden
www.scientology-malmo.org

STOCKHOLM

Church of Scientology of
Stockholm
Reimerschlomsgaten, 9-11
116 62 Stockholm, Sweden
www.scientology-stockholm.org

SWITZERLAND

BASEL

Church of Scientology of Basel
Herrengrabenweg 56
4054 Basel, Switzerland
www.scientology-basel.org

BERN

Church of Scientology of Bern
Muhlemattstrasse 31
Postfach 384
3000 Bern 14, Switzerland
www.scientology-bern.org

GENEVA

Church of Scientology of Geneva
12, rue des Acacias
1227 Carouge
Geneva, Switzerland
www.scientology-geneva.org

LAUSANNE

Church of Scientology of
Lausanne
10, rue de la Madeleine
1003 Lausanne, Switzerland
www.scientology-lausanne.org

ZURICH

Church of Scientology of Zurich
Freilagerstrasse 11
8047 Zurich, Switzerland
www.scientology-zurich.org

AUSTRALIA

ADELAIDE

Church of Scientology of Adelaide
18 Waymouth Street
Adelaide, South Australia
Australia 5000
www.scientology-adelaide.org

BRISBANE

Church of Scientology of Brisbane
106 Edward Street, 2nd Floor
Brisbane, Queensland
Australia 4000
www.scientology-brisbane.org

CANBERRA

Church of Scientology of
Canberra
Unit 4, 7-11 Botany St. Phillip
Canberra City, ACT 2606
Australia
www.scientology-canberra.org

MELBOURNE

Church of Scientology of
Melbourne
42–44 Russell Street
Melbourne, Victoria
Australia 3000
www.scientology-melbourne.org

PERTH

Church of Scientology of Perth
108 Murray Street, 1st Floor
Perth, Western Australia
Australia 6000
www.scientology-perth.org

SYDNEY

Church of Scientology of Sydney
201 Castlereagh Street
Sydney, New South Wales
Australia 2000
www.scientology-sydney.org

JAPAN

TOKYO

Scientology Tokyo
2-11-7, Kita-otsuka
Toshima-ku
Tokyo, Japan 170-004
www.scientology-tokyo.org

NEW ZEALAND

AUCKLAND

Church of Scientology of
New Zealand
532-534 Ellerslie/Panmure Highway
Panmure, Auckland
New Zealand
www.scientology-auckland.org

SOUTH AFRICA

CAPE TOWN

Church of Scientology of
Cape Town
185 Bree Street
Cape Town 8001, South Africa
www.scientology-capetown.org

DURBAN

Church of Scientology of Durban
20 Buckingham Terrace
Westville, Durban 3630
South Africa
www.scientology-durban.org

JOHANNESBURG

Church of Scientology of
Johannesburg
21 Kerk Avenue
Ruiterhof Ext. 2, Ferndale
Randburg, Johannesburg, 2194
South Africa
www.scientology.org.za

Church of Scientology
of Johannesburg North
No. 108 1st Floor,
Bordeaux Centre
Gordon Road, Corner Jan
Smuts Avenue
Blairgowrie, Randburg 2125
South Africa
www.scientology-johannesburgnorth.org

PORT ELIZABETH

Church of Scientology of
Port Elizabeth
2 St. Christopher's
27 Westbourne Road Central
Port Elizabeth 6001
South Africa
www.scientology-portelizabeth.org

PRETORIA

Church of Scientology of Pretoria
172 Brooklyn Road
Brooklyn, Pretoria 0181
South Africa
www.scientology-pretoria.org

ZIMBABWE

BULAWAYO

Church of Scientology of
Bulawayo
Southampton House, Suite 202
Main Street and 9th Avenue
Bulawayo, Zimbabwe
www.scientology-bulawayo.org

HARARE

Church of Scientology of Harare
No. 3 Seagrave Road
Mount Pleasant
Harare, Zimbabwe
www.scientology-harare.org

CELEBRITY CENTRES

CHURCH OF SCIENTOLOGY CELEBRITY CENTRE INTERNATIONAL

5930 Franklin Avenue
Hollywood, California 90028
www.celebritycentre.org

AUSTRIA

Church of Scientology
Mission of Vienna
Senefeldergasse 11/5
1100 Vienna, Austria
www.scientology-ccvienna.org

FRANCE

Spiritual Association of the
 Church of Scientology
Celebrity Centre Paris
69, rue Legendre
75017 Paris, France
www.scientology-ccparis.org

GERMANY

Church of Scientology
Celebrity Centre Rheinland e. V.
Luisenstraße 23
40215 Düsseldorf, Germany
www.scientology-ccduesseldorf.org

ITALY

Church of Scientology
Celebrity Centre Firenze
Via Salvestrina, 12
50129 Firenze

UNITED KINGDOM

Church of Scientology
Celebrity Centre London
42 Leinster Gardens
London, England W2 3AN
www.scientology-cclondon.org

UNITED STATES
DALLAS

Church of Scientology
Celebrity Centre Dallas
1850 North Buckner Boulevard
Dallas, Texas 75228
www.scientology-ccdallas.org

LAS VEGAS

Church of Scientology
Creative Mission of Las Vegas
4850 W. Flamingo Road, Suite 10
Las Vegas, Nevada 89103
www.scientology-cclasvegas.org

NASHVILLE

Church of Scientology
Celebrity Centre Nashville
1204 16th Avenue South
Nashville, Tennessee 37212
www.scientology-ccnashville.org

NEW YORK

Church of Scientology
Celebrity Centre New York
65 East 82nd Street
New York, New York 10028
www.scientology-ccnewyork.org

PORTLAND

Church of Scientology
Celebrity Centre Portland
708 S.W. Salmon Street
Portland, Oregon 97205
www.scientology-ccportland.org

ADVANCED ORGANIZATIONS

AUSTRALIA, NEW ZEALAND & OCEANIA

Church of Scientology
 Advanced Organization Saint Hill
 Australia, New Zealand and Oceania
19–37 Greek Stree, Glebe, New South Wales
Australia 2037

EUROPE & AFRICA

Church of Scientology Europe
 Advanced Organization
 Saint Hill
Jernbanegade 6
1608 Copenhagen V, Denmark

UNITED KINGDOM

Church of Scientology Advanced
 Organization Saint Hill
Saint Hill Manor
East Grinstead, West Sussex
England RH19 4JY

UNITED STATES

Church of Scientology
Western United States
Advanced Organization of
 Los Angeles
1306 L. Ron Hubbard Way
Los Angeles, California 90027

Church of Scientology
Western United States
American Saint Hill Organization
1413 L. Ron Hubbard Way
Los Angeles, California 90027

CHURCH OF SCIENTOLOGY FLAG SHIP SERVICE ORGANIZATION, INC.

c/o *Freewinds* Relay Office
118 N. Fort Harrison Avenue
Clearwater, Florida 33755-4013

CHURCH OF SCIENTOLOGY FLAG SERVICE ORGANIZATION, INC.

210 S. Fort Harrison Avenue
Clearwater, Florida 34616

To obtain any books or lectures by L. Ron Hubbard which are not available at your local organization, contact any of the following publishers:

NEW ERA PUBLICATIONS INTERNATIONAL ApS
Smedeland 20
2600 Glostrup, Denmark
Phone: (45) 33 73 66 66
Fax: (45) 33 73 66 33
e-mail:
books@newerapublications.com
www.newerapublications.com

NEW ERA PUBLICATIONS UK LTD
Saint Hill Manor
East Grinstead, West Sussex
England RH19 4JY
www.uk.newerapublications.com

NEW ERA PUBLICATIONS AUSTRALIA PTY LTD
16, Dorahy Street
Dundas, New South Wales
Australia 2117
www.au.newerapublications.com

CONTINENTAL PUBLICATIONS SOUTH AFRICA PTY LTD
PO Box 27080, Benrose
Johannesburg 2011, South Africa
www.sa.newerapublications.com

BRIDGE PUBLICATIONS, INC.
5600 E. Olympic Boulevard
Commerce, California 90022
Phone toll free: 1-800-722-1733
(in US and Canada)
Fax: 1-323-953-3328
e-mail: info@bridgepub.com
www.bridgepub.com

CONTINENTAL PUBLICATIONS LIAISON OFFICE
696 Yonge Street, Suite 705
Toronto, Ontario
Canada M4Y 2A7
www.can.bridgepub.com